Get the eBook FREE!

(PDF, ePub, Kindle, and liveBook all included)

We believe that once you buy a book from us, you should be able to read it in any format we have available. To get electronic versions of this book at no additional cost to you, purchase and then register this book at the Manning website.

Go to https://www.manning.com/freebook and follow the instructions to complete your pBook registration.

That's it!
Thanks from Manning!

Inside Deep Learning

Inside Deep Learning

Math, Algorithms, Models

Edward Raff

Foreword by Kirk Borne

MANNING

Shelter Island

Manning Publications Co.
20 Baldwin Road
PO Box 761
Shelter Island, NY 11964

Development editor:	Frances Lefkowitz
Technical development editor:	Kostas Passadis
Review editor:	Mihaela Batini
Production editor:	Andy Marinkovich
Copy editor:	Tiffany Taylor
Proofreader:	Keri Hales
Technical proofreader:	Al Krinker
Typesetter:	Benjamin Berg
Cover designer:	Marija Tudor

ISBN 9781617298639
Printed in the United States of America

This book is dedicated to my dad, Dr. Barry Raff,
whose first career was as a mechanical engineer before going
back to school to get his M.D. and becoming an internist.

You taught me about life but also instilled in me a deep desire
to explore, question, and understand. I would not be the man I am today
without you, and I promise to continue a legacy of delightfully bad and dry jokes.

brief contents

contents

foreword

From both a high-level "50,000-foot" perspective and a practical "in-your-hand" perspective, deep learning represents a remarkable technological convergence. Specifically, deep learning lives and thrives at the convergence of new, disruptive problem-solving approaches, scientific techniques, algorithmic methods, real-world applications, advanced mathematics, computational tools, computing resources, and the best minds in the computer and data sciences. Some would say that neural networks are not new. That's true. Some would say computer vision was around long before convolutional neural networks came to everyone's attention. That's also true. And some would say that machine learning and AI have already gone through multiple springs and winters over the past few decades. That's a winning hat trick for the naysayers. Right? I say, "Wrong!"

The ability to solve hard problems with computational algorithms and to automate those solutions is now possible at a depth and breadth we have never seen before. Previously insurmountably hard problems can now be solved, such as those required for safe operations of autonomous vehicles, or real-time language translation in live conversations, or conversational chatbots that come close to passing the Turing Test, or the relatively easy generation of textual and visual fakes that both entertain and frighten us. What makes all this possible is the convergence of the maturity and accessibility of advanced mathematical algorithms, ubiquitous fast computing resources, universally adoptable coding languages, and oceans of data, data, data everywhere!

Deep learning brings these many tools, techniques, and talents together (that's the convergence) in a myriad of diverse real-world applications (that's a healthy complement of divergence). Deep neural networks do a remarkable job of succinctly autoencoding the salient features in complex data (images, video, audio, documents, spoken language), which we may call *dimensionality reduction* or *explanatory feature generation*, and then applying those implicit (latent) hyper-patterns to inform decisions and actions fueled from those complex data sources. Whether the challenge is in image understanding, language understanding, or context understanding, the new deep learning techniques and components enable exciting functionalities in data-rich environments: object detection and recognition, behavior detection and recognition, anomaly detection, content (image, video, audio) generation, and relevance (attention) determination.

This excellent book guides us through the world of deep learning, from the fundamental building blocks to the advanced models that solve hard problems in data-drenched practical applications. We are introduced to the foundational concepts in a thoughtful and helpful sequence: learning, machine learning, neural networks, deep networks, deep learning, convolutional and recurrent networks, and beyond. All along the journey, we have thorough explanations, code snippets, sample problems and their solutions, evaluation techniques, exercises for the reader, and invaluable advice from one of the world's leading researchers and practitioners in the field. A theoretical book could never match the depth and applicability of this book, written by an author who has designed, developed, and delivered these solutions to clients in a large consulting organization and also presented award-winning research papers at machine learning and deep learning conferences. The evergreen wisdom, advice, practicality, and foundational strength represented in this book make it an invaluable resource in the current moment and also for years to come.

Readers will find great entry points into deep learning at all levels within this book. If you want to understand terminology like backpropagation, activation functions, or softmax (not just in words, but also in clear examples), you can learn it here. If you need to know the difference between CNN, RNN, LSTM, and GRU, you can explore them all here. If you want to build those things, you can learn how to do that. If you need to deep-dive into attention mechanisms, generative networks, autoencoding, or transfer learning, all of those are here, too. If deep learning is a construction project, this book provides all you need in one place: the foundations, building blocks, tools, expert advice, latest advances, deeply informative explanations, clear "show me how" examples, and metrics to evaluate the final product you build.

Pick up this book, and you won't be able to put it down (at least, not easily or quickly). It is a rich, engaging knowledgebase of deep learning math, algorithms, and models—just like the title says!

—Kirk Borne, PhD, Chief Science Officer, DataPrime.ai

I started my journey with machine and deep learning back in my undergrad days, during a semester abroad to England as part of my foreign language requirement (yes, you read that correctly). I immediately fell in love with the fundamental idea and the potential for ML to positively impact many disciplines and lives, but I found myself woefully unprepared for the math required by the subject.

Since then, I've forced myself to grow and learn to fill in those gaps: I obtained my PhD in the subject; I work as a chief scientist at Booz Allen Hamilton, leading multiple teams in ML and DL research; and I mentor PhD students as a visiting professor at the University of Maryland, Baltimore County. I get to help grow and mentor others who have the same passions and challenges I did, spawning the genesis of this book today. How can I help my employees, students, and colleagues obtain the knowledge they need more quickly and clearly, with less pain than I went through?

This book is a compilation of my knowledge in deep learning. It covers all the key topics I would like to be understood by an ideal candidate I would hire. These include a breadth of topic areas so you can begin to recognize and reuse patterns, positioning you to be effective in any area. It is critical to me that the book provides more than rote "use this model for this kind of problem" instruction. This book delves into why and how different models are selected. Hopefully, once you have finished reading this book, you will understand how the interplay between math, code, and intuition is built and grown, so you will be equipped to keep abreast of new developments in the field.

acknowledgments

I have been blessed by many people and opportunities in my life that I have not earned and for which I am very grateful, and I have insufficient space to acknowledge them all. Thank you to the many people at Booz Allen Hamilton who helped me reach his point, particularly David Capen, Drew Farris, Joshua Sullivan, and Steven Escaravage. I also thank the clients I have supported, who put faith in me when I had no special pedigree, and who fostered an environment of productivity, growth, and support.

My thanks to three years' worth of students in my "Modern and Practical Deep Learning" class at UMBC for reading initial drafts of this book: your feedback shaped it measurably. Thank you to my advisor, Charles Nicholas, for many lessons; to Ergun Simsek, for giving me the freedom to create the course; and to many other professors, students, and friends. Thank you to all the people who have reached out in various forms to provide feedback and to express their appreciation for this book, even in its earlier and less polished forms. Your voices carried more weight than you know and were an indispensable source of motivation for me to cross the finish line.

Thank you to the many professors at Purdue who helped shape my career in computer science and machine learning, and how I think about problems, especially Greg Frederickson, Jennifer Neville, Ananth Grama, Wojciech Szpankowski, and Charles Killian.

At Manning, the entire team has been wonderful to work with. My thanks particularly to Frances Lefkowitz for pushing, poking, prodding, and forcing me out of my writing comfort zone. You truly made me improve the writing and accessibility of this book.

Thank you to all the reviewers: Abdul Basit Hafeez, Adam Słysz, Al Krinker, Andrei Paleyes, Dze Richard Fang, Ganesh Swaminathan, Gherghe Georgios, Guillaume Alleon, Guillermo Alcantara Gonzalez, Gustavo A. Patino, Gustavo Velasco-Hernandez, Izhar Haq, Jeff Neumann, Levi D. McClenny, Luke Kupka, Marc-Philippe Huget, Mohana

Krishna, Nicole Königstein, Ninoslav Čerkez, Oliver Korten, Richard Vaughan, Sergio Govoni, Thomas Joseph Heiman, Tiklu Ganguly, Todd Cook, Tony Holdroyd, and Vishwesh Ravi Shrimali. Your suggestions helped make this a better book.

Finally, I'd like to thank my wife, Ashley, for listening to me kvetch about this process for years on end. And my thanks to my mom, Beryl, and Paul for encouraging my hubris in taking on this monumental task.

about this book

While writing this book, I tried to step back in time to when I was first learning: what did I find confusing, intimidating, and misleading? What helped me finally grasp a concept, get some code working, or realize that *no one knows* why it works? Then I thought about what I know today: what techniques tend to work best, and what skills do I wish my employees and students had? I've worked for the past three years to try to distill all these ideas down into one book for you. To do this, I've developed some key strategies used throughout the book:

- *Lots of code and visual results*—It's hard to stare at numbers all day, and math can be very abstract and difficult to reason about. Especially when you are learning for the first time, it's easier to see something visually and watch it change as you change your code. The book uses graphs and plots instead of dense tables, and I place a heavy focus on figures and image datasets where you can look at the data and results. The techniques you are learning are applicable to other kinds of data like audio or radio frequencies, but you don't need a unique background to understand them.

- *Multiple explanations*—Artificial Intelligence is a field born of many parents, with contributions from cognitive science, electrical engineering, computer science, psychology, and more. As such, there are often many different perspectives to understand the same approach. For this reason, I've tried to include multiple explanations or representations for many topics, especially complicated ones. This helps hammer home ideas and allows you to pick from the explanations that make the most sense to you.

- *Math for the rest of us*—If you can just read a new equation and "get it," you are a wizard. I am not a wizard, and I don't assume you are, either. Math is important to deep learning and understanding, so we talk about it, but I re-express the math in an easier-to-digest way. This includes rewriting equations as code, color-coding equations as sentences that describe the same functionality, mapping equations to NumPy expressions, and other strategies to help you truly understand the underlying approach, not just the code built atop it.

Who should read this book?

If you know the basics of machine learning and are comfortable getting things done using Python, you will be able to work through this book. This means you're familiar with standard ML concepts like training versus testing performance, overfitting and underfitting, and with bread-and-butter algorithms like logistic and linear regressions, k-means clustering, nearest neighbor searches, and principal component analysis (PCA). You should have used these as provided by scikit-learn and know the other tools in the ecosystem, like NumPy, pandas, and general object-oriented development. You don't need to know PyTorch, as we cover that in this book, but I encourage you to consult the PyTorch documentation (https://pytorch.org/docs/stable/index.html) as you read the chapters to get the nitty-gritty details.

   If you want to comprehend the mystery behind deep learning and start building an understanding of how it works, when to use it, and how to wield it with confidence, you should read this book! I've worked hard to find a happy medium between showing the code, practical details, and "on the job" knowledge with the math, statistics, and theoretical understanding that you need to separate yourself from the pack and keep pace with this fast-evolving field. If you stick with me, you will find each chapter challenging yet rewarding. The contents of this book should provide a strong foundation for any junior to mid-level ML engineer, data scientist, or researcher. Even the more senior researchers I work with have found this content useful, and I've used much of the code in production. Several of my PhD students have also found the code helpful in striking a balance between "usable" and "customizable," saving them time and helping them complete their research more quickly.

How this book is organized: A road map

This book has 2 parts and 14 chapters. Part 1 (chapters 1–6) focuses on the foundations of deep learning: the coding framework, the basic architecture types, the terminology for the different components, and techniques for constructing and training your neural networks. These are the basic tools from which you can build larger and more sophisticated systems. Then, in part 2 (chapters 7–14), we start adding new design choices or strategies. Each chapter helps to expand the utility of deep learning to a new kind of task or problem, broadening our scope for what DL can do and giving us new levers to adjust different design tradeoffs (e.g., speed versus accuracy).

While it may be tempting to jump to a chapter that sounds particularly relevant to your day job, this is not a book in which to skip chapters! The book is carefully constructed to be read in a linear order. Each chapter builds on a concept or technique introduced in the preceding chapter so that you slowly build a deep understanding with a broad repertoire of skills.

Part 1, "Foundational methods," has six chapters:

- Chapter 1 discusses PyTorch and the basics of how it works, showing you how to use the framework.

- Chapter 2 covers the most basic type of neural network—a fully connected network—and how to write code to train arbitrary networks in PyTorch. This includes a walk-through showing how a fully connected network is related to linear models.

- Chapter 3 introduces convolutions and how they enable convolutional neural networks that have dominated image-based deep learning.

- Chapter 4 introduces recurrent neural networks, how they encode sequential information, and how they can be used for text classification problems.

- Chapter 5 introduces newer training techniques that can be applied to any neural network to obtain higher accuracy in less time, and explains how they can achieve this goal.

- Chapter 6 develops the modern design patterns in common use today, bringing your knowledge of designing a neural network into the modern age.

Part 2, "Building advanced networks," has eight chapters:

- Chapter 7 introduces autoencoding as a technique for training a neural network without labeled data, allowing unsupervised learning.

- Chapter 8 introduces image segmentation and object detection as two techniques you can use to find multiple items within an image.

- Chapter 9 develops the generative adversarial network, an unsupervised approach that can produce synthetic data and is the foundation of many modern image-alteration and deep-fake techniques.

- Chapter 10 teaches you how to implement an attention mechanism, one of the most important recent advances in network priors. Attention mechanisms allow deep networks to selectively ignore irrelevant or unimportant parts of the input.

- Chapter 11 uses attention to build the seminal Seq2Seq model and shows how to build an English-to-French translator using the same approaches deployed in production systems.

- Chapter 12 introduces a new strategy for avoiding recurrent networks (due to their disadvantages) by rethinking how networks are designed. This includes the transformer architecture, a foundation of the best current tools for natural language processing.

■ Chapter 13 covers transfer learning, an approach that uses networks trained on one dataset to improve performance on another. This allows using less labeled data, making it one of the most useful tricks in real-world work.

■ Chapter 14 ends the book by revisiting some of the most fundamental components of a modern neural network and teaching you three recently published techniques that most practitioners still aren't aware of to build better models.

About the mathematical notations

Here are the most common notations and symbol styles used in the book, with their code equivalents, as a fast reference and primer.

Symbol	Meaning	Code
x or $x \in \mathbb{R}$	Lowercase letters are used to denote single floating-point values, and the $\in \mathbb{R}$ indicates explicitly that the value is "in the real numbers."	`x = 3.14` or `x = np.array(3.14)`
$\boldsymbol{x}$ or $\boldsymbol{x} \in \mathbb{R}^d$	The **bold** lowercase indicates a vector of d values.	`x = np.zeros(d)`
X or $\boldsymbol{x} \in \mathbb{R}^{r,c}$	CAPITALS indicate matrices or higher order tensors; the number of "," separated numbers/letters makes the number of axis explicit.	`X = np.zeros((r,c))`
$X^\top$ or $\boldsymbol{x}^\top$	Indicates a transposed matrix or vector.	`np.transpose(x)` or `np.transpose(X)`

$\displaystyle\sum_{i=start}^{end} f(i)$	Summation of an expression or function $f()$.	`result = 0`
		`for i in range(start, end+1):`
		`    result += f(i)`

$\displaystyle\prod_{i=start}^{end} f(i)$	Product of an expression or function $f()$.	`result = 1`
		`for i in range(start, end+1):`
		`    result *= f(i)`

$\lVert \boldsymbol{x} \rVert_2$	The 2-norm of a matrix or tensor, which indicates the "magnitude" of its values.	`result = 0`
		`for val in x:`
		`    result += val**2`
		`result = np.sqrt(result)`

About the exercises

Each chapter ends with a set of exercises to help you practice what you've learned. To encourage you to work out the problems on your own, no answers are provided. Instead, the author and publisher invite you to share and discuss your solutions with your fellow readers on the Manning online platform at Inside Deep Learning Exercises (https://liveproject.manning.com/project/945). Once you submit your own solution, you will be able to see the solutions submitted by other readers and see which ones the author judges to be the best.

About Google Colab

While deep learning really needs a GPU in order to work, I've designed every chapter to work in Google Colab: a platform that gives you access to GPU computing power for free, or for very little cost, depending on your usage. A good GPU will run you at least $600, so this way, you can educate yourself before making that investment. The appendix will help you get set up with Colab if you haven't used it before, but it's basically just a Jupyter notebook in the cloud.

About the code

Code is in a `fixed-width-font like this` and is often referenced in the text as normal English. For example, if we are talking about a "book" and we have a variable named `book`, we will use the fixed-width font to refer to both the concept and code simultaneously, and then we will switch back to normal fonts when we are talking about just the concept. So, I might talk about how `book` has a method to get `pages()` that you can read, to tie the concept of books to the code that implements the concept.

Very short code snippets occur in a similarly "fluent" style as just another paragraph of text, and longer code appears in a figure. Very long portions of code are broken up and can be found on GitHub at https://github.com/EdwardRaff/Inside-Deep-Learning. Sometimes the code isn't long, but a single line of the code is, so very long lines of code are wrapped around with a "continuity marker" (➥) that lets you know it's a single line of code split over more than one line.

liveBook discussion forum

Purchase of *Inside Deep Learning* includes free access to liveBook, Manning's online reading platform. Using liveBook's exclusive discussion features, you can attach comments to the book globally or to specific sections or paragraphs. To access the forum, go to https://livebook.manning.com/#!/book/inside-deep-learning/discussion. You can also learn more about Manning's forums and the rules of conduct at https://livebook.manning.com/#!/discussion.

Manning's commitment to our readers is to provide a venue where a meaningful dialogue between individual readers and between readers and the author can take place. It is not a commitment to any specific amount of participation on the part of the author, whose contribution to the forum remains voluntary (and unpaid). We suggest you try asking the author some challenging questions lest his interest stray! The forum and the archives of previous discussions will be accessible from the publisher's website as long as the book is in print.

Other online resources

I'll keep additional resources and updates to the book on my website, with a direct link to the book page: http://insidedeeplearningpytorch.com. As with all things in life, it can be good to get different perspectives, or you may find it easier to learn when concepts are explained in multiple ways. Toward that end, you may find Michael Nielsen's book (http://neuralnetworksanddeeplearning.com/) valuable for going deeper into some of the nitty-gritty details of simpler neural networks. I've personally learned a lot from Christopher Olah's blog (https://colah.github.io/), where he develops very thorough and insightful explanations of many advanced and new topics in deep learning. You can also follow me on Twitter @EdwardRaffML to learn more about deep learning.

about the author

Edward Raff, PhD, is a chief scientist at Booz Allen Hamilton, where he co-leads the machine learning research team in the Strategic Innovation Group. His work involves supervising internal research, recruiting and developing technical talent, collaborating with university partners, and business development specialized to high-end machine learning. Dr. Raff also assists several clients in conducting advanced research.

His enthusiasm for writing, developing, and teaching machine learning evolved from a desire to share his passion for any and all areas of machine learning. He is the author of the Java Statistical Analysis Tool (JSAT), a library for fast ML in Java. He currently supervises five Ph.D. students and has over 60 publications with three best-paper awards.

about the cover illustration

The figure on the cover of *Inside Deep Learning* is "Indien du Mexique," or "Mexican Indian," taken from a collection by Jacques Grasset de Saint-Sauveur, published in 1797. Each illustration is finely drawn and colored by hand.

In those days, it was easy to identify where people lived and what their trade or station in life was just by their dress. Manning celebrates the inventiveness and initiative of the computer business with book covers based on the rich diversity of regional culture centuries ago, brought back to life by pictures from collections such as this one.

Part 1

Foundational methods

Deep learning seems to be very new. Self-driving cars, computerized personal assistants, and chat bots are permeating our society—the applications and real-world impact of deep learning seemingly went from zero to ubiquitous in under a decade. So you want to dive right in and learn how to make your own self-driving robotic vacuum that will tell you where your cat hides the rubber bands and the socks that keep disappearing.

But if you really want to understand deep learning, you can't just drink from the firehose. The foundations are over six decades old—a tree whose fruit has finally ripened. You need to learn the basic techniques that serve as the foundation of modern deep learning, which we can then build on to grow your knowledge.

This part of the book steps through the key concepts and techniques, using modern frameworks to implement them. Chapter 1 introduces you to the specific framework, PyTorch, and the core concepts of automatic gradients and optimization. Chapter 2 shows you how to build your first simple deep learning networks. Chapters 3 and 4 explore how to extend a network with structure so it works better for images and textual data, respectively. Coming full circle, chapters 5 and 6 revisit optimization and how we design our networks, lifting the old style that we learned first into the modern era. This removes the mystery of why networks are designed the way they are and how the improvements work, and prepares you for more advanced designs in part 2 of the book.

The mechanics of learning

This chapter covers

- Using Google Colab for coding
- Introducing PyTorch, a tensor-based API for deep learning
- Running faster code with PyTorch's GPU acceleration
- Understanding automatic differentiation as the basis of learning
- Using the `Dataset` interface to prepare data

Deep learning, also called *neural networks* or *artificial neural networks*, has led to dramatic advances in machine learning quality, accuracy, and usability. Technology that was considered impossible 10 years ago is now widely deployed or considered technically possible. Digital assistants like Cortana, Google, Alexa, and Siri are ubiquitous and can react to natural spoken language. Self-driving cars have been racking up millions of miles on the road as they are refined for eventual deployment. We can finally catalog and calculate just *how much* of the internet is made of cat photos. Deep learning has been instrumental to the success of all these use cases and many more.

This book exposes you to some of the most common and useful techniques in deep learning today. A significant focus is how to use and code these networks and how and why they work at a deep level. With a deeper understanding, you'll be better equipped to select the best approach for your problems and keep up with advances in this rapidly progressing field. To make the best use of this book, you should be familiar with programming in Python and have some passing memory of calculus, statistics, and linear algebra courses. You should also have prior experience with machine learning (ML), although it is OK if you aren't an expert; ML topics are quickly introduced, but our goal is to move into details about deep learning.

Let's get a clearer idea of what deep learning is and how this book teaches about it. Deep learning is a subdomain of ML, which is a subdomain of artificial intelligence (AI). (Some may take offense at how I'm categorizing these groups. It's an oversimplification.) Broadly, we could describe AI as getting computers to make decisions that *look* smart. I say *look* because it is hard to define what *smart* or *intelligence* truly is; AI should be making decisions that we think are reasonable and what a smart person would do. Your GPS telling you how to get home uses some old AI techniques to work (these classic tried-and-true methods are sometimes called "good old-fashioned AI," or GOFAI), and taking the fastest route home is a smart decision. Getting computers to play video games has been accomplished with purely AI-based approaches: only the rules of the game are encoded; the AI does not need to be shown how to play a game of chess. Figure 1.1 shows AI as the outermost layer of these fields.

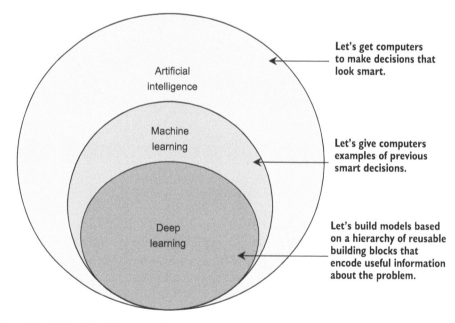

Figure 1.1   A (simplified) hierarchy of AI, ML, and deep learning

With ML, we start to give AI *examples* of previous smart and not-so-smart decisions. For example, we can improve our chess-playing AI by giving it example games played by chess grandmasters to learn from (each game has a winner and a loser—a smart and a not-as-smart set of decisions). This is a supervised-centric definition, but the critical component is that we have data that reflects the real world.

> NOTE A common saying is that data is truth, but that's also an oversimplification. Many biases can impact the data you receive, giving you a biased view of the world. That is an advanced topic for another book!

Deep learning, in turn, is not one algorithm, but *hundreds* of small algorithms that act like building blocks. Part of being a good practitioner is knowing what building blocks are available and which ones to stick together to create a larger model for *your* problem. Each building block is designed to work well for certain problems, giving the model valuable information. Figure 1.2 shows how we might combine blocks together to tackle three situations. One of the goals in this book is to cover a wide variety of building blocks so that you know and understand how they can be used for different kinds of problems. Some of the blocks are generic ("Data is a sequence" could be used for literally *any* kind of sequence), while others are more specific ("Data is an image" applies to only images), which impacts when and how you use them.

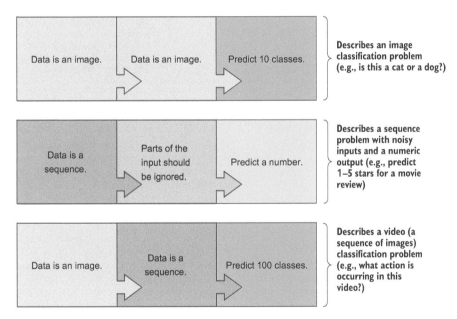

Figure 1.2 A defining characteristic of deep learning is building models from reusable blocks. Different blocks are useful for different kinds of data and can be mixed and matched to deal with different problems. The first row shows how blocks of the same type can be repeated to make a deeper model, which can improve accuracy.

The first row uses two "Data is an image" blocks to create a *deep* model. Applying blocks repeatedly is where the *deep* in *deep learning* comes from. Adding depth makes a model capable of solving more complex problems. This depth is often obtained by stacking the same kind of block multiple times. The second row in the figure shows a case for a sequence problem: for example, text can be represented as a sequence of words. But not all words are meaningful, and so we may want to give the model a block that helps it learn to *ignore* certain words. The third row shows how to describe new problems using the blocks we know about. If we want our AI to watch a video and predict what is happening (e.g., "running," "tennis," or "adorable puppy attack") we can use the "Data is an image" and "Data is a sequence" blocks to create a sequence of images—a video.

These building blocks define our model, but as in all ML, we also need data and a mechanism for learning. When we say *learning*, we are not talking about the way humans learn. In machine (and deep) learning, *learning* is the mechanical process of getting the model to make smart-looking predictions about data. This happens via a process called *optimization* or *function minimization*. Before we see any data, our model returns random outputs because all of the parameters (the numbers that control what is computed) are initialized to random values. In a common tool like linear regression, the regression coefficients are the parameters. By *optimizing* the blocks over the data, we make our models learn. This gives us the larger picture in figure 1.3.

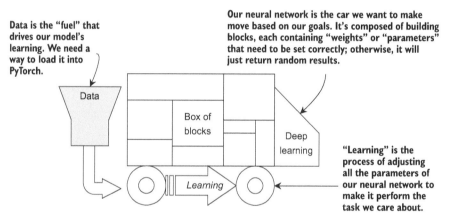

Figure 1.3 The "car" of deep learning. The car is built from many different building blocks, and we can use assortments of building blocks to build cars for different tasks. But we need fuel and wheels to make the car go. The wheels are the task of learning, which is done via a process called optimization; and the fuel is data.

In most chapters of this book, you learn about new building blocks that you can use to build deep learning models for different applications. You can think of each block as a kind of (potentially very simple) algorithm. We discuss the uses of each block and explain how or why they work and how to combine them in code to create a new model. Thanks to the nature of building blocks, we can ramp up from simple tasks (e.g., simple prediction problems you could tackle with a non-deep ML algorithm) to complex examples like machine translation (e.g., having a computer translate from English to French). We start with basic approaches and methods that have been used to train and build neural networks since the 1960s, but using a modern framework. As we progress through the book, we build on what we've learned, introducing new blocks, extending old blocks, or building new blocks from existing ones.

That said, this book is *not* a cookbook of code snippets to throw at any new problem. The goal is to get you comfortable with the language that deep learning researchers use to describe new and improved blocks so you can recognize when a new block may be useful. Math can often express complex changes succinctly, so I will be sharing the math behind the building blocks.

We won't *do* a lot of math—that is, *derive* or *prove* the math. Instead, I *show* the math: present the final equations, explain what they do, and attach helpful intuition to them. I'm calling it intuition because we go through the bare minimum math needed. Explaining the high-level idea of what is happening and showing why a result is the way it is would require more math than I'm asking you to have. As I show the equations, I interweave corresponding PyTorch code whenever possible so you can start to build a mental map between the equations and the deep learning code that implements them.

This chapter first introduces our compute environment: Google Colab. Next, we talk about PyTorch and tensors, which is how we represent information in PyTorch. After that, we dive into the use of graphics processing units (GPUs), which make PyTorch fast, and *automatic differentiation*, which is the "mechanics" that PyTorch uses to make neural network models learn. Finally, we quickly implement a dataset object that PyTorch needs to feed our data into the model for the learning process. This gives us the fuel and wheels to get our deep learning car moving, starting in chapter 2. From there on, we can focus on *just* the deep learning.

This book is designed to be read linearly. Each chapter uses skills or concepts developed in the preceding chapters. If you are already familiar with the concepts in a chapter, feel free to jump ahead to the next one. But if deep learning is new to you, I encourage you to proceed one chapter at a time instead of jumping to one that sounds more interesting, as these can be challenging concepts, and growing one step at a time will make it easier overall.

1.1 Getting started with Colab

We will use GPUs for *everything* we do with deep learning. It is, unfortunately, a computationally demanding practice, and GPUs are essentially a *requirement* for getting started, especially when you start to work on larger applications. I use deep learning all the time as part of my work and regularly kick off jobs that take a few *days* to train on multiple GPUs. Some of my research experiments can take *a month* of compute for each run.

Unfortunately, GPUs are expensive. Currently, the best option for most people who want to get started with deep learning is to spend \$600–\$1,200 on a higher-end NVIDIA GTX or Titan GPUs. That is, *if* you have a computer that can be expanded/upgraded with a high-end GPU. If not, you are probably looking at at least \$1,500–\$2,500 to build a nice workstation to put those GPUs in. That's a steep cost just to *learn* about deep learning.

Google's Colab (https://colab.research.google.com) provides a GPU for free for a limited amount of time. I've designed every example in this book to run within Colab's time limits. The appendix contains the instructions for setting up Colab. Once you have it set up, the common data science and ML tools like `seaborn`, `matplotlib`, `tqdm`, and `pandas` are all built-in and ready to go. Colab operates like a familiar Jupyter notebook, where you run code in cells that produce output directly below. This book is a Jupyter notebook, so you can run the code blocks (like the next one) to get the same results (I'll let you know if a code cell isn't meant to be run):

```
import seaborn as sns
import matplotlib.pyplot as plt
import numpy as np
from tqdm.autonotebook import tqdm
import pandas as pd
```

As we progress through this book, I do not repeatedly show all the imports, as that would be mostly a waste of paper. Instead, they are available online as part of the downloadable copy of the code, which can be found at https://github.com/EdwardRaff/Inside-Deep-Learning.

1.2   The world as tensors

Deep learning has been used on spreadsheets, audio, images, and text, but deep learning frameworks don't use classes or objects to distinguish between kinds of data. Instead, they work with one data type, and we must convert our data into this format. For PyTorch, this singular view of the world is through a *tensor* object. Tensors are used to represent both data, the inputs/outputs to any deep learning block, and the parameters that control the behavior of our networks. Two essential features are built into tensor objects: the ability to do fast parallel computation with GPUs and the ability to do some calculus (derivatives) automatically. With prior ML experience in Python, you should have prior experience with NumPy, which also uses the tensor concept. In this section, we quickly review the tensor concept and note how tensors in PyTorch differ from NumPy and form the foundation for our deep learning building blocks.

We begin by importing the `torch` library and discussing tensors, which are also called n-dimensional arrays. Both NumPy and PyTorch allow us to create n-dimensional arrays. A zero-dimensional array is called a *scalar* and is any single number (e.g., 3.4123). A one-dimensional array is a *vector* (e.g., [1.9, 2.6, 3.1, 4.0, 5.5]), and a two-dimensional array is a *matrix*. Scalars, vectors, and matrices are all tensors. In fact, any value of n for an n-dimensional array is still a tensor. The word *tensor* refers to the overall concept of an n-dimensional array.

We care about tensors because they are a convenient way to organize much of our data and algorithms. This is the first foundation that PyTorch provides, and we often convert NumPy tensors to PyTorch tensors. Figure 1.4 shows four tensors, their shapes, and the mathematical way to express the shape. Extending the pattern, a four-dimensional tensor could be written as (B, C, W, H) or as $\mathbb{R}^{B,C,W,H}$.

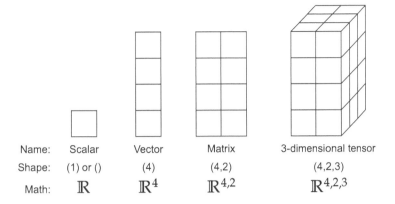

Name:	Scalar	Vector	Matrix	3-dimensional tensor
Shape:	(1) or ()	(4)	(4,2)	(4,2,3)
Math:	$\mathbb{R}$	$\mathbb{R}^4$	$\mathbb{R}^{4,2}$	$\mathbb{R}^{4,2,3}$

Figure 1.4 Examples of tensors, with more dimensions or axes as we move from left to right. A scalar represents a single value. A vector is a list of values and is how we often think about one datapoint. A matrix is a grid of values and is often used for a dataset. A three-dimensional tensor can be used to represent a dataset of sequences.

Tensor dimensions

When writing out the dimensions of a tensor like (B, C, W, H), we often use single-letter names with common notations or meanings behind the letters. This works as a useful shorthand, and you will see it frequently in code. Most are explained in more detail in later chapters, but some common dimension letters you will see include the following:

- B—The number of batches being used.
- D or H—The number of neurons/outputs in a hidden layer (sometimes N is also used for this).
- C—The number of channels in an input (e.g., think of "Red, Green, Blue" as three channels) or the number of classes/categories that a model could output.
- W and H—The width and height of an image (almost always in conjunction with a "C" dimension for the channels of an image).
- T—The number of items in a sequence (more on that in chapter 4).

We use common notation to associate math symbols with tensors of a specific shape. A capital letter like X or Q represents a tensor with two or more dimensions. If we are talking about a vector, we use a lowercase bold letter like $\boldsymbol{x}$ or $\boldsymbol{h}$. Last, we use a lowercase non-bold letter like x or h for a scalar.

In talking about and implementing neural networks, we often refer to a row in a larger matrix or a scalar in a larger vector. This is shown in figure 1.5 and is often called *slicing*. So if we have a matrix X, we can use $\boldsymbol{x}_i$ to reference the ith row of X. In code, that is x_i = X[i, :]. If we want the ith row and jth column, it becomes $x_{i,j}$, which is not bold because it is a reference to a single value—making it a scalar. The code version is x_ij = X[i,j].

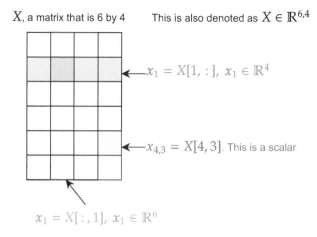

X, a matrix that is 6 by 4   This is also denoted as $X \in \mathbb{R}^{6,4}$

$x_1 = X[1, :], \; x_1 \in \mathbb{R}^4$

$x_{4,3} = X[4, 3]$. This is a scalar

$x_1 = X[:, 1], \; x_1 \in \mathbb{R}^6$

Figure 1.5   A tensor can be sliced to grab sub-tensors from a larger one. For example, in red, we grab a row-vector from the larger matrix; and in blue, we grab a column-vector from the matrix. Depending on what the tensor represents, this can let us manipulate different parts of the data.

To use PyTorch, we need to import it as the `torch` package. With it, we can immediately start creating tensors. Every time you nest a list within another list, you create a new dimension of the tensor that PyTorch will produce:

```
import torch

torch_scalar = torch.tensor(3.14)
torch_vector = torch.tensor([1, 2, 3, 4])
torch_matrix = torch.tensor([[1, 2,],
                             [3, 4,],
                             [5, 6,],
                             [7, 8,]])
torch_tensor3d = torch.tensor([
                  [
                  [ 1,   2,   3],
                  [ 4,   5,   6],
                  ],
                  [
                  [ 7,   8,   9],
                  [10,  11,  12],
                  ],
                  [
                  [13,  14,  15],
                  [16,  17,  18],
                  ],
                  [
                  [19,  20,  21],
                  [22,  23,  24],
                  ]
                   ])
```

You don't have to format it like I did; that's just for clarity.

If we print the shapes of these tensors, you should see the same shapes shown earlier. Again, while scalars, vectors, and matrices are different things, they are unified under the larger umbrella of tensors. We care about this because we use tensors of different shapes to represent different types of data. We get to those details later; for now, we focus on the mechanics PyTorch provides to work with tensors:

```
print(torch_scalar.shape)
print(torch_vector.shape)
print(torch_matrix.shape)
print(torch_tensor3d.shape)

torch.Size([])
torch.Size([4])
torch.Size([4, 2])
torch.Size([4, 2, 3])
```

If you have done any ML or scientific computing in Python, you have probably used the NumPy library. As you would expect, PyTorch supports converting NumPy objects into their PyTorch counterparts. Since both of them represent data as tensors, this is a painless process. The following two code blocks show how we can create a random matrix in NumPy and then convert it into a PyTorch `Tensor` object:

```
x_np = np.random.random((4,4))
print(x_np)

[[0.05095622 0.64330091 0.98293797 0.27355789]
 [0.37754388 0.51127555 0.29976254 0.97804978]
 [0.28363853 0.48929802 0.77875258 0.19889717]
 [0.23659932 0.21207824 0.25225453 0.54866766]]

x_pt = torch.tensor(x_np)
print(x_pt)

tensor([[0.0510, 0.6433, 0.9829, 0.2736],
        [0.3775, 0.5113, 0.2998, 0.9780],
        [0.2836, 0.4893, 0.7788, 0.1989],
        [0.2366, 0.2121, 0.2523, 0.5487]], dtype=torch.float64)
```

Both NumPy and torch support multiple different data types. By default, NumPy uses 64-bit floats, and PyTorch defaults to 32-bit floats. However, if you create a PyTorch tensor from a NumPy tensor, it uses the same type as the given NumPy tensor. You can see that in the previous output, where PyTorch let us know that `dtype=torch.float64` since it is not the default choice.

The most common types we care about for deep learning are 32-bit floats, 64-bit integers (`Longs`), and booleans (i.e., binary `True`/`False`). Most operations leave the tensor type unchanged unless we explicitly create or cast it to a new type. To avoid issues with types, you can specify explicitly what type of tensor you want to create when calling a function. The following code checks what type of data is contained in our tensor using the `dtype` attribute:

```
print(x_np.dtype, x_pt.dtype)

float64 torch.float64

x_np = np.asarray(x_np, dtype=np.float32)
x_pt = torch.tensor(x_np, dtype=torch.float32)
print(x_np.dtype, x_pt.dtype)

float32 torch.float32
```

◄——— **Let's force them to be 32-bit floats.**

The main exception to using 32-bit floats or 64-bit integers as the `dtype` is when we need to perform logic operations (like Boolean AND, OR, NOT), which we can use to quickly create *binary masks*.

A mask is a tensor that tells us which portions of another tensor are valid to use. We use masks in some of our more complex neural networks. For example, let's say we want to find every value greater than 0.5 in a tensor. Both PyTorch and NumPy let us use the standard logic operators to check for things like this:

```
b_np = (x_np > 0.5)
print(b_np)
print(b_np.dtype)

[[False True True False]
 [False True False True]
 [False False True False]
 [False False False True]]
bool

b_pt = (x_pt > 0.5)
print(b_pt)
print(b_pt.dtype)

tensor([[False,  True,  True, False],
        [False,  True, False,  True],
        [False, False,  True, False],
        [False, False, False,  True]])
torch.bool
```

While the NumPy and PyTorch APIs are not identical, they share many functions with the same names, behaviors, and characteristics:

```
np.sum(x_np)
```

[13]: 7.117571

```
torch.sum(x_pt)
```

[14]: tensor(7.1176)

While many functions are the same, some are not *quite* identical. There may be slight differences in behavior or in the arguments required. These discrepancies are usually because the PyTorch version has made changes that are particular to how these methods are used for neural network design and execution. Following is an example of the `transpose` function, where PyTorch requires us to specify which two dimensions to transpose. NumPy takes the two dimensions and transposes them without complaint:

```
    np.transpose(x_np)
[15]:  array([[0.05095622, 0.37754387, 0.28363854, 0.23659933],
              [0.6433009 , 0.51127553, 0.48929802, 0.21207824],
              [0.982938  , 0.29976255, 0.77875257, 0.25225455],
              [0.2735579 , 0.97804976, 0.19889717, 0.54866767]], dtype=float32)
    torch.transpose(x_pt, 0, 1)

[16]:  tensor([[0.0510, 0.3775, 0.2836, 0.2366],
               [0.6433, 0.5113, 0.4893, 0.2121],
               [0.9829, 0.2998, 0.7788, 0.2523],
               [0.2736, 0.9780, 0.1989, 0.5487]])
```

PyTorch does this because we often want to transpose dimensions of a tensor for deep learning applications, whereas NumPy tries to stay with more general expectations. As shown next, we can transpose two of the dimensions in our `torch_tensor3d` from the start of the chapter. Originally it had a shape of $(4, 2, 3)$. If we transpose the first and third dimensions, we get a shape of $(3, 2, 4)$:

```
print(torch.transpose(torch_tensor3d, 0, 2).shape)

torch.Size([3, 2, 4])
```

Because such differences exist, you should always double-check the PyTorch documentation at https://pytorch.org/docs/stable/index.html if you attempt to use a function you are familiar with but suddenly find it does not behave as expected. It is also a good tool to have open when using PyTorch. There are many different functions that can help you in PyTorch, and we cannot review them all.

1.2.1 PyTorch GPU acceleration

The first important functionality that PyTorch gives us beyond what NumPy can do is using a GPU to accelerate mathematical calculations. GPUs are hardware in your computer specifically designed for 2D and 3D graphics, mainly to accelerate videos (watching an HD movie) or play video games. What does that have to do with neural networks? Well, a lot of the math involved in making 2D and 3D graphics fast is tensor-based or at least tensor-related. For this reason, GPUs have been getting good at doing many things we want very quickly. As graphics, and thus GPUs, became better and more powerful, people realized they could also be used for scientific computing and ML.

At a high level, you can think of GPUs as giant tensor calculators. You should almost always use a GPU when doing anything with neural networks. It is a good pair-up since neural networks are compute-intensive, and GPUs are fast at the exact type of computations we need to perform. If you want to do deep learning in a professional context, you should invest in a computer with a powerful NVIDIA GPU. But for now, we can get by for *free* using Colab.

The trick to using GPUs effectively is to avoid computing on a *small* amount of data. This is because your computer's CPU must first move data to the GPU, then ask the GPU to perform its math, wait for the GPU to finish, and then copy the results back from the GPU. The steps in this process are fairly slow; and if we are only calculating a few things, using a GPU takes longer than the CPU would take to do the math.

What counts as "too small?" Well, that depends on your CPU, the GPU, and the math you are doing. If you are worried about this problem, you can do some benchmarking to see if using the CPU is faster. If so, you are probably working on too little data.

Let's test this with matrix multiplication—a basic linear algebra operation that is common in neural networks. If we have matrices $X^{n,m}$ and $Y^{m,p}$, we can compute a resulting matrix $C^{n,p} = X^{n,m}Y^{m,p}$. Note that C has as many rows as X and as many columns as Y. When implementing neural networks, we do lots of operations that change the *shape* of a tensor, like what happens when we multiply two matrices together. This is a common source of bugs, so you should think about tensor shapes when writing code.

We can use the `timeit` library: it lets us run code multiple times and tells us how long it took to run. We make a larger matrix X, compute XX several times, and see how long that takes to run:

```
import timeit
x = torch.rand(2**11, 2**11)
time_cpu = timeit.timeit("x@x", globals=globals(), number=100)
```

It takes a bit of time to run that code, but not too long. On my computer, it took 6.172 seconds to run, which is stored in the `time_cpu` variable. Now, how do we get PyTorch to use our GPU? First we need to create a `device` reference. We can ask PyTorch to give us one using the `torch.device` function. If you have an NVIDIA GPU, and the CUDA drivers are installed properly, you should be able to pass in `"cuda"` as a string and get back an object representing that device:

```
print("Is CUDA available? :", torch.cuda.is_available())
device = torch.device("cuda")

Is CUDA available? : True
```

Now that we have a reference to the GPU (device) we want to use, we need to ask PyTorch to move that object to the given device. Luckily, that can be done with a simple `to` function; then we can use the same code as before:

```
x = x.to(device)
time_gpu = timeit.timeit("x@x", globals=globals(), number=100)
```

When I run this code, the time to perform 100 multiplications is 0.6191 seconds, which is an instant 9.97× speedup. This was a pretty ideal case, as matrix multiplications are super-efficient on GPUs, and we created a big matrix. You should try making the matrix smaller and see how that impacts the speedup you get.

Be aware that this only works if every object involved is on the same device. Say you run the following code, where the variable x has been moved onto the GPU and y has not (so it is on the CPU by default):

```
x = torch.rand(128, 128).to(device)
y = torch.rand(128, 128)
x*y
```

You will end up getting an error message that says:

```
RuntimeError: expected device cuda:0 but got device cpu
```

The error tells you which device the first variable is on (cuda:0) but that the second variable was on a different device (cpu). If we instead wrote y*x you would see the error change to expected device cpu but got device cuda:0. Whenever you see an error like this, you have a bug that kept you from moving everything to the same compute device.

The other thing to be aware of is how to convert PyTorch data back to the CPU. For example, we may want to convert a tensor back to a NumPy array so that we can pass it to Matplotlib or save it to disk. The PyTorch tensor object has a .numpy() method that will do this, but if you call x.numpy(), you will get this error:

```
TypeError: can't convert CUDA tensor to numpy. Use Tensor.cpu()
to copy the tensor to host memory first.
```

Instead, you can use the handy shortcut function .cpu() to move an object back to the CPU, where you can interact with it normally. So you will often see code that looks like x.cpu().numpy() when you want to access the results of your work.

The .to() and .cpu() methods make it easy to write code that is suddenly GPU accelerated. Once on a GPU or similar compute device, almost *every* method that comes with PyTorch can be used and will net you a nice speedup. But sometimes we want to store tensors and other PyTorch objects in a list, dictionary, or other standard Python collection. To help with that, we can define this moveTo function, which goes recursively through the common Python and PyTorch containers and moves every object found onto the specified device:

```
def moveTo(obj, device):
    """
    obj: the python object to move to a device, or to move its
        contents to a device
    device: the compute device to move objects to
    """
    if isinstance(obj, list):
        return [moveTo(x, device) for x in obj]
    elif isinstance(obj, tuple):
        return tuple(moveTo(list(obj), device))
    elif isinstance(obj, set):
        return set(moveTo(list(obj), device))
    elif isinstance(obj, dict):
        to_ret = dict()
        for key, value in obj.items():
            to_ret[moveTo(key, device)] = moveTo(value, device)
```

```
        return to_ret
    elif hasattr(obj, "to"):
        return obj.to(device)
    else:
        return obj

some_tensors = [torch.tensor(1), torch.tensor(2)]
print(some_tensors)
print(moveTo(some_tensors, device))

[tensor(1), tensor(2)]
[tensor(1, device='cuda:0'), tensor(2, device='cuda:0')]
```

The first time we printed the arrays, we saw `tensor(1)` and `tensor(2)`; but after using the `moveTo` function, `device='cuda:0'` appeared. We won't have to use this function often, but when we do, it will make our code easier to read and write. With that, we now have the fundamentals to write *fast* code accelerated by GPUs.

> ### Why do we care about GPUs?
>
> Using a GPU is fundamentally about *speed*. It can literally be the difference between waiting *hours* or *minutes* for a neural network to train—and this is before we consider very large networks or huge datasets. I've tried to make every individual neural network that is trained in this book take 10 minutes or less, and in most cases under 5 minutes, when using a GPU. That means using toy problems and finagling them to show behavior that is representative of real life.
>
> Why not learn on real-world data and problems? Because real-world neural networks can take *days* or *weeks* to train. Some of the research I have done for my day job can take *a month* to train using *multiple* GPUs. The code we write is perfectly good and valid for real-world tasks, but we need to wait a little longer for the results.
>
> This long compute time also means you need to learn how to be productive while your model is training. One way is to develop new code for your next model on a spare machine or use the CPUs while your GPU is busy. You won't be able to train it, but you can push a tiny amount of data through to make sure no errors happen. This is also why I want you to learn how to map the math used in deep learning to code: so while your model is busy training, you can be reading about the latest and greatest deep learning tools that might help you.

1.3   *Automatic differentiation*

So far, we've seen that PyTorch provides an API similar to NumPy for performing mathematical operations on tensors, with the advantage of using a GPU (when available) to perform faster math operations. The second major foundation that PyTorch gives us is *automatic differentiation*: as long as we use PyTorch-provided functions, PyTorch can compute *derivatives* (also called *gradients*) automatically for us. In this section, we learn what that means and how automatic differentiation ties into the task of minimizing a function. In the next section, we see how to wrap it all up in a simple API provided by PyTorch.

Your first thought may be, "What is a derivative, and why do I care about that?" Remember from calculus that the derivative of a function $f(x)$ tells us how quickly the value of $f(x)$ is changing. We care about this because we can use the derivative of a function $f(x)$ to help us find an input x^* that is a *minimizer* of $f(x)$. The value x^* being a minimizer means the value of $f(x^*)$ is smaller than $f(x^* + z)$ for whatever value we set z to. The mathy way to say this is $f(x^*) \leq f(z), \forall x^* \neq z$:

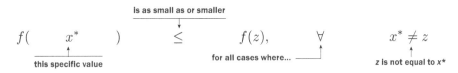

Another way to say this is that if I wrote the following code, I would be stuck waiting for an infinite loop:

```
while f(x_star) <= f(random.uniform(-1e100, 1e100)):
    pass
```

Why do we want to minimize a function? For all the kinds of ML and deep learning we discuss in this book, we train neural networks by defining a *loss function*. The loss function tells the network, in a numeric and quantifiable way, how *badly* it is doing at the problem. So if the loss is high, things are going poorly. A high loss means the network is losing the game, and badly. If the loss is zero, the network has solved the problem perfectly. We don't usually allow the loss to go negative because that gets confusing to think about.

When you read math about neural networks, you will often see the loss function defined as $\ell(x)$, where x are the inputs to the network and $\ell(x)$ gives us the loss the network received. Because of this, *loss functions return scalars*. This is important because we can compare scalars and say that one is definitively bigger or smaller than another, so it becomes unambiguous how bad a network is at the game. The derivative is generally defined with respect to a single variable, but our networks will have many variables (parameters). When getting the derivative with respect to multiple variables, we call it a *gradient*; you can apply the same intuition about derivatives and one variable to gradients over many variables.

We have stated that gradients are helpful, and perhaps you remember from a calculus class about minimizing functions using derivatives and gradients. Let's do a bit of a math reminder about how to find the minimum of a function using calculus.

Say we have the function $f(x) = (x - 2)^2$. Let's define that with some PyTorch code and plot what the function looks like:

```
def f(x):
    return torch.pow((x-2.0), 2)

x_axis_vals = np.linspace(-7,9,100)
y_axis_vals = f(torch.tensor(x_axis_vals)).numpy()

sns.lineplot(x=x_axis_vals, y=y_axis_vals, label='$f(x)=(x-2)^2$')
```

[22]:   <AxesSubplot:>

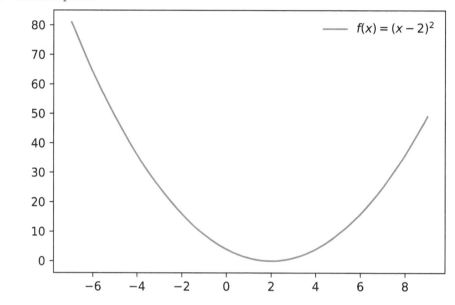

1.3.1   *Using derivatives to minimize losses*

We can clearly see that the minimum of this function is at $x = 2$, where we get the value $f(2) = 0$. But this is an intentionally easy problem. Let's say we can't plot it; we can use calculus to help us find the answer.

We denote the derivative of $f(x)$ as $f'(x)$, and we can get the answer (using calculus) that $f'(x) = 2 \cdot x - 4$. The minimum of a function (x^*) exists at *critical points*, which are points where $f'(x) = 0$. So let's find them by solving for x. In our case, we get

$$2 \cdot x - 4 = 0$$

$$2 \cdot x = 4$$

(add 4 to both sides)

$$x = 4/2 = 2$$

(divide each side by 2).

This required us to solve the equation for when $f'(x) = 0$. PyTorch can't quite do that for us because we are going to be developing more complicated functions where finding the *exact* answer is not possible. But say we have a current guess, $x^?$, that we are pretty sure is not the minimizer. We can use $f'(x^?)$ to help us determine how to adjust $x^?$ so that we move closer to a minimizer.

How is that possible? Let's plot $f(x)$ and $f'(x)$ at the same time:

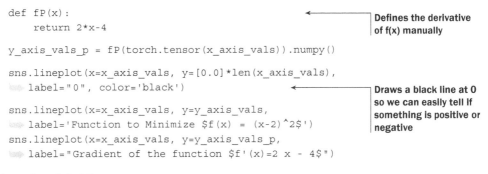

```
def fP(x):
    return 2*x-4                                              Defines the derivative
                                                              of f(x) manually

y_axis_vals_p = fP(torch.tensor(x_axis_vals)).numpy()

sns.lineplot(x=x_axis_vals, y=[0.0]*len(x_axis_vals),
    label="0", color='black')                                Draws a black line at 0
                                                              so we can easily tell if
                                                              something is positive or
sns.lineplot(x=x_axis_vals, y=y_axis_vals,                   negative
    label='Function to Minimize $f(x) = (x-2)^2$')
sns.lineplot(x=x_axis_vals, y=y_axis_vals_p,
    label="Gradient of the function $f'(x)=2 x - 4$")
```

```
[23]:   <AxesSubplot:>
```

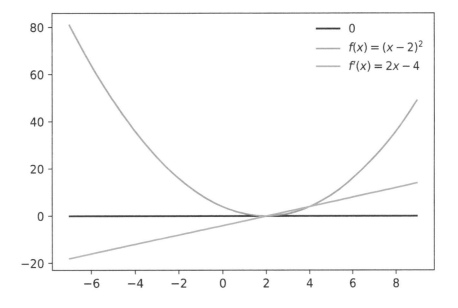

Look at the orange line. When we are too far to the left of the minimum $(x = 2)$, we see that $f'(x^?) < 0$. When we are to the right of the minimum, we instead get $f'(x) > 0$. Only when we are at a minimum do we see that $f'(x^?) = 0$. So if $f'(x^?) < 0$, we need to increase $x^?$; and if $f'(^?x) > 0$, we need to decrease the value of $x^?$. The *sign* of the gradient f' tells us which *direction* we should move to find a minimizer. This process of *gradient descent* is summarized in figure 1.6.

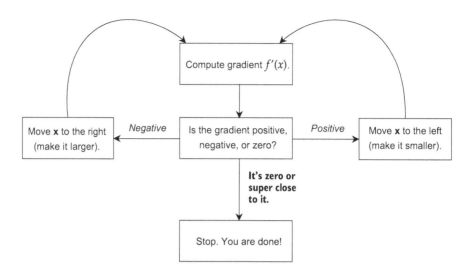

Figure 1.6   The process to minimize a function $f(x)$ **using its derivative** $f'(x)$ **is called gradient descent, and this figure shows how it is done. We iteratively compute** $f'(x)$ **to decide whether** x **should be larger or smaller to make the value of** $f(x)$ **as small as possible. The process stops when we are close enough to the gradient being zero. You can also stop early if you have done a lot of updates: "close enough is good enough" holds true for deep learning, and we rarely need to perfectly minimize a function.**

We also care about the *magnitude* of $f'(x^?)$. Because we are looking at a one-dimensional function, the magnitude just means the absolute value of $f'(x^?)$: i.e., $|f'(x^?)|$. The magnitude gives us an idea how far we are from the minimizer. So the sign of $f'(x^?)$ (<0 or >0) tells us which *direction* we should move, and the size ($|f'(x)|$) tells us how *far* we should move.

This is not a coincidence. It is *always* true for any function. If we can compute a derivative, we can find a minimizer. You may be thinking, "I don't remember my calculus all that well," or complaining that I skipped the steps about how to compute $f'(x)$. This is why we use PyTorch: automatic differentiation computes the value of $f'(x)$ for us. Let's use the toy example of $f(x) = (x-2)^2$ to see how it works.

1.3.2   *Calculating a derivative with automatic differentiation*

Now that we understand the concept of minimizing a function using its derivative, let's walk through the mechanics of doing it in PyTorch. First, let's create a new variable to minimize. We do this similar to before, but we add a new flag telling PyTorch to keep track of the gradient. This is stored in a variable called `grad`, which does not exist yet since we haven't computed anything:

```
x = torch.tensor([-3.5], requires_grad=True)
print(x.grad)
```

```
None
```

We see there is no current gradient. Let's try computing $f(x)$, though, and see if anything changes now that we set `requires_grad=True`:

```
value = f(x)
print(value)

tensor([30.2500], grad_fn=<PowBackward0>)
```

Now when we print the value of the returned variable, we get slightly different output. In the first part, the value 30.25 is printed, which is the correct value of $f(-3.5)$. But we also see this new `grad_fn=<PowBackward0>`. Once we tell PyTorch to start calculating gradients, it begins to keep track of *every* computation we do. It uses this information to go backward and calculate the gradients for everything that was used and had a `requires_grad` flag set to `True`.

Once we have a single *scalar* value, we can tell PyTorch to go back and use this information to compute the gradients. This is done using the `.backward()` function, after which we see a gradient in our original object:

```
value.backward()
print(x.grad)

tensor([-11.])
```

With that, we have now computed a gradient for the variable x. Part of the power of PyTorch and automatic differentiation is that you can make the function f(x) do almost anything, as long as it is implemented using PyTorch functions. The code we wrote for computing the gradient of x will not change. PyTorch handles all the details of how to compute it for us.

1.3.3 *Putting it together: Minimizing a function with derivatives*

Now that PyTorch can compute gradients for us, we can use the automatic differentiation of our PyTorch function $f(x)$ to numerically find the answer $f(2) = 0$. We are going to describe it first using mathematical notation and then in code.

We start with our current guess, $x_{cur} = -3.5$. I chose 3.5 arbitrarily; in real life, you would usually pick a random value. We also keep track of our previous guess using x_{prev}. Since we have not done anything yet, it is fine to set the previous step to any large value (e.g., $x_{prev} = x_{cur} * 100$).

Next, we compare whether our current and previous guesses are similar. We do this by checking whether $\|x_{cur} - x_{prev}\|_2 > \epsilon$. The function $\|z\|_2$ is called the *norm* or *2-norm*. Norms are the most common and standard ways of measuring *magnitude* for vectors and matrices. For one-dimensional cases (like this one), the 2-norm is the same as the absolute value. If we do not explicitly state what kind of norm we are talking about, you should always assume the 2-norm. The value ϵ is a common mathematical notation to refer to an arbitrary small value. So the way to read this is

the difference between our
previous and current solution

is greater than

a small value

$$\|x_{cur} - x_{prev}\|_2 \qquad > \qquad \epsilon$$

Now we know that $\|x_{cur} - x_{prev}\|_2 > \epsilon$ is how we check whether there are large ($> \epsilon$) magnitude ($\|\cdot\|_2$) changes ($x_{cur} - x_{prev}$) between our guesses. If this is false, $\|x_{cur} - x_{prev}\|_2 \le \epsilon$, which means the change was small and we can stop. Once we stop, we accept x_{cur} as our answer to the value of x that minimized $f(x)$ If not, we need a new, *better* guess.

To get this new guess, we move in the *opposite* direction of the derivative. This looks like this: $x_{cur} = x_{cur} - \eta \cdot f'(x_{cur})$. The value η is called the *learning rate* and is usually a small value like $\eta = 0.1$ or $\eta = 0.01$. We do this because the gradient $f'(x)$ tells us which way to move but only gives us a *relative* answer about how far away we are. It doesn't tell us exactly how far we should travel in that direction. Since we don't know how far to travel, we want to be conservative and go a little slower. Figure 1.7 shows why.

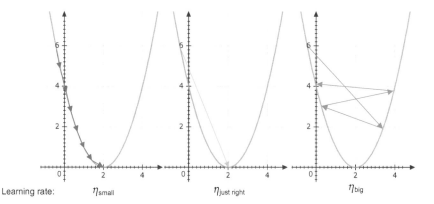

Figure 1.7   Three examples of how the learning rate η (also called step size) impacts learning. On the left, η is smaller than necessary. This still reaches the minimum but takes more steps than needed. If we knew the perfect value of η, we could set it just right, to take the smallest number of steps to the minimum value (middle). On the right, η is too big, which causes divergence. We never reach the solution!

By taking smaller steps in the current direction, we don't "drive past" the answer and have to turn around. Look at the previous example of our function to understand how that happens. If we have the *exactly* correct best value of η (middle image), we can take one step to the minimum. But we do not know what that value is. If we are instead conservative and choose a value that is likely smaller than we need, we may take more steps to get to the answer, but we eventually get there (left image). If we set our learning rate too high, we can end up shooting past the solution and bouncing around it (right image).

That might sound like a lot of scary math, but hopefully you will feel better about it when you look at the code that does the work. It is only a few lines long. At the end of the loop, we print the value of x_{cur} and see that it is equal to 2.0; PyTorch found the answer. Notice that when we define a PyTorch `Tensor` object, it has a child member `.grad` that stores the computed gradients for that variable, as well as a `.data` member that holds the underlying value. You usually shouldn't access either of these fields unless you have a specific reason to; for now, we are using them to demonstrate the mechanics of autograd:

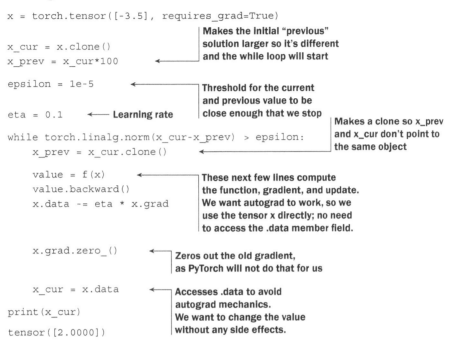

```
x = torch.tensor([-3.5], requires_grad=True)

x_cur = x.clone()
x_prev = x_cur*100          ◄─── Makes the initial "previous"
                                 solution larger so it's different
                                 and the while loop will start

epsilon = 1e-5              ◄─── Threshold for the current
                                 and previous value to be
eta = 0.1      ◄── Learning rate  close enough that we stop

while torch.linalg.norm(x_cur-x_prev) > epsilon:
    x_prev = x_cur.clone()  ◄───  Makes a clone so x_prev
                                  and x_cur don't point to
                                  the same object

    value = f(x)           ◄─── These next few lines compute
    value.backward()            the function, gradient, and update.
    x.data -= eta * x.grad      We want autograd to work, so we
                                use the tensor x directly; no need
                                to access the .data member field.

    x.grad.zero_()         ◄─── Zeros out the old gradient,
                                as PyTorch will not do that for us

    x_cur = x.data         ◄─── Accesses .data to avoid
                                autograd mechanics.
print(x_cur)                    We want to change the value
                                without any side effects.
tensor([2.0000])
```

What is this backpropagation I keep hearing about?

Many books begin their discussion of deep learning with an algorithm called *backpropagation*. This is the name of the original algorithm used to compute all the gradients in a neural network. Personally, I think backpropagation is a very intimidating place to start, as it involves a lot more math and drawing graphs, but it is fully encapsulated by automatic differentiation. With modern frameworks like PyTorch, you don't need to know about the mechanics of backpropagation to get started. If you want to understand backpropagation and how it works with automatic differentiation, I like the approach in chapter 6 of Andrew W. Trask's book, *Grokking Deep Learning* (Manning, 2019).

1.4 Optimizing parameters

What we just did, finding the minimum of a function $f(\cdot)$, is called *optimization*. Because we specify the goal of our network using a loss function $\ell(\cdot)$, we can optimize $f(\cdot)$ to minimize our loss. If we reach a loss $\ell(\cdot) = 0$, our network appears to have solved the problem. This is why we care about optimization and is foundational to how most

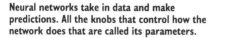

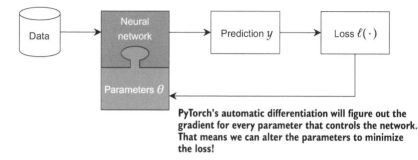

Figure 1.8 How neural networks use the loss $\ell(\cdot)$ and optimization process. The neural network is controlled by its parameters θ. To make useful predictions about the data, we need to alter the parameters. We do so by first computing the loss $\ell(\cdot)$, which tells us how badly the network is doing. Since we want to minimize the loss, we can use the gradient to alter the parameters! This gets the network to make useful predictions.

modern neural networks are trained today. Figure 1.8 shows a simplification of how it works.

Because of how important optimization is, PyTorch includes two additional concepts to help us: parameters and optimizers. A `Parameter` of a model is a value that we alter using an `Optimizer` to try to reduce our loss $\ell(\cdot)$. We can easily convert any tensor into a `Parameter` using the `nn.Parameter` class. To do that, let's re-solve the previous problem of minimizing $f(x) = (x - 2)^2$ with an initial guess of $x_{cur} = 3.5$. The first thing we do is create a `Parameter` object for the value of x, since that is what we are going to alter:

```
x_param = torch.nn.Parameter(torch.tensor([-3.5]), requires_grad=True)
```

The object `x_param` is now a `nn.Parameter`, which behaves the same way tensors do. We can use a `Parameter` anywhere we would use a tensor in PyTorch, and the code will work fine. But now we can create an `Optimizer` object. The simplest optimizer we use is called SGD, which stands for *stochastic gradient descent*. The word *gradient* is there because we are using the gradients/derivatives of functions. *Descent* means we are minimizing or *descending* to a lower value of the function that we are minimizing. We get to the *stochastic* part in the next chapter.

To use SGD, we need to create the associated object with a `list` of `Parameters` that we want to adjust. We can also specify the learning rate η or accept the default. The following code specifies η to match the original code:

```
optimizer = torch.optim.SGD([x_param], lr=eta)
```

Now we can rewrite the previous ugly loop into something cleaner that looks much closer to how we train neural networks in practice. We will loop over the optimization problem a fixed number of times, which we often call *epochs*. The `zero_grad` method does the cleanup we did manually before for every parameter passed in as an input. We compute our loss, call `.backward()` on that loss, and then ask the optimizer to perform one `.step()` of the optimization:

```
for epoch in range(60):
    optimizer.zero_grad()    ←— x.grad.zero_()
    loss_incurred = f(x_param)
    loss_incurred.backward()
    optimizer.step()    ←— x.data -= eta * x.grad
print(x_param.data)
```

The code prints out `tensor(2.0000)`, just like before. This will make our lives easier when we have literally *millions* of parameters in our network.

You'll notice a significant change in this code: we are not optimizing until we hit a gradient of zero or the difference between the previous and current solutions is very small. Instead, we are doing something dumber: a fixed number of steps. In deep learning, we rarely get to a loss of zero, and we would have to wait way too long for that to happen. So most people pick a fixed number of epochs that they are willing to wait for and then see what the results look like at the end. This way, we get an answer faster, and it's usually good enough to use.

Why PyTorch?

There are many deep learning frameworks, including TensorFlow and Keras, MXNet, others like fast.ai built on top of PyTorch, and newer ones like JAX. My opinion is that PyTorch sits at a better balance between "make things easy" and "make things accessible" than most of the other tools. The NumPy-like function calls make development fairly easy and, more importantly, easier to debug. While PyTorch has nice abstractions like the `Optimizer`, we have just seen how painless it is to switch between different levels of abstraction. This is another nice feature that makes debugging easier when you hit a strange bugs or want to try an exotic idea. PyTorch is also flexible for use outside classical deep learning tasks. The other platforms have their own strengths and weaknesses, but these are the reasons I've chosen PyTorch for this book.

1.5 Loading dataset objects

We have learned a little about the basic PyTorch tools. Now we want to start training a neural network. But first we need some data. Using the common notation of ML, we need a set of input data X and associated output labels y. In PyTorch, we represent that with a `Dataset` object. By using this interface, PyTorch provides efficient loaders that automatically handle using multiple CPU cores to pre-fetch the data and keep a limited amount of data in memory at a time. Let's start by loading a familiar dataset from scikit-learn: MNIST. We convert it from a NumPy array to the form PyTorch likes.

PyTorch uses a `Dataset` class to represent a dataset, and it encodes the information about how many items are in the dataset and how to get the nth item in the dataset. Let's see what that looks like:

```
from torch.utils.data import Dataset
from sklearn.datasets import fetch_openml

X, y = fetch_openml('mnist_784', version=1, return_X_y=True)
print(X.shape)

(70000, 784)
```

Loads data from https://www.openml.org/d/554

We have loaded the classic MNIST dataset with a total of 70,000 rows and 784 features. Now we will create a simple `Dataset` class that takes in `X, y` as input. We need to define a `__getitem__` method, which will return the data and label as a `tuple(inputs, outputs)`. The `inputs` are the objects we want to give to our model as inputs, and the `outputs` are used for the output. We also need to implement the `__len__` function that returns how large the dataset is:

```
class SimpleDataset(Dataset):

    def __init__(self, X, y):
        super(SimpleDataset, self).__init__()
        self.X = X
        self.y = y
    def __getitem__(self, index):
        inputs = torch.tensor(self.X[index,:], dtype=torch.float32)
        targets = torch.tensor(int(self.y[index]), dtype=torch.int64)
        return inputs, targets

    def __len__(self):
        return self.X.shape[0]
dataset = SimpleDataset(X, y)
```

This "work" could have gone in the constructor, but you should get into the habit of placing it in getitem.

Makes a PyTorch dataset

Notice that we do the minimal amount of work in the constructor and instead move it into the `__getitem__` function. This is intentional design and a habit you should emulate when doing deep learning work. In many cases, we need to do non-trivial preprocessing, preparation, and conversions to get our data into a form that a neural network can learn from. If you put those tasks into the `__getitem__` function, you get the benefit of PyTorch doing the work on an as-needed basis while you wait for your GPU to finish processing some other batch of data, making your overall process more compute efficient. This becomes really important when you work on larger datasets where preprocessing would cause a long delay up front or require extra memory, and doing the prep only when needed can save you a lot of storage.

> **NOTE** You may wonder why we use `int64` as the tensor type for the targets. Why not `int32` or even `int8`, if we know our labels are in a smaller range, or `uint32` if no negative values will occur? The unsatisfying answer is that for any situation where `int` types are required, PyTorch is hardcoded to work only with `int64`, so you just have to use it. Similarly, when floating-point values are needed, most of PyTorch will only work with `float32`, so you have to use `float32` instead of `float64` or other types. There are exceptions, but they are not worth getting into while learning the fundamentals.

Now we have a simple dataset object. It keeps the entire dataset in memory, which is OK for small datasets, but we want to fix it in the future. We can confirm that the dataset still has 70,000 examples, and each example has 784 features, as before, and quickly confirm that the length and index functions we implemented work as expected:

```
print("Length: ", len(dataset))
example, label = dataset[0]
print("Features: ", example.shape)     ←—— Returns 784
print("Label of index 0: ", label)

Length: 70000
Features: torch.Size([784])
Label of index 0: tensor(5)
```

MNIST is a dataset of hand-drawn numbers. We can visualize this by reshaping the data back into an image to confirm that our data loader is working:

```
plt.imshow(example.reshape((28,28)))
```

```
[34]:   <matplotlib.image.AxesImage at 0x7f4721b9fc50>
```

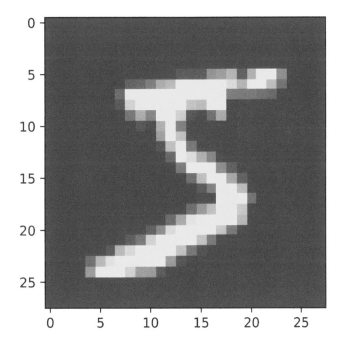

1.5.1   Creating a training and testing split

Now we have all of our data in one dataset. However, like good ML practitioners, we should create a training split and a testing split. In some cases, we have a dedicated training and testing dataset. If that is the case, you should create two separate `Dataset` objects—one for training and one for testing—from the respective data sources.

In this case, we have one dataset. PyTorch has a simple utility to break the corpus into train and test splits. Let's say we want 20% of the data to be used for testing. We can do that as follows using the `random_split` method:

```
train_size = int(len(dataset)*0.8)
test_size = len(dataset)-train_size

train_dataset, test_dataset = torch.utils.data.random_split(dataset,
     (train_size, test_size))
print("{} examples for training and {} for testing".format(
     len(train_dataset), len(test_dataset)))

56000 examples for training and 14000 for testing
```

Now we have train and test sets. In reality, the first 60,000 points are the standard training set for MNIST, and the last 10,000 are the standard test set. But the point was to show you the function for creating randomized splits yourself.

With that, we have learned about all of the foundational tools that PyTorch provides:

- A NumPy-like tensor API, which supports GPU acceleration

- Automatic differentiation, which lets us solve optimization problems

- An abstraction for datasets

We will build on this foundation, and you may notice that it starts to impact how you think about neural networks in the future. They do not magically do what is asked, but they try to numerically solve a goal specified by a loss function $\ell(\cdot)$. We need to be careful in how we define or choose $\ell(\cdot)$ because that will determine what the algorithm learns.

Exercises

Share and discuss your solutions on the Manning online platform at Inside Deep Learning Exercises (https://liveproject.manning.com/project/945). Once you submit your own answers, you will be able to see the solutions submitted by other readers, and see which ones the author judges to be the best.

1 Write a series of `for` loops that compute the average value in `torch_tensor3d`.

2 Write code that indexes into `torch_tensor3d` and prints out the value 13.

3 For every power of 2 (i.e., 2^i or `2**i`) up to 2^{11}, create a random matrix $X \in \mathbb{R}^{2^i, 2^i}$ (i.e., `X.shape` should give (`2**i`, `2**i`)). Time how long it takes to compute XX (i.e., `X @ X`) on a CPU and on a GPU, and plot the speedup. For what matrix sizes is the CPU faster than the GPU?

4 We used PyTorch to find the numeric solution to $f(x) = (x-2)^2$. Write code that finds the solution to $f(x) = \sin(x-2) \cdot (x+2)^2 + \sqrt{|\cos(x)|}$. What answer do you get?

5 Write a new function that takes two inputs, x and y, where

$$f(x, y) = \exp\left(\sin(x)^2\right) / (x-y)^2 + (x-y)^2$$

Use an Optimizer with initial parameter values of $x = 0.2$ and $y = 10$. What do they converge to?

6 Create a function libsvm2Dataset that takes a path to a libsvm dataset file (see https://www.csie.ntu.edu.tw/ cjlin/libsvmtools/datasets/ for many that you can download) and create a new dataset object. Check that it is the correct length and that each row has the expected number of features.

7 **Challenging**: Use NumPy's memmap functionality to write the MNIST dataset to disk. Then create a MemmapedSimpleDataset that takes the mem-mapped file as input, reading the matrix from disk to create PyTorch tensors in the __getitem__ method. Why do you think this would be useful?

Summary

- PyTorch represents almost everything using tensors, which are multidimensional arrays.

- Using a GPU, PyTorch can accelerate any operation done using tensors.

- PyTorch tracks what we do with tensors to perform automatic differentiation, which means it can calculate gradients.

- We can use gradients to minimize a function; the values altered by a gradient are parameters.

- We use a loss function to quantify how well a network is doing at a task and gradients to minimize that loss, which results in learning the parameters of the network.

- PyTorch provides a Dataset abstraction so that we can let PyTorch deal with some nuisance tasks and minimize memory usage.

Fully connected networks

This chapter covers

- Implementing a training loop in PyTorch
- Changing loss functions for regression and classification problems
- Implementing and training a fully connected network
- Training faster using smaller batches of data

Now that we understand how PyTorch gives us tensors to represent our data and parameters, we can progress to building our first neural networks. This starts with showing how *learning* happens in PyTorch. As we described in chapter 1, learning is based on the principle of optimization: we can compute a loss for how well we are doing and use gradients to minimize that loss. This is how the parameters of a network are "learned" from the data and is also the basis of many different machine learning (ML) algorithms. For these reasons, optimization of loss functions is the foundation PyTorch is built from. So to implement any kind of neural network in PyTorch, we must phrase the problem as an optimization problem (remember that this is also called *function minimization*).

In this chapter, we first learn how to set up this optimization approach to learning. It is a widely applicable concept, and the code we write will be usable for almost any neural network. This process is called a *training loop* and even works for simple bread-and-butter ML algorithms like linear and logistic regression. Since we are focusing on the mechanics of training, we will start with these two basic algorithms so we can stay focused on how training loops work in PyTorch for classification and regression.

The vector of weights that makes a logistic/linear regression is also called a *linear layer* or a *fully connected* layer. This means both can be considered a single layer model in PyTorch. Since neural networks can be described as a sequence of layers, we will modify our original logistic and linear models to become full-fledged neural networks. In doing so, you will learn the importance of a nonlinear layer and how logistic and linear regression are related to each other and to neural networks.

After mastering these concepts of a training loop, classification and regression loss functions, and defining a fully connected neural network, we will have covered the foundational concepts of deep learning that will reoccur in almost every model you will ever train. To round out the chapter, we will refactor our code into a convenient helper function and learn the practical utility of training on small groups of data called *batches* instead of using the entire dataset.

2.1 Neural networks as optimization

In chapter 1, we used PyTorch's *automatic differentiation* capability for optimizing (read, minimizing) a function. We defined a loss function to minimize and used the `.backward()` function to compute gradients, which told us how to alter the parameters to minimize the function. If we *make the input to the loss function a neural network*, we can use this exact same approach to train a neural network. This creates a process called a *training loop* with three major components: the training data (with correct answers), the model and loss function, and the update via gradients. These three components are outlined in figure 2.1.

2.1.1 Notation of training a neural network

Before we start, let's introduce some standard notation we reuse throughout this book. We use x to denote input features and $f()$ to denote a neural network model. The label associated with x is denoted with y. Our model takes in x and produces a prediction $\hat{y}$. Written out, this becomes $\hat{y} = f(x)$. This notation is widely used in deep learning papers, and getting familiar with it will help you stay up to date as new approaches are developed.

Our model needs parameters to adjust. Changing the parameters allows the network to alter its predictions to try to reduce the loss function. We will denote in abstract *all* the parameters of our model using Θ. If we want to be explicit, we might say $\hat{y} = f_\Theta(x)$ to state that the model's prediction and behavior depend on the value of its parameters Θ. You will also see Θ called the *state* of the model.

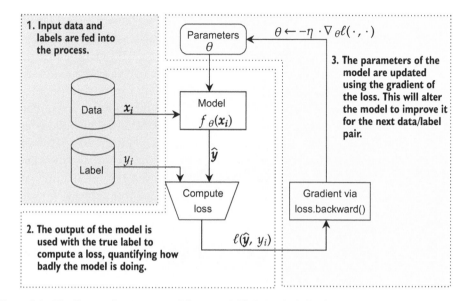

Figure 2.1   The three major steps to training a model in PyTorch. 1. The input data drives learning. 2. The model is used to make a prediction, and a loss scores how much the prediction and true label differ. 3. PyTorch's automatic differentiation is used to update the parameters of the model, improving its predictions.

We have a notation and language for describing our model, but we also need a way to frame the goal as function minimization. To do this, we use the concept of a *loss function*. The loss function *quantifies* how badly our model is doing at the goal of predicting the ground truth y. If y is our goal and $\hat{y}$ is the prediction, we will denote our loss function as $\ell(\hat{y}, y)$.

Now we have all we need to abstractly describe learning as a function minimization problem. Say we have a training set with N examples, which is trained by optimizing the equation $\min_{\Theta} \sum_{i=1}^{N} \ell(f_{\Theta}(\boldsymbol{x_i}), y_i)$. Let's write out what this equation says in English; we will color-code each English description to the math that says the same thing:

Alter the parameters θ to minimize the error/loss of the neural network's prediction against the correct predictions over the entire dataset.

$$\min_{\theta} \quad \sum_{i=1}^{N} \quad \ell\big(f_{\theta}(\boldsymbol{x_i}), \quad y_i \quad \big)$$

By looking at each piece of the math, we can see how this is just describing our goal and that the math allows us to convey a long sentence in less space. As code, it might instead look like this:[1]

```
def F(X, y, f, theta):
    total_loss = 0
    for i in range(N):
        total_loss += loss(f(X[i,:], theta), y[i])
    return total_loss
```

The summation ($\sum_{i=1}^{N}$) goes over all N pairs of input (x_i) and output (y_i) and determines how badly ($\ell(\cdot,\cdot)$) we are doing. This gets us the equation that computes the loss but doesn't minimize it. The big question is: how do we adjust Θ to do this minimization?

We do this by gradient descent, which is why PyTorch provides automatic differentiation. Suppose Θ_k is the *current* state of our model, which we want to improve. How do we find the next state Θ_{k+1}, which hopefully reduces our model's loss? The equation we want to solve is $\Theta_{k+1} = \Theta_k - \eta \cdot \frac{1}{N} \sum_{i=1}^{N} \nabla_{\Theta_k} \ell(f_{\Theta_k}(x_i), y_i)$. Again, let's write out what this equation says in English and map it back to the symbols:

The new parameters θ_{k+1} are equal to the old parameters θ_k minus the

gradient with respect to the old parameters of the error/loss of the

neural network's prediction against the correct predictions

averaged over the entire dataset, and down-weighted by the learning rate.

$$\theta_{k+1} = \theta_k - \eta \cdot \frac{1}{N}\sum_{i=1}^{N} \nabla_{\theta_k} \ell\left(f_{\theta_k}(x_i), \ y_i \ \right)$$

This equation shows the math for what is known as *gradient descent*. It looks almost exactly the same as what we did in chapter 1 to optimize a simple function. This biggest difference is the fancy new ∇ symbol. This *nabla* symbol ∇ is used to denote the *gradient*. In the last chapter, we used the terms *derivative* and *gradient* interchangeably because we had only *one* parameter. Since we have a set of parameters now, the gradient is the language we use to refer to the derivative with respect to every parameter. If we want to alter only a select subset z of the parameters, we write that as ∇_z. This means ∇ will be a tensor with one value for *every* parameter.

---

[1] A common convention in some ML research: when you have a larger function to optimize that is composed of the total loss over many smaller items, denote the larger function as F and the inner function as f. This is not hard and fast, but I like using common notations so you get familiar with them—even if they aren't very informative.

The gradient (∇) tells us how to adjust Θ, and just as before, we head in the opposite direction of the sign. The important thing to remember is that PyTorch provides automatic differentiation. That means if we use the PyTorch API and framework, we do not have to worry about how to compute ∇_Θ. We don't have to keep track of everything in Θ, either.

All we *need* to do is define what our model $f(\cdot)$ looks like and what our loss function $\ell(\cdot, \cdot)$ is. That will take care of almost all the work for us. We can write a function that performs this whole process.

2.1.2 *Building a linear regression model*

The framework we have described to train a model $f(\cdot)$ using gradient descent is widely applicable. The process demonstrated by figure 2.1 of iterating over the data and performing these gradient updates is the training loop. Using PyTorch and this approach, we can re-create many types of ML methods, like linear and logistic regression. To do so, we simply need to define $f(\cdot)$ in the correct manner. We will start by re-creating one of the bread-and-butter algorithms, linear regression, to introduce the code infrastructure that PyTorch provides for us to build into a larger neural network later.

The first thing to do is make sure we have all the needed standard imports. From PyTorch, this includes `torch.nn` and `torch.nn.functional`, which provide common building blocks that we use throughout this book. `torch.utils.data` has the tools for working with `Datasets`, and `idlmam` provides code we have written in previous chapters as we progress:

```
import torch
import torch.nn as nn
import torch.nn.functional as F
from torch.utils.data import *
from idlmam import *
```

2.1.3 *The training loop*

Now that we have those additional imports, let's start by writing a *training loop*. Assume we have a loss function `loss_func` ($\ell(\cdot, \cdot)$) that takes a `prediction` ($\hat{y}$) and a `target` (y), returning a single score for how well a `model` ($f(\cdot)$) has done. We need an iterator that loads the training data for us to train on.[2] This `training_loader` will gives us pairs of `inputs` with their associated `labels` for training.

Figure 2.2 shows the steps of a training loop. The yellow Prep section shows the object creation that needs to be done before training can start. We have to pick the device that will do all the computations (normally a GPU), define our model $f(\cdot)$, and create an optimizer for the model's parameters θ. The red regions indicate the start/repetition of the loop, which provides new data for us to train on. The blue region computes the

---

[2]   You could have all your data in a giant array, but that is a bad practice because you have your entire dataset in memory at all times. Iterators can load the data on the fly, which avoids excess memory usage. This is critical when you work with datasets larger than your computer memory.

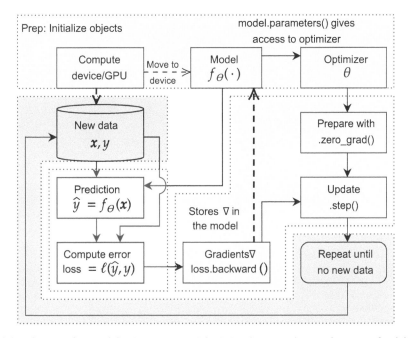

Figure 2.2 Diagram of the training loop process. It includes the same three major steps of training a model in PyTorch that we originally described, with matching color-coding. New is the initialization of objects that are reused in every training loop. Solid areas show steps, and dashed arrows show effects.

prediction $\hat{y}$ and loss $\ell(\hat{y}, y)$ for the model with its *current* parameters Θ. The green section takes the loss and computes the gradients and updates to alter the parameters Θ. Notice that the colors match the steps we saw in figure 2.1, but with a little more detail showing the PyTorch functions we need to call.

Using PyTorch, we can write a minimal amount of code that is enough to train many different kinds of neural networks. The `train_simple_network` function in the next code block follows all the parts of the figure 2.2 process. First we create an `optimizer` that takes in the model's `parameters()` Θ that will be altered. We then move the model to the correct compute `device` and repeat the optimization process for some number of `epochs`. Each epoch means we used every data point x_i *once*.

Each epoch involves putting the model into training mode with `model.train()`. The `training_loader` gives us our data in groups of tuples (x, y), which we move to the same compute `device`. The inner loop over these tuples cleans up the optimizer state with `zero_grad()` and then passes the `inputs` to the `model` to get a prediction `y_hat`. Our `loss_fun` takes in the prediction `y_hat` and the true `labels` to calculate a `loss`, describing how badly our network has done. Then we compute the gradients with `loss.backward()` and take a `step()` with the `optimizer`.

The code for the simple training loop is as follows:

Places the model on the correct compute resource (CPU or GPU)

Yellow step is done here. Creates the optimizer and moves the model to the compute device. SGD is stochastic gradient descent over the parameters Θ.

```
def train_simple_network(model, loss_func, training_loader,
    epochs=20, device="cpu"):
    optimizer = torch.optim.SGD(model.parameters(), lr=0.001)

    model.to(device)
```

The two for loops handle the red steps, iterating through all the data (batches) multiple times (epochs).

```
    for epoch in tqdm(range(epochs), desc="Epoch"):
        model = model.train()          ← Puts our model in training mode
        running_loss = 0.0

        for inputs, labels in tqdm(training_loader, desc="Batch", leave=False):
            inputs = moveTo(inputs, device)
            labels = moveTo(labels, device)
```

Moves the batch of data to the device we are using. This is the last red step.

```
            optimizer.zero_grad()
```

First a yellow step: prepare the optimizer. Most PyTorch code does this first to make sure everything is in a clean and ready state. PyTorch stores gradients in a mutable data structure, so we need to set it to a clean state before we use it. Otherwise, it will have old information from a previous iteration.

This line and the next perform the two blue steps. This line computes $f_\theta(x_i)$.

```
            y_hat = model(inputs)
```

Computes the loss

```
            loss = loss_func(y_hat, labels)
```

The remaining two yellow steps compute the gradient and ".step()" the optimizer. The call on this line computes ∇_Θ.

```
            loss.backward()

            optimizer.step()
```

Updates all the parameters
$$\Theta_{k+1} = \Theta_k \eta \cdot \nabla_{\Theta_k} \ell(\hat{y}, y)$$

```
            running_loss += loss.item()
```

Grabs information we would like to have

2.1.4   Defining a dataset

The code we have just described is sufficient to train almost all of the neural networks we design during this book. Now we need some data, a network, and a loss function to work with. Let's start by training a simple *linear regression* model. You should recall from a ML class or training that in *regression* problems, we want to predict a numeric value. For example, predicting the miles per gallon (mpg) of a car based on its features (e.g., weight in pounds, engine size, year produced) would be a regression problem because the mpg could be 20, 24, 33.7, or hypothetically even 178.1342 or almost any number.

Here we've created a synthetic regression problem with linear and nonlinear components, with some noise added to make it interesting. Because of how strong the linear component is, a linear model will do OK but won't be perfect:

```
X = np.linspace(0, 20, num=200)          ← Creates one-dimensional input
y = X + np.sin(X)*2 + np.random.normal(size=X.shape)          ← Creates output
sns.scatterplot(x=X, y=y)
```

`[6]:  <AxesSubplot:>`

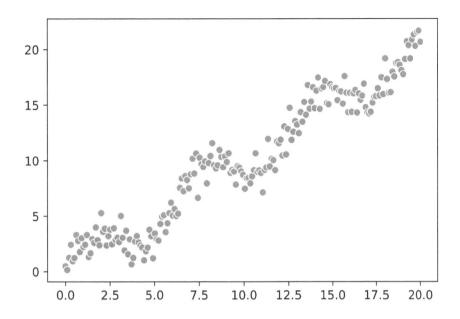

We have created a simple toy problem with a strong linear trend and a smaller but consistent oscillation up and down. We use toy problems like this one to do experiments so we can see the results and get a more intuitive understanding of what is happening. But we need the problem in a form that PyTorch will understand. The next code block creates a simple dataset object that knows we have a one-dimensional problem. The training data is shaped as an $(n, 1)$ matrix, where n is the number of data points. The labels (y) take a similar form. When we get an item, we grab the correct row of the dataset and return a PyTorch `tensor` object that is a `torch.float32` type, which is the default type for most things in PyTorch.

Along with the `Dataset`, we also need a `DataLoader`, which is already implemented for us by PyTorch. Whereas the `Dataset` defines how to get any specific data point, the `DataLoader` decides which data points to get. The standard approach is to pick the data points at random one at a time, which ensures that your model learns the data and not the order of the data.[3] There is a lot of built-in functionality with PyTorch's `DataLoader`, and we introduce some of it on an as-needed basis, but feel free to learn more in the documentation at https://pytorch.org/docs/stable/data.html. The most important feature to know about a `DataLoader` is that while your model is busy training on the GPU, your `DataLoader` is busy fetching the next data so the GPU is as busy as possible. (This type of performance optimization is often called *pipelining*.)

---

[3] There is some nice math that better justifies this, but we are not going to go there.

Here's the code:

```
class Simple1DRegressionDataset(Dataset):
    def __init__(self, X, y):
        super(Simple1DRegressionDataset, self).__init__()
        self.X = X.reshape(-1,1)
        self.y = y.reshape(-1,1)
    def __getitem__(self, index):
        return torch.tensor(self.X[index,:], dtype=torch.float32),
            torch.tensor(self.y[index], dtype=torch.float32)

    def __len__(self):
        return self.X.shape[0]
training_loader = DataLoader(Simple1DRegressionDataset(X, y),  shuffle=True)
```

How reshape works

The `reshape` function is important to understand because we use its behavior throughout this book. Suppose we have a tensor with six total values. That could be a vector
of length 6, a 2×3 matrix, 3×2, or a tensor with three dimensions where one dimension has a size of "1." As long as the total number of values stays the same, we can
reinterpret the tensor as having a different shape with the values moved around. The
following figure shows how this can be done. What is special about `reshape` is that it
lets us specify all but one of the dimensions, and it automatically puts the leftovers
into the unspecified dimension. This leftover dimension is denoted with –1; as we add
more dimensions, there are more ways we can ask NumPy or PyTorch to reshape a
tensor.

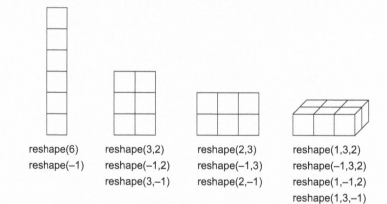

reshape(6)	reshape(3,2)	reshape(2,3)	reshape(1,3,2)
reshape(–1)	reshape(–1,2)	reshape(–1,3)	reshape(–1,3,2)
	reshape(3,–1)	reshape(2,–1)	reshape(1,–1,2)
			reshape(1,3,–1)

Four different tensor shapes that can be used to represent the same six values. The `reshape` function
takes as many arguments as you want axes in the resulting tensor. If you know the exact size, you can
specify it; or if you don't know the size for one axis, you can use –1 to indicate a leftover spot.

The `view` function has the same kind of behavior. Why have two functions with the
same behavior? Because `view` uses less memory and can be faster but can throw

errors if used inappropriately. You will learn the details with more advanced use of PyTorch; but for the sake of simplicity, you can *always* call `reshape` safely.

> **NOTE** If you have a total of N items in your tensor, you can reshape it into any new number of dimensions as long as the final number of items adds to N. So we can turn the $N = 6$ item tensor into a shape of $(3, 2)$ because $3 \times 2 = 6$. This also means we can have *any* number of total dimensions if we keep inserting dimensions of size 1. For example, we can turn the $N = 6$ values into a tensor with five dimensions by doing $(3, 1, 1, 2, 1)$ because $3 \times 1 \times 1 \times 2 \times 1 = 6$.

2.1.5 Defining the model

At this point, we have successfully created a training loop and a `Dataset` object to load our dataset. The last thing we are missing is a PyTorch model that implements the linear regression algorithm as a network. This is the Model box from figure 2.2, which I've isolated in figure 2.3.

Figure 2.3 The Model box denotes the neural network $f_\Theta(\cdot)$ that we want to train. This could be a small network or a very complex one. It is encapsulated into one model object with a single set of parameters Θ. The same process works for almost any network definition.

Defining the network we will use is very easy in this case. We want a simple linear function, and a linear function means a weight matrix W. Applying a weight matrix W to an input x means taking the matrix vector product. So we want a model $f(\cdot)$ that looks like this:

$$f(x) = x^\top \underbrace{}_{\substack{\text{dot product/matrix vector product} \\ \text{between input and linear layer.}}} W^{d,C} \leftarrow \left|\substack{\text{Linear layer/function that takes in} \\ \text{d inputs and produces C outputs.}}\right.$$

The vector x has all of our d features (in this case, $d = 1$), and the matrix W has a row for every feature and a column for every output. We use $W^{d,C}$ to be extra explicit that it is a tensor with d rows and C columns. That's a common notation we use in this book to be precise about the shapes of certain objects. Since we are predicting a single value, this means $C = 1$.

Notice, though, that this linear function is not quite complete. If $x = 0$, then $f(x) = 0$. That's a very strong constraint to have on a model. Instead, we add a *bias term* b that has no interaction with x:

$$f(x) = x^\top \underbrace{W^{d,C}}_{\text{nn.Linear (d,C)}} + b$$

Adding a bias term allows the model to shift its solution to the left or right as needed. Luckily for us, PyTorch has a `Module` that implements a linear function like this, which we can access using `nn.Linear(d, C)`. This creates a linear layer with d inputs and C outputs—exactly what we want.

> **NOTE**   The bias term is always a $+b$ on the side that does not interact with anything else. Because bias terms are almost always used but are annoying and cumbersome to write out, they are often dropped and assumed to exist implicitly. We do that in this book as well. Unless we state otherwise, assume the bias is implicitly there. If you see three weight matrices, assume there are three bias terms, one for each.

Modules are how PyTorch organizes the building blocks of modern neural network design. Modules have a `forward` function that takes inputs and produces an output (we need to implement this if we make our own `Module`), and a `backward` function (PyTorch takes care of this for us unless we have a reason to intervene). Many standard modules are provided in the `torch.nn` package, and we can build new ones out of tensors and `Parameter` and `torch.nn.functional` objects. Modules may also contain other modules, which is how we build larger networks.

2.1.6 *Defining the loss function*

So `nn.Linear` gives us our model $f(\boldsymbol{x})$, but we still need to decide on a loss function ℓ. Again, PyTorch makes this pretty simple for a standard regression problem. Say the ground truth is y, and our prediction is $\hat{y} = f(\boldsymbol{x})$. How do we quantify the difference between y and $\hat{y}$? We can just look at the absolute difference between them: $\ell(y, \hat{y}) = |y - \hat{y}|$.

Why the *absolute* difference? If we did not take the absolute value, $\hat{y} < y$ would produce a positive loss, encouraging the model $f(\boldsymbol{x})$ to make its prediction smaller. But if $\hat{y} > y$, then $y - \hat{y}$ would produce a *negative* loss. If it feels intimidating to reason about this using symbols like y and $\hat{y}$, try plugging in some actual values. So if $\hat{y} = 100$ and $y = 1$, and we computed the loss as $y - \hat{y} = 1 - 100 = -99$, we would end up with a loss of –99! A negative loss would be confusing (what would that be, profit?) and would encourage the network to make its predictions even larger when they were already too big. Our goal is $\hat{y} = y$, but since the network will blindly march forward trying to *minimize* the loss, it will learn to make $\hat{y}$ unrealistically large to exploit a negative loss. This is why we need our loss function to always return zero or a positive value. Otherwise, the loss will not make sense. Remember that the loss function is a penalty for errors, and negative penalties would mean encouragement.

Another option is to take the squared difference between y and $\hat{y}$: $\ell(y, \hat{y}) = (y - \hat{y})^2$. This again results in a function that is zero only if $y = \hat{y}$ and that grows only as y and $\hat{y}$ move farther away from each other.

Both of these options are pre-implemented in PyTorch. The former is called the $L1$ loss, as it corresponds to taking the 1-norm of the different (i.e., $\|y - \hat{y}\|_1$). The latter is popularly known as the mean squared error (MSE, also called $L2$) loss, and is the most popular, so we will use it going forward:

Loss function $\ell(y, \hat{y})$	PyTorch module
$\|y - \hat{y}\|$	`torch.nn.L1Loss`
$(y - \hat{y})^2$	`torch.nn.MSELoss`

Choosing between two loss functions

You have two loss functions, L1 and MSE, both of which are appropriate for a regression problem. How do you choose which one to use? We won't detour into the nuanced differences between loss functions because any one built into PyTorch will give reasonable results. You just need to know which loss functions are appropriate for which type of problem (like regression versus classification).

Getting comfortable with the meaning behind the math will help you to make these choices. In this case, the MSE loss has the squared term, which makes large differences grow larger (e.g., 100^2 will become 10,000); and L1 will keep differences the same (e.g., $|100| = 100$). So if the problem you are trying to solve is one where small differences are OK but large ones are really bad, the MSE loss might be a better choice. If your problem is such that being off by 200 is twice as bad as being off by 100, the L1 loss makes more sense. This is not a complete picture of how to choose between these two options, but it's a good way to make an initial choice.

2.1.7 *Putting it together: Training a linear regression model on the data*

We now have everything we need to create a linear regression: the `Dataset`, the `train_simple_network` function, a `loss_func` ℓ, and a `nn.Linear` model. The following code shows how we can quickly set it all up and pass it to our function to train a model:

```
in_features = 1
out_features = 1
model = nn.Linear(in_features, out_features)
loss_func = nn.MSELoss()

device = torch.device("cuda")
train_simple_network(model, loss_func, training_loader, device=device)
```

Did it work? Do we have a trained model? That's easy to find out, especially since this is a one-dimensional problem. We can just plot our model's prediction for all the data. We will use the `with torch.no_grad()`: context to get those predictions: it tells PyTorch that for any computation done within the scope of the `no_grad()` block, *do not calculate gradients.* We only want gradients to be computed during *training.* The gradient calculations take additional time and memory and can cause bugs if we want to train the model more after performing a prediction. So, good practice is to make sure we use the `no_grad()` block when making predictions. The following code block uses `no_grad()` to get the predictions:

```
with torch.no_grad():
    Y_pred = model(torch.tensor(X.reshape(-1,1), device=device,
 dtype=torch.float32)).cpu().numpy()
```

```
sns.scatterplot(x=X, y=y, color='blue', label='Data')  ◀── The data
sns.lineplot(x=X, y=Y_pred.ravel(), color='red', label='Linear Model') ◀──┐
```

[10]:   <AxesSubplot:>   **What our model learned** ┘

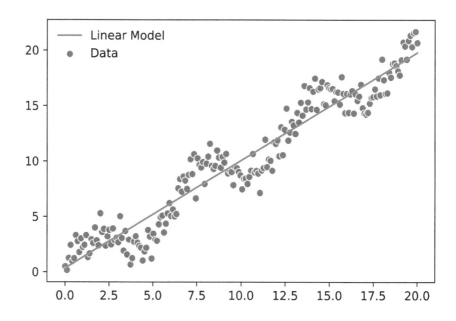

This code plots the result of our network, and it learned a good linear fit to the somewhat nonlinear data. This is exactly what we asked of the model, and the results look correct.

> **NOTE**   Making predictions on new data is also called *inference*. This is common jargon among ML practitioners—particularly in the deep learning community—because neural networks often require a GPU, so deploying a model is a bigger deal. Companies often buy GPUs designed for inference that have less RAM to be more cost-effective.

You have now used all the mechanics and tools for building neural networks. Each of the components we have described—a loss function ℓ, a Module for specifying our network, and the training loop—can be swapped in and out in a piecemeal fashion to build more powerful and complex models.

2.2 Building our first neural network

Now we have learned how to create a training loop and use gradient descent to modify a model so that it learns to solve a problem. This is the foundational framework we will use for all learning in this book. To train a neural network, we only need to replace the `model` object that we defined. The trick is knowing how to define these models. If we do a good job defining a neural network, it should be able to capture and model the nonlinear parts of the data. For our toy example, that means getting the smaller oscillations and not just the larger linear trend.

When we discuss neural networks and deep learning, we are usually talking about *layers*. Layers are the building blocks we use to define our `model`, and most of the PyTorch `Module` classes implement different layers that have different purposes. The linear regression model we just built could be described as having an *input* layer (the input data itself) and a *linear layer* (`nn.Linear`) that made the predictions.

2.2.1 Notation for a fully connected network

Our first neural network will be a simple *feed-forward fully connected* neural network. It's called *feed-forward* because every output from one layer flows directly into the next layer. So each layer has one input and one output and progresses sequentially. It is called *fully connected* because each network input has a connection to everything from the previous layer.

Let's start with what is called a *hidden layer*. The input x is consider the *input layer*, and a $\mathbb{R}^C$ (a vector with C outputs for C predictions) dimensional output is called the *output layer*. In our linear regression model, we essentially had only an input layer and an output layer. You can think of hidden layers as anything sandwiched between input and output.

How do we do that? Well, the easiest option is to stick another matrix between the input and output. So instead of

$$f(x) = x^\top W^{d \times C}$$

we add a second layer with a new matrix, giving us something like this:

$$f(x) = x^\top W^{d \times n}_{(h_1)} W^{n \times C}_{(\text{out})}$$

Notice the new value n of the matrix dimension. It's a new hyperparameter for us to tune and deal with. That means we get to decide what the value of n should be. It is called the *hidden layer size* or *number of neurons* in the first hidden layer. Why neurons?

If you draw every intermediate output as a *node* and draw arrows representing weights, you get what could be described as a *network*. This is shown in figure 2.4. The lines connecting the input to hidden nodes correspond to a `nn.Linear(3, 4)` layer, which is a matrix $W^{3 \times 4}$. Every column of that matrix corresponds to the inputs of one of the $n = 4$ neurons or outputs of that layer. Each row is an input's connection to each output. So if we wanted to know the strength of the connection from the second input

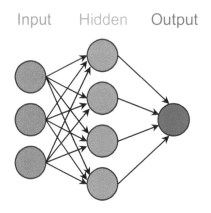

Input   Hidden   Output

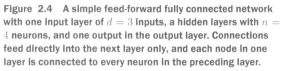

Figure 2.4 **A simple feed-forward fully connected network with one input layer of** $d = 3$ **inputs, a hidden layers with** $n = 4$ **neurons, and one output in the output layer. Connections feed directly into the next layer only, and each node in one layer is connected to every neuron in the preceding layer.**

to the fourth output, we would index `W[1,3]`. In the same fashion, the lines from hidden nodes to the output of the figure are a `nn.Linear(4, 1)` layer.

Notice that all the arrows connecting nodes/neurons to each other only move from left to right. That is the feed-forward property. Also note that each node in one layer is connected to every other node in the next layer. That is the fully connected property.

This network interpretation was in part inspired by how neurons in the brain work. A simple toy model of a neuron and its connections is shown in figure 2.5. On the left is a neuron, which has many *dendrites* that are connected to other neurons and act as the inputs. The dendrites get electrical signals when other neurons fire and carry those signals to the nucleus (center) of the neuron, which sums all the signals together. Finally, the neuron emits a new signal out from its *axon*.

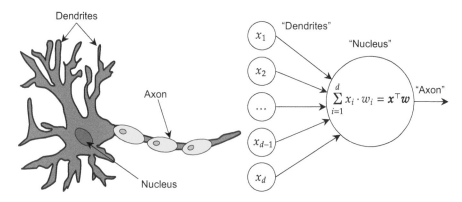

Figure 2.5 **Simplified diagram of biological neuron connectivity. By analogy, dendrites are connections/ weights between neurons, and the axon caries the result of the neuron forward. This is a loose inspiration and an oversimplification of how real neurons work.**

WARNING   Although neural networks were originally inspired by how neurons are connected and wired in the brain, do not let the analogy drag you too far in. The previous description is a *very* simplified model. A neural network's functionality is very far from what little we know about how the brain works in reality. You should take it as only a mild inspiration, not a literal analogy.

2.2.2 A fully connected network in PyTorch

According to these cool diagrams, and keeping with the idea of adding just one small change, we can insert two linear layers one after the other, we will have our first neural network. This is where the `nn.Sequential` Module comes into play. This is a Module that takes a list or sequence of Modules as its input. It then runs that sequence in a feed-forward fashion, using the output of one Module as the input to the next, until we have no more Modules. Figure 2.6 shows how we can do this for the toy network with three inputs and four hidden neurons.

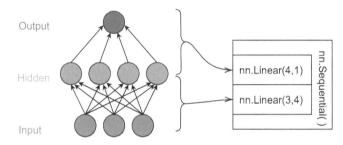

Figure 2.6 **Converting the conceptual feed-forward fully connected network into a PyTorch** `Module`. `nn.Sequential` **is a wrapper that takes two** `nn.Linear` **layers. The first** `nn.Linear` **defines the mapping from input to hidden layer, and the second** `nn.Linear` **defines the mapping from hidden layer to output.**

Rendering this to practice is easy because all the other code we have written will still work. The following code creates a new simple `model` that is a sequence of two `nn.Linear` layers. Then we just pass the `model` into the same `train_simple_network` function and continue as before. This model has one input, one output, and a single hidden layer with 10 neurons:[4]

```
model = nn.Sequential(          ◀──────── Input "layer" is implicitly the input.
    nn.Linear(1, 10),           ◀──────── Hidden layer
    nn.Linear(10, 1),           ◀──────── Output layer
)

train_simple_network(model, loss_func, training_loader)
```

> **NOTE** The `nn.Sequential` class provides the easiest way to specify neural networks in PyTorch, and we use it for *every* network in this book! So, it is worth getting familiar with. Eventually we will build more complex networks that can't be described *entirely* as a feed-forward process. Still, we will use the `nn.Sequential`

---

[4] The size is different from that in the figures because I need 10 neurons to get interesting results, but 10 is way too many to draw in a picture. It's also easier to plot functions with one input instead of three inputs. But I want the figure to show you that all inputs connect to all items in the next layer. A necessary inconsistency, and I apologize.

class to help us organize the subcomponents of a network that can be organized that way. This class is essentially your go-to tool for organizing models in PyTorch.

Now we can perform inference with our fancy neural network that has a hidden layer and see what we get. We use the exact same inference code as before. The only difference is our `model` object, which we've redesigned. You may notice a new NumPy function `ravel()` that is called to make the plot; using this function is the same as calling `reshape(-1)` on a PyTorch tensor, and we call it because `Y_pred` has an initial shape of $(N, 1)$:

```
with torch.no_grad():
    Y_pred = model(torch.tensor(X.reshape(-1,1),    ◀── Shape of (N, 1)
        dtype=torch.float32)).cpu().numpy()
sns.scatterplot(x=X, y=y, color='blue', label='Data')    ◀── The data
sns.lineplot(x=X, y=Y_pred.ravel(), color='red', label='Model')    ◀─┐
```
What our model learned

[12]:   <AxesSubplot:>

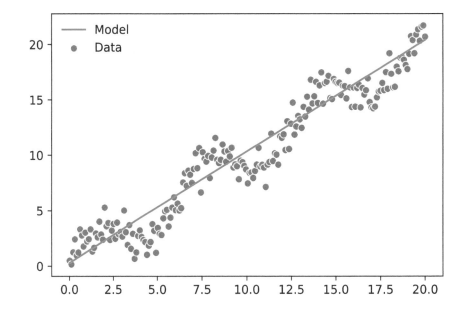

What gives? We made our `model` $f(\cdot)$ more sophisticated, training took longer, and it did about the same or maybe worse! A little linear algebra will explain why this happened. Recall that we defined

$$f(\boldsymbol{x}) = \boldsymbol{x}^\top \boldsymbol{W}_{(h_1)}^{d,n} \boldsymbol{W}_{(\text{out})}^{n,C}$$

Here $\boldsymbol{W}_{(h_1)}^{d \times n}$ is our hidden layer. Since we have one feature $d = 1$ and $n = 10$ hidden units, $\boldsymbol{W}_{(\text{out})}^{n \times C}$ is our output layer, where we still have the $n = 10$ hidden units from the previous layer and $C = 1$ total outputs. But we can simplify the two weight matrices. If we have a matrix with shape (a, b) and a second matrix with shape (b, c) and we multiply them together, we get a new matrix with shape (a, c). That means

$$W_{(h_1)}^{d \times n} W_{(\text{out})}^{n \times C} = \tilde{W}_{d,c}$$

and therefore

$$f(x) = x^\top W_{(h_1)}^{d \times n} W_{(\text{out})}^{n \times C} = x^\top \tilde{W}_{d,c}$$

That's equivalent to the linear model we started with. This shows that *adding any number of sequential linear layers is equivalent to using just one linear layer.* Linear operations beget linear operations and are usually redundant. Placing multiple linear layers one after the other is a common error I see in code written by novice or junior practitioners.

2.2.3 *Adding nonlinearities*

To get any kind of benefit, we need to introduce *nonlinearity* between every step. By inserting a nonlinear function after every linear operation, we allow the network to build up more complex functions. We call nonlinear functions that are used this way *activation functions.* The analogy from biology is that a neuron sums all of its inputs linearly and eventually *fires* or *activates*, sending a signal to other neurons in the brain.

What should we use as our activation functions? The first two we will look at are the *sigmoid* ($\sigma(\cdot)$) and *hyperbolic tangent* ($\tanh(\cdot)$) functions, which were two of the original activation functions and are still widely used.

The tanh function is an historically popular nonlinearity. It maps everything into the range $[-1, 1]$:

$$\tanh(x) = \frac{\sinh x}{\cosh x} = \frac{e^x - e^{-x}}{e^x + e^{-x}}$$

The sigmoid is the historical nonlinearity and is where the notation σ is most often used. It maps everything into the range $[0, 1]$:

$$\sigma(x) = \frac{e^x}{e^x + 1}$$

Let's quickly plot what these look like. The input is on the x-axis, and the activation is on the y-axis:

```
activation_input = np.linspace(-2, 2, num=200)
tanh_activation = np.tanh(activation_input)
sigmoid_activation = np.exp(activation_input)/(np.exp(activation_input)+1)
sns.lineplot(x=activation_input, y=activation_input,
    color='black', label="linear")
sns.lineplot(x=activation_input, y=tanh_activation,
    color='red', label="tanh(x)")
ax = sns.lineplot(x=activation_input, y=sigmoid_activation,
    color='blue', label="$\sigma(x)$")
```

```
ax.set_xlabel('Input value x')
ax.set_ylabel('Activation')
```

[13]: Text(0, 0.5, 'Activation')

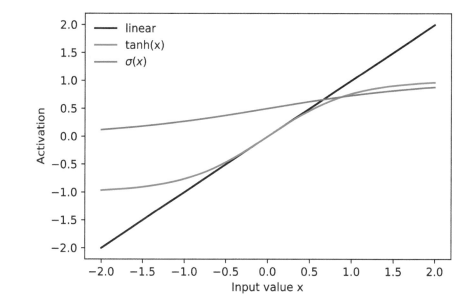

As promised, the sigmoid activation ($\sigma(x)$) maps everything to a minimum of 0 and a maximum of 1. The tanh function goes from –1 to 1. Notice how there is a range of input, around 0, where the tanh function *looks* linear but then diverges away: that's OK and can even be desirable. The important thing from a learning perspective is that neither $\tanh(\cdot)$ or $\sigma(\cdot)$ can be *perfectly* fit by a linear function.

We talk more about the properties of these functions in future chapters. For now, let's use the tanh function. We will define a new model that matches the following:

$$f(\boldsymbol{x}) = \tanh\left(\boldsymbol{x}^\top \boldsymbol{W}_{d\times n}^{(h_1)}\right) \boldsymbol{W}_{n\times C}^{(\text{out})}$$

Instead of stacking nn.Linear layers directly after one another, we call the tanh function after the first linear layer. When using PyTorch, we generally want to end our network with a nn.Linear layer. For this model, we have two nn.Linear layers, so we use $2 - 1 = 1$ activations. This is as simple as adding a nn.Tanh node to our sequential network specification, which PyTorch has built in. Let's see what happens when we train this new model:

```
model = nn.Sequential(
    nn.Linear(1, 10),        ◄──────── Hidden layer
    nn.Tanh(),               ◄──────── Activation
    nn.Linear(10, 1),        ◄──────── Output layer
)

train_simple_network(model, loss_func, training_loader, epochs=200)

with torch.no_grad():
    Y_pred = model(torch.tensor(X.reshape(-1,1),
        dtype=torch.float32)).cpu().numpy()

sns.scatterplot(x=X, y=y, color='blue', label='Data')   ◄──── The data
sns.lineplot(x=X, y=Y_pred.ravel(), color='red', label='Model')  ◄──┐
                                                          What our
                                                          model learned
```

`[15]:   <AxesSubplot:>`

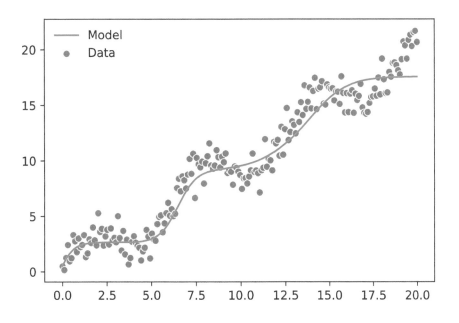

Reproducibility of numbers

At this point in the book, you may notice that you don't always get the *exact* same results I do. You may sometimes get *very* different-looking results. This is *normal* and *OK*. The initial weights for every neural network are random values, and a different set of initial random values may give you a different result. Don't let that scare you off; getting used to the variability in results can be valuable.

(continued)

If you know about random seeds, you may be thinking, "If you set a random seed so that you know what the random results will be, wouldn't that solve the problem?" This is correct at a high level, but unfortunately, the result of the layers in PyTorch are *not* always deterministic. They often exploit hardware-specific optimizations that can slightly alter the results and even change from run to run in odd circumstances. PyTorch is working on supporting more deterministic behavior, but it doesn't work for everything yet, and it doesn't work for all versions of CUDA. If I tried to enable it, it might make everything stop working for you. So, unfortunately, we are stuck with slightly different results every time you run the code.

Another option would be to run each experiment 5 to 15 times and plot the average result with error bars to show the variance of what can happen. But then the code samples would take 5 to 15 times longer to run. I've chosen to run things once to keep the time reasonable.

We can see that the network is now learning a nonlinear function, with bends that move and adapt to match the data's behavior. It's not perfect, though, especially for larger values of the input x on the right side of the plot. We also had to train for many more epochs than we did previously. That's also pretty common. This is part of why we use GPUs so much in deep learning: we have larger models, which means each update requires more computation; and the larger models need more updates to converge, resulting in longer training times.

In general, the more complex a function that needs to be learned, the more rounds of training we have to perform—and we may even get more data. However, there are many ways to improve the quality and rate at which our neural networks learn from the data, which we review in more detail later in the book. For now, our goal is to learn the basics.

2.3   Classification problems

You have now built your first neural network by extending a linear regression model, but what about classification problems? In this situation, you have C different *classes* that an input might belong to. For example, a car could be an SUV, sedan, coupe, or truck. As you may have guessed, you need an output layer that looks like nn.Linear(n, C), where again n is the number of hidden units in the previous layer and C is the number of classes/outputs. It would be difficult to make C predictions if we had fewer than C outputs.

Similar to how we can walk from linear regression to a nonlinear regression neural network, we can make the same walk from logistic regression to a nonlinear classification network. Recall that logistic regression is a popular algorithm for classification problems that finds a linear solution to try to separate C classes.

2.3.1 Classification toy problem

Before we can build a logistic model, we need a dataset. Getting our data loaded and into a `Dataset` object is always the first and most important step when using PyTorch. For this example, we use the `make_moons` class from scikit-learn:

```
from sklearn.datasets import make_moons
X, y = make_moons(n_samples=200, noise=0.05)
sns.scatterplot(x=X[:,0], y=X[:,1], hue=y, style=y)
```

[16]: <AxesSubplot:>

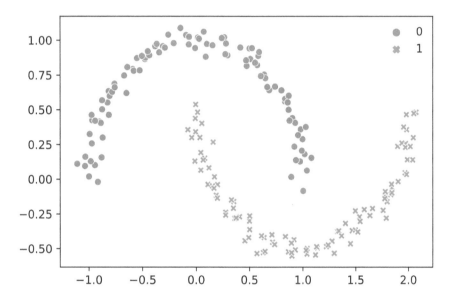

The moons dataset has $d = 2$ input features now, and the scatter plot shows the two classes as circles and crosses. This is a good toy problem since a linear classification model can do an *OK* job of separating circles from crosses but can't *perfectly* solve the problem.

To make our lives easier, we use the built-in `TensorDataset` object to wrap our current data. This only works if we can fit all of our data into RAM. But if you can, this is the easiest way to prepare data. You can use your favorite pandas or NumPy methods to load in the data and then start modeling.

We did make one important change, though. Our vector of labels y is now a `torch.long` rather than a `torch.float32`. Why? Because the labels are now classes, which start from 0 and go up to $C - 1$ to represent C different classes. There is no 0.25 class; only integers are allowed! For this reason, we use the long data type (a 64-bit integer) rather than a floating-point value since we only need to concern ourselves with integers. For example, if our classes were `cat`, `bird`, and `car`, we would use 0, 1, 2 to represent the three classes. You may recognize this as being very close to a one-hot encoding, where each class is given its own dimension. PyTorch does that last step for us under the hood to avoid wastefully representing all the non-present classes as one-hot encoding does:

```
classification_dataset = torch.utils.data.TensorDataset(
    torch.tensor(X, dtype=torch.float32), torch.tensor(y, dtype=torch.long))
training_loader = DataLoader(classification_dataset)
```

Now we define a linear classification model just as we did previously. In this case, we have two features, and we have two outputs (one for each class), so our model is *slightly* bigger. Notice that even though the *target* vector y is represented as a single integer, the network has C explicit outputs. This is because the labels are *absolute*: there is only one true class per data point. The network, however, must always consider all C classes as potential options and make a prediction for each class separately:

```
in_features = 2
out_features = 2
model = nn.Linear(in_features, out_features)
```

2.3.2 *Classification loss function*

The big question is, what do we use as our loss function? This was an easy question to answer when we did a regression problem. We had two inputs, and they were both floating-point values, so we could just subtract them to determine how far the two values were from each other.

This situation is different, though. Now our prediction is $\hat{y} \in \mathbb{R}^C$ because we need a prediction for each of our C different classes. But our labels are one value of a set of integers, $y \in \{0, 1, \ldots, C-1\}$. If we can define a loss function $\ell(\hat{y}, y)$ that takes in a vector of predictions $\hat{y} \in \mathbb{R}^C$ and compare it to a correct class y, we can reuse everything from the training loop in figure 2.2 and our previously defined neural network. Luckily this function already exists, but it's worth talking about in detail because of how foundational it is to everything we do in this book. We need two components: the softmax function and the cross-entropy, which combined are often just called the *cross-entropy loss*.

While many tutorials are happy to say "use cross-entropy" without explaining what it is, we will take a slightly involved detour and walk through the mechanics of cross-entropy so you can build a stronger mental foundation. The essence is to first convert some set of C scores (the values can be any number) into C probabilities (values must be between 0 and 1), and then calculate a loss based on the probability of the true class y. There are many statistical arguments for why it is done this way, and it's OK if you need to read this section more than once or come back to it later.

SOFTMAX

First, we intuitively want the dimension in $\hat{y}$ that has the largest value to correspond to the correct class label y (the same as if we used np.argmax). If we write this in math, we want:

$$y = \underset{i}{\text{argmax}}\, \hat{y}_i$$

$$\downarrow$$

$$\text{np.argmax}(\hat{\boldsymbol{y}})$$

We also want our predictions to be a sensible probability. Why? Suppose the correct class is $y = k$ and we succeed and have $\hat{y}_k$ as the largest value. How right or wrong is this? What if $\hat{y}_k - \hat{y}_j = 0.00001$? The difference is very small, and we want a way to tell the model that it should make the difference larger.

If we make $\hat{y}$ into probabilities, they have to sum up to 1. That means

$$\sum_{i=0}^{C-1} \hat{y}_i = 1$$

$$\downarrow$$

$$\text{np.sum}(\hat{\boldsymbol{y}})$$

This way we know a model is confident in its prediction when $\hat{y}_k = 1$, and all other values of $j \neq k$ result in $\hat{y}_j = 0$. If the model was less confident, we might see $\hat{y}_k = 0.9$; and if it was completely wrong, $\hat{y}_k = 0$. The constraint that $\hat{y}$ sums to 1 makes it easy for us to interpret the results.

But how do we ensure this? The values we get from the last nn.Linear layer could be anything, especially when we first start training and have not yet taught the model about what is correct. We will use the *soft maximum* (or *softmax*) function: it converts everything to a non-negative number and ensures that the values sum up to 1.0. The index k with the largest value will have the largest value afterward as well, *even if it is negative*, as long as every other index is an even smaller number. Smaller values also receive smaller but nonzero values. So softmax gives every value in $0, 1, \ldots, C-1$ a value in the range $[0, 1]$, such that they all sum to 1.

The following equation defines the softmax function, which I'm abbreviating in math as "sm" to make longer equations easier to read:

The probability of the *i*th item is the score of the *i*th item divided by the score of every item added together.

$$\text{sm}(\boldsymbol{x})_i = \frac{\exp(x_i)}{\sum_{j=1}^{d} \exp(x_j)}$$

Let's quickly look at the results of calling softmax on two different vectors:

$$\text{sm}(\boldsymbol{x} = \begin{bmatrix} 3, & \overset{\text{Largest}}{\underset{\downarrow}{4}}, & 1 \end{bmatrix}) = [0.259, \ 0.705, \ 0.036]$$

$$\text{sm}(\boldsymbol{x} = \begin{bmatrix} -3, & -4, & \overset{\text{Largest}}{\underset{\downarrow}{-1}} \end{bmatrix}) = [0.114, \ 0.042, \ 0.844]$$

In the first case, 4 is the largest value, so it receives the largest normalized score of 0.705. The second case (–1) is the largest value, and it receives a score of 0.844. Why does the second case result in a larger score even though –1 is smaller than 4? Because softmax is relative, 4 is only 1 larger than 3; the second case (–1) is 3 larger than –4, and because the difference is bigger, this case receives a bigger score.

Why is it called softmax?

Before we continue, I find it helpful to explain *why* the softmax function is called *softmax*. We can use this score to compute a "soft" maximum, where every value contributes a portion of the answer. If we take the dot product between the softmax scores and the original values, it is approximately equal to the maximum value. Let's look at how that happens:

$$
\begin{aligned}
\text{sm}(\boldsymbol{x} = \begin{bmatrix} 3, & 4, & 1 \end{bmatrix}) &= & [0.259, \ 0.705, \ 0.036] \\
\text{sm}(\boldsymbol{x})^\top \boldsymbol{x} &= & 0.259 \cdot 3 + 0.705 \cdot 4 + 0.036 \cdot 1 = \mathbf{3.633} \\
\max_i x_i &= & \mathbf{4}
\end{aligned}
$$

$$
\begin{aligned}
\text{sm}(\boldsymbol{x} = [-3, -4, -1]) &= & [0.114, \ 0.042, \ 0.844] \\
\text{sm}(\boldsymbol{x})^\top \boldsymbol{x} &= & 0.114 \cdot -3 + 0.042 \cdot -4 + 0.844 \cdot -1 = \mathbf{-1.354} \\
\max_i x_i &= & \mathbf{-1}
\end{aligned}
$$

The value of $\text{sm}(\boldsymbol{x})^\top \boldsymbol{x}$ is approximately equal ($\approx$) to finding the maximum value of $\boldsymbol{x}$. Because every value contributes to at least a portion of the answer, it is also the case that $\text{sm}(\boldsymbol{x})^\top \boldsymbol{x} \leq \max_i x_i$. So the softmax function can get close but only becomes equal to the maximum when *all* values are the same.

CROSS-ENTROPY

With the softmax function in hand, we have one of the two tools we need to define a good loss function for classification problems. The second tool we need is called the *cross-entropy* loss. If we have two probability distributions p and q, the cross-entropy between them is

The average number of bits needed to encode a message when you think it has a distribution q but it actually follows the distribution p (aka, how much do you need to repeat yourself because you (p) don't speak quite the same dialect as your friend (q)) is equal to

how often you expect to see token i multiplied by the log of how often you actually see token i

summed over all possible tokens i that you might see (and negated to make the number positive instead of negative).

$$\ell(p,q) = -\sum_{i=1}^{d} p_i \cdot \log(q_i)$$

Why cross-entropy? It's a statistical tool that tells us how much extra information it will take for us to encode information if we used the distribution defined by q when the data *actually* follows the distribution p. This is measured in bits (one-eighth of a byte), and the more bits it takes to encode something, the worse the fit between p and q. This explanation glosses over some of the precision of what the cross-entropy function is doing but gives you an intuitive idea at a high level. Cross-entropy boils down to telling us how different two distributions are.

Think of it as trying to minimize cost. Imagine we are ordering lunch for a group of people, and we expect 70% to eat chicken and 30% to eat turkey (see figure 2.7). That's the predicted distribution q. In reality, 5% want turkey and 95% want chicken. That's the true distribution p. In this scenario, we *think* we want to order more turkey than we actually need. But if we order all that turkey, we will be short on chicken and have wasted/unused turkey. If we knew what we actually needed, we wouldn't have so many leftovers. Cross-entropy is just a way to quantify how different these distributions are so that we can order the right amount of each thing.

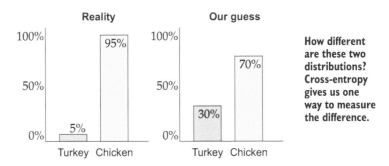

Figure 2.7 There are two different distributions: the real distribution on the left and our prediction on the right. To learn, we need a loss function to tell us precisely how different these distributions are. Cross-entropy solves that problem. In most cases, our label defines reality as being 100% for one class and 0% for all the others.

Now, with these two tools combined, we arrive at a simple loss function and approach. We first apply the softmax function ($sm(x)$), followed by computing the cross-entropy. If $\hat{y}$ is our vector output from the network and y is the correct class index, this simplifies to

> The loss between the prediction $\hat{y}$ (aka logits) and the correct class y is
>
> the negative log (makes it so that "good" values are smaller and "bad" are larger) of
>
> the predicted probability of the correct class.

$$\ell(\hat{y}, y) = -\log\left(sm(\hat{y})_y \right)$$

This may seem a bit mysterious, and that's OK. The result comes from simplifying the equations, and derivations are not the point of this book. We worked through the details because the softmax and cross-entropy functions are ubiquitous in deep learning research today, and some extra effort to understand what they do will make your life easier later in the book. The important thing is to know what a softmax function does (normalized inputs into probabilities) and that it can be used with cross-entropy to quantify how different two distributions (arrays of probabilities) are.

We use this loss function because it has a strong statistical grounding and interpretation. It ensures that we can interpret the results as being a probability distribution. For the case of a linear model, it results in the well-known algorithm *logistic regression*.

Using softmax followed by cross-entropy is so standard and well known that PyTorch integrates them into a single loss function `CrossEntropyLoss`, which performs both steps for us. This is good because implementing the softmax and cross-entropy functions manually can lead to tricky numerical stability issues and is not as direct as you might think.

2.3.3   *Training a classification network*

Now we can train a `model` and see how well it performs:

```
loss_func = nn.CrossEntropyLoss()
train_simple_network(model, loss_func, training_loader, epochs=50)
```

With our model trained, let's visualize the results. Since this is a 2D function, it's a little more complicated than our previous regression case. We use a contour plot to show the decision surface of our algorithm: dark blue represents the first class, dark red represents the second class, and the color transitions as the model's confidence decreases and increases. The original data points are shown as their respective blue and orange markers:

```
def visualize2DSoftmax(X, y, model, title=None):
    x_min = np.min(X[:,0])-0.5
    x_max = np.max(X[:,0])+0.5
    y_min = np.min(X[:,1])-0.5
    y_max = np.max(X[:,1])+0.5
    xv, yv = np.meshgrid(np.linspace(x_min, x_max, num=20),
        np.linspace(y_min, y_max, num=20), indexing='ij')
    xy_v = np.hstack((xv.reshape(-1,1), yv.reshape(-1,1)))
    with torch.no_grad():
        logits = model(torch.tensor(xy_v, dtype=torch.float32))
        y_hat = F.softmax(logits, dim=1).numpy()

    cs = plt.contourf(xv, yv, y_hat[:,0].reshape(20,20),
        levels=np.linspace(0,1,num=20), cmap=plt.cm.RdYlBu)
    ax = plt.gca()
    sns.scatterplot(x=X[:,0], y=X[:,1], hue=y, style=y, ax=ax)
    if title is not None:
        ax.set_title(title)

visualize2DSoftmax(X, y, model)
```

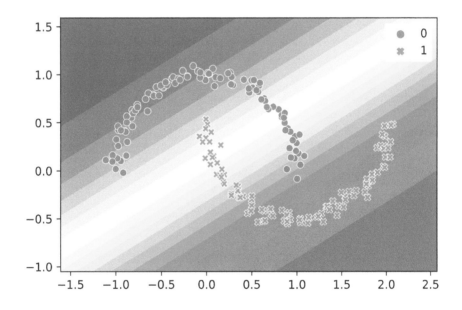

NOTE Notice that we call the PyTorch function `F.softmax` to perform the conversation from raw outputs into actual probability distributions. It is common jargon to call the value that goes into softmax the *logits* and the outputs $\hat{y}$ the probabilities. We will avoid using the term *logits* too much in this book, but you should be familiar with it. It often comes up when people are discussing the nitty-gritty details of an implementation or approach.

We can now see the results of our model on this data. Overall, it's a decent job: most of the blue circles are in the blue region, and the red crosses are in the red region. There is a middle ground where errors are being made because our problem cannot be fully solved with a linear model.

Now we do the same we did with our regression problem: add a hidden layer to increase the complexity of the neural network. In this case, we add two hidden layers just to show how easy it is. I've arbitrarily selected $n = 30$ hidden units for both hidden layers:

```
model = nn.Sequential(
    nn.Linear(2,  30),
    nn.Tanh(),
    nn.Linear(30,  30),
    nn.Tanh(),
    nn.Linear(30, 2),
)
train_simple_network(model, loss_func, training_loader, epochs=250)
```

You should notice that these models are starting to take some time to train: 250 `epochs` required 36 seconds when I ran this. The results appear to be worth it, though: if we look at a plot of our data, we see that the model has higher confidence for the regions that are unambiguously circles or crosses. You can also see that the threshold is starting to bend and curve as the neural network learns a nonlinear separation between the two classes:

```
visualize2DSoftmax(X, y, model)
```

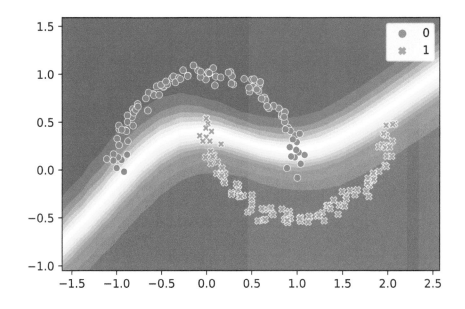

2.4 Better training code

We've now successfully trained fully connected networks for regression and classification problems. There is still a lot of room to improve our approaches. In particular, we have been training and evaluating visually on the same data. *This is not OK*: you can never judge how well your model works on *new* data by testing it on the *training* data. That gives the model a chance to cheat by memorizing the answers for each training datum instead of learning the underlying task. We also have another issue when dealing with classification problems: minimizing the cross-entropy loss is not really our goal. Our goal is to minimize errors, but we can't define errors in a differentiable way that will work with PyTorch, so we used cross-entropy as a proxy metric instead. Reporting the loss after every epoch for a classification problem is not as helpful because it is not our true goal.

We will talk about a number of changes we can make to our training code to give us much more robust tools. Like all good ML practitioners, we are making and using a *training* set and a *testing* set. We will also evaluate other metrics that we care about so we can track performance as we train.

2.4.1 Custom metrics

As mentioned, the metrics we care about (e.g., accuracy) may not be the same as the loss we used to train our model (e.g., cross-entropy). There are many ways these may *not* match perfectly, because a loss function must have the property of being *differentiable*, and most of the time our true goal does not have this property. So we often have two sets of scores: the metrics by which the developers and humans understand the problem and the loss function that lets the network understand the problem.

To help with this issue, we will modify our code so that we can pass in functions to compute different metrics from the labels and predicted values. We also want to know how these metrics vary across our training and validation datasets, so we will record multiple versions: one for each type of dataset.

To make our lives easier, we will make our code work well with most of the metrics provided by the scikit-learn library (https://scikit-learn.org/stable/modules/classes.html). To do this, let's assume we have an array y_true that contains the correct output label for every data point. We also need another array y_pred that contains the prediction of our model. If we are doing regression, each prediction is a scalar $\hat{y}$. If classification, each prediction is a vector $\hat{\boldsymbol{y}}$.

We need a way for the user (that's you) to specify which functions to evaluate and a place to store the results. For the score functions, let's use a dictionary score_funcs that takes the name of the metric as the key and a function reference as the value. That looks like

```
score_funcs={'Acc':accuracy_score, 'F1': f1_score}
```

if we use the functions provided by scikit-learn's `metrics` class (see https://scikit-learn.org/stable/modules/model_evaluation.html). This way, we can specify as many custom metrics as we want, as long as we implement a function `score_func(y_ture, y_pred)`. Then we just need a place to store the computed scores. After each epoch of the loop, we can use another dictionary `results` that maps strings as keys to a `list` of results. We'll use a list so we have one score for each epoch:

```
results[prefix+" loss"].append(np.mean(running_loss))
for name, score_func in score_funcs.items():
    results[prefix+" "+name].append(score_func(y_true, y_pred))
```

If we just used the `name` of each score function, we would not be able to differentiate between the score on the training set and the testing set. This is important because if there is a wide gap, it could indicate overfitting, and a small gap could indicate underfitting. So we use a `prefix` to distinguish between `train` and `test` scores.

> **NOTE**   If we are being proper in our evaluations, we should use only the validation/test performance to make adjustments and changes to our code, hyper-parameters, network architecture, etc. This is another reason we need to make sure we are distinguishing between training and validation performance. You should *never* use training performance to decide how well a model is doing.

2.4.2   *Training and testing passes*

We are modifying our training function to better support real-life work. That includes supporting a training epoch where we alter the model weights and a testing epoch where we only record our performance. It's essential that we make the testing epoch *never* adjust the weights of the model.

Performing one epoch of training or evaluation requires a *lot* of different inputs:

- `model`—The PyTorch `Module` to run for one epoch, which represents our model $f(\cdot)$
- `optimizer`—The object that updates the weights of the network and should be used only if we are performing a training epoch
- `data_loader`—The `DataLoader` object, which returns tuples of (input, label) pairs
- `loss_func`—The loss function $\ell(\cdot, \cdot)$, which takes two arguments, the `model` outputs $(\hat{y} = f(x))$ and the `labels` (y), and returns a loss to use for training
- `device`—The compute location to perform training
- `results`—A dictionary of strings to lists for storing results, as described previously
- `score_funcs`—A dictionary of scoring functions to use to evaluate the performance of the `model`, as described previously
- `prefix`—A string prefix for any scores placed in the `results` dictionary

Last, because neural networks can take a while to train, let's include an optional argument desc to provide a descriptive string for a progress bar. That will give us all the inputs we need for a function that processes one epoch, which we can give the following signature:

```
def run_epoch(model, optimizer, data_loader, loss_func, device,
              results, score_funcs, prefix="", desc=None):
```

At the start of this function, we need to allocate space to store results such as the losses, predictions, and the time we start computing:

```
running_loss = []
y_true = []
y_pred = []
start = time.time()
```

The training loop looks almost identical to the one we have used so far. The only thing we need to change is whether we use the optimizer. We can check this by looking at the model.training flag, which is True if our model is in training mode (model = model.train()) or False if it's in evaluation/inference mode (model = model.eval()). We can wrap the backward() call on the loss and optimizer calls into an if statement at the end of each loop:

```
if model.training:
    loss.backward()
    optimizer.step()
    optimizer.zero_grad()
```

Finally, we need to store the labels and predictions y_hat into y_true and y_pred, respectively. This can be done by calling .detach().cpu().numpy() to convert both from PyTorch tensors into NumPy arrays. Then we simply extend the lists of all labels by the current labels we are processing:

```
if len(score_funcs) > 0:
    labels = labels.detach().cpu().numpy()        ⟵──── Moves labels and predictions
    y_hat = y_hat.detach().cpu().numpy()                 back to CPU for later

    y_true.extend(labels.tolist())          ⟵─────────── Adds to predictions so far
    y_pred.extend(y_hat.tolist())
```

2.4.3 Saving checkpoints

The last modification we will make is the ability to save a simple checkpoint of the most recently completed epoch. In PyTorch, the torch.load and torch.save functions can be used for this purpose. While there is more than one way to use these methods, we recommend using the dictionary-style approach shown here, which lets us save the model, the optimizer state, and other information, all in one object:

```
torch.save({
    'epoch': epoch,
    'model_state_dict': model.state_dict(),
    'optimizer_state_dict': optimizer.state_dict(),
    'results' : results
    }, checkpoint_file)
```

The second argument `checkpoint_file` is a path to where we should save the file. We can put any picklable object into this dictionary to be saved. In our case, we denote the number of training epochs, the `model` state (the weights /parameters Θ), and any state used by the `optimizer`.

We need to be able to save our model so that when we are ready to use it, we do not have to retrain it from scratch. Saving after every epoch is a better idea, especially when you start to train networks that can take weeks to complete. Sometimes our code may fail after many epochs or a power failure may interrupt our job. By saving the model after every epoch, we can resume our training from the last epoch rather than starting from scratch.

2.4.4   *Putting it all together: A better model training function*

Now we have everything to build a better function for training our neural networks: not only the networks we have talked about (e.g., fully connected) but almost all the networks we discuss in this book. The signature for this new function looks like this:

```
def train_simple_network(model, loss_func, train_loader,
    test_loader=None, score_funcs=None, epochs=50,
    device="cpu", checkpoint_file=None):
```

The arguments are as follows:

- `model`—The PyTorch `Module` to run for one epoch, which represents our model $f(\cdot)$
- `loss_func`—The loss function $\ell(\cdot, \cdot)$, which takes two arguments, the `model` outputs ($\hat{y} = f(x)$) and the `labels` (y), and returns a loss to use for training
- `train_loader`—The `DataLoader` object that returns tuples of (input, label) pairs used for training the model
- `test_loader`—The `DataLoader` object that returns tuples of (input, label) pairs used for evaluating the model
- `score_funcs`—A dictionary of scoring functions to use to evaluate the performance of the `model`, as described earlier
- `device`—The compute location to perform training
- `checkpoint_file`—A string indicating the location to save model checkpoints to disk

The gist of this new function is shown next, and you can find the full version in the idlmam.py file that comes with the book:

```
optimizer = torch.optim.SGD(model.parameters(), lr=0.001)  ←── Performs bookkeeping
                                                                 and setup; prepares
                                                                 the optimizer

                                                  ┌─ Places the model on
                                                  │  the correct compute
                                                  │  resource (CPU or GPU)
model.to(device)          ←───────────────────────┘

for epoch in tqdm(range(epochs), desc="Epoch"):

    model = model.train()      ←──────────── Puts our model in training mode

    total_train_time += run_epoch(model, optimizer, train_loader,
        loss_func, device, results, score_funcs,
        prefix="train", desc="Training")

    results["total time"].append( total_train_time )
    results["epoch"].append( epoch )
                                              Saves a checkpoint if
    if test_loader is not None:   ←────────── checkpoint_file is not None
        model = model.eval()
        with torch.no_grad():
            run_epoch(model, optimizer, test_loader, loss_func, device,
                results, score_funcs, prefix="test", desc="Testing")
```

We use the `run_epoch` function to perform a training step after putting the model into the correct mode, and that function records the results from training. Then, if `test_loader` is given, we switch to `model.eval()` mode and enter the `with torch.no_grad()` context so we do not alter the model in any way and can examine its performance on the held-out data. We use the prefixes `"train"` and `"test"` for the results from the training and testing runs, respectively.

Finally, we have this new training function convert the results into a pandas `DataFrame`, which will make it easy for us to access and view them later:

```
return pd.DataFrame.from_dict(results)
```

With this new and improved code, let's retrain our model on the moons dataset. Since accuracy is what we really care about, we import the accuracy metrics from scikit-learn. Let's include the F1 score metrics to demonstrate how the code can handle two different metrics at the same time:

```
from sklearn.metrics import accuracy_score
from sklearn.metrics import f1_score
```

We also want to do a better job of evaluating and including a validation set. Since the moons data is synthetic, we can easily create a new dataset for validation. Rather than performing 200 epochs of training like before, let's generate a larger training set:

```
X_train, y_train = make_moons(n_samples=8000, noise=0.4)
X_test, y_test = make_moons(n_samples=200, noise=0.4)
train_dataset = TensorDataset(torch.tensor(X_train, dtype=torch.float32),
    torch.tensor(y_train, dtype=torch.long))
test_dataset = TensorDataset(torch.tensor(X_test, dtype=torch.float32),
    torch.tensor(y_test, dtype=torch.long))
```

```
training_loader = DataLoader(train_dataset, shuffle=True)
testing_loader = DataLoader(test_dataset)
```

We have everything we need to train our model again. We will use model.pt as the location to save our model's results. All we need to do is declare a new `model` object and call our new `train_simple_network` function:

```
model = nn.Sequential(
    nn.Linear(2, 30),
    nn.Tanh(),
    nn.Linear(30, 30),
    nn.Tanh(),
    nn.Linear(30, 2),
)
results_pd = train_simple_network(model, loss_func, training_loader,
    epochs=5, test_loader=testing_loader, checkpoint_file='model.pt',
    score_funcs={'Acc':accuracy_score,'F1': f1_score})
```

Time to look at some results. First, let's see that we can load our checkpoint `model` rather than use the one we already trained. To load a `model`, we first need to define a *new* `model` that has all the same sub-modules as the original, and they all need to be the same size. This is necessary so the weights all match up. If we saved a model with 30 neurons in the second hidden layer, we need to have a new model with 30 neurons; otherwise, there will be too few or too many, and an error will occur.

One reason we use the `torch.load` and `torch.save` functions is the `map_location` argument that they provide. This handles loading a model from the data to the correct compute device for us. Once we load in the dictionary of results, we can use the `load_state_dict` function to restore the states of our original model into this new object. Then we can apply the model to the data and see that we get the same results:

```
model_new = nn.Sequential(
    nn.Linear(2, 30),
    nn.Tanh(),
    nn.Linear(30, 30),
    nn.Tanh(),
    nn.Linear(30, 2),
)

visualize2DSoftmax(X_test, y_test, model_new, title="Initial Model")
plt.show()

checkpoint_dict = torch.load('model.pt', map_location=device)

model_new.load_state_dict(checkpoint_dict['model_state_dict'])

visualize2DSoftmax(X_test, y_test, model_new, title="Loaded Model")
plt.show()
```

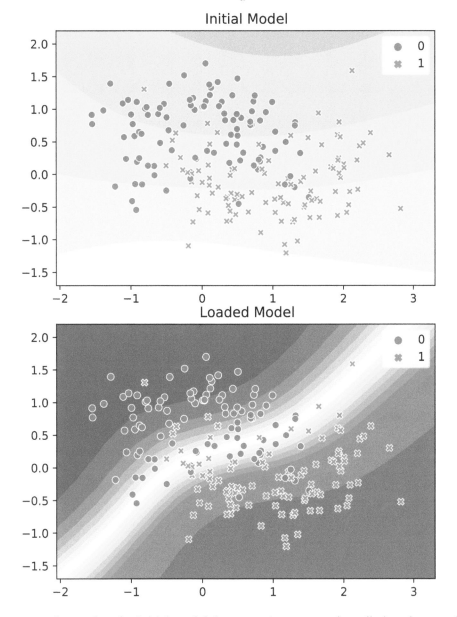

You can easily see that the initial model does not give very good predictions because its weights are random values and untrained. If you run the code several times, you should see many slightly different but equally unhelpful results. But after we load the previous `model` state into the `model_new`, we get the nice crisp results we expect.

NOTE   In this example, we only load the model's state because we only made pre-dictions; you don't need the optimizer unless you want to continue training. If you do want to continue training, you'll want to add a `optimizer.load_state_dict` `(checkpoint['optimizer_state_dict'])` line to your code.

Our new training function was written to return a pandas `DataFrame` object with information about the model after every epoch. This gives us some valuable information that we can easily visualize. For example, we can quickly plot the training and validation accuracy as a function of the finished epoch:

```
sns.lineplot(x='epoch', y='train Acc', data=results_pd, label='Train')
sns.lineplot(x='epoch', y='test Acc', data=results_pd, label='Test')
```

[29]:   <AxesSubplot:xlabel='epoch', ylabel='train Acc'>

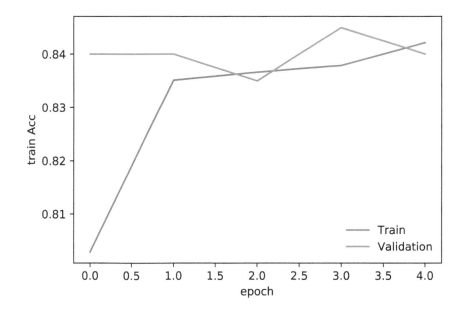

It's now easy to see that by using more data, it took about two epochs for our model to top out on the noisier training data. Two score functions were provided, so let's look at the F1 score as a function of the literal amount of training time in seconds. This will become more useful in the future if we want to compare how quickly two different models can learn:

```
sns.lineplot(x='total time', y='train F1', data=results_pd, label='Train')
sns.lineplot(x='total time', y='test F1', data=results_pd, label='Test')
```

[30]:   <AxesSubplot:xlabel='total time', ylabel='train F1'>

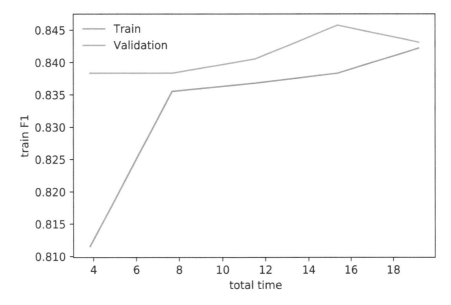

For this toy dataset, F1 and Accuracy give very similar scores because both classes have similar behavior and are balanced in size. A more interesting trend you should notice is that the training accuracy increases and then stabilizes, but the validation accuracy has more asperity as it moves up and down with each epoch of training. *This is normal.* The model will start to overfit the training data, which makes its performance look stable, and slowly inch upward as it finishes learning and starts to memorize the more challenging data points. Because the validation data is separate, these small changes that may be good or bad for new data are unknown to the model, so it cannot adjust to get them consistently correct. It's essential that we keep a separate validation or test set so that we can see this less biased view of how the model will actually perform on new data.

2.5 *Training in batches*

If you look at the x-axis of the previous graph, when we plot the F1 score as a function of training time, you may notice that it took almost a minute to train a model on just 8,000 data points with only $d = 2$ features. Given this long training time, how could we ever hope to scale up to larger datasets?

We need to train on *batches* of data. A batch of data is just a larger group of data. Let's say we have the following dataset of $N = 4$ items:

$$
X^{4 \times 2} = \begin{bmatrix} \boldsymbol{x_1} = [1,2] \\ \boldsymbol{x_2} = [3,4] \\ \boldsymbol{x_3} = [5,6] \\ \boldsymbol{x_4} = [7,8] \end{bmatrix}, y = \begin{bmatrix} 0 \\ 1 \\ 1 \\ 0 \end{bmatrix}
$$

Our current code, over one epoch, will perform four updates: one for each item in the dataset. This is why it is called *stochastic gradient descent* (SGD). The word *stochastic* is jargon that means "random" but usually with some underlying purpose or invisible hand driving the randomness. The stochastic part of the name SGD comes from us using only a portion of the shuffled data to compute the gradient instead of the entire dataset. Because it is shuffled, we get a different result every time.

If we push all N data points through the model and compute the loss over the entire dataset, $\nabla \sum_{i=1}^{N} \ell(f(\boldsymbol{x}_i), y_i)$, we get the *true* gradient. This can also make our training more *computationally efficient* by processing all of the data at once instead of one datum at a time. So instead of passing in a vector with a shape of (d) as the input to a model $f(\cdot)$, we pass in a matrix of shape (N, d). PyTorch modules are designed for this situation by default; we just need a way to tell PyTorch to group our data into a larger batch. It turns out the DataLoader has this functionality built in with the optional batch_size argument. If a value is unspecified, it defaults to batch_size=1. If we set this to batch_size=len(train_dataset), we perform true gradient descent:

```
training_loader = DataLoader(train_dataset, batch_size=len(train_dataset),
    shuffle=True)
testing_loader = DataLoader(test_dataset, batch_size=len(test_dataset))
model_gd = nn.Sequential(
    nn.Linear(2, 30),
    nn.Tanh(),
    nn.Linear(30, 30),
    nn.Tanh(),
    nn.Linear(30, 2),
)
results_true_gd = train_simple_network(model_gd, loss_func,
    training_loader, epochs=5, test_loader=testing_loader,
    checkpoint_file='model.pt',
    score_funcs={'Acc':accuracy_score,'F1': f1_score})
```

Five epochs of training just happened in 0.536 seconds. Clearly, training on *more* data at one time has allowed us to benefit from the parallelism available in a modern GPU. But if we plot the accuracy, we see that training the gradient descent $(B = N)$ has produced a less accurate model:

```
sns.lineplot(x='total time', y='test Acc', data=results_pd,
    label='SGD, B=1')
sns.lineplot(x='total time', y='test Acc', data=results_true_gd,
    label='GD, B=N')
```

```
[32]:   <AxesSubplot:xlabel='total time', ylabel='test Acc'>
```

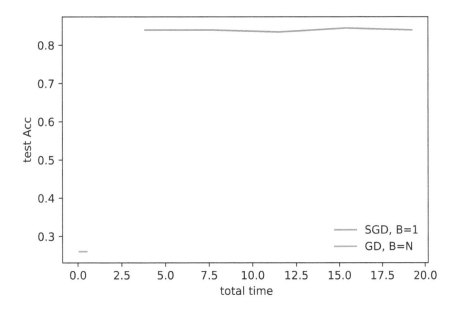

Let's look at a toy example to explain why this is happening. Figure 2.8 shows a function that we are optimizing, and if we are using gradient descent (which looks at *all* the data), we take steps leading us in the correct direction. But each step is expensive, so we can only take a few steps. This example shows us taking four total updates/steps corresponding to four epochs.

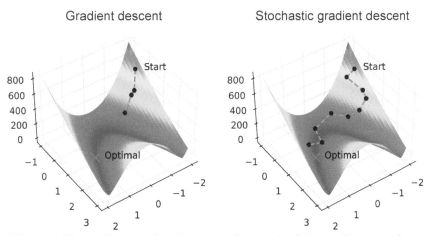

Figure 2.8 The left image shows gradient descent over four epochs of the data. That means it can make only four steps of progress, but each step is headed in the right direction. On the right, SGD makes multiple updates per epoch by looking at just some of the data. This means each step is noisy and not always in the correct direction, but it is usually in a useful direction, so SGD can often make more progress toward the goal in fewer epochs.

When we use SGD, we perform N updates per epoch, so we get more updates or steps for a fixed number of epochs. But because of the *stochastic* or random behavior of using just one data point for each update, the steps we take are noisy. They don't always head in the correct direction. The larger total number of steps eventually gets us closer to the answer, but the cost is an increase in runtime because we lose the computational efficiency of processing all the data at once.

The solution we use in practice is to balance between these two extremes. Let's choose a batch size big enough to use the GPU more efficiently but small enough that we still get to perform many more updates per epoch. We use B to denote the batch size; for most applications, you will find $B \in [32, 256]$ is a good choice. Another good rule of thumb is to make the batch size as large as you can fit into GPU memory and to add more training epochs until the model converges. This requires a bit more work because as you develop your network and make changes, the largest batch size you can fit onto your GPU may change.

> **NOTE**   Because we only use the validation data to *evaluate* how our model is doing and not to update the weights of the model, the batch size used to validate the data has no particular tradeoff. We can just increase the batch size to whatever runs fastest and go with that. The results will be the same regardless of the batch size used for the test data. In practice, most people use the same batch size for training and testing data for simplicity.

Here's the code:

```
training_loader = DataLoader(train_dataset, batch_size=32, shuffle=True)
model_sgd = nn.Sequential(
    nn.Linear(2, 30),
    nn.Tanh(),
    nn.Linear(30, 30),
    nn.Tanh(),
    nn.Linear(30, 2),
)
results_batched = train_simple_network(model_sgd, loss_func,
    training_loader, epochs=5, test_loader=testing_loader,
    checkpoint_file='model.pt',
    score_funcs={'Acc':accuracy_score,'F1': f1_score})
```

Now, if we plot the results as a function of time, we see the green line giving us the best of both worlds. It runs in only 1.044 seconds and gets nearly the same accuracy. You will find that using batches of data like this has almost no downside and is the preferred approach in modern deep learning.

```
sns.lineplot(x='total time', y='test Acc', data=results_pd, label='SGD, B=1')
sns.lineplot(x='total time', y='test Acc', data=results_true_gd,
    label='GD, B=N')
sns.lineplot(x='total time', y='test Acc', data=results_batched,
    label='SGD, B=32')
```

`[35]:` `<AxesSubplot:xlabel='total time', ylabel='test Acc'>`

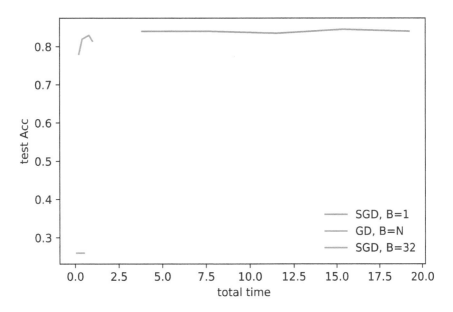

Exercises

Share and discuss your solutions on the Manning online platform at Inside Deep Learning Exercises (https://liveproject.manning.com/project/945). Once you submit your own answers, you will be able to see the solutions submitted by other readers, and see which ones the author judges to be the best.

1   The input range of data can have a large impact on a neural network. This applies to inputs *and* outputs, as for regression problems. Try applying scikit-learn's `StandardScaler` to the targets y of the toy regression problem at the start of this chapter, and train a new neural network on it. Does changing the scale of the outputs help or hurt the model's predictions?

2   The area under the curve (AUC) metric does not follow the standard pattern in scikit-learn, as it requires y_pred to be a vector of shape (N) instead a matrix of shape $(N, 2)$. Write a wrapper function for AUC that makes it compatible with our `train_simple_network` function.

3   Write a new function `resume_simple_network` that loads a `checkpoint_file` from disk, restores both the `optimizer` and `model` states, and continues training to a specified total number of epochs. So if the model is saved after 20 epochs, and you specify 30 epochs, it should perform only 10 more epochs of training.

4   When performing experiments, we may want to go back and try versions of our model from different epochs, especially if we are trying to determine when some

weird behavior started to occur. Modify the `train_simple_network` function to take a new argument `checkpoint_every_x` that saves a version of the model every x epochs with different filenames. That way, you can go back and load a specific version without filling your hard drive with a model for *every* epoch.

5   The *deep* part of deep learning refers to the number of layers in a neural network. Try adding more layers (up to 20) to the models we used for the `make_moons` classification problem. How do more layers impact performance?

6   Try changing the number of neurons used in the hidden layers of the `make_moons` classification problem. How does it impact performance?

7   Use scikit-learn to load the breast cancer Wisconsin dataset (https://scikit-learn.org/stable/modules/generated/sklearn.datasets.load_breast_cancer.html), convert it into a `TensorDataset`, and then split it into 80% for training and 20% for testing. Try to build your own classification neural network for this data.

8   We saw results on the `make_moons` dataset with a batch size of $B = \{1, 32, N\}$. Write a loop to train a new model on that same dataset for every power-of-two batch size less than N (i.e., $B = \{2, 4, 8, 16, 32, 64, \ldots\}$), and plot the results. Do you notice any trends in terms of accuracy and/or training time?

Summary

- The `train_simple_network` function abstracts away details and can be reused for almost any neural network.
- `CrossEntropyLoss` is for classification problems, and `MSE` and `L1` losses are for regression problems.
- The `nn.Linear` layer can be used to implement linear and logistic regression.
- Fully connected networks can be seen as extensions to linear and logistic regression by adding more `nn.Linear` layers with *nonlinearities* inserted between each layer.
- The `nn.Sequential Module` can be used to organize sub-`Module`s to create larger networks.
- We can trade compute efficiency versus number of optimization steps by using the `batch_size` option in a `DataLoader`.

Convolutional neural networks

This chapter covers

- How tensors represent spatial data
- Defining convolutions and their uses
- Building and training a convolutional neural network (CNN)
- Adding pooling to make CNNs more robust
- Augmenting image data to improve accuracy

Convolutional neural networks (CNNs) revitalized the field of neural networks while simultaneously ushering in a new branding of deep learning starting in 2011 and 2012. CNNs are still at the heart of many of the most successful applications of deep learning, including self-driving cars, speech recognition systems used by smart devices, and optical character recognition. All of this stems from the fact that *convolutions* are powerful yet simple tools that help us encode information about the problem into the design of our network architecture. Instead of focusing on feature engineering, we spend more time engineering the *architectures* of our networks.

The success of convolutions comes from their ability to learn spatial patterns, which has made them the default method to use for any data resembling an image. When you apply a convolution to an image, you can learn to detect simple patterns like horizontal or vertical lines, changes in color, or grid patterns. When you stack convolutions in layers, they begin to recognize more complex patterns, building upon the simpler convolutions that came before.

Our goal in this chapter is to teach you all the basics needed to build your own CNNs for new image-classification problems. First, we discuss how images are represented to a neural network. That images are 2D is an important structure or meaning we will encode into the specific way we organize data in our tensors. You should always care about the structure of your data because picking the right architecture to match the structure is the best way to improve the accuracy of your model. Next, we remove the mystery of what a convolution is, show how convolutions can detect simple patterns, and explain why they're a good approach for data structured like an image. Then, we'll create a convolutional layer, which can act as a replacement for the nn.Linear layer we used in the previous chapter. Finally, we build some CNNs and discuss a few additional tricks to improve their accuracy.

3.1   *Spatial structural prior beliefs*

As of now, you know how to build and train a very simple neural network. What you have learned applies to any kind of tabular (also called *columnar*) data, where your data and features may be organized in a spreadsheet. However, other algorithms (e.g., random forests and XGBoost) are usually better for such data. If all you have is columnar data, you probably do not want to use a neural network.

Neural networks are really useful and start to out-perform other methods when we use them to impose a *prior belief*. We use the words *prior belief* in a very literal way: there is something we *believe* is true about how the data/problem/world works *prior* to ever looking at the data.[1] Specifically, deep learning has been most successful at imposing *structural* priors. By how we design the network, we impart some knowledge about the intrinsic nature or structure of the data. The most common types of structure encoded into neural networks are spatial correlation (i.e., images in this chapter) and sequential relationships (e.g., weather changes from one day to the next). Figure 3.1 shows some of the cases where you want to use a CNN.

There are several ways to encode structure that we know (or believe) about the problem into a neural network, and the list is growing all the time. For now, we will talk about CNNs, which have dominated the image-based world. First we need to learn how an image and its structure are encoded in PyTorch as tensors so that we can understand how a convolution can use this structure. Previously, we had input with no structure. Our data could be represented by an (N, D) matrix with N data points and D features. We could have rearranged the order of the features, and doing so would not have changed the meaning behind the data because there was no structure or importance to how the data was organized. All that mattered was that if column j corresponded to a

---

[1]   If you have any friends who call themselves Bayesian, they might take offense at this definition, but that's OK. We are not being Bayesians today. Bayesian statistics often involves a more precise definition of a prior; see http://mng.bz/jjJp (Scott Lynch, 2007) for an introduction.

specific feature, we'd always put that feature's value in column j (i.e., we just needed to be consistent).

Columnar data: Fully connected layers   **Audio data:** Use a 1D *CNN*   **Image data:** Use a 2D *CNN*

Feature 1	Feature 2	...	Feature d
1	Yes	...	2
8.2	No	...	5123
7	Yes	...	542

Figure 3.1 Columnar data (data that could go in a spreadsheet) should use fully connected layers, because there is no structure to the data and fully connected layers impart no prior beliefs. Audio and images have spatial properties that match how CNNs see the world, so you should almost always use a CNN for those kinds of data. It is hard to listen to a book, so we'll stick with images instead of audio.

Images, however, are structured. There is an order to the pixels. If you shuffled the pixels around, you would fundamentally change the meaning of a picture. In fact, you would probably end up with an incomprehensible image if you did that. Figure 3.2 shows how this works.

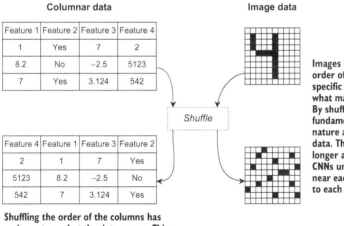

Columnar data

Feature 1	Feature 2	Feature 3	Feature 4
1	Yes	7	2
8.2	No	−2.5	5123
7	Yes	3.124	542

Shuffle

Feature 4	Feature 1	Feature 3	Feature 2
2	1	7	Yes
5123	8.2	−2.5	No
542	7	3.124	Yes

Shuffling the order of the columns has no impact on what the data means. This is because the data has no fundamental structure.

Image data

Images have structure: the order of the data implies a specific relationship. That's what makes it an image. By shuffling the pixels, we fundamentally change the nature and meaning of the data. This "4" digit is no longer a digit after shuffling. CNNs understand that values near each other are related to each other.

Figure 3.2 Shuffling your data will destroy the structure in your data. Left: For columnar data, shuffling has no real impact because the data has no special structure. Right: When an image is shuffled, it is no longer recognizable. It is the structural nature of images that pixels near each other are related to each other. CNNs encode the idea that items located near each other are related, making CNNs a good fit for images.

Suppose we have N images, and each has a height H and a width W. As a starting point, we might consider a matrix of image data to have the shape

$$(N, W, H)$$

which gives us a three-dimensional tensor. This would be fine if we had black-and-white images only. But what about color? We need to add some *channels* to our representation. Every channel has the same width and height but represents a different perceptual concept. Color is usually represented with red, green, and blue (RGB) *channels*, and we interpret the mixture of red, green, and blue to create a final color image. This is shown in figure 3.3.

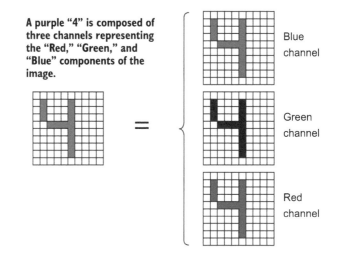

A purple "4" is composed of three channels representing the "Red," "Green," and "Blue" components of the image.

Blue channel

Green channel

Red channel

Figure 3.3   Color images are represented by three sub-images of the same size, called channels. Each channel represents a different concept, the most common being red, green, and blue (RGB). In general, every channel represents a different kind of feature at different locations.

To include color, we need to add a dimension to the tensor for the channels:

$$(N, C, W, H)$$

Now we have a four-dimensional tensor with structure. By *structure,* we mean that the axes of the tensor and the order in which we access data have specific meanings (we can't shuffle them). If x is a batch of color images, x[3,2,0,0] says, "From the fourth image ($N = 3$), grab the blue value ($C = 2$) of the upper-left pixel $(0, 0)$." Or, we could grab the red, green, and blue values using x[3,:,0,0]. This means we are processing the pixel values at locations i and j; we know we need to access the index x[:,:,i,j]. More importantly, we need to know something about the *neighboring pixel at the bottom right,* which we can access using x[:,:,i+1,j+1]. Thanks to the input being *structured,* this is true regardless of the values of i and j. Convolutions use this approach so that when a convolution looks at pixel location i, j in an image, it can also consider the neighboring pixel locations.

> **NOTE** RGB is the most common standard for images, but it is not the only option. Other popular ways to represent data use hue, saturation, and value (HSV) and cyan, magenta, yellow, and key (that is, black) (CMYK). These standards are often called *color spaces*.

3.1.1 Loading MNIST with PyTorch

While it has become a bit cliché, we will start exploring what all this means using the ubiquitous MNIST dataset. It's a collection of black-and-white images of the digits 0 through 9; each is 28 pixels wide and 28 pixels tall. PyTorch has a convenient loader for this dataset in a package called `torchvision`. If you are doing *anything* with images and PyTorch, you almost certainly want to use this package. Although MNIST is a toy problem, we will work with it in most chapters because it allows us to run examples in just a few minutes, whereas real datasets take hours to *weeks* for a *single run*. I've designed these chapters so that the approaches and lessons you will learn transfer to real problems.

We load the `torchvision` package as follows:

```
import torchvision
from torchvision import transforms
```

Now we can load the MNIST dataset using the following code. The first argument, `"./data"`, tells PyTorch where we would like the data stored, and `download=True` says to download the dataset if it's not already there. MNIST has a predefined training and testing split, which we can obtain by setting the `train` flag to `True` or `False`, respectively:

```
mnist_data_train = torchvision.datasets.MNIST("./data", train=True,
    download=True)
mnist_data_test = torchvision.datasets.MNIST("./data", train=False,
    download=True)
x_example, y_example = mnist_data_train[0]
type(x_example)
```

```
[5]: PIL.Image.Image
```

Now you will notice that the `type` of the data returned is *not* a tensor. We get a `PIL.Image.Image` (https://pillow.readthedocs.io/en/stable) because the dataset *is* images. We need to use a `transform` to convert the images to tensors, which is why we import the `transforms` package from `torchvision`. We can simply specify the `ToTensor` transform, which converts a Python Imaging Library (PIL) image into a PyTorch tensor where the minimum possible value is 0.0 and the max is 1.0, so it's already in a pretty good numerical range for us to work with. Let's redefine these dataset objects to do that right now. All it takes is adding `transform=transforms.ToTensor()` to the method call, as shown next, where we load the train and test splits and print the shape of the first example of the training set:

```
mnist_data_train = torchvision.datasets.MNIST("./data", train=True,
    download=True, transform=transforms.ToTensor())
mnist_data_test = torchvision.datasets.MNIST("./data", train=False,
    download=True, transform=transforms.ToTensor())
x_example, y_example = mnist_data_train[0]
print(x_example.shape)
```

```
torch.Size([1, 28, 28])
```

We have accessed a single example from the dataset, and it has a shape of $(1, 28, 28)$ for $C = 1$ channels (it's black and white) and a width and height of 28 pixels. If we want to visualize a tensor representation of an image that is grayscale, `imshow` expects it to have only a width and height (i.e., a shape of (W, H)). The `imshow` function also needs us to tell it explicitly to use grayscale. Why? Because `imshow` is meant for a wider class of scientific visualization where you might want other options, instead:

```
imshow(x_example[0,:], cmap='gray')
```

```
[7]:  <matplotlib.image.AxesImage at 0x7f6a1fea3090>
```

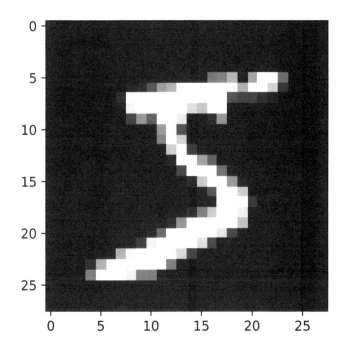

OK, clearly that is the digit 5. Since we are learning how images are presented as tensors, let's do a color version. If we stack three copies of the same digit on top of each other, we will have a tensor of shape $(3, 28, 28)$. Because the *structure* of the tensor has meaning, this instantaneously makes it a color image by virtue of having three channels. The following code does exactly that, stacking the first grayscale image three times and printing its shape:

```
x_as_color = torch.stack([x_example[0,:], x_example[0,:], x_example[0,:]],
     dim=0)
print(x_as_color.shape)
```

```
torch.Size([3, 28, 28])
```

Now let's visualize the color version. Here we need to be a little careful. In PyTorch, an image is represented as (N, C, W, H),[2] but `imshow` expects a single image as (W, H, C). So we need to *permute* the dimensions when using `imshow`. If our tensor has r dimensions, the `permute` function takes r inputs: the indexes $0, 1, \ldots, r-1$ of the original tensor in the *new order* in which we want them to appear. Since our image has (C, W, H) right now, maintaining that order means $(0, 1, 2)$. We want the channel at index 0 to become the last dimension, width first, and height second, which is $(1, 2, 0)$. Let's try it:

```
imshow(x_as_color.permute(1,2,0))
```

[9]:   <matplotlib.image.AxesImage at 0x7f6b681c60d0>

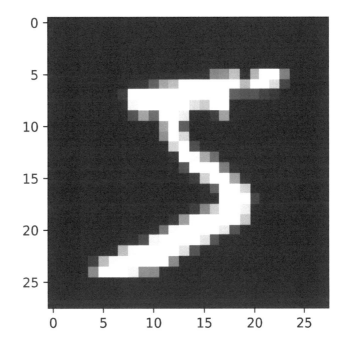

---

[2] Different frameworks support different orderings for a variety of nuanced reasons that we are not going to get into. Let's focus on the basics and default PyTorch behavior.

Why is this *color* image still black and white? Because the original image was black and white. We have the same value copied in the red, green, and blue channels, which is how you represent a black-and-white image in color. If we zero out the red and blue channels, we get a green number:

```
x_as_color = torch.stack([x_example[0,:], x_example[0,:], x_example[0,:]])
x_as_color[0,:] = 0            ←── No Red. We're leaving Green alone.
x_as_color[2,:] = 0            ←── No Blue
imshow(x_as_color.permute(1,2,0))
```

[10]:   <matplotlib.image.AxesImage at 0x7f6a1fc8b810>

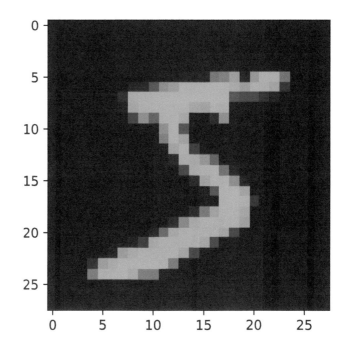

Changing the color of this image is an example of

- How the different channels impact what the data represents
- What it means for this to be a *structured* data representation

Just to make sure these two points are clear, let's stack three different images together into one color image. We will reuse the same numeral 5 as in the first image in the stack. It will go into the red channel, so we should see a red 5 mixed with two other digits that are green and blue, respectively:

```
x1, x2, x3 = mnist_data_train[0], mnist_data_train[1],
       mnist_data_train[2]                          ←——— Grabs 3 images

x1, x2, x3 = x1[0], x2[0], x3[0]                     ←— Drops the labels

x_as_color = torch.stack([x1[0,:], x2[0,:], x3[0,:]], dim=0)
imshow(x_as_color.permute(1,2,0))
```

[11]:   <matplotlib.image.AxesImage at 0x7f6a1fc00650>

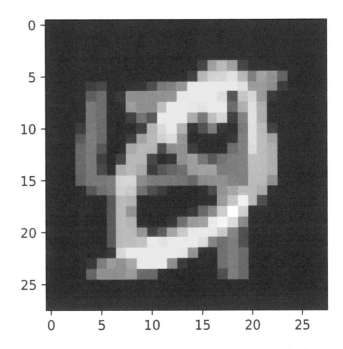

You should see a red 5, a green 0, and a blue 4. Where two of the images overlap, the colors blend because they were placed in separate color channels. For example, in the middle, the 4 and 5 intersect, and red + blue = purple. The order of the data has meaning, and we can't arbitrarily reorder things without potentially destroying the structure and thus the data.

Let's look at this more explicitly. What happens if we shuffle the data within a channel? Does it have the same important structured meaning? Let's look at the digit 5 one last time but randomly shuffle the values in the tensor:

```
rand_order = torch.randperm(x_example.shape[1] * x_example.shape[2])
x_shuffled = x_example.view(-1)[rand_order].view(x_example.shape)
imshow(x_shuffled[0,:], cmap='gray')
```

`[12]:   <matplotlib.image.AxesImage at 0x7f6a1fb72cd0>`

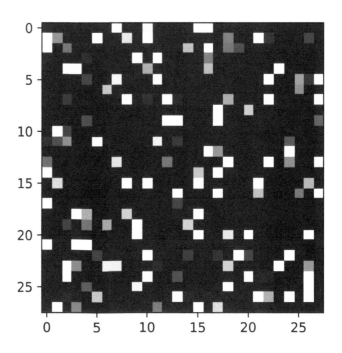

As you can see, this has *completely* changed the meaning of the image. Instead of being a 5, it's . . . nothing, really. The locations of a value and its *nearby values* are intrinsically part of that value's meaning. The value of one pixel cannot be separated from its neighbors. This is the *structural spatial prior* we try to capture in this chapter. Now that we have learned how to represent the structure of images with tensors, we can learn about convolutions to exploit that structure.

3.2   *What are convolutions?*

What do we change now that we have our data shaped like an image? We would like to put a *prior* into our model: the *spatial relationship*. The prior that convolutions encode is that *things near each other are related, and things far from each other have no relationship*. Think about the pictures of the digit 5 in the previous section. Pick any black pixel: most of its neighboring pixels are also black. Pick any white pixel: most of its neighbors are white or a shade of white. This is a kind of spatial correlation. It doesn't really matter where in the image this happens because it tends to happen *everywhere* by the nature of this *being an image.*

A *convolution* is a mathematical function with two inputs. Convolutions take an *input* image and a *filter* (also called a *kernel*) and output a new image. The goal is for the filter to recognize certain patterns from the input and highlight them in the output. A convolution can be used to impose a spatial prior on any tensor with r dimensions; a simple example is shown in figure 3.4. Right now, we are just trying to understand what a convolution does—we get to how it works in a moment.

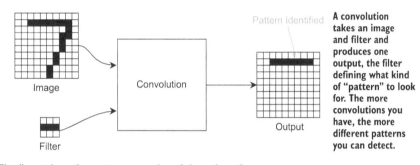

An "image" is any tensor with a shape of (BatchSize, Channels, *), where * can be any number of additional dimensions. We use a simple 2D image because its easy to "picture," literally.

Pattern Identified

A convolution takes an image and filter and produces one output, the filter defining what kind of "pattern" to look for. The more convolutions you have, the more different patterns you can detect.

Image

Convolution

Output

Filter

A "filter" must have the exact same number of channels as the "images" coming into it. A filter's size (e.g, width/height) defines how spatially far away correlated patterns may be.

Figure 3.4 Example of a convolution. An input image and a filter are combined by the convolution. The output is a new image that has been altered. The purpose of the filter is to identify or recognize certain patterns in the input. In this example, the filter identifies the horizontal line at the top of a numeral 7.

While we keep referring to *images*, convolutions are not constrained to only working on two-dimensional data. To help us understand how convolutions work, we will start with a one-dimensional example because it makes the math easier to walk through. Once we understand 1D convolutions, the 2D version we use for images will follow very quickly. Because we want to create multiple layers of convolutions, we will also learn about *padding*, which is necessary for that purpose. Finally, we will talk about weight sharing, which is a different way of thinking about convolutions that re-emerges throughout the book.

3.2.1 1D convolutions

To understand how a convolution works, let's talk about a one-dimensional image first, as it is easier to show the details in 1D than 2D. A 1D image has a shape of (C, W) for the number of channels and the width. There is no height because we are talking about just 1D, not 2D. For a 1D input with (C, W) shape, we can define a filter with a shape of (C, K). We get to choose the value of K, and we need C to match up between the image and the filter. Since the number of channels must *always* match, we call this a "filter of size K" for short. If we apply a filter of size K to an input of shape (C, W), we get an output that has shape $(C, W - 2 \cdot \lfloor K/2 \rfloor).$[3] Let's look at how that works in figure 3.5.

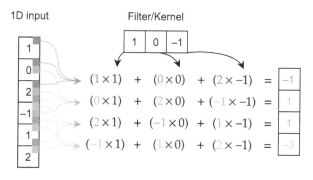

Figure 3.5   A 1D input "1, 0, 2, –1, 1, 2" is convolved with the filter "1, 0, –1". This means we take every subsequence of three input items, multiply those items with the filter values, and then add the results together.

An input of shape $(1, 6)$ is on the left, and we are applying a filter of size 3 that has the values $[1, 0, -1]$. The output is on the right. For each output, you can see arrows coming in for the *spatially relevant* inputs for that output. So for the first output, -1, only the first three inputs are relevant; nothing else in the input impacts that specific output. Its value is calculated by multiplying the first three inputs with the three values in the kernel and then summing them. The second value of the output is computed by using the second set of three input values. Notice it is *always* the same three values from the filter, applied to *every* position in the input. The following code shows how to implement this in raw Python:

```
filter = [1, 0, -1]
input = [1, 0, 2, -1, 1, 2]
output = []
for i in range(len(input)-len(filter)):        ←—— Slides the filter over the input
    result = 0
    for j in range(len(filter)):               ←————— Applies the filter at this location
        result += input[i+j]*filter[j]
    output.append(result)                      ←————— The output is ready to use.
```

In effect, we are *sliding* the filter across every location in the input, computing a value at each location, and storing it in the output. That's what a convolution is. The size of the output shrinks by $2 \cdot \lfloor 3/2 \rfloor$ because we run out of values at the edges of the input. Next we'll show how to make this work in 2D, and then we'll have the foundation of CNNs.

---

[3] $\lfloor x \rfloor$ is the floor function that rounds a value down: e.g., $\lfloor 9.9 \rfloor = 9$. The ceiling function is $\lceil 9.1 \rceil = 10$.

3.2.2 *2D convolutions*

As we increase the number of dimensions r in our tensor, the idea of convolutions and how they work stays the same: we slide a filter around the input, multiply the values in the filter with each area of the image, and then take the sum. We simply make the filter shape match accordingly. Let's look at a 2D example that aligns with the images we will try to process: figure 3.6 introduces the $\circledast$ operator, which means *convolve*.

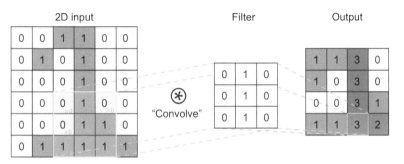

Figure 3.6 An image of a numeral 1 convolved with a 2D filter. The green region shows the part of the image currently being convolved, with the values from the filter shown in light blue. The result in the output is shown in orange. By sliding the green/orange areas together over the entire image, you produce the output result.

Again, the 2D output results from multiplying the filter values (pairwise) at each location and summing them all. The highlighted regions of the input are used to create the values in the output. In the bottom-right corner of the input cells, you see the filter value we are multiplying by. In deep learning, we almost always use square filters, meaning all r dimensions of the filter have the same number of values. So, in this case, we would call this a 2D filter of size K, or just size K for short. In this case, $K = 3$. The code for a 2D convolution doubles the number of loops:

```
filter = [[0, 1, 0], [0, 1, 0], [0, 1, 0]]
input = [[0,0,1,1,0,0],
         [...],
         [0,1,1,1,1,1]
        ]
height, width = len(input), len(input[0])
output = []
for i in range(height-len(filter)):        ⟵── Slides the filter over the rows
    row_out = []
    for j in range(width-len(filter)):     ⟵── Slides the filter over the columns
        result = 0
        for k_i in range(len(filter)):     ⟵── Applies the filter at this location
            for k_j in range(len(filter)):
                result += input[i+k_i][j+k_j]*filter[k_i][k_j]

        row_out.append(result)             ⟵────── Builds up a row of the output

    output.append(row_out)                 ⟵────── Adds the row to the final output.
                                                    The output is ready for use.
```

Since this 2D input has a shape of $(1, 6, 6)$ and the kernel has a shape of $(1, 3, 3)$, we shrink the width and height by $2 \cdot \lfloor 3/2 \rfloor = 2$. That means the height is 6 pixels $-2 = 4$ pixels, and we get the same result for the width: $6 - 2 = 4$ pixels wide. We now have the exact operation that is the foundation of CNNs for image classification.

3.2.3   Padding

Notice that every time we apply a convolution, the output becomes skinnier and shorter than the original input. That means if we kept applying convolutions over and over again, we would eventually be left with nothing. This is not something we want, because we will create multiple layers of convolutions. Most modern deep learning design practices keep the input and output the same size so that we can more easily reason about the shapes of our networks and make them as deep as we like without worrying about the input disappearing. The solution is called *padding*. You should almost always use padding by default so you can change your architecture without changing the shapes of your tensors. Figure 3.7 shows how this works for the same 2D image.

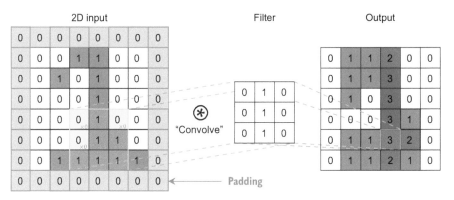

Figure 3.7   **The same convolution as before, with the same input and filter—but the input is padded with the value 0 to make the image larger by one pixel in each direction. This causes the output image to become the same width and height as the original image.**

We add an imaginary row/column of zeros all the way around the image and process it as if it was larger than it actually is. This specific example is called *zero padding by one* because we're adding one value to all the edges of the image, and the value was filled with 0. If we use a convolutional filter of size K, we can use padding of $\lfloor K/2 \rfloor$ to make sure our output stays the same size as our input. Again, even though the height and width can be padded to different degrees, we generally use the same amount of padding in each dimension because our filters have the same size in each dimension.

3.2.4 Weight sharing

There is another way to think about convolutions, which introduces an important concept called *weight sharing*. Let's look at the 1D case again because it is simpler to write code for. Imagine you have a neural network $f_\Theta(\cdot)$ with parameters (or *weights*) Θ, which takes in an input vector z with K features, $z \in \mathbb{R}^K$. Now let's say we have a larger input x with $C = 1$ channels and D features, where $D > K$. We can't use $f_\Theta(\cdot)$ on x because the shapes $D \neq K$ do not match.

One way we could apply the network $f_\Theta(\cdot)$ to this larger dataset would be to *slide* the network across slices of the input and *share* the weights Θ for each position. Some Python pseudocode looks like this:

```
x = torch.rand(D)                    ⟵──────── Some input vector
output = torch.zeros(D-K//2*2)
for i in range(output.shape[0]):
    output[i] = f(x[i:i+K], theta)
```

Now, if we defined our network as `f = nn.Linear(K, 1)`, it will implement *exactly a 1D convolution*. This insight can teach us some important properties about convolutions and how to use them to design deep neural networks. Right now, the primary thing this teaches us is that *convolutions are linear operations that work spatially*. As with the `nn.Linear` layer from the last chapter, a convolution followed by a second convolution is equivalent to just one slightly different convolution. That means:

- Never repeat convolutions, because doing so is redundant.

- Include a nonlinear activation function after using convolutions.

NOTE If we had a rectangular kernel of size $(1, 3, 5)$, the width of the output image would be $2 \cdot \lfloor 3/2 \rfloor = 2$ smaller than the input. The height of the output would be $2 \cdot \lfloor 5/2 \rfloor = 4$, removing *two* from each side. While rectangular kernels are possible, they are rarely used. Also notice that we have been sticking with kernels that have an *odd* size—nothing divisible by two. This is mostly for representational convenience because the filter is using an exact center from the input to produce each output. Like rectangular kernels, filters with even sizes are possible but are rarely used.

3.3 How convolutions benefit image processing

We have spent a lot of time talking about what convolutions are. Now it's time to see what they can do. Convolutions have a rich history of use in computer vision applications; this simple operation can define many useful things, as long as we select the appropriate kernel.

To start, let's again look at a *specific* image of the digit 4 from MNIST. We load the SciPy `convolve` function and define the `img_index` so you can change what image you are processing and see how these convolutions work across other inputs:

```
from scipy.signal import convolve
img_indx = 58
img = mnist_data_train[img_indx][0][0,:]
plt.imshow(img, vmin=0, vmax=1, cmap='gray')
```

[13]:   <matplotlib.image.AxesImage at 0x7f6a1f963b50>

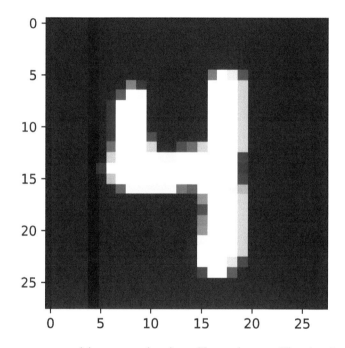

One common computer vision operation is to *blur* an image. Blurring involves taking a local average pixel value and replacing every pixel with the average of its neighbors. This can be useful to wash out small noisy artifacts or soften a sharp edge. It's done with a *blur kernel*, where

$$\text{Image} \quad \circledast \frac{1}{9} \begin{bmatrix} 1 & 1 & 1 \\ 1 & 1 & 1 \\ 1 & 1 & 1 \end{bmatrix} = \text{Blurred image}$$

We can take this math and convert it directly into code. The matrix is an `np.asarray` call, we've already loaded the image, and the convolution ⊛ is done with the `convolve` function. When we show the output image, we get a blurry version of the digit 4:

```
blur_filter = np.asarray([[1,1,1],
                          [1,1,1],
                          [1,1,1]
                         ])/9.0

blurry_img = convolve(img, blur_filter)
plt.imshow(blurry_img, vmin=0, vmax=1, cmap='gray')
plt.show()
```

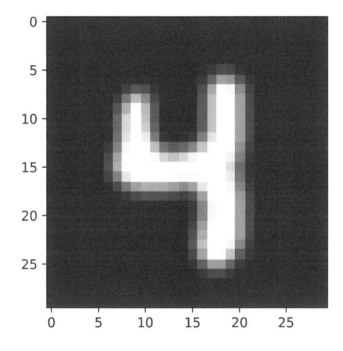

An especially common application of convolutions is to perform *edge detection*. In any computer vision application, it's good to know where the edges are. They can help you determine where the edges of a road are (you want your car to stay in its lane) or find objects (edges in different shapes are easy to recognize). In the case of this 4, the edges are the outline of the digit. So if all the pixels in a local area of the image are the *same*, we want everything to cancel out and result in no output. We only want there to be an output when there is a local change. Again, this can be described as a kernel where everything around the current pixel is negative, and the center pixel counts for the same weight as all its neighbors:

$$\text{Image} \quad \circledast \quad \begin{bmatrix} -1 & -1 & -1 \\ -1 & 8 & -1 \\ -1 & -1 & -1 \end{bmatrix} = \text{Edge image}$$

This filter is maximized when everything around a pixel is different than itself. Let's see what happens:

```
edge_filter = np.asarray([[-1,-1,-1],
                          [-1, 8,-1],
                          [-1,-1,-1]
                          ])
```

We can find edges by focusing on the difference between a pixel and its neighbors.

```
edge_img = convolve(img, edge_filter)
plt.imshow(edge_img, vmin=0, vmax=1, cmap='gray')
plt.show()
```

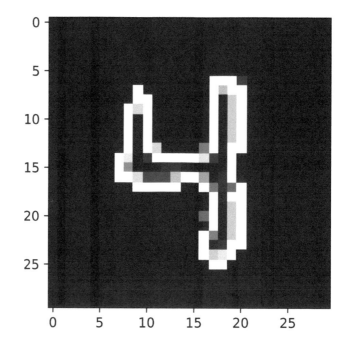

As promised, the filter found the edges of the digit. The response occurs only at the edges because that's where the most changes are. Outside the digit, there is no response because the high center weight cancels out all the neighbors, which is also true for the *inside* region of the digit. Thus, we have now found all the edges in the image.

We also may want to look for edges at a specific angle. If we constrain ourselves to a 3×3 kernel, it is easiest to find horizontal or vertical edges. Let's create one for horizontal edges by making the kernel values change signs across the horizontal of the filter:

$$\text{Image} \quad \circledast \begin{bmatrix} -1 & -1 & -1 \\ 0 & 0 & 0 \\ 1 & 1 & 1 \end{bmatrix} = \text{Horizontal edge image}$$

```
h_edge_filter = np.asarray([[-1,-1,-1],          ←────  We could look for
                            [0, 0,0],                   only horizontal edges.
                            [1, 1, 1]
                           ])
```

```
h_edge_img = convolve(img, h_edge_filter)
plt.imshow(h_edge_img, vmin=0, vmax=1, cmap='gray')
plt.show()
```

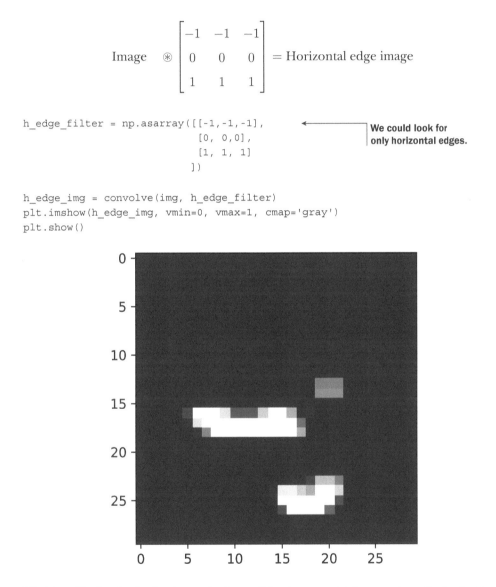

We identified only the horizontal edges of the image, which are primarily the bottom bar of the 4. As we define more useful kernels, you can imagine how we might compose a *combination* of filters to start recognizing higher-level concepts. Imagine if we only had the vertical and horizontal filters: we would not be able to classify all 10 digits, but figure 3.8 shows how we could narrow down the answer.

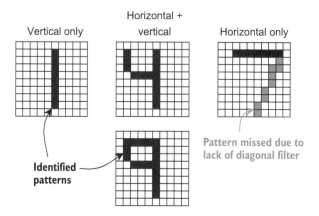

Figure 3.8   Example where we have only a vertical and a horizontal edge filter. If only the vertical filter turns on, we are probably looking at the digit 1. If only the horizontal filter turns on, we could be looking at a 7, but we would like an additional diagonal filter to help us confirm. If both the horizontal and vertical filters respond, we could be looking at a 4 or a 9; it's hard to tell without more filters.

Designing all the filters you might need by hand was a big part of computer vision for many decades. Convolutions on top of convolutions could also identify larger concepts: for example, after we identified horizontal and vertical edges, a new filter might take those as input and look for an empty space in the center with horizontal edges on top and vertical edges on the side. This would get us an O-like shape that could tell the difference between a 9 and a 4.

Thanks to deep learning, though, we don't have to go through the mental effort of imagining and testing all the filters we might need. Instead, we can let the neural network learn the filters itself. That way, we save ourselves from a labor-intensive process, and the kernels are optimized for the specific problem we care about.

3.4   *Putting it into practice: Our first CNN*

Now that we have discussed what a convolution is, let's look at some mathematical symbols and PyTorch code. We've seen that we can take an image $I \in \mathbb{R}^{C,W,H}$ and apply a convolution using a filter $g \in R^{C,K,K}$ to get a new result image $\mathbb{R}^{W',H'}$. We can write this in math as

That means each filter looks at all C input channels on its own. Figure 3.9 shows that using the 1D input example since it is easier to visualize.

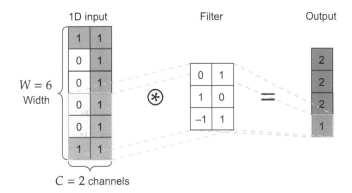

Figure 3.9 **Example of a 1D convolution with two channels. Because there are two channels, the 1D input looks like a matrix and has two axes. The filter also has two axes, one for each channel. This filter slides from top to bottom and produces one output channel. One filter always produces one output channel, regardless of however many input channels there are.**

Because the input has a shape of (C, W), the filter has a shape of (C, K). So when the input has multiple channels, the kernel will have a value for each channel separately. That means for a color image, we could have a filter that looks for "red horizontal lines, blue vertical lines, and no green" all in one operation. But it also means that after applying *one filter*, we get *one output*.

3.4.1 *Making a convolutional layer with multiple filters*

Considering the previous examples, we probably want more than one filter. We want C_{out} different filters; and let's use C_{in} to indicate the number of channels in the input. In this case, we have a tensor that represents all the filters as $G \in \mathbb{R}^{C_{\text{out}}, C_{\text{in}}, K, K}$, so we get a new result $R \in \mathbb{R}^{K, W', H'}$ when we write $R = I \circledast G$.

How do we convert this math notation to convolving input image I with a set of multiple filters G? PyTorch provides the nn.Conv1d, nn.Conv2d, and nn.Conv3d functions for handling this for us. Each of these implements a convolutional layer for one-, two-, and three-dimensional data. Figure 3.10 shows what is happening as a mechanical process.

The same process is used by all three standard convolution sizes: Conv1d works on tensors that are (Batch, Channels, Width), Conv2d does (Batch, Channels, Width, Height), and Conv2d does (Batch, Channels, Width, Height, Depth). The number of channels in the input is C_{in}, and the convolutional layer is made of C_{out} filters/kernels. Since each of these filters produces one output channel, the output of this layer has C_{out} channels. The value K defines the size of the kernel being used.

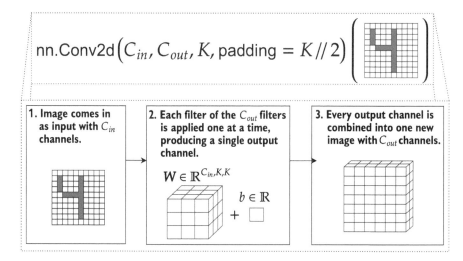

Figure 3.10   The `nn.Conv2d` functions defines a convolutional layer and works in three steps. First, it takes the input image, which has C_{in} channels. As part of the construction, `nn.Conv2d` takes the number of filters to use: C_{out}. Each filter is applied to the input. one at a time, and the results are combined. So the input tensor's shape is (B, C_{in}, W, H), and the output tensor has a shape of (B, C_{out}, W, H).

3.4.2   *Using multiple filters per layer*

To help drive home how this works, let's dive a little deeper and show the full process in detail. Figure 3.11 shows all the steps and math for an input image with $C_{in} = 3$, $C_{out} = 2$, and $K = 3$.

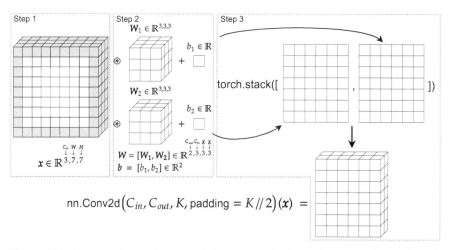

Figure 3.11   Example showing how convolutions are applied to multiple channels of a single image. Left: The input image, with padding shown in red. Middle: The parameters of two filters, W_1 and W_2 (with their associated bias terms, b_1, b_2). Each filter is convolved with the input to produce one channel. Right: The results are stacked to create a new image that has two channels, one for each filter. This whole process is done for us by the PyTorch `nn.Conv2d` class.

The input image has $C_{\text{in}} = 3$ channels, and we will process it using `nn.Conv2d(C_in, C_out, 3, padding=3//2)(x)` `= output`. Since $C_{\text{out}} = 2$, that means we process the input with two *different* filters, add the bias terms for every location, and get two resulting images that have the same height and width as the original image (because we used padding). The results are stacked into one larger single image with two channels because we specified $C_{\text{out}} = 2$.

3.4.3 *Mixing convolutional layers with linear layers via flattening*

When we had a fully connected layer, we wrote something like figure 3.12 for a single hidden layer with n hidden units/neurons. The mathematical notation we would use to describe a network with one *convolutional* hidden layer is very similar:

$$f(x) = \tanh \left(\underbrace{x_{C_{\text{in}},W,H} \circledast \overbrace{W^{(h_1)}_{C_{\text{out}},C_{\text{in}},K,K}}^{\text{nn.Conv2d}(C_{\text{in}},C_{\text{out}},K)} + b^{(h_1)}}_{\text{Input image}} \right) \overbrace{W^{(\text{out})}_{(C_{\text{out}}\cdot w \cdot h),C}}^{\text{nn.Linear}(C_{\text{out}}\cdot w \cdot h, C)} + b^{(\text{out})}$$

$$f(x) = \tanh \left(x^\top W^{(h_1)}_{d \times n} + b^{(h_1)} \right) W^{(\text{out})}_{n \times \text{classes}} + b^{(\text{out})}$$

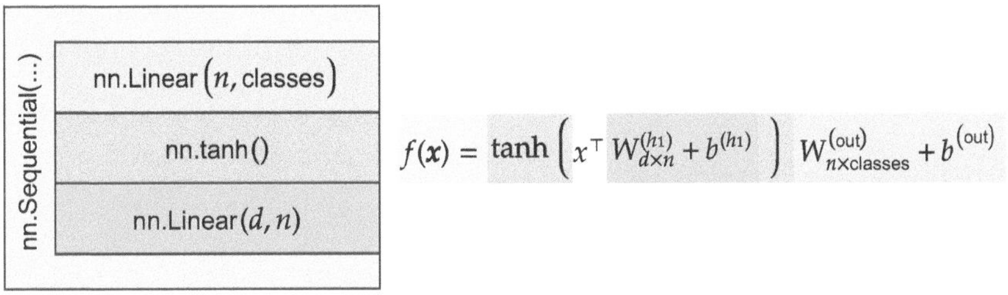

Figure 3.12 **One hidden layer in a fully connected network. Left: The PyTorch** `Modules` **that match the equation on the right. Colors show which** `Module` **maps to which part of the equation.**

That equation may look a little scary, but if we slow down, it's not that bad. It's intimidating because we have included the shape of each tensor in the equation and annotated where our fancy new `nn.Conv2d module` comes into play. We've included the shape information so you can see how we are processing different sized inputs—if we remove those extra details, it's not as scary-looking:

$$f(x) = \tanh \left(x \circledast W^{(h_1)} + b^{(h_1)} \right) W^{(\text{out})} + b^{(\text{out})} \tag{3.1}$$

Now it's clear that the only thing we have changed is replacing the dot product (a linear operation denoted by $\{\}^\top$) with convolution (a spatially linear operation denoted by $\circledast$).

This is *almost* perfect, but we have one issue: the output of the convolution has a shape of (C, W, H), but our linear layer ($W^{(\text{out})} + b^{(\text{out})}$) expects something of shape $(C \times W \times H)$—that's *one* dimension with all three original dimensions collapsed into it. Essentially, we need to *reshape* the output of our convolutions to remove the spatial interpretation so our linear layer can process the result and compute some predictions; see figure 3.13.

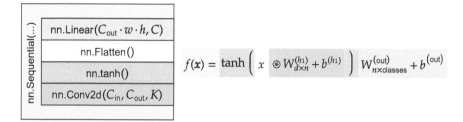

Figure 3.13   One hidden layer in a convolutional network. Left: The PyTorch `Modules` that match the equation on the right. Colors show which `Module` maps to which part of the equation.

This is called *flattening* and is a common operation in modern deep learning. We can consider equation 3.1 on the previous page to have implicitly used this flatten operation. PyTorch provides a `module` to do this called `nn.Flatten`. We often write this with implicit bias terms as $f(\boldsymbol{x}) = \tanh\left(\boldsymbol{x} \circledast \boldsymbol{W}^{(h_1)}\right) \boldsymbol{W}^{(\text{out})}$.

3.4.4   PyTorch code for our first CNN

Let's finally define some code for training this CNN-based model. First we need to grab the CUDA compute device and create a `DataLoader` for the training and testing sets. We use a batch size B of 32:

```
if torch.cuda.is_available():
  device = torch.device("cuda")
else:
  device = torch.device("cpu")

B = 32
mnist_train_loader = DataLoader(mnist_data_train, batch_size=B, shuffle=True)
mnist_test_loader = DataLoader(mnist_data_test, batch_size=B)
```

Now we will define some variables. Again, because PyTorch works in batches of data, when we think in a PyTorch context, our tensor shapes begin with B; and since the input consists of images, the initial shape is (B, C, W, H). We have $B = 32$ because we defined that and $C = 1$ because MNIST is black and white. We'll define a few helper variables like `K` to represent our filter size and `filters` for how many filters we want to build.

The first model is `model_linear` because it uses only `nn.Linear` layers. It begins with calling `nn.Flatten()`. Notice the specific comment we put into the code `#(B, C, W, H) -> (B, C*W*H) = (B,D)`: this is to remind us that we are changing the shape of the tensor using this operation. The original shape (B, C, W, H) is on the left, and the new shape $(B, C \times W \times H)$ is on the right. Since we have the variable D to represent the total number of features, we also include a note of the value it is equal to: `= (B,D)`. It is very easy to lose track of the shapes of tensors when writing code, and this is one of the easiest ways to introduce bugs. I always include comments like this when the shape is altered by a tensor.

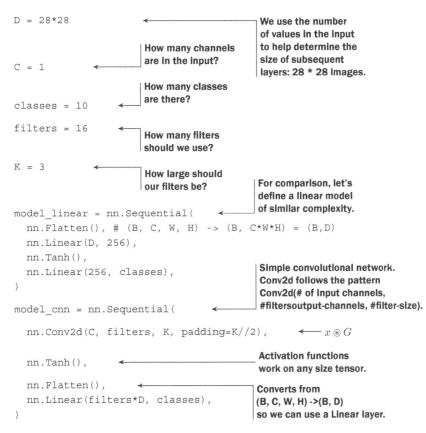

```
D = 28*28
```
We use the number of values in the input to help determine the size of subsequent layers: 28 * 28 images.

How many channels are in the input?
```
C = 1
```

How many classes are there?
```
classes = 10
```

```
filters = 16
```
How many filters should we use?

```
K = 3
```
How large should our filters be?

For comparison, let's define a linear model of similar complexity.
```
model_linear = nn.Sequential(
    nn.Flatten(), # (B, C, W, H) -> (B, C*W*H) = (B,D)
    nn.Linear(D, 256),
    nn.Tanh(),
    nn.Linear(256, classes),
)
```

Simple convolutional network. Conv2d follows the pattern Conv2d(# of input channels, #filtersoutput-channels, #filter-size).
```
model_cnn = nn.Sequential(

    nn.Conv2d(C, filters, K, padding=K//2),
```
$x \circledast G$

Activation functions work on any size tensor.
```
    nn.Tanh(),
```

Converts from (B, C, W, H) ->(B, D) so we can use a Linear layer.
```
    nn.Flatten(),
    nn.Linear(filters*D, classes),
)
```

`model_linear` is a simple fully connected layer for us to compare against. Our first CNN is defined by `model_cnn`, where we use the `nn.Conv2d` module to input a convolution. Then we can apply our nonlinear activation function tanh just like before. We only flatten the tensor once we are ready to use a `nn.Linear` layer to reduce the tensor to a set of predictions for each class. That's why the `nn.Flatten()` module occurs right before the call to `nn.Linear`

Does a CNN perform better than a fully connected model? Let's find out. We can train both a CNN and a fully connected model, measure accuracy on the test set, and look at the accuracy after each epoch:

```
loss_func = nn.CrossEntropyLoss()
cnn_results = train_simple_network(model_cnn, loss_func,
    mnist_train_loader, test_loader=mnist_test_loader,
    score_funcs={'Accuracy': accuracy_score}, device=device, epochs=20)
fc_results = train_simple_network(model_linear, loss_func,
    mnist_train_loader, test_loader=mnist_test_loader,
    score_funcs={'Accuracy': accuracy_score}, device=device, epochs=20)
```

```
sns.lineplot(x='epoch', y='test Accuracy', data=cnn_results, label='CNN')
sns.lineplot(x='epoch', y='test Accuracy', data=fc_results,
    label='Fully Connected')
```

[20]:   <AxesSubplot:xlabel='epoch', ylabel='test Accuracy'>

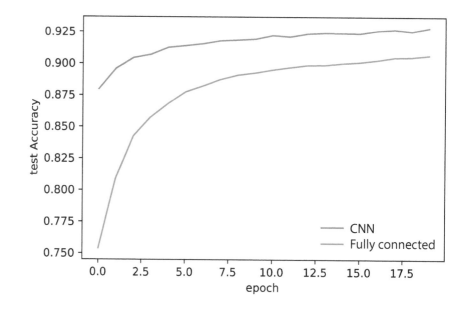

One epoch of training our CNN has *better accuracy* than our fully connected network ever achieves. While our CNN is about $1.138\times$ slower to train, the results are well worth it. Why does it perform so much better? Because we have given the network information about the problem (convolutions) via the structure of the domain (data consists of images). This does not mean CNNs are always better: if the assumptions for a CNN are not true or accurate, they will not perform well. Remember that convolutions impart the prior belief that things located near each other are related, but things far from each other are not related.

3.5   *Adding pooling to mitigate object movement*

Like feed-forward networks, we can make convolutional networks more powerful by stacking more layers with nonlinearities inserted in between. But before we do that, there is a special type of layer we like to use with CNNs called a *pooling* layer.

Pooling helps us solve the issue that we aren't fully exploiting the spatial nature of our data. That may seem confusing: we just significantly increased our accuracy with a simple switch to nn.Conv2d, and we spent a lot of time talking about how convolutions encode this spatial prior by sliding a set of weights over the input and applying them at every location. The problem is that we *eventually* switch to using a fully connected layer, which does not understand the spatial nature of the data. For this reason, the nn.Linear layer learns to look for values (or objects) at *very specific* locations.

This is not a huge problem for MNIST because all the digits are aligned so they are in the center of the image. But imagine a digit that is not perfectly center-aligned with your image. This is a very real potential problem—and pooling helps us solve it. Let's quickly grab an image from the MNIST dataset and create two altered versions by moving the content *ever so slightly* up or down by one pixel:

```
img_indx = 0
img, correct_class = mnist_data_train[img_indx]
img = img[0,:]
img_lr = np.roll(np.roll(img, 1, axis=1), 1, axis=0)      ← Moves to the lower right,
img_ul = np.roll(np.roll(img, -1, axis=1), -1, axis=0)      then upper left

f, axarr = plt.subplots(1,3)                               ← Plots the images
axarr[0].imshow(img, cmap='gray')
axarr[1].imshow(img_lr, cmap='gray')
axarr[2].imshow(img_ul, cmap='gray')
plt.show()
```

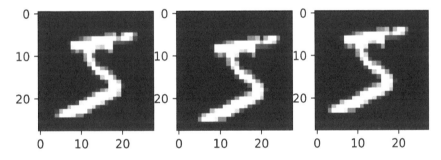

Clearly, all three versions of the image are the same digit. It does not matter that we shifted the content up or down, left or right, by just a few pixels. *But our model does not know this.* If we classify different versions of image, there is a good chance we will get it wrong.

Let's quickly put this model into eval() mode and write a function to get the predictions for a single image. That happens with the below pred function, which takes an image as input:

```
model = model_cnn.cpu().eval()          ← eval mode since
                                          we are not training

def pred(model, img):                     Always turn off gradients
    with torch.no_grad():                 ← when evaluating.

        w, h = img.shape                  ← Finds the width/
                                            height of the image
```

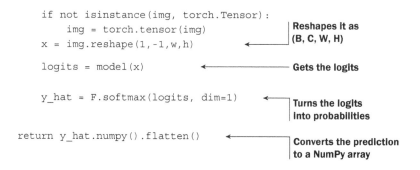

```
    if not isinstance(img, torch.Tensor):
        img = torch.tensor(img)
    x = img.reshape(1,-1,w,h)
```
Reshapes it as (B, C, W, H)

```
    logits = model(x)
```
Gets the logits

```
    y_hat = F.softmax(logits, dim=1)
```
Turns the logits into probabilities

```
    return y_hat.numpy().flatten()
```
Converts the prediction to a NumPy array

This is a simple way to apply a model to *single* images. PyTorch always expects things to be in batches, so we reshape the input to have a batch dimension, which is equal to 1 since there are no other images. The `if not isinstance` check is some defensive code you can add to make sure your code works for both NumPy and PyTorch input tensors. Also remember that the `CrossEntropy` loss we used handles softmax implicitly. So when we use a model trained with `CrossEntropy`, we need to call `F.softmax` to transform the outputs into probabilities.

With that out of the way, we can get predictions for all three images to see if tiny changes to the image can significantly change the network's prediction. Remember, each image differs by shifting the image to the lower right or upper left by one pixel. Intuitively, we expect very little to change:

```
img_pred = pred(model, img)
img_lr_pred = pred(model, img_lr)
img_ul_pred = pred(model, img_ul)

print("Org Img Class {} Prob: ".format(correct_class),
      img_pred[correct_class])
print("Lower Right Img Class {} Prob: ".format(correct_class),
      img_lr_pred[correct_class])
print("Uper Left Img Class {} Prob: ".format(correct_class),
      img_ul_pred[correct_class])

Org Img Class 5 Prob: 0.78159285
Lower Right Img Class 5 Prob: 0.44280732
Uper Left Img Class 5 Prob: 0.31534675
```

Clearly, we want all three examples to receive the same classification. They are *essentially* the same image, yet the outputs swing from a reasonably confident and correct 78.2% down to an erroneous 31.5%. The problem is that a small shift or translation causes the predictions to change significantly.

What we desire is a property called *translation invariance*. Being invariant to property X means our output does not change based on changes to X. We do not want translations (shifting up/down) to change our decisions—we want to be translation invariant.

Pooling can enable us to obtain partial translation invariance. Specifically, we will look at *max pooling*. What is max pooling? Similar to convolution, we apply the same function to multiple locations in an image. We generally stick to even-sized pooling filters. As the name implies, we slide the max function around the image. You can describe this as having a kernel size K, which is the size of the window from which to select the maximum. The big difference here is that we move the max function by K pixels at a time, where we moved only 1 pixel at a time when performing a convolution (see figure 3.14).

2D input channel

Channel output

1	3	4	7	-5	2
2	-9	3	2	8	8
5	7	6	2	1	6
8	4	9	3	2	5
-5	2	7	6	4	5
3	1	-4	1	-8	2

nn.MaxPool2d(2)

3	7	8
8	9	6
3	7	5

1	3	4	7	-5	2
2	-9	3	2	8	8
5	7	6	2	1	6
8	4	9	3	2	5
-5	2	7	6	4	5
3	1	-4	1	-8	2

nn.MaxPool2d(3)

7	8
9	6

Figure 3.14 Example of max pooling for $K = 2$ (top) and $K = 3$ (bottom). Each region of the input (left) has a color indicating the group of pixels participating in the pooling, and the output (right) shows which value was selected from the input region. Note that the output is smaller than the input by a factor of K.

The choice of how many pixels to slide by is called the *stride*. By default, practitioners tend to use stride=1 for convolutions so that *every* possible location is evaluated. We use stride=K for pooling so the input is shrunk by a factor of K. For any operation, if you use stride=z for any (positive integer) value of Z, the result will be smaller by a factor of Z along each dimension.

The intuition behind pooling is that it gives us more robustness to slight changes in values. Consider the upper-left part of figure 3.14 if you shifted every value over to the right by one position. Five of the output values *would not change*, giving the pooling operation a minor degree of *invariance* to *translating* the image by one pixel. This is not perfect, but it helps reduce the impact of such alterations. If we accumulate this effect through multiple rounds of pooling, we can make the effect stronger.

Just like before, PyTorch provides `nn.MaxPool1d`, `nn.MaxPool2d`, and `nn.MaxPool3d` for almost all your needs. The function takes the kernel size as input, which is also the stride. Having a stride of K means we shrink the size of each shape dimension by a factor of K. So if our input has a shape of (B, C, W, H), the output of `nn.MaxPool2d(K)` will be a shape of $(B, C, W/K, H/K)$. Since C remains the same, we apply this simple operation to every channel independently. If we do max pooling with a 2×2 filter (the norm for most applications), we end up with an image one-fourth the size (half as many rows and half as many columns).

3.5.1   CNNs with max pooling

It's easy to add pooling to our model's definition: just insert `nn.MaxPool2d(2)` into `nn.Sequential`. But *where* should we use max pooling? First, let's talk bout *how many times* to apply max pooling. Every time pooling is applied, we shrink the width (and height, if 2D) by a factor of K. So n rounds of pooling means shrinking by a factor of K^n, which will make the image very small very quickly. For MNIST, we only have 28 pixels of width, so we can do at most four rounds of pooling with a size of $K = 2$. That's because five rounds would give us $28/2^5 = 28/32$, which is *less than a pixel of output*.

Does doing four rounds of pooling make more sense? Try to imagine if it was a problem *you* were asked to solve. Four rounds of pooling means shrinking the image to just $28/2^4 = 28/16 = 1.75$ pixels tall. If you could not guess what digit was being represented with 1.75 pixels, your CNN probably couldn't either. Visually shrinking your data is a good way to estimate the maximum amount of pooling you should apply to most problems. Using two or three rounds of pooling is a good initial lower bound or estimate for images up to 256×256 pixels.

> **NOTE**   Most modern applications of CNNs are on images smaller than 256×256. That's very large to process with modern GPUs and techniques. In practice, if your images are larger than that, the first step is to resize them to have at most 256 pixels along any dimension. If you really *need* to process at a larger resolution, you probably want someone on your team with relevant experience, because the tricks of working at that scale are unique and often require very expensive hardware.

Every application of pooling shrinks the image by a factor of K, which also means the network has less data to process after every round of pooling. If you are working with very large images, pooling can help reduce the time it takes to train larger models and the memory costs of training. If neither of these is a problem, common practice is to increase the number of filters by $K \times$ after every round of pooling so that the total computation done at every layer remains roughly the same (i.e., twice as many filters on half as many rows/columns about balances out).

Let's quickly try this on our MNIST data. The following code defines a deeper CNN with multiple layers of convolution and two rounds of max pooling:

```
model_cnn_pool = nn.Sequential(
    nn.Conv2d(C, filters, 3, padding=3//2),
    nn.Tanh(),
    nn.Conv2d(filters, filters, 3, padding=3//2),
    nn.Tanh(),
    nn.Conv2d(filters, filters, 3, padding=3//2),
    nn.Tanh(),
    nn.MaxPool2d(2),
    nn.Conv2d(filters, 2*filters, 3, padding=3//2),
    nn.Tanh(),
    nn.Conv2d(2*filters, 2*filters, 3, padding=3//2),
    nn.Tanh(),
    nn.Conv2d(2*filters, 2*filters, 3, padding=3//2),
    nn.Tanh(),
    nn.MaxPool2d(2),

    nn.Flatten(),
    nn.Linear(2*filters*D//(4**2), classes),    ⬅
)
```

Why reduce the number of units into the Linear layer by a factor of 4^2? Because pooling a 2×2 grid down to one value means going from four values to one, and we do this twice.

```
cnn_results_with_pool = train_simple_network(model_cnn_pool, loss_func,
    mnist_train_loader, test_loader=mnist_test_loader,
    score_funcs={'Accuracy': accuracy_score}, device=device, epochs=20)
```

Now, if we run the same shifted test image through our model, we should see different results. Max pooling is not a *perfect* solution to the translation problem, so the scores for each shifted version of the image still change. But they don't change *as much*. That is overall a good thing because it makes our model more *robust* to real-life issues. Data will not always be perfectly aligned, so we want to make the model resilient to the kinds of issues we expect to see in real-life test data:

```
model = model_cnn_pool.cpu().eval()
img_pred = pred(model, img)
img_lr_pred = pred(model, img_lr)
img_ul_pred = pred(model, img_ul)

print("Org Img Class {} Prob: ".format(correct_class),
    img_pred[correct_class])
print("Lower Right Img Class {} Prob: ".format(correct_class),
    img_lr_pred[correct_class])
print("Uper Left Img Class {} Prob: ".format(correct_class),
    img_ul_pred[correct_class])

Org Img Class 5 Prob: 0.7068047
Lower Right Img Class 5 Prob: 0.71668524
Uper Left Img Class 5 Prob: 0.7311974
```

Finally, we can look at the accuracy of this new and larger network we trained, which is shown in the following plot. Adding more layers causes our network to take *much* longer to converge, but once it does, it can eke out a little better accuracy:

```
sns.lineplot(x='epoch', y='test Accuracy', data=cnn_results,
    label='Simple CNN')
sns.lineplot(x='epoch', y='test Accuracy', data=cnn_results_with_pool,
    label='CNN w/ Max Pooling')
```

[27]: <AxesSubplot:xlabel='epoch', ylabel='test Accuracy'>

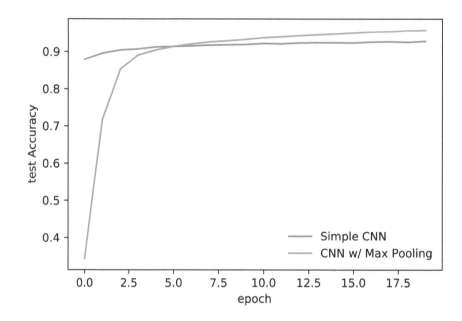

It is common for using more layers to cause training to take longer to converge *and* longer to process for each epoch. This double whammy is offset only by the fact that using more layers—making models *deeper*—is how we tend to obtain the best possible accuracy. If you continued to train this deeper model for more epochs, you will see it continue to climb higher than we could achieve with our first model that contained only one nn.Conv2d layer.

> WARNING   Just like ice cream, you can have too much of a good thing and make a network too deep to learn. In chapters 5 and 6, you'll learn improved techniques that can help you build networks with as many as 100 to 200 layers—and that's about the limit on how deep we can train networks today while still obtaining some benefit. Note that 5 to 20 layers are often good enough, and depth is always a tradeoff between compute cost and diminishing returns.

As we continue in this book, we'll learn about newer and better approaches that help resolve these issues and make convergence faster and better. But I want to take you on this slower and somewhat more painful path so you understand *why* these newer techniques were developed and what problems they solve. This deeper understanding will help you be better prepared for the more advanced techniques we tackle by the time you finish the book.

3.6 Data augmentation

It may seem a little anticlimactic, but you now know everything you need to start training and building CNNs for new problems. All it took to implement a CNN in PyTorch was replacing `nn.Linear` layers with `nn.Conv2d`, followed by a `nn.Flatten` before the end. But there is one more big secret to applying CNNs in practice: using *data augmentation*. In general, neural networks are data-hungry, meaning they learn best when you have a *huge* amount of *diverse* data. Since it takes time to obtain data, we will instead *augment* our real data by creating new, fake data based on the real data.

The idea is simple. If we are working with 2D images, we can apply many transforms to an image that do not change the meaning of its content but alter the pixels. For example, we can rotate the image by a few degrees without altering what the content means. PyTorch provides a number of transforms in the `torchvision.transforms` package; let's take a look at some of them:

```
                                              Built-in transformations
                                              given aggressive values
sample_transforms = {                         to make their impact obvious

    "Rotation" : transforms.RandomAffine(degrees=45),
    "Translation" : transforms.RandomAffine(degrees=0, translate=(0.1,0.1)),
    "Shear": transforms.RandomAffine(degrees=0, shear=45),
    "RandomCrop" : transforms.RandomCrop((20,20)),
    "Horizontal Flip" : transforms.RandomHorizontalFlip(p=1.0),
    "Vertical Flip": transforms.RandomVerticalFlip(p=1.0),
    "Perspective": transforms.RandomPerspective(p=1.0),
    "ColorJitter" : transforms.ColorJitter(brightness=0.9, contrast=0.9)
}
pil_img = transforms.ToPILImage()(img)         Converts the Tensor image back
                                               to a PIL image using a transform

f, axarr = plt.subplots(2,4)                   Plots a random application
                                               of each transform

for count, (name, t) in enumerate(sample_transforms.items()):
    row = count % 4
    col = count // 4
    axarr[col,row].imshow(t(pil_img), cmap='gray')
    axarr[col,row].set_title(name)
plt.show()
```

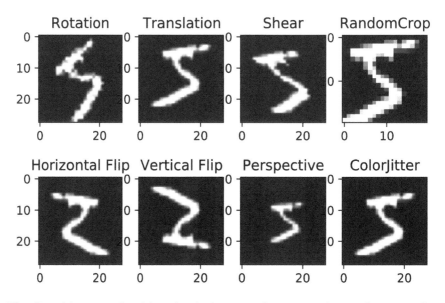

The first thing you should notice is that transforms are almost always *randomized*, and every time we apply one, it gives a different result. These new results are our augmented data. For example, specifying `degrees=45` says the maximum rotation is ±45° degrees, and the amount applied is a randomly chosen value in that range. This is done to increase the *diversity* of inputs our model sees. Some transforms do not always apply themselves and offer the `p` argument to control the probability of being chosen. We set these as `p=1.0` so you would definitely see them have an impact on the test image. For real use, you probably want to pick a value of `p=0.5` or `p=0.15`. Like many things, the specific value to use will depend on your data.

Not every transform should *always* be used. Make sure that your transforms preserve the essence or meaning of your data. For example, horizontal and vertical flips are not a good idea for the MNIST dataset: a vertical flip applied to the digit 9 could turn it into a 6, and that *changes the meaning of the image.* Your best bet for selecting a good set of transforms is to apply them to data and *look at the results yourself;* if you can't tell what the correct answer is anymore, chances are your CNN can't either.

But once you select a set of transforms you are comfortable with, this is a simple and powerful approach to improve your model's accuracy. Following is a short example of using the `Compose` transform to create a sequence of transforms in a larger pipeline, which we can apply to augment training data on the fly. All the image-based datasets PyTorch provides have the `transform` argument so that you can perform these alterations:

```
train_transform = transforms.Compose([
    transforms.RandomAffine(degrees=5, translate=(0.05, 0.05),
        scale=(0.98, 1.02)),
    transforms.ToTensor(),
])

test_transform = transforms.ToTensor()
```

```
mnist_train_t = torchvision.datasets.MNIST("./data", train=True,
    transform=train_transform)
mnist_test_t = torchvision.datasets.MNIST("./data", train=False,
    transform=test_transform)
mnist_train_loader_t = DataLoader(mnist_train_t, shuffle=True,
    batch_size=B, num_workers=5)
mnist_test_loader_t = DataLoader(mnist_test_t, batch_size=B,
    num_workers=5)
```

> **NOTE** A new and important optional argument has been specified in the
> `DataLoader` class: the `num_workers` flag controls how many threads are used to
> *preload* batches of data for training. While the GPU is busy crunching a batch of
> data, each thread can prepare the next batch to be ready to go when the GPU is
> done. You should always use this flag because it helps you use your GPU more
> efficiently. It's essential when you start using transforms because the CPU will have
> to spend time processing the images, which keeps your GPU idly waiting.

Now we can redefine the same network we used to show max pooling and call the same
training method. The data augmentation happens automatically by defining these new
data loaders. A simple `ToTensor` transform is all we use for the test set because we want
the test set to be *deterministic*—that means if we run the same model five times on the
test set, we get the same answer five times:

```
model_cnn_pool = nn.Sequential(
    nn.Conv2d(C, filters, 3, padding=3//2),
    nn.Tanh(),
    nn.Conv2d(filters, filters, 3, padding=3//2),
    nn.Tanh(),
    nn.Conv2d(filters, filters, 3, padding=3//2),
    nn.Tanh(),
    nn.MaxPool2d(2),
    nn.Conv2d(filters, 2*filters, 3, padding=3//2),
    nn.Tanh(),
    nn.Conv2d(2*filters, 2*filters, 3, padding=3//2),
    nn.Tanh(),
    nn.Conv2d(2*filters, 2*filters, 3, padding=3//2),
    nn.Tanh(),
    nn.MaxPool2d(2),
    nn.Flatten(),
    nn.Linear(2*filters*D//(4**2), classes),
)

cnn_results_with_pool_augmented = train_simple_network(model_cnn_pool,
    loss_func, mnist_train_loader_t, test_loader=mnist_test_loader_t,
    score_funcs={'Accuracy': accuracy_score}, device=device, epochs=20)
```

We can now plot the result showing the difference in validation accuracy. With a careful
choice of augmentation, we helped our model learn faster and converge to a better-
quality solution, 96.2% accuracy instead of 95.7%:

```
sns.lineplot(x='epoch', y='test Accuracy', data=cnn_results_with_pool,
    label='CNN w/ Max Pooling')
sns.lineplot(x='epoch', y='test Accuracy',
    data=cnn_results_with_pool_augmented,
    label='CNN w/ Max Pooling + Augmentation')
```

[31]:   <AxesSubplot:xlabel='epoch', ylabel='test Accuracy'>

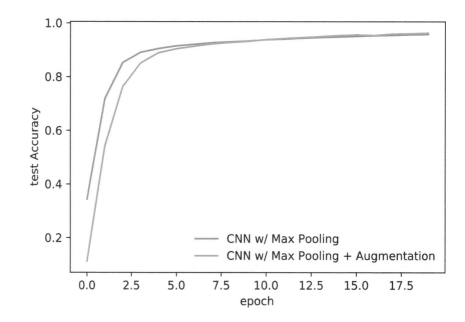

Designing good data augmentation pipelines is the feature engineering counterpart to deep learning. If you do it well, it can have a massive impact on your results and be the difference between success and failure. Because PyTorch uses PIL images as its foundation, you can also write custom transforms to add into the pipeline. This is where you can import tools like scikit-image that provide more advanced computer vision transforms that you can apply. The impact of good data augmentation will also grow as we learn how to build more sophisticated networks and when you work on more complex datasets than MNIST. Data augmentation also increases the value of training for more epochs. Without augmentation, each epoch revisits the exact same data; with augmentation, your model sees a different variant of the data that helps it better generalize to new data. Our 10 epochs aren't enough to see the full benefit.

Despite the importance of good data augmentation, you can go far in deep learning without it. We will not use data augmentation for most of this book: part of the reason is to keep our examples simpler without having to explain the choices of data augmentation pipelines for every new dataset, and the other reason is that augmentation is *domain-specific*. What works for images *only* works for images. You need to come up with a new set of transforms for audio data, and text is a difficult realm in which to perform augmentation. Most of the techniques we will learn in this book can be applied to a fairly broad class of problems.

Exercises

Share and discuss your solutions on the Manning online platform at Inside Deep Learning Exercises (https://liveproject.manning.com/project/945). Once you submit your own answers, you will be able to see the solutions submitted by other readers, and see which ones the author judges to be the best.

Note that these exercises are intentionally *exploratory* in nature. The goal is for you to learn about and discover a number of common trends and properties for working with CNNs through your own code and experience.

1 Try training all the networks in this chapter for 40 epochs instead of 10. What happens?

2 Load the CIFAR10 dataset from `torchvision`, and try to build your own CNN. Try using 2 to 10 layers of convolutions and 0 to 2 rounds of max pooling. What seems to work best?

3 Go through the transforms provided and see which makes sense for CIFAR10 via visual inspection. Do any transforms work for CIFAR10 that do not make sense for MNIST?

4 Train a new CIFAR10 model with the transforms you selected. What impact does this have on accuracy?

5 Try altering the size of the convolutional filters in CIFAR10 and MNIST. What impact does it have?

6 Create a new custom `Shuffle` transform that applies the same fixed reordering of the pixels in an image. How does using this transform impact your CIFAR10 model? *Hint:* Look at the `Lambda` transform to help you implement this.

Summary

- To represent images in a PyTorch tensor, we use multiple channels, where the channel describes something of a different nature about the image (e.g., red, green, and blue channels).

- Convolution is a mathematical operation that takes a kernel (a small tensor) and applies a function over every location in a larger input tensor to produce an output. This makes convolutions *spatial* in nature.

- A convolutional layer learns multiple different kernels to apply to the input to create multiple outputs.

- Convolutions don't capture translation (shifts up or down) invariance, and we can use pooling to make our models more robust to translations.

- Both convolutions and pooling have a stride option that dictates how many pixels we move when sliding across the image.

- When our data is spatial (e.g., images), we can embed a prior (convolutions are spatial) into our network to learn faster and better solutions.

- We can augment our training data by selecting a set of transformations to apply to the data, improving our model's accuracy.

Recurrent neural networks

The previous chapter showed us how to develop neural networks for a particular type of spatial structure: spatial locality. Specifically, we learned how the convolution operator endowed our neural network with a prior that items near each other are related but items far from each other have *no* relationship. This allowed us to build neural networks that learned faster and provide more accurate solutions for classifying images.

Now we want to develop models that can handle a new type of structure: *sequences* with T items that occur in a specific order. For example, the alphabet—a, b, c, d, . . .—is a sequence of 26 characters. Each sentence in this book can be thought of as a sequence of words *or* a sequence of characters. You could use the temperature every hour as a sequence to try to predict the temperature in the future. As long as each item in the sequence can be represented as a vector x, we can use a sequence-based

111

model to learn over it. For example, videos can be treated as a sequence of images; you could use a convolutional neural network (CNN) to convert each image into a vector.[1]

In all these cases, the structure is uniquely different compared to the images and convolution from chapter 3. Sequences can have a *variable* number of items. For example, the two previous sentences have variable length: 18 and 8 words, respectively. By comparison, images are *always* the exact same width and height. This is not too restricting for images since it is easy to resize them without changing their meaning. But we can't just "resize" a sequence, so we need an approach that can handle this new problem of variable-length data.

That is where recurrent neural networks (RNNs) come into play. They give us a different prior for our model: *inputs follow a sequence, and order matters.* RNNs are particularly useful because they can handle inputs with differing sequence lengths. When talking about sequences and RNNs, we will often refer to the sequence as a *time series* and the ith item in the sequence as the ith *step in time* (using t and i to denote a specific item or point in time is common, and we will use both). This comes from a view of RNNs as processing a sequence of events at a regular interval. This terminology is prevalent, so we'll use T for *time* to refer to the number of items in the input sequence. Using the first two sentences from the last paragraph again, that would be $T = 18$ for 18 words in the first sentence and $T = 8$ for 8 words in the second sentence.

Using an RNN, we learn in this chapter how to create networks for sequence classification problems. Examples include the following:

- *Sentiment detection*—Is this sequence of words (e.g., a sentence, tweet, or paragraph) indicating a positive, negative, or neutral impression? For example, I might run sentence detection on Twitter to find out if people like this book.

- *Vehicle maintenance*—Your car may store daily or weekly information about how many miles have been driven, miles per gallon while driving, engine temperature, and more. This could be used to predict whether a car will need repairs in the next 3, 6, or 12 months, often called *predictive maintenance*.

- *Weather prediction*—Every day, you can record the high, mean, and low temperature, humidity, wind speed, and so on. Then you can predict tons of things like the temperature the next day, how many people will go to the mall (companies would love to know that), and if traffic will be normal, bad, or good.

RNNs are often challenging for people to grasp when diving into deep learning, and many materials treat them as magic black boxes that take in sequences and output new sequences. For this reason, we will carefully build our way up to understanding what an RNN actually is. This is one of the two most challenging chapters in the book, and it's OK if it doesn't all make sense on the first read. RNNs are an intrinsically mind-bending concept—it took me several years to wrap my head around them. To help you understand the concepts in this chapter, I recommend using pen and paper

---

[1] This is a real type of model, but it tends to take a long time to train. We won't do any examples that are quite that complex.

to draw the processes and figures yourself, starting with a sequence of T=1, then adding a second and a third, and so on.

Before diving into problems, in section 4.1 we slowly work our way up to defining what a RNN is via the concept of *weight sharing*. This is the foundation of how RNNs work, so we start by talking about weight sharing for a simple fully connected network to understand the concept and then show how that concept is applied to produce a RNN. Once we have the mental picture in place, section 4.2 moves into the mechanics of loading sequence classification problems and defining a RNN in PyTorch. A common problem with RNNs in PyTorch is that the sequences you want to train on have variable lengths, but the `Tensor` object does not have any flexibility: all dimensions must have the same length. Section 4.3 resolves this `Tensor`/sequence problem with a technique called *padding* that allows PyTorch to run correctly when sequences in a batch have variable length. Section 4.4 closes out the new material with two modifications to RNNs that improve their accuracy.

4.1 Recurrent neural networks as weight sharing

Before we get into the new topic of recurrent neural networks (RNNs), let's talk a bit more about a concept from the last chapter: *weight sharing*. To make sure you are familiar with this fundamental idea, we walk through solving a contrived problem. That way, we can show the mechanics of the process before diving into the more complex RNN. Figure 4.1 is a quick reminder of the weight sharing concept, where we reuse a layer in multiple locations. PyTorch handles the tricky math of learning correctly when reusing a layer.

Normal situation: Each block that processes the input is a different function, with different knobs and parameters. Training alters the parameters of each individual box to produce a desired output.

Weight sharing: Some blocks are reused exactly in multiple locations. The block always has the same parameters even though it is used in multiple locations. Training learns how to set the parameters to be useful in multiple locations.

Figure 4.1 Outline of how weight sharing works. Boxes represent any kind of neural network or PyTorch module. Boxes have an input/output relationship, and normally each layer of our network is a different box. If we reuse the same box multiple times, we are effectively sharing the same weights between multiple layers.

When using a CNN, the convolution operation is like having a single small linear network that we slide across the image, applying the *same function to every spatial position*. This is an implicit property of a CNN that we made explicit with this small bit of code:

```
x = torch.rand(D)                    ←——————— Input vector
output = torch.zeros(D-K//2*2)
for i in range(output.shape[0]):
    output[i] = f(x[i:i+K], theta)
```

This code reuses the same weights Θ for multiple inputs. Our CNN does this implicitly. To help understand RNNs and how they work, we explicitly apply weight sharing to show how we can use it in different ways. Then we can adjust how we use weight sharing to arrive at the original RNN algorithm.

4.1.1   Weight sharing for a fully connected network

Let's imagine that we want to create a fully connected network with three hidden layers for a classification problem. Figure 4.2 shows what this network looks like as a sequence of PyTorch modules.

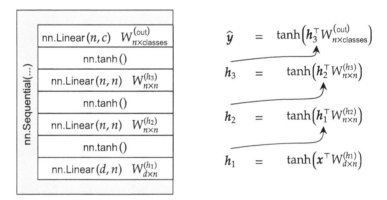

Figure 4.2   A simple network with three hidden layers and one output layer. The `nn.Sequential` layer is shown wrapping the sequence of layers in the order they are used (first on the bottom, last at the top).

To make sure we are learning how to read and write network definitions as both code and math, the same network, written as equations, is shown next. The linear layers W are also referenced in figure 4.2 so that we can map the parts to each other:

$$f(x) = \tanh\left(\tanh\left(\tanh\left(x^\top W_{d\times n}^{(h_1)}\right) W_{n\times n}^{(h_2)}\right) W_{n\times n}^{(h_3)}\right) W_{n\times \text{classes}}^{(\text{out})}$$

I've decided to be explicit with this equation and show the shape of each linear layer. We have d input features according to this equation, n neurons in each hidden layer, and classes outputs. This explicit detail will become important in a moment. Let's quickly implement this network for MNIST:

```
mnist_data_train = torchvision.datasets.MNIST("./data", train=True,
    download=True, transform=transforms.ToTensor())
mnist_data_test = torchvision.datasets.MNIST("./data", train=False,
    download=True, transform=transforms.ToTensor())

mnist_train_loader = DataLoader(mnist_data_train, batch_size=64, shuffle=True)
mnist_test_loader = DataLoader(mnist_data_test, batch_size=64)
```

```
D = 28*28         ◄──────  How many values are in
                            the input? We use this to
                            help determine the size
                            of subsequent layers.

n = 256           ◄──────  Hidden layer size

C = 1             ◄──────  How many channels
                            are in the input?

classes = 10      ◄──────  How many classes are there?

model_regular = nn.Sequential(   ◄──  Creates our regular model
    Flatten(),
    nn.Linear(D, n),
    nn.Tanh(),
    nn.Linear(n, n),
    nn.Tanh(),
    nn.Linear(n, n),
    nn.Tanh(),
    nn.Linear(n, classes),
)
```

This is a simple fully connected model since we use `nn.Linear` layers. To train this as a classification problem, we again use the `train_simple_network` function. (This should all be familiar from chapters 2 and 3.) We can train this model and get the following result, which is nothing new:

```
loss_func = nn.CrossEntropyLoss()
regular_results = train_simple_network(model_regular, loss_func,
    mnist_train_loader, test_loader=mnist_test_loader,
    score_funcs={'Accuracy': accuracy_score}, device=device, epochs=10)
```

Now, let's *pretend* that this is a very large network—so large that we can't fit the weights for all three hidden layers $\boldsymbol{W}^{(h_1)}_{d \times n}$, $\boldsymbol{W}^{(h_2)}_{n \times n}$, and $\boldsymbol{W}^{(h_3)}_{n \times n}$. But we *really* want a network with three hidden layers. One option is to *share* the weights between some of the layers. We can do this mathematically by simply replacing h_3 with h_2, which is the same as defining one object and reusing that object twice in our definition. Figure 4.3 shows how to do this with the second and third hidden layers because they have the same shape.

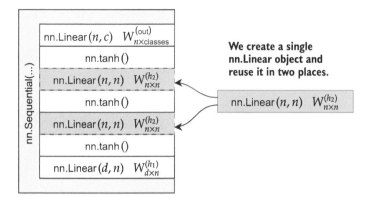

Figure 4.3 **A simple feed-forward network with weight sharing. Before creating the** `nn.Sequential`
object, we define a single `nn.Linear(n,n)` **layer that is used as both the second and third hidden
layers. PyTorch figures out how to learn with that setup, and the second and third layers share the same
weights.**

The mathematical way to express this is to change our previous equation to the following:

$$f(\boldsymbol{x}) = \tanh\left(\tanh\left(\tanh\left(\boldsymbol{x}^{\top}\boldsymbol{W}_{d\times n}^{(h_1)}\right)\boldsymbol{W}_{n\times n}^{(h_2)}\right)\boldsymbol{W}_{n\times n}^{(h_2)}\right)\boldsymbol{W}_{n\times\text{classes}}^{(\text{out})}$$

The only thing that has changed (in red) is that we are reusing the weights $\boldsymbol{W}^{(h_2)}$ in
two different locations. *This is weight sharing*, reusing the weights of a layer. It's called
this because we can pretend the two different usages of $\boldsymbol{W}^{(h_2)}$ are different layers in
the network that share the same weights. How do we implement this in PyTorch? It's
simple. If we think of that linear layer as an object, we *reuse the layer object*. Everything
else works exactly the same.

> **NOTE** You may also hear weight sharing called *tied* weights. This is the same
> concept, just a different analogy for the name: the weights are tied together. Some
> people prefer this terminology if the weights are used slightly differently. For
> example, one layer may use W while the other uses the transposed weights $W^{\top}$.

The following code shows the same fully connected network but with weight sharing for
the second and third hidden layers. We declare the `nn.Linear` layer we want to share as
an object named `h_2` and insert it twice in the `nn.Sequential` list. So, the `h_2` is used as
both the second and third hidden layers, and PyTorch will correctly train the network
using the very same function—no changes needed:

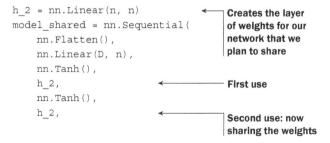

```
h_2 = nn.Linear(n, n)                      Creates the layer
model_shared = nn.Sequential(              of weights for our
    nn.Flatten(),                          network that we
    nn.Linear(D, n),                       plan to share
    nn.Tanh(),
    h_2,                                   First use
    nn.Tanh(),
    h_2,                                   Second use: now
                                           sharing the weights
```

```
        nn.Tanh(),
        nn.Linear(n, classes),
)
```

That this code works may seem trivial from a coding perspective. It's a very object-oriented design: we create an object, and the object is used in two places. But making the math work out is not a simple matter. Luckily, PyTorch handles this for you, and the same training function handles this weight sharing just fine:

```
shared_results = train_simple_network(model_shared, loss_func,
    mnist_train_loader, test_loader=mnist_test_loader,
    score_funcs={'Accuracy': accuracy_score}, device=device, epochs=10)
```

With the new weight-shared network, we can plot the validation accuracy of both to see what PyTorch *really* learn with shared weights and what the results look like:

```
sns.lineplot(x='epoch', y='test Accuracy',
    data=regular_results, label='Normal')

sns.lineplot(x='epoch', y='test Accuracy',
    data=shared_results, label='Shared')
```

Plots the results and compares them

[10]: <AxesSubplot:xlabel='epoch', ylabel='test Accuracy'>

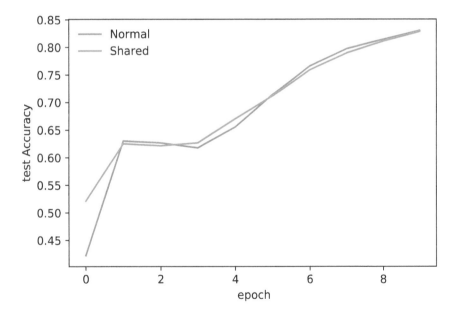

Using weight sharing doesn't take any longer to train, and we don't lose any accuracy (that is *not* a guarantee). We do get a nice benefit of slightly reduced memory, but what we have done here is rarely used. Better approaches exist to reduce memory usage, and the purpose of this problem was just to demonstrate the weight sharing. We care about weight sharing because it is the foundation for creating and training RNNs.

4.1.2 *Weight sharing over time*

Now that we understand weight sharing, we can talk about how it is used to create RNNs. The goal of an RNN is to summarize every item in a sequence of items, using just a single item. The process is shown in figure 4.4. The RNN takes in two items: a tensor h_{t-1} that represents everything seen so far in the order it has seen, and a tensor x_t that represents the newest/next item in the sequence. The RNN combines the historical summary (h_{t-1}) and the new information (x_t) to create a *new* summary of everything seen thus far (h_t). To make a prediction about the entire sequence of T items, we can use the output after T inputs (h_T) because it represents the Tth item and every preceding item.

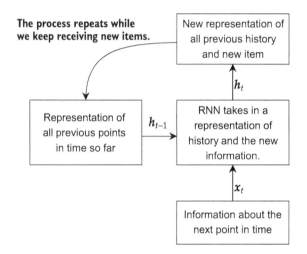

Figure 4.4   Diagram of the RNN process. We use t to represent the current point in time (the tth item in a sequence). The RNN takes in a single representation of all previous content h_{t-1} and information about the newest item in the sequence x_t. The RNN merges these into a new representation of everything seen so far h_t, and the process repeats until we reach the end of the sequence.

The idea is that an RNN loops over all the items in the input. Let's make sure we give some mathematical notation to all the parts of this discussion. We have T total units of time. Instead of a single input $x \in \mathbb{R}^d$, we have T inputs $x_1, x_2, \ldots, x_{T-1}, x_T$. Each input is a vector of the same size (i.e., $x_j \in \mathbb{R}^d$). Remember that each $x_1, x_2, \ldots, x_{T-1}, x_T$ is a vector representation of something sequential. For example, the weather could have a vector with the high, low, and average temperature each day ($x_t = [\text{high}, \text{low}, \text{mean}]$), and the days must occur in their natural order (no time-traveling allowed).

How do we process something over time? If we have a network module A, where $A(x) = h$, we can use weight sharing to apply the network module A to every item independently. So, we get T outputs, $h_i = A(x_i)$. We will eventually use one of these outputs h as the input to a linear layer, but first we need to work our way to an RNN. The naive approach of applying $A(\cdot)$ independently is shown in figure 4.5.

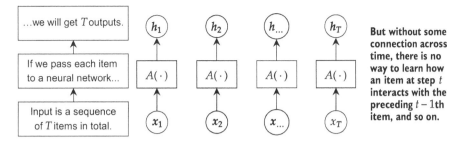

Figure 4.5 A naive solution using a network module A to process T different inputs in a sequence in-dependently. Each item in the sequence x_i is processed independently of every other sequence. This approach does not recognize the sequential nature of the data, because there is no path connecting x_t and x_{t+1}.

We use weight sharing to apply the same function/layer $A(\cdot)$ to each item over time. But we don't do anything to connect information *over* time. We need our RNN function A to take in both a history and the input so we can have code that looks something like this:

```
history_summary = 0     ⟵ h₀
inputs = [...]     ⟵ x₁, x₂, ..., xₜ
for t in range(T):
    new_summary = RNN(history_summary, inputs[t])     ⟵ hₜ = A(hₜ₋₁, xₜ)
    history_summary = new_summary
```

That way, the RNN takes in both the history and the new item. This is done by giving A a *recurrent* weight. We've used h_t to indicate the result from time step t, so let's incorporate that into our model. First, let's look at the equation with some light annotation—the kind you might see in a paper or online. Take a few minutes to try to parse the parts on your own; this will help you grow your skills in reading this kinds of deep learning math:

$$\underset{\text{history summary}}{\underset{\text{new summary}}{h_t}} = A(\ h_{t-1}\ ,\ \underset{\text{new item}}{x_t}\ ) = \tanh(\ \underset{\text{update history summary}}{h_{t-1}^\top W_{n\times n}^{\text{prev}}} + \underset{\text{incorporate new information}}{x_t^\top W_{d\times n}^{\text{cur}}}\ )$$

$$\underbrace{\qquad\qquad\qquad\qquad\qquad}_{\text{combine into new summary}}$$

Now let's look at a heavily annotated version of this same equation:

The current vector h_t is a summary of all t items that have been seen so far. To make this summary, a RNN takes in a summary of everything previously seen and the tth new item x_t. This is done by having a linear layer process the previous history and a second linear layer process the new input and then mixing them together. A nonlinearity is applied afterward, making the new summary h_t.

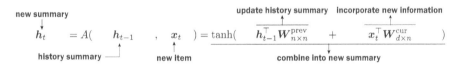

We have one set of weights $(\boldsymbol{W}_{d \times n}^{\text{cur}})$ that takes in the *current* time step $(\boldsymbol{x}_i)$ added to a second set of weights $(\boldsymbol{W}_{n \times n}^{\text{prev}})$ for the *previous* time step's result $(\boldsymbol{h}_{i-1})$. By reusing this new function at each time step, we get information across time. This is all shown in figure 4.6.

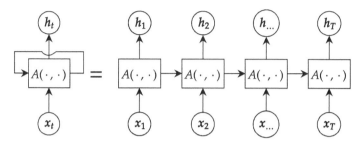

Figure 4.6 The network A is defined to take in two inputs: the previous hidden state h_{t-1} and the current input x_t. This allows us to unroll the network and share information across time, dealing effectively with the sequential nature of the data.

This approach to sharing information across time defines a basic RNN. The idea is that we are reusing the *same function and weights A* at every time step. At time step t, the model gets information about the past from the hidden state $\boldsymbol{h}_{t-1}$. Because $\boldsymbol{h}_{t-1}$ is computed from $\boldsymbol{h}_{t-2}$, it has information from the past *two* time steps. And since $\boldsymbol{h}_{t-2}$ depends on $\boldsymbol{h}_{t-3}$, it's *three* previous steps. Keep following this back to the default value of $\boldsymbol{h}_0$, and you can see how $\boldsymbol{h}_{t-1}$ has information from every previous time step based on the order of those time steps. That's how RNNs capture information over time. But what do we do at the start of time $(i = 1)$ when we need $\boldsymbol{h}_0$, which does not exist? Implicitly, we assume that $\boldsymbol{h}_0 = \vec{0}$ (i.e., a vector of all zeros) to make things complete. It can be helpful to draw this out more explicitly, as shown in figure 4.7; this is often called *unrolling* the RNN over time.

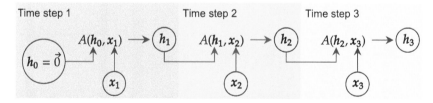

Figure 4.7 An example of unrolling the RNN for $T = 3$ time steps. Here we explicitly draw out each input (x_t) and hidden activation (h_t) in the process. The initial hidden state h_0 is always set to a vector of all zero values. Notice that it now looks like a feed-forward model.

Notice how it is starting to look eerily similar to a fully connected network. The only difference is that we have multiple inputs, $\boldsymbol{x}_1, \ldots, \boldsymbol{x}_T$, one for each time step. For simple classification problems, we will use the last activation $\boldsymbol{h}_T$ as the result from which to make a prediction because $\boldsymbol{h}_T$ has information from every previous time step, and it is the last time step. This makes $\boldsymbol{h}_T$ the only step with information about the *entire* sequence. The fact that we can unroll an RNN like this is why we can use the same algorithms to train it. Unrolling an RNN so that we are applying the same function (weight sharing) over and over, just changing the inputs, is the essence of what an RNN is.

4.2 RNNs in PyTorch

Now that we know what an RNN is, we need to figure out how to use one in PyTorch. While a lot of code is provided for us to accomplish this goal, we still need to build a lot of code ourselves. Like everything in this book, the first step is to create a `Dataset` that represents our data and loads it, followed by a `model` that uses the PyTorch `nn.Module` class that takes the input data and produces a prediction.

But for RNNs, we need vectors, and most of the data we use is *not* naturally represented as a vector. We need to do some extra work to fix that. Figure 4.8 shows the steps to get this working.

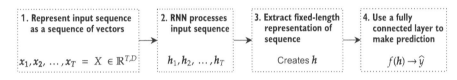

Figure 4.8 Four high-level steps for making a prediction based on an input sequence of length T. We need to create a representation of the sequence as vectors, pass that representation to an RNN to produce T hidden states, reduce to one hidden state, and then use a fully connected layer to make a prediction.

To represent sequence data for an RNN in PyTorch, we use a three-dimensional input representation:

$$(B, T, D)$$

As before, B tells us how many items in a batch (i.e., how many data points) we will use. T gives us the total number of time steps, and D is how many features are present per time step. Because time is represented in the tensor object itself, it's easy to specify the model.

Let's start by creating a many-to-one classification problem. What do I mean by this? We will have many inputs (every time step), but we will have only *one* output: the class label we are trying to predict.

4.2.1 A simple sequence classification problem

To create a model, we first need data. This gets us to step 1 of figure 4.8. To keep things simple, we will borrow the task from the PyTorch RNN tutorial (http://mng.bz/nrKK): identifying the language a name comes from. For example, "Steven" is an English name. Note that this problem can't be solved perfectly—for example, "Frank" could be English or German—so we should expect some errors due to these issues and oversimplification. Our goal is to make code that embodies the process shown in figure 4.9.

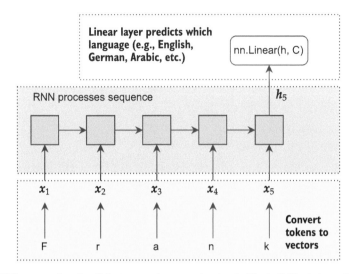

Figure 4.9   RNN process for classifying a name's source language. The individual characters of a name make the sequence that is fed into the RNN. We learn how to convert each character into a vector and how to get an RNN to process that sequence and return a final activation h_T, and we end with a linear layer that produces a prediction.

The following code downloads the dataset and extracts all the files. Once complete, the folder structure is names/[LANG].txt, where [LANG] indicates the language (which is also the label for this problem), and the content of the text file is a list of names that occur in that language:

```
zip_file_url = "https://download.pytorch.org/tutorial/data.zip"

import requests, zipfile, io
r = requests.get(zip_file_url)
z = zipfile.ZipFile(io.BytesIO(r.content))
z.extractall()
```

Since this dataset is pretty small, we load all of it into memory. The data is stored in a dictionary `namge_language_data`, which maps the language name (e.g., English) to a list of all the names. To simplify our lives, `unicodeToAscii` removes non-ASCII characters from each name. The dictionary `alphabet` contains all the characters we expect to see and *maps every item to a unique integer*, starting from 0 and increasing sequentially. This is important. Our computers have no idea what any character or item in your sequence means. Unless your data naturally exists as numeric values (e.g., the temperature outside), a conversion step is needed. We get to *how* that conversion is done in a moment, but we standardize this process by mapping every unique item that may occur in a sequence to a unique integer value.

Here's the code:

```
namge_language_data = {}

import unicodedata
import string

all_letters = string.ascii_letters + " .,;'"
n_letters = len(all_letters)
alphabet = {}
for i in range(n_letters):
    alphabet[all_letters[i]] = i

def unicodeToAscii(s):
    return ''.join(
        c for c in unicodedata.normalize('NFD', s)
        if unicodedata.category(c) != 'Mn'
        and c in all_letters
    )

for zip_path in z.namelist():

    if "data/names/" in zip_path and zip_path.endswith(".txt"):
        lang = zip_path[len("data/names/"):-len(".txt")]
        with z.open(zip_path) as myfile:
            lang_names = [unicodeToAscii(line).lower()
                for line in
                str(myfile.read(), encoding='utf-8').strip().split("\ n")]
            namge_language_data[lang] = lang_names
        print(lang, ": ", len(lang_names))
```

Removes UNICODE tokens to make life easy for us processing-wise: e.g., converts "Ślusàrski" to "Slusarski"

Turns a Unicode string into plain ASCII

Loops through every language, opens the zip file entry, and reads all the lines from the text file

Prints out the name of each language

```
Arabic : 2000
Chinese : 268
Czech : 519
Dutch : 297
English : 3668
French : 277
German : 724
Greek : 203
Irish : 232
Italian : 709
Japanese : 991
Korean : 94
Polish : 139
Portuguese : 74
Russian : 9408
Scottish : 100
Spanish : 298
Vietnamese : 73
```

Now we have created a dataset, which you may notice is not well balanced: there are *far more* Russian names than any other language. This is something we should be on the lookout for when evaluating our model.

With our data loaded in memory, we can now implement a `Dataset` to represent it. The `data` list contains each name, and an associated index in the `labels` list indicates which language the name came from. A `vocabulary` dictionary maps every unique item to an integer value:

```
class LanguageNameDataset(Dataset):
    def __init__(self, lang_name_dict, vocabulary):
        self.label_names = [x for x in lang_name_dict.keys()]
        self.data = []
        self.labels = []
        self.vocabulary = vocabulary
        for y, language in enumerate(self.label_names):
            for sample in lang_name_dict[language]:
                self.data.append(sample)
                self.labels.append(y)
    def __len__(self):
        return len(self.data)
    def string2InputVec(self, input_string):
        """
        This method will convert any input string into a vector of long
        ➥ values,
        according to the vocabulary used by this object.
        input_string: the string to convert to a tensor
        """
        T = len(input_string)
        name_vec = torch.zeros((T), dtype=torch.long)

        for pos, character in enumerate(input_string):
            name_vec[pos] = self.vocabulary[character]
        return name_vec
    def __getitem__(self, idx):
        name = self.data[idx]
        label = self.labels[idx]
        label_vec = torch.tensor([label], dtype=torch.long)

        return self.string2InputVec(name), label
```

Creates a new tensor to store the result → `name_vec = torch.zeros((T), dtype=torch.long)`

How many characters long is the string? → `T = len(input_string)`

Iterates through the string and places the appropriate values in the tensor

Converts the correct class label into a tensor for PyTorch

NOTE   The concept of a vocabulary is common in machine learning and deep learning. You will often see the math symbol Σ used to denote the vocabulary. For example, we could ask, "Is the word *cheese* in the vocabulary?" more succinctly by writing "cheese" $\in \Sigma$. If we write "blanket" $\notin \Sigma$, we are indicating that the item "blanket" is not in the vocabulary. We can also denote the size of the vocabulary using $|\Sigma|$.

The `__len__` function is straightforward: it returns the total number of data points in the `Dataset`. The first interesting function is the helper function `string2InputVec`, which takes an `input_string` and returns a new `torch.Tensor` as the output. The tensor's length is the number of characters as the `input_string`, and it has the `torch.long` type (also known as `torch.int64`). The values in the tensor indicate which unique token was present in the `input_string` and their order. This gives us a new tensor-based representation that PyTorch can use.

This `string2InputVec` is then reused in our `__getitem__` method. We grab the original string from the `self.data[idx]` member and convert it into the tensor representation PyTorch needs using `string2InputVec`. The returned value is a tuple following the pattern (input, output). For example,

```
(tensor([10, 7, 14, 20, 17, 24]), 0)
```

indicates that a name with six characters should be classified as the first class (Arabic). The original string was converted to a tensor of integers by our `string2InputVec` function so that PyTorch can understand it.

With that, we can create a new dataset to determine the language of a given name. The following code snippet creates a train/test split, with 300 items in the test split. We use a batch size of 1 in the loaders (we come back to this nuance later in the chapter):

```
dataset = LanguageNameDataset(namge_language_data, alphabet)

train_data, test_data = torch.utils.data.random_split(dataset,
    (len(dataset)-300, 300))
train_loader = DataLoader(train_data, batch_size=1, shuffle=True)
test_loader = DataLoader(test_data, batch_size=1, shuffle=False)
```

Stratified sampling for class imbalance

Our dataset has an issue of *class imbalance* that we are not tackling at the moment. This occurs when the ratio of classes is uneven. In this setting, the model may sometimes learn to simply reiterate the most common class label. For example, imagine you are trying to predict whether someone has cancer. You can make a model that is 99.9% accurate by *always* predicting "no cancer," because, thankfully, most people do not have cancer at a given moment in time. But this approach is not useful for a model.

Solving class imbalance is its own niche topic area, and we will not go into much detail about it. But one simple improvement is to use *stratified* sampling to create the train/test split. It's a common tool and available in scikit-learn (http://mng.bz/v4VM). The idea is that you want to *force* the sampling to maintain the class ratios in the splits. So if the original data is 99% A and 1% B, you want your stratified splits to have the same percentages. With random sampling, you could easily end up with 99.5% A and 0.5% B. Normally, this is not a huge issue, but class imbalance can significantly skew your perception of how well a model is doing.

With the dataset loaded, we can talk about the remaining parts of our RNN model in PyTorch.

4.2.2 *Embedding layers*

Step 1 of figure 4.8 requires us to represent the input sequence as a sequence of vectors. We have the `LanguageNameDataset` object to load our data, which converts each character/token (e.g., "Frank") to a unique integer using a vocabulary (Σ). The last thing we need is a way to map each integer to a corresponding vector, which is accomplished using an *embedding* layer. This is shown at a high level in figure 4.10. Note that this is standard terminology used in the deep learning community, and you should become familiar with it.

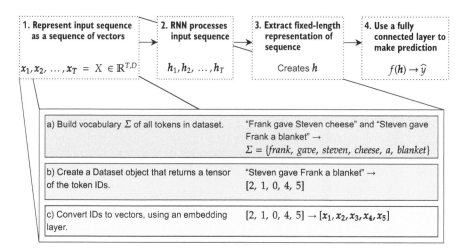

Figure 4.10 Subsets (a) and (b) are both accomplished by the `LanguageNameDataset` we have implemented. The final subset (c) is done by an `nn.Embedding` layer.

Embedding layers are lookup tables designed to map each integer value to a specific vector representation. You tell the embedding layer how large the vocabulary is (i.e., how many unique items exist) and how large you want the output dimension to be. Figure 4.11 shows how this process works at a conceptual level.

In this toy example, the vocabulary contains both characters and words. The vocabulary does not need to be strings, as long as you can consistently map the items to an integer value. `nn.Embedding`'s first argument is 5 to indicate that the vocabulary has five unique items. The second argument 3 is the output dimension. You should think of this like the `nn.Linear` layer, where the second argument tells you how many outputs will exist. We can increase or decrease the output size based on how much information we think the model needs to be able to pack into each vector. In most applications, you want to try values in the range of $[64, 256]$ for the number of output dimensions.

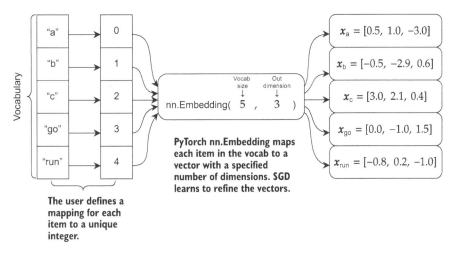

Figure 4.11 Embedding layer designed to take in a vocabulary of five unique items. You have to write the code that maps objects (like strings) into integers. The embedding maps each integer to its own d-dimensional vector $x \in \mathbb{R}^d$.

Egad, embeddings everywhere!

Embeddings as a concept are highly leveraged in practical work. Mapping each word to a vector and trying to predict nearby words is the essence behind ubiquitous tools like word2vec (https://en.wikipedia.org/wiki/Word2vec) and Glove (https://nlp.stanford.edu/projects/glove), but that goes down a deeper rabbit hole about natural language processing than we have time for. In short, learning to represent items as vectors so that you can use other tools is an effective approach to tackle real-world problems.

Once you have embeddings, you can use a nearest-neighbor search to implement a search engine or "did you mean" functionality, throw them into Uniform Manifold Approximation and Projection (UMAP) (https://umap-learn.readthedocs.io/en/latest) for visualization, or run your favorite non-deep algorithm to do some prediction or clustering. At other points in the book, I'll note approaches that can be used to create embeddings.

The nn.Embedding layer is designed to work with sequences of things. That means the sequence can contain repetitions. For example, the following code snippet creates a new input sequence with $T = 5$ items but a vocabulary of only 3 items. This is OK because the input sequence $[0, 1, 1, 0, 2]$ has repetitions (0 and 1 occur twice). The embd object is created with a dimension of $d = 2$ and processes the input to create a new representation x_seq:

```
with torch.no_grad():
    input_sequence = torch.tensor([0, 1, 1, 0, 2], dtype=torch.long)
    embd = nn.Embedding(3, 2)
    x_seq = embd(input_sequence)
```

```
    print(input_sequence.shape, x_seq.shape)
    print(x_seq)
torch.Size([5]) torch.Size([5, 2])
tensor([[ 0.7626,    0.1343],
        [ 1.5189,    0.6567],
        [ 1.5189,    0.6567],
        [ 0.7626,    0.1343],
        [-0.5718,    0.2879]])
```

This x_seq is the tensor representation that is now compatible with all the standard tools of deep learning. Notice that its shape is $(5, 2)$, with random values filled in—that's because the Embedding layer initializes everything to random, and these values are altered by gradient descent as the network is trained. But the first and fourth rows of the matrix have the same values, as do the second and third. This is because the order in the output matches the order in the input. The unique item denoted by "0" was at the first and fourth positions, so the same vector is used in both places. The same is true for the unique item denoted by "1," which is repeated as the second and third items.

When working with strings or any other content that does not naturally exist as vectors, you almost always want to use an embedding layer as your first step. This is the standard tool for converting these abstract concepts to representations we can work with and completes step 1 of figure 4.8.

4.2.3 Making predictions using the last time step

The task of using an RNN in PyTorch is quite easy, as PyTorch provides implementations of the standard RNN algorithm. The trickier part is extracting the last time step h_T after it's processed by the RNN. We want to do this because the last time step is the *only* one that carries information from all T inputs based on the input's order. This way, we can use h_T as a fixed-length summary of the input data for a fully connected sub-network. This works because h_T has the same shape and size no matter how long the input sequence is. So if our RNN layer has 64 neurons, h_T will be a 64-dimension vector represented as a tensor of shape $(B, 64)$. It does not matter if our sequence has one item $T = 1$ or $T = 100$ items; it will always be the case that h_T will have shape $(B, 64)$. This process is shown in figure 4.12.

We need to implement a new Module that extracts the last time step before we can specify a RNN architecture in PyTorch. There are a few idiosyncrasies to deal with in how PyTorch stores this information. We need to know two things: the number of layers and whether the model is bidirectional. This is because the RNN will return enough information to extract the result from any layer, giving us the flexibility to implement other models that we will discuss later. We also talk about what *bidirectional* means later in this chapter.

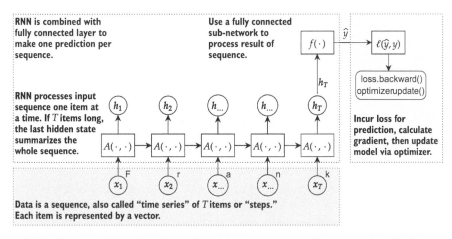

Figure 4.12 Parts of applying a RNN to predict a label for a sequence. The output of the RNN is a sequence of hidden states $h_1, h_2, \ldots, h_T$. The last time step h_T contains information about the entire sequence, so we want to use it as a representation for the whole sequence. That way, it can go into a normal fully connected network $f(\cdot)$.

The following code is based on content from PyTorch's documentation and does the work to extract the LastTimeStep h_T from a RNN. Depending on the specific RNN we use (more on that in chapter 6), the output of an RNN Module is a tuple of two tensors or a nested tuple of three tensors, with the last time step's activation stored in the second item of the tuple:

```
class LastTimeStep(nn.Module):
    """
    A class for extracting the hidden activations of the last time step
    following
    the output of a PyTorch RNN module.
    """
    def __init__(self, rnn_layers=1, bidirectional=False):
        super(LastTimeStep, self).__init__()
        self.rnn_layers = rnn_layers
        if bidirectional:
            self.num_directions = 2
        else:
            self.num_directions = 1
    def forward(self, input):
        rnn_output = input[0]

        last_step = input[1]

        if(type(last_step) == tuple):
          last_step = last_step[0]
        batch_size = last_step.shape[1]

        last_step = last_step.view(self.rnn_layers,
            self.num_directions, batch_size, -1)
```

Result is either a tuple (out,h_t) or a tuple (out, (h_t, c_t))

This is h_t unless it's a tuple, in which case it's the first item in the tuple.

Per the docs, shape is '(num_layers * num_directions, batch, hidden_size)'

Reshapes so everything is separate

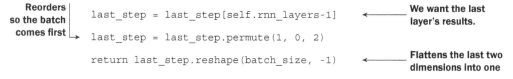

```
last_step = last_step[self.rnn_layers-1]
```
Reorders so the batch comes first
```
last_step = last_step.permute(1, 0, 2)

return last_step.reshape(batch_size, -1)
```
We want the last layer's results.

Flattens the last two dimensions into one

The output of a RNN in PyTorch is a tuple of shape $(out, \boldsymbol{h}_T)$ or $(out, (\boldsymbol{h}_T, \boldsymbol{c}_T))$. The *out* object has information about *every* time step, and $\boldsymbol{h}_T$ contains information about only the *last* time step but for *every* layer. So we check if the second item is a `tuple` and extract the right $\boldsymbol{h}_T$ object. The value $\boldsymbol{c}_T$ is an extract context tensor, which is part of a more advanced RNN that we discuss in chapter 6.

Once we have $\boldsymbol{h}_T$, PyTorch provides it as an input that has been `flatten()`ed. We can use the `view` function to reshape the tensor with information about the layers, bidirectional content (again, we will talk about that soon), batch size, and number of neurons d in the hidden layer. We know we want the last layer's results so we can index in and then use the `permute` function to move the batch dimension to the front.

That gives us what we need to extract the last layer of a RNN so we have the tools to implement steps 2 and 3 from figure 4.8. The fourth step is to use a fully connected layer, which we already know how to do using a `nn.Linear` layer. The following code does the work of all four steps. The variable `D` is the size of the `nn.Embedding` result, `hidden_nodes` is the number of neurons in the RNN, and `classes` is the number of classes we are trying to predict (in this application, the number of different languages a name may have come from):

```
D = 64
vocab_size = len(all_letters)
hidden_nodes = 256
classes = len(dataset.label_names)

first_rnn = nn.Sequential(
    nn.Embedding(vocab_size, D),                    # (B, T) -> (B, T, D)

    nn.RNN(D, hidden_nodes, batch_first=True),      # (B, T, D) -> ( (B,T,D) , (S, B, D) )

    LastTimeStep(),
```
The tanh activation is built into the RNN object, so we don't need to do it here. We take the RNN output and reduce it to one item, (B, D).
```
    nn.Linear(hidden_nodes, classes),               # (B, D) -> (B, classes)
)
```

When working with RNNs, we often have a lot of complex tensor shapes occurring at once. For this reason, I always include a comment on each line indicating how the tensor shapes are changing due to each operation. The input batch is processing B items with a length of up to T, so the input has a shape of (B, T). The `nn.Embedding` layer converts this to a shape of (B, T, D), adding the `D` dimensions from the embedding.

The RNN takes inputs of shape (B, T, D) only if we specify that `batch_first=True`. While the rest of PyTorch assumes batch first, RNNs and sequence problems often assume that the batch dimension comes third. In early implementations, having the tensors shaped this way made them significantly faster due to low-level technical details that we are not going to get into. While that representation order can still be faster, the gap is not as big today. So, I prefer to use the `batch_first` option to make it more consistent with the rest of PyTorch.

> **NOTE** The RNN classes in PyTorch apply nonlinear activation functions on their own. They are implicit in this case. This is another situation where the behavior of PyTorch for RNNs is different from the rest of the framework. For this reason, you should *not* apply a nonlinear activation function afterward, because it has already been done for you.

The RNN returns a `tuple` of at least two tensors, but our `LastTimeStep` module is designed to take this and return a fixed-length vector by extracting h_T from the last time step. Since $h_T \in \mathbb{R}^D$ and we are processing B items in a batch, that gives us a tensor of shape (B, D). This is the same shape that our fully connected networks expect. That means we can now use standard fully connected layers. In this case, we can use one to create a linear layer that makes the final prediction. With that, we can again use the `train_simple_network` function to train our first RNN:

```
loss_func = nn.CrossEntropyLoss()
batch_one_train = train_simple_network(first_rnn, loss_func,
    train_loader, test_loader=test_loader,
    score_funcs={'Accuracy': accuracy_score}, device=device, epochs=5)

sns.lineplot(x='epoch', y='test Accuracy', data=batch_one_train, label='RNN')
```

```
[19]:   <AxesSubplot:xlabel='epoch', ylabel='test Accuracy'>
```

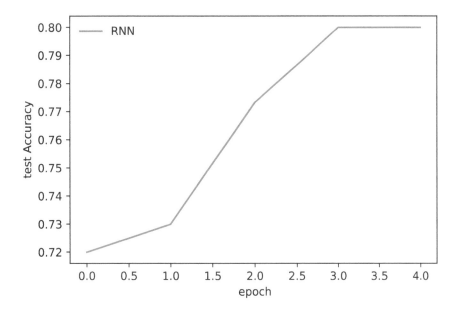

Now that we have trained our model, we can play around with it. Let's try typing in a few names and see what the model thinks of them. Remember, we converted all names to lowercase, so don't use any capital letters:

```
pred_rnn = first_rnn.to("cpu").eval()
with torch.no_grad():
    preds = F.softmax(pred_rnn(
        dataset.string2InputVec("frank").reshape(1,-1)), dim=-1)
    for class_id in range(len(dataset.label_names)):
        print(dataset.label_names[class_id], ":",
            preds[0,class_id].item()*100 , "
```

```
Arabic : 0.002683540151338093 %
Chinese : 0.2679025521501899 %
Czech : 10.59301644563675 %
Dutch : 7.299012690782547 %
English : 36.81915104389191 %
French : 0.5335223395377398 %
German : 37.42799460887909 %
Greek : 0.018611310224514455 %
Irish : 0.7783998735249043 %
Italian : 1.1141937226057053 %
Japanese : 0.00488687728648074 %
Korean : 0.421459274366498 %
Polish : 1.1676722206175327 %
Portuguese : 0.08807195699773729 %
Russian : 1.2793921865522861 %
Scottish : 1.6346706077456474 %
Spanish : 0.14639737782999873 %
Vietnamese : 0.40296311490237713 %
```

For a name like "Frank," we get the largest response for English and German as the source languages, both of which are reasonable answers. Frank is a common name in English and has German origins. You should try other names yourself and see how the behavior changes. This also shows how we can apply our RNN to variable-length inputs. Regardless of the length of the input string, you still get a prediction at the end, whereas in our previous examples with fully connected or convolutional layers, the input had to *always* be the same size. This is one of the reasons we use RNNs is to resolve these kinds of issues.

A note about classification and ethics

The example we have been working with is an oversimplification of reality. Names do not necessarily come from *one* specific language, which our model implies because each name is labeled with one correct answer. This is an example of our model simplifying the world to make our lives as modelers easier.

This is a good, if simplified, example to learn on, but it also presents a good opportunity to talk about some of the ethics involved in machine learning. Simplifying assumptions can be useful and help solve real problems, but they can also alter how you think about the problem and how the eventual users of your model think about the world. For this reason, you should note why you make these assumptions when modeling, what the model is for, and how it is validated. These are often called *model cards*.

For example, imagine someone using our language model to try to determine a user's background and alter content displayed based on their name. Would this be OK? Probably not. One name may come from several sources, and people form their identity in many ways other than their name and place of birth, so there is a good chance that using this model in such a scenario isn't the best idea.

Another common introductory problem is *sentiment classification*, where you attempt to determine whether a sentence or document is conveying a positive, negative, or neutral sentiment. This technique can be useful and valid. For instance, a food or beverage brand may want to monitor Twitter to see if people are mentioning products with a negative sentiment so that the company can investigate potential product failures or bad customer experiences. At the same time, positive, negative, and neutral are not the only sentiments, and a message can convey more complex thoughts. Consider making sure your users are aware of such limitations, and think about these kinds of choices. If you want to learn more about the ethics and impact of such decisions, Kate Crawford (https://www.katecrawford.net) is an expert in this space who has some accessible readings on her website.

4.3 Improving training time with packing

When building this model, we used a batch size of 1. This is not a very efficient way to train a model. What happens if you change the batch size to 2? Go on, try it.

You should get an error message. The problem is that each name is a different length, so by default, it is very hard to represent as a tensor. Tensors need all dimensions to be consistent and the same, but our *time* dimension (in this case, how many characters long each name is) is not consistent. This is what causes the error: we have two different sequences with different lengths.

We saw in chapter 2 that training on batches of data can reduce the training time significantly by making better use of our GPU's compute, so we have a real reason to increase the batch size. Yet we appear to be stuck using an inefficient batch size of 1 due to inputs with differing sizes.

This is an *abstraction* problem because fundamentally, nothing prevents an RNN from working with inputs of varying lengths of time. To fix this, PyTorch provides the *packed sequence* abstraction (http://mng.bz/4KYV). All types of RNNs available in PyTorch support working on this class.

Figure 4.13 shows conceptually what is happening when we pack six different sequences of varying lengths. PyTorch organizes them by length and begins by including the *first* time step of all sequences in one *batch over time*. As time progresses, the shorter sequences reach their end, and the batch size is reduced to the number of sequences that have not reached their end.

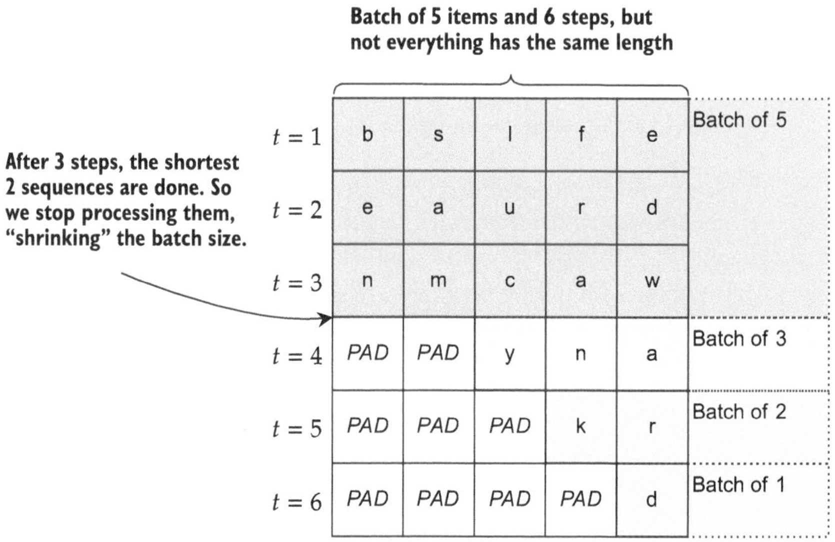

**Batch of 5 items and 6 steps, but
not everything has the same length**

Figure 4.13   Example of packing a batch of five items with sequence lengths of 3, 3, 4, 5, and 6. For the first three steps, we process all five sequences. On the fourth step $t = 4$, two of the sequences have run out, so we drop them and continue the batch on only the sequences that have a length ≥ 4. Packing organizes the data by length to make this fast and efficient.

Let's talk through what is happening in this example. We are trying to train on a batch of five names: "ben," "sam," "lucy," "frank," and "edward." The packing process has sorted them from shortest to longest. There will be a total of $T = 6$ steps in this sequence because "edward" is the longest name at six characters. This means our RNN will perform six iterations in total. Now let's see what happens at each step:

1 In the first iteration, all five items are processed together in one large batch.

2 All five items are again processed together in one large batch.

3 All five items are again processed, but we have reached the end of the first two items, "ben" and "sam." We record their final hidden states from *this* step h_3, since that's when they were finished being processed.

4 A batch of only *three items* is processed, containing "lucy," "frank," and "edward," because the first two items are done. PyTorch adaptively *shrinks* the effective batch size to what remains. "lucy" is finished, and its final state saved as h_4.

5 A batch of only *two items* is processed. "frank" is finished after this step, so h_5 is saved for "frank."

6 The last step processes only one item, "edward," bringing us to the end of the batch and the final hidden state: h_6.

Processing this way ensures that we get the correct hidden state h_T for each item even though they have different lengths. It also makes PyTorch run faster. We do more efficient batched computation as much as possible and shrink that batch as needed so we only work on the still-valid data.

4.3.1 Pad and pack

Packing actually involves two steps: *padding* (make everything the same length) and *packing* (store information about how much padding was used). To implement both padding and packing, we need to override the *collate function* used by the `DataLoader`. This function's job is to collate lots of independent data points into one larger batch of items. The default collate function can handle tensors as long as all tensors have the same shape. Our data comes in as a tuple $(\boldsymbol{x}_i, y_i)$ with shapes (T_i) and (1), respectively. T_i can be different for each item, which is normally a problem, so we need to define a new function called `pad_and_pack`. It's a two-step process that is outlined in figure 4.14.

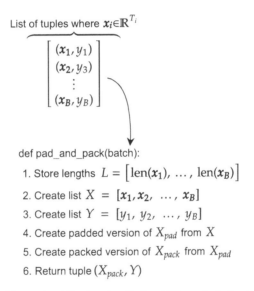

List of tuples where $\boldsymbol{x}_i \in \mathbb{R}^{T_i}$

$$\begin{bmatrix} (\boldsymbol{x}_1, y_1) \\ (\boldsymbol{x}_2, y_3) \\ \vdots \\ (\boldsymbol{x}_B, y_B) \end{bmatrix}$$

def pad_and_pack(batch):

1. Store lengths $L = \left[\text{len}(\boldsymbol{x}_1), \ldots, \text{len}(\boldsymbol{x}_B) \right]$

2. Create list $X = [\boldsymbol{x}_1, \boldsymbol{x}_2, \ldots, \boldsymbol{x}_B]$

3. Create list $Y = [y_1, y_2, \ldots, y_B]$

4. Create padded version of X_{pad} from X

5. Create packed version of X_{pack} from X_{pad}

6. Return tuple (X_{pack}, Y)

Figure 4.14 Steps of packing and padding input so that an RNN can be trained on batches of data that have different lengths

The input is passed to our function as list objects. Every item in the tuple comes *directly* from the `Dataset` class. So if you alter the `Dataset` to do something unique, this is how you update the `DataLoader` to work with it. In our case, the `Dataset` returns a tuple of (input, output), so our `pad_and_pack` function takes in a list of tuples. The steps are as follows:

1. Store the length of every item.

2. Create new lists of *just* the inputs and *just* the output labels.

3 ⟶ Create a *padded* version of the input list. This makes all the tensors the same size, with a special token appended to the shorter items. PyTorch can do this using the pad_sequence function.

4 ⟶ Create the *packed* version of the input using PyTorch's pack_padded_sequence function. This takes the padded version as input, along with the list of lengths, so that the function knows how long each item was originally.

That's the high-level idea. The following code implements this process:

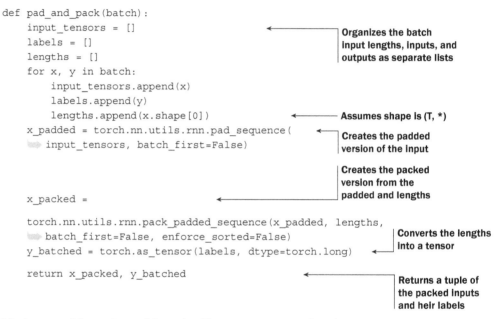

```
def pad_and_pack(batch):
    input_tensors = []
    labels = []
    lengths = []
    for x, y in batch:
        input_tensors.append(x)
        labels.append(y)
        lengths.append(x.shape[0])
    x_padded = torch.nn.utils.rnn.pad_sequence(
        input_tensors, batch_first=False)

    x_packed =

torch.nn.utils.rnn.pack_padded_sequence(x_padded, lengths,
        batch_first=False, enforce_sorted=False)
    y_batched = torch.as_tensor(labels, dtype=torch.long)

    return x_packed, y_batched
```

Organizes the batch input lengths, inputs, and outputs as separate lists

Assumes shape is (T, *)

Creates the padded version of the input

Creates the packed version from the padded and lengths

Converts the lengths into a tensor

Returns a tuple of the packed inputs and heir labels

Notice two things about this code. First, we set an optional argument batch_first= False because our input data does not yet have a batch dimension; it just has the length. If we had a batch dimension, and it was stored as the first dimension (the norm for most code), we would set this value to True.

Second, for the packing step, we have the flag enforce_sorted=False because we have chosen not to presort the input batches by length. If we set enforce_sorted=True, we would get an error because our inputs are not sorted. Older versions of PyTorch required you to do this sorting yourself, but the current version works fine on unsorted inputs. It still avoids unnecessary computations and is generally just as fast, so we chose this easier option.

4.3.2 *Packable embedding layer*

We need one more item before we can build a RNN that can be trained in batches. It turns out the nn.Embedding layer from PyTorch does not handle packed inputs. I find it's easiest to create a new wrapper Module that takes an nn.Embedding object in the constructor and fixes it to handle packed inputs. This is shown in the following code:

```
class EmbeddingPackable(nn.Module):
    """
    The embedding layer in PyTorch does not support Packed Sequence
    objects.
    This wrapper class will fix that. If a normal input comes in, it will
    use the regular Embedding layer. Otherwise, it will work on the packed
    sequence to return a new Packed sequence of the appropriate result.
    """

    def __init__(self, embd_layer):
        super(EmbeddingPackable, self).__init__()
        self.embd_layer = embd_layer
    def forward(self, input):
        if type(input) == torch.nn.utils.rnn.PackedSequence:
            sequences, lengths =
              torch.nn.utils.rnn.pad_packed_sequence(          ◄──── Unpacks the input
              input.cpu(), batch_first=True)
            sequences = self.embd_layer(sequences.to(         ◄──── Embeds it
              input.data.device))
            return torch.nn.utils.rnn.pack_padded_sequence(   ◄──┐ Packs it into a
              sequences, lengths.cpu(),                          │ new sequence
              batch_first=True, enforce_sorted=False)
        else:                                                   ┌─ Applies to
            return self.embd_layer(input)          ◄────────────┘  normal data
```

The first step is to check whether the input is a `PackedSequence`. If it is packed, we need to first *unpack* the input sequence. Now we have an unpacked tensor because either it was provided as unpacked or we unpacked it ourselves, so we can call the original `embd_layer` that we saved. Notice that because our data is a packed *batch* and the batch dimension is the *first* dimension, we have to set the `batch_first=True` flag. Unpacking gives us the original *padded* `sequences` as well as their respective `lengths`. The next line performs the standard embedding on the unpacked `sequences`, making sure to move the `sequences` to the same compute device that the original `input.data` was on. We call `pack_padded_sequence` to again create a packed version of the now-embedded inputs.

4.3.3 *Training a batched RNN*

With our `EmbeddingPackable` module in hand and our new collation function `pad_and_pack`, we are ready to train an RNN on batches of data at a time. First we need to create new `DataLoader` objects. This looks the same as previously, except that we specify the optional argument `collate_fn=pad_and_pack` so it uses the `pad_and_pack` function to create batches of training data:

```
B = 16
train_loader = DataLoader(train_data, batch_size=B, shuffle=True,
  collate_fn=pad_and_pack)
test_loader = DataLoader(test_data, batch_size=B, shuffle=False,
  collate_fn=pad_and_pack)
```

In this case, we have chosen to use a batch of 16 data points at a time. The next step is to define our new RNN module. We use the `nn.Sequential` to build our model out of the `EmbeddingPackable` to perform the embedding, `nn.RNN` to create a RNN layer, `LastTimeStep` to extract the final hidden states, and a `nn.Linear` to perform a classification based on the input:

```
rnn_packed = nn.Sequential(
    EmbeddingPackable(nn.Embedding(vocab_size, D)),      ⟵  (B, T) -> (B, T, D)
    nn.RNN(D, hidden_nodes, batch_first=True),           ⟵  (B, T, D) -> ( (B,T,D) , (S, B, D) )
    LastTimeStep(),                                       ⟵
                                                              Takes the RNN output and
                                                              reduces it to one item, (B, D)
    nn.Linear(hidden_nodes, classes),                    ⟵  (B, D) -> (B, classes)
)

rnn_packed.to(device)
```

Finally we can train this model. It works by calling our `train_simple_network` because we have abstracted all the issues of packing and padding into `collate_fn` and the `EmbeddingPackable` objects. Batch training is also much more efficient, so we train for 20 epochs—four times as many as before:

```
packed_train = train_simple_network(rnn_packed, loss_func,
    train_loader, test_loader=test_loader,
    score_funcs={'Accuracy': accuracy_score}, device=device, epochs=20)
```

If we look at the accuracy of this model, it is overall very similar to the model trained with a batch size of 1, but perhaps a little worse. This is not unusual behavior for training a RNN—the weight sharing over time and multiple inputs can make it difficult to learn RNNs in general. For this reason, people often keep batch sizes for RNNs relatively smaller to improve performance, but in the next two chapters we'll learn about techniques that help solve this problem.

Here's the plot:

```
sns.lineplot(x='epoch', y='test Accuracy', data=batch_one_train,
    label='RNN: Batch=1')
sns.lineplot(x='epoch', y='test Accuracy', data=packed_train,
    label='RNN:Packed Input')
```

```
[26]:    <AxesSubplot:xlabel='epoch', ylabel='test Accuracy'>
```

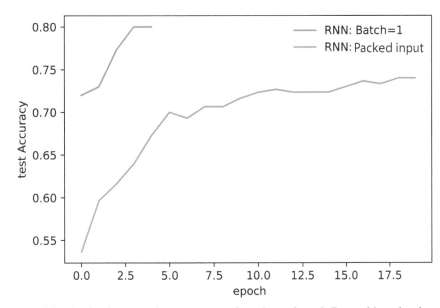

However, this plot looks at performance as a function of *epoch*. By packing the data into a larger batch, it is *much* faster to train. If we look at accuracy as a function of the total time we had to wait, packing becomes much more competitive:

```
sns.lineplot(x='total time', y='test Accuracy', data=batch_one_train,
    label='RNN: Batch=1')
sns.lineplot(x='total time', y='test Accuracy', data=packed_train,
    label='RNN:Packed Input')
```

[27]:   <AxesSubplot:xlabel='total time', ylabel='test Accuracy'>

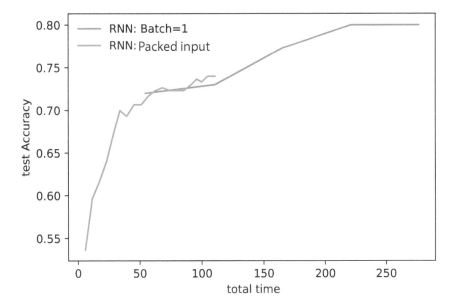

4.3.4   *Simultaneous packed and unpacked inputs*

The way we wrote our code has given us a sneaky but small benefit that makes the code more flexible for different scenarios. The RNN layers take in packed sequence objects *or* normal tensors. Our new `EmbeddingPackable` also supports both types of inputs. The `LastTimeStep` function we have been using always returns a normal tensor because there is no reason or value to the last time step being packed. For this reason, the same code we just wrote will work with *both* packed and non-packed inputs. We can confirm this by trying to see if we can predict the linguistic origin of some new names:

```
pred_rnn = rnn_packed.to("cpu").eval()

with torch.no_grad():
    preds = F.softmax(pred_rnn(dataset.string2InputVec(
        "frank").reshape(1,-1)), dim=-1)
    for class_id in range(len(dataset.label_names)):
        print(dataset.label_names[class_id], ":",
            preds[0,class_id].item()*100 , "%")
```

```
Arabic : 0.586722744628787 %
Chinese : 0.5682710558176041 %
Czech : 15.79725593328476 %
Dutch : 5.215919017791748 %
English : 42.07158088684082 %
French : 1.7968742176890373 %
German : 13.949412107467651 %
Greek : 0.40299338288605213 %
Irish : 2.425672672688961 %
Italian : 5.216174945235252 %
Japanese : 0.3031977219507098 %
Korean : 0.7202120032161474 %
Polish : 2.772565931081772 %
Portuguese : 0.9149040095508099 %
Russian : 4.370814561843872 %
Scottish : 1.0111995041370392 %
Spanish : 1.2703102082014084 %
Vietnamese : 0.6059217266738415 %
```

This makes it easier to reuse the same code for both training (on a batch of data) and making predictions (where we may not want to wait for a batch of data). The code is also easier to reuse in other code that may or may not support packed inputs.

This inconsistent support stems from RNNs and sequences being more complex to work with. We put in a lot of extra effort to get the code to work with batches of data, and much of the code online has not bothered to do so. When you learn about a new technique for training or using RNNs, it may not support packed inputs as this code does. By writing the code the way we did, you get the best of both worlds: faster batch training with standard tools, and compatibility with other tools that may not have put in the same effort.

4.4   *More complex RNNs*

More complex RNNs are available: in particular, we can make RNNs with multiple layers and RNNs that process information from right to left in addition to left to right. Both of these changes improve the accuracy of the RNN model. It may seem overwhelming that we have two new concepts to learn about with RNNs, but PyTorch makes both of them easy to add with minimal effort.

4.4.1   *Multiple layers*

Like other approaches we have learned about, you can stack multiple layers of RNNs. However, due to the computational complexity of training RNNs, PyTorch provides highly optimized versions. Rather than manually insert multiple `nn.RNN()` calls in a sequence, you can pass in an option telling PyTorch how many layers to use. Figure 4.15 shows a diagram of an RNN with two layers.

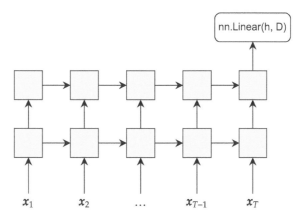

Figure 4.15 **Example of an RNN with two layers. The arrows show connections from one RNN cell to another. Blocks with the same color in a layer share weights. The input vectors come in from the bottom, and the last RNN's output can go to a fully connected layer to produce a prediction.**

Adding multiple layers to a RNN repeats the pattern of hidden units taking input from the previous RNN at the *same* level and the result from the current time step from the *preceding* level. This is as simple as adding `num_layers=3` to our `RNN` and `LastTimeStep` objects if we want a model with three recurrent layers:

```
rnn_3layer = nn.Sequential(
    EmbeddingPackable(nn.Embedding(vocab_size, D)),              ⟵————— (B, T) -> (B, T, D)
    nn.RNN(D, hidden_nodes, num_layers=3, batch_first=True),    ⟵⎤(B, T, D) ->
                                                                 ⎦((B,T,D),(S, B, D))
    LastTimeStep(rnn_layers=3),              ⟵———— Takes the RNN output and
                                                  reduces it to one item, (B, D)
    nn.Linear(hidden_nodes, classes),    ⟵——— (B, D) -> (B, classes)
)

rnn_3layer.to(device)
rnn_3layer_results = train_simple_network(rnn_3layer, loss_func,
```

```
        train_loader, test_loader=test_loader, lr=0.01,
        score_funcs={'Accuracy': accuracy_score}, device=device, epochs=20,
)
```

Plotting the accuracy of a three-layer approach shows that it *usually* performs better but generally not worse. Some of this again relates to the trickiness of RNNs. My recommendation is to look at using two or three layers of the recurrent components in your architecture. While more can do better, it becomes very expensive, and the difficulties of training RNNs can get in the way of gains from depth. We learn about other techniques that can give more of an advantage later in this book.

Here's the plot:

```
sns.lineplot(x='epoch', y='test Accuracy', data=packed_train,
    label='RNN: 1-Layer')
sns.lineplot(x='epoch', y='test Accuracy', data=rnn_3layer_results,
    label='RNN: 3-Layer')
```

[30]: <AxesSubplot:xlabel='epoch', ylabel='test Accuracy'>

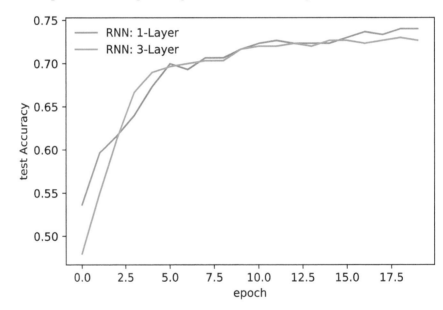

4.4.2 *Bidirectional RNNs*

A more sophisticated improvement is to create a *bidirectional* RNN. You may have noticed that our RNNs always go from left to right, but this can make learning challenging. What if the information we need occurs near the front of the input sequence? The RNN has to make sure information survives multiple time steps, where each time step is an opportunity for noise to be introduced or for other information to otherwise obscure the past.

A good way to think about why retaining information over time is difficult is to imagine an extreme scenario. Say you have only 32 neurons in your RNN layer, but the time series is *1 billion steps long*. The information in an RNN exists entirely within the universe of only 32 values, which is simply not enough to keep that information intact after a billion operations.

To make it easier for the RNN to get the information it needs from long sequences, we can have the RNN traverse the input in *both* directions at once and *share* this information with the next layer of the RNN. This means at the second layer of the RNN, time step 1 has *some* information about time step T. Information about time accumulates more evenly through the RNN, which can make learning easier. The connections for this kind of RNN are shown in figure 4.16.

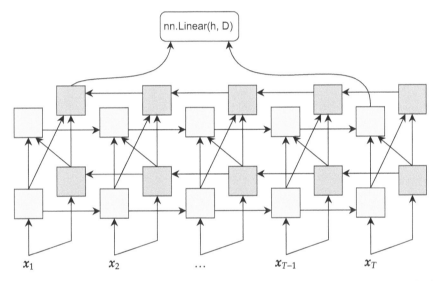

Figure 4.16   Bidirectional RNN. The output of each step in time goes to two RNNs: one processing input from left to right (green) and the other from right to left (red). The output of the two RNNs is combined (via concatenation) to create one new item at each step. This item then goes to two outputs.

Notice that the *last* time step now comes partially from the leftmost and rightmost items in the sequence. Our `LastTimeStep` function already handles that, which is why we did the work of implementing it. It allows us to seamlessly handle this new feature.

Implementing bidirectional RNNs efficiently and accurately is no easy task. Luckily, PyTorch again makes it easy: simply set the `bidirectional=True` flag. Note, though, that the final hidden state is *twice as large* now because we have the final activations from *each* direction, so our `LastTimeStep` has twice as many values as expected. As long as we remember to multiply the `hidden_nodes*2` in the final `nn.Linear` layer, this will still work with little changes. The new code is as follows:

```
rnn_3layer_bidir = nn.Sequential(
    EmbeddingPackable(nn.Embedding(vocab_size, D)),      ← (B, T) -> (B, T, D)
    nn.RNN(D, hidden_nodes, num_layers=3,
        batch_first=True, bidirectional=True),           ← (B, T, D) -> ( (B,T,D) , (S, B, D) )
    LastTimeStep(rnn_layers=3, bidirectional=True),      ← Takes the RNN output
                                                           and reduces it to one
                                                           item, (B, D)
```

```
    nn.Linear(hidden_nodes*2, classes),         ←——————— (B, D) -> (B, classes)
)

rnn_3layer_bidir.to(device)
rnn_3layer_bidir_results = train_simple_network(rnn_3layer_bidir,
    loss_func, train_loader, test_loader=test_loader,
    score_funcs={'Accuracy': accuracy_score}, device=device,
    epochs=20, lr=0.01)

sns.lineplot(x='epoch', y='test Accuracy', data=packed_train,
    label='RNN: 1-Layer')
sns.lineplot(x='epoch', y='test Accuracy', data=rnn_3layer_results,
    label='RNN: 3-Layer')
sns.lineplot(x='epoch', y='test Accuracy', data=rnn_3layer_bidir_results,
    label='RNN: 3-Layer BiDir')
```

```
[32]:  <AxesSubplot:xlabel='epoch', ylabel='test Accuracy'>
```

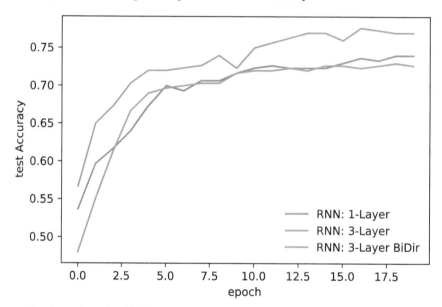

The results show that the bidirectional RNN has a clear advantage. Whenever possible, use a bidirectional RNN, as it makes learning the access information across time much easier for the network. This has led to an increase in accuracy for our simple problem. But there will be cases where you do not want to or can't use a bidirectional version; such examples come later in the book.

Exercises

Share and discuss your solutions on the Manning online platform at Inside Deep Learning Exercises (https://liveproject.manning.com/project/945). Once you submit your own answers, you will be able to see the solutions submitted by other readers, and see which ones the author judges to be the best.

1 Modify LanguageNameDataset so the vocabulary object in the constructor does not need to be passed in as an argument but instead can be *inferred* from the input dataset. This means you need to iterate through the dataset and create a dictionary with all the characters *actually seen*. One way to implement this is to create a default value vocabulary=None and use is vocabulary None: to change behavior.

2 Update LanguageNameDataset with a flag in the constructor for unicode=False. Change any of the code you need to so that when unicode=True, Language-NameDataset instead keeps all the Unicode characters seen when vocabulary=None (this depends on exercise 1). Train a new RNN classifier with unicode=True. How does it impact the results?

3 Update LanguageNameDataset with a new min_count=1 argument in the constructor. If vocabulary=None, it should replace any character that occurs too few times with a special "UNK" token, indicating an unknown value. How is the size of the vocabulary impacted by setting min_count=300, and what happens to the results?

4 The original training/test split for this task was created by randomly sampling the dataset. Create your own function that performs *stratified* splitting: selecting a test set that has the same proportions of each class. How does this impact your apparent results?

5 Replace the last output layer nn.Linear(hidden_nodes, classes) from the RNN implementation with a fully connected network with two hidden layers and one output layer. How does this impact the accuracy of the model?

6 You can use the collation function to implement interesting features. To get a better handle on how it works, implement your own collate_fn that removes half the items from a batch of training data. Does training with two epochs of this model obtain the same results as training with one epoch of a normal collate_fn? Why or why not?

7 Compare training a three-layer bidirectional RNN with batch sizes of $B = \{1, 2, 4, 8\}$ for five epochs. Which batch size seems to give the best balance between speed and accuracy?

Summary

- Recurrent neural networks (RNNs) are used for processing data that comes in as a sequence (e.g., text).

- RNNs work by using weight sharing, so the same weights are reused for every item in the sequence. This lets them process sequences of variable length.

- Text problems require a vocabulary of tokens. An embedding layer converts those tokens to vectors for the RNN's input.

- The hidden state is passed to the next step of the sequence and passed up to the next layer. The hidden state at the top-right (last layer, last item being processed) is a representation of the entire sequence.

- To train on batches of sequences, we pad them to have the same length and use the packing functions so that only the valid parts of the input are processed.

- RNN accuracy can be improved by processing data bidirectionally: left to right and right to left.

Modern training
techniques

This chapter covers

- Improving long-term training using a learning rate schedule
- Improving short-term training using optimizers
- Combining learning rate schedules and optimizers to improve any deep model's results
- Tuning network hyperparameters with Optuna

At this point, we have learned the basics of neural networks and three types of architectures: fully connected, convolutional, and recurrent. These networks have been trained with an approach called stochastic gradient descent (SGD), which has been in use since at least the 1960s. Newer improvements to learning the parameters of our network have been invented since then, like momentum and learning rate decay, which can improve *any neural network for any problem* by converging to better solutions in fewer updates. In this chapter, we learn about some of the most successful and widely used variants of SGD in deep learning.

Because there are no constraints on a neural network, they often end up with complex optimization problems with many local minima, as shown figure 5.1. The minima appear to reduce the loss by the most possible, which would mean our model has learned, but

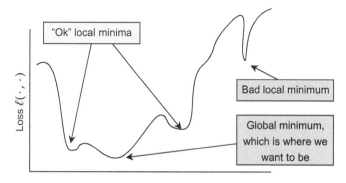

Figure 5.1 Example of a loss landscape that a neural network might encounter. The loss on the y-axis is what we want to minimize, but there are many local minima. There is one global minima that is the best solution, with two local minima that are almost as good—and one bad minima that will not work well.

the global context reveals that other minima may be better. Not all local minima are "bad"; if a minimum is sufficiently close to the global minimum, we will probably get good results. But some local minima are just not going to give us a model with the predictive accuracy we want. Because gradient descent makes its decisions "locally," once we hit a local minimum, we have no idea how "good" that minimum is or which direction to head if we want to try to find a new one.

In this chapter, we learn about *learning rate schedules* and *optimizers* that can help us reach better minima faster, resulting in neural networks that reach higher accuracies in fewer epochs. Again, this applies to *every* network you will ever train and are ubiquitous in modern designs.

To do this, we do a quick review of gradient descent and see how it can be broken up into two parts: the gradient and the learning rate *schedule*. PyTorch has special classes for both of these, so we write a new `train_network` function that will replace the `train_simple_network` function we have seen through the book that incorporates both of these abstractions. These new abstractions will be covered in section 5.1. Then we start filling in the details of these abstractions and how they work, first with the learning rate schedule in section 5.2 followed by gradient update strategies in section 5.3.

There is a *second* optimization problem we have been ignoring, which is how to choose all these hyperparameters like the number of layers, the number of neurons in each layer, and so on. In section 5.4, we are going to learn about how to select hyperparameters using a tool called Optuna. Optuna has special features that make it great at setting hyperparameters even when we have a lot of them and to avoid the full cost of training many different networks to try the parameters.

This chapter is a bit longer because we explain why these newer techniques for using gradients reduce the number of epochs you need to get a good solution, where many other materials just jump right to using these improved methods. This is also important because researchers are constantly working on improved strategies, and the extra work we do to go from the original SGD to modern approaches will help you appreciate the potential for future improvements and to reason about why they may be helping. The Optuna section in particular may seem odd because we will not use this topic in other chapters, as it can get in the way of learning about other techniques. But Optuna and its approach to tuning hyperparameters is a critical real-world skill in deep learning that will help keep you productive and building more accurate solutions.

5.1 Gradient descent in two parts

So far, we have been using and thinking about learning via gradient descent as one monolithic equation and process. We pick a loss function ℓ and a network architecture f, and gradient descent just goes and updates the weights. Because we want to improve how gradient descent works, we first need to recognize and understand its two components. By recognizing that these two components have different behaviors, we can develop strategies for improving each one to get our networks to learn more accurate solutions in fewer epochs. Let's start with a quick review of how gradient descent works.

Remember that everything we do in deep learning works by treating the network as one giant function $f_\Theta(x)$, where we need to use the gradient (∇) with respect to the parameters (Θ) of f to adjust its weights. So we perform

$$\Theta_{t+1} = \Theta_t - \eta \cdot \underbrace{\nabla_{\Theta_t} \ell(f_{\Theta_t}(x), y)}_{\text{the gradient } g^t}$$

This is called *gradient descent* and is the basis for how all modern training of neural networks is done. However, there is room for significant improvement in how we perform this critical step. We use g^t as shorthand for the gradient since we talk about it a *lot* in this section. Notice that we included this ^{t} superscript as if it was part of a sequence. That's because when we learn, we get a new gradient for every batch of data we process, so our model is learning from a sequence of gradients. We use this to our advantage later.

With this shorthand, it becomes clearer that there are just two parts to this process: the gradient g^t and the learning rate η, as we can see here. Those are the only two parts we can alter to try to improve this:

The new parameters θ_{t+1} are equal to   the old parameters θ_t minus the

learning rate times   the gradient over the batch

$$\theta_{t+1} = \quad \theta_t - \quad \eta \cdot \quad g^t$$

5.1.1   *Adding a learning rate schedule*

Let's discuss the problems with the earlier update equation. First, there is an issue with the learning rate η. We choose *one* learning rate for *every batch of every epoch of training*. This can be an unreasonable expectation. Consider, as an analogy, a train traveling from one city to another. The train does not travel *full speed* and then instantaneously come to a stop once it reaches the destination. Instead, the train slows down as it approaches the destination. Otherwise, the train would go barreling past the destination.

So, the first type of improvement we can discuss is to alter the learning rate η as a function of how far along we are in the optimization process (t). Let's call this function L and give it an *initial* learning rate η_0 and the current iteration step t as inputs:

$$\underbrace{\Theta_{t+1}}_{\text{new parameters}} = \underbrace{\Theta_t}_{\text{old parameters}} - \underbrace{L(\eta_0, t)}_{\text{learning rate schedule}} \cdot \underbrace{\boldsymbol{g}^t}_{\text{gradient}}$$

We review the details of how we define $L(\eta_0, t)$ shortly. Right now, the important thing is to understand that we have created an abstraction for altering the learning rate, and this abstraction is called a *learning rate schedule*. We can use this to replace L with different schedules based on our needs or problem. Before we start showing this with code, we need to discuss a second part of the update equation that is tightly coupled with the learning rate schedule $L(\cdot, \cdot)$ in PyTorch.

5.1.2   *Adding an optimizer*

This part does not have a satisfying name; PyTorch calls it the optimizer, but that also describes the process as a whole. Still, we will use that name since it's the most common—and it's how we *use* the gradient $\boldsymbol{g}^t$. All of the information and learning come from $\boldsymbol{g}^t$; it controls what the network learns and how well it learns. The learning rate η simply controls how quickly we follow that information. But the gradient $\boldsymbol{g}^t$ is only as good as the data we use to train the model. If our data is noisy (and it almost always is), our gradients will also be noisy.

These noisy gradients and how they impact learning are shown in figure 5.2 with three other situations. One is the ideal gradient descent path, which almost never happens. The other two are real problems. Say, for example, that we sometimes get a gradient $\boldsymbol{g}^t$ that is just *too large*. This can happen when we add hundreds of layers to our network and is a common problem called an *exploding gradient*. Mathematically, that would be a situation where $\|\boldsymbol{g}^t\|_2 \to \infty$. If we use that gradient, we may take a far larger step than we ever intended (even with a small η), which can degrade performance or even completely prevent us from learning. The opposite situation occurs too; the gradient could be too small $\|\boldsymbol{g}^t\|_2 \to 0$, causing us to make no progress toward training (even with a large η). This is called a *vanishing* gradient and can occur in almost any architecture but is particularly common when we use the tanh($\cdot$) and $\sigma(\cdot)$ activation functions.[1] When looking at these four situations, remember that optimization also

---

[1]   More on that in the chapter 6.

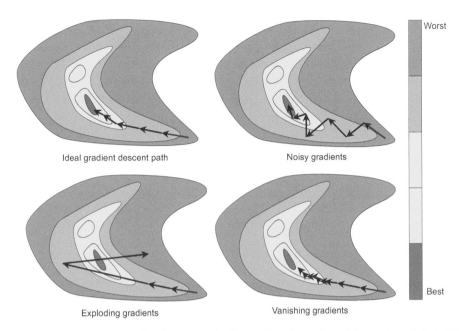

Figure 5.2 A toy example showing three scenarios for gradient descent. Each is a contour plot of a 2D optimization going from red (high values, bad) to dark green (low values, good). The ideal case is at the top left, where each gradient heads exactly toward the solution. The top right shows noisy gradients that cause the descent to head in not quite the correct direction, requiring more steps. The bottom left shows exploding gradients, where we begin to take steps that are far too large and head away from the solution. The bottom right shows vanishing gradients, where the gradient becomes so small that we have to take an excessive number of steps to get to the solution.

means *minimization*, so the process of going from a high value (red) down to a low value (green) is literally how a neural network "learns."

In these situations, naively using the raw gradient g^t could mislead us. Again, we probably want to introduce an abstraction that takes g^t in as input and do something more clever to avoid these situations. We call that function G that *alters* the gradient to make it better behaved and help accelerate the learning. So now we again update our equation and get:

The new parameters θ_{t+1} are equal to   the old parameters θ_t minus the learning rate that has adapted during training (so that we slow down or speed up as needed) multiplied by   the gradient over the batch, processed by a function $G(\cdot)$ that tries to exploit any similarities to previous gradients.

$$\theta_{t+1} = \theta_t - L(\eta_0, t) \cdot G(g^t)$$

Now we have a new gradient descent equation. It has all the base components as before, plus some extra abstractions to make it more flexible. These two strategies—adjusting the learning rate and gradient—are ubiquitous in modern deep learning. As such, they both have interfaces in PyTorch. So let's define a new version of our `train_simple_network` function we have been using that allows for these two kinds of improvements. We can then use this new function to compare the effect of the new techniques and continue to use them later.

The interplay between $L(\cdot, \cdot)$ and $G(\cdot)$

The learning rate schedule and gradient updates ultimately tackle similar goals, so why have both instead of picking one? You can think of them as working on two time scales. The learning rate schedule $L(\cdot, \cdot)$ operates *once per epoch* to adjust the global rate of progress. The gradient update functions $G(\cdot)$ operate on *every* batch, so if you have millions of data points, you may be calling $G(\cdot)$ millions of times but calling $L(\cdot, \cdot)$ at most a few hundred times. So you can think of these things as balancing between long-term and short-term strategies to minimize a function. Like most things in life, it's better to play the balance than focus purely on short- or long-term goals.

5.1.3 *Implementing optimizers and schedulers*

PyTorch provides two interfaces for us to implement the $L(\cdot, \cdot)$ and $G(\cdot)$ functions we have described. First is the `torch.optim.Optimizer` class that you have already been using. We've been using a naive `SGD` optimizer thus far. We start replacing the `SGD` object, but with other optimizers that use the same interface, so almost no code has to change. The new class is `_LRScheduler`, which has several options for us to choose from. To implement our `train_network` function, we'll make just a few modifications to the `train_simple_network` code. Figure 5.3 shows the high-level process, which has only one new step in yellow, with a slight change to the update step to use $G(\cdot)$ to denote that we can change how gradients are used.

UPDATING THE TRAINING CODE

Now let's talk about the three changes we need to make to the `train_simple_network` code. The first thing we change is the function signature so there are two new options available: the optimizer and scheduler. The new signature is shown here, with `optimizer` for $G(\cdot)$ and `lr_schedule` for $L(\cdot, \cdot)$, respectively:

```
def train_network(model, loss_func, train_loader, val_loader=None,
    test_loader=None, score_funcs=None, epochs=50, device="cpu",
    checkpoint_file=None, optimizer=None, lr_schedule=None):
```

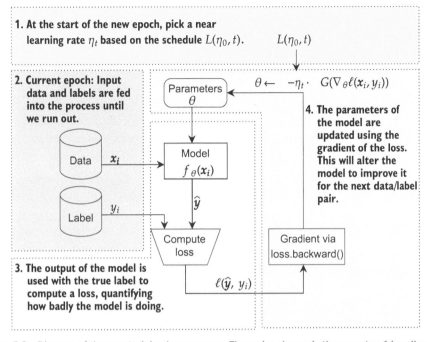

1. At the start of the new epoch, pick a near learning rate η_t based on the schedule $L(\eta_0, t)$. $L(\eta_0, t)$

2. Current epoch: Input data and labels are fed into the process until we run out.

Parameters θ

$\theta \leftarrow \quad -\eta_t \cdot \quad G(\nabla_\theta \ell(x_i, y_i))$

4. The parameters of the model are updated using the gradient of the loss. This will alter the model to improve it for the next data/label pair.

Data x_i

Model $f_\theta(x_i)$

$\widehat{y}$

Label y_i

Compute loss

Gradient via loss.backward()

3. The output of the model is used with the true label to compute a loss, quantifying how badly the model is doing.

$\ell(\widehat{y}, y_i)$

Figure 5.3   Diagram of the new training loop process. The major change is the new step 1 in yellow, showing that we have a learning rate schedule $L(\cdot, \cdot)$. The schedule determines the learning rate η_t used by the process in step 4. Everything else remains the same as before.

Notice that we set both to have a None default value. Specifying a schedule is *always* optional, and you may want to change the schedule used, depending on the task at hand. Some problems take just a few epochs, others take hundreds to thousands, and both of these factors change based on how much data you have. For these reasons, I don't like *requiring* a learning rate schedule to *always* be used. I like to work without one first and then add one based on the problem at hand. However, we must *always* use some kind of optimizer. So if none is given, we add the following code to use a good default (we get to how it works later in this chapter):

```
if optimizer == None:
    optimizer = torch.optim.AdamW(model.parameters())
```

AdamW is a good default optimizer.

Surprisingly, we are halfway done with the new code. We do not need to make any changes to the run_epoch method because it is customary to alter the learning rate after each *epoch* rather than each *batch* (and an epoch is made up of many batches). So after our run_epoch function is done, we can add the following code:

```
if lr_schedule is not None:
    if isinstance(lr_schedule, ReduceLROnPlateau):
        lr_schedule.step(val_running_loss)
    else:
        lr_schedule.step()
```

In PyTorch, the convention is to update the learning rate after every epoch.

Again, we learn about `ReduceLROnPlateau` in a moment. It is an idiosyncratic and special member of the learning rate scheduler family that requires an extra argument. Otherwise, we simply call the `step()` function at the end of each epoch, and the learning rate schedule is updated automatically. You may recognize this as the same approach we use for the `Optimizer` class inside of `run_epoch`, which calls `optimizer.step()` at the end of every batch. This is an intentional design choice to make the two closely coupled classes consistent. You can find the complete function definition in the code in the idlmam.py file (https://github.com/EdwardRaff/Inside-Deep-Learning/blob/main/idlmam.py).

USING THE NEW TRAINING CODE

That is all it takes to prepare our code for some new and improved learning. Now that we have a new loading function implemented, let's train a neural network. We use the Fashion-MNIST dataset because it is slightly more challenging while retaining the same size and shape as the original MNIST corpus, which will let us accomplish some testing in a reasonable time.

Here we load Fashion-MNIST, define a multilayer fully connected network, and then train it in a manner equivalent to using our old `train_simple_network` method. To do this, we need slightly more ceremony by specifying the SGD optimizer ourselves:

```
epochs = 50            ◀── 50 epochs of training
B = 256                ◀── A respectable average batch size

train_data = torchvision.datasets.FashionMNIST("./data", train=True,
    transform=transforms.ToTensor(), download=True)
test_data = torchvision.datasets.FashionMNIST("./data", train=False,
    transform=transforms.ToTensor(), download=True)

train_loader = DataLoader(train_data, batch_size=B, shuffle=True)
test_loader = DataLoader(test_data, batch_size=B)
```

Now we write some more familiar code, a fully connected network with three hidden layers:

```
                       ┌ How many values are
                       │ in the input? We use this
                       │ to help determine the
D = 28*28          ◀──┘ size of subsequent layers.
n = 128                ◀── Hidden layer size
C = 1                  ◀── How many channels are in the input?
classes = 10           ◀── How many classes are there?

fc_model = nn.Sequential(
    nn.Flatten(),
    nn.Linear(D,  n),
    nn.Tanh(),
    nn.Linear(n,  n),
    nn.Tanh(),
    nn.Linear(n,  n),
    nn.Tanh(),
    nn.Linear(n, classes),
)
```

Last, we need to settle on a default starting learning rate η_0. If we do not provide any kind of learning rate schedule $L(\cdot, \cdot)$, then η_0 will be used for every epoch of training. We'll use $\eta_0 = 0.1$, which is more aggressive (read, *large*) than you usually want. I chose this larger value to make it easier to show the impacts of the schedules we can choose from. Under normal use, different optimizers tend to have different preferred defaults, but using $\eta_0 = 0.001$ is usually a good starting point:

```
eta_0 = 0.1
```

With that in place, we can define a naive SGD optimizer the same as we did before. We just need to explicitly call `torch.optim.SGD` and pass it in ourselves, which you can see in the following code. Notice that we set the default learning rate η_0 in the `optimizer`'s constructor. This is the standard process in PyTorch, and any `LRSchedule` object we might use will reach into the `optimizer` object to alter the learning rate:

```
loss_func = nn.CrossEntropyLoss()

fc_results = train_network(fc_model, loss_func, train_loader,
    test_loader=test_loader, epochs=epochs,
    optimizer=torch.optim.SGD(fc_model.parameters(), lr=eta_0),
    score_funcs={'Accuracy': accuracy_score}, device=device)
```

Just like before, we can use seaborn with the return `fc_results` pandas dataframe to quickly plot the results. The following code and output show the kinds of results we get, clearly learning with more training but having occasional regressions. This is because our learning rate is a bit too aggressive, but it's the kind of behavior you often see on real-world problems with non-aggressive learning rates (like $\eta_0 = 0.001$):

```
sns.lineplot(x='epoch', y='test Accuracy', data=fc_results, label='Fully
    Connected')
```

```
[12]:   <AxesSubplot:xlabel='epoch', ylabel='test Accuracy'>
```

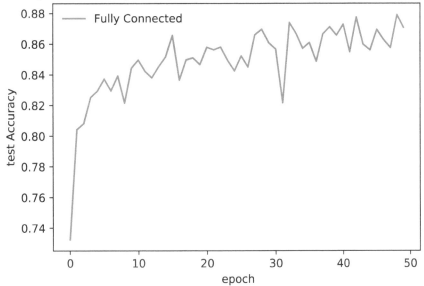

5.2   *Learning rate schedules*

Now let's talk about ways to implement the learning rate adjustment $(L(\eta_0, t))$ we described earlier. In PyTorch, these are called *learning rate schedulers*, and they take the `optimizer` object as an input because they directly alter the learning rate η used within the `optimizer` object. The high-level approach is shown in figure 5.4. The *only* thing we need to change is the equation used for $L(\eta_0, t)$ to switch between schedules.

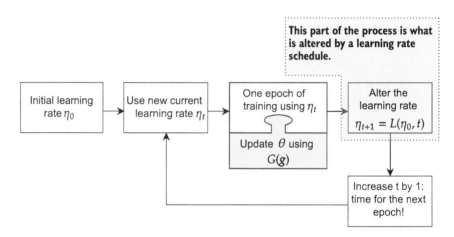

Figure 5.4   General process for every learning rate schedule. We set up before training starts with initial values, do one epoch of training, and then alter η_{t+1}, which is used by the next epoch. The gradient optimizer $G(\cdot)$ is used multiple times per epoch and operates independently of the learning rate schedule.

We will talk about four approaches to adjusting the learning rate that you should be aware of. Each of these schedules has different pros and cons. You may select your schedule to try to stabilize a model that isn't training consistently (accuracy oscillating up and down between epochs), reduce the number of epochs needed to train to save time, or maximize the accuracy of your final model. For most of the content of this book, we are using very few training iterations (10 to 50) to make sure the run in a reasonable amount of time. When you work on a problem in real life, it is common to train for 100 to 500 epochs. The more epochs of training you perform, the bigger the impact a learning rate schedule can have, because there are more opportunities to alter the learning rate. So while we may not use these heavily in the rest of this book, you should still be aware of them.

   We first talk about four of the most fundamental learning rate schedules in modern use and the kinds of minimization issues they help resolve, and how. We'll talk about these at an *intuitive* level, as proving them is more math than we want to do in this book. Once we have reviewed the four approaches, we'll do a bake-off to compare their results.

5.2.1   *Exponential decay: Smoothing erratic training*

The first approach we discuss may not be the most common but is one of the simplest. It is called an *exponential decay rate*. The exponential decay rate is a good choice if your model behaves erratically, with loss or accuracy increasing and decreasing by large amounts. You can use the exponential decay to help stabilize the training and get a more consistent result. We pick a value $0 < \gamma < 1$ that is multiplied by our learning rate after every epoch. It is defined by the following function, where t represents the current epoch:

$$\underset{\text{current learning rate}}{\eta_t} \quad = L_\gamma(\eta_0, t) = \quad \underset{\text{initial learning rate}}{\eta_0} \quad \cdot \quad \underset{\text{the decay rate}}{\gamma^t}$$

PyTorch provides this using the `torch.optim.lr_scheduler.ExponentialLR` class. Because we usually do many epochs, it is important to make sure γ is not set too aggressively: it's a good idea to start with a desired *final* learning rate and call that η_{min}. Then, if you train for a total of T epochs, you can set

$$\gamma = \sqrt[T]{\eta_{min}/\eta_0}$$

to ensure that you pick a value of γ that reaches your desired minimum and results in learning throughout.

For example, say the initial learning rate is $\eta_0 = 0.001$, you want the minimum to be $\eta_{min} = 0.0001$, and you train for $T = 50$ epochs. You need to set $\gamma \approx 0.91201$. The following code simulates this process and shows how to write the code to calculate γ:

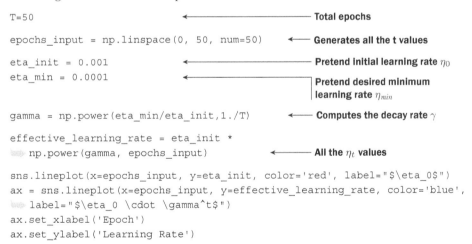

```
T=50                                                    ◀────────────────── Total epochs

epochs_input = np.linspace(0, 50, num=50)    ◀──── Generates all the t values

eta_init = 0.001                              ◀──────────────── Pretend initial learning rate η₀
eta_min = 0.0001                              ◀─────────────┐
                                                            │ Pretend desired minimum
                                                            │ learning rate ηₘᵢₙ

gamma = np.power(eta_min/eta_init,1./T)       ◀──── Computes the decay rate γ

effective_learning_rate = eta_init *
    np.power(gamma, epochs_input)             ◀──────── All the ηₜ values

sns.lineplot(x=epochs_input, y=eta_init, color='red', label="$\eta_0$")
ax = sns.lineplot(x=epochs_input, y=effective_learning_rate, color='blue',
    label="$\eta_0 \cdot \gamma^t$")
ax.set_xlabel('Epoch')
ax.set_ylabel('Learning Rate')
```

```
[13]:  Text(0, 0.5, 'Learning rate')
```

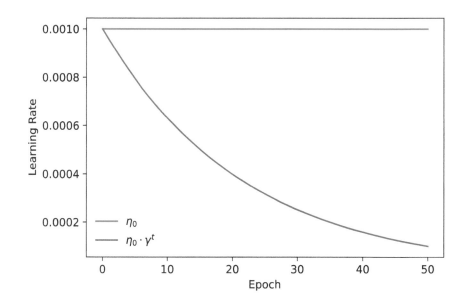

The exponential decay rate smoothly and consistently decreases the learning rate every epoch. At a high level, there are many ways to do this. Some people use linear decay $(\eta_0/(\gamma \cdot t))$ instead of exponential $(\eta_0 \cdot \gamma^t)$, and a variety of other approaches achieve the same goal; no one can give you a definitive playbook or flowchart to choose between exponential decay and its related family members. They all follow a similar intuition for why they work, which we will walk through.

In particular, the exponential learning rate schedule helps solve the problem of getting *near* the solution but not quite making it *to* the solution. Figure 5.5 shows how this happens. The black lines show the path that the parameters Θ take as they are altered from one step to the next. The initial weights are random, so we start with a bad set of weights Θ, and initially, updates move us toward the local minima. But as we get closer, we start bouncing around the minimum—sometimes getting closer than a previous step and sometimes moving farther away—which causes the loss to fluctuate up and down.

Returning to our analogy of a train traveling to its destination, going *fast* is great when you are *far* from your goal because it gets you closer faster. But once you are near your destination, it's a good idea to *slow down*. If the station was only 100 feet away and the train was going 100 miles per hour, the train would barrel past the station. You want the train to start slowing down so it can reach a precise location, and that's what the exponential learning rate does; an example is shown in figure 5.6.

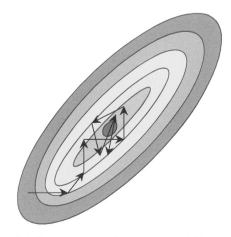

Figure 5.5 Example of the minimization problem that an exponential learning rate helps solve. When you are far from the solution, a large η helps you get to the right area faster. But once you are in the right area, η is too large to reach the best solution. Instead, it keeps overshooting the local minima (in this case, it's the only minima and so also the global minima).

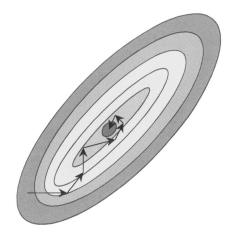

Figure 5.6 Shrinking η at every step causes the optimization to slow down as it gets closer to the destination. This helps it converge to the local minimum instead of bouncing around it.

The trick to using the exponential learning rate well is setting η_{min}. I usually recommend making it 10 to 100 times smaller than η_0. A reduction of 10 to 100$\times$ is normal in machine learning and a theme you will see across the schedules we use. The following code shows how we can create the exponential decay schedule by passing in the `optimizer` as an argument at construction. We also use the first line to reset the learned weights to be random so we don't have to keep re-specifying the same neural network over and over again:

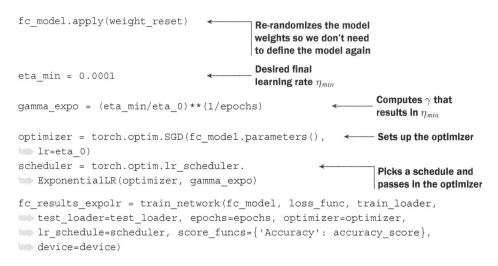

```
fc_model.apply(weight_reset)  ◄───  Re-randomizes the model
                                    weights so we don't need
                                    to define the model again

eta_min = 0.0001              ◄───  Desired final
                                    learning rate η_min

gamma_expo = (eta_min/eta_0)**(1/epochs)  ◄───  Computes γ that
                                                results in η_min

optimizer = torch.optim.SGD(fc_model.parameters(),  ◄───  Sets up the optimizer
    lr=eta_0)
scheduler = torch.optim.lr_scheduler.              ◄───  Picks a schedule and
    ExponentialLR(optimizer, gamma_expo)                 passes in the optimizer

fc_results_expolr = train_network(fc_model, loss_func, train_loader,
    test_loader=test_loader, epochs=epochs, optimizer=optimizer,
    lr_schedule=scheduler, score_funcs={'Accuracy': accuracy_score},
    device=device)
```

5.2.2 Step drop adjustment: Better smoothing

The second strategy is an especially popular variant of the exponential decay we just discussed. The *step drop* approach has the same motivation and is also useful to stabilize learning but usually delivers improved accuracy after training. What is the difference between step drop and exponential decay? Instead of constantly adjusting the learning rate ever so slightly, we let it stay fixed for a while and then drop it dramatically just a few times. This is shown in figure 5.7.

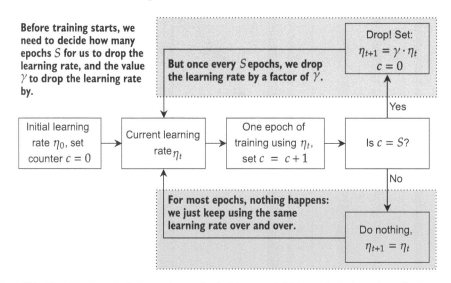

Figure 5.7   The step drop strategy requires us to decide on an initial learning rate, a decay factor γ, and a frequency S. Every S epochs of training, we decrease the learning rate by a factor of γ.

The logic behind this approach is that early in the optimization, we are still far from the solution, so we should go as fast as possible. For the first S epochs, we head toward the solution at the maximum speed η_0. This is (hopefully) better than exponential decay because the exponential decay starts slowing down *immediately* and is therefore counterproductive (at least in the beginning). Instead, let's keep going at our maximum speed and simply drop the learning rate instantaneously once or twice. That way, we go maximum speed for as long as possible but eventually slow down to converge on the solution.

We can also express this strategy in a more mathematical notation. If we want to drop the learning rate every S epochs, we obtain

If you compare this equation to the exponential day, you should notice that they look *almost identical* and are deeply connected. If we set the step drop strategy to drop every epoch ($S = 1$), we get $\gamma^{\lfloor t/1 \rfloor} = \gamma^t$, which is *exactly* exponential decay. So the step drop strategy reduces the frequency at which we decrease the learning rate and balances that out by instead increasing the amount by which we decay.

The same rule of thumb about a 10 to $100\times$ drop from η_0 to η_{min} applies, so we usually set γ to a value in the range of $0.1, 0.5$ and set S such that the learning rate is adjusted only two or three times during training. Again, PyTorch provides this using the `StepLR` class. The following code shows what a StepLR might look like compared to the exponential decay; you can see that it has a higher learning rate for *most* of the epochs but a lower learning rate for longer at the end of training:

```
[15]: Text(0, 0.5, 'Learning Rate')
```

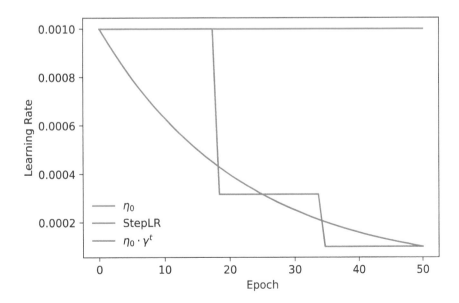

As with all learning rate schedules, we pass in the `optimizer` at construction time. This is shown in the following code, where we train with four drops in learning rate, each by a factor of $\gamma = 0.3$. The last drop happens in the last few epochs, and we have far fewer total epochs, which means the first three are much more important. Although four drops equal a $1/0.3^4 \approx 123\times$ reduction in the learning rate, most of the training happens with a $1/0.3^3 \approx 37\times$ drop (or less):

```
fc_model.apply(weight_reset)

optimizer = torch.optim.SGD(fc_model.parameters(), lr=eta_0)
scheduler = torch.optim.lr_scheduler.StepLR(optimizer,
    epochs//4, gamma=0.3)
```

Tells it to step down by a factor f γ every epochs //4 so this happens four times total.

```
fc_results_steplr = train_network(fc_model, loss_func, train_loader,
    test_loader=test_loader, epochs=epochs, optimizer=optimizer,
    lr_schedule=scheduler, score_funcs={'Accuracy': accuracy_score},
    device=device)
```

5.2.3 Cosine annealing: Greater accuracy but less stability

The next learning rate is odd but effective: *cosine annealing*. Cosine annealing has a different logic and strategy than exponential decay and the step learning rate. The latter two only decrease the learning rate, but cosine annealing decreases and increases the learning rate. This approach is very effective for getting the best possible results but does not provide the same degree of stabilization, so it might not work on poorly behaved datasets and networks.

Cosine annealing also has an initial learning rate η_0 and a minimum rate η_{min}; the difference is that we alternate between the minimum and maximum learning rates. The math follows this equation, where T_{max} is the number of epochs between cycles:

$$\eta_t = \eta_{min} + (\eta_0 - \eta_{min}) \cdot \frac{1}{2}\left(1 + \cos\left(\frac{t}{T_{max}} \cdot \pi\right)\right)$$

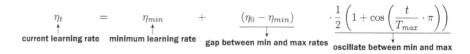

current learning rate   minimum learning rate   gap between min and max rates   oscillate between min and max

The cos term fluctuates up and down like the cosine function normally does, and we rescale its cosine to have a maximum at η_0 instead of 1 and a minimum at η_{min} instead of –1. PyTorch provides this with the `CosineAnnealingLR` class. The value T_{max} becomes a new hyperparameter for the model. I like to set T_{max} so we have 10 to 50 oscillation dips total, and we want to always end on a dip (to end by slowing down for the destination). For example, if we want S dips, we use $T_{max} = T/(S \cdot 2 - 1)$. The following code shows two dips of oscillation in the cosine schedule by setting $T_{max} = T/(2 \cdot 2 - 1)$:

**Computes the cosine schedule
η_t for every value of t**

```
cos_lr = eta_min +
0.5*(eta_init-eta_min)*(1+np.cos(epochs_input/(T/3.0)*np.pi))   ←
sns.lineplot(x=epochs_input, y=eta_init, color='red', label="$\eta_0$")
sns.lineplot(x=epochs_input, y=cos_lr, color='purple', label="$\cos$")
sns.lineplot(x=epochs_input, y=[eta_init]*18+[eta_init/3.16]*16 +
    [eta_init/10]*16, color='green', label="StepLR")    %
ax = sns.lineplot(x=epochs_input, y=effective_learning_rate, color='blue',
    label="$\eta_0 \cdot \gamma^t$")
ax.set_xlabel('Epoch')
ax.set_ylabel('Learning Rate')
```

[17]: Text(0, 0.5, 'Learning Rate')

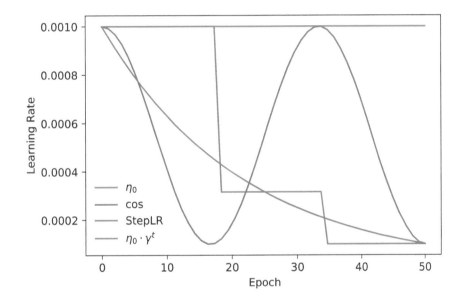

At first glance, this cosine schedule does not make sense. Why would we want to fluctuate the learning rate up and down? It makes more sense when we remember that neural networks are not *convex*. A convex function has only one local minimum, and *every* gradient leads us to the optimal solution. But neural networks are non-convex and can have many local minima, which may not be a good solution. If our model first heads towards one of these local minima, and we decrease only the learning rate, we may get stuck in this sub-optimal area.

Figure 5.8 shows what can go wrong when training a neural network that has multiple minima. The network starts in a bad position (because initial weights Θ are random) and makes progress toward a local minimum. It's an OK solution, but a better one exists nearby. Optimization is hard, and we have no way of knowing how good our minima are or how many exist; so we end up stuck in a sub-optimal position.

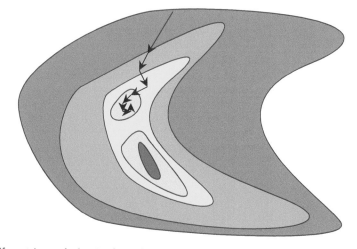

Figure 5.8   If we get an unlucky starting point (because it leads to a sub-optimal minimum), our search may take us to the sub-optimal minimum (light green). If we shrink the learning rate, our search may get stuck. The only way to escape is to increase the learning rate.

There is a sliver of hope, though. Through experimentation (and hard math that we aren't going to look at), there is a common phenomenon that sub-optimal local minima exist on the way toward a better minimum (figure 5.8 shows this). So if we shrink and then later increase the learning rate η, we can give our model a chance to escape the current local minimum and find a new alternative minimum. The larger learning rate hopefully gets us to a new and better area, and the decay again allows us to hone in on a more refined solution. Figure 5.9 shows how this works with cosine annealing.

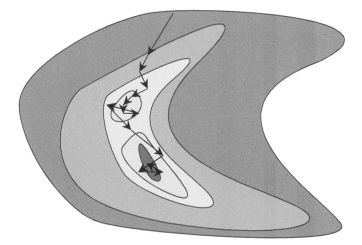

Figure 5.9   Gradient descent first takes us to the sub-optimal minimum, but as the learning rate increases again, we bounce out of that area and toward a better solution. The search continues to bounce around the better solution until the cosine schedule again decreases the learning rate, allowing the model to converge toward a more precise answer.

You may wonder what stops us from bouncing out of a better solution into a worse one. Technically, nothing stops that from happening. However, researchers have developed a lot of theory about neural networks that gives us some confidence that bouncing out of a good solution is unlikely. The gist of these results is that gradient descent likes to find wide basins as good solutions, and it would be difficult for the optimization to bounce out because the solution is wide. This gives us a little more confidence that this crazy cosine schedule is a good idea, and empirically it has performed well on a number of tasks (image classification, natural language processing, and many more). In fact, cosine annealing has been so successful that there have been dozens of proposed alternatives.

The code to implement this approach again is very similar to the previous learning rate schedules. This example uses `epochs//3` for the T_{max} value, which means it performs two dips. I always stick with an odd number for the divisor of epochs so the learning ends with a dip down to a small learning rate. It is also important that the number of dips be no more than one-quarter the number of epochs—otherwise, the learning rate will fluctuate too much from one epoch to the next. Here's the code:

```
fc_model.apply(weight_reset)

optimizer = torch.optim.SGD(fc_model.parameters(), lr=eta_0)
scheduler = torch.optim.lr_scheduler.CosineAnnealingLR(optimizer, epochs//3,
    eta_min=0.0001)
```

Tells the cosine to go down, then up, and then down (that's three). If we were doing more than 10 epochs, I would push this higher.

```
fc_results_coslr = train_network(fc_model, loss_func, train_loader,
    test_loader=test_loader, epochs=epochs, optimizer=optimizer,
    lr_schedule=scheduler, score_funcs={'Accuracy': accuracy_score},
    device=device)
```

Many friends and flavors of cosine annealing

Cosine annealing is an effective learning rate schedule on its own, but its original design was for a slightly different purpose. You may recall from your prior work or training in machine learning that *ensembling* is a great way to improve predictive accuracy on a task: train a bunch of models, and average your predictions to get a final, better, answer. But training 20 to 100 neural networks just to average them together is very expensive. That's where cosine annealing comes in. Instead of training 20 models, train 1 model with cosine annealing. Every time the learning rate bottoms out in a dip, take a copy of those weights and use that as one of your models. So if you want an ensemble of 20 networks and you are doing T epochs of training, you use $T_{max} = T/(20 \cdot 2 - 1)$. This results in exactly 20 dips in the learning rate.

(continued)

Since PyTorch 1.6, an even fancier version of this idea called *stochastic weight averaging* (SWA) is built in (https://pytorch.org/docs/stable/optim.html#stochastic-weight-averaging). With SWA, you can *average* the parameters Θ from each dip, giving you *one* model that is closer in accuracy to an ensemble of models. This is a rare best of both worlds, where you get the benefits of ensembling at the cost and storage of just one model.

5.2.4   *Validation plateau: Data-based adjustments*

None of the learning rate schedules we have talked about so far rely on external information. All you need to know is an initial learning rate η_0, a minimum rate η_{min}, and not much else. None of them use information about *how well the learning is going*. But what information do we have available to use, and how should we use it? The primary information we have is the loss ℓ for each epoch of training, and we can add it into our approach to try to maximize the accuracy of our final model. This is what the plateau-based strategy does, and it will often get you the best possible accuracy for your final model. Let's look at the training and testing set loss from the baseline network `fc_model`:

```
sns.lineplot(x='epoch', y='test loss',
    data=fc_results, label='Test Loss')
sns.lineplot(x='epoch', y='train loss',
    data=fc_results, label='Train Loss')
```

```
[19]:   <AxesSubplot:xlabel='epoch', ylabel='test loss'>
```

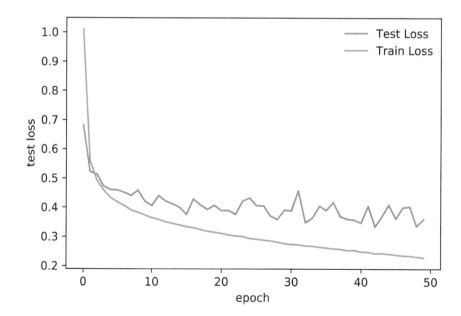

The training loss consistently heads down, which is normal since neural networks rarely underfit the data. When our model trains on a specific set of data and sees the same data over and over (that's what an epoch is: seeing all the data once), the model gets *unreasonably* good at predicting the right answer for the training data. That's classic overfitting, which occurs to different degrees depending on how big your network is. We expect the training loss to always go down, so it isn't a good source of information about how well the learning is going. But if we look at the test loss, we see that it does *not* consistently get better with each epoch. The test loss begins to stabilize or plateau after a certain point.

If the test loss has stabilized, that would be a good time to reduce the learning rate.[2] If we are already at an optimal location, reducing the learning rate will not hurt anything. If we are bouncing around a better solution, reducing the learning rate can help us improve based on the same logic we used to justify exponential decay. But now we are reducing the learning rate *when doing so appears necessary based on the data*, rather than based on a fixed arbitrary schedule.

This is the idea behind the *reduce learning rate on plateau* schedule, implemented by the ReduceLROnPlateau class in PyTorch. This is also why the step function needs the last validation loss passed in as an argument in our code, which looks like lr_schedule.step(results["val loss"][-1]). That way, the ReduceLROnPlateau class can compare the current loss to the recent history of losses.

ReduceLROnPlateau has three primary arguments to control how well it works. First is patience, which tells us how many epochs of no improvement we want to see before reducing the learning rate. A value of 10 is common, as you don't want to drop the learning rate prematurely. Instead, you want some consistent evidence that no more progress is being made before changing speed.

The second argument is threshold, which defines what counts as not improving. A threshold of exactly 0 says that we are improving if there is *any* amount lower than the previous best loss in the past patience epochs. That might be *too* pedantic because the loss could be decreasing by tiny but meaningless amounts every epoch. If we use a threshold of 0.01, we are saying that the loss needs to decrease by more than 1% to count as an improvement. But that could also be a little too loose: when you train for hundreds of epochs, you could be making slow but steady progress, and *reducing* the learning rate is unlikely to speed up convergence. It can take some work to setting this *just* right, so we stick the default value of 0.0001, but this is a hyperparameter worth playing with if you want to squeeze out the maximum possible performance.

---

[2] If the test loss starts increasing, which indicates more severe overfitting, that is another good reason to slow down learning. That helps slow the overfitting. But ideally, the test loss has stabilized.

The last parameter is the `factor` by which we want to drop the learning rate η every time we determine that we have hit a plateau. This works the same way γ does for the `StepLR` class. Again, values in the range of 0.1 to 0.5 are all reasonable choices.

But we need to recognize one critical thing before using the `ReduceLROnPlateau` schedule: you can't use the test data to choose when to alter the learning rate. Doing so *will* cause overfitting because you are using information about the test data to make decisions and then using the test data to evaluate your results. Instead, you need to have training, validation, and testing splits. Our normal code has been using validation as the test data, which was fine because we were not *looking* at the validation data to make decisions while training. The process of `ReduceLROnPlateau` with this important detail is summarized in figure 5.10.

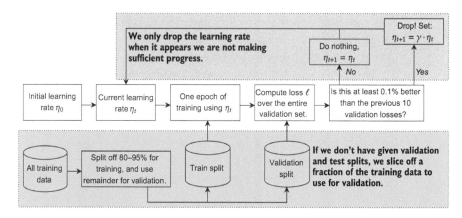

Figure 5.10   Plateau-based learning rate schedule strategy. The bottom part, in red, shows us slicing off a portion of the training data to use as our validation set. Doing this, or having a special validation set along with a test set, is necessary to avoid overfitting. The upper part, in green, shows how we reduce only the learning rate η when our validation loss is not reducing.

The following code shows how to do this properly. First, we use the `random_split` class to create an 80/20 split of the *training* data. The 20% split will become our validation set, which `ReduceLROnPlateau` uses to check whether we should drop the learning rate; and the 80% is used to train the model parameters Θ. Pay attention to the call to *train_network*, where we use the `train_loader`, `val_loader`, and `test_loader` to set each of the three components properly. In the results of this model, we need to make sure we are looking at the *test* results and not the *val* results. Other than these careful precautions, this code is not much different from before:

```
fc_model.apply(weight_reset)
```

Resets the weights again so we don't have to define a new model

```
train_sub_set, val_sub_set = torch.utils.data.random_split(train_data,
    [int(len(train_data)*0.8),
    int(len(train_data)*0.2)])
```

Creates training and validation subsets since we do not have explicit validation and test sets

```
train_sub_loader = DataLoader(train_sub_set,
    batch_size=B, shuffle=True)
val_sub_loader = DataLoader(val_sub_set, batch_size=B)

optimizer =torch.optim.SGD(fc_model.parameters(), lr=eta_0)
```

Creates loaders for the train and validation subsets. Our test loader stays the same—never alter your test data!

```
scheduler =torch.optim.lr_scheduler.ReduceLROnPlateau(
    optimizer, mode='min', factor=0.2, patience=10)
```

Sets up our plateau schedule using gamma=0.2

```
fc_results_plateau = train_network(fc_model, loss_func, train_loader,
    val_loader=val_sub_loader, test_loader=test_loader, epochs=epochs,
    optimizer=optimizer, lr_schedule=scheduler, score_funcs={'Accuracy':
    accuracy_score}, device=device)
```

Train up the model!

Don't shoot yourself in the foot!

Plateau-based adjustments to the learning rate are a *very* popular and successful strategy. Using information about how well the current model appears to be doing gets the best results on many problems. *But* you should not blindly use it in all circumstances. There are two particular cases where ReduceLROnPlateau may perform poorly or even mislead you into an overconfident result.

First is the case where you don't have much data. The ReduceLROnPlateau strategy requires training and validation sets to work and thus reduces the amount of data you have for learning the model parameters. If you have only 100 training points, it may be painful to use 10 to 30% for validation. You need enough data both to estimate the parameters Θ and tell whether the learning has plateaued—and if you don't have a lot of data, that may be too tall an order to fill.

The second case is when your data strongly violates the identically and independently distributed (IID) assumption. For example, if your data includes multiple samples from the same person, or events that depend on the date they occur (e.g., if you want to predict the weather, you can't have data from the future!), naively applying a random split to create the validation set can lead to poor results. In this situation, you need

(continued)

to make sure your training, validation, and testing splits don't have any accidental leakage from one to the other. Using the weather example, you might want to make sure your training split has data from *only* the years 1980 through 2004, validation data 2005 through 2010, and test data 2011 through 2016. This way, no accidental time traveling will occur, which would be a big IID violation.

5.2.5   *Comparing the schedules*

Now that we have trained four common learning rate schedules, we can compare their results and see which performed best. The results are shown in the following plot, with the test accuracy on the y-axis. Some trends are quickly obvious and worth talking about. The vanilla SGD does fine but constantly fluctuates up and down from epoch to epoch. Every learning rate schedule we are looking at provides *some* kind of benefit:

```
sns.lineplot(x='epoch', y='test Accuracy', data=fc_results, label='SGD')
sns.lineplot(x='epoch', y='test Accuracy',
    data=fc_results_expolr, label='+Exponential Decay')
sns.lineplot(x='epoch', y='test Accuracy',
    data=fc_results_steplr, label='+StepLR')
sns.lineplot(x='epoch', y='test Accuracy',
    data=fc_results_coslr, label='+CosineLR')
sns.lineplot(x='epoch', y='test Accuracy',
    data=fc_results_plateau, label='+Plateau')
```

```
[22]:  <AxesSubplot:xlabel='epoch', ylabel='test Accuracy'>
```

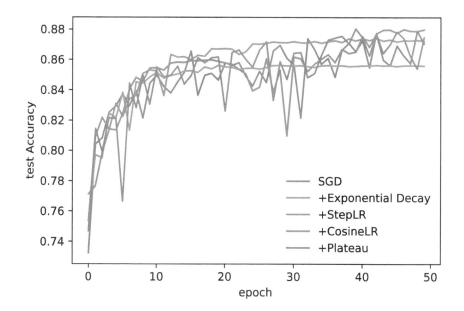

Exponential decay has the benefit of being *smooth and consistent*: from epoch to epoch, it has almost identical behavior. Unfortunately, it trends toward the lower side of accuracy and does a little worse than naive SGD. But consistency has value, and if we ended one epoch sooner, SGD would perform worse.

The StepLR schedule is very similar to the exponential one in behavior, with a bit more asperity in the beginning as it goes fast before slowing down and stabilizing later in training. This ends up on the higher end of SGD in performance.

The cosine schedule ultimately does even better, reaching the highest accuracy of naive SGD, StepLR, or exponential decay. About 27 epochs in, performance drops suddenly as the learning rate ramps back up; then performance restabilizes at a higher accuracy when the learning rate decays again. This is why I recommend setting the cosine approach so that it ends on a dip.

The Plateau approach also does a good job, and happens to just get second place in this set of tests. With more epochs, the Plateau would self-stabilize by dropping the learning rate further. Using feedback from how the model is actually doing, rather than assuming behavior, can help get every last bit of accuracy out of your model.

Table 5.1 summarizes the pros and cons and when you might want to use each method. Unfortunately, no one size fits all, and each will have cases where it doesn't pan out. That depends heavily on your data, and you won't know until you train the data and find out. This is why I like to start with no learning rate schedule and then add one of these four based on what happens.

Table 5.1 Flow control statements

	Exponential decay	StepLR	CosineLR	Plateau
Pros	Very consistent results. Little tuning needed.	Consistent results. Little tuning needed. Often improves accuracy.	Often improves accuracy. Advanced versions can significantly improve accuracy.	Often improves accuracy significantly and reduces epochs of training.
Cons	Can modestly reduce final accuracy.	Most helpful when training for 100+ epochs.	Requires some parameter tuning; doesn't always work.	Not all data is used for training. More risk of overfitting.
When to use	Training the same model, but with different initial weights, can give wildly different results. Exponential decay can help fix stabilize training.	You want to improve your final model's accuracy with minimal work.	You want to squeeze out maximum performance without too much extra work, and ideally you have enough time to do a few extra training runs.	You want to squeeze out maximum performance without too much extra work, and ideally you have a lot of data.

Despite how well the plateau approach does, we won't use it much in this book. Part of the reason is that it requires extra code that can be distracting when we are trying to focus on new concepts. Also, sometimes we will set up learning problems in a *specific* way so you see real-world behavior for problems that take only a few minutes to run instead of hours or more, and the plateau approach makes it harder to set up some of these scenarios. But these initial results show that you should keep it in mind as a powerful tool in your arsenal.

5.3   *Making better use of gradients*

We now know several ways to alter the learning rate η to improve how quickly our model learns and allow it to learn more accurate solutions. We did this by defining different learning rate schedules $L(\cdot, \cdot)$, which look at the long term. Think of $L(\cdot, \cdot)$ as setting the desired speed for the journey. But detours, potholes, and other obstacles in the short term may require a change in speed. This is why we also want to modify the gradient $\boldsymbol{g}$ with a function $G(\cdot)$. We focus on gradient update schemes on their own first and then combine them with learning rate schedules to get improved results. First, we talk about some broad motivations and then dive into the most common approaches. All three approaches are one-line changes to your code with PyTorch (they are built in) and can dramatically improve the accuracy of your models.

Remember that we are using $\boldsymbol{g}^t$ to indicate the tth gradient that we are receiving to update the network. Because we are doing stochastic gradient descent in batches, this is a noisy gradient. Even with the noise in $\boldsymbol{g}^t$, there is valuable information in $\boldsymbol{g}^t$ that we are not fully utilizing. Consider the jth parameter's gradient $\boldsymbol{g}_j^t$. What if it's consistently almost the same value every time? Mathematically, that would be a situation where

$$\boldsymbol{g}_j^t \approx \boldsymbol{g}_j^{t-1} \approx \boldsymbol{g}_j^{t-2} \approx \boldsymbol{g}_j^{t-3} \approx \dots$$

This tells us the jth parameter needs to be moved in the same direction each time. Figure 5.11 shows such a situation.

We don't necessarily want to increase the learning rate η, because other dimensions may have different behavior. Every network parameter gets its own gradient value, and networks can have millions of parameters. So if the gradient at index j is consistently the same, maybe we should be increasing how far we step (i.e., increase learning rate η) for *just* index j. We would need to ensure that this was done only with respect to index j, because the gradient for a different index i might not be as consistent.

So, we would like to have a global learning rate η and individualized learning rates η_j for all of the parameters. While the global learning rate stays fixed (unless we use a learning rate schedule), we let some algorithms adjust each of the η_j values to try to improve convergence. Most gradient update schemes work by rescaling the gradient $\boldsymbol{g}^t$, which is equivalent to giving each parameter its own personalized learning rate η_j.

5.3.1   *SGD with momentum: Adapting to gradient consistency*

We want to increase the learning rate if the gradient for parameter j consistently heads in the same direction. We can describe this as wanting the gradient to build momentum. If the gradient in one direction keeps returning similar values, it should start taking

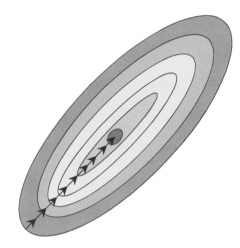

Figure 5.11 Example where the gradient value could consistently return the same value over and over. We are heading on a direct path toward the solution, but we could get there faster if we used a larger learning rate.

bigger and bigger steps in the same direction. Figure 5.12 shows an example problem that momentum can help fix.

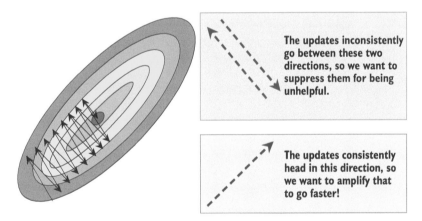

The updates inconsistently go between these two directions, so we want to suppress them for being unhelpful.

The updates consistently head in this direction, so we want to amplify that to go faster!

Figure 5.12 The naive optimization is almost stuck oscillating between the top-left and bottom-right directions, but it is slowly and consistently making progress in the top-right direction that leads to the solution. If we could build some momentum in that direction, we would not need so many steps.

This momentum strategy was one of the first developed for improving SGD and solving the problem shown in the figure and is still widely used today. Let's talk about the math of how it works.

Our normal gradient update equation, again, looks like this:

$$\Theta_{t+1} = \Theta_t - \eta \cdot \boldsymbol{g}^t$$

The initial version of the momentum idea is to have a momentum weight μ, which has some value in the range $(0, 1)$ (i.e., $\mu \in (0, 1)$).[3] Next, we add a velocity term called v, which accumulates our momentum. So our velocity v contains a fraction (μ) of our previous gradient step, as detailed in the following equation:

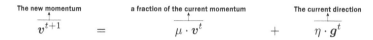

$$
\underset{\substack{\uparrow \\ \text{The new momentum}}}{v^{t+1}} \quad = \quad \underset{\substack{\uparrow \\ \text{a fraction of the current momentum}}}{\mu \cdot v^t} \quad + \quad \underset{\substack{\uparrow \\ \text{The current direction}}}{\eta \cdot g^t}
$$

Because our velocity depends on our previous velocity, it takes into account all of our previous gradient updates. Next, we simply use v in place of g to perform the gradient update:

$$
\Theta^{t+1} = \Theta^t - v^{t+1}
$$

The amazing shrinking history

The equation for momentum relies heavily on the fact that μ is a value smaller than 1. This is because it has a shrinking effect on old gradients. One way to look at this is to write out what happens to the equations as we repeatedly apply momentum. Let's write this out in detail.

The following table shows what happens to the velocity v as we keep applying momentum μ. The left-most column is the new value of Θ, and we start with Θ_1 as the initial random weights. There is no previous velocity v yet, so nothing happens. Starting with the second round, we can expand the velocity term, as shown on the right.

$$\Theta_2 = \Theta_1 - \underset{\substack{\downarrow \\ \text{this is the new momentum } v_1}}{(\eta \cdot g_1)}$$

$$\Theta_3 = \Theta_2 - \underset{\substack{\downarrow \\ v_3}}{(\mu \cdot v_2 + \eta \cdot g_2)} = \Theta_2 - \underset{\substack{\downarrow \\ v_3}}{\left(\underset{\substack{\overbrace{\mu \cdot \eta \cdot g_1}}^{\text{This is } \mu \cdot v_2} + \eta \cdot g_2} \right)}$$

$$\Theta_4 = \Theta_3 - \underset{\substack{\downarrow \\ v_4}}{(\mu \cdot v_3 + \eta \cdot g_3)} = \Theta_3 - \underset{\substack{\downarrow \\ v_4}}{\left(\underset{\substack{\overbrace{\mu^2 \cdot \eta \cdot g_1 + \mu \cdot \eta \cdot g_2}}^{\text{This is } \mu \cdot v_3} + \eta \cdot g_3} \right)}$$

$$\Theta_5 = \Theta_4 - \underset{\substack{\downarrow \\ v_5}}{(\mu \cdot v_4 + \eta \cdot g_4)} = \Theta_4 - \underset{\substack{\downarrow \\ v_5}}{\left(\underset{\substack{\overbrace{\mu^3 \cdot \eta \cdot g_1 + \mu^2 \cdot \eta \cdot g_2 + \mu \cdot \eta \cdot g_3}}^{\text{This is } \mu \cdot v_4} + \eta \cdot g_4} \right)}$$

Notice that every time we update with momentum, *every previous gradient* contributes to the current update! Also notice that the exponents above μ get larger every time we apply another round of momentum. This makes the contributions of very old gradients become essentially zero as we keep updating. If we use a standard momentum of

---

[3] I think using μ for momentum is confusing, but it's the most common notation, so I'm sticking with it so you can learn it.

$\mu = 0.9$, old gradients contribute less than 0.01% of their value after just 88 updates. Since we often do thousands to hundreds of thousands of updates per epoch, this is a very short-term effect.

You may look at the previous equations and be concerned: if we are taking into account all of our old gradients, what if some of them are no longer useful? That's why we keep the momentum term $\mu \in (0, 1)$. If we are currently at update t, and we think about the past gradient from k steps ago, its contribution is $\mu^k g^t$, which quickly becomes small. If we have $\mu = 0.9$, the gradient 40 steps ago is contributing a weight of only $0.9^{40} \approx 0.01$ to the current velocity v. The value μ helps us forget past gradients so that learning can adapt and is able to grow larger if we are always heading in the same direction.

This strategy is a simple way to significantly improve your model's accuracy and training time. It can solve both problems we have looked at; figure 5.13 shows the solutions.

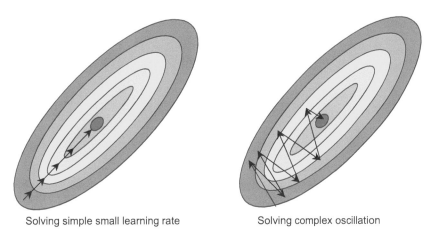

Solving simple small learning rate   Solving complex oscillation

Figure 5.13   On the left, momentum solves the problem of a small learning rate. The direction is consistent, so the momentum builds and increases the effective learning rate. On the right, the momentum builds consistently—but initially, slowly—in the top-right direction. The oscillation may continue, but fewer steps are needed to reach the minimum.

If you want to get the *best possible* accuracy from your network, SGD with some form of momentum is still considered one of the best options. The downside is that finding the combination of μ and η values that gives the *absolute best results* is not easy and requires training many models. We talk about smarter ways to search for μ and η in the last section of this chapter.

NESTEROV MOMENTUM: ADAPTING TO CHANGING CONSISTENCY

A second flavor of momentum exists and is worth mentioning, as it often performs better in practice. This version is called *Nesterov momentum*.

In normal momentum, we take the gradient with respect to the current weights (that is, g^t) and then move in the direction of our gradient and velocity combined. If we have built up a *lot* of momentum, it can be difficult to make turns during the optimization. Let's look at a toy example of what can go wrong in figure 5.14.

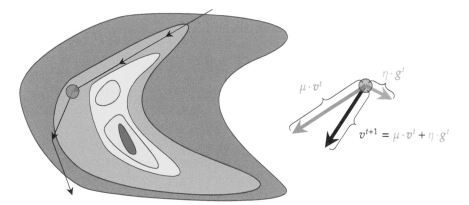

Figure 5.14   Imagine that it has taken a long time to reach this point, so the optimizer has built up a large momentum (i.e., $\|v^t\|_2 > 0$). When we reach the purple point, the momentum causes us to swerve around the desired area because the momentum, even after decay, is larger than the gradient. Since it is larger, it carries the weights more in the same direction rather than a new direction.

Technically, this problem shows momentum behaving correctly: the momentum is carrying Θ_{t+1} in a consistent direction. It's just not a good idea anymore, and it will take a few iterations for the momentum to be corrected and start heading toward the actual solution.

In Nesterov momentum, we instead decide to be patient. Normal momentum at step t immediately calculates the new gradient g^t and adds the velocity v^t. Nesterov first acts on the velocity and *then* calculates a new gradient *after* letting the momentum move us. This way, if we are moving in the *wrong* direction, Nesterov will likely have a larger gradient to push us back in the correct direction sooner. This looks like the following sequence of equations, where I'm using t' to denote the patient steps.

First we compute $\Theta^{t'}$ based only on the previous velocity. We don't look at the new data yet, meaning this could be a bad direction if things are changing (or it could be good—we don't know because we haven't looked at the data):

Second, we finally look at the new data x using our modified weights $\Theta^{t'}$. This is like peeking at the near future so we can change or correct our answer about how we want to update the parameters. If the velocity was in the correct direction, nothing really changes. But if the velocity was going to take us in a bad direction, we can change course and counteract the effect more quickly:

Finally, we modify $\Theta^{t'}$ again using the new velocity that contains the fresh gradient, giving us the ultimate updated weights Θ^{t+1}:

To recap: the first equation alters the parameters Θ based on *only* the current velocity (no new batch and no new information). The second equation computes a *new* velocity using the old velocity and the gradient *after* having altered Θ from the first equation. Finally, the third equation takes a step based on these results. While this looks like extra work, there is a clever way to organize it so that it takes exactly the same amount of time as normal momentum (which we won't go into because it's a little confusing). Figure 5.15 shows how Nesterov momentum affects the previous example.

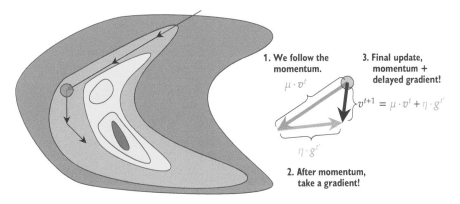

Figure 5.15 At the same purple point, the right side shows how the update is calculated. Instead of computing g^t at the starting point, we first follow the momentum, which is in the wrong direction. This causes the gradient at this new location to be larger back in the correct direction. Combined, we get a smaller step that is closer to the solution. The original standard momentum result is shown faded in black.

Let's reason through another scenario to exercise our mental model of what is happening. Try drawing a diagram of this yourself to help you follow along.

Consider the standard momentum case where our momentum has been useful, allowing us to head in the correct direction, and assume that we have just reached our goal. We are at the function's minimum, and the problem is solved. But, *we don't ever know for sure that we are at the minimum*, so we run the next step of the optimization process. Because of the momentum we have built up, we are about to roll past the minimum. In normal momentum, we compute the gradient—and if we are at the solution, the gradient $g^t = 0$, so there is no change. Then we add the velocity v^t, and it carries us away.

Now, think about this scenario under Nesterov momentum. We are at the solution, and first we follow the velocity, pushing us away from the goal. Then we calculate the gradient, which recognizes that we need to head back in the opposite direction and thus move toward the goal. When we add these two together, they almost cancel out (we take a smaller step forward or backward, depending on which has a larger magnitude, g^t or v^t). In one step, we have started to change the direction in which our optimizer is headed, whereas normal momentum would take two steps.

This is the intuition and reasoning for why Nesterov momentum is usually the preferred version of momentum. Now that we've talked about the ideas, we can turn them into code. The SGD class simply requires us to set the momentum flag to a nonzero value if we would like momentum and nesterov=True if we want it to be Nesterov momentum. The following code trains our network with both versions.

```
fc_model.apply(weight_reset)

optimizer = torch.optim.SGD(fc_model.parameters(), lr=eta_0,
    momentum=0.9, nesterov=False)

fc_results_momentum = train_network(fc_model, loss_func, train_loader,
    test_loader=test_loader, epochs=epochs, optimizer=optimizer,
    score_funcs={'Accuracy': accuracy_score}, device=device)


fc_model.apply(weight_reset)

optimizer = torch.optim.SGD(fc_model.parameters(), lr=eta_0,
    momentum=0.9, nesterov=True)

fc_results_Nesterov = train_network(fc_model, loss_func, train_loader,
    test_loader=test_loader, epochs=epochs, optimizer=optimizer,
    score_funcs={'Accuracy': accuracy_score}, device=device)
```

COMPARING SGD WITH MOMENTUMS

Here we plot the results from vanilla SGD and both flavors of momentum. Both momentum versions perform dramatically better, learning faster and giving more accurate solutions. But you won't usually see one version of momentum perform dramatically better or worse than the other. While Nesterov does solve a real problem, normal momentum will *eventually* correct itself after more gradient updates. Still, I prefer to use the Nesterov flavor because in my experience, if one momentum is better by a nontrivial amount, it is usually Nesterov:

```
sns.lineplot(x='epoch', y='test Accuracy', data=fc_results, label='SGD')
sns.lineplot(x='epoch', y='test Accuracy', data=fc_results_momentum,
    label='SGD w/ Momentum')
sns.lineplot(x='epoch', y='test Accuracy', data=fc_results_nestrov,
    label='SGD w/ Nesterov Momentum')
```

[25] : `<AxesSubplot:xlabel='epoch', ylabel='test Accuracy'>`

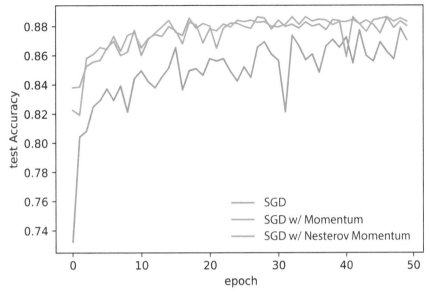

5.3.2 Adam: Adding variance to momentum

One of the currently most popular optimization techniques is called *adaptive moment estimation*, or Adam for short. Adam is strongly related to the SGD with momentum that we just described. Adam is my current favorite approach because it has default parameters that just work, so I don't have to spend time tuning them. This is not true for SGD with momentum (normal or Nesterov flavored). We have to rename a few terms to make the math consistent with how you will read about it elsewhere: the velocity v becomes m, and the momentum weight μ becomes β_1. Now we can describe the first step of Adam, which has one major change shown in red:

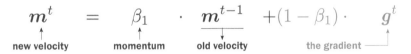

$$m^t = \beta_1 \cdot m^{t-1} + (1 - \beta_1) \cdot g^t$$

This describes the momentum update equation, but we are now down-weighting the *current* gradient g^t by $(1 - \beta_1)$. This makes m^t a *weighted average* between the previous velocity and the current gradient. More specifically, because we added the $(1 - \beta_1)$ term, this is now called an *exponential moving average*. It's called *exponential* because the gradient from z steps ago g^{t-z} has an exponentiated contribution of β_1^z, and it's a *moving average* because it is computing a kind of weighted average where most of the weight is on the most recent items, so the average moves with the most recent data.

Since we are now discussing momentum as an *average* or *mean* gradient over multiple updates, we can talk about the *variance* of the gradient as well. If one parameter g_j^t has high variance, we probably don't want to let it contribute too much to the momentum because it will likely change again. If a parameter g^t_j has *low* variance, it's a reliable direction to head in, so we should give it *more* weight in the momentum calculation.

To implement this idea, we can calculate information about the variance over time by looking at squared gradient values. Normally, for variance, we would subtract the mean before squaring, but that is hard to do in this scenario. So we use the squared values as an *approximation* of the variance and keep in mind that it does not provide perfect information. Using $\odot$ to denote the elementwise multiplication between two vectors ($a \odot b = [a_1 \cdot b_1, a_2 \cdot b_2, \ldots]$) leads to this equation for variance of velocity v:

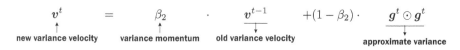

$$v^t \qquad = \qquad \beta_2 \qquad \cdot \qquad v^{t-1} \qquad +(1-\beta_2)\cdot \qquad g^t \odot g^t$$

new variance velocity   variance momentum   old variance velocity   approximate variance

We save m^t and v^t, but we perform one more alteration before using them. Why? Because when we are early in the optimization process, meaning t is a small value, m^t and v^t give us biased estimates of the mean and variance. They are biased because they are initialized to zero (i.e., $m^0 = v^0 = \vec{0}$), so the early estimates will be *too small* if we use them naively.

Think about when $t = 1$. In that case, the value of $m^1 = (1-\beta_1)\cdot g$. The true average is just g, but instead we have discounted it by a factor of $1 - \beta_1$. To fix this, we just adjust as so:

$$\hat{m} = \frac{m^t}{1 - \beta_1^t}$$

$$\hat{v} = \frac{v^t}{1 - \beta_2^t}$$

Now we have $\hat{m}$ and $\hat{v}$, which give us the unbiased estimates of the mean and variance, respectively, and we use them together to update our weights Θ:

The new parameters θ_{t+1} are equal to   the old parameters θ_t minus the

learning rate times momentum and gradient (what currently looks best)

but adjust how much we trust the direction by how consistently we've been going in the same direction over time.

$$\theta_{t+1} = \theta_t - \eta \cdot \frac{\hat{m}}{\sqrt{\hat{v}}+\epsilon}$$

What is going on here? The numerator $\eta \cdot \hat{m}$ is computing the SGD with momentum term, but now we are normalizing each dimension by the variance. That way, if a parameter has naturally large swings in its value, we won't adjust as quickly to a new large swing—because it usually is quite noisy. If a parameter usually has a small variance and is very consistent, we adapt quickly to any observed change. The ϵ term is a very small value so we never end up dividing by zero.

That gives you the intuition behind Adam. The original authors proposed using the following values: $\eta = 0.001$, $\beta_1 = 0.9$, $\beta_2 = 0.999$, and $\epsilon = 10^{-8}$.

Personally, I recommend using Adam or one of its descendants as the default choice for any optimization problem. Why? Because it's an optimizer that, using the default values, usually performs well with no further alteration. It may not get you the *best possible* performance, and you can often improve results by adjusting the parameters, but the defaults usually work well. And if they don't work, other parameter settings usually won't, either.

Most optimizers don't share this property, or not to the degree that Adam exhibits it. For example, SGD is very sensitive to the momentum and learning rate terms, and you usually need to do some tuning to get good performance out of normal SGD. Since Adam does not *require* this finicky tuning, you don't have to do as much experimentation to figure out what works. Thus, you can save a detailed optimization process until after you have settled on your final architecture and are ready to squeeze out every last drop of accuracy. Ultimately, this makes Adam a great time saver: spend the time on your architecture, and leave the optimizer changes for the end.

Other flavors of Adam

The original paper for the Adam algorithm contained a mistake, but the proposed algorithm still worked well for the vast majority of problems. A version that fixes this mistake is called `AdamW` and is the default we use in this book.

Another extension of Adam is NAdam, where the *N* stands for Nesterov. As you might guess, this version adapts Adam to use Nesterov momentum rather than standard momentum. A third flavor is AdaMax, which replaces some of the multiplication operations in Adam with max operations to improve the algorithm's numerical stability. All of these flavors have pros and cons that are beyond the scope of this book, but any Adam variant will serve you well.

Now that we have learned about Adam, let's try it. The following code again resets the weights for the neural network we have been training over and over, but using `AdamW` this time:

> We don't set the learning rate for Adam because you should always use the default, and Adam can be more sensitive to large changes in the learning rate.

```
fc_model.apply(weight_reset)

optimizer = torch.optim.AdamW(fc_model.parameters())    ◄──

fc_results_adam = train_network(fc_model, loss_func, train_loader,
    test_loader=test_loader, epochs=epochs, optimizer=optimizer,
    score_funcs={'Accuracy': accuracy_score}, device=device)
```

Now we can plot `AdamW` along with the three versions of SGD we have already looked at. The result shows that AdamW performs as well as SGD with either flavor of momentum, but its behavior is a bit more stable when the dips down are not as frequent or dramatic:

```
sns.lineplot(x='epoch', y='test Accuracy', data=fc_results, label='SGD')
sns.lineplot(x='epoch', y='test Accuracy', data=fc_results_momentum,
    label='SGD w/ Momentum')
sns.lineplot(x='epoch', y='test Accuracy', data=fc_results_nestrov,
    label='SGD w/ Nestrov Momentum')
sns.lineplot(x='epoch', y='test Accuracy', data=fc_results_adam,
    label='AdamW')
```

```
[27]:  <AxesSubplot:xlabel='epoch', ylabel='test Accuracy'>
```

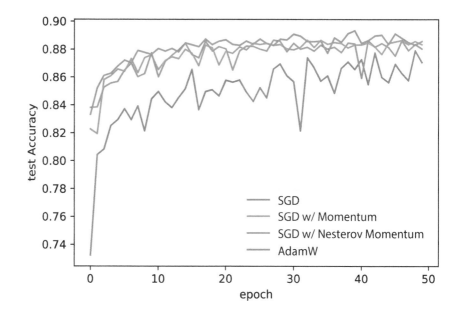

We can also combine these new optimizers with the learning rate schedules we have learned about. Here, we train Adam and SGD with Nesterov momentum combined with the cosine annealing schedule:

```
fc_model.apply(weight_reset)                              Adam with cosine
optimizer = torch.optim.AdamW(fc_model.parameters())  ←  annealing

scheduler = torch.optim.lr_scheduler.
    CosineAnnealingLR(optimizer, epochs//3)
fc_results_adam_coslr = train_network(fc_model, loss_func, train_loader,
    test_loader=test_loader, epochs=epochs, optimizer=optimizer,
    lr_schedule=scheduler, score_funcs={'Accuracy': accuracy_score},
    device=device)

fc_model.apply(weight_reset)
optimizer = torch.optim.SGD(fc_model.parameters(),
    lr=eta_0, momentum=0.9, nesterov=True)  ←          SGD+Nesterov with
                                                       cosine annealing
```

```
scheduler = torch.optim.lr_scheduler.
    CosineAnnealingLR(optimizer, epochs//3)
fc_results_nesterov_coslr = train_network(fc_model, loss_func,
    train_loader, test_loader=test_loader, epochs=epochs,
    optimizer=optimizer, lr_schedule=scheduler,
    score_funcs={'Accuracy': accuracy_score}, device=device)
```

Now we can compare the results with and without the cosine schedule in the following code and plot. Again we see a similar trend, that adding the learning rate schedule gives a bump to accuracy and that the version with AdamW is *slightly* better behaved:

```
sns.lineplot(x='epoch', y='test Accuracy', data=fc_results_nesterov,
    label='SGD w/ Nesterov')
sns.lineplot(x='epoch', y='test Accuracy', data=fc_results_nesterov_coslr,
    label='SGD w/ Nesterov+CosineLR')
sns.lineplot(x='epoch', y='test Accuracy', data=fc_results_adam,
    label='AdamW')
sns.lineplot(x='epoch', y='test Accuracy', data=fc_results_adam_coslr,
    label='AdamW+CosineLR')
```

```
[29]:   <AxesSubplot:xlabel='epoch', ylabel='test Accuracy'>
```

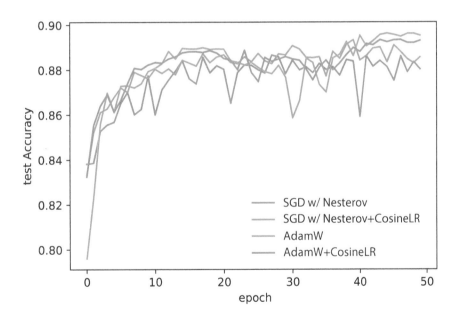

5.3.3 Gradient clipping: Avoiding exploding gradients

We have one last trick to talk about, which is compatible with both optimizers like Adam and SGD as well as learning rate schedules. It is called *gradient clipping*, and it helps us solve the exploding gradient problem. Unlike all the mathematical intuition and logic that went into everything we have discussed so far, gradient clipping is refreshingly simple: if any (absolute) value in a gradient is larger than some threshold z, just set it to a maximum value of z. So if we use $z = 5$ and our gradient is $g = [1, -2, 1000, 3, -7]$, the clipped version becomes $\text{clip}_5(g) = [1, -2, 5, 3, -5]$. The idea is that any value larger than our threshold z clearly indicates the *direction*; but it is set to an unreasonable *distance*, so we forcibly clip it to something reasonable.

The following code shows how to add gradient clipping to any neural network. We grab the parameters Θ using the `model.parameters()` function and use `register_hook` to register a callback that is executed every time the gradients are used. In this case, we simply take the tensor `grad` that represents the gradients and use the `clamp` function that returns a new version of `grad` where nothing is smaller than `-5` or larger than `5`. That's all it takes:

```
fc_model.apply(weight_reset)

for p in fc_model.parameters():
    p.register_hook(lambda grad: torch.clamp(grad, -5, 5))

optimizer = torch.optim.AdamW(fc_model.parameters())
scheduler = torch.optim.lr_scheduler.CosineAnnealingLR(optimizer, epochs//3)
fc_results_nesterov_coslr_clamp = train_network(fc_model, loss_func,
    train_loader, test_loader=test_loader, epochs=epochs,
    optimizer=optimizer, lr_schedule=scheduler,
    score_funcs={'Accuracy': accuracy_score}, device=device)
```

Plotting the results, you see that they are *usually* the same. In this case, they are a little worse, but they could have been better, instead. It depends on the problem:

```
sns.lineplot(x='epoch', y='test Accuracy', data=fc_results_nesterov_coslr,
    label='AdamW+CosineLR')
sns.lineplot(x='epoch', y='test Accuracy',
    data=fc_results_nesterov_coslr_clamp, label='AdamW+CosineLR+Clamp')
```

[31]: `<AxesSubplot:xlabel='epoch', ylabel='test Accuracy'>`

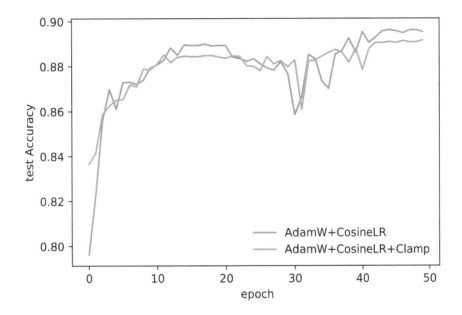

Exploding gradients are usually a *catastrophic* problem. If your model has them, it's probably learning a degenerate solution or not converging at all. Since this dataset and network don't have that problem, gradient clipping isn't beneficial.

In most applications, I don't use gradient clipping unless my models are not learning well to begin with. If they learn well, I probably don't have exploding gradients, so I focus on other changes. If the model isn't good, I test gradient clipping to see if that fixes the problem. If I'm working with recurrent neural networks, I *always* use gradient clipping because the recurrent connections tend to cause exploding gradients, making them a common issue in that scenario. But if you want to always include clipping, doing so is an equally valid strategy. Using a clip value of $z = 5$ or $z = 10$ is common and works well for most problems.

5.4 Hyperparameter optimization with Optuna

Now that we have improved how to do training, we will reuse many of these techniques throughout the book because they are useful for *any and every* neural network you will ever train. The improvements so far have focused on optimizing when we have gradients. But hyperparameters are things we would like to optimize for which we do not have any gradients, such as the initial learning rate η to use and the value of the momentum term μ. We would also like to optimize the architecture of our networks: should we use two layers or three? How about the number of neurons in each hidden layer?

The first hyperparameter tuning method most people learn in machine learning is called *grid search*. While valuable, grid search works well only for optimizing one or two variables at a time due to its exponential cost as more variables are added. When training a neural network, we usually have at least three parameters we want to optimize (number of layers, number of neurons in each layer, and learning rate η). We instead use a newer approach—Optuna—to tuning hyperparameters, which works much better. Unlike grid search, it requires fewer decisions, finds better parameter values, can handle more hyperparameters, and can be adapted to your computational budget (i.e., how long you are willing to wait).

With all that said, hyperparameter tuning is still very expensive, and these examples can't run in a few minutes because they require training tens of models. In the real world, there could even be hundreds of models. This makes Optuna impractical for use in future chapters because we do not have the time, but using it is still a critical skill for you to know.

5.4.1 *Optuna*

To perform a smarter type of hyperparameter optimization, we use a library called Optuna. Optuna can be used with any framework, as long as you can describe the goal as a single numeric value. Luckily for us, we have the accuracy or error as our goal, so we can use Optuna. Optuna does a better job of hyperparameter optimization by using a Bayesian technique to model the hyperparameter problem as its own machine learning task. We could spend a whole chapter (or more) on the technical details of how Optuna works: in short, it trains its own machine learning algorithm to predict a model's accuracy (the label) based on its hyperparameters (the features). Optuna then sequentially tries new models based on what it predicts to be good hyperparameters, trains the model to find out how well it did, adds that information to improve the model, and then selects a new guess. But for now, let's focus on how to use Optuna as a tool.

To start, let's see a little about how Optuna works. Similar to PyTorch, it has a "define by run" concept. For Optuna, we define a function that we want to minimize (or maximize), which takes as input a `trial` object. This `trial` object is used to get `guesses` for each parameter we want to tune and returns a score at the end. The returned values are floats and integers, just as we would use ourselves, making it easy to use. Figure 5.16 shows how this works.

Let's look at a toy function that we want to minimize: $f(x, y) = \text{abs}((x - 3) \cdot (y + 2))$. It's easy to tell that one minimum exists at $x = 3$ and $y = -2$. But can Optuna figure that out? First we need to import the Optuna library, which is a simple `pip` command:

```
!pip install optuna
```

Now we can import Optuna:

```
import optuna
```

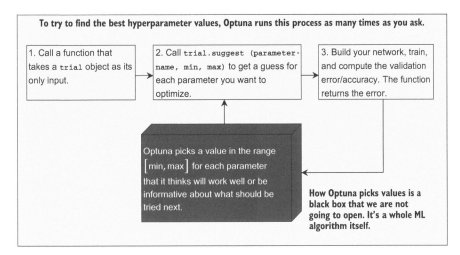

Figure 5.16 You supply Optuna with a function that does the three steps outlined in this diagram. Optuna uses its own algorithm to pick values for each hyperparameter, which you tell Optuna about using the `trial.suggest` functions; this function also informs Optuna about the minimum and maximum values you want to consider. You tell Optuna how many times to do this process, and each time it does, the black box gets better at picking new values to try.

Next we need to define the function to be minimized. `toyFunc` takes in the `trial` object. Optuna figures out how many hyperparameters exist by means of us using the `trial` object to obtain a guess for each parameter. This happens with the `suggest_uniform` function, which requires us to provide a range of possible values (something we must do for any hyperparameter optimization approach):

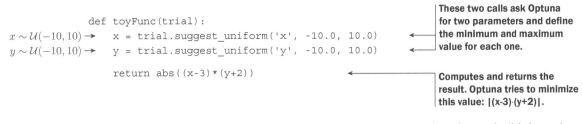

```
def toyFunc(trial):
    x = trial.suggest_uniform('x', -10.0, 10.0)
    y = trial.suggest_uniform('y', -10.0, 10.0)

    return abs((x-3)*(y+2))
```

$x \sim \mathcal{U}(-10, 10) \rightarrow$
$y \sim \mathcal{U}(-10, 10) \rightarrow$

These two calls ask Optuna for two parameters and define the minimum and maximum value for each one.

Computes and returns the result. Optuna tries to minimize this value: $|(x\text{-}3)\cdot(y\text{+}2)|$.

That's all we needed to do. Now we can use the `create_study` function to build the task and call `optimize` with the number of trials we want to let Optuna have to minimize the function:

```
study = optuna.create_study(direction='minimize')
study.optimize(toyFunc, n_trials=100)
```

If you use direction='maximize', Optuna will try to maximize the value returned by toyFunc.

Tells Optuna which function to minimize and that it gets 100 attempts to do so

When you run the code, you should see a long list of output something like this:

```
Finished trial#12 with value: 2.285 with parameters:
{'x': 0.089, 'y': -2.785}.
Best is trial#9 with value: 0.535.
Finished trial#13 with value: 3.069 with parameters:
{'x': -1.885, 'y': -2.628}.
Best is trial#9 with value: 0.535.
Finished trial#14 with value: 0.018 with parameters:
{'x': -3.183, 'y': -1.997}.
Best is trial#14 with value: 0.018.
```

When I ran this code, Optuna got a very precise answer: $5.04 \cdot 10^{-5}$ is very close to the true minimum of zero. The values it returned were also close to what we knew was the true answer. We can access these using `study.best_params`, which contains a `dict` object mapping the hyperparameters to the values that, in combination, gave the best result:

This dictionary holds the parameter values Optuna found to be best.

```
print(study.best_params)
```
```
{'x': 2.984280340674378, 'y': -1.8826725682225192}
```

We can also use the `study` object to get information about the optimization process that happened. Optuna is powerful because it uses machine learning to explore the space of parameter values. By specifying the parameters with min and max values, we give Optuna the constraints—and it attempts to balance exploring the space to understand what it looks like and minimizing the score based on its current understanding of the space.

We can use a contour plot to see an example:

```
fig = optuna.visualization.plot_contour(study)
```

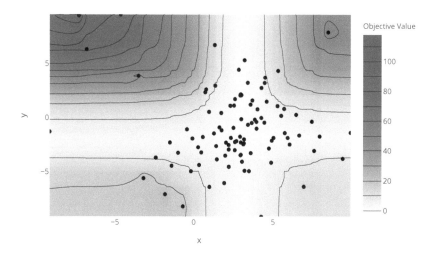

Notice how Optuna has spent most of its effort testing values near the minimum and very little in the larger, extreme areas of the space. Optuna quickly figures out that there is no way to find a better solution in these parts of the space and stops exploring those areas. This allows it to spend more time looking for the best solution and to better handle more than just two parameters.

5.4.2 Optuna with PyTorch

You now know all the basics of using Optuna; it's time to combine it with PyTorch to do some advanced parameter searching. We'll define a new function for Optuna to optimize our neural network. We do not want to go crazy, as optimizing without any gradients is still very difficult and Optuna is not a magic bullet. But we can use Optuna to help us make some decisions. For example, how many neurons should we have in each layer, and how many layers? Figure 5.17 shows how we can define a function to do this:

1 Create train/validation splits (we did that with the plateau schedule).

2 Ask Optuna to give us three critical hyperparameters.

3 Define our model using the parameters.

4 Compute and return the result from the validation split.

```
def objective(trial):
```

Create train and validation splits with respective loaders t_loader and v_loader.

This purple code asks Optuna to set three hyperparameters. Notice _int and _loguniform, which change how samples are returned. We don't want 2.5 layers!

```
n=trial.suggest_int('neurons_per_layer',16,256)
layers=trial.suggest_int('hidden_layers',1,6)
eta_global=trial.suggest_loguniform('learning_rate',1e-5,1e-2)
```

Define model, learning rate schedule, and optimizer using the above hyperparameters

We end by training the model and returning the validation results from the last epoch.

```
results = train_network(fc_model, loss_func, t_loader,
    val_loader=v_loader, epochs=10, optimizer=optimizer,
    lr_schedule=scheduler, score_funcs={'Accuracy': accuracy_score},
    device=device, disable_tqdm=True)
return results['val Accuracy'].iloc[-1]
```

Figure 5.17 The four steps of defining an `objective` function that Optuna can use to optimize our neural network training. The two most important steps shown as code are getting the hyperparameters and computing the result!

An important thing to note here is that we have to create new training and validation splits using only the original training data. Why? Because we will reuse the validation set multiple times, and we do not want to overfit to the specifics of our validation data.

So, we create a new validation set and save our original validation data until the very end. That way, we only use the true validation data once to determine how well we did at optimizing our network architecture.

This function has very little *new* code; most of it is the same code we have used for several chapters to create data loaders, construct a network `Module`, and call our `train_network` function. Some significant PyTorch changes are that we set `disable_tqdm=True` because Optuna does not play nicely with progress bars in the function it is trying to optimize.

ADDING A DYNAMIC NUMBER OF LAYERS

It may not be obvious at first, but we can very easily use the variable number of layers with our `nn.Sequential` object to adapt to what Optuna tells us to use. The code is as follows:

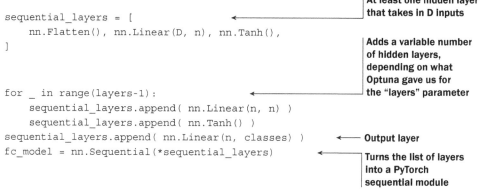

```
sequential_layers = [
    nn.Flatten(), nn.Linear(D, n), nn.Tanh(),
]


for _ in range(layers-1):
    sequential_layers.append( nn.Linear(n, n) )
    sequential_layers.append( nn.Tanh() )
sequential_layers.append( nn.Linear(n, classes) )
fc_model = nn.Sequential(*sequential_layers)
```

At least one hidden layer that takes in D inputs

Adds a variable number of hidden layers, depending on what Optuna gave us for the "layers" parameter

Output layer

Turns the list of layers into a PyTorch sequential module

This breaks up the model specification into a few parts so that the number of hidden layers is a variable filled in with a `for` loop, `for _ in range(layers-1):`. It's a little more verbose for small networks but makes the same code able to handle a variety of layers, and it's less code if we want to add more layers.

GETTING SUGGESTIONS FROM OPTUNA

The other changes are different `suggest` functions that Optuna provides via the `trial` object. There is `suggest_int` for integers, which makes sense for links like the number of neurons (76.8 neurons does not make sense) and the number of layers. We already saw `suggest_uniform`, which works for float values that are covered by a simple random range (like the momentum term μ, which should be between 0 and 1). The other important option is `suggest_loguniform`, which gives *exponentially spaced* random values. This is the function you should use for parameters that are altered by orders of magnitude, like the learning rate ($\eta = 0.001, 0.01,$ and 0.1 differ by a factor of 10). The next code snippet shows how we can get three hyperparameter suggestions from Optuna by specifying the appropriate `suggest` function and providing minimum and maximum values that we are willing to consider:

```
n = trial.suggest_int('neurons_per_layer', 16, 256)
layers = trial.suggest_int('hidden_layers', 1, 6)
```

```
eta_global = trial.suggest_loguniform('learning_rate', 1e-5, 1e-2)
```

This ends by simply training our network and taking the validation accuracy from the last epoch. You must remember that this is a *validation split* and that we have not used the test set. We should only use the test set *after* the hyperparameters have been found, to determine the overall accuracy. The following code searches for the hyperparameters for this problem:

```
study = optuna.create_study(direction='maximize')
study.optimize(objective, n_trials=10)

print(study.best_params)
```

Normally we would do more like 50 to 100 trials, but we are using fewer so this notebook runs in a reasonable amount of time.

```
{'neurons_per_layer': 181, 'hidden_layers': 3, 'learning_rate':
0.005154640793181943}
```

You can see the parameters that Optuna selected. Now that we have trained our network, an exercise for you is to train a new model with this information to determine what final validation accuracy you get on the true validation set. Doing so completes the entire hyperparameter optimization process, which is outlined in figure 5.18.

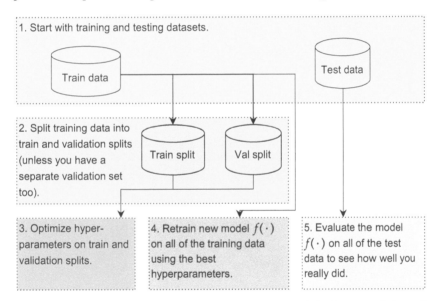

Figure 5.18 All the steps you need to follow to do hyperparameter optimization correctly. It may be tempting to merge or skip some of these steps, but doing so could give you misleading results about how well your model will actually do.

VISUALIZING OPTUNA RESULTS

Beyond just looking at the *final* answer, we can also look at the progress Optuna made over time and other views of the optimization process. Doing so can help us build some intuition about the range of "good" parameters. This information can be helpful when we set up new experiments so that we can hopefully start the optimization process closer to the true solution and thus reduce the number of optimization attempts required.

The following is one of the simplest options: plotting the validation accuracy (and individual trials) based on how many trials have been attempted. The red line on top shows the current best result, and each blue dot shows the result from one experiment. If big improvements in accuracy are still occurring (red line going up), we have a good reason to increase the number of trials we let Optuna run. If accuracy has plateaued for a long time, we can reduce the number of trials in the future:

```
fig = optuna.visualization.plot_optimization_history(study)
fig.show()
```

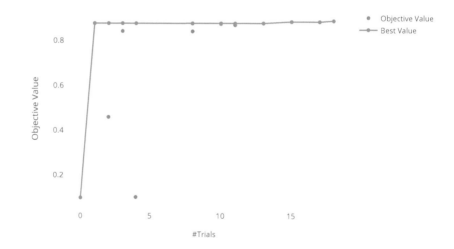

We might also want to get an idea of how each hyperparameter performs with respect to the objective (accuracy). That can be done with a *slice plot*. The following example makes a scatter plot for each hyperparameter, with the objective on the y-axis; the color of the dot indicates which trial the result came from. This way, you can see if any one hyperparameter has a particularly strong relationship with your objective and how long it took Optuna to figure it out. In this specific example, in most cases, three to six hidden layers perform well, and learning rates above $\eta > 0.001$ are also consistently good. This kind of information can help us reduce the search range in future trials or even eliminate a hyperparameter if it seems to have little impact on the objective.

Both of these will help Optuna converge to solutions with fewer attempts in future runs. Here's the code:

```
fig = optuna.visualization.plot_slice(study)
fig.show()
```

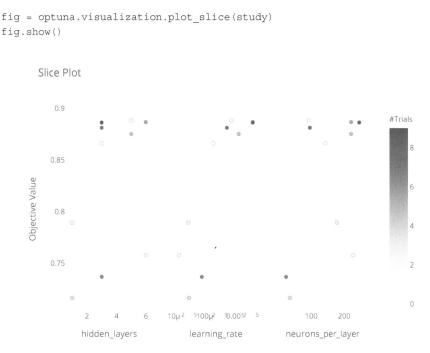

Optuna can also help you understand the interactions between hyperparameters. One option is the `plot_contour()` function, which creates a grid showing how every combination of two different hyperparameters impacts the results. The other option is the `plot_parallel_coordinate()` function, which shows all the results of every trial in one graph. Both of these are a little harder to read and require more trials to produce really interesting results, so I recommend trying them on your own when you have a chance to do 100 trials for a model.

5.4.3 Pruning trials with Optuna

Another feature that Optuna supports that is particularly useful when training neural networks is *pruning* trials early. The idea is that optimizing a neural network is iterative: we take multiple epochs through the dataset, and we (hopefully) improve with every epoch. This is valuable information we are not using. If we can determine early in the process that a model won't pan out, we can save a lot of time.

Say we start testing a set of parameters, and learning fails from the start, with terrible results on the first few epochs. Why continue training until the end? The model is *very unlikely* to start as degenerate and later become one of the best performers. If we report intermediate results to Optuna, Optuna can prune out trials that look bad based on the trials that have already completed.

We can accomplish this by replacing the last two lines of code from the `def objective(trial):` function. Instead of calling `train_network` once with 10 epochs, we call it 10 times in a loop for 1 epoch each. After each epoch, we use the `report` function of the `trial` object to let Optuna know how we are *currently* doing and ask Optuna if we should stop. The revised code looks like this:

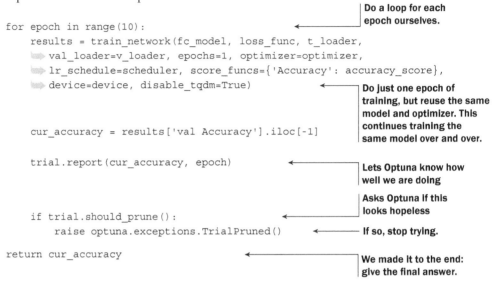

```
for epoch in range(10):                                    Do a loop for each
                                                           epoch ourselves.
    results = train_network(fc_model, loss_func, t_loader,
        val_loader=v_loader, epochs=1, optimizer=optimizer,
        lr_schedule=scheduler, score_funcs={'Accuracy': accuracy_score},
        device=device, disable_tqdm=True)                  Do just one epoch of
                                                           training, but reuse the same
                                                           model and optimizer. This
                                                           continues training the
    cur_accuracy = results['val Accuracy'].iloc[-1]        same model over and over.


    trial.report(cur_accuracy, epoch)                      Lets Optuna know how
                                                           well we are doing

                                                           Asks Optuna if this
                                                           looks hopeless
    if trial.should_prune():
        raise optuna.exceptions.TrialPruned()              If so, stop trying.

return cur_accuracy                                        We made it to the end:
                                                           give the final answer.
```

With this code change, I'm going to run a new trial with Optuna but intentionally set the number of neurons to go down to 1 (way too small) and the learning rate to go up to $\eta = 100$ (way too big). This will create some *really* bad models that are easy to prune out, just to show off this new pruning feature. All of these changes only needed to happen in the `objective` function: we call the same `create_study` and `optimize` functions and get pruning automatically. The following snippet shows this, but I set `n_trials=20` to give pruning more opportunities to occur since it depends on the best *current* models found by Optuna (it does not know what a bad run looks like until it sees a good run to compare against):

```
study2 = optuna.create_study(direction='maximize')
study2.optimize(objectivePrunable, n_trials=20)
```

Now you should see several `TrialState.PRUNED` logs from Optuna when you run this code. When I ran it, 10 of the 20 trials were pruned early. How many epochs into training were these models before they got pruned? We can have Optuna plot the results of all the trials with their intermediate values to help us understand that better. This is done with the `plot_intermediate_values()` function, as shown next:

```
fig = optuna.visualization.plot_intermediate_values(study2)
fig.show()
```

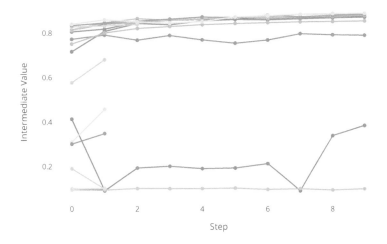

It looks like all 10 trials were pruned after just 1 or 2 epochs through the dataset. That's very early in the process: Optuna has reduced the number of effective trials almost by half. We also see some cases where models that did not perform well were allowed to run until completion, even though "better" models were pruned early. This happens because pruning is based on the best models Optuna has seen *so far*. Early on, Optuna lets bad models run to completion because it does not yet know they are bad models. Only after more trials and seeing much better models does it learn that the original ones could have been pruned. So pruning does not avoid *all* bad models, but it can avoid many of them.

Looking at the graph carefully, you should be able to see some cases where Optuna pruned models that were diverging (getting worse) and some that looked like they would improve but were not doing well enough that they would become competitive with what Optuna had already seen. These are also good cases for pruning and part of how Optuna saves us time.

> **NOTE** While Optuna is one of my favorite tools, we won't use it again in this book. This is purely a computational concern, as I want to stick with examples that run in just a few minutes. Optuna needs to train multiple networks, which means *multiplying* training time. Just 10 trials is not a lot, but an example that would take 6 minutes with no hyperparameters would take an hour or more with Optuna. However, when you are working on the job, you should *definitely* use Optuna to help you build your neural networks.

Exercises

Share and discuss your solutions on the Manning online platform at Inside Deep Learning Exercises (https://liveproject.manning.com/project/945). Once you submit your own answers, you will be able to see the solutions submitted by other readers, and see which ones the author judges to be the best.

1   Modify the `train_network` function to accept `lr_schedule="ReduceLROnPlateau"` as a valid argument. If the `train_network` function gets this string argument, it should check whether validation and test sets have been provided and, if so, set up the `ReduceLROnPlateau` scheduler appropriately.

2   Rerun the experiments with `AdamW`, SGD with Nesterov momentum, and the cosine annealing schedule using batch sizes of $B = 1, 4, 32, 64, 128$. How does the change in batch size impact the effectiveness and accuracy of these three tools?

3   Write code that creates a neural network with $n = 256$ neurons and an argument to control how many hidden layers are in the network. Then train networks with 1, 6, 12, and 24 hidden layers using naive SGD and again using `AdamW` with cosine annealing. How do these new optimizers impact your ability to learn these deeper networks?

4   Retrain the three-layer bidirectional RNN from the last chapter with each of the new optimizers from this chapter. How do they impact the results?

5   Add gradient clipping to the experiments from exercise 4. Does it help or hurt the RNN?

6   Write your own function that uses Optuna to optimize the parameters of a fully connected neural network. Once it's done, create a new network with those hyper-parameters, train it using all of the training data, and test it on the held-out test set. What results do you get on FashionMNIST, and how close is Optuna's guess at the accuracy compared to your test-set performance?

7   Redo exercise 6, but replace the hidden layers with convolutional ones and add a new argument that controls how many rounds of max pooling to perform. How does it perform on FashionMNIST compared with your results from exercise 6?

Summary

- The two main components of gradient descent are how we use gradients (optimizers) and how fast we follow them (learning rate schedules).

- By using information about the history of gradients, we can increase how quickly our models learn.

- Adding momentum to optimizers allows training even when gradients become very small.

- Gradient clipping mitigates exploding gradients, allowing training even when gradients become very large.

- By altering the learning rate, we can ease the optimization view of learning for further improvements.

- Instead of grid search, we can use powerful tools like Optuna to find the hyper-parameters of a neural network such as the number of layers and number of neurons.

- By checking the results after each epoch, we can accelerate the hyperparameter tuning process by pruning bad models early.

Common design
building blocks

This chapter covers

- Adding new activation functions
- Inserting new layers to improve training
- Skipping layers as a useful design pattern
- Combining new activations, layers, and skips into new approaches more powerful than the sum of their parts

At this point, we have learned about the three most common and fundamental types of neural networks: fully connected, convolutional, and recurrent. We have improved all of these architectures by changing the optimizer and learning rate schedule, which alter how we update the parameters (weights) of our models, giving us more accurate models almost for free. All of the things we have learned thus far also have a long shelf life and have taught us about problems that have existed for decades (and continue). They give you a good foundation to speak the language of deep learning and some very fundamental building blocks that larger algorithms are made from.

Now that we have these better tools for training our models, we can learn about newer approaches to designing neural networks. Many of these newer methods *would not work* without the improvements to learning like Adam (discussed in the last chapter), which is why we are only talking about them now! Most of the ideas in this chapter are less than 10 years old and have a lot of utility—but are also still evolving. In another four years, some may be supplanted by newer options. But now that we have some shared vernacular to talk about the mechanics of deep learning, we can examine why the techniques in this chapter help build better models. Anything that works better will likely be tackling the same underlying problems, so the lessons should remain timeless.[1]

This chapter gives you some of the most widely used building blocks for model training in production today. For this reason, we spend time talking about *why* these new techniques work so that you can learn to recognize the logic and reasoning behind them and start to develop your intuition about how you might make your own changes. It is also important to understand these techniques because many new methods that are developed are variants of the ones we learn about in this chapter.

We discuss five new methods in this chapter that work for feed-forward models and one new improvement to RNNs. We introduce the first five methods roughly in the order that they were invented, as each tends to use the preceding techniques in their design. Individually, they improve accuracy and speed up training; but combined, they are greater than the sum of their parts. The first method is a new activation function called a *rectified linear unit* (ReLU). Then we sandwich a new type of normalization layer between our linear/convolution layers and our nonlinear activation layers. After that, we learn about two types of design choices, *skip connections* and 1×1 *convolution*, that reuse the layers we already know about. The same way vinegar is terrible on its own but amazing in a larger recipe, skip connections and 1×1 convolution are combined to create the fifth method, a *residual layer*. Residual layers provide one of the largest improvements in accuracy for CNNs.

We end by introducing the *long short-term memory* (LSTM) layer, which is a type of RNN. The original RNN we talked about is not widely used anymore because of how difficult it is to get working, but it is much easier to explain how RNNs work in general. LSTMs have been successfully used for over 20 years and are a great vehicle to explain how many of the lessons in this chapter can be recombined into a new kind of solution. We'll also briefly mention a "diet" version of the LSTM that is a little less memory hungry, and we'll use it to keep our models in an envelope that can safely run in Colab's lower-end free GPUs.

GETTING SET UP WITH A BASELINE

The following code loads the Fashion-MNIST dataset again, since using it is hard enough for us to see improvements but easy enough that we don't have to wait a long time for the results. We use this dataset to create a baseline—a model showing what we can accomplish with our current methods—that we can compare against to see the impact our new techniques have on accuracy:

---

[1] You can learn a lot by reading papers on neural networks from the 1990s. Even if they are not used today, the creativity of past solutions may give you good lessons and intuition for solving modern problems. As I'm writing this book, I'm working on research enabled by some mostly forgotten work from 1995.

```
train_data = torchvision.datasets.FashionMNIST("./", train=True,
    transform=transforms.ToTensor(), download=True)
test_data = torchvision.datasets.FashionMNIST("./", train=True,
    transform=transforms.ToTensor(), download=True)

train_loader = DataLoader(train_data, batch_size=128, shuffle=True)
test_loader = DataLoader(test_data, batch_size=128)
```

In this chapter, we train fully connected and convolutional networks for almost every example, because the code for some of the techniques looks a little different for each type of network. You should compare how the code changes between the fully connected and CNN models to understand what parts are related to the fundamental idea and which are artifacts of the type of network we are implementing. This will help you to apply these techniques to other models in the future!

Let's define some basic hyperparameters and details that we reuse throughout the chapter and the book. Here we have the code specifying our features, the number of hidden neurons for the fully connected layers, the number of channels and filters for the convolutional network, and the total number of classes:

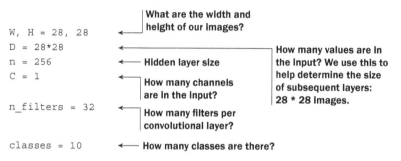

```
W, H = 28, 28        ←┤ What are the width and
                       │ height of our images?
D = 28*28            ←──────────────────────────  How many values are in
n = 256              ←── Hidden layer size          the input? We use this to
C = 1                                               help determine the size
                       ┌ How many channels           of subsequent layers:
                       │ are in the input?          28 * 28 images.
n_filters = 32       ←─┘
                       ┌ How many filters per
                       │ convolutional layer?
classes = 10         ←── How many classes are there?
```

A FULLY CONNECTED AND CONVOLUTIONAL BASELINE

Finally, we can define our models. We add a few more layers for each fully connected and CNN compared to what we used in previous chapters. As we introduce new approaches to building a network in this chapter, we'll compare to these simpler starting models. First we define the fully connected network here. Thanks to the simplicity of fully connected networks, it is easy to use list unpacking with the * operator to make the same code work for almost any number of hidden layers. We can unpack a list comprehension [define_block for _ in range(n)] to create n layers of define_block layers:

```
                                                  Now that each remaining
                                                  layer has the same input/
fc_model = nn.Sequential(                         output sizes, we can make
    nn.Flatten(),                First hidden layer  them with a list unpacking.
    nn.Linear(D, n), nn.Tanh(),          ←──────┘
    *[nn.Sequential(nn.Linear(n, n),nn.Tanh()) for _ in range(5)],  ←───
    nn.Linear(n, classes),
)
```

We define our CNN layer next. We could write nicer code if we were making the model deeper, but the approaches we have learned so far aren't good enough to learn a deep CNN. So we kept the CNN fairly shallow to make it easier to compare against. But once you learn about the techniques in this chapter, you'll be able to make deeper networks that reliably converge to more accurate solutions! Here's the code:

```
cnn_model = nn.Sequential(
    nn.Conv2d(C, n_filters, 3, padding=1),              nn.Tanh(),
    nn.Conv2d(n_filters, n_filters, 3, padding=1),      nn.Tanh(),
    nn.Conv2d(n_filters, n_filters, 3, padding=1),      nn.Tanh(),
    nn.MaxPool2d((2,2)),
    nn.Conv2d(  n_filters, 2*n_filters, 3, padding=1), nn.Tanh(),
    nn.Conv2d(2*n_filters, 2*n_filters, 3, padding=1), nn.Tanh(),
    nn.Conv2d(2*n_filters, 2*n_filters, 3, padding=1), nn.Tanh(),
    nn.MaxPool2d((2,2)),
    nn.Conv2d(2*n_filters, 4*n_filters, 3, padding=1), nn.Tanh(),
    nn.Conv2d(4*n_filters, 4*n_filters, 3, padding=1), nn.Tanh(),
    nn.Flatten(),
    nn.Linear(D*n_filters//4, classes),
)
```

We use our new `train_network` function to train all of the models from this point forward. Remember that we modified this method to use the `AdamW` optimizer by default, so we don't have to specify that:

```
loss_func = nn.CrossEntropyLoss()
fc_results = train_network(fc_model, loss_func, train_loader,
    test_loader=test_loader, epochs=10,
    score_funcs={'Accuracy': accuracy_score}, device=device)
cnn_results = train_network(cnn_model, loss_func, train_loader,
    test_loader=test_loader, epochs=10,
    score_funcs={'Accuracy': accuracy_score}, device=device)
```

Finally, a small change: we'll use the `del` command to delete some of our neural networks once we are done with them in this chapter. If you are unlucky and get one of the lower-end GPUs from Colab, you might run out of memory running these examples. Let's be explicit and tell Python we are finished so we can get back the GPU memory and avoid such annoyances:

```
del fc_model
del cnn_model
```

Now let's look at the initial results, plotted with seaborn (this should be very familiar by this point). We are comparing the performance of our two initial models and the future enhancements we will add. That way, we can see that these improvements apply to more than just one type of network. Unsurprisingly, the CNN performs much better than the fully connected network. We expect this because we are working with images, and as we learned in chapter 3, convolutional layers are a powerful way of encoding the "structural prior" about pixels and their relationships into our network:

```
sns.lineplot(x='epoch', y='test Accuracy', data=fc_results,
    label='Fully Connected')
sns.lineplot(x='epoch', y='test Accuracy', data=cnn_results,
    label='CNN')
```

[12]:   <AxesSubplot:xlabel='epoch', ylabel='test Accuracy'>

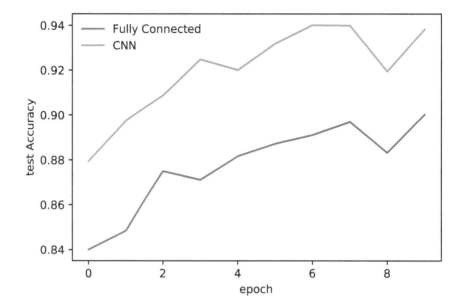

With these results in hand, we can dive into the rest of this chapter! We spend each section talking about a new kind of `Module` you can use in your neural networks and the intuition or reason for using it, and then apply it to our baseline networks.

6.1   Better activation functions

We have been relying very heavily on the $\tanh(\cdot)$ activation function and, to a smaller degree, the sigmoid function $\sigma(\cdot)$, throughout this book. They are two of the original activation functions used for neural networks, but they are not the only options. Currently, we as a community don't know definitively what makes one activation function better than another, and there isn't any one option you should always use. But we have learned about some things that are usually undesirable in an activation function. Both $\tanh(\cdot)$ and $\sigma(\cdot)$ can lead to a problem called *vanishing gradients*.

6.1.1   Vanishing gradients

Remember that every architecture we define learns by treating the network as one giant function $f_\Theta(\boldsymbol{x})$, where we need to use the gradient (∇) with respect to the parameters (Θ) of f to adjust its weights according to a loss function $\ell(\cdot, \cdot)$. So, we perform

$$\Theta_{t+1} = \Theta_t - \eta \cdot \nabla_{\Theta_t} f_{\Theta_t}(\boldsymbol{x})$$

But what if $\nabla_\Theta f_\Theta(x)$ is very small? If that happens, there will be almost no change in the value of Θ, and thus no learning:

$$\Theta_{t+1} = \Theta_t - \eta \cdot \underbrace{\nabla_{\Theta_t} f_{\Theta_t}(x)}_{\approx 0}$$

$$\Theta_{t+1} \approx \Theta_t - \eta \cdot 0 = \Theta_t$$

While momentum (discussed in chapter 5) can help with this problem, it would be better if the gradients never vanished in the first place. This is because as the math shows us, if we get too close to zero, there is nothing to do.

How do the tanh and sigmoid activations result in this vanishing gradient problem? Let's plot both of these functions again:

```
def sigmoid(x):
    return np.exp(activation_input)/(np.exp(activation_input)+1)

activation_input = np.linspace(-5, 5, num=200)
tanh_activation = np.tanh(activation_input)
sigmoid_activation = sigmoid(activation_input)

sns.lineplot(x=activation_input, y=tanh_activation, color='red',
    label="tanh(x)")
sns.lineplot(x=activation_input, y=sigmoid_activation, color='blue',
    label="$\sigma(x)$")
```

[13]:   <AxesSubplot:>

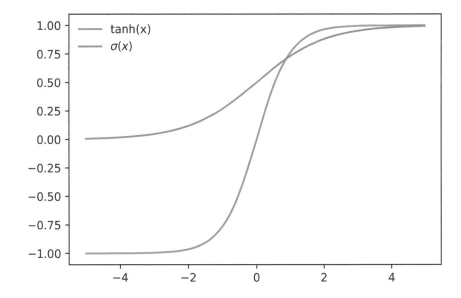

Both activations have a property called *saturation*, which is when the activation stops changing as the input keeps changing. For both tanh($\cdot$) and $\sigma(\cdot)$, if the input x keeps getting larger, both activations saturate at the value 1.0. If the input to the activation is 100 and you double the input value, you still get a value of (almost) 1.0 from the output. That's what saturation is. Both of these activations also saturate on the left-hand side of the plot, so when the input x becomes very small, tanh($\cdot$) will saturate at -1.0 and $\sigma(\cdot)$ will saturate at 0.

Let's plot the derivatives of these functions—we see that saturation has an undesirable result:

```
def tanh_deriv(x):
    return 1.0 - np.tanh(x)**2
def sigmoid_derivative(x):
    return sigmoid(x)*(1-sigmoid(x))

tanh_deriv = tanh_deriv(activation_input)
sigmoid_deriv = sigmoid_derivative(activation_input)

sns.lineplot(x=activation_input, y=tanh_deriv, color='red',
    label="tanh'(x)")
sns.lineplot(x=activation_input, y=sigmoid_deriv, color='blue',
    label="$\sigma'(x)$")
```

[14]:   <AxesSubplot:>

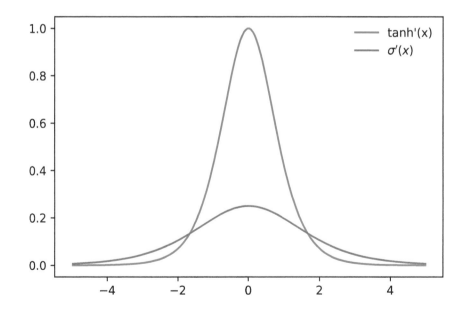

Do you see the problem in the plot? As the activation *begins to saturate, its gradient begins to vanish.* This happens with *any* activation function that saturates. Since our weight changes based on the value of the gradient ∇, our network will stop learning if too many neurons begin saturating.

This does not mean that you should never use tanh(·) and $\sigma(\cdot)$; there are some cases where you want saturation (we'll see an example at the end of this chapter with the LSTM). If you don't have a specific reason why you *want* saturation, I recommend avoiding activation functions that saturate—which is the next thing we learn to do.

> **NOTE** Saturating activations are not the only cause of vanishing gradients. You can check whether your gradients are vanishing by looking at a histogram of them (using the .grad member variable). If you are using an activation function that can saturate, you can also plot a histogram of the activation functions to check whether that is the cause of vanishing gradients. For example, if you are using $\sigma(\cdot)$ as your activation function, and a histogram says 50% of your activations are within 0.01 of 1.0 or 0.0, you know saturation is the source of the problem.

6.1.2 *Rectified linear units (ReLUs): Avoiding vanishing gradients*

Now we know that an activation function that saturates, by default, is probably not a great activation function to use. What should we use instead? The most common approach to fix this is to use an activation function known as the *rectified linear unit* (ReLU),[2] which has a very simple definition:

$$\text{ReLU}(x) = \max(0, x)$$

That's all the ReLU does. If the input is positive, the return is unaltered. If the input is negative, the return is zero, instead. This may seem surprising, as we have harped on the importance of having a nonlinearity. But it turns out almost *any* nonlinearity is sufficient to learn from. Choosing a simple activation function like this also leads to a simple derivative:

$$\text{ReLU}'(x) = \begin{cases} 1, & \text{if } x > 0 \\ 0, & \text{otherwise} \end{cases}$$

And that's all it takes. For half of all possible inputs, the ReLU has a constant value as its derivative. For most use cases, simply replacing tanh(·) or $\sigma(\cdot)$ with the ReLU activation will allow your model to converge to a more accurate solution in fewer epochs. However, the ReLU often performs worse for very small networks.

---

[2] V. Nair and G. E. Hinton, "Rectified linear units improve restricted Boltzmann machines," *Proceedings of the 27th International Conference on Machine Learning*, pp. 807–814, 2010.

Why? Instead of having a *vanishing* gradient, the ReLU has *no* gradient for $x <= 0$. If you have a lot of neurons, it is OK if some of them "die" and stop activating; but if you don't have enough extra neurons, it becomes a serious problem. This can again be solved with a simple modification: instead of returning 0 for negative inputs, let's return something else. This leads us to what is called the *leaky ReLU*.[3] The leaky ReLU takes a "leaking" factor α, which is supposed to be small. Values in the range $\alpha \in [0.01, 0.3]$ are often used, and the specific value has relatively little impact in most cases.

What is the mathematical definition of the leaky ReLU? Again, it is a simple change that reduces negative values by a factor of α. This new activation and derivative can be succinctly defined as follows:

$$\text{LeakyReLU}(x) = \max(\alpha \cdot x, x)$$

$$\text{LeakyReLU}'(x) = \begin{cases} 1, & \text{if } x > 0 \\ \alpha, & \text{otherwise} \end{cases}$$

Saying the same thing in code, we have

```
def leaky_relu(x, alpha=0.1):        ←── Activation function converted to code
    return max(alpha*x, x)
def leaky_reluP(x, alpha=0.1):       ←── Derivative of the activation function,
    if x > 0:                            where x is the original input to which
        return 1                         the activation was applied
    else:
        return alpha
```

The intuition to an improved ReLU is that there is a hard "floor" when $x <= 0$. Because there is no change at this floor's level, there is no gradient. Instead, we would like the floor to "leak" so that it changes—but slowly. If it changes even just a little, we can get a gradient. Let's plot all of these activations and see what they look like:

```
activation_input = np.linspace(-5, 5, num=200)
relu_activation = np.maximum(0,activation_input)
leaky_relu_activation = np.maximum(0.3*activation_input,activation_input)

sns.lineplot(x=activation_input, y=tanh_activation, color='red',
    label="tanh(x)")
sns.lineplot(x=activation_input, y=sigmoid_activation, color='blue',
    label="$\sigma(x)$")
sns.lineplot(x=activation_input, y=relu_activation, color='green',
    label="ReLU(x)")
sns.lineplot(x=activation_input, y=leaky_relu_activation, color='purple',
    label="LeakyReLU(x)")
```

---

[3]   A. L. Maas, A. Y. Hannun, and A. Y. Ng, "Rectifier nonlinearities improve neural network acoustic models," *Proceedings of the 30th International Conference on Machine Learning*, vol. 28, p. 6, 2013.

[15]: <AxesSubplot:>

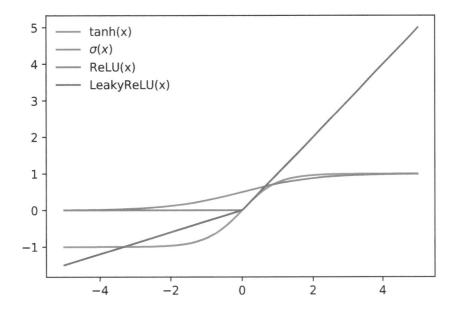

We can see that to the right, as the input gets larger, ReLU and LeakyReLU behave linearly, just increasing with the input. To the left, as the input gets smaller, both are *still* linear, but the ReLU is stuck at zero and the LeakyReLU is decreasing. The nonlinearity for both is simply changing the slope of the line, which is enough. Now let's plot gradients with a little more code:

```
relu_deriv = 1.0*(activation_input > 0)
leaky_deriv = 1.0*(activation_input > 0) + 0.3*(activation_input <= 0)

sns.lineplot(x=activation_input, y=tanh_deriv, color='red',
    label="tanh'(x)")
sns.lineplot(x=activation_input, y=sigmoid_deriv, color='blue',
    label="$\sigma'(x)$")
sns.lineplot(x=activation_input, y=relu_deriv, color='green',
    label="ReLU'(x)")
sns.lineplot(x=activation_input, y=leaky_deriv, color='purple',
    label="LeakyReLU'(x)")
```

```
[16]:   <AxesSubplot:>
```

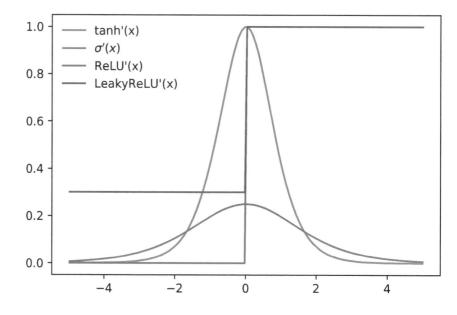

So the LeakyReLU has gradient values that will *never* vanish on their own, but the inter-action between layers could still cause an exploding or vanishing gradient. We'll tackle that problem later in this chapter with residual layers and LSTMs, but the LeakyReLU at least does not contribute to the problem like the $\tanh(\cdot)$ and $\sigma(\cdot)$ activations do.

6.1.3 *Training with LeakyReLU activations*

Now that we understand why we want to use the LeakyReLU, let's check how good it is by testing training with it and see if accuracy improves. We'll train new versions of our models with the LeakyReLU, which we usually find equals or outperforms the standard ReLU due to its slightly better behavior (lack of hard zeros in activation and gradient). First we define the leak rate to use. PyTorch uses a default of $\alpha = 0.01$, a fairly conservative value that works just well enough to avoid a zero gradient for a normal ReLU. We use $\alpha = 0.1$, which is my preferred default value, but this is not a critical choice:

```
leak_rate = 0.1
```

How much we want LeakyReLU to leak. Anything in [0.01, 0.3] would be fine.

Next we define a new version of both architectures, only changing the nn.Tanh() function to nn.LeakyReLU. First is the fully connected model, still just five lines of code:

```
fc_relu_model = nn.Sequential(
    nn.Flatten(),
    nn.Linear(D, n), nn.LeakyReLU(leak_rate),
    *[nn.Sequential(nn.Linear(n, n), nn.LeakyReLU(leak_rate))
      for _ in range(5)],
```

```
        nn.Linear(n, classes),
)
```

The CNN model can be done the same way, but the function name is getting long to type and read. Let's see another way to organize code. We define a `cnnLayer` function that takes in the input and output size of each layer and returns the combination of `Conv2d` and the activation function that makes a complete layer. This way, when we experiment with new ideas, we can just change this function, and the rest of our code will change with it; we don't have to make as many edits. We can also add niceties like computing the padding size automatically, using common defaults like the kernel size, and keeping the output the same size as the input:

```
def cnnLayer(in_filters, out_filters=None, kernel_size=3):
    """
    in_filters: how many channels are coming into the layer
    out_filters: how many channels this layer should learn / output, or 'None'
if we want to have the same number of channels as the input.
    kernel_size: how large the kernel should be
    """
    if out_filters is None:              This is a common pattern, so let's
    out_filters = in_filters           ◄── automate it as a default if not asked.

    padding=kernel_size//2             ◄── Padding to stay the same size

    return nn.Sequential(              ◄── Combines the layer and activation
                                            into a single unit

    nn.Conv2d(in_filters, out_filters, kernel_size, padding=padding),
    nn.LeakyReLU(leak_rate)
)
```

Now our CNN's code is more concise and easier to read. The `cnnLayer` function also makes it easier to use list unpacking as we did with the fully connected model. The following is our generic CNN code block. Ignoring the object name, this code block can be re-purposed for many different styles of CNN hidden layers by changing the definition of the cnnLayer function:

```
cnn_relu_model = nn.Sequential(
    cnnLayer(C, n_filters), cnnLayer(n_filters), cnnLayer(n_filters),
    nn.MaxPool2d((2,2)),
    cnnLayer(n_filters, 2*n_filters),
    cnnLayer(2*n_filters),
    cnnLayer(2*n_filters),
    nn.MaxPool2d((2,2)),
    cnnLayer(2*n_filters, 4*n_filters), cnnLayer(4*n_filters),
    nn.Flatten(),
    nn.Linear(D*n_filters//4, classes),
)
```

We are ready to train both models. As always, PyTorch's modular design means we don't have to alter anything else:

```
fc_relu_results = train_network(fc_relu_model, loss_func, train_loader,
    test_loader=test_loader, epochs=10,
    score_funcs={'Accuracy': accuracy_score}, device=device)
del fc_relu_model
cnn_relu_results = train_network(cnn_relu_model, loss_func, train_loader,
    test_loader=test_loader, epochs=10,
    score_funcs={'Accuracy': accuracy_score}, device=device)
del cnn_relu_model
```

Let's compare our new `relu_results` and our original `fc_results` and `cnn_results`. You should see that the LeakyReLU easily outperforms its tanh counterpart for both the CNN and fully connected networks. Not only is it more accurate, but it is also numerically nicer and easier to implement. The exp() function that is required to compute tanh requires a decent amount of compute, but ReLUs only have simple multiplication and max() operations, which are faster. Here's the code:

```
sns.lineplot(x='epoch', y='test Accuracy', data=fc_results, label='FC')
sns.lineplot(x='epoch', y='test Accuracy', data=fc_relu_results,
    label='FC-ReLU')
sns.lineplot(x='epoch', y='test Accuracy', data=cnn_results,
    label='CNN')
sns.lineplot(x='epoch', y='test Accuracy', data=cnn_relu_results,
    label='CNN-ReLU')
```

```
[22]: <AxesSubplot:xlabel='epoch', ylabel='test Accuracy'>
```

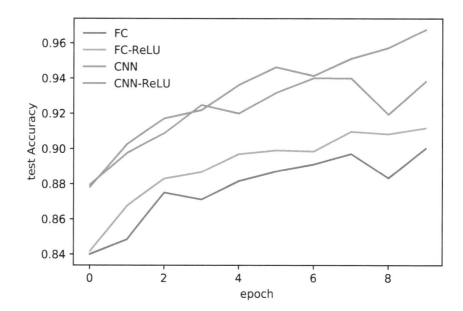

ReLU variants

So the ReLU family gives better accuracy, is a little faster, and is less code when implemented from scratch. For these reasons, the ReLU has quickly become the default favorite among many in the community; it is a good practical choice since it has been used successfully in most modern neural networks for several years now.

There are *many* other flavors of the ReLU activation function, several of which are built into PyTorch. There is the PReLU, which attempts to learn what α should be for the LeakyReLU, removing it as a hyperparameter. ReLU6 introduces an intentional saturation for the odd scenario where you want that kind of behavior. There are also "smooth" extensions to the ReLU like CELU, GELU, and ELU, which have been derived to have certain properties. Those are just the ones already in PyTorch; you can find even more variants and alternatives to the ReLU online (http://mng.bz/VBeX). We don't have time or space to go into all of these, but the improvement from $\tanh(\cdot)$ to ReLUs is not as big as the difference from ReLU and its leaky variant to these other new flavors. If you want to learn more about these other activation functions, they are worth trying, as we have seen it can make a big difference. But you'll generally be safe and in good company using any ReLU variants as your default choice.

6.2 *Normalization layers: Magically better convergence*

To explain a *normalization layer* and how it works, let's talk about how you might handle normalizing a normal dataset $X = \{x_1, x_2, \ldots, x_n\}$ that has n rows and d features. Before you start feeding the matrix X into your favorite ML algorithm, you usually *normalize* or standardize the features in some way. This could be making sure the values are all within the range of $[0, 1]$, or subtracting the mean μ and dividing by the standard deviation σ.[4] Standardizing by removing the mean and dividing by the standard deviation is something you have probably done before, given its ubiquity, but let's write out the three steps (where ϵ is a tiny value like 10^{-15} to avoid division by zero if everything has the same value):

$$\mu = \frac{1}{n} \sum_{1=1}^{n} x_i$$

$$\sigma = \sqrt{\epsilon + \frac{1}{n} \sum_{1=1}^{n} (\mu - x_i) \odot (\mu - x_i)} = \sqrt{\epsilon + \frac{1}{n} \sum_{1=1}^{n} (\mu - x_i)^2}$$

$$\hat{X} = \{\ldots, \frac{x_i - \mu}{\sigma}, \ldots\}$$

This results in the data $\hat{X}$ having a mean of zero and a standard deviation of 1. We do this because most algorithms are sensitive to the *scale* of the input data. This scale sensitivity means if you multiply every feature in your dataset by 1,000, it changes what

---

[4] Annoyingly, σ is used for denoting both standard deviation and the sigmoid activation function. You'll have to use context to make sure you differentiate them.

your models end up learning. By performing normalization or standardization, we ensure that our data is in a reasonable numeric range (–1 to 1 is a good place to be), making it easier for our optimization algorithms to run.

6.2.1 Where do normalization layers go?

Before we train our neural networks, we again usually do normalization or standardization before passing the data into the first layer of our network. But what if we applied this normalization process before *every* layer of a neural network? Would this allow the network to learn even faster? If we include a few extra details, it turns out that the answer is yes! The organization of our new network with normalization layers is shown in figure 6.1.

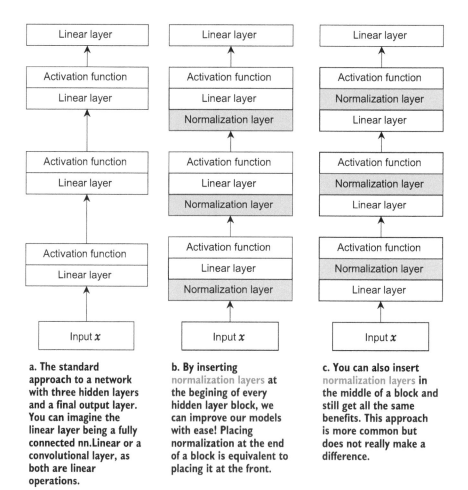

a. The standard approach to a network with three hidden layers and a final output layer. You can imagine the linear layer being a fully connected nn.Linear or a convolutional layer, as both are linear operations.

b. By inserting normalization layers at the begining of every hidden layer block, we can improve our models with ease! Placing normalization at the end of a block is equivalent to placing it at the front.

c. You can also insert normalization layers in the middle of a block and still get all the same benefits. This approach is more common but does not really make a difference.

Figure 6.1   Three versions of a network with three hidden layers and one output layer: (a) the normal approach we have learned thus far; (b) and (c) two different ways to add a normalization layer

Let's use x_l to denote the input to the lth layer and, similarly, μ_l and σ_l for the mean and standard deviation of the lth layer's inputs. Normalization layers are applied at every layer with one extra trick: let's let the network *learn* how to scale the data instead of assuming that a mean of 0 and standard deviation of 1 are the best choices. This takes the form

> Normalize the lth layer's inputs   and then let the network learn
>
> to alter the scale of the data (change the standard deviation)
>
> and learn to shift the input left/right (change the average).

$$\frac{x_l - \mu_l}{\sigma_l} \cdot \gamma_l + \beta_l$$

The first term is the same kind we had before: the mean is removed from the data and divided by the standard deviation. The crucial additions here are γ, which lets the network change the scale of the data, and β, which lets the network shift the data left/right. Since the network controls γ and β, they are learned parameters (so γ and β are included in the set of all parameters Θ). It is common to initialize $\gamma = \vec{1}$ and $\beta = \vec{0}$ so that at the start, each layer is doing a simple standardization. As training progresses, gradient descent allows us to scale (alter γ) or shift (alter β) the result as desired.

Normalization layers have been extraordinarily successful, and I often describe them as "magic pixie dust": you sprinkle some normalization layers into your network, and suddenly it starts converging faster to more accurate solutions. Even networks that would not train at all suddenly start working. We'll talk about two normalization layers that are the most widely used: *batch* and *layer*.[5] Once we have discussed each type, we can explain when to pick one over the other (but you should almost always use some form of normalization layer). The only difference between the two approaches is what goes into computing the mean μ and standard deviation σ at each layer; they both use the same equations and follow the diagram in figure 6.1.

6.2.2 Batch normalization

The first and most popular type of normalization layer is *batch normalization* (BN). BN is applied differently depending on the structure of the input data. If we are working with fully connected layers (PyTorch dimension (B, D)), we take the average and standard deviation of the feature values D over the B items in the batch. Hence, we *normalize over the data features in a given batch.* This means μ, σ, γ, and β have a shape of (D), and each item in the batch is normalized by the mean and standard deviation *of just that batch of data.*

---

[5] Yes, the names are confusing. I don't like them either.

To make this clear, let's look at some hypothetical Python code that computes μ and σ based on a tensor with shape (B, D). We make the for loops explicit to make it clear. If you implement this for real use, you should try to use functions like torch.sum and torch.mean to make this run quickly:

```
B, D = X.shape                          This BN example uses explicit loops:
μ = torch.zeros((D))                    you wouldn't write torch code like this
σ = torch.zeros((D))                    for real! X is shape (B, D) for this example.

for i in range(B):                      Goes over every item in the batch
    μ += X[i,:]                         Averages the features
μ /= B
for i in range(B):                      Handles standard deviation the same way
    σ += (X[i,:]-μ)*(X[i,:]-μ)
σ += 1e-5
σ = torch.sqrt(σ)
```

Because it averages over the batch dimension of the tensor, BN is sensitive to the batch size during training and is impossible to use with a batch size of 1. It also takes some cleverness to use at inference/prediction time because you don't want your predictions to depend on the other data being available! To resolve this, most implementations keep a running estimate of the mean and standard deviation across all previously seen batches and use that single estimate for all predictions once training is done. PyTorch has already handled this for you.

What if we have one-dimensional data of shape (B, C, D)? In this case, we normalize the *channels* over the batch. This means μ, σ, γ, and β each have a shape of (C). This is because we want to treat each of the D values in a channel as having the same nature and structure, so the average is over the $B \times D$ values in the channel across all B batches. We then apply the same scale γ and shift β to all the values in each channel. What if we have 2D data of shape (B, C, W, H)? Similar to the 1D case, μ, σ, γ, and β have a shape of (C). For any z-dimensional structured data where we have channels, we always use BN over the channels. The following table summarizes which PyTorch module you should be looking for depending on the tensor shape:

Tensor shape	PyTorch module
(B, D)	torch.nn.BatchNorm1d(D)
(B, C, D)	torch.nn.BatchNorm1d(C)
(B, C, W, H)	torch.nn.BatchNorm2d(C)
(B, C, W, H, D)	torch.nn.BatchNorm3d(C)

If we were to apply BN to an input tensor X at inference time, it might look something like this in code:

```
BN = torch.tensor((B, C, W, H))
for j in range(C):
    BN[:,j,:,:] = (X[:,j,:,:]-μ[j]/σ[j])*γ[j] + β[j]
```

6.2.3   *Training with batch normalization*

When we created our data loaders for Fashion-MNIST, we used a batch size of 128, so we should have no issue applying BN to our architectures. Following the previous table, we add `BatchNorm1d` after each `nn.Linear` layer of our fully connected network—that is the only change we need to make! Let's see what that looks like in the next code snippet. I put BN after the linear layer instead of before to match what most people do, so that when you read this in other code, it looks familiar:[6]

```
fc_bn_model = nn.Sequential(
    nn.Flatten(),
    nn.Linear(D, n), nn.BatchNorm1d(n), nn.LeakyReLU(leak_rate),
    *[nn.Sequential(nn.Linear(n, n), nn.BatchNorm1d(n),
      nn.LeakyReLU(leak_rate)) for _ in range(5)],
    nn.Linear(n, classes),
)
```

Thanks to how we organized our CNNs, we can redefine the `cnnLayer` function in the next code block to change its behavior. All we have to do is add `nn.BatchNorm2d` after each `nn.Conv2d` layer of our CNN. Then we run the exact same code that defined `cnn_relu_model` but rename it as our `cnn_bn_model` this time:

```
def cnnLayer(in_filters, out_filters=None, kernel_size=3):

    if out_filters is None:            ┐ This is a common pattern,
        out_filters = in_filters       │ so let's automate it as a
                                       ┘ default if not asked.

    padding=kernel_size//2      ←──────  Padding to stay the same size

                                       ┐ Combines the layer and
    return nn.Sequential(       ←──────┘ activation into a single unit

        nn.Conv2d(in_filters, out_filters, kernel_size, padding=padding),

        nn.BatchNorm2d(out_filters),   ←── The only change: adding
        nn.LeakyReLU(leak_rate)            BatchNorm2d after our
    )                                      convolution!
```

Next is our familiar code block to train this new batch norm based fully connected and CNN models, respectively:

```
fc_bn_results = train_network(fc_bn_model, loss_func, train_loader,
    test_loader=test_loader, epochs=10,
    score_funcs={'Accuracy': accuracy_score}, device=device)
del fc_bn_model
```

---

[6] I prefer to put BN before the linear layer, as I think it tracks better with the intuition we've laid out. There are also niche cases with thousands of activations where BN before linear layers can perform better in my experience. But these are nitpicky details. I'd rather show you what is common than take a stand on obtuse particulars.

```
cnn_bn_results = train_network(cnn_bn_model, loss_func, train_loader,
    test_loader=test_loader, epochs=10,
    score_funcs={'Accuracy': accuracy_score}, device=device)
del cnn_bn_model
```

The results of our new network are shown next, plotted against our previous best result from adding the ReLU activation. Again we see an improvement in accuracy across the board, *especially* for our CNN:

```
sns.lineplot(x='epoch', y='test Accuracy', data=fc_relu_results,
    label='FC-ReLU')
sns.lineplot(x='epoch', y='test Accuracy', data=fc_bn_results,
    label='FC-ReLU-BN')
sns.lineplot(x='epoch', y='test Accuracy', data=cnn_relu_results,
    label='CNN-ReLU')
sns.lineplot(x='epoch', y='test Accuracy', data=cnn_bn_results,
    label='CNN-ReLU-BN')
```

```
[27]: <AxesSubplot:xlabel='epoch', ylabel='test Accuracy'>
```

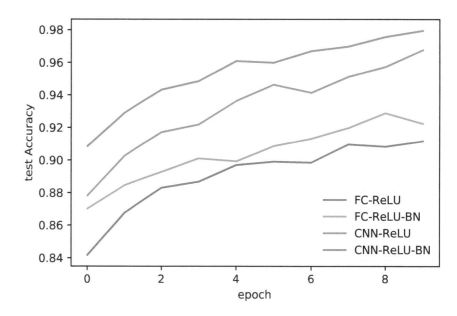

NOTE   Looking at the difference in improvement between the fully connected and CNN-based models, we might infer that the fully connected architecture is starting to reach the best it can do without being made larger or deeper. That's not important right now, but I mention it as an example of using multiple models to infer hypotheses about your data.

Why does BN work so well? The best intuition I can give you is the logic we walked through earlier: normalizing helps to ensure that our literal numeric values after each layer are in a generically "good" range; and through γ and β, the network can *decide* precisely where that range is. But getting to the root of why this works is an active research area in deep learning! Unfortunately, no one has a truly definitive answer yet.

6.2.4   *Layer normalization*

Another popular type of normalization approach is (confusingly) called *layer normalization* (LN), where we look at the average activation *over features* instead of over batches. This means every example in a batch gets its own μ and σ values but shares a γ and a β that are learned. Again, we can look at an example with explicit code to make this clear:

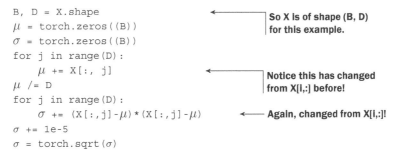

```
B, D = X.shape
μ = torch.zeros((B))
σ = torch.zeros((B))
for j in range(D):
    μ += X[:, j]
μ /= D
for j in range(D):
    σ += (X[:,j]-μ)*(X[:,j]-μ)
σ += 1e-5
σ = torch.sqrt(σ)
```

So X is of shape (B, D) for this example.

Notice this has changed from X[i,:] before!

Again, changed from X[i,:]!

The only difference between LN and BN is thus *what* we are averaging over! With LN, it does not matter how many examples are present in a batch B, so we can use LN when batches are smaller.

With that, we can dive into our repeated example of applying this new method to our same network architecture. Unlike BN, which has a different class in PyTorch for each kind of tensor shape, LN has one class for *all* architectures. There are some nuanced reasons that relate to certain kinds of problems where LN is preferred over BN and that require extra flexibility.

6.2.5   *Training with layer normalization*

The `nn.LayerNorm` class takes a single argument that is a *list* of integers. If you are working on fully connected layers with tensors of shape (B, D), you use `[D]` as the list, giving you `nn.LayerNorm([D])` as the layer construction. Here you can see the code for our fully connected network that uses LN. For fully connected layers, simply replace the BN with LN:

```
fc_ln_model = nn.Sequential(
    nn.Flatten(),
    nn.Linear(D, n), nn.LayerNorm([n]), nn.LeakyReLU(leak_rate),
    *[nn.Sequential(nn.Linear(n, n), nn.LayerNorm([n]),
        nn.LeakyReLU(leak_rate)) for _ in range(5)],
    nn.Linear(n, classes),
)
```

Why does LN take a list of integers? This list tells LN, from right to left, which values to average over. So if we have a 2D problem with tensors of shape (B, C, W, H), we give LN the last three dimensions as a list [C, W, H]. That covers *all the features*, which is what we want LN to normalize over. This makes LN a little trickier for CNNs because we also need to pay attention to how large the width and height are, and they change every time we apply max pooling.

Following is the new cnnLayer function that works around this. We add a pool_factor argument that keeps track of how many times pooling has been applied. After, is an LN object with a list [out_filters, W//(2**pool_factor), H//(2**pool_factor)] where we shrink with width and height based on how many times pooling has been applied.

> **NOTE**   This is also *another* reason to use padding with our convolutional layers. By padding the convolution so that the output has the same width and height as the input, we simplify the things we need to keep track of. Right now, we need to divide by 2 for each round of pooling. The code would be *far* more complicated if we also had to keep track of how many times we did convolutions. That would also make it much harder to make changes to our network's definition.

Here's the code:

```
def cnnLayer(in_filters, out_filters=None, pool_factor=0,kernel_size=3):

    if out_filters is None:
        out_filters = in_filters          ←——— This is a common pattern,
                                                 so let's automate it as
                                                 a default if not asked.

    padding=kernel_size//2                ←——————— Padding to stay the same siz

    return nn.Sequential(                 ←——— Combines the layer and
                                                 activation into a single unit

        nn.Conv2d(in_filters, out_filters, kernel_size, padding=padding),
        nn.LayerNorm([out_filters,
        ➥ W//(2**pool_factor), H//(2**pool_factor)]),  ←—— The only change:
        nn.LeakyReLU(leak_rate)                              switching to LayerNorm
    )                                                        after our convolution!
```

Now that we have our new cnnLayer function, we can create a cnn_ln_model that uses LN. The following code shows its creation, since we have to add the pool_factor argument after we've performed pooling:

```
cnn_ln_model = nn.Sequential(
    cnnLayer(C, n_filters),
    cnnLayer(n_filters),
    cnnLayer(n_filters),
    nn.MaxPool2d((2,2)),                  ←——————— We've done one round of
                                                    pooling, so pool_factor=1.
    cnnLayer(n_filters, 2*n_filters, pool_factor=1),
    cnnLayer(2*n_filters, pool_factor=1),
    cnnLayer(2*n_filters, pool_factor=1),
```

```
    nn.MaxPool2d((2,2)),                              ←——————  Now we've done two rounds
                                                               of pooling, so pool_factor=2.
    cnnLayer(2*n_filters, 4*n_filters, pool_factor=2),
    cnnLayer(4*n_filters, pool_factor=2),
    nn.Flatten(),
    nn.Linear(D*n_filters//4, classes),
)
```

It's a little more work, but nothing too painful. We can now train these two new models:

```
fc_ln_results = train_network(fc_ln_model, loss_func, train_loader,
    test_loader=test_loader, epochs=10,
    score_funcs={'Accuracy': accuracy_score}, device=device)
del fc_ln_model
cnn_ln_results = train_network(cnn_ln_model, loss_func, train_loader,
    test_loader=test_loader, epochs=10,
    score_funcs={'Accuracy': accuracy_score}, device=device)
del cnn_ln_model
```

Let's plot the results with LN, BN, and the ReLU-based models that have no normalization layers. The magic pixie dust powers don't appear to be as strong in LN. For the CNN, LN is an improvement over *no* normalization but worse than BN. For the fully connected layers, LN appears to be more in line with the non-normalized variant:

```
sns.lineplot(x='epoch', y='test Accuracy', data=fc_relu_results,
    label='FC-ReLU')
sns.lineplot(x='epoch', y='test Accuracy', data=fc_bn_results,
    label='FC-ReLU-BN')
sns.lineplot(x='epoch', y='test Accuracy', data=cnn_relu_results,
    label='CNN-ReLU')
sns.lineplot(x='epoch', y='test Accuracy', data=cnn_bn_results,
    label='CNN-ReLU-BN')
sns.lineplot(x='epoch', y='test Accuracy', data=fc_ln_results,
    label='FC-ReLU-LN')
sns.lineplot(x='epoch', y='test Accuracy', data=cnn_ln_results,
    label='CNN-ReLU-LN')
```

```
[32]:  <AxesSubplot:xlabel='epoch', ylabel='test Accuracy'>
```

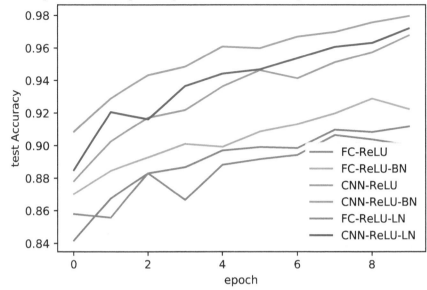

At first blush, LN does not look as helpful. Its code is clunkier to include, and it does not perform quite as well in terms of the model's accuracy. The clunkier code does have a purpose, though. BN is really only useful for fully connected layers and convolutional models, so PyTorch can easily hardcode it to the two tasks. LN can be helpful for almost any architecture (e.g., RNNs), and the list of integers telling LN explicitly what to normalize over allows us to use the same `Module` for these varieties of use cases.

6.2.6   *Which normalization layer to use?*

While normalization layers have been around for a few years, fully understanding them and when to use them is an active research problem. For non-recurrent networks, using BN is a good idea *provided* you can train on batches $B \geq 64$. If your batch isn't big enough, you won't get a good estimate of μ and σ, and your results could suffer. If your problem fits this situation of larger batches, BN will *usually* improve your results, but there are instances where it does not. So if you have difficulty getting your model to train, it's worth testing a version of your model without BN to see if you are in the odd situation where BN *hurts* instead of helping. Fortunately these situations are rare, so I still default to including BN if I have CNNs and large batches.

LN has been particularly popular for recurrent architectures and is worth adding to your RNN. LN should be your first pick whenever you reuse a subnetwork with weight sharing: BN's statistics assume *one* distribution, and when you do weight sharing, you get *multiple* distributions, which can cause problems. LN can also be effective when you have small batch sizes $B \leq 32$, although it does not usually provide the same level of improvement as BN for CNNs and fully connected networks. This can be a factor if it looks like enlarging your network will improve performance but you can't make it any larger without having to shrink the batch size due to a lack of RAM.

While BN and LN are the two most popular and widely used normalization layers, they are far from the only ones being developed and used. It's worth keeping your eye out for new approaches to normalization layers; using them is often an easy change to make to your code.

6.2.7 A peculiarity of layer normalization

Given how important LN has become, I'd like to share a deeper insight about what makes normalization layers particularly unusual and sometimes confusing to think about. Let's talk about the *strength* or, more technically, the *capacity* of a network.

I'm using these words a little loosely to refer to how complex a problem or neural network is.[7] A good mental model is to think of complexity as random-looking or erratic; some examples are shown in figure 6.2. The more complex a function is, the more complex or powerful our neural network must be to be able to approximate it. Things get interesting when we talk about the model, because two different factors are interacting:

- What does the model technically have the capacity to represent (i.e., if an oracle could tell you the perfect parameters for a given model)?

- What can our optimization process *actually learn*?

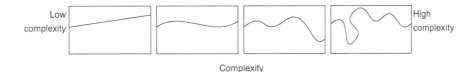

Figure 6.2 We can think of the complexity of a function as how squiggly and erratic it looks. This diagram shows a very low-complexity function on the left (linear); complexity increases as you move to the right.

We saw in chapter 5 that our optimization approach is not perfect, so it is always the case that what a model can learn must be less than or equal to what it can represent. Whenever we add an additional layer or increase the number of neurons in a layer, we increase the network's capacity.

We can describe underfitting the data as having a model with less capacity than the complexity of the problem we are trying to solve. It's like trying to use a microwave to cater a wedding: you don't have the capacity to meet the needs of the situation. This, along with two more important situations, is shown in figure 6.3. The first situation could cause overfitting, but that does mean we can solve the problem. This is nice because we have tools to tackle it (e.g., making the model smaller or adding regularization). We can easily check if we are in the second situation by giving all the data points random labels: if the training loss goes down, the model has enough capacity to memorize the entire dataset.

---

[7] Defining what *complexity* or *capacity* means is possible, but it gets very technical very quickly. It is a rabbit hole too deep for this book.

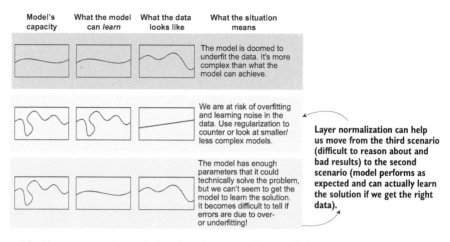

Figure 6.3   Three common types of situations that occur when specifying a neural network. Focus on the relative comparisons of complexity, not the exact type shown. The first situation is common when our model is too small. The second and third are both common when we make our model larger, but the third is much harder to reason about. Normalization layers help move us from the bad third to the better second situation.

The third situation in figure 6.3 is the most nefarious, and we do not have any good ways to check if that's the problem we are experiencing. Usually it's discovered only when something better is invented (e.g., going from SGD to SGD with momentum). Normalization layers are unique in that they *do not increase capacity*. Said another way, their representational capacity does not change, but what they can learn improves.

Normalization layers are fairly unique in this regard, and we as a community are still trying to figure out *why* they work so well. Because they do not increase capacity, many practitioners and researchers are vexed by this behavior. It would be nicer if we did not have to include these normalization layers since they do not impact capacity, but currently, they are too valuable to live without.

Proof that batch norm does not add representational power

It may seem odd that I say that normalization layers do not add any representational power to the network. We've added a new kind of layer, and adding more layers generally makes a network capable of representing more complex functions. So why are normalization layers different?

We can answer that with a little algebra! Remember that we said normalization layers take the form of

$$\frac{x - \mu}{\sigma} \cdot \gamma + \beta$$

(continued)

but that x value is the result of a linear layer. So we can rewrite this as

$$\frac{(x^\top W + b) - \mu}{\sigma} \cdot \gamma + \beta$$

Using algebra, we can take the following steps to simplify this. First, the order of operations in the numerator doesn't change with or without the parentheses, so let's remove them:

$$\frac{x^\top W + b - \mu}{\sigma} \cdot \gamma + \beta$$

Now let's move γ to the left and apply it to the terms in the numerator. We group the two shifts of the bias term b and the mean μ:

$$\frac{x^\top W \cdot \gamma + (b - \mu) \cdot \gamma}{\sigma} + \beta$$

Next we apply the division by σ to each term independently:

$$\frac{x^\top W \cdot \gamma}{\sigma} + \frac{(b - \mu) \cdot \gamma}{\sigma} + \beta$$

The left-most term involves the vector matrix product of $x^\top W$, so we can move all the element-wise operations with γ and σ onto just W and make x something that happens afterward (the result is the same):

$$x^\top \left(\frac{W \cdot \gamma}{\sigma}\right) + \frac{(b - \mu) \cdot \gamma}{\sigma} + \beta$$

Do you see the answer in sight? We have the same situation we talked about in chapters 2 and 3. Normalization is a *linear operation*, and *any consecutive sequence of linear operations is equivalent to one linear operation*! The sequence of linear layers followed by BN is *equivalent* to a different, single `nn.Linear` layer with weights $\tilde{W}$ + and biases $\tilde{b}$:

$$x^\top \underbrace{\left(\frac{W \cdot \gamma}{\sigma}\right)}_{\tilde{W}} + \underbrace{\frac{(b - \mu) \cdot \gamma}{\sigma}}_{\tilde{b}} + \beta = x^\top \tilde{W} + \tilde{b}$$

If you use convolutional layers, you get the same kind of result. This has caused some deep learning researchers and even practitioners consternation because BN is so effective, but its utility is so enormous it's hard to turn down.

6.3   *Skip connections: A network design pattern*

Now that we have learned about some new `Modules` that improve our networks, let's turn to learning about new *designs* that we can incorporate into our networks. The first is called a *skip connection*. With a normal feed-forward network, an output from one layer goes directly to the next layer. With skip connections, this is still true, but we also "skip" the next layer and connect to a preceding layer as well. There are *many* ways to do this, and figure 6.4 shows a few options.

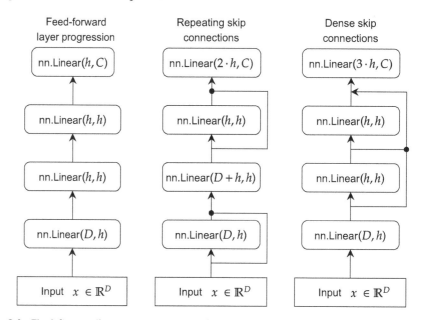

Figure 6.4   The left-most diagram shows a normal feed-forward design. The right two diagrams show two different ways to implement skip connections. The black dots on the connections indicate concatenation of the outputs from all of the inputs. Only linear layers are shown, for simplicity, but the networks would also contain normalization and activation layers.

The left image is a normal network like we have been using. The second shows one strategy of having every other layer "skip" to the next one. When this happens, the number of inputs to every second layer increases based on the size of the outputs from the two preceding layers' inputs. The idea is that every solid dot in the diagram indicates concatenation of outputs. So if x and h connect in the diagram, they input to the next layer: $[x, h]$. In code, this would be something like `torch.cat([x, h], dim=1)`. That way, the two inputs x and h have shapes (B, D) and (B, H). We want to stack the features so the result will have shape $(B, D + H)$. The third example in the figure shows multiple inputs skipping to one specific layer, giving it three times as many inputs. This causes the final layer's input size to triple based on the three layers coming into it, all having an output size of h.

Why use skip connections? Part of the intuition is that skip connections can make the optimization process easier. Said another way, skip connections can shrink the gap between a network's capacity (what it could represent) and what it can learn (what it learns to represent). Figure 6.5 highlights this fact. Consider the normal network example on the left. The gradient contains the information we need to learn and adjust every parameter. On the left side, the first hidden layer requires waiting for three other layers to process and pass along a gradient before obtaining any information. But every step is also an opportunity for noise, and if we had too many layers, learning would become ineffective. The network on the right will, for very deep networks, reduce the path of the gradient by half.

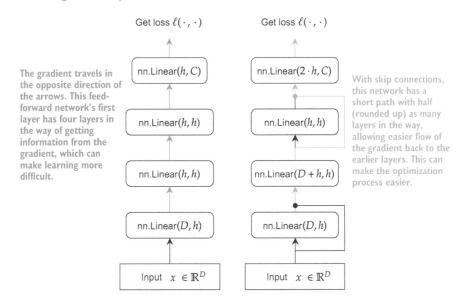

Figure 6.5 Every operation done makes the network more complex, but also makes the gradient more complex, creating a tradeoff between depth (capacity) and learnability (optimization). Skip connections create a short path with fewer operations, and can make the gradient easier to learn. Only linear layers are shown for simplicity, but would also contain normalization and activation layers.

A more extreme option is to connect every hidden layer to the output layer with a skip connection. This is shown in figure 6.6. Every hidden layer gets some amount of information about the gradient directly from the output layer, giving more direct access to the gradient, and the gradient is also processed from the longer path going layer by layer. This more direct feedback can make learning easier. It can also have benefits for certain applications that require high- and low-level details. Imagine you are trying to tell the difference between mammals: high-level details like shape can easily tell apart a whale and dog, but low-level details like the style of fur are important for differentiating between different dog breeds.

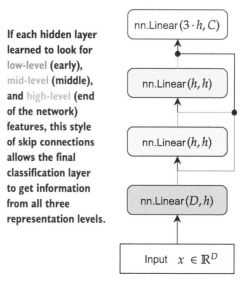

If each hidden layer learned to look for low-level **(early)**, mid-level **(middle)**, and high-level **(end of the network)** features, this style of skip connections allows the final classification layer to get information from all three representation levels.

Figure 6.6 Creating dense skip connections where everything connects to the output layer significantly reduces the length of the path from the output gradient back to each layer. It can also be helpful when different layers learn different types of features. Only linear layers are shown, for simplicity, but a real network would also contain normalization and activation layers.

A noisy definition of noise

Here, and many times throughout the book, we use a very broad definition of *noise*. Noise could be literal noise added to the network, or it could be vanishing or exploding gradients, but often it is just means *hard to use*. The gradient is not magic; it is a greedy process looking for the best current choice.

Imagine playing a game of telephone, trying to communicate a message from one person to the next. Each person in the telephone progression greedily listens to and passes along the message to the next person. But when the message makes its way back to the start of the telephone chain, it is often a garbled version of what was originally said. The more people in the telephone line, the more likely that errors happen in the message. If each person was a hidden layer in the network, we would have the same issue with our training! The gradient is the message, and each hidden layer alters the message as it tries to pass it back. If it is too deep, the message becomes too distorted by the telephone game to be useful.

However, having every layer connect directly to the output can be overkill and eventually make the learning problem more difficult. Imagine if you had 100 hidden layers, all connected directly to the output layer—that would be a *huge* input for the output layer to deal with. That said, this approach has been used successfully[8] by organizing "blocks" of dense skip connections.

---

[8] The most prominent example is a network called DenseNet (https://github.com/liuzhuang13/DenseNet).

6.3.1 Implementing fully connected skips

Now that we've talked about skip connections, let's implement one for a fully connected network. This example shows how to create the second style of skip connection from figure 6.6, where a large number of layers skip to one final layer. Then we can reuse this layer multiple times to create a hybrid strategy of shortcuts every other layer to implement the first style from figure 6.5.

Figure 6.7 shows show this works. Each set of skip connections makes one block defined by a `SkipFC Module`. By stacking multiple blocks, we re-create the style of network used in figure 6.6. Figure 6.5 could be re-created using a single `SkipFC(6, D, N)`.

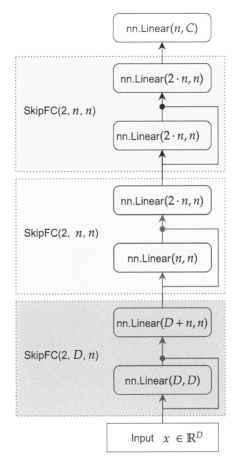

Figure 6.7 The architecture we define for our fully connected network with skip connections. Each dashed block shows a block of dense connections and is created using one `SkipFC` object that we define.

To do this, we need to store a list of hidden layers. In PyTorch, this should be done using the `ModuleList` class. Computer scientists are not very creative when they name things, so as the name implies, it is a `list` that stores only objects of the `Module` class type. This is important so PyTorch knows that it should search through the `ModuleList` for more `Module` objects. That way, it still works to use automatic differentiation and grab all the parameters using a single `.parameters()` function.

The following PyTorch module defines a class for creating skip connections. It creates one larger block of multiple layers in a dense-style skip connection containing `n_layers` total. Used on its own, it can create dense networks; or, used sequentially, it can create staggered skip connections:

```python
class SkipFC(nn.Module):
    def __init__(self, n_layers, in_size, out_size, leak_rate=0.1):
        """
        n_layers: how many hidden layers for this block of dense skip
          connections
        in_size: how many features are coming into this layer
        out_size: how many features should be used for the final layer of
          this block.
        leak_rate: the parameter for the LeakyReLU activation function.
        """

        super().__init__()
        l = n_layers-1
        self.layers = nn.ModuleList([
            nn.Linear(in_size*l, out_size) if i == l
            else nn.Linear(in_size, in_size)
            for i in range(n_layers)])
        self.bns = nn.ModuleList([
            nn.BatchNorm1d(out_size) if i == l
            else nn.BatchNorm1d(in_size)
            for i in range(n_layers)])
        self.activation = nn.LeakyReLU(leak_rate)
```

The final layer will be treated differently, so let's grab its index to use in the next two lines.

The linear and batch norm layers are stored in layers and bns, respectively. A list comprehension creates all the ayers in one line each. "if i == l" allows us to single out the last layer, which needs to use out_size instead of in_size.

Since we are writing our own forward function instead of using nn.Sequential, we can use one activation object multiple times.

```python
    def forward(self, x):
        activations = []

        for layer, bn in zip(self.layers[:-1], self.bns[:-1]):
            x = self.activation(bn(layer(x)))
            activations.append( x )
        x = torch.cat(activations, dim=1)

        return self.activation(self.bns[-1](
            self.layers[-1](x)))
```

First, we need a location to store the activations from every layer (except the last one) in this block. All the activations will be combined as the input to the last layer, which is what makes the skips!

Zips the linear and normalization layers into paired tuples, using [:-1] to select all but the last item in each list.

Concatenates the activations together, making the input for the last layer

We manually use the last linear and batch-norm layer on this concatenated input, giving us the result.

With the `SkipFC` class, we can easily create networks that contain skip connections. Figure 6.7 showed how to use three of these objects followed by a linear layer to define a network, which we do in the next block of code. Notice that we are still using the `nn.Sequential` object to organize all this code, which now proceeds in a feed-forward manner; and the non-feed-forward skips are encapsulated by the `SkipFC` object. This helps keep our code shorter and easier to read and organize. This approach of encapsulating the non-feed-forward parts into a custom `Module` is my preferred approach to organize custom networks:

```
fc_skip_model = nn.Sequential(
    nn.Flatten(),
    SkipFC(2, D, n),
    SkipFC(2, n, n),
    SkipFC(2, n, n),
    nn.Linear(n, classes),
)

fc_skip_results = train_network(fc_skip_model, loss_func, train_loader,
    test_loader=test_loader, epochs=10,
    score_funcs={'Accuracy': accuracy_score}, device=device)
del fc_skip_model
```

With that done, we can look at the results of this new network. The following code calls seaborn to plot only the fully connected networks we have trained so far. The results are middling at best, with skip connections not clearly better or worse than a network without BN:

```
sns.lineplot(x='epoch', y='test Accuracy', data=fc_relu_results,
    label='FC-ReLU')
sns.lineplot(x='epoch', y='test Accuracy', data=fc_bn_results,
    label='FC-ReLU-BN')
sns.lineplot(x='epoch', y='test Accuracy', data=fc_skip_results,
    label='FC-ReLU-BN-Skip')
```

```
[35]:   <AxesSubplot:xlabel='epoch', ylabel='test Accuracy'>
```

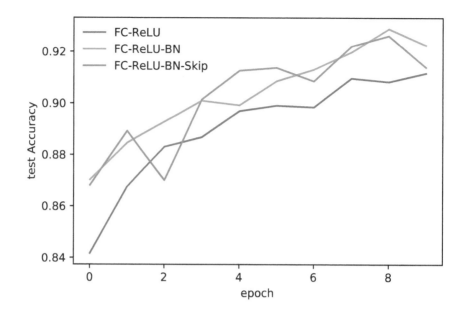

Everything I explained about skip connections helping with learning and gradient flow is still true, but it's not the whole story. Part of the issue is that skip connections were more effective on their own before normalization layers were invented to help tackle the same problem. Since our networks both have BN, the skip connections are a little redundant. Part of the problem is that our network isn't that deep, so the difference isn't that big.

6.3.2 *Implementing convolutional skips*

Because skip connections are so widely used, despite what we've seen thus far, let's repeat this exercise for the convolutional network. This will be a quick excursion as the code is almost identical. I'm repeating this because of how important and widely used skip connections are as a component in larger solutions.

We replace our SkipFC class with a new SkipConv2d class in the following code. The forward function is identical. The only difference is that we define a few helper variables for things like the kernel size and padding, which don't exist for fully connected layers, and we replace the contents of lns and bns with Conv2d and BatchNorm2d:

```
class SkipConv2d(nn.Module):
    def __init__(self, n_layers, in_channels, out_channels,
        kernel_size=3, leak_rate=0.1):

        super().__init__()

        l = n_layers-1
        f = (kernel_size, kernel_size)
        pad = (kernel_size-1)//2
```

Simple helper values ⟶ (l, f, pad lines)

The last convolution will have a different number of inputs and output channels, so we still need that index. ⟵

```
        self.layers = nn.ModuleList([
            nn.Conv2d(in_channels*l, out_channels,
            kernel_size=f, padding=pad) if i == l
            else nn.Conv2d(in_channels, in_channels,
            kernel_size=f, padding=pad)
            for i in range(n_layers)])
        self.bns = nn.ModuleList([
            nn.BatchNorm2d(out_channels) if i == l
            else nn.BatchNorm2d(in_channels)
            for i in range(n_layers)])

        self.activation = nn.LeakyReLU(leak_rate)


def forward(self, x):
    activations = []

    for layer, bn in zip(self.layers[:-1], self.bns[:-1]):
        x = self.activation(bn(layer(x)))
        activations.append( x )




    x = torch.cat(activations, dim=1)




    return self.activation(self.bns[-1](self.layers[-1](x)))
```

Defines the layers used, altering the construction of the last layer using the same "if l == l" list comprehension. We will combine convolutions via their channels, so the in and out channels change for the last layer.

This code is identical to the SkipFC class, but it's worth highlighting the most important line that could change . . .

. . . which is the concatenation of all the activations. Our tensors are organized as (B, C, W, H), which is the default in PyTorch. But you can change that, and sometimes people use (B, W, H, C). In that situation, the C channel would be at index 3 instead of 1, so you'd use cat=3. This is also how you can adapt this code to work with RNNs.

Now we can define a CNN `Module` that uses skip connections. But there is a significant problem: our input has only three channels. That's too few for the network to learn something useful. To fix that, we insert a single `Conv2d` layer at the start with *no activation function*. This makes it mathematically redundant, but our code is easier to organize because `SkipConv2d` starts constructing a larger set of filters:

```
cnn_skip_model = nn.Sequential(
    nn.Conv2d(C, n_filters, (3,3), padding=1),
    SkipConv2d(3, n_filters, 2*n_filters),
    nn.MaxPool2d((2,2)),
    nn.LeakyReLU(),
    SkipConv2d(3, 2*n_filters, 4*n_filters),
    nn.MaxPool2d((2,2)),
    SkipConv2d(2, 4*n_filters, 4*n_filters),
    nn.Flatten(),
    nn.Linear(D*n_filters//4, classes),
)
```

```
cnn_skip_results = train_network(cnn_skip_model, loss_func, train_loader,
    test_loader=test_loader, epochs=10,
    score_funcs={'Accuracy': accuracy_score}, device=device)
del cnn_skip_model
```

Also notice that we can't do skips across the `MaxPool2d` layer. Pooling changes the width and height of the image, and we would get an error if we tried to concatenate two tensors of shape (B, C, W, H) and $(B, C, W/2, H/2)$, because the axes have different sizes. The only tensor axis that can have a different size when we concatenate is the axis on which we are concatenating! So we can do (B, C, W, H) and $(B, C/2, W, H)$ if we are concatenating on the C axis (`dim=1`).

The next chunk of code plots the results for the skip CNN and the previous ones and results in the same story we just saw. But it was important to do this exercise to make sure you are comfortable with skip connections and prime you with the two issues we just saw—needing to adjust the number of channels for skip connections, and the difficulty skipping past pooling layers (we address the first of these items in the next two sections, and the second pooling issue is good to understand):

```
sns.lineplot(x='epoch', y='test Accuracy', data=cnn_relu_results,
    label='CNN-ReLU')
sns.lineplot(x='epoch', y='test Accuracy', data=cnn_bn_results,
    label='CNN-ReLU-BN')
sns.lineplot(x='epoch', y='test Accuracy', data=cnn_skip_results,
    label='CNN-ReLU-BN-Skip')
```

```
[38]:  <AxesSubplot:xlabel='epoch', ylabel='test Accuracy'>
```

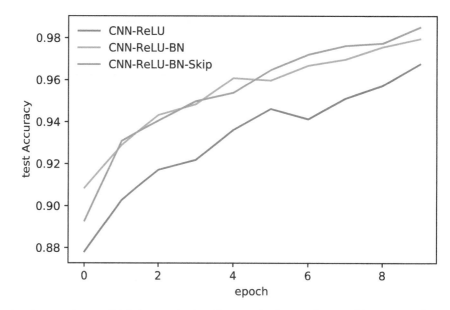

Again, the results are fairly inconclusive. In practical experience, skip connections can sometimes make a big difference on their own, but it's very problem-dependent. So why are we learning about them? Combined with one more trick, skip connections form one of the basic building blocks of a more powerful and routinely successful technique called a *residual layer* that is reliably more effective. But we need to build our way up to this more sophisticated approach to understand the foundation it is built on. Let's learn about one more ingredient we can combine with skip connections to create this fabled "residual" layer that I keep hyping.

6.4 *1 × 1 Convolutions: Sharing and reshaping information in channels*

Everything we have done with convolutions thus far has been to capture *spatial* information, and we have said that the point of convolutions is to capture this spatial *prior* that values near each other (spatially) are related to each other. As such, our convolutions have a kernel with some size k so we can capture information about our $\lfloor k/2 \rfloor$ neighbors.

But what if we set $k = 1$? This gives us *no* information about our neighbors and thus captures *no spatial information*. At first glance, this seems to make a convolution a useless operation. However, there can be valuable reasons to use a convolution with this kind of neighbor blindness. One particular application is as a computationally cheap operation to change the number of channels at a given layer. This would have been a better choice for the first layer of our CNN-based skip connection. We didn't want a fully hidden layer; we just wanted the number of channels C to be a more convenient value. Using $k = 1$ is often called a 1×1 convolution, and doing so is $\approx 9\times$ faster ($3^2/1 = 9$, ignoring overheads) than the normal 3×3 layer we used and requires less memory.

This is possible because we have C_{in} input channels and C_{out} output channels when we perform a convolution. So a convolution with $k = 1$ is looking not at spatial neighbors but at spatial *channels* by grabbing a stack of C_{in} values and processing them all at once. You can see this in figure 6.8, which shows applying a 1×1 convolution to an image with three channels.

In essence, we are giving the network a new prior: that it should try to share information across channels, rather than looking at neighboring locations. Another way to think about this is that if each channel has learned to look for a different kind of pattern, we are telling the network to *focus on the patterns found at this location* instead of having it try to build new spatial patterns.

For example, say we are processing an image, and one channel has learned to identify horizontal edges, another vertical edges, another edges at a 45-degree angle, and so on. If we want a channel to learn to identify *any* edge, we can accomplish that by looking just at the channel values (i.e., have *any* of these angle-dependent edge-detecting filters fired?) without considering the neighboring pixels. If such identifications are useful, $k = 1$ convolutions can help improve learning and reduce computational cost!

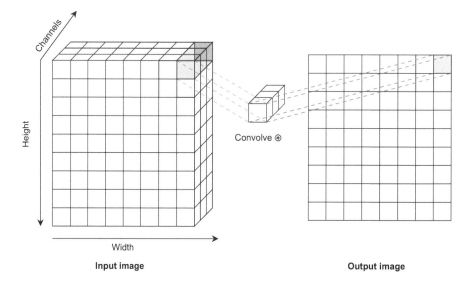

Figure 6.8   Example of a 1×1 **convolution applied to an image. The filter in the middle looks like a stick because it has a width and height of 1. It is applied to every pixel location alone, without looking at any neighboring pixels.**

6.4.1   *Training with 1 $\times$ 1 convolutions*

Such convolutions are easy to implement: we add a second helper function named `infoShareBlock` in conjunction with the `cnnLayer` function we used for batch normalization. This new function takes the number of input filters and applies a 1×1 convolution to maintain the size of the output and hopefully perform useful learning along the way:

```
def infoShareBlock(n_filters):
    return nn.Sequential(
        nn.Conv2d(n_filters, n_filters, (1,1), padding=0),
        nn.BatchNorm2d(n_filters),
        nn.LeakyReLU())
```

The following code implements the new approach by adding the `infoShareBlock` once per block of hidden layers. I've chosen to do it after two rounds of normal hidden layers. The `infoShareBlocks` are fairly cheap, so it's OK to sprinkle them around. I sometimes add one per region of the network (e.g., once per pooling); others add them more regularly. You can experiment with it for your problem to see if it's useful and find what works:

```
cnn_1x1_model = nn.Sequential(
    cnnLayer(C, n_filters),
    cnnLayer(n_filters),
    infoShareBlock(n_filters),          ◄──── First info block after 2x cnnLayers
    cnnLayer(n_filters),
    nn.MaxPool2d((2,2)),
```

```
            cnnLayer(n_filters, 2*n_filters),
            cnnLayer(2*n_filters),
            infoShareBlock(2*n_filters),
            cnnLayer(2*n_filters),
            nn.MaxPool2d((2,2)),
            cnnLayer(2*n_filters, 4*n_filters),
            cnnLayer(4*n_filters),
            infoShareBlock(4*n_filters),
            nn.Flatten(),
            nn.Linear(D*n_filters//4, classes),
)
```

> **Trains up
> this model**

```
cnn_1x1_results = train_network(cnn_1x1_model, loss_func,  ◄─┘
     train_loader, test_loader=test_loader, epochs=10,
     score_funcs='Accuracy': accuracy_score, device=device)
del cnn_1x1_model
```

When we plot the results, we see that we did not improve our accuracy much. Why is that? Well, the example we gave about information sharing *can be done by larger filters anyway*. So this process has not necessarily allowed us to learn something we could not learn before:

```
sns.lineplot(x='epoch', y='test Accuracy', data=cnn_relu_results,
     label='CNN-ReLU')
sns.lineplot(x='epoch', y='test Accuracy', data=cnn_bn_results,
     label='CNN-ReLU-BN')
sns.lineplot(x='epoch', y='test Accuracy', data=cnn_1x1_results,
     label='CNN-ReLU-BN-1x1')
```

```
[42]:  <AxesSubplot:xlabel='epoch', ylabel='test Accuracy'>
```

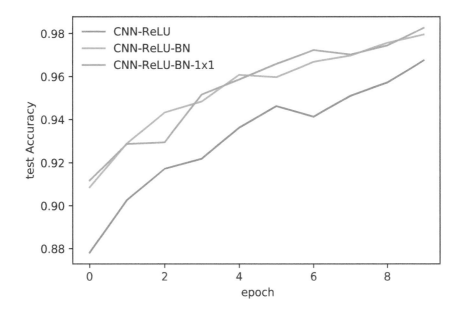

While 1×1 convolutions are cheaper to run, we can't just always use them and expect better results. They are a more strategic tool, and it takes a mix of experience and intuition to learn when they are worth adding to your model. As mentioned at the start of this section, one of their most common uses is as a fast and easy way to change the number of channels at a given layer. This is the critical function they provide for implementing residual layers in the next section.

6.5   *Residual connections*

We have learned about two approaches that, on their own, don't seem to be all that useful. Sometimes they do better, sometimes worse. But if we combine skip connections and 1×1 convolutions in just the right way, we get an approach called a *residual connection* that converges faster to more accurate solutions. The specific design pattern called a residual connection is exceptionally popular, and you should almost always use it as your default approach to specifying a model architecture when working with fully connected or convolutional layers. The strategy, ideas, and intuition behind the residual connection reoccur in this chapter and multiple times in this book, and the residual connection has become a widely used design component. It is broken into two types of connections: the standard block and the bottleneck variant.

6.5.1   *Residual blocks*

The first connection type is a *residual block*, shown in figure 6.9. The block is a kind of skip connection where two layers combine at the end, creating long and short paths. However, in a residual block, the short path has *no operations*. We simply leave the input unaltered! Once the long path has computed its result h, we add it to the input x to get the final result $x + h$. We often denote the long path as a subnetwork $F(\cdot) = h$, and we can describe all residual connections as follows:

> The residual layer's output is
>
> the original input to the layer plus
>
> the result of a sub-network $F(\cdot)$ processing the input.

$$f(x) = \quad x + \quad F(x)$$

When we start combining multiple residual blocks one after another, we create an architecture with a very interesting design. You can see that in figure 6.10, where we end up with a *long* path and a *short* path through the network. The short path makes it easier to learn deep architectures by having as few operations as possible. Fewer operations means less chance of noise in the gradient, making it easy to propagate a useful gradient back farther than would otherwise be possible. The long path then performs the actual work, learning units of complexity that are added back in via the skip connections (using addition instead of concatenation).

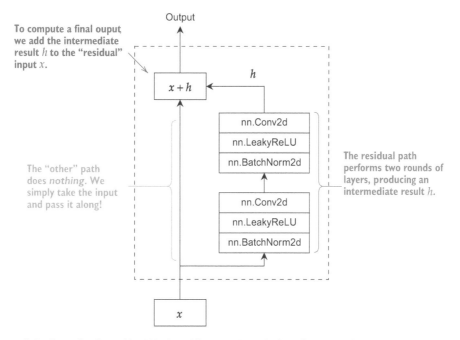

To compute a final ouput we add the intermediate result h to the "residual" input x.

Output

$x + h$

h

nn.Conv2d

nn.LeakyReLU

nn.BatchNorm2d

nn.Conv2d

nn.LeakyReLU

nn.BatchNorm2d

x

The "other" path does *nothing*. We simply take the input and pass it along!

The residual path performs two rounds of layers, producing an intermediate result h.

Figure 6.9 Example of a residual block architecture. The left side of the block is the short path, which performs no operations or alterations to the input. The right side of the block is a residual connection and performs a skip connection with two rounds of BN/linear activation to produce an intermediate result h. The output is the sum of the input x and h.

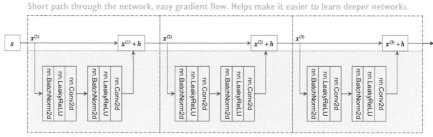

Short path through the network, easy gradient flow. Helps make it easier to learn deeper networks.

Long path through the network. Allows for depth and learning complex functions of the input.

Figure 6.10 An architecture with multiple layers of residual blocks. This creates a long path and a short path through the network. The short path on top makes it easy to get the gradient to propagate back to many layers, allowing for more depth by avoiding as much work as possible. The long path does the actual work, letting the network learn complex functions one piece at a time.

This kind of residual block can easily be converted to a fully connected counterpart. But when we are working with images, we like to do a few rounds of max pooling to help build some translation invariance and then double the number of channels after each round of pooling to do a consistent amount of computation and work at each layer of the network. But the residual block *requires* that the input and output have the *exact same shape* because we are using addition instead of concatenation. This is where the bottleneck layer helps, as we see shortly.

6.5.2   Implementing residual blocks

The residual block we have described is called *Type E* and is one of the favored residual setups. As you might have guessed from the name, people have tried tons of different reorderings on the normalization, convolution, and number of layers in each residual block. They all tend to work well, but we'll stick with Type E for simplicity. Notice how we can use `nn.Sequential` to organize our code the same way our math reads, helping us keep the definition simple and easy to check for correctness:

```
class ResidualBlockE(nn.Module):
    def __init__(self, channels, kernel_size=3, leak_rate=0.1):
        """
        channels: how many channels are in the input/output to this layer
        kernel_size: how large of a filter should we use
        leak_rate: parameter for the LeakyReLU activation function
        """
        super().__init__()
        pad = (kernel_size-1)//2
        self.F = nn.Sequential(
            nn.Conv2d(channels, channels, kernel_size, padding=pad),
            nn.BatchNorm2d(channels),
            nn.LeakyReLU(leak_rate),
            nn.Conv2d(channels, channels, kernel_size, padding=pad),
            nn.BatchNorm2d(channels),
            nn.LeakyReLU(leak_rate),
        )
    def forward(self, x):
        return x + self.F(x)
```

How much padding will our convolutional layers need to maintain the input shape?

Defines the conv and BN layers we use in a subnetwork: just two hidden layers of conv/BN/activation

F() has all the work for the long path: we just add it to the input.

6.5.3   Residual bottlenecks

The residual layer is a simple extension of the skip connection idea that works by making the short path do as little work as possible to help with the gradient flow and minimize noise. But we need a way to handle different numbers of channels after we do pooling. The solution is 1×1 convolutions. We can use the 1×1 layer to do the minimum amount of work to simply change the number of channels in the input, increasing or decreasing the number of channels as we see fit. The preferred approach is to create a *residual bottleneck*, as shown in figure 6.11. The short path is still short and has no activation function but simply performs a 1×1 convolution followed by BN to change the original number of channels C into the desired number C'.

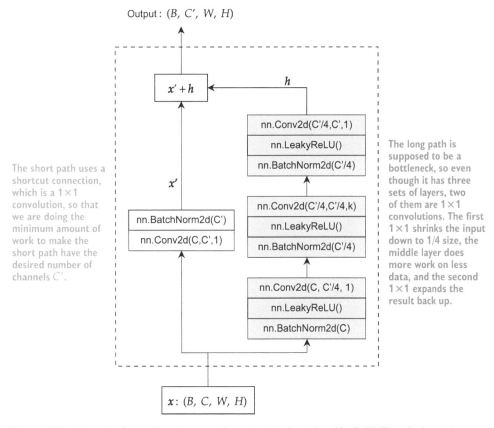

Output : (B, C', W, H)

$x' + h$

h

nn.Conv2d(C'/4,C',1)

nn.LeakyReLU()

nn.BatchNorm2d(C'/4)

x'

nn.Conv2d(C'/4,C'/4,k)

nn.BatchNorm2d(C')

nn.LeakyReLU()

nn.Conv2d(C,C',1)

nn.BatchNorm2d(C'/4)

nn.Conv2d(C, C'/4, 1)

nn.LeakyReLU()

nn.BatchNorm2d(C)

The short path uses a shortcut connection, which is a 1×1 convolution, so that we are doing the minimum amount of work to make the short path have the desired number of channels C'.

The long path is supposed to be a bottleneck, so even though it has three sets of layers, two of them are 1×1 convolutions. The first 1×1 shrinks the input down to 1/4 size, the middle layer does more work on less data, and the second 1×1 expands the result back up.

x : (B, C, W, H)

Figure 6.11 Example of a bottleneck connection where the input has (B, C, W, H) as its input shape and the goal is to have an output shape of (B, C', W, H). The short path has to change shape, so a 1×1 convolution is used to do the minimum work needed to change the number of channels. The long path is supposed to be a bottleneck that encourages compression, so it starts with a 1×1 convolution to shrink the number of channels, followed by a normal convolution and ending with another 1×1 convolution to expand the number of channels back up to the desired size C'.

The approach is called a bottleneck because of the long path $F(\cdot)$ on the right that has three hidden layers. The first hidden layer uses another 1×1 convolution to shrink the number of channels C before doing a normal hidden layer in the middle, followed by a final 1×1 convolution to expand the number of channels back up to the original count. There are two reasons and interpretations behind the bottleneck.

The first is a design choice of the original authors of the residual network. They wanted to make their networks deeper as a way to increase their capacity. Making the bottlenecks shrink and then expand keeps the number of parameters down, saving valuable GPU memory for adding more layers! The authors used this to train a network with a total of 152 layers. At the time, this was an obscenely deep network and set a new record for results on the seminal ImageNet dataset (widely used as a benchmark by researchers).

The second reason draws on the concept of compression: making things smaller. An entire area of machine learning studies compression as a tool to make models learn interesting things. The idea is that if you force a model to go from a large number of parameters to a small number, you force the model to create more meaningful and compact representations. As a loose analogy, think about how you can simply say "cat" to communicate a specific species of animal with a particular shape, dietary habits, and more with just three letters. If you say "the orange house cat," you quickly narrow down the mental image of what you are talking about with very little information given. That is the idea behind compression: being able to compress implies some level of intelligence.

6.5.4   *Implementing residual bottlenecks*

Let's convert the idea of a residual bottleneck into code. It looks very similar to `ResidualBlockE`. The main difference is that we have two subnetworks: first is the long path, encoded in `self.F`; the short path gets a member variable `self.shortcut`. We do this with a little trick: if the bottleneck is *not* changing the number of channels, we use the `Identity` function to implement it. This function simply returns the input as the output. If the number of channels *does* change, we override the definition with a small `nn.Sequential` that does the 1×1 followed by BN:

```
class ResidualBottleNeck(nn.Module):
    def __init__(self, in_channels, out_channels,
    ➥ kernel_size=3, leak_rate=0.1):

        super().__init__()
        pad = (kernel_size-1)//2
        bottleneck = max(out_channels//4, in_channels)



        self.F = nn.Sequential(
            nn.BatchNorm2d(in_channels),
            nn.LeakyReLU(leak_rate),
            nn.Conv2d(in_channels, bottleneck, 1, padding=0),

            nn.BatchNorm2d(bottleneck),
            nn.LeakyReLU(leak_rate),

            nn.Conv2d(bottleneck, bottleneck, kernel_size, padding=pad),

            nn.BatchNorm2d(bottleneck),
            nn.LeakyReLU(leak_rate),
            nn.Conv2d(bottleneck, out_channels, 1, padding=0)
        )


        self.shortcut = nn.Identity()
        if in_channels != out_channels:
```

How much padding will our convolutional layers need to maintain the input shape?

The bottleneck should be smaller, so output /4 or input. You could also try changing max to min; it's not a major issue.

Compresses down

Defines the three sets of BN and convolution layers we need. Notice that for the 1×1 convs, we use padding=0, because 1×1 will not change shape!

Normal layer doing a full conv

Expands back up

By default, our shortcut is the Identity function, which simply returns the input as the output.

If we need to change the shape, let's turn the shortcut into a small layer with 1×1 conv and BM.

```
            self.shortcut = nn.Sequential(
                nn.Conv2d(in_channels, out_channels, 1, padding=0),
                nn.BatchNorm2d(out_channels)
            )

    def forward(self, x):
        return self.shortcut(x) + self.F(x)
```

"shortcut(x)" plays the role of "x"; we do as little work as possible to keep the tensor shapes the same.

Now we can define a residual network! It is difficult to make this exactly the same as our original network because each residual layer includes two or three rounds of layers as well, but the following definition gets us to something reasonably close. Since our network is on the small side, we added a LeakyReLU after rounds of residual blocks. You do not have to include this, because the long path through the residual layers has activation functions in it. For very deep networks (30+ blocks), I recommend not including the activation between blocks, to help get information through all those layers. This is not a critical detail, though, and the approach will work well either way. You can always try it and see which way works best for your problem and network size. Also notice how defining our own blocks as a Module lets us specify this very complex network in relatively few lines of code:

BottleNeck to start because we need more channels. It's also common to start with just one normal hidden layer before beginning residual blocks.

Inserts an activation after each residual. This is optional.

```
cnn_res_model = nn.Sequential(
    ResidualBottleNeck(C, n_filters),
    nn.LeakyReLU(leak_rate),
    ResidualBlockE(n_filters),
    nn.LeakyReLU(leak_rate),
    nn.MaxPool2d((2,2)),
    ResidualBottleNeck(n_filters, 2*n_filters),
    nn.LeakyReLU(leak_rate),
    ResidualBlockE(2*n_filters),
    nn.LeakyReLU(leak_rate),
    nn.MaxPool2d((2,2)),
    ResidualBottleNeck(2*n_filters, 4*n_filters),
    nn.LeakyReLU(leak_rate),
    ResidualBlockE(4*n_filters),
    nn.LeakyReLU(leak_rate),
    nn.Flatten(),
    nn.Linear(D*n_filters//4, classes),
)

cnn_res_results = train_network(cnn_res_model, loss_func, train_loader,
    test_loader=test_loader, epochs=10,
    score_funcs={'Accuracy': accuracy_score}, device=device)
```

Now, if we plot the results, we should *finally* see consistent improvement! While the difference is not big for this dataset, it will be more dramatic for larger and more challenging problems. Fashion-MNIST just does not have much room for improvement.

We are hitting over 98% accuracy, a significant improvement from the 93% we started with:

```
sns.lineplot(x='epoch', y='test Accuracy', data=cnn_results, label='CNN')
sns.lineplot(x='epoch', y='test Accuracy', data=cnn_relu_results,
    label='CNN-ReLU')
sns.lineplot(x='epoch', y='test Accuracy', data=cnn_bn_results,
    label='CNN-ReLU-BN')
sns.lineplot(x='epoch', y='test Accuracy', data=cnn_res_results,
    label='CNN-ReLU-BN-Res')
```

[47]:   <AxesSubplot:xlabel='epoch', ylabel='test Accuracy'>

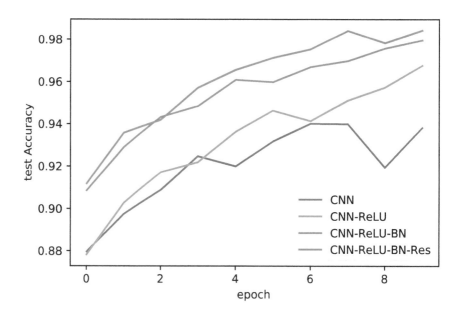

With that said, it is hard to overstate how large an impact residual connections have had on modern deep learning, and you should almost always default to implementing a residual-style network. You will often see people refer to *ResNet-X*, where the *X* stands for the total number of layers in a specific residual network architecture. This is because thousands of researchers and practitioners like to start with ResNet as their baseline and add or remove a few parts to customize it to their problem. In many cases, using ResNet with no change except to the output layer gives a strong result on an image classification problem. As such, it should become one of your go-to tools when tackling real-life problems.

6.6   *Long short-term memory RNNs*

The RNN we described in chapter 4 is rarely used in practice. It is notoriously difficult to train and get working on complex problems. Many different variants of RNNs have been published, but the tried-and-true option that always works well is called a *long short-term memory* (LSTM) *network.* LSTMs are a type of RNN architecture originally developed in 1997. Despite their age (and a small tune-up in 2006), LSTMs have continued to be one of the best options available for a recurrent architecture.

6.6.1 *RNNs: A fast review*

Let's quickly recall what a simple RNN looks like with figure 6.12 and equation 6.1. We can describe it succinctly with its inputs x_t and the previous hidden state h_t being concatenated together into one larger input. They are processed by a nn.Linear layer and go through the tanh nonlinearity, and that becomes the output:

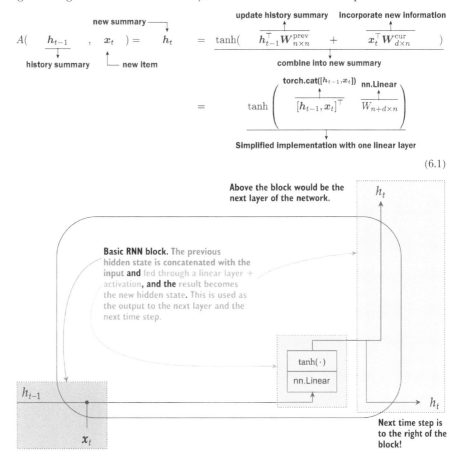

(6.1)

Figure 6.12 A simple RNN that we learned about in chapter 4. Information over time is captured in the hidden activations h_t that are fed into the next RNN layer and used as the output to any following layers. Small black dots denote concatenation.

One of the challenges with learning an RNN is that, when unrolled through time, many operations are performed on the same tensor. It is hard for the RNN to learn how to use this finite space to extract information it needs from the fixed-sized representation of a variable number of timesteps, and then to also add information to that representation.

This problem is similar to what residual layers tackle: it's easy for the gradient to send information back when there are fewer operations on it. If we have a sequence with 50 steps, that's like trying to learn a network with 50 layers with 50 more opportunities for gradient noise to get in the way.

6.6.2 LSTMs and the gating mechanism

The difficulty of getting a gradient to carry a signal back many time steps is one of the primary issues an LSTM tries to solve. To do this, the LSTM creates two sets of states: a hidden state h_t and a context state C_t. h_t does the work and tries to learn complex functions, and the context C_t tries to simply hold valuable information for use later. You can think of C_t as focusing on *long-term* information and h_t as working on *short-term* information; hence, we get the name *long short-term memory*.

LSTMs use a strategy called *gating* to make this happen. A gating mechanism produces a value in the range of $[0, 1]$. That way, if you multiply by the result of a gate, you can remove everything (the gate returned 0 and anything time 0 is 0) or allow everything to pass through (the gate returned 1). LSTMs are designed with three gates:

- The *forget gate* allows us to forget what is in our context C_t.

- The *input gate* controls what we want to add or input into C_t.

- The *output gate* is how much of the context C_t we want to include in the final output h_t.

Figure 6.13 shows what this looks like at a high level.

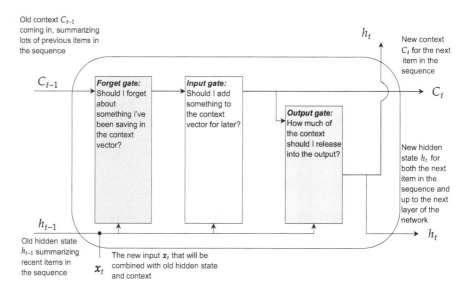

Figure 6.13 The strategy of an LSTM involves three gates that operate sequentially and allow interaction between the short term h_t and the long term C_t. The forget gate is red, the input gate is blue, and the output gate is green.

This gating is accomplished using the sigmoid $\sigma(\cdot)$ and $\tanh(\cdot)$ activation functions. Implementing gating mechanisms is a situation where you *want saturation* because you need your outputs to be in a very specific range of values so you can create a prior that *some inputs need to be allowed, and some need to be stopped.* The sigmoid activation function $\sigma(\cdot)$ produces a value in the range of $[0, 1]$. If we take another value α and multiply it with the result of the sigmoid, we get $z = \alpha \cdot \sigma(\cdot)$. If $\sigma(\cdot) = 0$, then we have essentially closed the gate on z containing any information about α. If $\sigma(\cdot) = 1$, we have $z = \alpha$ and have essentially let all the information flow through the gate. For values in between, we end up regulating how much information/content from α gets to flow through the network. We can see how an LSTM uses this gating approach in figure 6.14.

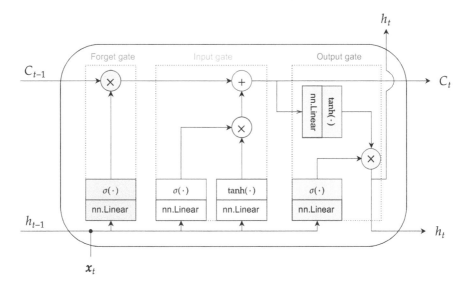

Figure 6.14 Diagram showing the detailed operations of an LSTM and how each gate is implemented and connected. The $\times$ indicates two values being multiplied together, and the $+$ shows values being added together. The same color coding applies (red for the forget gate, blue for the input gate, and green for the output gate).

The context vector is on the top half and the short-term hidden states on the bottom. The setup has some properties reminiscent of the residual network we just learned about. The context C_t acts kind of like a short path: few (and simple) operations are performed on it, making it easier for the gradient to flow back over very long sequences. The bottom half of the LSTM does the heavy lifting (like the residual path) with linear layers and nonlinear activation functions and attempts to learn more complex functions that are necessary but also make it harder for the gradient to propagate through to the beginning.

This idea of gating and having short and long paths is the main secret to making LSTMs work well and better than the simple RNN we learned about. Just like all RNNs, the LSTM also uses weight sharing over time. So we have looked at the LSTM cell for one input in time, and the same weights are reused for every item over time.

A very thorough description and explanation of LSTMs by Chris Olah is available at https://colah.github.io/posts/2015-08-Understanding-LSTMs; he also describes some of the deeper details about *peephole connections*, which are a standard improvement in modern LSTMs. The idea behind the peephole is to also concatenate the old context C_{t-1} into the nn.Linear layers that decide the forget fate and input gate, the idea being that you really should know what you are about to forget before deciding to forget it. Similarly, adding it to the input gate helps you avoid adding redundant information you already have. Following this train of logic, one more peephole connection adds C_t to the last nn.Linear layer which gates the output, the idea being you should know what you are looking at outputting before deciding if you should output it.

There are *tons* of variants on the LSTM, including another popular RNN called the *Gated Recurrent Unit* (GRU). The GRU has the same inspiration as the LSTM but tries to get the hidden state h_t to do double-duty as the short- and long-term memory. This makes the GRU faster, use less memory, and is easier to write code with, which is why we use it. The downside is that the GRU is not always as accurate as the LSTM. By contrast, the LSTM with peephole connections has been a tried-and-true method that is hard to beat and is what people are usually referring to when they say an "LSTM."

6.6.3   *Training an LSTM*

Now that we have talked about what an LSTM is, let's implement one and try it. We'll reuse the dataset and problem from chapter 4, where we tried to predict the original language a name might have come from. The first thing we do is set up that problem again using the same code and our LanguageNameDataset class. Briefly, here's a review of the block creating the data loader objects:

```
dataset = LanguageNameDataset(namge_language_data, alphabet)

train_lang_data, test_lang_data = torch.utils.data.random_split(dataset,
    (len(dataset)-300, 300))
train_lang_loader = DataLoader(train_lang_data, batch_size=32,
    shuffle=True, collate_fn=pad_and_pack)
test_lang_loader = DataLoader(test_lang_data, batch_size=32,
    shuffle=False, collate_fn=pad_and_pack)
```

Reuses our code from chapter 4

Let's set up a new RNN as our baseline. I'm using a three-layer one, but I'm not making it bidirectional. While bidirectional layers help with the problem of getting information across time, I want to make that problem *worse* so that we can better see the benefit of an LSTM:

```
rnn_3layer = nn.Sequential(                        ← Simple old-style RNN
    EmbeddingPackable(
        nn.Embedding(len(all_letters), 64)),       ← (B, T) -> (B, T, D)
        nn.RNN(64, n, num_layers=3, batch_first=True),  ← (B, T, D) ->
                                                        ( (B,T,D) , (S, B, D) )

    LastTimeStep(rnn_layers=3),                    ← We need to take the RNN
                                                     output and reduce it to
                                                     one item, (B, D).
```

```
        nn.Linear(n, len(namge_language_data)),        ←———— (B, D) -> (B, classes)
)
```

                                                         Applies gradient clipping
                                                         to maximize its performance

```
for p in rnn_3layer.parameters():                   ←————
    p.register_hook(lambda grad: torch.clamp(grad, -5, 5))

rnn_results = train_network(rnn_3layer, loss_func, train_lang_loader,
    test_loader=test_lang_loader,
    score_funcs={'Accuracy': accuracy_score}, device=device, epochs=10)
```

Next we implement an LSTM layer. Since the LSTM is built directly into PyTorch, it's very easy to incorporate. We can just replace every nn.RNN layer with an nn.LSTM! We are also reusing the LastTimeStep layer from chapter 4: if you go back and look at the code, you now know why we had this comment: "Result is either a tuple (out, h_t) or a tuple (out, (h_t, c_t))." It's because when we use an LSTM, we get the hidden states h_t and the context states c_t! That addition in chapter 4 made our code a little more future-proof for the LSTM we are now using. The LSTM version of the network is as follows, and we had to change only one line to make it happen:

```
lstm_3layer = nn.Sequential(
    EmbeddingPackable(nn.Embedding(len(all_letters), 64)), ←—— (B, T) -> (B, T, D)

    nn.LSTM(64, n, num_layers=3,                      ←————
        batch_first=True),
```
                                                         nn.RNN became
                                                         nn.LSTM, and now
                                                         we are upgraded to
                                                         LSTMs w/(B, T, D) ->
                                                         ((B,T,D) , (S, B, D)).
```
    LastTimeStep(rnn_layers=3),                       ←————
```
                                                         We need to take the
                                                         RNN output and reduce
                                                         it to one item, (B, D).
```
    nn.Linear(n, len(namge_language_data)),           ←———— (B, D) -> (B, classes)
)
```
                                                         We still want to use
                                                         gradient clipping with
                                                         every kind of RNN,
```
for p in lstm_3layer.parameters():                  ←———— including LSTMs.
    p.register_hook(lambda grad: torch.clamp(grad, -5, 5))

lstm_results = train_network(lstm_3layer, loss_func, train_lang_loader,
    test_loader=test_lang_loader,
    score_funcs={'Accuracy': accuracy_score}, device=device, epochs=10)
```

If we plot the results, we can see that the LSTM helps improve them over the RNN. We also have some evidence of the LSTM starting to overfit after about four epochs. If we were trying to train for real, we might want to reduce the number of neurons to prevent overfitting or use a validation step to help us learn that we need to stop after four epochs:

```
sns.lineplot(x='epoch', y='test Accuracy', data=rnn_results,
    label='RNN: 3-Layer')
sns.lineplot(x='epoch', y='test Accuracy', data=lstm_results,
    label='LSTM: 3-Layer')
```

[53]:   `<AxesSubplot:xlabel='epoch', ylabel='test Accuracy'>`

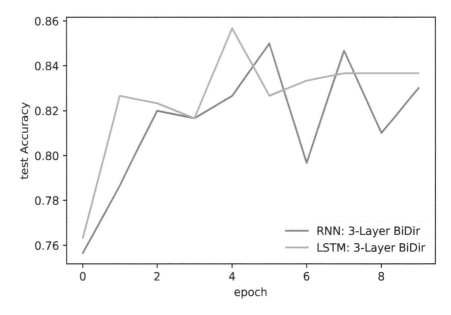

The LSTM is one of the few tried-and-true deep learning methods that has lasted for *decades* without much change. If you need an RNN, the LSTM is a good default choice. The gated recurrent unit (GRU) we mentioned is also a good choice, particularly if you need something that requires less computational resources. We won't go into the details of the GRU, but it's an intentional simplification of the LSTM design: it is simpler in that it does not need the context state C_t and instead tries to get the hidden state h_t to do double duty as the hidden and context. This explaining the details a bit more involved, but I like the example at https://blog.floydhub.com/gru-with-pytorch if you want to learn more. If you have shorter and simpler data or if compute limitations are a concern, the GRU is worth checking out because it requires less memory. I like using the GRU because its code is a little simpler, since there is only the hidden state, but there are definitely applications where the LSTM performs better. You can use either a GRU or LSTM and get good results, but the best will probably come from tuning (e.g., with Optuna) an LSTM.

Exercises

Share and discuss your solutions on the Manning online platform at Inside Deep Learning Exercises (https://liveproject.manning.com/project/945). Once you submit your own answers, you will be able to see the solutions submitted by other readers, and see which ones the author judges to be the best.

1 Try replacing the LeakyReLU with the `nn.PReLU` activation function in the various CNNs we have trained. Does it perform better or worse?

2 Write a `for` loop to train CNN models with 1 to 20 sets of hidden layers, once with BN layers and one without. How does BN impact the ability to learn deeper models?

3 *MATH*: We used algebra to show that a linear layer followed by BN is equivalent to one linear layer. Try doing the same kind of math to show that BN followed by a linear layer *also* is equivalent to one different linear layer.

4 Re-implement the `ResidualBlockE` for fully connected layers instead of convolutional layers. Does making the fully connected model use residual connections still improve performance?

5 Write a `for` loop to train a residual model with progressively more combinations of `ResidualBlockE` layers. Do the residual blocks allow you to train even deeper models?

6 Try creating a bidirectional LSTM layer. Do you get better or worse results?

7 Try training various LSTM and GRU networks with varying numbers of layers and neurons, and compare them in terms of the time to reach a desired accuracy level. Do you see any relative pros or cons of each?

Summary

- A family of activation functions called rectified linear units requires fewer epochs to reach better accuracies.

- Inserting a normalization layer between every linear layer and activation function provides another boost.

- Batch normalization works well for most problems, but with weight sharing (like recurrent architectures) and small batch sizes.

- Layer normalization is not always as accurate but is almost always a safe addition to any network design.

- Skip connections provide a different strategy for combining layers that can create long and short paths through a network.

- A 1×1 convolution can be used to adjust a convolutional layer's number of channels.

- A design pattern called residual layers allows us to build deeper networks that improve accuracy by mixing skip connections and 1×1 convolutions.

- The $\tanh(\cdot)$ and $\sigma(\cdot)$ activation functions are useful for creating gating mechanisms, which encode a new kind of prior.

- Gating is a strategy of forcing a neuron's activation to be between 0 and 1 and then multiplying another layer's output by this value.

- RNNs can be improved by using an approach called long short-term memory (LSTM), which is a careful application of gating.

Part 2

Building advanced networks

To a lay carpenter like myself, a hammer is but a blunt instrument to put nails through wood, crack open a tough watermelon, and smash my thumb while adding intentional and tasteful post-modernist holes to my drywall. To a professional carpenter, it is a multifaceted tool that, in concert with a few others, can be used to construct beautiful furniture and art or even create new tools. In part 1 of the book, you learned about the tools; now we will build you into a craftsperson. Part 2 focuses less on new deep learning methods and more on how to combine the methods you already know to build beautiful new architectures to solve different kinds of problems, and new tools you can use to work faster and expand your abilities.

Each of the first few chapters focuses on a new kind of task. Chapter 7 shows you how to do unsupervised learning with a neural network. Chapter 8 lets you make multiple predictions per image so that you can detect individual objects and their locations. Chapter 9 takes unsupervised learning one step further to generative models, where the model can create or alter images. Chapters 10 and 11 work in concert to teach you how to predict an entire sequence, so that you can build a model that translates text from English to French.

The last three chapters follow a theme of revisiting and improvement. Chapter 12 provides alternatives to RNNs with varying tradeoffs, working up to the Transformer architecture that has fast become critical to modern natural language processing. Chapter 13 explores the trick of transfer learning, providing higher accuracy in less time to solve real-world problems. Finally, chapter 14 covers three cutting-edge improvements to training a deep neural network that are not just useful but also show how far you've come: from zero to understanding some of the latest advancements and research in the field.

Autoencoding and self-supervision

You now know several approaches to specifying a neural network for classification and regression problems. These are the classic machine learning problems, where for each data point x (e.g., a picture of a fruit), we have an associated answer y (e.g., fresh or rotten). But what if we do not have a label y? Is there any useful way for us to learn? You should recognize this as an *unsupervised* learning scenario.

People are interested in self-supervision because *labels are expensive.* It is often much easier to get lots of data, but knowing *what* each data point is requires a lot of work. Think about a sentiment classification problem where you try to predict if a sentence is conveying a positive notion (e.g., "I love this deep learning book I'm reading.") or a negative one (e.g., "The author of this book is bad at making jokes."). It's not *hard* to read the sentence, make a determination, and save that information. But if you want to build a *good* sentiment classifier, you might want to label hundreds of thousands to millions of sentences. Do you really want to spend days or weeks labeling so many sentences? If we could somehow learn without needing these labels, it would make our lives much easier.

One strategy for unsupervised learning that has become increasingly common in deep learning is called *self-supervision*. The idea behind self-supervision is that we use a regression or classification loss function ℓ to do the learning, and we predict something about the input data x itself. In these cases, the labels come *implicitly with the data* and allow us to use the same tools we have already learned to use. Coming up with clever ways to get implicit labels is the trick to self-supervision.

Figure 7.1 shows three of the many ways self-supervision can be done: *inpainting*, where you obscure part of the input and then try to predict what was hidden; *image sorting*, where you break the image into multiple parts, shuffle them, and then try to put them back in the right order; and *autoencoding*, where you're given the input image and predict the input. Using self-supervision, we can train models without labels and then use what the model has learned to do data clustering, perform tasks like identifying noisy/bad data, or build useful models with less data (the latter will be demonstrated in chapter 13).

There are numerous ways to create a self-supervised problem, and researchers are coming up with new approaches all the time. In this chapter, we focus on one specific kind of self-supervision called *autoencoding*, the third example in figure 7.1, because the key to autoencoding is *predicting the input from the input*. This may seem like an insane idea at first. Surely it is a trivial problem for the network to learn to return the input as it was given. This would be like defining a function as

```
def superUsefulFunction(x):
    return x
```

This `superUsefulFunction` would implement a *perfect* autoencoder. So if the problem is so easy, how can it be useful? That's what we learn in this chapter. The trick is to *constrain* the network, giving it a handicap so that it is unable to learn the trivial solution. Think of it like a test in school, where the teacher has given you 100 questions on an open book exam. If you had all the time in the world, you could simply read the book, find the answers, and write them down. But if you are *constrained* to complete the exam in just an hour, you don't have time to search the book for everything. Instead, you are forced to learn the *underlying concepts* that help you reconstruct the answers to all the questions. The constraints help encourage learning and understanding. The same idea is at work with autoencoders: with the trivial solution off the table, the network is forced to learn something more useful (underlying concepts) to solve the problem.

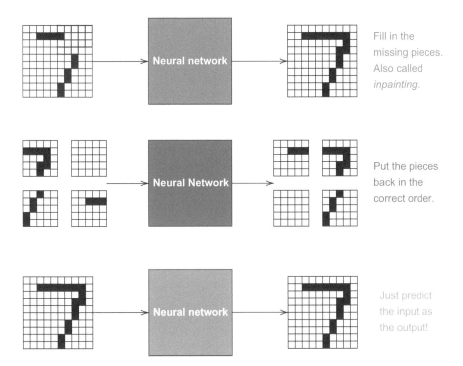

Figure 7.1 Three different types of self-supervised problems: inpainting, image sorting, and autoencoding. In each case, we do not need to know what the image is of because the network will try to predict the original image no matter what. In the first case (red), we randomly block out a portion of the image and ask the network to fill in the missing piece. In the second case, we break the image into pieces, shuffle them, and ask the network to put them back in the correct order. In the last case, we simply ask the network to predict the original image from the original image.

This chapter explains the concept of autoencoding further and shows that bread-and-butter principal component analysis (PCA) works by secretly being an autoencoder. We'll make small changes to a PyTorch version of PCA to change it into a fully fledged autoencoding neural network. As we make an autoencoding network larger, it becomes more important to constrain it well, which we demonstrate with the *denoising* strategy. Finally we apply these concepts to sequential models like RNNs, which gives the *autoregressive* model.

7.1 How autoencoding works

Let's first describe the idea of autoencoding in a little more detail. Autoencoding means we generally learn *two* functions/networks: first a function $f^{in}(x) = z$, which transforms the input x into a new representation $z \in \mathbb{R}^{D'}$, and then a function $f^{out}(z) = x$, which converts the new representation z back into the original representation. We call these two functions the *encoder* f^{in} and the *decoder* f^{out}, and the process is summarized in figure 7.2. Without any labels, the new representation z is learned in such a way that it captures useful information about the structure of the data in a compact form that is friendly to ML algorithms.

This assumes that there is a representation z to be found that somehow captures information about the data x but is unspecified. We don't know what z should look like because we have never observed it. For this reason, we call it a *latent* representation of the data because it is not visible to us but emerges from training the model.[1]

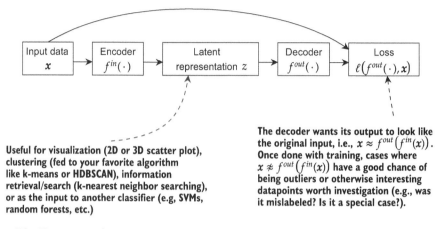

Figure 7.2   The process of autoencoding. The input goes through an encoder that produces a new representation of the data z. The representation z can be useful for lots of tasks like clustering, search, and even classification. The decoder attempts to reconstruct the original input x from the encoding z.

This may seem very silly at first glance. Couldn't we just learn a function f^{in} that does not do anything and returns the input as output? That would trivially solve the problem, but it's like taking out a loan from the bank only to *immediately* pay it back. You have *technically* satisfied all the explicit goals, but you didn't accomplish anything by doing it. This silliness is the dangerous shortcut that we want to avoid. The trick is to set up the problem so the network can't cheat like this. There are a number of different approaches to doing this, and we learn about two of them in this chapter: bottlenecks and denoising. Both of these work by constraining the network so that it is impossible to learn the naive solution.

7.1.1   *Principle component analysis is a bottleneck autoencoder*

This block of the chapter is a little more challenging to work through, but it's worth it. You'll gain a new perspective on a classic algorithm that will help you further bridge how existing tools that aren't generally thought of as deep learning are actually deeply related.

To exemplify how you can constrain a network so that it can't learn the naive `superUsefulFunction` approach, we first talk about a famous algorithm you probably know about but may not be aware is secretly an autoencoder: the feature engineering and dimensionality reduction technique known as *principle component analysis* (PCA).

---

[1]   *Latent* generally means something that isn't (easily) visible but does exist and/or can be enhanced. For example, a latent infection exists but has no symptoms, so you can't see it. But untreated, it will emerge and become more visible. *Latent* in our context is fortunately not as morbid.

PCA is used to convert a feature vector in a D-dimensional space down to a lower dimension D', which one might call an *encoder*. PCA also includes a seldom-used *decoder* step, where you can convert back (approximately) to the original D dimensional space. The following annotated equation defines the optimization problem that PCA solves:

Alter the weights W so that   the difference between   the original data

and the decoded version of   the encoded data   is as small as possible

(and please make sure the encoder is capturing as much variance in the data as possible).

$$\underset{W}{\text{minimize}} \left\| \mathbf{X} - \mathbf{X}W\ W^\top \right\|_2^2$$

subject to $W^\top W = I$

PCA is an important and widely used algorithm, so if you want to use it, you should use one of the existing implementations. But PyTorch is flexible enough for us to implement PCA ourselves. If you look closely at the equation, PCA is a *regression* problem. How? Let's look at the main part of the equation and try to annotate it again with deep learning style equations:

$$\left\| \underset{\text{label } y \in \mathbb{R}^D}{\mathbf{X}} - \mathbf{X} \overset{f(X)}{\underset{\text{encoder}}{W} \underset{\text{decoder}}{W^\top}} \right\|_2^2$$

We have one weight matrix W acting as the encoder, and its transpose $W^\top$ is acting as the decoder. That means PCA is using *weight sharing* (remember that concept from chapters 3 and 4?). The original input is on the left, and we have the 2-norm ($\|\cdot\|_2^2$), which is used by the mean squared error loss. The "subject to" part of the equation is a *constraint* requiring the weight matrix to behave in a particular way. Let's rewrite this equation in the same manner we have been doing for our neural networks:

Alter the weights W so that   the difference between   the original data

and the decoded version of the encoded data   is as small as possible

(and please make sure the encoder is capturing as much variance in the data as possible).

$$\|W^\top W - I\|_2^2 + \sum_{i=1}^{n} \ell\left(\frac{f(x_i)}{f^{out}(f^{in}(x_i))} , \frac{x_i}{y_i} \right)$$

$\|WW^\top - I\|_2^2$ is a regularization penalty based on the "subject to" constraint. Personally, I think re-expressing PCA as an autoencoder using a loss function helps make it easier to understand it. It's also more explicit that we are using $f(\cdot)$ as a single network that encompasses the sequence of the encoder $f^{in}(\cdot)$ and decoder $f^{out}(\cdot)$.

Now we have written our PCA as a loss function over all our data points. We know PCA works, and if PCA is an autoencoder, then the idea of autoencoding can't be as crazy as it first seems. So how does PCA make it work? The insight that PCA provides is that we make the *intermediate representation too small*. Remember that the first thing PCA does it go from D dimensions down to $D' < D$. Imagine if $D = 1,000,000$ and $D' = 2$. There is *no possible way* to save enough information about 1 million features in just 2 features to be able to reconstruct the input perfectly. So the best that PCA can do is learn the best 2 features possible, which then forces PCA to learn something useful. This is the primary trick to make autoencoding work: push your data into a smaller representation than you started with.

7.1.2   *Implementing PCA*

Now that we understand how PCA is an autoencoder, let's work on converting it into PyTorch code. We need to define our network function $f(x)$, given by the following equation. But how do we implement the rightmost $W^\top$ part?

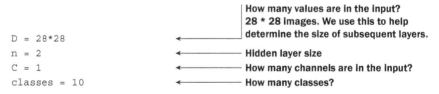

The main trick we need to implement this is to reuse the weight from a `nn.Linear` layer in PyTorch. We walk through implementing PCA in PyTorch here to hammer home the fact that *PCA is an autoencoder*. Once we have implemented PCA, we will make a few changes to convert it into a deep autoencoder, similar to how we moved from linear regression into a neural network in chapter 2. First, let's quickly define some constants for the number of features we are working with, how large our hidden layers should be, and other standard items we want:

```
D = 28*28              ←————————  How many values are in the input?
                                  28 * 28 images. We use this to help
                                  determine the size of subsequent layers.
n = 2                  ←————————  Hidden layer size
C = 1                  ←————————  How many channels are in the input?
classes = 10           ←————————  How many classes?
```

Next, let's implement this missing layer to represent $W^\top$. We call this new layer a *transpose layer*. Why? Because the mathematical operation we are using is called a *transpose*. We also add some logic to have a custom bias term for the weight transposed layer because the input layer has a matrix with shape $W \in \mathbb{R}^{D \times D'}$ and a bias vector $\boldsymbol{b} \in \mathbb{R}^{D'}$. That means $W^\top \in \mathbb{R}^{D' \times D}$, but we can't really take a meaningful transpose of $\boldsymbol{b}$. So if someone wants a bias term, it has to be a new separate one.

Our new `TransposeLinear` module follows. This class implements the `Transpose` operation $W^\top$. The matrix to transpose W must be passed in as the `linearLayer` in the constructor. This way, we can share weights between an original `nn.Linear` layer and this transposed version of that layer.

```
class TransposeLinear(nn.Module):
    def __init__(self, linearLayer, bias=True):
        """
        linearLayer: is the layer that we want to use the transpose of to
            produce the output of this layer. So the Linear layer represents
            W, and this layer represents W^T. This is accomplished via
            weight sharing by reusing the weights of linearLayer
        bias: if True, we will create a new bias term b that is learned
            separately from what is in
        linearLayer. If false, we will not use any bias vector.
        """

        super().__init__()
        self.weight = linearLayer.weight

        if bias:
            self.bias = nn.Parameter(torch.Tensor(
                linearLayer.weight.shape[1]))

        else:
            self.register_parameter('bias', None)

    def forward(self, x):
        return F.linear(x, self.weight.t(), self.bias)
```

Our class extends nn.Module. All PyTorch layers must extend this.

Creates a new bias vector. By default, PyTorch knows how to update Modules and Parameters. Since tensors are neither, the Parameter class wraps the Tensor class so PyTorch knows that the values in this tensor need to be updated by gradient descent.

Creates a new variable weight to store a reference to the original weight term

The Parameter class can't take None as an input. So if we want the bias term to exist but be potentially unused, we can use the register_parameter function to create it. The important thing here is that PyTorch always sees the same parameters regardless of the arguments for the Module.

The F directory of PyTorch contains many functions used by Modules. For example, the linear function performs a linear transform when given an input (we use the transpose of our weights) and a bias (if None, it knows to not do anything).

The forward function is the code that takes an input and produces an output.

Now that we have our `TransposeLinear` layer completed, we can implement PCA. First is the architecture, which we break into the encoder and decoder portions. Because PyTorch `Modules` are also built from `Modules`, we can define the encoder and decoder as separate parts and use both as components in a final `Module`.

Note that because the input comes in as an image with shape $(B, 1, 28, 28)$, and we are using linear layers, we first need to flatten the input into a vector of shape $(B, 28*28)$. But in the decode step, we want to have the same shape as the original data. We can use the `View` layer I've provided to convert it back. It works just like the `.view` and `.reshape` functions on tensors, except as a `Module`, for convenience:

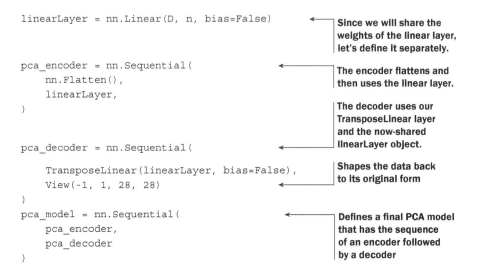

```
linearLayer = nn.Linear(D, n, bias=False)
```
Since we will share the weights of the linear layer, let's define it separately.

```
pca_encoder = nn.Sequential(
    nn.Flatten(),
    linearLayer,
)
```
The encoder flattens and then uses the linear layer.

The decoder uses our TransposeLinear layer and the now-shared linearLayer object.

```
pca_decoder = nn.Sequential(

    TransposeLinear(linearLayer, bias=False),
    View(-1, 1, 28, 28)
)
```
Shapes the data back to its original form

```
pca_model = nn.Sequential(
    pca_encoder,
    pca_decoder
)
```
Defines a final PCA model that has the sequence of an encoder followed by a decoder

PCA INITIALIZATION AND LOSS FUNCTION

We have everything we need to train up this autoencoder. But to make it *truly* PCA, we need to add the $WW^\top = I$ constraint. This constraint has a name: *orthogonality*. We won't go into the derivation of *why* PCA has this, but we will include it as a good exercise. We start our model in the right place by giving it an initial *random* set of orthogonal weights using the nn.init.orthogonal_ function. That just takes one line of code:

```
nn.init.orthogonal_(linearLayer.weight)
```

We aren't going to strictly enforce orthogonality during training because the code to do that would be a little uglier than I want. Instead, we take a common and simple approach to *encourage* orthogonality but not *require* it.[2] This is done by converting the equality $W^T W = I$ into a *penalty* or *regularizer* $\|WW^\top - I\|_2^2$. This works because if the penalty is 0, then W is orthogonal; and if the penalty is nonzero, it will increase the loss, and thus gradient decent will try to make W more orthogonal.

It is not hard to implement this. We are using the mean square error (MSE) loss function $\ell_{MSE}(f(\boldsymbol{x}), \boldsymbol{x})$ to train the self-supervision part. We can just augment this loss function with the loss over the penalty:

$$\underbrace{\ell_{MSE}(f(\boldsymbol{x}), \boldsymbol{x})}_{\text{Please learn to be a good autoencoder}} \quad + \quad \underbrace{\ell_{MSE}(WW^\top, \boldsymbol{I})}_{\text{and try to keep your weights orthogonal}}$$

The following block of code does this. As an additional step, we decrease the strength of the regularizer by a factor of 0.1 to reinforce that the autoencoding portion is more important than the orthogonality portion:

---

[2] Technically, that means we aren't learning the PCA algorithm—but we are learning something *very* similar to it. Close enough is good enough.

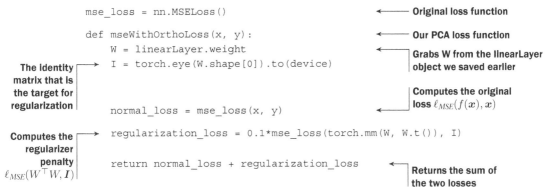

```
mse_loss = nn.MSELoss()                                    ← Original loss function

def mseWithOrthoLoss(x, y):                                ← Our PCA loss function
    W = linearLayer.weight                                 ← Grabs W from the linearLayer
    I = torch.eye(W.shape[0]).to(device)                     object we saved earlier

    normal_loss = mse_loss(x, y)                           ← Computes the original
                                                             loss ℓ_MSE(f(x), x)

    regularization_loss = 0.1*mse_loss(torch.mm(W, W.t()), I)

    return normal_loss + regularization_loss              ← Returns the sum of
                                                             the two losses
```

The identity matrix that is the target for regularization

Computes the regularizer penalty $\ell_{MSE}(W^\top W, I)$

7.1.3 Implementing PCA with PyTorch

Now we want to create a wrapper for the MNIST datasets. Why? Because the default MNIST dataset will return data in pairs (x, y) for the input and label, respectively. But in our case, the *input is the label* because we are trying to predict the output from the input. So we extend the PyTorch Dataset class to take the original tuple x, y and instead return a tuple x, x. This way, our code keeps the convention that the first item in the tuple is the input, and the second item is the desired output/label:

```
class AutoEncodeDataset(Dataset):
    """Takes a dataset with (x, y) label pairs and converts it to (x, x) pairs.
    This makes it easy to reuse other code"""

    def __init__(self, dataset):
        self.dataset = dataset

    def __len__(self):
        return len(self.dataset)

    def __getitem__(self, idx):
        x, y = self.dataset.__getitem__(idx)          ← Throws away the
        return x, x                                      original label
```

NOTE   If you were implementing an autoencoder for a real-world problem, you would have code that looks more like x = self.dataset.__getitem__(idx), because you wouldn't know the label y. Then you could return x, x.

With this AutoEncodeDataset wrapper in hand, we can load the original MNIST dataset and wrap it with AutoEncodeDataset, and we'll be ready to start training:

```
train_data = AutoEncodeDataset(torchvision.datasets.MNIST("./", train=True,
    transform=transforms.ToTensor(), download=True))
test_data_xy = torchvision.datasets.MNIST("./", train=False,
    transform=transforms.ToTensor(), download=True)
test_data_xx = AutoEncodeDataset(test_data_xy)

train_loader = DataLoader(train_data, batch_size=128, shuffle=True)
test_loader = DataLoader(test_data_xx, batch_size=128)
```

Now we can train this PCA model the same way we have been training other neural networks. The `AutoEncodeDataset` makes the input also act as the label, `pca_model` combines the sequence of encoding and decoding the data, and `mseWithOrthoLoss` implements a PCA-specific loss function that combines: 1) making the output look like the input $\ell_{MSE}(f(x), x)$, and 2) maintaining the orthogonal weights that PCA desires ($\|W^\top W - I\|_2^2 = 0$):

```
train_network(pca_model, mseWithOrthoLoss, train_loader,
    test_loader=test_loader, epochs=10, device=device)
```

7.1.4   *Visualizing PCA results*

You may have noticed that we used the hidden layer size $n = 2$. This was intentional because it lets us *plot* the results and build some good visual intuition about how autoencoders work. This is because we can use PCA to visualize our data in two dimensions when $n = 2$. This is a very common use case for PCA. Even if we used a larger target dimension, projecting the data down can make it faster and/or more accurate to search for similar data. So it is useful to have a function that will take a dataset and encode it all to the lower-dimensional space. The following function does that and copies the labels so that we can look at our results compared to the ground truth of the MNIST test data:

```
def encode_batch(encoder, dataset_to_encode):
    """
    encoder: the PyTorch network that takes in a dataset and converts it to
        a new dimension
    dataset_to_encode: a PyTorch 'Dataset' object that we want to convert.

    Returns a tuple (projected, labels) where 'projected' is the encoded
        version of the dataset, and 'labels' are the original labels
        provided by the 'dataset_to_encode'
    """
    projected = []                                 ⟵┐ Creates space to store
    labels = []                                      │ the results

    encoder = encoder.eval()                       ⟵── Switches to eval mode
    encoder = encoder.cpu()                        ⟵┐ Switches to CPU mode
                                                     │ for simplicity, but
                                                     │ you don't have to

                                                   ⟵┐ We don't want to train,
    with torch.no_grad():                            │ so torch.no_grad!
        for x, y in DataLoader(dataset_to_encode, batch_size=128):
            z = encoder(x.cpu())                          ⟵── Encodes the original data
            projected.append( z.numpy() )           ⟵┐ Stores the encoded
            labels.append( y.cpu().numpy().ravel() ) │ version and label

    projected = np.vstack(projected)                ⟵┐ Turns the results into
                                                      │ single large NumPy arrays
    labels = np.hstack(labels)
    return projected, labels                        ⟵──────── Returns the results
projected, labels = encode_batch(pca_encoder, test_data_xy)  ⟵── Projects our data
```

Using the `encode_batch` function, we have now applied PCA to the dataset, and we can plot the results with seaborn. This should look like a very familiar PCA plot: some classes have decent separation from the others, while some are clumped together. The following code has this odd bit: `hue=[str(l) for l in labels]`, `hue_order=[str(i) for i in range(10)]`, which is included to make the plot easier to read. If we used `hue=labels`, the code would work fine, but seaborn would give all the digits similar colors and that would be hard to read. By making the labels strings (`hue=[str(l) for l in labels]`), we get seaborn to give each class a more distinct color, and we use the `huge_order` to make seaborn plot the classes in the order we expect:

```
sns.scatterplot(x=projected[:,0], y=projected[:,1],
    hue=[str(l) for l in labels],
    hue_order=[str(i) for i in range(10)], legend="full")
```

`[15]:` `<AxesSubplot:>`

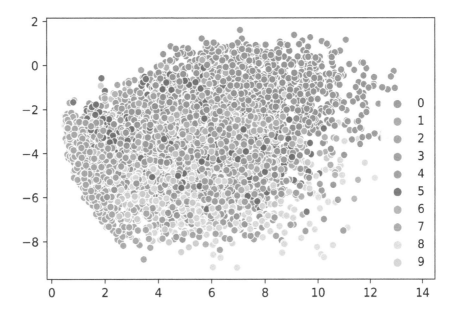

From this plot, we can get some ideas about the quality of the encoding. For example, it's probably easy to differentiate the 0 and 1 classes from all the others. Some of the others might be much harder, though; and in a truly unsupervised scenario, where we don't know the true labels, we won't be able to easily discover the distinct concepts. Another thing we can use to help judge this is the encode/decode process. If we did a good job, the output should be the same as the input. First, we define a simple helper function to plot the original input x on the left and the encoded-decoded version on the right:

```
def showEncodeDecode(encode_decode, x):
    """

    encode_decode: the PyTorch Module that does the encoding and decoding
    ➡ steps at once
    x: the input to plot as is, and after encoding & decoding it
    """

    encode_decode = encode_decode.eval()
    encode_decode = encode_decode.cpu()
    with torch.no_grad():
        x_recon = encode_decode(x.cpu())
    f, axarr = plt.subplots(1,2)
    axarr[0].imshow(x.numpy()[0,:])
    axarr[1].imshow(x_recon.numpy()[0,0,:])
```

Switches to eval mode

Always no_grad if you are not training

Moves things to the CPU so we don't have to think about what device anything is on and because this function is not performance-sensitive

Uses Matplotlib to create a side-by-side plot with the original on the left

We reuse this function throughout this chapter. First let's look at some input-output combinations for a few different digits:

```
showEncodeDecode(pca_model, test_data_xy[0][0])
showEncodeDecode(pca_model, test_data_xy[2][0])
showEncodeDecode(pca_model, test_data_xy[10][0])
```

Shows the input (left) and output (right) for three data points

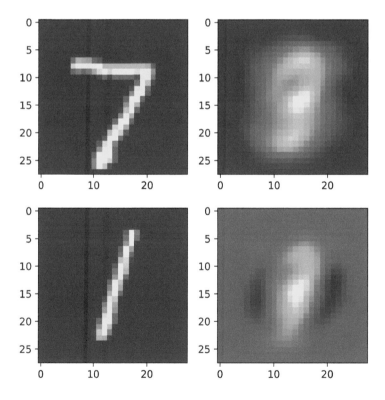

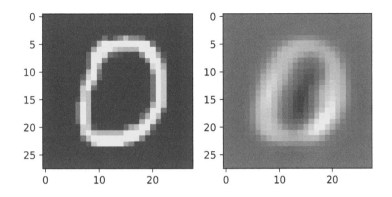

These results match what we expected based on the 2D plot. The 0 and 1 classes look kind of like a 1 and 0 after we encode and decode them. The 7 . . . not so much. Why? Well, we are converting 784 dimensions down to 2. That's a *lot* of information compression—much more than we can reasonably expect poor PCA to be able to do.

7.1.5 *A simple nonlinear PCA*

PCA is one of the simplest autoencoders we could design because it is a completely linear model. What happens if we just add a little of what we have learned about? We can add a single nonlinearity and remove the weight sharing to turn this into a small nonlinear autoencoder. Let's see how that looks:

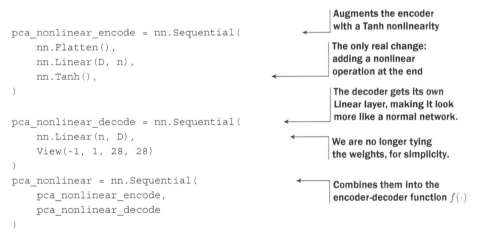

```
pca_nonlinear_encode = nn.Sequential(
    nn.Flatten(),
    nn.Linear(D, n),
    nn.Tanh(),
)

pca_nonlinear_decode = nn.Sequential(
    nn.Linear(n, D),
    View(-1, 1, 28, 28)
)
pca_nonlinear = nn.Sequential(
    pca_nonlinear_encode,
    pca_nonlinear_decode
)
```

Augments the encoder with a Tanh nonlinearity

The only real change: adding a nonlinear operation at the end

The decoder gets its own Linear layer, making it look more like a normal network.

We are no longer tying the weights, for simplicity.

Combines them into the encoder-decoder function $f(\cdot)$

Since we are no longer sharing weights between the encoder and decoder, we do not care if the weights are orthogonal. So when we train this model, we use the normal MSE loss:

```
train_network(pca_nonlinear, mse_loss, train_loader,
    test_loader=test_loader, epochs=10, device=device)
```

In the following blocks of code, we again plot all the 2D encodings and our three encoded-decoded images to see visually what has changed. This lets us look subjectively to see if the quality is better:

```
projected, labels = encode_batch(pca_nonlinear_encode, test_data_xy)
sns.scatterplot(x=projected[:,0], y=projected[:,1],
    hue=[str(l) for l in labels],
    hue_order=[str(i) for i in range(10)], legend="full" )
```

[20]:   <AxesSubplot:>

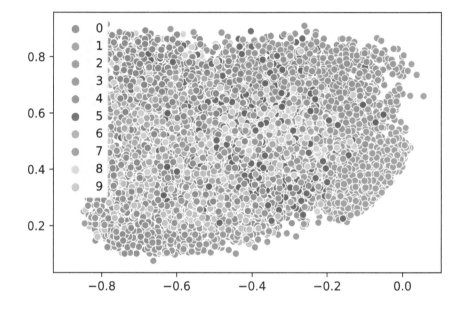

```
showEncodeDecode(pca_nonlinear, test_data_xy[0][0])
showEncodeDecode(pca_nonlinear, test_data_xy[2][0])
showEncodeDecode(pca_nonlinear, test_data_xy[10][0])
```

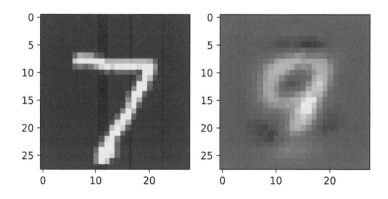

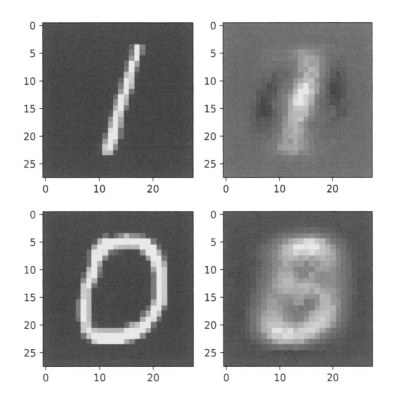

Overall, the change is noticeable but not clearly different. The 2D plot still has a lot of overlap. The encode-decode images show a few artifacts: 0, 1, and 7 are qualitatively similar but with different styles. What was the point? We have turned PCA into an autoencoder with one nonlinearity, so we have modified the PCA algorithm; and because we did so in PyTorch, it trained up and worked out of the box. Now we can try to make bigger changes to get a better result. As a theme of deep learning, if we make this model deeper by adding more layers, we should be able to successfully improve the results.

7.2 Designing autoencoding neural networks

PCA is a very popular method for dimensionality reduction and visualization, and any situation where you would use PCA is one where you may want to instead use an *autoencoding network*. An autoencoding network is the same idea, but we will make the encoder and decoder larger networks with more layers so they can learn more powerful and complex encoders and decoders. Since we have seen that PCA is an autoencoder, an autoencoding network may be a more accurate choice by being able to learn more complex functions.

Autoencoding networks are also useful for *outlier detection*. You want to detect outliers so that you can have them manually reviewed, because an outlier is unlikely to be handled well by a model. An autoencoder can detect outliers by looking at how well it reconstructed the input. If you can reconstruct the input well, the data probably looks like normal data you've seen. If you *cannot* successfully reconstruct the input, it is probably *unusual* and thus an outlier. This process is summarized in figure 7.3. You can use this approach to find potentially bad data points in your training data or validate user-submitted data (e.g., if someone uploads a picture of their face to an application that looks for ear infections, you should detect the face as an outlier and not make a diagnosis).

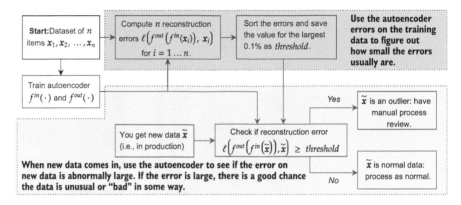

Figure 7.3 **Example application of autoencoders to detect outliers. A dataset is used to train the autoencoder, and then you compute all the reconstruction errors. Assuming that 0.1% of the data is abnormal, it should be the most difficult to reconstruct. If you find the threshold for the top 0.1% of errors, you can apply that threshold to new data to detect outliers. Outliers are often ill-behaved, and it may be better to treat them differently or give them an extra review. Outlier detection can be done on training data or new testing data. You can change the 0.1% to match what you believe is happening in your dataset.**

Now let's talk about how to set up a deep learning-based autoencoder. The standard approach is to make a symmetric architecture between the encoder and decoder: keep the same number of layers in each and put them in the reverse order (encoder goes from big to small, and decoder goes from small to big). We also use a *bottleneck* style encoder, meaning the layers have progressively fewer neurons. This is shown in figure 7.4.

Autoencoders do not *have* to be symmetric. They work *just fine* if they are not. This is done purely to make it easier to think and reason about the network. This way, you are making half as many decisions about how many layers are in the network, how many neurons are in each layer, and so on.

The bottleneck in the encoder *is* important, though. Just as PCA did, by pushing down to a smaller representation, we make it impossible for the network to cheat and learn the naive solution of immediately returning the input as the output. Instead, the network must learn to identify high-level concepts like "there is a circle located at the center," which could be used for encoding (and then decoding) the numbers 6 and 0. By learning multiple high-level concepts, the network is forced to start learning useful representations.

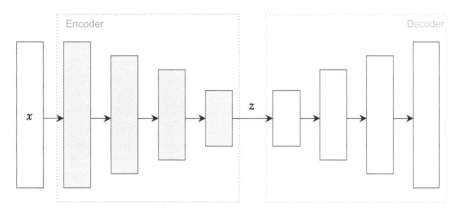

Figure 7.4 Example of a standard autoencoder design. The input comes in on the left. The encoder starts out large and tapers down the size of the hidden layers at each step. Because autoencoders are usually symmetric, our decoder will receive the small representation z and begin expanding it back to the original size.

NOTE The autoencoder can also be seen as a way to produce embeddings. The encoder part of the network in particular makes an excellent candidate for an embedding construction. The approach is unsupervised, so you don't need labels, and the encoder's lower-dimensional output works better with common tools for visualization and nearest-neighbor search.

7.2.1 Implementing an autoencoder

Since we have gone through the pain of implementing PCA, the autoencoder should be easier and more straightforward when done in this style, primarily because we do not share any weights across layers and no longer need the orthogonal constraint on the weights. For simplicity, we focus on fully connected networks for autoencoders, but the concepts are widely applicable. To start, let's define another helper function getLayer that creates a single hidden layer for us to place in a network, similar to what we did in chapter 6:

```
def getLayer(in_size, out_size):
    """
    in_size: how many neurons/features are coming into this layer
    out_size: how many neurons/outputs this hidden layer should produce
    """
    return nn.Sequential(                    ← Organizes the conceptual
        nn.Linear(in_size, out_size),          "block" of a hidden layer
        nn.BatchNorm1d(out_size),              into a Sequential object
        nn.ReLU())
```

With this helper function in hand, the following code shows how easy it is to implement an autoencoder using the more advanced tools we have learned about, like batch normalization and ReLU activations. It uses a simple strategy of decreasing the number of neurons in each hidden layer by a fixed pattern. In this case, we divide the number of neurons by 2, then 3, then 4, and so on until the last layer of the decoder, where we jump straight to the target size D'. The pattern used to decrease the number of layers is not that important, as long as the size of the layers consistently decreases:

```
auto_encoder = nn.Sequential(
    nn.Flatten(),
    getLayer(D, D//2),
    getLayer(D//2, D//3),
    getLayer(D//3, D//4),
    nn.Linear(D//4, n),
)
```

← Dividing by 2, 3, 4, etc., is one of many patterns that can be used.

← Each layer has a smaller output size than the previous one.

← Jumps down to the target dimension

← Decoder does the same layers/sizes in reverse to be symmetric

```
auto_decoder = nn.Sequential(
    getLayer(n, D//4),
    getLayer(D//4, D//3),
    getLayer(D//3, D//2),

    nn.Linear(D//2, D),
    View(-1, 1, 28, 28)
)
auto_encode_decode = nn.Sequential(
    auto_encoder,
    auto_decoder
)
```

← Each layer increases in size because we are in the decoder.

← Reshapes to match the original shape

← Combines into a deep autoencoder

As always, we can train this network using the exact same function. We stick with the mean squared error, which is very common in autoencoders:

```
train_network(auto_encode_decode, mse_loss, train_loader,
    test_loader=test_loader, epochs=10, device=device)
```

7.2.2   *Visualizing autoencoder results*

How did our new autoencoder do? The 2D plot shows *much* more separation in the projected dimension z. Classes 0, 6, and 3 are *very* well separated from all the others. In addition, the middle area where there are more classes next to each other at least has more continuity and uniformity in the class present. The classes have distinct homes in the middle area, rather than being smeared on top of each other:

```
projected, labels = encode_batch(auto_encoder, test_data_xy)
sns.scatterplot(x=projected[:,0], y=projected[:,1],
    hue=[str(l) for l in labels],
    hue_order=[str(i) for i in range(10)], legend="full")
```

`[25]:  <AxesSubplot:>`

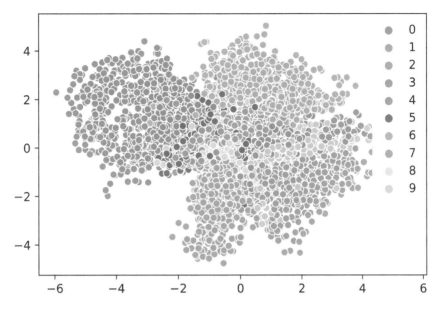

This is also one way to use autoencoders to explore unknown data. If we did not know the class labels, we might have concluded from this projection that there were likely at least two to four different subpopulations in the data.

We can also look at some examples of the encode-decode cycle. Unlike before, the reconstructions are now crisp, with much less blur. But it's not perfect: class 4 is usually hard to separate from others and has low-quality reconstructions:

```
showEncodeDecode(auto_encode_decode, test_data_xy[0][0])
showEncodeDecode(auto_encode_decode, test_data_xy[2][0])
showEncodeDecode(auto_encode_decode, test_data_xy[6][0])
showEncodeDecode(auto_encode_decode, test_data_xy[23][0])
```

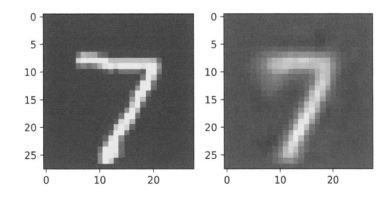

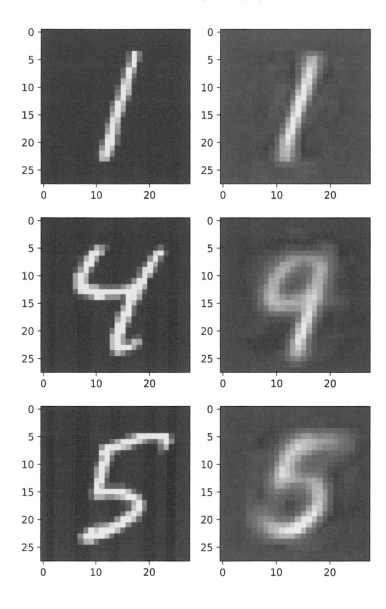

Try playing with the code and looking at the results for different data points. If you do, you may start to notice that the reconstructions do not always maintain the *style* of the inputs. This is more obvious with the 5 here: The reconstruction is smoother and more pristine than the original input. Is this a good thing or a bad thing?

From the perspective of how we trained the model, it's a bad thing. The reconstruction *is different* from the input, and the goal was to *exactly* reconstruct the input.

However, our true goal is not to just learn to reconstruct inputs from themselves. We already have the input. Our goal was to learn a useful representation of the data without needing to know the data labels. From this perspective, the behavior is a good thing: it means there are multiple different potential "5"'s that could be the input and would be mapped to the same "5" reconstruction. In this sense, the network has on its own learned that there is a *canonical* or *prototypical* 5, without being explicitly told about the concept of 5 or even that there are distinct numbers present.

But the example of the digit 4 is a bad failure case. The network reconstructed a completely different digit because the restriction is *too strong*: the network was forced down to just two dimensions and couldn't learn all the complexity in the data with such little space. This meant forcing out the concept of a 4. Similar to PCA, if you give the network a larger bottleneck (more features to use), the reconstructions will steadily improve in quality. Using two dimensions is great for visualization in scatterplots, but for other applications, you probably want to use a few more features. (This, like most things in ML, is problem-specific. You should make sure you have a way to test your results to compare them, and then use that test to determine how many features you should use).

7.3 Bigger autoencoders

All the autoencoding we have done so far has been based on projecting down to two dimensions, which we have already said makes the problem exceptionally hard. Your intuition should tell you that if we make the target dimension size D' a little larger, our reconstructions should improve in quality. But what if we made the target size *larger* than the original input? Would this work? We can easily modify our autoencoder to try this and see what happens. In the following block of code, we simply jump up to $D' = 2 \cdot D$ right after the first layer of the encoder and stay at that number of neurons for the entire process:

```
auto_encoder_big = nn.Sequential(
    nn.Flatten(),
    getLayer(D, D*2),
    getLayer(D*2, D*2),
    getLayer(D*2, D*2),
    nn.Linear(D*2, D*2),
)

auto_decoder_big = nn.Sequential(
    getLayer(D*2, D*2),
    getLayer(D*2, D*2),
    getLayer(D*2, D*2),
    nn.Linear(D*2, D),
    View(-1, 1, 28, 28)
)

auto_encode_decode_big = nn.Sequential(
    auto_encoder_big,
    auto_decoder_big
)
```

```
train_network(auto_encode_decode_big, mse_loss, train_loader,
    test_loader=test_loader, epochs=10, device=device)
```

We can't make a 2D plot since we have too many dimensions. But we can still do the encode/decode comparisons on the data to see how our new autoencoder performs. If we plot some examples, it becomes clear that we now have *very good* reconstructions, which include even minute details from the original input. For example, the following 7 has a slight uptick at the top left and a slightly thicker ending at the bottom, which are present in the reconstruction. The 4 that was completely mangled previously has a lot of unique curves and styles that are also faithfully preserved:

```
showEncodeDecode(auto_encode_decode_big, test_data_xy[0][0])
showEncodeDecode(auto_encode_decode_big, test_data_xy[6][0])
showEncodeDecode(auto_encode_decode_big, test_data_xy[10][0])
```

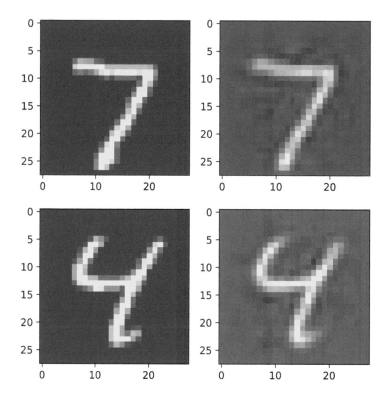

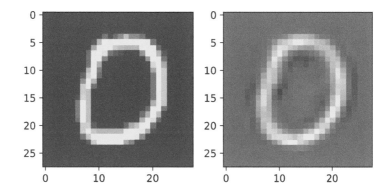

So the question is, is this a better autoencoder than the previous one? Have we learned a useful representation? It's a hard question to answer because we are using the input reconstruction as the loss of the network, but it is not what we truly care about. We want the network to learn *useful* representations. This is a variant of the classic unsupervised learning problem: if you don't know what you are looking for, how do you know if you are doing a good job?

7.3.1 Robustness to noise

To help us answer the question about which autoencoder is better, $D' = 2$ or $D' = 2 \cdot D$, we will add some noise to our data. Why? One intuition we can use is that if a representation is good, it should be *robust*. Imagine if the clean data we have been using was like a road, and our model was the car. If the road is pristine and smooth, the car will handle well. But what if there are potholes and cracks (read, noise) in the road? A good car should still be able to drive successfully. Similarly, if we have noisy data, an ideal model will still perform well.

There are *many* different ways we could make our data noisy. One of the easiest is to add noise from a normal distribution. We denote the normal distribution as $N(\mu, \sigma)$, where μ is the mean value returned and σ is the standard deviation. If s is a value sampled from the normal distribution, we denote that as $s \sim N(\mu, \sigma)$.

To make our data noisy, we use PyTorch to construct an object that represents the normal distribution and perturbs the input data such that we get $\tilde{x} = x + s$, where $s \sim N(\mu, \sigma)$. To represent the normal distribution $N(\mu, \sigma)$, PyTorch provides the `torch.distributions.Normal` class:

```
normal = torch.distributions.Normal(0, 0.5)
```

First argument is the mean μ; second is the standard deviation σ

This class has a `sample` method that performs the $s \sim$ step. We use the `sample_shape` argument to tell it that we want a tensor with a shape of `sample_shape` to be filled with random values from this distribution. The following function takes an input x and sample noise that is the same shape as x so we can add it, creating our noisy sample $\tilde{x} = x + s$:

```
def addNoise(x, device='cpu'):
    """
    We will use this helper function to add noise to some data.
    x: the data we want to add noise to
    device: the CPU or GPU that the input is located on.
    """
    return x + normal.sample(sample_shape=
      torch.Size(x.shape)).to(device)    ←—— $x + s$
```

With our simple `addNoise` function in place, we can try it with our big model. We have intentionally set the amount of noise to be fairly large to make the changes and differences between models obvious. For the following input data, you should see that the reconstructions are garbled, with extraneous lines. Since the noise is random, you can run the code multiple times to see different versions:

```
showEncodeDecode(auto_encode_decode_big, addNoise(test_data_xy[6][0]))
showEncodeDecode(auto_encode_decode_big, addNoise(test_data_xy[23][0]))
```

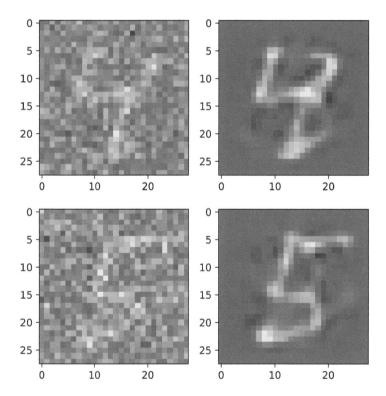

This would seem to indicate that our large autoencoder with $D' = 2 \cdot D$ is not very robust. What happens if we apply the same noisy data to our original autoencoder, which uses $D = 2$? You can see that next. The 5 is reconstructed almost exactly as it was before: a little blurry, but clearly a 5:

```
showEncodeDecode(auto_encode_decode, addNoise(test_data_xy[6][0]))
showEncodeDecode(auto_encode_decode, addNoise(test_data_xy[23][0]))
```

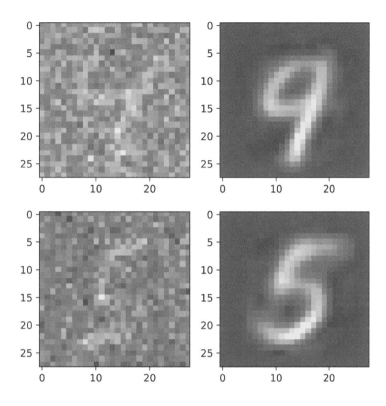

If you run the 4 through multiple times, sometimes you get a 4 back out of the decoder, and sometimes you get something else. This is because the noise is different every time, and our 2D plot showed that the 4 was being conflated with many other classes.

Based on this experiment, we can see that as we make the encoding dimension D' smaller, the model becomes *more robust*. If we let the encoding dimension become too large, it may be good at performing reconstructions on easy data, but it is not robust to changes and noise. Part of this is because when $D' \geq D$, it becomes easy for the model to learn a simple approach. It has more than enough capacity to copy the input and learn to regurgitate what it was given. By constraining the model with a smaller capacity ($D' \leq D$), the only way it can learn to solve the task is by creating a more compact representation of the input data. Ideally, you try to find a dimension D' that fits a balance between reconstructing the data well but using as small an encoding dimension as possible.

7.4   Denoising autoencoders

It is not easy to balance having D' small enough to be robust but large enough to do well at reconstruction. But there is a trick we can play that will allow us to have large $D' > D$ *and* learn a robust model. The trick is to create what is called a *denoising autoencoder*. A denoising autoencoder adds noise to the encoder's input while still expecting the decoder to produce a clean image. So our math goes from $\ell(f(\boldsymbol{x}), \boldsymbol{x})$ to $\ell(f(\tilde{\boldsymbol{x}}), \boldsymbol{x})$. If we do this, there is no naive solution of just copying the input, because we perturb it before giving it to the network. The network must learn how to remove the noise, or denoise, the input and thus allows us to use $D' > D$ while still obtaining robust representations.

Denoising networks have a lot of practical usages. If you can make synthetic noise that is realistic to the issues you might see in real life, you can create models that remove the noise and improve the accuracy by making the data cleaner. Libraries like scikit-image (https://scikit-image.org) are available with many transforms that can be used to make noisy images, and I've personally used this approach to improve fingerprint recognition algorithms.[3] How I used a denoising autoencoder is shown in figure 7.5, which is also a summary of how denoising autoencoders are typically set up. The original (or sometimes very clean) data comes in at the start, and we apply noise-generating processes to it. The more that noise looks like the kinds of issues you see in real data, the better. The noisy/corrupted version of the data is given as the input to the autoencoder, but the loss is computed against the original clean data.

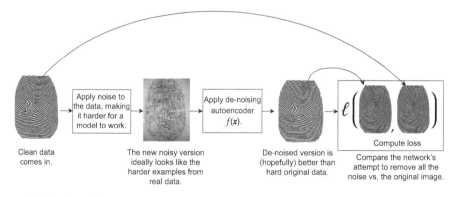

Figure 7.5   The denoising autoencoder processes applied to fingerprint images. This used special software that generates hyper-realistic fingerprint images, with the goal of removing that noise to make fingerprint processing less error prone. You can still get good results with simpler and unrealistic noise.

---

[3]   E. Raff, "Neural fingerprint enhancement," in *17th IEEE International Conference on Machine Learning and Applications (ICMLA)*, 2018, pp. 118–124, https://doi.org/10.1109/ICMLA.2018.00025.

7.4.1 Denoising with Gaussian noise

We will make only one change to our previous `auto_encoder_big` model: we will add a new layer at the beginning of the encoder subnetwork, which adds noise to the input *only when we are training*. The assumption is usually that our training data is relatively clean and prepared, and we are adding noise to make it more robust. If we are then *using* the model, and no longer training, we want to get the best answer we can—which means we want the cleanest data possible. Adding noise at that stage would make our lives more difficult, and if the input already had noise, we would just compound the problem.

So the first code we need is a new `AdditiveGaussNoise` layer. It takes the input x in. If we are in training mode (denoted by `self.training`), we add noise to the input; otherwise we return it unperturbed:

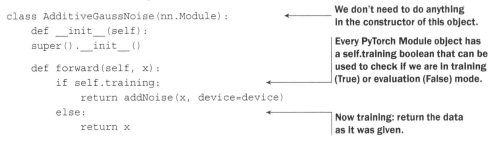

```
class AdditiveGaussNoise(nn.Module):          ◄────  We don't need to do anything
    def __init__(self):                             in the constructor of this object.
        super().__init__()
                                                     Every PyTorch Module object has
    def forward(self, x):                            a self.training boolean that can be
        if self.training:                            used to check if we are in training
            return addNoise(x, device=device)  ◄──── (True) or evaluation (False) mode.
        else:
            return x                           ◄──── Now training: return the data
                                                     as it was given.
```

Next, we redefine the same large autoencoder as before, where $D' = 2 \cdot D$. The only difference is that we insert the `AdditiveGaussNoise` layer at the start of the network:

```
dnauto_encoder_big = nn.Sequential(
    nn.Flatten(),
    AdditiveGaussNoise(),          ◄────  Only addition! We hope
    getLayer(D, D*2),                     inserting noise here helps.
    getLayer(D*2, D*2),
    getLayer(D*2, D*2),
    nn.Linear(D*2, D*2),
)

dnauto_decoder_big = nn.Sequential(
    getLayer(D*2, D*2),
    getLayer(D*2, D*2),
    getLayer(D*2, D*2),
    nn.Linear(D*2, D),
    View(-1, 1, 28, 28)
)

dnauto_encode_decode_big = nn.Sequential(
    dnauto_encoder_big,
    dnauto_decoder_big
)
train_network(dnauto_encode_decode_big, mse_loss, train_loader,
    test_loader=test_loader, epochs=10, device=device)  ◄──── Trains as usual
```

How well does it do? Following, we can see the same data reconstructed when there is and is not noise. The new denoising model is clearly the best at creating reconstructions of all the models we have developed so far. In both cases, the denoising autoencoder captures most of the style of the individual digits. The denoising approach still misses small details, likely because they are so small that the model isn't sure if they are a real part of the style or part of the noise. For example, the flourishes on the bottom of the 4 and the top of the 5 are missing after reconstruction:

```
showEncodeDecode(dnauto_encode_decode_big, test_data_xy[6][0])
showEncodeDecode(dnauto_encode_decode_big, addNoise(test_data_xy[6][0]))
```

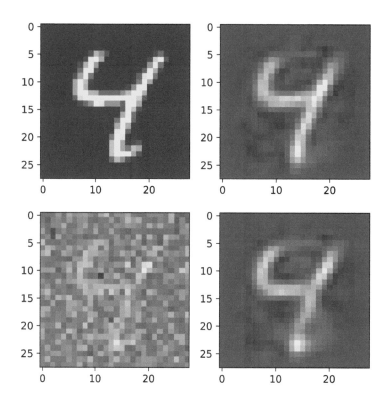

```
showEncodeDecode(dnauto_encode_decode_big, test_data_xy[23][0])
showEncodeDecode(dnauto_encode_decode_big, addNoise(test_data_xy[23][0]))
```

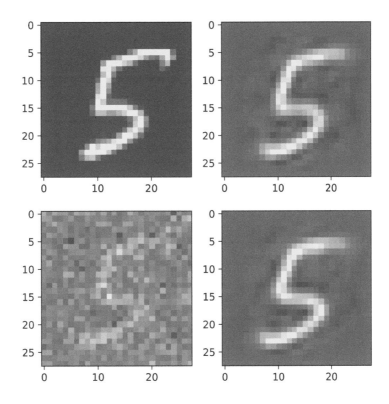

The denoising approach is very popular for training autoencoders, and the trick of introducing your own perturbations into the data is widely used to build more accurate and robust models. As you learn more about deep learning and different applications, you will find many forms and spins on this approach.

Beyond helping learn more robust representations, the denoising approach can itself be a useful model. Noise can naturally occur in many situations. For example, when performing optical character recognition (OCR) to convert an image into searchable text, you can get noise from damage to the camera, damage to the document (e.g., water or coffee stains), changes in lighting, objects casting shadows, and so on. Many OCR systems have been improved by learning to add noise that looks like the noise seen in real life and asking the model to learn in spite of it.

DENOISING WITH DROPOUT

Adding Gaussian noise can be cumbersome because we need to figure out exactly how much noise to add, which can change from dataset to dataset. A second, more popular approach is to use *dropout*.

Dropout is a very simple idea: with some probability p, zero out any given feature value. This forces the network to be robust because it can *never* rely on any specific feature or neuron value, since $p\%$ of the time, the feature or value will not be there. Dropout is a very popular regularizer that can be applied to both the *input* of a network and to the *hidden layers*.

The following code block trains up a dropout-based denoising autoencoder. By default, dropout uses $p = 50\%$, which is fine for hidden layers but on the aggressive size for the input. So for the input, we apply only $p = 20\%$:

```
dnauto_encoder_dropout = nn.Sequential(
    nn.Flatten(),
    nn.Dropout(p=0.2),          ⟵   For the input, we usually drop
                                     only 5 to 20% of the values.
    getLayer(D, D*2),
    nn.Dropout(),               ⟵
    getLayer(D*2, D*2),              By default, dropout uses 50%
                                     probability to zero out values.
    nn.Dropout(),
    getLayer(D*2, D*2),
    nn.Dropout(),
    nn.Linear(D*2, D*2)
)

dnauto_decoder_dropout = nn.Sequential(
    getLayer(D*2, D*2),
    nn.Dropout(),
    getLayer(D*2, D*2),
    nn.Dropout(),
    getLayer(D*2, D*2),
    nn.Dropout(),
    nn.Linear(D*2, D),
    View(-1, 1, 28, 28)
)

dnauto_encode_decode_dropout = nn.Sequential(
    dnauto_encoder_big,
    dnauto_decoder_big
)
train_network(dnauto_encode_decode_dropout, mse_loss,   ⟵   Trains as usual
    train_loader, test_loader=test_loader, epochs=10,
    device=device)
```

Now that the model is trained, let's apply it to some of the test data. Dropout can encourage a large degree of robustness, which we can show off by applying it to both dropout noise and Gaussian noise. The latter is something the network has never seen before, but that does not stop the autoencoder from faithfully determining an accurate reconstruction:

```
showEncodeDecode(dnauto_encode_decode_dropout,
    test_data_xy[6][0])
showEncodeDecode(dnauto_encode_decode_dropout,
    addNoise(test_data_xy[6][0]))
showEncodeDecode(dnauto_encode_decode_dropout,
    nn.Dropout()(test_data_xy[6][0]))
```

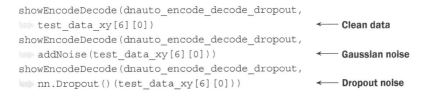

←——— **Clean data**

←——— **Gaussian noise**

←——— **Dropout noise**

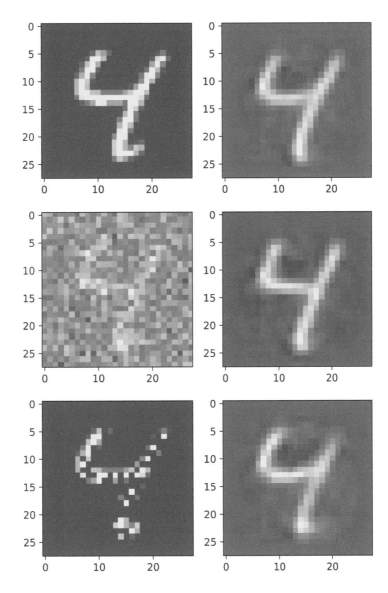

The rise and fall of dropout

The origins of dropout began with denoising autoencoders way back in 2008[a] but was applied to only the input. Later it was developed into a more general-purpose regularizer[b] and played a significant role in the rebirth of neural networks as a field and research area.

Like most regularizers, dropout had the goal of improving generalization and reducing overfitting. It was quite good at it and had an attractive and intuitive story about how it worked. For many years, dropout was a critical tool for getting good results, and implementing a network without it was almost impossible. Dropout still works as a regularizer and is useful and used, but it is not ubiquitous as it once was. The tools we have learned thus far, like normalization layers, better optimizers, and residual connections, give us most of the benefits of dropout.

Using dropout is not a *bad* thing, and I'm being hyperbolic by referring to "the fall of dropout." The technique has simply become less popular over time. My unsubstantiated theory as to why is that first, it is a little slower to train, requiring lots of random numbers and increased memory use when we can get most of its benefits now without those costs. Second, dropout is applied differently at training versus test time. During training, you lose ~50% of your neurons, making the network effectively smaller. But during validation, you get all 100% of your neurons. This can cause the confusing situation where testing performance looks better than training performance because train and test are being evaluated in different ways. (Technically, the same is true of batch normalization, but the inversion isn't as common.) I think people opted for the slightly less expensive and less perplexing results of other methods. That said, dropout is still a great default choice to use as a regularizer for new architectures where you are not sure what does or does not work.

---

[a]   P. Vincent, H. Larochelle, Y. Bengio, and P.A. Manzagol, "Extracting and composing robust features with denoising autoencoders," in *Proceedings of the 25th International Conference on Machine Learning*, New York: Association for Computing Machinery, 2008, pp. 1096–1103, https://doi.org/10.1145/1390156.1390294.

[b]   N. Srivastava, G. Hinton, A. Krizhevsky, I. Sutskever, and R. Salakhutdinov, "Dropout: a simple way to prevent neural networks from overfitting," *The Journal of Machine Learning Research*, vol. 15, no. 1, pp. 1929–1958, 2014.

7.5   *Autoregressive models for time series and sequences*

The autoencoding approach has been very successful for images, signals, and even fully connected models with tabular data. But what if our data is a sequence problem? Especially if our data is in a language represented by discrete tokens, it's hard to add meaningful noise to things like a letter or word. Instead, we can use an *autoregressive model*, which is an approach specifically designed for time-series problems.

You can use an autoregressive model for basically all the same applications for which you might use an autoencoding one. You can use the representation an autoregressive model learns as the input to another ML algorithm that doesn't understand sequences. For example, you could train an autoregressive model on book reviews of *Inside Deep*

Learning and then a clustering algorithm like k-means or HDBSCAN to cluster those reviews.[4] Since these algorithms do not naturally take text as input, the autoregressive model is a nice way to quickly expand the reach of your favorite ML tools.

Let's say you have t steps of your data: $x_1, x_2, \ldots, x_{t-1}, x_t$. The goal of an autoregressive model is to predict x_{t+1} given all the previous items in the sequence. The mathy way to write this would be $\mathbb{P}(x_{t+1}|x_1, x_2, \ldots, x_t)$, which is saying

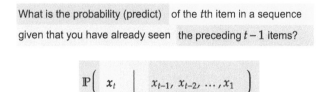

The autoregressive approach is still a form of self-supervision because the next item in a sequence is a trivial component of having the data in the first place. If you treat the sentence "This is a sentence" as a sequence of characters, you, by definition, know that T is the first item, h the second, i the third, and so on.

Figure 7.6 illustrates how autoregressive models happen at a high level. A sequence-based model is shown in the green blocks and takes in an input x_i. The prediction at the ith step is thus $\hat{x}_i$. We then use the loss function ℓ to compute the loss between the current prediction $\hat{x}_i$ and the *next input* x_{i+1}, $\ell(\hat{x}_i, x_{i+1})$. So for an input with T time steps, we have $T - 1$ loss calculations: the last time step T can't be used as an input because there is no $T + 1$th item to compare it against.

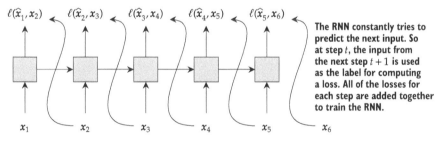

Every item in the sequence gets processed one at a time in the correct order. When training, future inputs $(t + 1)$ are used as the labels for current inputs (t).

Figure 7.6 Example of an autoregressive setup. The inputs are at the bottom, and the outputs are at the top. For an input x_i, the prediction from the autoregressive model is $\hat{x}_i$, and the label $y_i = x_{i+1}$.

---

[4] You should look up "topic modeling" algorithms if you want to maximize your results with text data. There are deep topic models, but they are a bit beyond what we cover in this book. That said, I have seen people be reasonably successful with this autoregressive approach, which is more flexible with new situations and types of data than topic models are.

You may have guessed from the look of this diagram that we will use a recurrent neural network to implement our autoregressive models. RNNs are great for sequence-based problems like this one. The big change compared to our previous use of RNNs is that we will make a prediction at *every* step, instead of just the *last* step.

A type of autoregressive model popularized by Andrej Karpathy (http://karpathy.github.io) is called *char-RNN* (character RNN). This is an autoregressive approach where the inputs/outputs are characters, and we'll show a simple way to implement a char-RNN model on some Shakespeare data.

> **NOTE** While RNNs are an appropriate and common architecture to use for autoregressive models, bidirectional RNNs are not. This is because an autoregressive model is making predictions about the future. If we used a bidirectional model, we would have information about the future content in the sequence, and knowing the future is cheating! Bi-directional RNNs were useful when we wanted to make a prediction about the *whole* sequence, but now that we are making predictions about the input, we need to enforce a no-bidirectional policy to make sure our models do not get to peek at information they should not see.

7.5.1 *Implementing the char-RNN autoregressive text model*

The first thing we need is our data. Andrej Karpathy has shared some text from Shakespeare online that we will download. There are about 100,000 characters in this text, so we store the data in a variable called `shakespear_100k`. We use this dataset to show the process of training an autoregressive model, as well as its generative capabilities:

```
from io import BytesIO
from zipfile import ZipFile
from urllib.request import urlopen
import re

all_data = []
resp = urlopen(
➥    "https://cs.stanford.edu/people/karpathy/char-rnn/shakespear.txt")
shakespear_100k = resp.read()
shakespear_100k = shakespear_100k.decode('utf-8').lower()
```

Now we will build a vocabulary Σ of all the characters in this dataset. One change you could make is to not use the `lower()` function to convert everything to lowercase. As we are exploring deep learning, these early decisions are important for how our model will eventually be used and how useful it will be. So, you should learn to recognize choices like this *as choices*. I've chosen to use all lowercase data, and as a result, our vocabulary is smaller. This reduces the difficulty of the task but means our model can't learn about capitalization.

Here's the code:

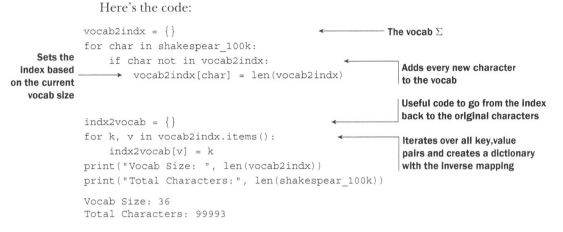

```
vocab2indx = {}                                    ←——————— The vocab Σ
for char in shakespear_100k:
    if char not in vocab2indx:                     ←———
        vocab2indx[char] = len(vocab2indx)              Adds every new character
                                                        to the vocab

                                                        Useful code to go from the index
                                                        back to the original characters
indx2vocab = {}
for k, v in vocab2indx.items():                    ←———
    indx2vocab[v] = k                                   Iterates over all key,value
print("Vocab Size: ", len(vocab2indx))                  pairs and creates a dictionary
print("Total Characters:", len(shakespear_100k))        with the inverse mapping

Vocab Size: 36
Total Characters: 99993
```

Sets the index based on the current vocab size

Next we take a very simple approach to build an autoregressive dataset. We have the original 100,000 characters in one long sequence since they are taken from one of Shakespeare's plays. If we break this sequence into chunks that are sufficiently long, we can almost guarantee that each chunk will contain a few complete sentences. We obtain each chunk by indexing into a position `start` and grabbing a slice of the text `[start:start+chunk_size]`. Since the dataset is autoregressive, our *labels* are the tokens starting one character over. This can be done by grabbing a new slice shifted by one, `[start+1:start+1+chunk_size]`. This is shown in figure 7.7.

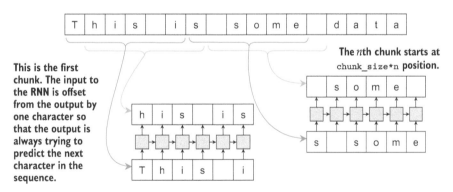

This is the first chunk. The input to the RNN is offset from the output by one character so that the output is always trying to predict the next character in the sequence.

The *n*th chunk starts at `chunk_size*n` position.

Figure 7.7   Red shows grabbing the input, and yellow the output, using chunks of six characters. This makes it easy to create the dataset for the model where every batch size has the same length, simplifying our code and ensuring maximum GPU utilization (no work done on padded inputs/outputs).

The following code uses this strategy to implement the dataset for autoregressive problems from a large text corpus. We assume the corpus exists as one long string, and it is OK to concatenate multiple files together into one long string since our chunks are smaller than most documents. While we are giving our model the difficulty of having to learn *starting at a random position that is probably part-way into a word*, it makes it very easy for us to implement all of the code:

```python
class AutoRegressiveDataset(Dataset):
    """
    Creates an autoregressive dataset from one single, long, source
    sequence by breaking it up into "chunks".
    """

    def __init__(self, large_string, max_chunk=500):
        """
        large_string: the original long source sequence that chunks will
        be extracted from
        max_chunk: the maximum allowed size of any chunk.
        """
        self.doc = large_string
        self.max_chunk = max_chunk

    def __len__(self):
        return (len(self.doc)-1) // self.max_chunk

    def __getitem__(self, idx):
        start = idx*self.max_chunk

        sub_string = self.doc[start:start+self.max_chunk]
        x = [vocab2indx[c] for c in sub_string]
        sub_string = self.doc[start+1:start+self.max_chunk+1]
        y = [vocab2indx[c] for c in sub_string]
        return torch.tensor(x, dtype=torch.int64), torch.tensor(y,
            dtype=torch.int64)
```

The number of items is the number of characters divided by chunk size.

Computes the starting position for the idx'th chunk

Converts the substring into integers based on our vocab

Grabs the input substring

Grabs the label substring by shifting over by 1

Converts the label substring into integers based on our vocab

Now comes the tricky part: implementing an autoregressive RNN model. For this we use a gated recurrent unit (GRU) instead of long short-term memory (LSTM), because the code will be a little easier to read since the GRU has only the hidden states h_t and does not have any context states c_t. The high-level strategy for our implementation is given in figure 7.8.

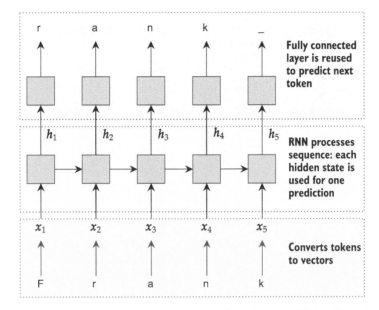

Figure 7.8 Autoregressive RNN design. The input (starting from the bottom) is in yellow, where an `nn.Embedding` layer converts each character into a vector. These vectors are fed into an RNN layer, shown in green, which sequentially processes each character. Then a set of fully connected layers processes each RNN hidden state h_t independently (via weight sharing) to make a prediction about the next token.

DEFINING AN AUTOREGRESSIVE CONSTRUCTOR

Our constructor takes some familiar arguments. We want to know the size of the vocabulary `num_embeddings`, how many dimensions in the embedding layer `embd_size`, the number of neurons in each hidden layer `hidden_size`, and the number of RNN layers `layers=1`:

```
class AutoRegressive(nn.Module):

    def __init__(self, num_embeddings, embd_size, hidden_size, layers=1):
        super(AutoRegressive, self).__init__()
        self.hidden_size = hidden_size
        self.embd = nn.Embedding(num_embeddings, embd_size)
```

Our first major change to our architecture is that we do not use the normal `nn.GRU` module. The normal `nn.RNN`, `nn.LSTM` and `nn.GRU` modules take in *all* the time steps at once and return *all the outputs* at once. You can use these to implement an autoregressive model, but we are instead going to use the `nn.GRUCell` module. The `GRUCell` processes sequences *one item at a time*. This is slower but can make it easier to handle inputs with an unknown and variable length. This approach is summarized in figure 7.9. The `Cell` classes will be useful once we are finished training the model, but I don't want to ruin the surprise—we will come back to *why* we are doing it this way in a moment.

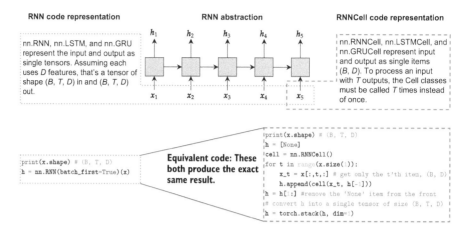

Figure 7.9 Example demonstrating the primary difference between the RNN and cell classes in PyTorch. Left: Normal RNNs process the entire sequence in a single operation, making them faster but requiring all data to be available at once. Right: Cell classes process items one at a time, making them slower but easier to use when you don't have all the inputs already available.

If we want multiple `layers` of an RNN, we have to manually specify and run them ourselves. We can do this by using a `ModuleList` to specify multiple modules in a group. This means our initialization code after `self.embd` looks like this:

```
self.layers = nn.ModuleList([nn.GRUCell(embd_size, hidden_size)] +
    [nn.GRUCell(hidden_size, hidden_size) for i in range(layers-1)])
self.norms = nn.ModuleList(
    [nn.LayerNorm(hidden_size) for i in range(layers)])
```

We broke up the specification of `GRUCell` layers into two parts. First is a list of one item for the first layer since it has to go from `embd_size` inputs to `hidden_size` outputs. Second is all remaining layers with `[nn.GRUCell(hidden_size, hidden_size) for i in range(layers-1)]`, which works because each of these layers has the same input and output size. For fun, I've also included a `LayerNorm` normalization layer for each RNN result.

The last thing we need in our constructor is the purple layers that take in the hidden states h_t and output a prediction for the class. This is done with a small fully connected network:

```
self.pred_class = nn.Sequential(
    nn.Linear(hidden_size, hidden_size),          ⟵ (B, *, D)
    nn.LeakyReLU(),
    nn.LayerNorm(hidden_size),                     ⟵ (B, *, D)
    nn.Linear(hidden_size, num_embeddings)         ⟵ (B, *, D) -> B(B, *, VocabSize)
)
```

Notice that we define a component of this module as an entire network. This will help us compartmentalize our design and make our code easier to read. If you ever want to go back and change the subnetwork that goes from hidden RNN states to predictions, you can change just the `pred_class` object, and the rest of the code will work fine.

IMPLEMENTING THE AUTOREGRESSIVE FORWARD FUNCTION

The `forward` function of the module will organize the work done by two other helper functions. First we embed the input tokens into their vector forms, as this can all be done at once. Because we are using a `GRUCell` class, we need to keep track of the hidden states ourselves. So we use a `initHiddenStates(B)` function that creates the initial hidden states $h_0 = \vec{0}$ for each GRU layer. Then we use a `for` loop to grab each of the t items and process them one step at a time using a `step` function that takes the inputs x_t and a list of the GRU hidden states `h_prevs`. The GRU hidden states are stored in a list `last_activations` to get the predictions at every time step. Finally, we can return a single tensor by `stacking` the results together:

```
def forward(self, input):                    ←—— Input should be (B, T).
    B = input.size(0)                         ←—— What is the batch size?
    T = input.size(1)                         ←—┐ What is the maximum
                                                 │ number of time steps?

    x = self.embd(input)                      ←—— (B, T, D)

    h_prevs = self.initHiddenStates(B)        ←—— Initial hidden states

    last_activations = []
    for t in range(T):
        x_in = x[:,t,:]                       ←—— (B, D)
        last_activations.append(self.step(x_in, h_prevs))

    last_activations = torch.stack(last_activations, dim=1)    ←—— (B, T, D)

    return last_activations
```

`initHiddenStates` is easy to implement. We can use the `torch.zeros` function to create a tensor of all zero values. We just have the argument `B` for how large the batch is, and then we can grab the `hidden_size` and number of `layers` from the object's members:

```
def initHiddenStates(self, B):
    """
    Creates an initial hidden state list for the RNN layers.

    B: the batch size for the hidden states.
    """
    return [torch.zeros(B, self.hidden_size, device=device)
        for _ in range(len(self.layers))]
```

The `step` function is a little more involved. First we check the shape of the input, and if it has only one dimension, we assume that we need to embed the token values to make vectors. Then we check the hidden states `h_prevs` and, if they are not provided, initialize them using `initHiddenStates`. These are both good defensive code steps to make sure our function can be versatile and avoid errors:

```
def step(self, x_in, h_prevs=None):
    """

    x_in: the input for this current time step and has shape (B)
    if the values need to be embedded, and (B, D) if they
    have already been embedded.

    h_prevs: a list of hidden state tensors each with shape
    (B, self.hidden_size) for each layer in the network.
    These contain the current hidden state of the RNN layers
    and will be updated by this call.
    """

    if len(x_in.shape) == 1:
        x_in = self.embd(x_in)

    if h_prevs is None:
        h_prevs = self.initHiddenStates(x_in.shape[0])

    for l in range(len(self.layers)):
        h_prev = h_prevs[l]
        h = self.norms[l](self.layers[l](x_in, h_prev))

        h_prevs[l] = h
        x_in = h
    return self.pred_class(x_in)
```

Annotations:
- **Preps all three arguments to be in the final form. First, (B); we need to embed it.**
- **Now (B, D)**
- **Processes the input**
- **Pushes in the current input with previous hidden states**
- **Makes predictions about the token**

After those defensive coding steps, we simply loop through the number of layers and process the results. `x_in` is the input to a layer, which is passed into the current layer `self.layers[l]` and then the normalization layer `self.norms[l]`. After that, we do the minor bookkeeping of storing the new hidden state `h_prevs[l] = h` and setting `x_in = h` so that the next layer has its input ready to process. Once that loop is done, `x_in` has the result from the last RNN layer, so we can feed it directly to the `self.pred_class` object to go from the RNN hidden state to a prediction about the next character.

A shortcut for linear layers over time

You may notice a comment in this code about the tensor shapes with (B, D). This is because nn.Linear layers have a special trick that allows them to be applied to multiple inputs *independently* at the same time. We have always used a linear model over a tensor with shape (B, D), and the linear model can take in D inputs and return D' outputs. So we would go from $(B, D) \rightarrow (B, D')$. If we have T items in a sequence, we have a tensor of shape (B, T, D). Applying a linear model to *each* time step naively would require a for loop and look like this:

```
def applyLinearLayerOverTime(x):
    results = []        ◄── Place to store result for each step
    B, T, D = x.shape
    for t in range(T):
        results.append(linearLayer(x[:,t,:]))    ◄── Gets the result for each step
    return torch.stack(results, dim=0).view(B, T, -1)    ◄── Stacks everything into one tensor and shapes it correctly
```

That is more code than we would like, *and* it will run slower because of the for loop. PyTorch has a simple trick that nn.Linear layers are applied to the *last* axis of a tensor *regardless of the number of axes*. That means this whole function can be replaced with just linearLayer, and you will get the *exact same result*. That is less code *and* faster. This way, any fully connected network can be used on single time steps or groups of time steps, without having to do anything special. Still, it's good to keep comments like (B, D) and (B, T, D) so that you can remind yourself *how* you are using your networks.

With our model defined, we are almost finished. Next we quickly create our new AutoRegressiveDataset with the shakespear_100k data as the input, and we make a data loader using a respectable batch size. We also create our AutoRegressive model with 32 dimensions for the embedding, 128 hidden neurons, and 2 GRU layers. We include gradient clipping because RNNs are sensitive to that issue:

```
autoRegData = AutoRegressiveDataset(shakespear_100k, max_chunk=250)
autoReg_loader = DataLoader(autoRegData, batch_size=128, shuffle=True)

autoReg_model = AutoRegressive(len(vocab2indx), 32, 128, layers=2)
autoReg_model = autoReg_model.to(device)

for p in autoReg_model.parameters():
    p.register_hook(lambda grad: torch.clamp(grad, -2, 2))
```

IMPLEMENTING AN AUTOREGRESSIVE LOSS FUNCTION

The last thing we need is a loss function ℓ. We are making a prediction at every step, so we want to use the CrossEntropyLoss that is appropriate for classification problems. *However*, we have *multiple* losses to compute, one for every time step. We can solve this by writing our own loss function CrossEntLossTime that computes the cross-entropy for each step. Similar to our `forward` function, we slice each prediction `x[:,t,:]` and a corresponding label `y[:t]` so that we end up with the standard (B, C) and (B) shapes for the prediction and labels, respectively, and can call `CrossEntropyLoss` directly. Then we add the losses from every time step to get a single total loss to return:

```
def CrossEntLossTime(x, y):
    """
    x: output with shape (B, T, V)
    y: labels with shape (B, T)
    """
    cel = nn.CrossEntropyLoss()

    T = x.size(1)

    loss = 0

    for t in range(T):              ←── For every item in the sequence . . .
        loss += cel(x[:,t,:], y[:,t])   ←── . . . compute the sum of the prediction errors.

    return loss
```

Now we can finally train our autoregressive model. We use our same `train_network` function but pass in our new `CrossEntLossTime` function as the loss function ℓ—and everything just works:

```
train_network(autoReg_model, CrossEntLossTime, autoReg_loader, epochs=100,
    device=device)
```

7.5.2 *Autoregressive models are generative models*

We saved one last detail for the end because it's easier to *see* it than it is to explain. Autoregressive models are not only self-supervised; they also fall into a class known as *generative models*. This means they can *generate* new data that looks like the original data it was trained on. To do this, we switch our model to `eval` mode and create a tensor `sampling` that stores our generated output. Any output generated from a model can be called a *sample*, and the process of generating that sample is called *sampling*, if you want to sound cool (and this is good terminology for you to remember):

```
autoReg_model = autoReg_model.eval()
sampling = torch.zeros((1, 500), dtype=torch.int64, device=device)
```

To sample from an autoregressive model, we usually need to give the model a *seed*. This is some original text that the model is *given*; then the model is asked to make predictions about what comes next. The code for setting a seed is shown next, where "EMILIA:" is our initial seed, as if the character Emilia is about to speak in the play:

```
seed = "EMILIA:".lower()
cur_len = len(seed)
sampling[0,0:cur_len] = torch.tensor([vocab2indx[x] for x in seed])
```

The sampling process of an autoregressive model is shown in figure 7.10. Our seed is passed in as the initial inputs to the model, and we *ignore* the predictions being made. This is because our seed is helping to build the hidden states h of the RNN, which contain information about every previous input. Once we have processed the entire seed, we have no more inputs. After the seed has run out of inputs, we use the *previous* output of the model $\hat{x}_t$ as the *input* for the next time step $t + 1$. This is possible because the autoregressive model has *learned to predict what comes next.* If it does a good job at this, its predictions can be used as inputs, and we end up *generating* new sequences in the process.

When using an already trained autoregressive model (i.e., "testing"), current outputs (t) are used as future inputs ($t + 1$). The usage is swapped based on if you are training or testing the autoregressive model.

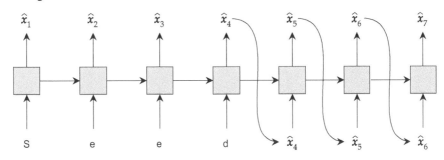

Figure 7.10 A seed is given to the model, and we ignore the predictions being made. Once the seed runs out, we use the predictions at time step t as the input to the next step $t + 1$.

But how do we use a prediction as an input? Our model is making a prediction about the probability of seeing *every* different character as the next possible output. But the next input needs to be a *specific* character. This can be done by *sampling* the predictions based on the model's output probabilities. So if the character *a* has a 100% prediction of being next, the model *will* return *a*. If instead we have 80% *a*, 10% *b*, and 10% *c*, we will *probably* select *a* as the next class, but we could also pick *b* or *c*. The following code does just that:

```
for i in tqdm(range(cur_len, sampling.size(1))):
    with torch.no_grad():
        h = autoReg_model(sampling[:,0:i])        ⟵ Processes all the previous items
        h = h[:,-1,:]                              ⟵ Grabs the last time step
        h = F.softmax(h, dim=1)                    ⟵ Makes probabilities
        next_tokens = torch.multinomial(h, 1)      ⟵ Samples the next prediction
        sampling[:,i] = next_tokens                ⟵ Sets the next prediction
        cur_len += 1                               ⟵ Increases the length by one
```

NOTE Just as autoencoders make great embeddings, so do autoregressive models. The hidden state h in the previous code can be used as an embedding that summarizes the entire sequence processed thus far. This is a good way to go from word embeddings to sentence or paragraph embeddings.

Now we have a new sequence that we have predicted, but what does it look like? That is why we saved an *inverse mapping* from tokens back to our vocabulary with the indx2vocab dict: we can use that to map each integer back to a character, and then join them together to create an output. The following code converts our generative sample back into text we can read:

```
s = [indx2vocab[x] for x in sampling.cpu().numpy().flatten()]
print("".join(s))

emilia:
to hen the words tractass of nan wand,
no bear to the groung, iftink sand'd sack,
i will ciscling
bronino:
if this,
so you you may well you and surck, of wife where sooner you.


corforesrale:
where here of his not but rost lighter'd therefore latien ever
un'd
but master your brutures warry:
why,
thou do i mus shooth and,
rity see! more mill of cirfer put,
and her me harrof of that thy restration stucied the bear:
and quicutiand courth, for sillaniages:
so lobate thy trues not very repist
```

You should notice a few things about the output of our generation. While it kind of looks Shakespearian, it quickly devolves. This is because with each step of the data, we get further from *real* data, and our model *will* make unrealistic choices that thus become errors and negatively impact future predictions. So the longer we generate, the lower the quality will become.

7.5.3   *Changing samples with temperature*

The model rarely gives a probability of *zero* for any token, which means we will eventually select an incorrect or unrealistic next token. If you are 99% sure that the next character should be *a*, why give the model the 1% opportunity to pick something that is likely wrong? To encourage the model to go with the most likely predictions, we can add a *temperature* to the generation process. The temperature is a scalar that we divide the model's prediction by before computing the softmax to make probabilities. This is shown in figure 7.11, where you can push the temperature to extreme values like infinity or zero. Something with infinite temperature will result in uniformly random behavior (not what we want), and something with zero temperature is frozen solid and returns the same (most likely) thing over and over again (also not what we want).

Adding the temperature into the computation is just dividing every logit z (logit is just what goes into the exp function) by a specific value.

$$\mathbb{P}(BBQ) = \frac{\exp(z_{BBQ}/temp)}{\exp(z_{Seafood}/temp) + \exp(z_{BBQ}/temp) + \exp(z_{Pasta}/temp)}$$

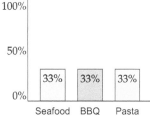

Infinite Temperature

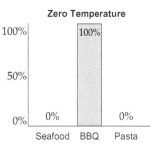

Zero Temperature

If everything is infinitely hot, it is like a bunch of boiling water atoms bouncing around and looks completely random.

If the temperature is zero, it is like a frozen block of ice. It is solid and consistent: you get the same thing every time you look at it. No randomness.

$$\frac{\exp(z_{BBQ}/\infty)}{\exp(z_{Seafood}/\infty) + \exp(z_{BBQ}/\infty) + \exp(z_{Pasta}/\infty)}$$

$$\approx \frac{\exp(z_{BBQ}\cdot 0)}{\exp(z_{Seafood}\cdot 0) + \exp(z_{BBQ}\cdot 0) + \exp(z_{Pasta}\cdot 0)}$$

$$= \frac{1}{1+1+1} = 1/3, \text{ aka uniformly random}$$

Figure 7.11 What food is Edward going to eat? If the temperature is set very high, Edward's selection will be random, regardless of what the initial probabilities are. If the temperature is at or near zero, Edward will always pick BBQ because it is more likely than any other option. More temperature = more randomness, and no negative temperatures are allowed.

Instead of using these extremes, we can instead focus on adding a small effect by making the temperature a value slightly larger or smaller than 1.0. The default value of temperature=1.0 causes no change in the probabilities and so is the same as what we already did: compute the original probabilities and sample a prediction based on those probabilities. But if you use a temperature < 1, then items that originally had a larger chance of being selected (like BBQ) will get an even bigger advantage and increase their probability (think, "the rich get richer"). If we make temperature > 1, we end up giving lower-probability items more of a chance to be selected, at the cost of the originally higher probabilities. The effect of temperature is summarized in figure 7.12 with an example of picking my next meal.

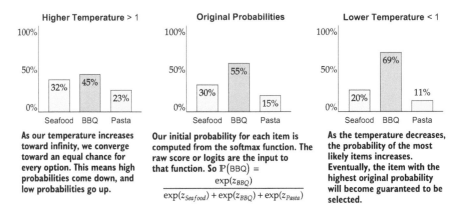

As our temperature increases, we converge toward an equal chance for every option. This means high probabilities come down, and low probabilities go up.

Our initial probability for each item is computed from the softmax function. The raw score or logits are the input to that function. So $\mathbb{P}(\text{BBQ}) =$

$$\frac{\exp(z_{BBQ})}{\exp(z_{Seafood}) + \exp(z_{BBQ}) + \exp(z_{Pasta})}$$

As the temperature decreases, the probability of the most likely items increases. Eventually, the item with the highest original probability will become guaranteed to be selected.

Figure 7.12   Example of how temperature impacts the probability of selecting my next meal. I'm most likely to eat BBQ by default because it is delicious. Raising the temperature encourages diversity, eventually selecting each item at random if we went to the extreme minimum temperature (zero). Lowering temperature reduces diversity, eventually selecting only the most likely original item at the extreme highest possible temperature (toward infinity).

In practice, a value of 0.75 is a good default[5] (I usually see 0.65 at the low end and 0.8 at the high end) because it maintains diversity but avoids picking items that were more unlikely originally (e.g., BBQ is my favorite food group, but some diversity is good for you and is more realistic). The following code adds the temperature to the sampling process:

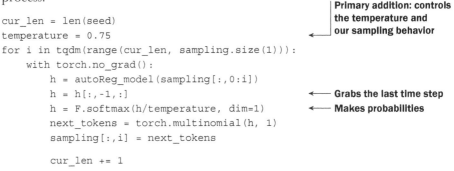

```
cur_len = len(seed)
temperature = 0.75                          Primary addition: controls
                                            the temperature and
for i in tqdm(range(cur_len, sampling.size(1))):   our sampling behavior
    with torch.no_grad():
        h = autoReg_model(sampling[:,0:i])
        h = h[:,-1,:]                       Grabs the last time step
        h = F.softmax(h/temperature, dim=1) Makes probabilities
        next_tokens = torch.multinomial(h, 1)
        sampling[:,i] = next_tokens

        cur_len += 1
```

Why is temperature called temperature?

The analogy you should go with is a pot of water, and the temperature is literally the temperature of the water. If the temperature is very high, the water begins to boil, and the water's atoms are in random positions as they bounce around. As the temperature decreases, the water begins to freeze, and the atoms stay still in an organized pattern. High temperature = chaotic (read, random), and low temperature is still (read, no randomness).

---

[5]   A good default for text generation, that is. Other tasks may need you to play around with the temperature to select a better value.

If we print out our predictions, we should see something that feels a little more reasonable. It is not perfect, and a bigger model with more epochs of training can help improve that. But adding a `temperature` is a common trick to help control the generation process:

```
s = [indx2vocab[x] for x in sampling.cpu().numpy().flatten()]
print("".join(s))

emilia:
therefore good i am to she prainns siefurers.

king ford:
beor come, sir, i chaed
to me, the was the strong arl and the boy fear mabber lord,,
coull some a clock dightle eyes, agaary must her was flord but the hear fall
the cousion a tarm:
i am a varstiend the her apper the service no that you shall give yet somantion,
and lord, and commind cure, i why had they helbook.

mark ars:
who her throw true in go speect proves of the wrong and further gooland, before
but i am so are berether, i
```

So you may be thinking, why not lower the temperature even further? Should we not *always* want to go with the most likely prediction? This gets to some deep issues about the difficulty of evaluating generative and autoregressive models, especially when the input is something like human text, which is not all that predictable to begin with. If I told you I could *perfectly* predict what someone was going to say, you would likely be incredulous. How could that be possible? We should always apply that same standard to our model. If we *always* select the most likely prediction, we are assuming the model can *perfectly* predict what a person would say next. We can try that by setting the temperature to a very low value like 0.05:

```
cur_len = len(seed)
temperature = 0.05                                  ◄────── Very low temp: will
for i in tqdm(range(cur_len, sampling.size(1))):            almost always pick the
    with torch.no_grad():                                   most likely items
        h = autoReg_model(sampling[:,0:i])
        h = h[:,-1,:]                               ◄────── Grabs the last time step
        h = F.softmax(h/temperature, dim=1)         ◄────── Makes probabilities
        next_tokens = torch.multinomial(h, 1)
        sampling[:,i] = next_tokens

        cur_len += 1
s = [indx2vocab[x] for x in sampling.cpu().numpy().flatten()]
print("".join(s))
```

```
emilia:
i will straight the shall shall shall be the with the shall shall shall shall
be the with the shall be the with the shall shall shall be the shall shall
shall she shall shall shall shall shall be the with the shall shall shall
shall be the shall be the shall shall shall shall shall shall shall shall be
the prove the will so see and the shall be the will the shall shall shall
shall shall shall be the with the shall shall shall shall be the shall be the
with the shall shall shall be the wi
```

The model has become *very* repetitive. This is what usually happens when you select the most likely token as the next one; the model devolves to selecting a sequence of the most common words/tokens over and over and over again.

Hot alternatives to temperature

Adjusting the temperature is but one of many possible techniques for selecting the generated output in a more realistic-looking manner. Each has pros and cons, but you should be aware of three alternatives: beam search, top-k sampling, and nucleus sampling. The fine folks at Hugging Face have a good blog post that introduces these at a high level (https://huggingface.co/blog/how-to-generate).

7.5.4 *Faster sampling*

You may have noticed that the sampling process takes a surprisingly long time—about 45 to 50 seconds to generate 500 characters—yet we could train over 100,000 characters in just seconds per epoch. This is because each time we make a prediction, we needed to refeed the entire generated sequence far back into the model to get the next prediction. Using Big O notation means we are doing $O(n^2)$ work to generate a sequence of $O(n)$ length.

The GRUCell that processes sequences one step at a time makes it easy for us to solve this problem. We break our for loop up into two parts, each using the step function directly instead of the forward function of the module. The first loop pushes the seed into the model, updating an explicitly created set of hidden states h_prevs. After that, we can write a new loop that generates the new content and calls the step function to update the model after sampling the next character. This process is shown in the following code:

```
seed = "EMILIA:".lower()                          ◄────┤ Sets up our seed and
cur_len = len(seed)                                     │ the location to store the
                                                        │ generated content

sampling = torch.zeros((1, 500), dtype=torch.int64, device=device)
sampling[0,0:cur_len] = torch.tensor([vocab2indx[x] for x in seed])

temperature = 0.75                                 ◄──────── Picks a temperature
with torch.no_grad():
    h_prevs = autoReg_model.initHiddenStates(1)    ◄──── Initializes the hidden state
    for i in range(0, cur_len):                          to avoid redundant work
        h = autoReg_model.step(sampling[:,i], h_prevs=h_prevs)
```

Pushes the seed through

```
          for i in tqdm(range(cur_len, sampling.size(1))):
              h = F.softmax(h/temperature, dim=1)
              next_tokens = torch.multinomial(h, 1)
              sampling[:,i] = next_tokens
              cur_len += 1
              h = autoReg_model.step(sampling[:,i], h_prevs=h_prevs)
```

Generates new text one character at a time

Makes probabilities

Now pushes only the new sample into the model

This new code runs in less than a second. This is much faster, and it gets faster the longer the sequence we want to generate, because it has a better Big O complexity of $O(n)$ to generate $O(n)$ tokens. Next we print out the generated result, which you can see is qualitatively the same as before:

```
s = [indx2vocab[x] for x in sampling.cpu().numpy().flatten()]
print("".join(s))
```

```
emilia:
a-to her hand by hath the stake my pouse of we to more should there had the
would break fot his good, and me in deserved
to not days all the wead his to king; her fair the bear so word blatter with
my hath thy hamber--

king dige:
it the recuse.

mark:
wey, he to o hath a griec, and could would there you honour fail;
have at i would straigh his boy:
coursiener:
and to refore so marry fords like i seep a party. or thee your honour great
way we the may her with all the more ampiled my porn
```

With that, you now know all the basics of autoencoders and autoregressive models, two related approaches that share the same fundamental idea: use the input data as the target output. These can be especially powerful techniques to mimic/replace expensive simulations (have the network learn to predict what happens next), clean up noisy data (inject realistic noise and learn how to remove it), and generally train useful models without any labeled data. The latter note will become important in chapter 13 when you learn how to do transfer learning, a technique allowing you to use unlabeled data to improve results on a smaller labeled dataset.

Exercises

Share and discuss your solutions on the Manning online platform at Inside Deep Learning Exercises (https://liveproject.manning.com/project/945). Once you submit your own answers, you will be able to see the solutions submitted by other readers, and see which ones the author judges to be the best.

1. Create a new version of the MNIST dataset that does not contain the numbers 9 and 5, and train one of the autoencoders on this dataset. Then run the autoencoder on the test dataset, and record the average error (MSE) for each of the 10 classes.

Do you see any patterns in the results, and can the autoencoder identify 9 and 5 as outliers?

2 Train the bottleneck-style autoencoder with a target size $D' = 64$ dimensions. Then use k-means (https://scikit-learn.org/stable/modules/clustering.html#k-means) to create $k = 10$ clusters on the original version of MNIST and the version encoded using $D' = 64$ dimensions. Use the homogeneity score from scikit-learn (http://mng.bz/nYQV) to evaluate these clusters. Which method does best: k-means on the original images or k-means on the encoded representations?

3 Use the denoising approach to implement a denoising convolutional network. This can be done by not having any pooling operations so that the input stays the same size.

4 Sometimes people train deep autoencoders with weight sharing between the encoder and decoder. Try implementing a deep bottleneck autoencoder that uses the TransposeLinear layer for all of the decoder's layers. Compare the weight shared versus the non-weight shared network when you have only n=1,024, 8,192, 32,768, and all 60,000 samples from MNIST.

5 **Challenging:** Train an asymmetric denoising autoencoder for MNIST where the encoder is a fully connected network and the decoder is a convolutional network. *Hint:* You will need to end the encoder with a View layer that changes the shape from (B, D) to $(B, C, 28, 28)$, where D is the number of neurons in the last nn.LinearLayer of the encoder and $D = C \cdot 28 \cdot 28$. Do the results of this network look better or worse than the fully connected network in the chapter, and how do you think intermixing architectures impacts that result?

6 **Challenging:** Reshape the MNIST dataset as a sequence of pixels, and train an autoregressive model over the pixels. This requires using real-valued inputs and outputs, so you will not use an nn.Embedding layer, and you will need to switch to the MSE loss function. After training, try generating multiple digits from this autoregressive pixel model.

7 Convert the GRUCells in the autoregressive model to LSTMCells, and train a new model. Which one do you think has better generated output?

8 The AutoRegressiveDataset can start an input in the middle of a sentence since it naively grabs subsequences of the input. Write a new version that will only select the start of a sequence at the start of a new line (i.e., after a carriage return '\n') and then returns the next max_chunk characters (it's OK if there is some overlap between chunks). Train a model on this new version of the dataset. Do you think it changes the characteristics of the generated output?

9 After training your autoregressive model on sentences, use the LastTimeStep class to extract a feature vector representing each sentence. Then feed these vectors into your favorite clustering algorithm and see if you can find any groups of similar

styles or types of sentences. *Note:* You may want to sub-sample a smaller number of sentences to make your clustering algorithm run faster.

Summary

- Self-supervision is a means of training a neural network by using parts of the input *as the labels* we are trying to predict.

- Self-supervision is considered unsupervised because it can be applied to any data and does not require any kind of process or human to manually label the data.

- Autoencoding is one of the most popular forms of self-supervision. It works by having the network predict the input as the output but somehow constrains the network so that it can't naively return the original input.

- Two popular constraints are a bottleneck design that forces the dimension to shrink before expanding back out and a denoising approach where the input is altered before being given to the network, but the network still must predict the unaltered output.

- If we have a sequence problem, we can instead use autoregressive models, which look at every previous input in a sequence to predict the next input.

- Autoregressive approaches have the benefit of being *generative*, which means we can create synthetic data from the model!

Object detection

Imagine this: you want to build a system that counts the different kinds of birds in a park. You point a camera at the sky, and for each bird in this photograph, you want to know its species name. But what if there are no birds in the picture? Or just 1? Or 12? To accommodate these situations, you need to first detect each bird in the image and then classify each detected bird. This two-step process is known as *object detection*, and it comes in many forms. Broadly, they all involve identifying the subcomponents of an image. So instead of generating one prediction per image, which is what our models have done so far, the system generates many predictions from a single image.

Even when improved with data augmentation, better optimizers, and residual networks, the image classification models we built earlier all assume that the image is of a desired class. By this, we mean the image content matches the training data. For example, our MNIST model assumes that an image *always* contains a digit, and the digit is one of 0 through 9. Our normal CNN models simply do not have the concept that an image could be empty or have multiple digits. To handle these cases, our model needs to be able to detect what is contained in a single image, and where in that image those things are located. Object detection is how we handle this problem.

In this chapter, we learn about two approaches used for object-detection tasks. First we go into the details of *image segmentation*, which is an expensive but simpler approach. Similar to how the autoregressive models in chapter 7 made a prediction for *every* item in a sequence, image segmentation makes a prediction for *every* pixel in an image. Image segmentation is expensive because you need someone to label every individual pixel in an image. The expense can often be justified by the effectiveness of the results, ease of implementing segmentation models, and applications that need that level of detail. To improve image segmentation, we learn about a *transposed* convolution operation that allows us to undo the shrinking effect of pooling so that we can get the benefits of pooling and still make a prediction at every pixel. With this in hand, we build a foundational architecture called *U-Net* that has become a de facto design approach for image segmentation.

The second half of this chapter moves beyond per-pixel predictions to a variable number of predictions. This is done with an option that is less precise but also less expensive to label: *bounding box*-based object detection. Bounding box labels are boxes that are *just* large enough to capture a whole object within an image. This is easier to label: you only need to click and drag a box (sometimes crudely) around the object. But effective object-detection models are difficult to implement and expensive to train. Since object detection is so challenging to implement from scratch, we learn about the *region proposal*-based detector that is built into PyTorch. The region proposal approach is widely used and readily available, so we cover the details about *how* it works that generalize to other approaches. We'll skip the minute details that make a specific implementation, but I'll provide references if you want to learn more.

8.1 Image segmentation

Image segmentation is a simple approach to finding objects in an image. Image segmentation is a classification problem, but instead of classifying the whole image (what we have been doing with MNIST), we classify *every pixel*. So a 200×200 image will have $200 \times 200 = 40,000$ classifications. The classes in image segmentation tasks are usually different kinds of objects we could detect. For instance, the image in figure 8.1 has a horse, a person, and some cars as class objects.

The goal is to produce the *ground truth*, where *every pixel* is classified as belonging to either a person, a horse, a car, or the background. We have a classification problem with four unique classes; it just happens to be that a single input involves making many predictions. So if we have a 128×128 image, we have $128^2 = 16,384$ classifications to perform.

Input   Label

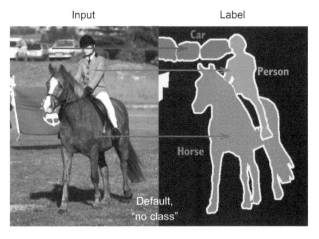

Figure 8.1   **Example of an input image (on the left) with the segmented ground-truth labels (on the right) from the PASCAL VOC 2012 dataset. Every pixel has been given a class, with a default "no class" or "background" class given to pixels that are not part of a labeled object.**

If we can successfully segment an image, we can then perform object detection. For figure 8.1, we can find the person blob (pink pixels connected together) to determine that a person exists in the image and where they exist within it. Segmentation can also be the goal in and of itself. For example, medical[1] doctors may want to identify the percentage of tumor cells in an image of a cell biopsy to determine how someone's cancer is progressing (larger percentage than before means it's growing and getting worse; smaller percentage means the cancer is shrinking and the treatment is working). Another common task in medical research is to manually label the number of different types of cells in an image and use the relative numbers of cell types to determine a patient's overall health or other medical properties. In these tasks, we don't just want to know where objects are: we also want to know precisely how big they are and their relative proportions within an image.

The task of image segmentation is a great opportunity to use a convolutional neural network. A CNN is designed to produce *local* outputs for a *local* region of the input. So our strategy for designing an image segmentation network will use convolutional layers as the output layer, too, instead of an nn.Linear layer as we did before. When we design a network that contains only convolutional layers (in addition to nonlinearity and normalization layers), we call that network *fully convolutional.*[2]

8.1.1   *Nuclei detection: Loading the data*

For our first introduction to image segmentation, we will use data from the 2018 Data Science Bowl (https://www.kaggle.com/c/data-science-bowl-2018). The goal of this

---

[1]   I use the "medical" qualifier in purely self-interested justification that I too am a doctor, just not a particularly helpful one. But someday a machine learning emergency will happen on a plane, and I'll be ready!

[2]   Some people get upset when you call a model fully convolutional but still use pooling layers. I consider this nitpicking. In general, any network that uses only convolutions and has no nn.Linear layers (or some other non-convolutional layer like an RNN) can be called fully convolutional.

competition was to detect nuclei of cells and their respective sizes. But we will just segment the image for now. We will download this dataset, set up a `Dataset` class for the problem, and then specify a fully convolutional network to make predictions about the entire image. When you download the data and extract it, all the files should be in a stage1/train folder.

The data is organized into a number of paths. So if we have the path/folder data0, an image of a cell under a microscope is found in the path data0/images/some_file_name.png. For every nucleus in the image, there is a file under data0/masks/name_i.png. The `Dataset` object loads that in so we can get started. To make things simple for now, we do some normalization and prep in the `Dataset` class. We remove an alpha channel that comes with these images (usually for transparent images), reorder the channels to be the first dimension as PyTorch likes, and compute the label for each input. The way we prepare this data is summarized in figure 8.2.

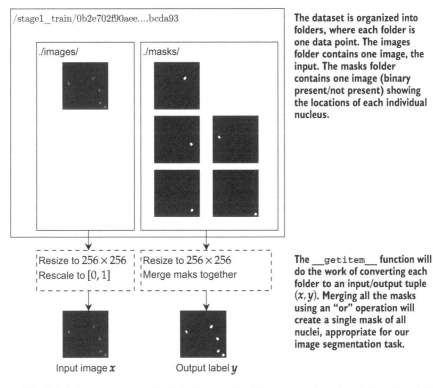

Figure 8.2 This is how we process the Data Science Bowl data for image segmentation. Each folder under the root directory has several subfolders: an images folder with one image (I know, confusing) and a masks folder that has a binary mask for each nucleus. The masks are separated for object detection (we'll get to that later), so we merge them all into one image that indicates where masks are (class 1) and are not (class 0).

All the images in a subdirectory are the exact same size, as shown in figure 8.2, but they have different sizes *between* directories. So for the sake of simplicity, we'll resize everything to 256×256. That way, we don't have to worry about padding images to make them the same size. To build a label, we want an image that is the same shape, with 0 for no class or 1 for a nucleus being present. We can do this by converting each image to an array of binary values called a *mask*, where 1 = True = nuclei present. Then we can do a logical or operation on the masks to get one final mask that has a 1 at every pixel where a nucleus was present.

The following code is the class for the 2018 Data Science Bowl dataset. Our `Dataset` class goes through every mask and ors them together so we get a single mask showing every pixel that contains an object. This is done in `__getitem__`, which returns a tuple with the input image followed by the mask we want to predict (i.e., all pixels that contain nuclei):

```
class DSB2018(Dataset):
    """Dataset class for the 2018 Data Science Bowl."""
    def __init__(self, paths):
        """paths: a list of paths to every image folder in the dataset"""
        self.paths = paths
    def __len__(self):
        return len(self.paths)
    def __getitem__(self, idx):
        img_path = glob(self.paths[idx] + "/images/*")[0]
        mask_imgs = glob(self.paths[idx] + "/masks/*")
        img = imread(img_path)[:,:,0:3]
        img = np.moveaxis(img, -1, 0)
        img = img/255.0

        a_different_nuclei/ masks = [imread(f)/255.0
            for f in mask_imgs]

        final_mask = np.zeros(masks[0].shape)
        for m in masks:
            final_mask = np.logical_or(final_mask, m)
        final_mask = final_mask.astype(np.float32)

        img, final_mask = torch.tensor(img),
            torch.tensor(final_mask).unsqueeze(0)

        img = F.interpolate(img.unsqueeze(0), (256, 256))
        final_mask = F.interpolate(final_mask.unsqueeze(0), (256, 256))

        return img.type(torch.FloatTensor)[0],
            final_mask.type(torch.FloatTensor)[0]
```

The image shape is (W, H, 4). The last dimension is an unused alpha channel. We trim off the alpha to get (W, H, 3).

We want this to be (3, W, H), the normal shape for PyTorch.

Last step for the image: rescale it to the range [0, 1].

There is only one image in each images path, so we grab the first thing we find with [0] at the end.

But there are multiple mask images in each mask path.

Since we want to do simple segmentation, we create a final mask that contains all nuclei pixels from every mask.

Every mask image has the shape (W, H), which has a value of 1 if the pixel is of a nucleus and a value of 0 if the image is background.

Not every image in the dataset is the same size. To simplify the problem, we resize every image to be (256, 256). First we convert them to PyTorch tensors.

The interpolate function can be used to resize a batch of images. We make each image a "batch" of 1.

The shapes are (B=1, C, W, H). We need to convert them back to FloatTensors and grab the first item in the batch. This will return a tuple of (3, 256, 256), (1, 256, 256).

8.1.2 *Representing the image segmentation problem in PyTorch*

Now that we can load the dataset, let's visualize some of the data . The corpus has cell images from a variety of sources: some look like they are black and white, while others have color from the dye used. The next block of code loads the data and displays the original image on the left and, on the right, the mask that shows exactly where all the nuclei are:

```
dsb_data = DSB2018(paths)                          ←—— Creates the Dataset class object

plt.figure(figsize=(16,10))
plt.subplot(1, 2, 1)                               ←—— Plots the original image

plt.imshow(dsb_data[0][0].permute(1,2,0).numpy())

plt.subplot(1, 2, 2)                               ←—— Plots the mask

plt.imshow(dsb_data[0][1].numpy()[0,:], cmap='gray')
```

```
[7]:   <matplotlib.image.AxesImage at 0x7fd24a8a5350>
```

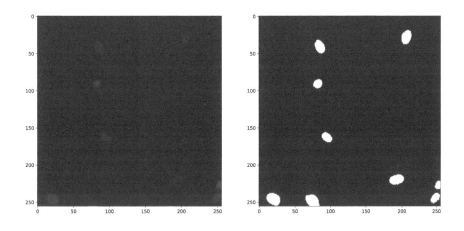

```
plt.figure(figsize=(16,10))                        ←——————— Let's plot a second
plt.subplot(1, 2, 1)                                         image that is in color.
plt.imshow(dsb_data[1][0].permute(1,2,0).numpy())
plt.subplot(1, 2, 2)
plt.imshow(dsb_data[1][1].numpy()[0,:], cmap='gray')
```

[8]:   <matplotlib.image.AxesImage at 0x7fd24a7eb6d0>

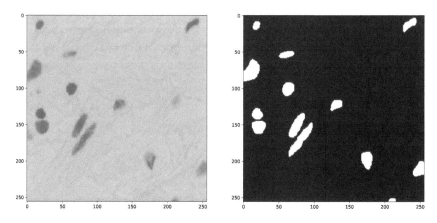

As we can see, there are many types of input image slices. Some have many nuclei, some have few, and the nuclei can be close to each other or far apart. Let's quickly create training and testing splits to work with, using a smaller batch size of 16 images. We're using smaller batches because these images are larger—256×256 instead of just 28×28—and I want to make sure the batches fit onto your GPU even if Colab gives you one of the smaller instances:

```
train_split, test_split = torch.utils.data.random_split(dsb_data,
  [500, len(dsb_data)-500])
train_seg_loader = DataLoader(train_split, batch_size=16, shuffle=True)
test_seg_loader = DataLoader(test_split, batch_size=16)
```

Since these are color images, we use $C = 3$ channels for our input: red, green, and blue. I've arbitrarily chosen 32 filters for our convolutional layers. The last setup item in the following code is to use `BCEWithLogitLoss` instead of `CrossEntropyLoss`. The `BCE` part of the name stands for *binary* cross-entropy. It's a specialized version of `CrossEntropyLoss` that only works for two-class problems. Because we *know* there are only two classes (nuclei and background), the output of our network can be 1 neuron per pixel for a Yes/No style prediction. If we used `CrossEntropyLoss`, we would need two outputs per pixel, and that's a little uglier for our code:

How many channels are in the input? ⟶
Smallest value of filters you should usually consider. If we wanted to try to optimize the architecture, we could use Optuna to pick a better number of filters.

```
C = 3
n_filters = 32          ⟵
loss_func = nn.BCEWithLogitsLoss()
```

BCE loss implicitly assumes a binary problem.

NOTE When you have only two classes, binary cross-entropy using `BCEWithLogitLoss` and `CrossEntropyLoss` will converge to the same result. They are *mathematically equivalent*, so the choice is coding preference. I prefer to use `BCEWithLogitLoss` for two-class problems because it makes it obvious that I'm working with a binary output/prediction the moment I see the loss function, which tells me a little more about the problem. In general, it's good to give your classes names and write your code in ways that tell you about what is happening in your code. At some point, you will have to go back and look at the old code you wrote, and these details will help you remember what is going on.

8.1.3 Building our first image segmentation network

Because we need to make predictions for *every* pixel, our network's output $f(\cdot)$ must have a shape with the same height and width as our original inputs. So if our input is (B, C, W, H), our output needs to be $(B, class, W, H)$. The *number of channels can change* based on the number of classes. In general, we will have one channel for every class we could predict the input as. In this case, we have two classes, so we can use one output channel with the binary cross-entropy loss. Thus we have an output of shape $(B, 1, W, H)$. If we *end* our network with a convolutional layer that has *only one filter*, our model's final output will have only one channel. So, we use a convolutional layer as the last layer.

The easiest way to keep the same W and H values is to *never* use pooling and to always use padding so the output is the same size as the input. Remember from chapter 3 that using a filter size of k means setting padding $= \lfloor \frac{k}{2} \rfloor$ will ensure that the height and width of the output are the same as the input. We also use that constraint in defining our network.

The following code incorporates both of these choices into a simple neural network. It follows our usual pattern of repeating convolutions, normalization, and then a nonlinearity:

```
def cnnLayer(in_filters, out_filters, kernel_size=3):        ←── Defines our helper
    """                                                           function that creates a
                                                                  hidden layer for a CNN
    in_filters: how many channels are in the input to this layer
    out_filters: how many channels should this layer output
    kernel_size: how large should the filters of this layer be
    """
    padding = kernel_size//2
    return nn.Sequential(
        nn.Conv2d(in_filters, out_filters, kernel_size, padding=padding),
        nn.BatchNorm2d(out_filters),
        nn.LeakyReLU(),                      ←──────── We aren't setting the leak value,
    )                                                  to make the code shorter.
segmentation_model = nn.Sequential(          ←──────── Specifies a model for
    cnnLayer(C, n_filters),                            image segmentation
```

The first layer changes the number of channels to the large number. `──→`

Creates five more hidden layers →
```
    *[cnnLayer(n_filters, n_filters) for _ in range(5)],
    nn.Conv2d(n_filters, 1, (3,3), padding=1),    ←
)
seg_results = train_network(segmentation_model,
    ⤷ loss_func, train_seg_loader, epochs=10,
    ⤷ device=device, val_loader=test_seg_loader)
```
Makes a prediction for every location. We use one channel out since we have a binary problem and are using BCEWithLogitsLoss as our loss function. The shape is now (1, W, H).

Trains the segmentation model

Now that we have trained a model, let's visually inspect some of the results. The following code shows how we can grab an item from the test dataset, push it through the model, and get a prediction. Since we use the binary cross-entropy loss, we need to use the `torch.sigmoid` (σ) function to convert the raw outputs (also called *logits*) into the right form. Remember that the sigmoid maps everything into the range $[0, 1]$, so the threshold of 0.5 tells us if we should go with a final answer of "nuclei present" or "not present." Then we can plot the results showing the raw input (left), ground truth (center), and prediction (right) for the image:

Picks a specific example from the dataset that shows a particular result. Change this to look at other entries from the dataset.

Pushes a test datapoint through the model. Remember, the raw outputs are called the logits.

```
index = 6
```

We don't want gradients if we aren't training, so no gradients please! →
```
with torch.no_grad():
    logits = segmentation_model(test_split[index][0].
        ⤷ unsqueeze(0).to(device))[0].cpu()
    pred = torch.sigmoid(logits) >= 0.5
```
Applies σ to the logits to make predictions and then applies a threshold to get a prediction mask.

Plots the input, ground truth, and prediction. →
```
plt.figure(figsize=(16,10))
plt.subplot(1, 3, 1)
plt.imshow(test_split[index][0].permute(1,2,0).numpy(),
    ⤷ cmap='gray')
plt.subplot(1, 3, 2)
plt.imshow(test_split[index][1].numpy()[0,:], cmap='gray')
plt.subplot(1, 3, 3)
plt.imshow(pred.numpy()[0,:], cmap='gray')
```
First plots the original input to the network.

Second is the ground truth.

Third is the prediction our network made.

```
[12]:  Text(-240, -50, 'Error: Phantom object')
```

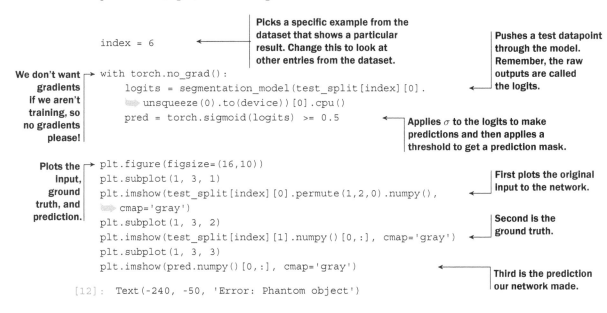

Overall, the results are very good. We even get most of the literal edge cases (nuclei at the border of the image) correct. Objects that occur on the edges of images are often harder to predict correctly. But there are some errors: for the really big nuclei, our segmentation model put a hole that does not belong. We also detected some nuclei that don't exist. I've annotated the output with red arrows to highlight these mistakes.

Part of the issue may be that our receptive field for the network is too small to accurately handle large nuclei. For each layer of convolution, the *maximal* range is increased by $\lceil \frac{k}{2} \rceil$. Since we have six convolutional layers, that gets us just barely $2 \cdot 6 = 12$ pixels of width. While the simple option would be to add more layers or increase the width of the convolutions, those can get expensive. On reason it's so expensive may be that we are never doing any pooling, so each time we add a layer or double the number of filters, we increase the total memory used by our approach.

8.2   Transposed convolutions for expanding image size

We prefer to somehow use pooling so that we get the benefits of a smaller output (less memory) and larger receptive field, and then later *expand back up* to a larger form. We can do this with what is called a *transposed* convolution. In a normal convolution, the value of *one output* is determined by *multiple inputs*. Because each output has multiple inputs, the output is *smaller* than the input so each output gets its full contribution. An easy way to think about transposed convolutions is to imagine that *one input* contributes to *multiple outputs*. This is shown in figure 8.3 applied to a small 2×2 image. Because the transposed version has one input to multiple outputs, we need to make the output *larger than the original input* so each output that an input contributes to is represented.

Figure 8.4 shows an example of convolution on top and transposed convolution on the bottom. Both are using the same image and filter in their respective patterns. Like a normal convolution, the transposed version adds together all of the contributions at each location to reach a final value. For this reason, notice that the *inside* area shown with a red dashed border has an *identical* result between normal and transposed convolution. The difference is how we interpret border cases: regular convolution shrinks, and transposed convolutions expand. Every transposed convolution has an equivalent regular convolution that has simply changed the amount of padding and other parameters applied.

The important thing to remember here is that transposed convolutions give us a way to expand back up in size. In particular, we can add a *stride* to cause a doubling effect to reverse the halving effect caused by pooling. A *stride* is how much we slide our filter by when applying a convolution. By default, we use a stride $s = 1$, meaning we slide the filter over one position at a time. Figure 8.5 shows what happens when we use a stride $s = 2$. A regular convolution takes steps of 2 on the *input*, while a transposed one takes steps of 2 on the *output*. So a stride 2 *convolution halves the size*, and a stride 2 *transposed convolution doubles the size*.

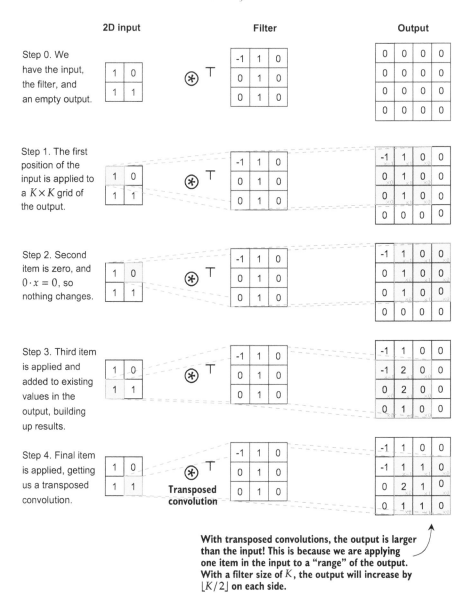

Figure 8.3 Step-by-step calculation of a transposed convolution. The green region on the left shows which part of the input is being used, and the orange on the right shows which part of the output is being altered. At every step, the input is multiplied by the filter and added to the output at the given location. Because the input expands by the size of the filter, the size of the output is larger than that of the input.

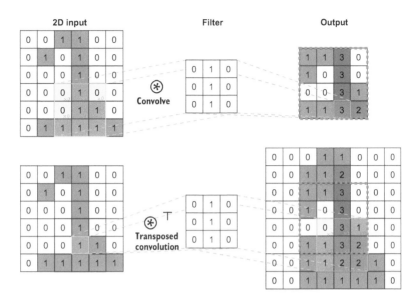

Figure 8.4 Example of a regular convolution (top) and transposed convolution (bottom) when applied to the same input image with the same filter. The regular convolution shrinks the output by the size of the filter, and the transposed version extends the output by the size of the kernel.

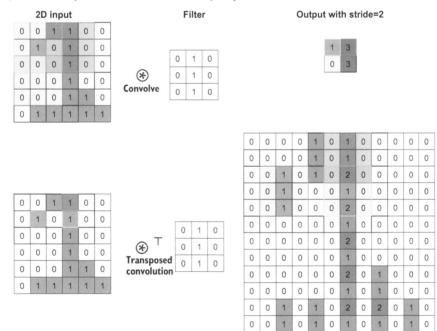

Figure 8.5 Example of how a stride of $s = 2$ impacts a regular and transposed convolution. The shaded regions show the input/output mappings. For convolution, the input moves the filter by two positions, making the output smaller. Transposed convolution still uses every input position, but the output is moved by two positions.

The way we incorporate transposed convolution into our architecture is that every few layers, we would do a round of pooling. If we do pooling in a 2×2 grid (the standard), we double the width of the model's receptive field. Each time we perform pooling, we end up looking at a higher-level view of the image. Once we reach halfway through the network, we start to perform transposed convolutions to get back up to the correct size. The layers after transposed convolutions give the model a chance to refine the high-level view. Similar to how we designed our autoencoders from the last chapter, we make the pooling and transpose rounds symmetric.

8.2.1   *Implementing a network with transposed convolutions*

With a transposed convolution, we can expand a network's output, which means we can use pooling and then undo the reduction in width and height later. Let's try it to see if this provides any real value to our model. In the interest of keeping these examples small and allowing them to run quickly, we do only one round of pooling and transposed convolution; but if you did more, you might see better results. The following code redefines our network with one round of max pooling and later one round of transposed convolution:

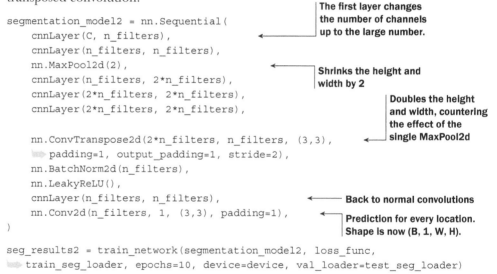

```
segmentation_model2 = nn.Sequential(
    cnnLayer(C, n_filters),                          ← The first layer changes
    cnnLayer(n_filters, n_filters),                    the number of channels
    nn.MaxPool2d(2),                                   up to the large number.
    cnnLayer(n_filters, 2*n_filters),
    cnnLayer(2*n_filters, 2*n_filters),              ← Shrinks the height and
    cnnLayer(2*n_filters, 2*n_filters),                width by 2

                                                       Doubles the height
                                                       and width, countering
                                                       the effect of the
    nn.ConvTranspose2d(2*n_filters, n_filters, (3,3), ← single MaxPool2d
        padding=1, output_padding=1, stride=2),
    nn.BatchNorm2d(n_filters),
    nn.LeakyReLU(),
    cnnLayer(n_filters, n_filters),                  ← Back to normal convolutions
    nn.Conv2d(n_filters, 1, (3,3), padding=1),       ← Prediction for every location.
)                                                      Shape is now (B, 1, W, H).

seg_results2 = train_network(segmentation_model2, loss_func,
    train_seg_loader, epochs=10, device=device, val_loader=test_seg_loader)
```

Now that we have trained this new model, let's try it on the same data and see what happens:

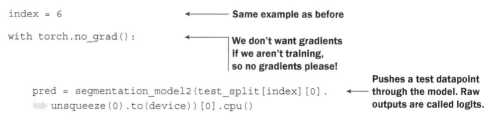

```
index = 6                              ← Same example as before

with torch.no_grad():                  ← We don't want gradients
                                         if we aren't training,
                                         so no gradients please!

                                                       Pushes a test datapoint
    pred = segmentation_model2(test_split[index][0].   ← through the model. Raw
        unsqueeze(0).to(device))[0].cpu()                outputs are called logits.
```

```
        pred = torch.sigmoid(pred) >= 0.5
```
◄─ **Applies** σ **to the logits to make predictions and then applies a threshold to get a prediction mask**

```
plt.figure(figsize=(16,10))
plt.subplot(1, 3, 1)
```
◄─ **Plots the input, ground truth, and prediction**

```
plt.imshow(test_split[index][0].permute(1,2,0).numpy(), cmap='gray')
plt.subplot(1, 3, 2)
```
◄─ **First plots the original input to the network**

```
plt.imshow(test_split[index][1].numpy()[0,:], cmap='gray')
plt.subplot(1, 3, 3)
```
◄─ **Second is ground truth**

```
plt.imshow(pred.numpy()[0,:], cmap='gray')
```
◄─ **Third is the prediction our network made**

```
[15]:  <matplotlib.image.AxesImage at 0x7fd24804e1d0>
```

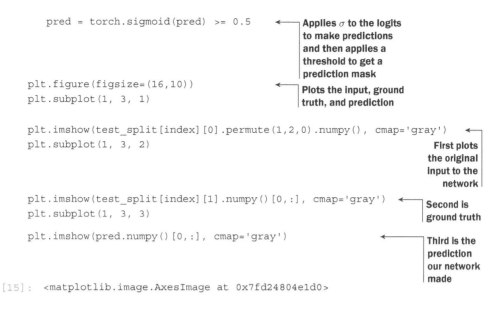

The hole has been patched; the nuclei object detection shows nice solid regions of white. The network has also done a slightly better job with some of the edge cases. Working on a smaller representation (the rounds after pooling) helps to encourage softer and smoother masks in our output. But we should never look at just a single image to decide if we've made an improvement, so let's check the validation loss:

```
sns.lineplot(x='epoch', y='val loss', data=seg_results, label='CNN')
sns.lineplot(x='epoch', y='val loss', data=seg_results2,
       label='CNN w/ transposed-conv')
```

[17]:   <AxesSubplot:xlabel='epoch', ylabel='val loss'>

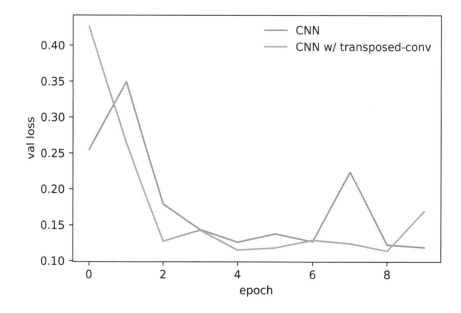

According to the validation error, we have overall done a *slightly* better job than before. Something that is often just as important is learning speed, and we can see that this approach was able to make faster progress in fewer epochs of training. This faster learning is a significant benefit, and its importance grows as we work on harder and larger problems.

8.3   U-Net: Looking at fine and coarse details

Right now, we have two ways to model the image segmentation problem. The first approach, from section 8.1, uses no pooling and performs many rounds of convolutional layers. This makes a model that can look at minute fine-grained details but can literally miss the forest for the trees.

The second, from section 8.2, uses rounds of max pooling followed by transposed convolution layers at the end of the architecture. You can think of this approach as progressively looking at higher-level regions of the image. The more rounds of pooling you do, the higher the model looks to make decisions.

Max pooling/up-sampling works well for detecting larger objects and broad borders, and the fine-grained model works better for small objects and nuanced object borders. We want a way to get the best of both worlds, capturing both fine details and high-level things simultaneously.

We can achieve this best-of-both-worlds by including *skip connections* (from chapter 6) into our approach. Doing so creates an architecture approach known as *U-Net*,[3] where we create three subnetworks to process the input:

- An input subnetwork that applies hidden layers to the full-resolution (lowest level of features) input.

- A bottleneck subnetwork that is applied after max pooling, allowing it to look at a lower resolution (higher-level features), and then uses a transposed convolution to expand its results back up to the same width and height as the original input.

- An output subnetwork that combines the results from the two proceeding networks. This lets it get the best of both worlds, looking at low- and high-level details simultaneously.

Figure 8.6 shows a single block of the U-Net style approach.

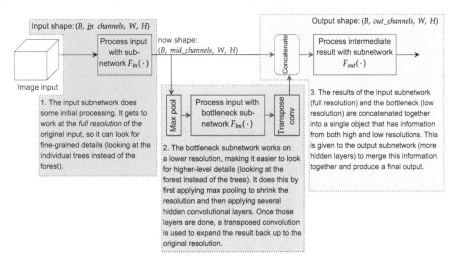

Figure 8.6 Design of a U-Net block, which is divided into three subnetworks. Each subnetwork has multiple convolutional hidden layers. The result of the first subnetwork goes to two locations: the second bottleneck subnetwork (after going through max pooling), and the third subnetwork after being combined with the second's result.

Expanding this into a larger U-Net architecture is done by repeatedly making the bottleneck subnetwork be *another* U-Net block. This way, you get a network that learns to look at multiple different resolutions at once. When you draw the diagram of inserting U-Net blocks into U-Net blocks, you end up with a U shape as shown in figure 8.7. This diagram also shows that each time we shrink the resolution by a factor of $2\times$, we tend to increase the number of filters by a factor of $2\times$. This way, each level of the network has a roughly comparable amount of work and computation to perform.

---

[3] O. Ronneberger, P. Fischer, and T. Brox, "U-Net: convolutional networks for biomedical image segmentation," in *Medical Image Computing and Computer-Assisted Intervention—MICCAI 2015*, N. Navab, J. Hornegger, W.M. Wells, and A.F. Frangi, eds., Springer International Publishing, 2015, pp. 234–241.

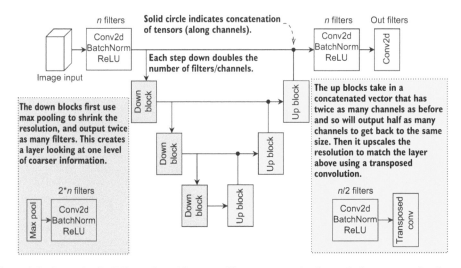

Figure 8.7   Example of a U-Net style architecture. After some rounds of convolution, max pooling is used to shrink the image several times. Eventually, a transposed convolution up-samples the results, and every up-sample includes a skip connection to the previous result before pooling. The results are concatenated together and proceed to a new output round of convolutions. The architecture makes a U-like shape.

Figure 8.7 shows one group of Conv2d, BatchNorm, and ReLu activation per input/ output pair, but you could have any number of hidden layer blocks. While U-Net refers to both a *specific* architecture and a *style* of architecture, I'm going to refer to the style overall. In the next section, we define some code for implementing U-Net style models.

8.3.1   *Implementing U-Net*

To make our implementation simpler, we take in the number of in_channels and use mid_channels as how many filters should be used in the convolutions. If we want the output to have a different number of channels, we use a 1×1 convolution to change mid_channels to out_channels. Since each block can have multiple layers, we make that an argument as well. The last thing we need is the sub_network used as the bottleneck. So our constructor documentation looks like this:

> Our class extends nn.Module;
> all PyTorch layers must extend this.

```
class UNetBlock2d(nn.Module):
    def __init__(self, in_channels, mid_channels, out_channels=None,
        layers=1, sub_network=None, filter_size=3):
        """
        in_channels: the number of channels in the input to this block
        mid_channels: the number of channels to have as the output for each
            convolutional filter
        out_channels: if not 'None', ends the network with a 1x1
            convolution to convert the number of output channels to a
            specific number.
        layers: how many blocks of hidden layers to create on both the
            input and output side of a U-Net block
```

```
        sub_network: the network to apply after shrinking the input by a
            factor of 2 using max pooling. The number of output channels
            should be equal to `mid_channels`
        filter_size: how large the convolutional filters should be
    """

        super().__init__()
```

Now let's walk through the constructor's contents. The input to a block (step 1) will always have shape $(B, \text{in\_channels}, W, H)$ and produce a shape $(B, \text{mid\_channels}, W, H)$. But the output portion from step 3 will have two possible shapes: either $(B, 2 \cdot \text{mid\_channels}, W, H)$, because it combines the results from step 1 and step 2, giving it $2\times$ the number of channels; or $(B, \text{mid\_channels}, W, H)$ if there is no bottleneck. So we need to check whether we have a sub_network and change the number of inputs to the output block accordingly. Once that is done, we can build the hidden layers for steps 1 and 3. For step 2, we use a subnetwork self.bottleneck to represent the model that is applied on the shrunken version of the image after nn.MaxPool2d is applied. The next block of code shows all of this and organizes step 1 into self.in_model, step 2 into self.bottleneck, and step 3 into out_model:

```
in_layers = [cnnLayer(in_channels, mid_channels, filter_size)]      ◄─┐ Starts preparing
                                                                       │ the layers used to
if sub_network is None:          ◄──────────  If we have a subnetwork, │ process the input
    inputs_to_outputs = 1                     we double the number
else:                                         of inputs to the output. ┌ Prepares the layers
    inputs_to_outputs = 2                     So let's figure that out now. │ used to make the
                                                                       │ final output, which
out_layers = [cnnLayer(mid_channels*inputs_to_outputs,                │ has extra input
    mid_channels, filter_size)]              ◄──────────────────────── │ channels from
                                                                       └ any subnetwork
```

```
for _ in range(layers-1):
    in_layers.append(cnnLayer(mid_channels, mid_channels, filter_size))
    out_layers.append(cnnLayer(m
id_channels, mid_channels, filter_size))          Uses 1 × 1 convolutions
                                                   to ensure a specific
if out_channels is not None:          ◄───────────  output size
    out_layers.append(nn.Conv2d(mid_channels, out_channels, 1, padding=0))
```

Makes the additional hidden layers used for the input and output

```
self.in_model = nn.Sequential(*in_layers)      ◄──┐ Defines our three total subnetworks.
                                                   │ 1) in_model performs the initial
                                                   │ rounds of convolution.
```

```
if sub_network is not None:          ◄────────────┐ 2) Our subnetwork works on the
    self.bottleneck = nn.Sequential(              │ max pooled result. We add the
    nn.MaxPool2d(2),                              │ pooling and up-scaling
    sub_network,                                  │ directly into the submodel.
    nn.ConvTranspose2d(mid_channels, mid_channels,
        filter_size, padding=filter_size//2,
        output_padding=1, stride=2)
    )
```

Shrinks →

Processes the smaller resolution →

Expands back up →

```
else:
    self.bottleneck = None
self.out_model = nn.Sequential(*out_layers)
```

3) The output model that processes the concatenated result, or just the output from in_model if no subnetwork was given

That gets all the hard coding out of the way. The last step is to implement the `forward` function that uses it. By organizing all of our parts into different `nn.Sequential` objects, this last step is fairly painless. We get the full-scale result by applying `in_model` on the input x. Next, we check whether a `bottleneck` is present, and if so, we apply it and concatenate that result with the full-scale one. Finally, we apply the `out_model`:

```
def forward(self, x):
    full_scale_result = self.in_model(x)

    if self.bottleneck is not None:
        bottle_result = self.bottleneck(full_scale_result)

        full_scale_result = torch.cat(
            [full_scale_result, bottle_result], dim=1)

    return self.out_model(full_scale_result)
```

Computes the convolutions at the current scale. (B, C, W, H)

Checks if we have a bottleneck to apply

(B, C, W, H) shape because bottleneck does both the pooling and expansion

Shapes (B, 2*C, W, H)

Computes the output on the concatenated (or not!) result

This gives us a single U-Net block represented by the `UNetBlock2d` class. With this one `UNetBlock2d` module, we can implement an entire U-Net architecture by specifying that the `sub_network` itself be another `UNetBlock2d`. We can then just repeat this as many times as we like. The following code nests three `UNetBlock2d`s together, followed by one round of convolution to reach our desired output size:

```
unet_model = nn.Sequential(
    UNetBlock2d(3, 32, layers=2, sub_network=
        UNetBlock2d(32, 64, out_channels=32, layers=2, sub_network=
            UNetBlock2d(64, 128, out_channels=64, layers=2)
        ),
    ),
    nn.Conv2d(32, 1, (3,3), padding=1),    ← Shape is now (B, 1, W, H)
)

unet_results = train_network(unet_model, loss_func, train_seg_loader,
    epochs=10, device=device, val_loader=test_seg_loader)
```

Now that we have trained this model, let's plot the results compared to our first two segmentation models. Notice that the U-Net approach is the best of both worlds, giving us both lower total loss and learning faster than either the fine- or coarse-grained models from earlier. U-Net converges to the same or better accuracy faster than the other approaches. It is also useful because we don't have to guess exactly how many layers of pooling to use. We can simply pick a slightly larger number of rounds of pooling (U-Net blocks) than we think is necessary and let U-Net learn on its own if it should use the lower-resolution results. This is possible because U-Net maintains information from every level of resolution via the concatenation and output subnetworks from each block:

```
sns.lineplot(x='epoch', y='val loss', data=seg_results, label='CNN')
sns.lineplot(x='epoch', y='val loss', data=seg_results2,
    label='CNN w/ transposed-conv')
sns.lineplot(x='epoch', y='val loss', data=unet_results, label='UNet')
```

```
[20]:  <AxesSubplot:xlabel='epoch', ylabel='val loss'>
```

The U-Net approach is a strong starting point for any image segmentation problem or any related tasks where you need to make a prediction about multiple points within an image. It is also a repetition of some similar concepts we have already learned: combining skip connections and 1×1 convolutions allows us to build a more expressive and powerful model. This also shows how we can adjust these concepts to apply certain kinds of priors to the data we are working on. We believed that we wanted small local details and coarser higher-level details to make better decisions, and we used skip connections and transposed convolution to embed that prior into the design of our architecture. Learning to recognize these opportunities and following through on them will make the biggest difference in your results compared to almost anything else you might do.

8.4 *Object detection with bounding boxes*

Image segmentation is conceptually simple, a single network running once to get predictions for every pixel, but getting every pixel labeled is expensive. We'll now learn how a more involved approach, with multiple components working together, can perform bounding-box-based object detection. This strategy finds objects in one pass, and a second step determines what specific object is present at a location. That makes the labeling easier, but the network is more technically complicated.

In particular, we go over an algorithm called *Faster R-CNN*,[4] which has become the de facto baseline for object detection. Most other approaches are variations on Faster R-CNN. Like most object detectors, Faster R-CNN uses the idea of *bounding boxes* for labels and prediction. Figure 8.8 shows a potential bounding box label and prediction for a stop sign. The bounding box approach is often preferred because it is cheaper and easier to label. You simply need software to annotate a box around an image (you can find some freely available online at https://github.com/heartexlabs/awesome-data-labeling#images), which is much easier than painstakingly marking *every pixel* as required by image segmentation.

Figure 8.8   A stop sign as the target for bounding-box-based object detection. The green box shows the ground truth, a box just large enough to contain the entire object. The red box shows a potential predic-tion, which is close but not quite correct. Water doesn't obey the whimsical desires of the lowly stop sign.

We want the model to detect objects by drawing a box around any object of interest. Since objects could be at weird sizes or angles, the goal is that the box should bound the object, so the box should be *just* big enough to fit the entire object within the box. We do not want the box to be any larger, because then we could cheat by marking a box the size of the image. We also don't want the box to be any smaller because then it will miss part of the object, and we don't want a single object to have multiple boxes.

Getting a model to predict boxes around objects is tricky. How do we represent the box as a prediction? Does each pixel get its own box predicted? Won't that lead to tons of false positives? How do we do it efficiently without writing a lot of horrendous `for` loops? There are many different approaches to these issues, but we'll focus on Faster R-CNN. This algorithm's high-level strategy is a good basis for understanding other more sophisticated object detectors and is built into PyTorch by default.

---

[4] Yes, "Faster" is part of the name. It is good marketing!

8.4.1 Faster R-CNN

Let's say we have a self-driving car, and we want the car to stop at stop signs because we don't want to go to jail for developing a car that plows through intersections. We need as many images as possible that both include and do not include stop signs and where the stop signs have had a box drawn around them. Faster R-CNN is a complicated algorithm with many parts, but by this point you've learned enough to understand all the parts that make the whole. Faster R-CNN approaches this problem in three steps:

1 Process the image and extract features.

2 Use those features to detect potential/proposed objects.

3 Take each potential object and decide what object it is, or if it isn't an object at all.

Figure 8.9 gives an overview of the Faster R-CNN algorithm; we go into the details in a moment. The three steps we described can be broken into three subnetworks: a *backbone network* to extract feature maps, a *region proposal network* (RPN) to find objects, and a *region of interest pooling* (RoI pooling or just RoI) network that predicts what type of object is being looked at. Faster R-CNN is an extension of what we have learned because the backbone network is a fully convolutional network like we used for image segmentation, except we have the final convolution layer output some number of C' channels instead of just 1 channel.

We will not implement Faster R-CNN from scratch because it has a number of important details and takes hundreds of lines of code to implement in total. But we'll review all the critical components because so many other object detectors build on this approach. Faster R-CNN is also built into PyTorch, so you don't have to do as much work to use it yourself. The following sections summarize how the backbone, region proposal, and region of interest subnetworks work, in the order used.

BACKBONE

The backbone network is essentially *any* neural network that works like the object-segmentation network we just defined. It takes in an image with a width, height, and number of channels (C, W, H) and outputs a new feature map (C', W', H'). The backbone can have a different width and height as its output, as long as the output height and width are always a multiple of the input height and width (i.e., if $W' = W \cdot z$ then $H' = H \cdot z$, you have to maintain the ratio between width and height). These extra details are shown in figure 8.10.

The goal of the backbone is to *do all of the feature extraction* so the other subnetworks can be smaller and don't need to be very complex. This makes it faster to run (only one big network to run once) and helps coordinate the two other subnetworks (they are working from the same representation). The backbone is an excellent location to use a U-Net style approach so that you can detect and distinguish between high-level objects (e.g., a car versus a cat doesn't need much detail) and similar objects that can only be distinguished by looking at finer, low-level details (e.g., different breeds of dog, like the Yorkshire terrier and the Australian terrier).

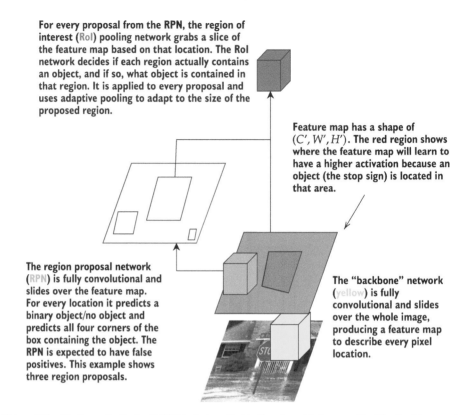

For every proposal from the RPN, the region of interest (RoI) pooling network grabs a slice of the feature map based on that location. The RoI network decides if each region actually contains an object, and if so, what object is contained in that region. It is applied to every proposal and uses adaptive pooling to adapt to the size of the proposed region.

Feature map has a shape of (C', W', H'). The red region shows where the feature map will learn to have a higher activation because an object (the stop sign) is located in that area.

The region proposal network (RPN) is fully convolutional and slides over the feature map. For every location it predicts a binary object/no object and predicts all four corners of the box containing the object. The RPN is expected to have false positives. This example shows three region proposals.

The "backbone" network (yellow) is fully convolutional and slides over the whole image, producing a feature map to describe every pixel location.

Figure 8.9   Diagram of a Faster R-CNN being applied to the stop sign from earlier. The backbone network scans the image and is the largest network, doing the heavy lifting to produce good features for the rest of the algorithm. The region proposal network comes next and is also fully convolutional but very small. It reuses the work of the backbone's feature map to make predictions or proposals for where objects may be in the image. Finally, a region of interest network takes every subregion of the feature map that corresponds to one of the proposals and makes a final determination about whether an object is present—and, if so, what object it is.

REGION PROPOSAL NETWORK (RPN)

Once the backbone has given us a feature-rich representation of our image as a (C', W', H') tensor, the RPN determines whether an object exists at a specific location in the image. It does this by predicting two things:

- A bounding box with four locations (top left, top right, bottom left, and bottom right)

- A binary prediction to classify the box as "has object" or "does not have object"

In this case, it does not matter how many classes we are trying to predict or what specific object is present—the only goal is to determine whether an object exists and where the object is. Essentially, all the classes of the problem are merged into one superclass of "has object."

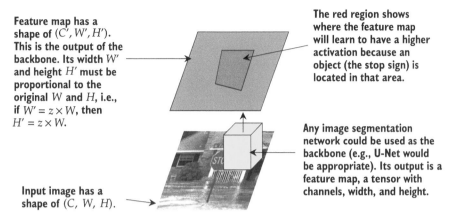

Feature map has a shape of (C', W', H'). **This is the output of the backbone. Its width** W' **and height** H' **must be proportional to the original** W **and** H, **i.e., if** $W' = z \times W$, **then** $H' = z \times W$.

The red region shows where the feature map will learn to have a higher activation because an object (the stop sign) is located in that area.

Any image segmentation network could be used as the backbone (e.g., U-Net would be appropriate). Its output is a feature map, a tensor with channels, width, and height.

Input image has a shape of (C, W, H).

Figure 8.10 The backbone takes in the original image and creates a new image that is the feature map. It has multiple channels C' (a user-defined value) and a new width W' and height H'. The backbone is the only large network in Faster R-CNN and is meant to do all the heavy lifting so the other networks can be smaller and faster.

To make the model even more robust, we can make these six total predictions (4 box coordinates + 2 has object/no object) k times.[5] The idea is to give the model k chances to predict the correct box shape during learning. A common default is to use $k = 9$ guesses. This allows the RPN to have multiple predictions about the size or shape of an object at a given location within the image and is a common optimization that is included in most implementations. The overall process of the RPN is shown in figure 8.11.

Because we are making k predictions per location, we *know* that there will be more false positives than necessary (if an object is at that location, only one of those k predictions will be the closest, and the others become false positives). This is part of why the predictions are called *proposals* instead of predictions. We expect that many more proposals will exist than actual objects, and later in the process, we will do more work to clean up these false positives.

The RPN *could* be implemented with a single convolutional layer, using `nn.Conv2d(C', 6*k, 1)`, which would slide over every location in the image and make six predictions. This is a trick to use a one-by-one convolution to make local predictions. In real implementations, this is usually done with two layers instead, something like this:

```
nn.Sequential(
    nn.Conv2d(C', 256, (1,1)),    ← One layer for nonlinearities
    nn.BatchNorm2d(256),
    nn.LeakyReLU(),
    nn.Conv2d(256, 6*k, (1,1)),
  ...                              Some code is added here to split the
)                                  output into one group of four and another
                                   group of two. The approach depends
                                   on the implementation strategy.
```

---

[5] This could also be done as 4 boxes + 1 by training has object/no object as a binary. Most papers and resources online use the +2 approach, though, so I'm sticking with that for my description.

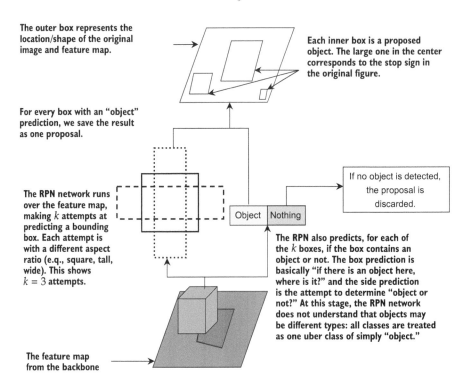

The outer box represents the location/shape of the original image and feature map.

Each inner box is a proposed object. The large one in the center corresponds to the stop sign in the original figure.

For every box with an "object" prediction, we save the result as one proposal.

The RPN network runs over the feature map, making k attempts at predicting a bounding box. Each attempt is with a different aspect ratio (e.q., square, tall, wide). This shows $k = 3$ attempts.

Object   Nothing

If no object is detected, the proposal is discarded.

The RPN also predicts, for each of the k boxes, if the box contains an object or not. The box prediction is basically "if there is an object here, where is it?" and the side prediction is the attempt to determine "object or not?" At this stage, the RPN network does not understand that objects may be different types: all classes are treated as one uber class of simply "object."

The feature map from the backbone

Figure 8.11 Further details on how the region proposal network (RPN) works. It takes in the feature map from the backbone and makes multiple predictions at every location. It is predicting multiple boxes and, for each box, whether it contains an object. Boxes that receive an "object" prediction become the outputs of the RPN: a list of regions in the original input that may contain objects.

Adding just one extra layer gives the model some nonlinear capability to make better predictions. We can use such a small network because the backbone network has already done the heavy lifting. So a small, fast, barely nonlinear RPN network runs on top of the backbone. The RPN's job is to make predictions about *where* objects are and *what their shape is.*

REGION OF INTEREST (ROI) POOLING

The last step is RoI pooling. The outputs of the RPN give us the locations for $W' \cdot H' \cdot k$ total potential regions of interest. The RoI pooling takes each proposal from the RPN and grabs the corresponding region of the feature map (produced by the backbone) as its input. But each of these regions may be a different size, and regions may overlap. At training, we need to make predictions for all of these regions so that the model can learn to suppress false positives and detect false negatives. At test time, we only need to make predictions for the proposals that received larger scores from the RPN subnetwork. In both training and testing, we have an issue that the *size of the proposals is variable.* So we need to devise a network that can handle *variable-sized* inputs and still make a single prediction.

To achieve this, we use *adaptive pooling*. In normal pooling, we say how much we want to shrink the input by (e.g., we usually shrink the image by a factor of 2). In adaptive pooling, we state how large we want the output to be, and adaptive pooling adjusts the shrinkage factor based on the input's size. For example, if we want a 3×3 output, and the input is 6×6, adaptive pooling would be done in a 2×2 grid ($6/2 = 3$). But if the input was 12×12, the pooling would be done in a 4×4 grid to get $12/4 = 3$. That way, we *always* get the same size output. The RoI pooling process is shown in more detail in figure 8.12.

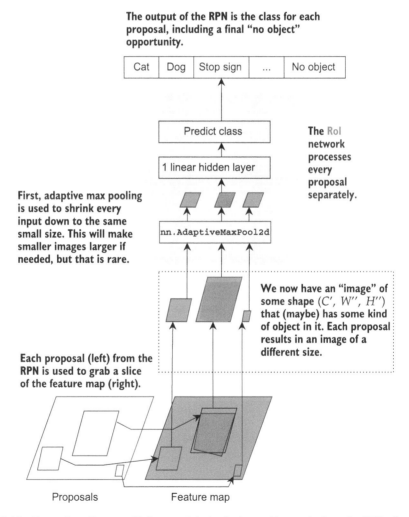

The output of the RPN is the class for each proposal, including a final "no object" opportunity.

| Cat | Dog | Stop sign | ... | No object |

Predict class

The RoI network processes every proposal separately.

1 linear hidden layer

First, adaptive max pooling is used to shrink every input down to the same small size. This will make smaller images larger if needed, but that is rare.

`nn.AdaptiveMaxPool2d`

We now have an "image" of some shape (C', W'', H'') that (maybe) has some kind of object in it. Each proposal results in an image of a different size.

Each proposal (left) from the RPN is used to grab a slice of the feature map (right).

Proposals   Feature map

Figure 8.12 The region of interest (RoI) network is the final step. The results from the RPN tell us which regions of the feature map may contain an object. Slices of these regions are extracted, resized to a standard small shape using `nn.AdaptiveMaxPool2d`, and then a small, fully connected hidden layer makes a prediction for each proposal. This is the final determination of what specific object is present.

The code for this RoI subnetwork might look something like this:

```
nn.Sequential(
    nn.AdaptiveMaxPool2d((7,7)),          ◄─┐ For an input of any W and H
    nn.Flatten(),                            │ to have a shape of (B, C, 7, 7)
    nn.Linear(7*7, 256),                  ◄──── now (B, C*7*7)
    nn.BatchNorm1d(256),                  ◄─┐
    nn.LeakyReLU(),                          │ Assuming C=1 and 256
    nn.Linear(256, classes),                 │ hidden neurons
)
```

The RoI network starts with adaptive pooling to enforce a particular size for all predictions. This is an aggressively small 7×7 to make the RoI network small and fast to run since we have many proposals to process. It is so small that we follow it with just two rounds of nn.Linear layers instead of convolutional ones because it's been shrunken so much. We can then apply this network to every region identified by the RPN network, regardless of the size, and get a prediction.

8.4.2   *Using Faster R-CNN in PyTorch*

The details of implementing Faster R-CNN are not trivial, and it's a tough algorithm to get completely right. (If you want the minutia, check out the article "Object Detection and Classification using R-CNNs" at http://mng.bz/RqnK.) Lucky for us, PyTorch has Faster R-CNN built in. Training it is expensive, though, so we'll create a toy problem from MNIST to show its basics.

Our toy dataset will be a larger 100×100 image containing a random number of MNIST digits in random locations. The goal will be to detect where these images are and classify them correctly. Our dataset will return a tuple. The first item in the tuple is the 100×100 image on which we want to perform object detection. The second item in the tuple is a dictionary with two subtensors.

The first subtensor is indexed by the name boxes. If there are k objects in the image, this have a shape of $(k, 4)$ and store float32 values, giving the four corners of the box. The second item is indexed by labels and is only necessary to perform training. This tensor looks more like the ones we have used before, with a shape of (k) int64 values giving the class ID for each of the k objects to be detected.

IMPLEMENTING A R-CNN DATASET

The following code block shows our Dataset class that implements our toy MNIST detector. Note the comments for computing the offset, as the bounding box corners are all absolute locations, so we need to compute two of the corners based on their relative distance to the starting corners:

```python
class Class2Detect(Dataset):
    """This class is used to create a simple convesion of a dataset from
    a classification problem, to a detection problem. """

    def __init__(self, dataset, toSample=3, canvas_size=100):
        """
        dataset: the source dataset to sample items from as the "objects"
        to detect
        toSample: the maximum number of "objects" to put into any image
        canvas_size: the width and height of the images to place objects
        inside of.
        """
        self.dataset = dataset
        self.toSample = toSample
        self.canvas_size = canvas_size

    def __len__(self):
        return len(self.dataset)

    def __getitem__(self, idx):
        boxes = []
        labels = []

        final_size = self.canvas_size
        img_p = torch.zeros((final_size,final_size),
            dtype=torch.float32)
        for _ in range(np.random.randint(1,self.toSample+1)):
            rand_indx = np.random.randint(0,len(self.dataset))
            img, label = self.dataset[rand_indx]
            _, img_h, img_w = img.shape

            offsets = np.random.randint(0,final_size -
                np.max(img.shape),size=(4))
            offsets[1] = final_size - img.shape[1] - offsets[0]
            offsets[3] = final_size - img.shape[2] - offsets[2]

            with torch.no_grad():
                img_p = img_p + F.pad(img, tuple(offsets))

            xmin = offsets[0]
            xmax = offsets[0]+img_w

            ymin = offsets[2]
            ymax = offsets[2]+img_h

            boxes.append( [xmin, ymin, xmax, ymax] )
            labels.append( label )
        target = {}
        target["boxes"] = torch.as_tensor(boxes, dtype=torch.float32)
        target["labels"] = torch.as_tensor(labels, dtype=torch.int64)

        return img_p, target
```

Samples up to self.toSample objects to place into the image. We are calling the PRNG, so this function is not deterministic.

Creates a larger image that will store all the "objects" to detect

Picks an object at random from the original data-set, and its label

Gets the height and width of that image

Changes the padding at the end to make sure we come out to a specific 100,100 shape

Picks a random offset of the x- and y-axis, essentially placing the image at a random location

xmax is the offset plus the image's width.

Creates the values for the "boxes." All of these are in absolute pixel locations. xmin is determined by the randomly selected offset.

y min/max follows the same pattern.

Adds to the box with the right label

IMPLEMENTING A R-CNN COLLATE FUNCTION

The Faster R-CNN implementation of PyTorch does not take input batches using the pattern we have used thus far (one tensor with everything padded to be the same size). The reason is that Faster R-CNN is designed to work with images of highly variable size, so we would not have the same W and H values for every item. Instead, Faster R-CNN wants a list of tensors and a list of dictionaries. We have to use a custom collate function to make that happen. The following code creates our training and test sets along with the needed collate function and loader:

```
train_data = Class2Detect(torchvision.datasets.MNIST("./", train=True,
    transform=transforms.ToTensor(), download=True))
test_data = Class2Detect(torchvision.datasets.MNIST("./", train=False,
    transform=transforms.ToTensor(), download=True))

def collate_fn(batch):
    """
    batch is going to contain a python list of objects. In our case, our
        data loader returns (Tensor, Dict) pairs
    The FasterRCNN algorithm wants a List[Tensors] and a List[Dict]. So we
        will use this function to convert the
    batch of data into the form we want, and then give it to the Dataloader
        to use
    """
    imgs = []
    labels = []
    for img, label in batch:
        imgs.append(img)
        labels.append(label)
    return imgs, labels

train_loader = DataLoader(train_data, batch_size=128, shuffle=True,
    collate_fn=collate_fn)
```

EXAMINING THE MNIST DETECTION DATA

Now we have all our data set up. Let's look at some of the data to get a sense of it:

```
x, y = train_data[0]    ◀—— Grabs an image with its labels
imshow(x.numpy()[0,:])
```

[24]: <matplotlib.image.AxesImage at 0x7fd248227510>

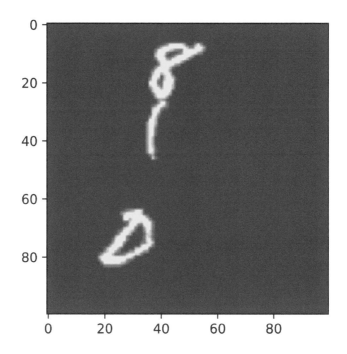

This image has three items in random locations: in this case, 8, 1, and 0. Let's look at the label object, y. It's a Python `dict` object so we can see the keys and values and index the `dict` to look at the individual items it contains.

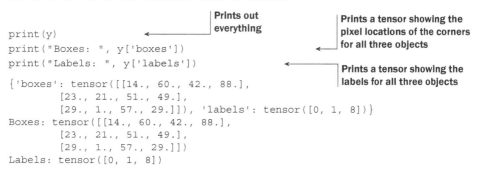

```
print(y)                                    Prints out
                                            everything
print("Boxes: ", y['boxes'])
                                                        Prints a tensor showing the
print("Labels: ", y['labels'])                          pixel locations of the corners
                                                        for all three objects
{'boxes': tensor([[14., 60., 42., 88.],
         [23., 21., 51., 49.],                          Prints a tensor showing the
         [29.,  1., 57., 29.]]), 'labels': tensor([0, 1, 8])}   labels for all three objects
Boxes: tensor([[14., 60., 42., 88.],
         [23., 21., 51., 49.],
         [29.,  1., 57., 29.]])
Labels: tensor([0, 1, 8])
```

All three outputs look sensible. The `boxes` component of y has shape $(3, 4)$, and `labels` has shape (3). If we compare the first row of `boxes` with the previous image, we can see that on the x-axis, it starts at around 30 and goes out near 60, which corresponds to the values in the `boxes` tensor. The same holds for the height values (y coordinates), which start near 10 and go down near 30.

The important thing here is that the boxes and the labels occur in a consistent order. Label 4 could be the first label as long as the first row of `boxes` has the correct location of object 4.

DEFINING A FASTER R-CNN MODEL

With this in place, let's build a small backbone network to use. We simply iterate a number of "Conv, BatchNorm, ReLU" in blocks and slowly increase the number of filters. The last thing we need to do is add a `backbone.out_channels` value to the network we create. This tells the Faster R-CNN implementation the value of C', which is the number of channels in the feature map produced by the backbone network. This is used to set up the RPN and RoI subnetworks for us. Both the RPN and RoI networks are so small that there aren't many parameters for us to tune, and we don't want to make them bigger because then training and inference would be very expensive. Here's the code:

```
C = 1                        ←—— How many channels are in the input?
classes = 10                 ←—— How many classes are there?
n_filters = 32               ←—— How many filters in our backbone?

backbone = nn.Sequential(
    cnnLayer(C, n_filters),
    cnnLayer(n_filters, n_filters),
    cnnLayer(n_filters, n_filters),
    nn.MaxPool2d((2,2)),
    cnnLayer(n_filters, 2*n_filters),
    cnnLayer(2*n_filters, 2*n_filters),
    cnnLayer(2*n_filters, 2*n_filters),
    nn.MaxPool2d((2,2)),
    cnnLayer(2*n_filters, 4*n_filters),
    cnnLayer(4*n_filters, 4*n_filters),    Lets Faster R-CNN know
)                                          exactly how many output
backbone.out_channels = n_filters*4    ←— channels to expect
```

Now we can define our Faster R-CNN model. We give it the backbone network and tell it how many classes exist and how to normalize the image (if your image values are in the range of $[0, 1]$, a mean of 0.5 and deviation of 0.23 are good defaults for most images). We also tell Faster R-CNN the minimum and maximum image sizes. To make this run faster, we are setting them both to the only image size of 100. But for real data, this is used to try to detect objects at multiple scales; that way it can handle objects that are up close or far away. However, that requires more computation to run and even more to train.

> NOTE   How should you set the min and max size for Faster R-CNN on real problems? Here's a rule of thumb: if it's too small for a human to do it, the network probably can't do it, either. In your data, try looking for the objects you care about at different image resolutions. If the smallest resolution at which you can find your object is 256×256, that's a good minimum size. If the largest resolution you need to make your images to spot the objects is 1024×1024, that is a good maximum size.

As of PyTorch 1.7.0, you must also specify some information about the RPN and RoI networks when using your own backbone. This is done with the `AnchorGenerator` and `MultiScaleRoIAlign` objects, respectively. The `AnchorGenerator` controls the number of proposals made by the RPN, generating them at different aspect ratios (e.g., 1.0 is a square, 0.5 is a rectangle twice as wide as it is tall, 2 is a rectangle twice as tall as it is wide), and how many pixels tall those predictions should be (i.e., how big or small might your objects be? You might use between 16 and 512 pixels for real-world problems). `MultiScaleRoIAlign` needs us to tell `FasterRCNN` which part of the backbone provides the feature maps (it supports multiple feature maps as a fancy feature), how large the RoI's network will be, and how to handle fractional pixel locations predicted from the RPN. The following code has all of this put together:

How many proposals k should be generated? Every aspect ratio will be one, and the process will be repeated for multiple image sizes. To make this run faster, we're telling PyTorch to look only for square images that are 32×32 in size.

```
anchor_generator = AnchorGenerator(sizes=((32),),
    aspect_ratios=((1.0),))

roi_pooler = torchvision.ops.MultiScaleRoIAlign(
    featmap_names=['0'], output_size=7,
    sampling_ratio=2)

model = FasterRCNN(backbone, num_classes=10,
    image_mean = [0.5], image_std = [0.229],
    min_size=100, max_size=100,
    rpn_anchor_generator=anchor_generator,
    box_roi_pool=roi_pooler)
```

Tells PyTorch to use the final output of the backbone as the feature map (['0']); uses adaptive pooling down to a 7×7 grid (output_size=7). sampling_ratio is poorly named: it controls details on how the RoI grabs slices of the feature map when a fractional pixel location is predicted (e.g., 5.8 instead of 6). We are not going into those low-level details; 2 is a reasonable default for most work.

Creates the FasterRCNN object. We give it the backbone network, number of classes, min and max size at which to process images (we know all our images are 100 pixels), a mean and standard deviation to subtract from the images, and the anchor generation (RPN) and RoI objects.

IMPLEMENTING A FASTER R-CNN TRAINING LOOP

Because of the unusual use of lists of tensors and lists of dictionaries, we can't use our standard `train_network` function to handle this case. So, we write a minimal training loop to do that training for us. The main trick is to move every item in each list (inputs and labels) to the compute device we want to use. This is because the `.to(device)` method only exists for PyTorch `nn.Module` classes and the standard list and dictionary in Python don't have these functions. Luckily, we defined a `moveTo` function early on that does this and works on lists and dictionaries.

The second oddity is that the `FasterRCNN` object behaves differently in training mode and evaluation model. In training mode, it expects the labels to be passed in with the inputs so that it can compute the loss of every prediction. It also returns a list of every individual prediction loss instead of a single scalar. So, we need to add all of these individual losses to get a final total loss. The following code shows a simple loop for training one epoch of `FasterRCNN`:

```
model = model.train()
model.to(device)
optimizer = torch.optim.AdamW(model.parameters())

for epoch in tqdm(range(1), desc="Epoch", disable=False):
    running_loss = 0.0
    for inputs, labels in tqdm(train_loader, desc="Train Batch",
        leave=False, disable=False):
        inputs = moveTo(inputs, device)        ◄─── Moves the batch to
        labels = moveTo(labels, device)              the device we are using

        optimizer.zero_grad()
        losses = model(inputs, labels)         ◄─── RCNN wants model(inputs, labels),
        loss = 0                                     not just model(inputs).
        for partial_loss in losses.values():
            loss += partial_loss
        loss.backward()                        ◄─────── Proceed as usual.

        optimizer.step()

        running_loss += loss.item()
```

Computes the loss. RCNN gives us a list of losses to add up.

That's all it takes to use the Faster R-CNN implementation provided by PyTorch. Now let's see how well it did. First, set the model to `eval` mode, which changes how the Faster R-CNN implementation takes inputs and returns outputs:

```
model = model.eval()
model = model.to(device)
```

Next, let's quickly grab an item from the test dataset and see what it looks like. In this case, we see it has three objects, 8, 0, and 4:

```
x, y = test_data[0]
print(y)                        ◄─────── This is the ground truth
                                         we want to get back.
{'boxes': tensor([[31., 65., 59., 93.],
        [10., 36., 38., 64.],
        [64., 24., 92., 52.]]), 'labels': tensor([8, 0, 4])}
```

Let's make a prediction. Since we are in `eval` mode, PyTorch wants a `list` of images to make predictions on. It also no longer needs a `labels` object to be passed in as a second argument, which is good because if we already knew where all the objects were, we wouldn't be doing this:

```
with torch.no_grad():
    pred = model([x.to(device)])
```

EXAMINING THE RESULTS

And now we can look at our results. PyTorch's implementation returns a `list` of `dicts` containing three items: `boxes` for the locations of predicted items, `labels` for the class predicted for each item, and `scores` for a confidence associated with each prediction. The following code shows the content of `pred` for this image:

```
print(pred)

[{'boxes': tensor([[31.9313, 65.4917, 59.7824, 93.3052],
        [64.1321, 23.8941, 92.0808, 51.8841],
        [70.3358, 26.2407, 96.2834, 53.7900],
        [64.9917, 24.2980, 92.9516, 52.2016],
        [30.9127, 65.1308, 58.6978, 93.3224]], device='cuda:0'), 'labels':
tensor([8, 4, 1, 9, 5], device='cuda:0'), 'scores': tensor([0.9896, 0.9868,
0.1201, 0.0699, 0.0555], device='cuda:0')}]
```

Each dictionary has a `boxes` tensor with $(k', 4)$ shape for k' predictions. The `labels` tensor has (k') shape, giving the label it predicted for each object. Last, the `scores` tensor also has (k') shape, and it returns a score in the range of $[0, 1]$ for each returned prediction. These scores are the "object" scores from the RPN subnetwork.

In this case, the model is confident it found an 8 and a 4 (≥ 0.9 scores) but less confident about other classes. It's easier to understand these results by printing them into a picture, so we quickly define a function to do that:

```
import matplotlib.patches as patches

def plotDetection(ax, abs_pos, label=None):
    """
    ax: the matplotlib axis to add this plot to
    abs_pos: the positions of the bounding box
    label: the label of the prediction to add
    """
    x1, y1, x2, y2 = abs_pos
    rect = patches.Rectangle((x1,y1),x2-x1,y2-y1,
        linewidth=1,edgecolor='r',facecolor='none')     ◄─── Make a rectangle
    ax.add_patch(rect)                                        for the bounding box.
    if label is not None:                                ◄───────── Add the label if given.
        plt.text(x1+0.5, y1, label, color='black',
            bbox=dict(facecolor='white', edgecolor='white', pad=1.0))

    return

def showPreds(img, pred):
    """
    img: the image to show the bounding box predictions for
    pred: the Faster R-CNN predictions to show on top of the image
    """
    fig,ax = plt.subplots(1)
    ax.imshow(img.cpu().numpy()[0,:])                    ◄─────────── Plot the image.
    boxes = pred['boxes'].cpu()                          ◄─────────── Grab the predictions.
    labels = pred['labels'].cpu()
    scores = pred['scores'].cpu()

    num_preds = labels.shape[0]
    for i in range(num_preds):                           ◄─────────  For each prediction,
        plotDetection(ax, boxes[i].cpu().numpy(),                    plots if it has a high
            label=str(labels[i].item()))                             enough score.

    plt.show()
```

With this code in hand, we can plot the result of Faster R-CNN on this image. We can clearly see that the network did a good job on the 4 and 8 but completely missed the 0. We also have spurious predictions from the network identifying subparts of the 4 and 8 as other digits. For example, look at the right half of the 4. If you weren't paying attention to the left half, you might say it was the digit 1—or you could be looking at the entire image and think it's an incomplete 9. The 8 has similar issues. If you ignore the loop at the top-left, it looks like a 6; and if you ignore the right half of the 8, you could be forgiven for calling it a 9:

```
showPreds(x, pred[0])
```

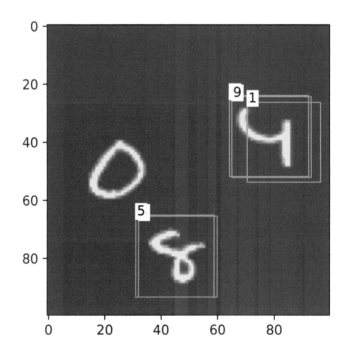

Spurious overlapping objects are a common problem with object detectors. Sometimes these overlapping objects are predictions of the same object (e.g., identifying several 8s) or mislabeled predictions as we see here.

8.4.3   *Suppressing overlapping boxes*

A simple and effective solution to this problem is to *suppress* overlapping boxes. How do we know which boxes to suppress? We want to make sure we pick the *correct* box to use, but we also don't want to throw away boxes that are correctly predicting an adjacent object.

A simple approach called *non-maximum suppression* (NMS) can be used to do this. NMS uses the *intersection over union* (IoU) between two boxes to determine if they overlap *too* much. The IoU is a score: 1 indicates that the boxes have the exact same location, and 0 indicates no overlap. Figure 8.13 shows how it is computed.

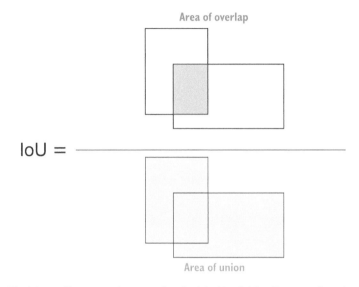

Figure 8.13 The intersection over union score is calculated by dividing the area of overlap between two boxes by the area of the union between two boxes.

IoU divides the size of the intersection of two boxes by the area of the two boxes. This way, we get a size-sensitive measure of how similar two boxes' positions are. NMS works by taking every pair of boxes that have an IoU greater than some specified threshold and keeping only the one with the *largest* score from the RPN network.

Let's quickly see how the NMS method works on our data. We can import it from PyTorch as the nms function:

```
from torchvision.ops import nms
```

Let's remind ourselves of the boxes we have and their associated scores by printing out these fields from the pred returned by our model:

```
print(pred[0]['boxes'])

tensor([[31.9313, 65.4917, 59.7824, 93.3052],
        [64.1321, 23.8941, 92.0808, 51.8841],
        [70.3358, 26.2407, 96.2834, 53.7900],
        [64.9917, 24.2980, 92.9516, 52.2016],
        [30.9127, 65.1308, 58.6978, 93.3224]], device='cuda:0')


print(pred[0]['scores'])

tensor([0.9896, 0.9868, 0.1201, 0.0699, 0.0555], device='cuda:0')
```

The nms function happily takes the tensor of boxes as the first argument and the tensor of scores as the second. The third and final argument is the threshold for calling two boxes different objects. The following code says that if the IoU between two boxes is 50% or more, they are the same item, and we should keep the box with the highest score:

```
print(nms(pred[0]['boxes'], pred[0]['scores'], 0.5))

tensor([0, 1], device='cuda:0')
```

We use a threshold of 50% overlap, and nms returns a tensor of an equal or smaller size, telling us which indices should be kept. In this case, it says to keep boxes 0 and 1, which had the highest scores.

Let's modify our prediction function to use NMS to clean up the output from Faster R-CNN. We also add a min_score flag, which we can use to suppress predictions that are unlikely to be meaningful:

```
def showPreds(img, pred, iou_max_overlap=0.5, min_score=0.05,
    label_names=None):
    """
    img: the original image object detection was performed on
    pred: the output dictionary from FasterRCNN for evaluation on img
    iou_max_overlap: the iou threshold at which non-maximum suppression
        will be performed
    min_score: the minimum RPN network score to consider an object
    """
    fig,ax = plt.subplots(1)
    img = img.cpu().numpy()
    if img.shape[0] == 1:
        ax.imshow(img[0,:])
    else:
        ax.imshow(np.moveaxis(img, 0, 2))
    boxes = pred['boxes'].cpu()
    labels = pred['labels'].cpu()
    scores = pred['scores'].cpu()

    selected = nms(boxes, scores, iou_max_overlap).cpu().numpy()

    for i in selected:
        if scores[i].item() > min_score:
            if label_names is None:
                label = str(labels[i].item())
            else:
                label = label_names[labels[i].item()]
            plotDetection(ax, boxes[i].cpu().numpy(), label=label)

    plt.show()
```

Next, we again plot this image using our improved `showPreds` function, and we see a better and cleaner result: just the 4 and 8 on their own. Alas, the 0 is still undetected, and there is nothing we can do to fix that besides more data and more epochs of training:

```
showPreds(x, pred[0])
```

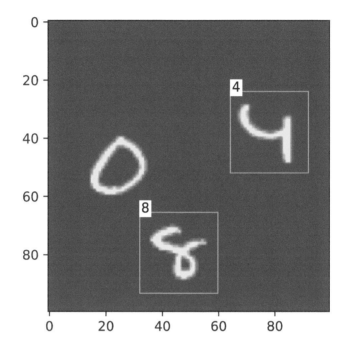

8.5 Using the pretrained Faster R-CNN

PyTorch also provides a pretrained Faster R-CNN model. It's trained on a dataset called COCO, and we can instantiate it and see the class names used for this model:

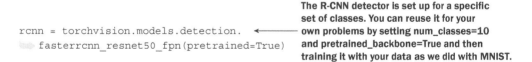

```
rcnn = torchvision.models.detection.
    fasterrcnn_resnet50_fpn(pretrained=True)
```

The R-CNN detector is set up for a specific set of classes. You can reuse it for your own problems by setting num_classes=10 and pretrained_backbone=True and then training it with your data as we did with MNIST.

We set this model in `eval` mode since it does not need training, and we also define the following `NAME` list that contains the class names for all the objects that this pretrained R-CNN knows how to detect:

```
rcnn = rcnn.eval()
```

COCO_INSTANCE_CATEGORY_NAMES.
These come from the PyTorch
documentation:
pytorch.org/vision/0.8/models.html.

```
NAME = [ ◄
    '__background__', 'person', 'bicycle', 'car', 'motorcycle', 'airplane',
    'bus', 'train', 'truck', 'boat', 'traffic light', 'fire hydrant',
    'N/A', 'stop sign', 'parking meter', 'bench', 'bird', 'cat', 'dog',
    'horse', 'sheep', 'cow', 'elephant', 'bear', 'zebra', 'giraffe',
    'N/A', 'backpack', 'umbrella', 'N/A', 'N/A', 'handbag', 'tie',
    'suitcase', 'frisbee', 'skis', 'snowboard', 'sports ball', 'kite',
    'baseball bat', 'baseball glove', 'skateboard', 'surfboard',
    'tennis racket', 'bottle', 'N/A', 'wine glass', 'cup', 'fork',
    'knife', 'spoon', 'bowl', 'banana', 'apple', 'sandwich', 'orange',
    'broccoli', 'carrot', 'hot dog', 'pizza', 'donut', 'cake', 'chair',
    'couch', 'potted plant', 'bed', 'N/A', 'dining table', 'N/A', 'N/A',
    'toilet', 'N/A', 'tv', 'laptop', 'mouse', 'remote', 'keyboard',
    'cell phone', 'microwave', 'oven', 'toaster', 'sink',
    'refrigerator', 'N/A', 'book', 'clock', 'vase', 'scissors',
    'teddy bear', 'hair drier', 'toothbrush'
]
```

Let's try downloading some images from the internet and see how well our model does. Keep in mind that random images contain lots of things this algorithm has *never* seen before. This will give you some ideas about how you might be able to use Faster R-CNN models in the future and interesting ways in which they can fail. The following code imports some libraries for grabbing images from a URL, as well as three URLs to get some images in which to try to detect objects. Feel free to change which URL is used or add your own URLs to try the object detector on something different:

```
from PIL import Image
import requests
from io import BytesIO

urls = [
    "https://hips.hearstapps.com/hmg-prod.s3.amazonaws.com/images/
        10best-cars-group-cropped-1542126037.jpg",
    "https://miro.medium.com/max/5686/1*ZqJFvYiS5GmLajfUfyzFQA.jpeg",
    "https://www.denverpost.com/wp-content/uploads/2018/03/
        virginia_umbc_001.jpg?w=910"
]

response = requests.get(urls[0])
img = Image.open(BytesIO(response.content))
```

Once we have loaded the image, we reformat it the way PyTorch's pretrained model wants. This includes normalizing the pixel values to the range $[0, 1]$ and reordering the dimensions to be channel, width, height. That's done in the following code, after which we make our prediction:

```
img = np.asarray(img)/256.0
img = torch.tensor(img, dtype=torch.float32).permute((2,0,1))

with torch.no_grad():
    pred = rcnn([img])    ←——— Passes the image to the model
```

Now we can check out the results. You may find that you need a different `nms` threshold or `min_score` for each image to get the best results. Tuning these parameters can be very problem-dependent. It depends on the relative cost of false positives versus false negatives, the difference between the training images in style/content versus the testing images, and ultimately *how* you will be using your object detector:

```
showPreds(img, pred[0], iou_max_overlap=0.15, min_score=0.15,
    label_names=NAME)
```

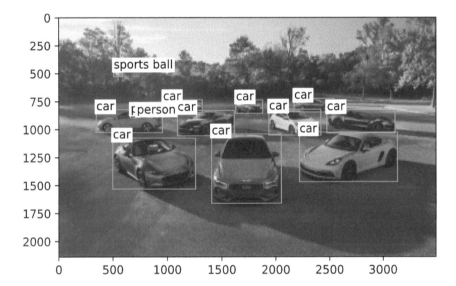

Exercises

Share and discuss your solutions on the Manning online platform at Inside Deep Learning Exercises (https://liveproject.manning.com/project/945). Once you submit your own answers, you will be able to see the solutions submitted by other readers, and see which ones the author judges to be the best.

1. Now that you know how to enlarge a tensor after pooling, you can implement a convolutional autoencoder using only the bottleneck approach. Go back to chapter 7 and reimplement a convolutional autoencoder by using two rounds of pooling in the encoder countered by two rounds of transposed convolutions in the decoder.

2 You may have noticed that a transposed convolution can create unevenly spaced *artifacts* in its output, which occur in our example diagram. These are not always a problem, but you can do better. Implement your own `Conv2dExpansion(n_filters_in)` class that takes the following approach: first, up-sample the image using `nn.Upsample` to expand the tensor width and height by a factor of 2. If you are off by a pixel, use `nn.ReflectionPad2d` to pad the output to the desired shape. Finally, apply a normal `nn.Conv2d` to perform some mixing and change the number of channels. Compare this new approach with transposed convolution and see if you can identify any pros and cons.

3 Compare a network that has three rounds of pooling and transposed convolution and a network with three rounds of pooling and `Conv2dExpansion` on the Data Science Bowl dataset. Do you see any difference in the results? Why do you think you do or do not?

4 Strided convolution can be used to shrink an image as an alternative to max pooling. Modify the U-Net architecture to create a truly fully convolutional model by replacing all pooling with strided convolutions. How does the performance change?

5 Modify the residual network from chapter 6 to use `nn.AdaptiveMaxPooling` followed by a `nn.Flatten()`, a linear hidden layer, and then a linear layer to make predictions. (*Note:* The number of `nn.MaxPool2d` classes should not change.) Does this improve your results on Fashion-MNIST? Try comparing the original residual network and your adaptive pooling variant on the CIFAR-10 dataset and see if there is a greater difference in performance.

6 Modify the Faster R-CNN training loop to include a test-pass that computes a test loss over a test set after each epoch of training. *Hint:* You will need to keep the model in `train` mode since its behavior changes when in `eval` mode.

7 Try implementing a network with residual connections for the backbone of the Faster R-CNN detector. Does it get better or worse performance?

8 Our bounding boxes for `Class2Detect` are loose because we assumed the digit takes up the entire image. Modify this code to find a tight bounding box on the digits, and retrain the detector. How does this change the results you see on some test images?

9 **Challenging:** Use an image-search engine to download at least 20 images of cats and 20 images of dogs. Then find software online for labeling images with bounding boxes, and create your own cat/dog-detecting Faster R-CNN. You will need to write a `Dataset` class for whichever labeling software you use.

Summary

- With image segmentation, we make a prediction for *every* pixel in an image.

- Object detection uses a backbone similar to an image segmentation model and augments it with two smaller networks to *propose* the locations of objects and *decide what object is present*, respectively.

- You can upscale an image with transposed convolutions, which are often used to reverse the impact of max pooling.

- A residual-like block for object detection called a U-Net block combines max pooling and transposed convolutions to create full-scale and low-resolution paths, allowing more accurate models with less work.

- Adaptive max pooling converts any size input image into a target of a specific size and is useful for designing networks that can train and predict on arbitrarily sized inputs.

- Object detection's false positives can be reduced using non-maximum suppression.

Generative adversarial networks

Most of what we have learned thus far has been a *one-to-one* mapping. Every input has one correct class/output. The dog can only be a "dog"; the sentence is only "positive" or "negative." But we can also encounter *one-to-many* problems where there is more than one possible answer. For example, we may have the concept of "seven" as input and need to create several different kinds of pictures of the digit 7. Or, to colorize an old black-and-white photograph, we could produce multiple possible color images that were all equally valid. For one-to-many problems, we can use a *generative adversarial network* (GAN). Like other unsupervised models such as the autoencoder, we can use the representation a GAN learns as the input to other AI/ML algorithms and tasks. But the representation a GAN learns is often more meaningful, allowing us to manipulate our data in new ways. For example, we could take a picture of a frowning person and have the algorithm alter the image so the person is smiling.

GANs are currently one of the most successful types of *generative models*: models that can create new data that looks like the training data without just making naive copies. If you have enough data and GPU compute, you can create some *very* realistic images with GANs. Figure 9.1 shows an example of what the latest and greatest GANs can achieve. As a GAN gets better at generating content, it often becomes better at manipulating content as well. We could, for example, use a GAN to change the person's hair color in figure 9.1 or give them a frown. The website https://thispersondoesnotexist.com shows more examples of what a high-end GAN can do.

Figure 9.1 This person does not actually exist! The image was generated using a GAN called StyleGAN (https://github.com/lucidrains/stylegan2-pytorch).

Similar to autoencoders, GANs learn in a self-supervised fashion, so we do not *need* labeled data to create a GAN. There are ways to make GANs use labels, though, so they can also be supervised models, depending on what you want to do. You could use a GAN for anything you might use an autoencoder for, but GANs tend to be the go-to tool for making realistic-looking synthetic data (e.g., visualizing a product for a user), manipulating images, and solving one-to-many problems that have multiple valid outputs. GANs have become so effective that hundreds of specialized variants exist for different kinds of problems like text generation, image manipulation, audio, data augmentation, and more. This chapter focuses on the fundamentals of how GANs work and fail, to give you a good foundation for understanding other specialized versions.

First, we learn how GANs work through an adversarial game played between two competing neural networks, a *discriminator* and a *generator*. The first GAN we build will follow the original approach so we can show the most common issue with GANs, *mode collapse*, which can prevent them from learning. Then we learn about an improved approach to training GANs that helps reduce (but not solve) this problem. The mode-collapse issue can't be *solved*, but it can be reduced, and we show how using an improved Wasserstein GAN. The Wasserstein GAN makes it easier to learn a reasonable GAN, which we then use to show how you can make a *convolutional* GAN for image generation and a conditional GAN that includes label information. The last technical concept we discuss about GANs is manipulating the content a GAN produces by altering the latent space it produces. We end this chapter with a brief discussion of the many things that can be done with GANS and the ethical responsibilities involved in using such a powerful approach.

9.1   Understanding generative adversarial networks

When we talk about a GAN, there are usually two subnetworks: G, which is called the *generator* network; and D, the *discriminator* network. These networks have competing goals, making them adversaries. Figure 9.2 shows how they interact. The generator wants to create new data that looks realistic, and the discriminator wants to determine if an input came from the *real* dataset or is a *fake* provided by the generator.

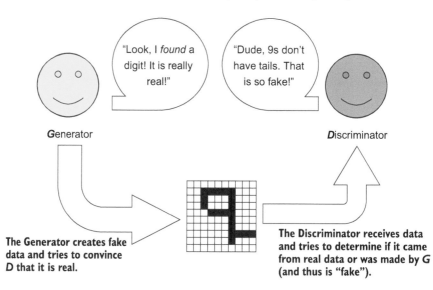

Figure 9.2   A high-level example of how the generator and discriminator interact. The generator has a goal of generating fake data and giving it to the discriminator. The discriminator has the goal of determining whether an image came from the GAN.

The generator takes in random data and tries to convert it into something that looks realistic. The dimensions m and d could be tensors too. For images, d would be something like $d = (C, W, H)$ and m could be $m = (C', W', H')$.

| Create a vector of random numbers $z \in \mathbb{R}^m$. | → | Generator takes in z and outputs a vector $\tilde{x} \in \mathbb{R}^d$. | → | Add label y_{fake} because $\tilde{x}$ is not real data. |

| Generator gets an error $loss_G$ for the *Discriminator's* non-errors and no error for *Discriminator's* errors. |

| Take turns picking real and fake data. | | Discriminator predicts if the item is real or fake. |

| Dataset with data $x \in \mathbb{R}^d$ | → | Add label y_{real} because x came from real data. |

| D does not know if real or fake data was chosen. | | Discriminator gets an error $loss_D$ for mispredicting fake/real data. |

The tensor shape d should match your real data, and setting m requires some trial and error.

G and D have opposing losses. D's loss is a normal classification loss, predicting the "class" of real/fake data. G's loss is the opposite of D's loss, essentially swapping y_{real} and y_{fake} when computing the loss. This is possible because autograd keeps track of G's output, going into D and then all the way through D's output.

Figure 9.3 Diagram of how GANs are generally trained. The generator G learns to assign meaning to random values z to produce meaningful outputs $\tilde{x}$. The discriminator receives real and fake data but doesn't know which—and tries to learn the difference in a standard classification problem. Then G's loss is computed on D's output but is the inverse. G gets an error when D does not, and G gets no error when D does.

GANs can get pretty complex, so we will start at a high level and expand the details one level at a time. Our next level of this detail is shown in figure 9.3, and we will walk through it slowly.

G works by taking in a *latent* vector $z \in \mathbb{R}^m$ and predicting an output the same size and shape as the real data. We get to choose the number of dimensions m (it's a hyperparameter) for the latent vector z: it should be large enough to represent different concepts in our data (which takes some manual trial and error). For example, some latent properties we might want to learn are smile/frown, hair color, and hairstyle. The values of z are called *latent* because we never observe what they actually are: the model has to infer them from the data. If we do a good job, the generator G can use this latent representation z as a smaller and more compact representation of the data—kind of like a lossy form of compression. You can think of the generator as a sketch artist who has to take in a description (the latent vector z) and, from that, construct an accurate picture for the output! The same way a sketch artist's drawing is a product of how they *interpret* your description, the meaning of these latent vectors depends on how the generator G interprets them. In practice, we use a simple representation of each latent variable being sampled from a Gaussian distribution (i.e, $z_i \sim N(0, 1)$). This makes it easy to sample new values of z so that we can produce and control synthetic data. It is up to the generator to learn how to make something meaningful out of these values.

D has the goal of determining whether an input is from *real* data or *fake* data. So D's job is a simple classification problem. If the input $x \in \mathbb{R}^d$ came from real data, the label

$y = 1 = y_1$ = real. If the input $\boldsymbol{x}$ came from the generator G, the label is $y = 0 = y_0$ fake. This is similar to an autoencoder where we use a supervised loss function, but the labels are trivial. We are essentially using all of the training data to define the real class, and anything output by G belongs to the fake class.

9.1.1   The loss computations

This last part may seem complicated: D and G are both computing their loss from D's output, and G's loss is somehow the opposite of D's. Let's be explicit about what is involved. We use $\ell(\cdot, \cdot)$ to represent our classification loss (binary cross entropy of softmax, which we have used many times). There are two models (G and D) with two classes (y_{real} and y_{fake}), giving the four combinations in this table:

	Real data x	Fake data z
$loss_D =$	$\ell(D(\boldsymbol{x}), y_{real})$ +	$\ell\left(D\left(\overbrace{G(\boldsymbol{z})}^{\text{fake data}}\right), y_{fake}\right)$
$loss_G =$	0 +	$\ell\left(D\left(\overbrace{G(\boldsymbol{z})}^{\text{fake data}}\right), y_{real}\right)$

When working on D's loss $loss_D$, we have real data and fake data. For real data, we want to say that it looks real. It's pretty straightforward, but let's annotate the equation anyway:

The discriminator wants to say real data looks like real data   to compute its loss.

$$\ell\Big(\ D(\boldsymbol{x})\ ,\quad y_{real}\ \Big)$$

That gives us D's loss on real data. Its loss on fake data is also a straightforward classification, except we replace the real data $\boldsymbol{x}$ with the generator's output $G(\boldsymbol{z})$, and we use y_{fake} as the target because the input to D is fake data from G. Again, let's annotate this:

The generator's output is given to the distriminator, which wants to say that the result looks fake to compute D's loss.

$$\ell\Big(\ D\big(\ G(z) \ \big) \ , \ y_{fake} \ \Big)$$

On to the generator G's loss. For real data, it is easy: G does not care what D says about real data, so nothing happens to G when real data is used. But for fake data, G does care about what D says. It wants D to call its fake data real, because that means it has successfully tricked D. This involves swapping the label. Let's annotate that equation, too:

The generator's output is given to the discriminator. G wants to trick into saying that the result looks real to compute G's loss.

$$\ell\Big(\ D\big(\ G(z) \ \big) \ , \ y_{real} \ \Big)$$

PUTTING THE LOSSES TOGETHER

Now that we know how to compute all the components of the loss, we can combine them. We have to keep them listed as two losses because we are training two different networks. First we have the discriminator's loss:

$$loss_D = \frac{1}{n} \overbrace{\sum_{i=1}^{n} \ell(D(\boldsymbol{x}), y_{real})}^{} + \frac{1}{n} \sum_{i=1}^{n} \ell(D(G(\ \overbrace{z \sim \mathcal{N}(0,1)}^{\text{Pick a new random vector each time.}}\ )), y_{fake})$$

D says the real data looks real. D says random outputs of G look fake.

This is a simple combination of the two values from the table on the previous page. We've just been a little more explicit that this loss is computed over all the data n (which will become batches instead of the entire dataset). Since a `for` loop is involved with the summation Σ, we also write $z \sim \mathcal{N}(0,1)$ to be explicit that a different random vector z is used each time.

We have the generator's loss, which has only one summation symbol because G does not care what D says about real data. G only cares about the fake data, and G is successful if it tricks D into calling fake data real. This gets us the following:

$$loss_G = \sum_{i=1}^{n} \ell(D(G(\ \overbrace{z \sim \mathcal{N}(0,1)}^{\text{Pick a new random vector each time.}}\ )), y_{real})$$

D says random outputs of G look real.

Expectation

You may notice something odd about the equations involving the random data z. We are summing n items but never access anything. It does not matter how big the dataset is; we could sample half as many values of z or twice as many. We would never get an index out of bounds unless we kept increasing the value of n.

This is because we are approximating what we could call an *expectation*. The equation $\frac{1}{n}\sum_{i=1}^{n} \ell(D(G(z \sim \mathcal{N}(0,1)), y_{real})$ basically asks, "What do we expect the average value of $\ell(D(G(z), y_{real})$ to be if $z \sim \mathcal{N}(0,1)$? Another way to write this is

$$loss_G = \underset{z \sim \mathcal{N}(0,1)}{\mathbb{E}} \ell(D(G(z)), y_{real})$$

which is the mathematical way to ask what the exact answer is if you set $n = \infty$. Obviously, we don't have time to sample forever, but this expectation-based symbol is very common when reading about GANs. For this reason, it's worth spending a little extra time getting familiar with this symbol so you are prepared to read other materials.

The symbol $\mathbb{E}$ in the previous equation stands for *expectation*. If you have a distribution p and a function f, writing: $\mathbb{E}_{z \sim p} f(z)$ is a fancy way of saying "If I sample values z from the distribution p *forever*, what is the average value of $f(z)$?" Sometimes we can use math to prove what the expectation will be and compute the result directly—but that is not going to happen here. Instead, we can do something like sample one value for every item in a batch. This approach is an *approximation* of the expectation because we sample for a *finite* number of steps instead of an *infinite* number.

Let's close out this detour by rewriting the $loss_D$ using the expectation symbol. We have a summation for D's predictions on real data, because there is a finite amount of real data. We have an expectation for D's predictions on fake data, because there is infinite fake data. This gets us the following equation:

$$loss_D = \frac{1}{n} \underbrace{\sum_{i=1}^{n} \ell(D(x), y_{real})}_{D \text{ says the all real data looks real.}} + \underbrace{\underset{z \sim \mathcal{N}(\vec{0}, I)}{\mathbb{E}} \ell(D(G(z)), y_{fake})}_{D \text{ says all random outputs of } G \text{ look fake.}}$$

9.1.2 The GAN games

We have talked about how the two losses $loss_D$ and $loss_G$ are computed for the discriminator and generator, respectively. How do we train two networks with two losses? By taking turns computing $loss_D$ and $loss_G$, updating both networks from their respective losses, and repeating. This turns the training procedure into a kind of game between G and D. Each gets its own score for how well it's doing at the game, and each tries to improve its score to the detriment of the other.

The game (training process) starts with the generator producing horrible, random-looking results, which are easy for the discriminator to separate from real data (see figure 9.4). D tries to predict the source (training data or G) based on the image and gets a loss computed from both real and fake data. G's loss is computed over only the fake data and is the same setup as D's loss but with the label swapped. The label is swapped because G wants D to say real instead of fake for G's work.

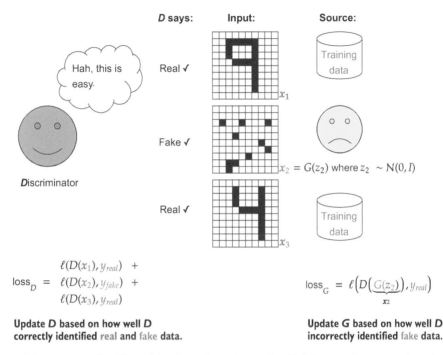

$$\text{loss}_D = \begin{array}{l} \ell(D(x_1), y_{real}) \ + \\ \ell(D(x_2), y_{fake}) \ + \\ \ell(D(x_3), y_{real}) \end{array}$$

$$\text{loss}_G = \ell\left(D\left(\underbrace{G(z_2)}_{x_2}\right), y_{real}\right)$$

Update D based on how well D correctly identified real and fake data.

Update G based on how well D incorrectly identified fake data.

Figure 9.4   The start of training a GAN. D receives a batch of multiple images. Some come from the real training data, and others are fake (created by G). For every prediction, D receives a loss based on whether it was correct or not about the source of the image (real versus fake). G's loss is computed only from the discriminator's prediction.

Because G's loss is based on what the discriminator D says, it learns to alter its predictions to look more like what D thinks real data looks like. As the generator G improves, the discriminator D needs to improve how it distinguishes between real and fake data. The cycle repeats forever (or until convergence). Figure 9.5 shows how the results might evolve over multiple rounds of this game.

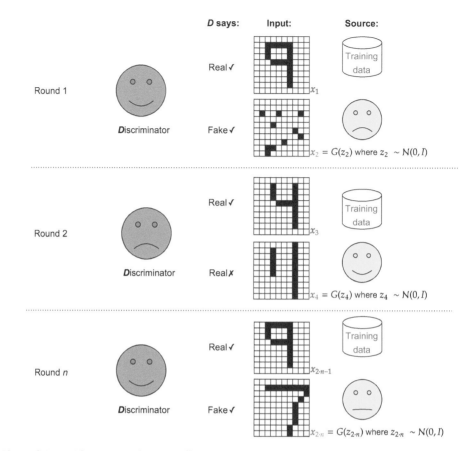

Figure 9.5   Multiple rounds of training G and D together. Early on, D has an easy time because the fake data looks random. Eventually G gets better and tricks D. D learns to better distinguish fake data, which lets G get better at making more realistic data. Eventually, both D and G are pretty good at their jobs.

We've given the complete description of how to set up a GAN for training. There is another detail about how to consider or interpret the GAN setup called *min-max*. If we think of D as returning the probability that an input comes from real data, we want to alter D to *maximize D's probability on real data* while simultaneously altering G to *minimize D's performance on fake data*. This useful concept comes with a scary-looking equation:

$$\min_{G} \max_{D} \quad \underbrace{\mathbb{E}_{\boldsymbol{x}\sim\text{Data}} \big[\log(D(\boldsymbol{x}))\big]}_{D \text{ thinks the real data looks real.}} \quad + \quad \underbrace{\mathbb{E}_{\boldsymbol{z}\sim\mathcal{N}(\vec{0},I)} \big[\log(1 - D(G(\boldsymbol{z})))\big]}_{D \text{ thinks fake data looks real.}}$$

I don't like this equation for explaining GANs at a practical level—it looks scarier than I think it needs to be. I include it because you will see that equation a lot when reading about GANs. But if you look carefully, this is the same equation we started with. You can replace the expectations $\mathbb{E}$ with summations Σ, and you can replace $\log(D(\boldsymbol{x}))$ with

$\ell(D(\boldsymbol{x}), y_{real})$, and $\log(1 - D(G(\boldsymbol{z})))$ with $\ell(D(G(\boldsymbol{z})), y_{fake})$. That gets you exactly what we had at the start. We solve this min-max game by taking turns optimizing D and G for their respective goals. I also like writing it using loss functions ℓ because then it's a little more obvious that we could change the loss functions to change the behavior of our GAN. Changing the loss ℓ in a GAN is extremely common, so it's an important detail I don't want to hide.

9.1.3 *Implementing our first GAN*

Now that we understand the game played by a generator G and discriminator D, we can begin to implement it. We need to define `Modules` for both D and G, writing a new training loop that takes turns updating D and G, respectively and some extra helper code to record useful information and visualize our results. First, let's predefine some values: the `batch_size` B, the number of `neurons` for our hidden layers, and the number of epochs `num_epochs` for training our GAN. Two new things are `latent_d` and `out_shape`.

The variable `latent_d` is the number of dimensions in our latent variable $\boldsymbol{z}$. We can make this smaller or larger; it is a new hyperparameter for our model. If we have too few or too many dimensions, we have difficulty training. My recommendation is to start out at 64 or 128 and keep increasing the dimension until you get results that look good. We also have a variable `out_shape` that is used purely to reshape the output of our network to the given dimensions. It starts with `-1` for the batch dimension. This way, the results from the generator will be whatever shape we want. This will be more important later when we make a convolutional GAN; for now, we start with fully connected networks. The `fcLayer` function gives us a shorthand for building the models in this chapter.

Here's the code:

```
batch_size = 128
latent_d = 128
neurons = 512
out_shape = (-1, 28, 28)     ◄── You could also do (-1, 1, 28, 28) for
num_epochs = 10                  one channel, but that makes NumPy
                                 code a little more cumbersome later.

def fcLayer(in_neurons, out_neurons, leak=0.1):   ◄── Our helper function
    """
    in_neurons: how many inputs to this layer
    out_neurons: how many outputs for this layer
    leak: the leaky relu leak value.
    """
    return nn.Sequential(
        nn.Linear(in_neurons, out_neurons),
        nn.LeakyReLU(leak),
        nn.LayerNorm(out_neurons)
    )
```

DEFINING THE D AND G NETWORKS

Next, we implement a function that defines both the generator G and the discriminator D. The generator needs to know latent_d because that will be the input size. Both G and D need to know the out_shape because it is the output of the generator *and* the input to the discriminator. I've also included an optional flag sgimoidG to control when the generator should end with a nn.Sigmoid activation $\sigma(\cdot)$. For some of the GANs we train in this chapter, we want to apply $\sigma(\cdot)$ at the end so the output is constrained to be in the range $[0, 1]$ because our MNIST data is also constrained to $[0, 1]$. But we also do an example problem where there is no such constraint. I've also arbitrarily defined a few hidden layers with a LeakyReLU and layer normalization (LN).

Here's the code:

```
def simpleGAN(latent_d, neurons, out_shape, sigmoidG=False, leak=0.2):
    """
    This function will create a simple GAN for us to train. It will return
    a tuple (G, D), holding the generator and discriminator network
    respectively.
    latent_d: the number of latent variables we will use as input to the
    generator G.
    neurons: how many hidden neurons to use in each hidden layer
    out_shape: the shape of the output of the discriminator D. This should
    be the same shape as the real data.
    sigmoidG: true if the generator G should end with a sigmoid activation,
    or False if it should just return unbounded activations
    """

    G = nn.Sequential(
        fcLayer(latent_d, neurons, leak),
        fcLayer(neurons, neurons, leak),
        fcLayer(neurons, neurons, leak),
        nn.Linear(neurons, abs(np.prod(out_shape)) ),      ◄──
        View(out_shape)                                    ◄──
    )



    if sigmoidG:                                           ◄──
        G = nn.Sequential(G, nn.Sigmoid())
    D = nn.Sequential(
        nn.Flatten(),
        fcLayer(abs(np.prod(out_shape)), neurons, leak),
        fcLayer(neurons, neurons, leak),
        fcLayer(neurons, neurons, leak),
        nn.Linear(neurons, 1 )                             ◄──
    )
    return G, D
```

np.prod multiplies each value in the shape, giving us the total number of needed outputs. abs removes the impact of "−1" for the batch dimension.

Reshapes the output to whatever D expects

Sometimes we do or don't want G to return a sigmoid value (i.e., [0,1]), so we rap it in a conditional.

D has one output for a binary classification problem.

With this function, we can quickly define a new G and D model by calling the simpleGAN function:

```
G, D = simpleGAN(latent_d, neurons, out_shape, sigmoidG=True)
```

A starting recipe for GANs

GANs are notorious for being difficult to train. The first attempt often does not work well, and it can take a lot of manual fiddling to get them to work and produce nice crisp results like the example at the start of this chapter. There are a lot of tricks online for getting GANs to train well, but some of them are specific to certain types of GANs. Others are more reliable and work well for multiple architectures. Here are my recommendations when trying to build any GAN:

- Use the LeakyReLU activation function with a large leak value like $\alpha = 0.1$ or $\alpha = 0.2$. It is extra important that our discriminator not have vanishing gradients, because the gradient for training G must first go all the way through D! The larger leak values help avoid this problem.

- Use LN instead of batch normalization (BN). Some have found that they get their best results with BN. In other cases we can *prove* that BN causes problems. So I prefer to start with LN, which has more consistent and reliable performance when training GANs. If I'm struggling to get that last ounce of performance, I try replacing LN with BN in *only* the generator.

- Use the Adam optimizer specifically with the learning rate $\eta = 0.0001$ and $\beta_1 = 0$ and $\beta_2 = 0.9$. This is slower than Adam's normal defaults but works better for GANs. This is the last thing I would change to try to get better results.

IMPLEMENTING THE GAN TRAINING LOOP

How do we train our two networks? Each network G and D has its own optimizer, and we will take turns using them! For this reason, we *do not* use the same `train_network` function that we have used for most of the book. This is one reason it is important to learn the framework and the tools it provides: not everything can be easily abstracted away and work with *every* type of neural network you might want to train in the future.

First let's do some setup. Let's move our models to the GPU, specify our binary cross-entropy loss function (because real versus fake is a binary problem), and set up our two different optimizers for each network:

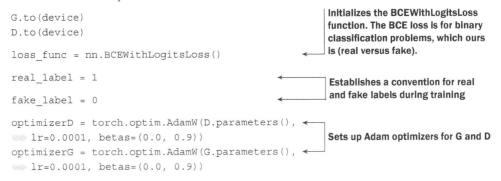

```
G.to(device)
D.to(device)

loss_func = nn.BCEWithLogitsLoss()          Initializes the BCEWithLogitsLoss
                                             function. The BCE loss is for binary
                                             classification problems, which ours
                                             is (real versus fake).

real_label = 1                               Establishes a convention for real
                                             and fake labels during training
fake_label = 0

optimizerD = torch.optim.AdamW(D.parameters(),
    lr=0.0001, betas=(0.0, 0.9))             Sets up Adam optimizers for G and D
optimizerG = torch.optim.AdamW(G.parameters(),
    lr=0.0001, betas=(0.0, 0.9))
```

Next we grab MNIST as our dataset. We won't really use the test set in this chapter since we are focusing on generating new data:

```
train_data = torchvision.datasets.MNIST("./", train=True,
    transform=transforms.ToTensor(), download=True)
test_data = torchvision.datasets.MNIST("./", train=False,
    transform=transforms.ToTensor(), download=True)

train_loader = DataLoader(train_data, batch_size=batch_size, shuffle=True,
    drop_last=True)
test_loader = DataLoader(test_data, batch_size=batch_size)
```

Now we need to train this GAN. We break the process into two steps, one for D and one for G, as shown in figure 9.6.

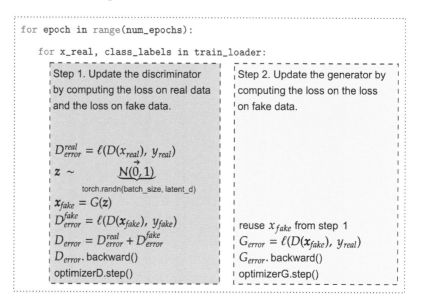

Figure 9.6   Steps for training the GAN. For several epochs, we run both steps. In step 1, we compute the discriminator loss on real and fake data, then update the weights of D using its optimizer. In step 2, we update the generator. Since both steps need an output from G, we reuse $G(z)$ between the two steps.

Hopefully, by this point you are starting to feel comfortable mixing code and math notation. This diagram specifies almost every detail we need to successfully implement a GAN! Let's translate it into complete code. First we have the `for` loops and some setup. We use two arrays to store the loss at each batch so we can look at it after training. The loss function can be particularly informative for GANs. We also create y_{real} and y_{fake}, which that are used in both steps and move the data onto the right device. That's shown in the following code:

```
G_losses = []
D_losses = []

for epoch in tqdm(range(num_epochs)):
    for data, class_label in tqdm(train_loader, leave=False):
        real_data = data.to(device)
        y_real = torch.full((batch_size,1), real_label,
            dtype=torch.float32, device=device)
        y_fake = torch.full((batch_size,1), fake_label,
            dtype=torch.float32, device=device)
```

Preps the batch and makes labels

Now we can move on to step 1: updating the discriminator. Implementing this does not take much work. We call `backward` after each error component is computed, as a mild efficiency optimization. But we still add the errors together later to save the combined error. The big trick here that you should pay attention to is the use of `fake.detach()` when passing the fake image into D. The `detach()` method returns a new version of the same object that will not pass a gradient back any further. We do this because the `fake` object was computed using G, so naively using the `fake` object in our calculation would cause us to input a gradient for G that *benefits the discriminator* because we are computing the discriminator's loss! Since step 1 is only supposed to alter D and a gradient for G at this point would be counterproductive to G's goals (it wants to beat the discriminator!), we call `.detach()` so G does not get any gradient.

Here's the code:

```
D.zero_grad()
errD_real = loss_func(D(real_data), y_real)
errD_real.backward()

z = torch.randn(batch_size, latent_d, device=device)

fake = G(z)

errD_fake = loss_func(D(fake.detach()), y_fake)

errD_fake.backward()

errD = errD_real + errD_fake

optimizerD.step()
```

Real data

Trains with an all-fake batch and generates a batch of latent vectors $z \sim \mathcal{N}(\vec{0}, 1)$.

Calculate D's loss on the all-fake batch; note the use of fake.detach(). $\ell(D(x_{real}), y_{real})$

$x_{fake} = G(z)$

Generates a fake image batch with G and classifies the fake batch with D. We save this to reuse in step 2.

Calculates the gradients for this batch

Adds the gradients from the all-real and all-fake batches

Updates D

The final part of our loop body is step 2: updating the generator G. We reuse the `fake` object so we don't have to create a new one, which saves us time. Since we also *want* to alter G, we use the original `fake` object directly—no call to `.fake()`. Very little code is needed here, and we append the errors of G and D into a list so we can plot them afterward:

```
G.zero_grad()
errG = loss_func(D(fake), y_real)
errG.backward()
optimizerG.step()
```

Calculates G's loss based on this output: $\ell(D(x_{fake}), y_{real})$

Calculates gradients for G

Updates G

```
G_losses.append(errG.item())
D_losses.append(errD.item())
```

INSPECTING THE RESULTS

Running that code successfully trains a GAN. Because the latents z come from a Gaussian distribution ($z \sim \mathcal{N}(\vec{0}, I)$), we can easily sample them and compute $G(z)$ to get synthetic data. We can also look at the value of $D(G(z))$ to see what the discriminator thinks about each sample's realism. The way we trained the model, a value of 1 would indicate that the discriminator thinks the input is definitely real, and 0 would indicate that the discriminator thinks it is definitely fake. The following code samples some new latents into a variable called noise, which is another common name you will see for the latent object in a GAN. We make our fake digits with G and compute the scores for how real they look with D:

```
with torch.no_grad():
    noise = torch.randn(batch_size, latent_d, device=device)    ⟵ z ~ 𝒩(0⃗, I)
    fake_digits = G(noise)
    scores = torch.sigmoid(D(fake_digits))
    fake_digits = fake_digits.cpu()
    scores = scores.cpu().numpy().flatten()
```

Next is some Matplotlib code to plot all of the generated images, with the score in red above each digit. The plot automatically resizes based on the batch size we are using. The code quickly computes the largest square of images that can be filled from the given batch. We make scores an optional argument, as our future GANs won't have the same kind of score:

```
def plot_gen_imgs(fake_digits, scores=None):
    batch_size = fake_digits.size(0)                          This code assumes
    fake_digits = fake_digits.reshape(-1,          ⟵——— we are working with
      fake_digits.size(-1), fake_digits.size(-1))             black-and-white images.
    i_max = int(round(np.sqrt(batch_size)))
    j_max = int(np.floor(batch_size/float(i_max)))
    f, axarr = plt.subplots(i_max,j_max, figsize=(10,10))
    for i in range(i_max):
        for j in range(j_max):
            indx = i*j_max+j
            axarr[i,j].imshow(fake_digits[indx,:].numpy(), cmap='gray',
              vmin=0, vmax=1)
            axarr[i,j].set_axis_off()
            if scores is not None:
                axarr[i,j].text(0.0, 0.5, str(round(scores[indx],2)),
                  dict(size=20, color='red'))
plot_gen_imgs(fake_digits, scores)
```

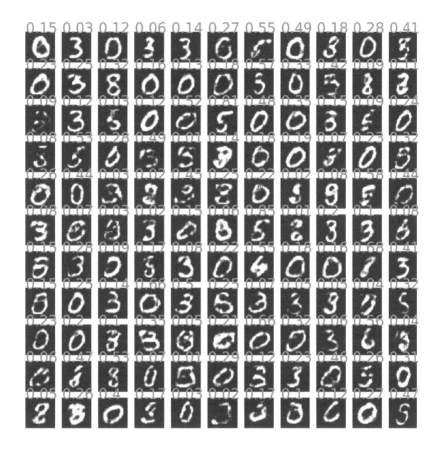

We've generated synthetic data, and some of it looks quite good! Some of the samples don't look realistic, which is OK. The problem of learning a generative model is intrinsically more challenging than learning a discriminative model. If you run this code again, you should get new results and start noticing some issues.

The first pattern you might notice is that the generator likes a few digits more than others. When I run this, I usually see a lot of 0s, 3s, and 8s generated. Other digits are much rarer. Second, the discriminator is almost always correct in calling the generated samples fake. These two issues are related.

The repetition of a few digits is a problem because it means our generator is not modeling the *whole* distribution. This makes its outputs as a whole less realistic, even if individual digits look good. The discriminator being very good at detecting fakes is a potential problem because we use the binary cross entropy (BCE) loss! Since BCE involves a sigmoid, if D gets *too* good and predicts 0% that a sample is malicious, it will cause a vanishing gradient for G. This is because G's gradient comes from the opposite of D's predictions. If D does a perfect job predicting, G can't learn.

The risk that D might win the game with perfect predictions is important because the game between D and G is unfair. What do I mean by unfair? Let's look at the loss of the discriminator and generator over the training. We can quickly plot the loss for G and D and compare them to see how they are doing:

```
plt.figure(figsize=(10,5))
plt.title("Generator and Discriminator Loss During Training")
plt.plot(G_losses,label="G")
plt.plot(D_losses,label="D")
plt.xlabel("iterations")
plt.ylabel("Loss")
plt.legend()
plt.show()
```

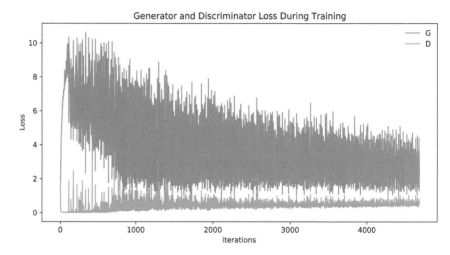

While the generator has improved significantly, it always does worse than D. The discriminator starts at and stays near a loss of zero the entire time because it has an intrinsically easier problem to solve. Discrimination is always easier than generation! Thus, it becomes easy for D to win the game against the generator G. This is part of why the generator tends to focus on a few digits and ignore the rest. Early on, the generator G finds that some digits are easier to trick D with than others. There is no penalty for G other than fooling D, so it puts all its effort into whatever seems to be working best.

Why is discrimination easier than generation?

Let's take a quick detour, which you can skip if you are happy to simply trust that discrimination is easier. A little math will show *why* it is easier. Let's start with a quick refresher on Bayes's rule:

The probability of class y given features x is equal to

the probability of having features x and having class y divided by

the probabilities of having x for every possible class added together.

$$\mathbb{P}(y \mid x) = \frac{\mathbb{P}(x, y)}{\sum_{y \in Y} \mathbb{P}(x, y)}$$

If we wanted to write out the problem in terms of statistics, the generator G is trying to learn what is called the *joint distribution*. There is real data x with labels y, and the joint distribution is denoted as $\mathbb{P}(x, y)$. If you can sample from the joint distribution, you have a generative model. If it is doing a good job, you should get all the different classes that y might indicate exist.

The discriminator's task is a conditional distribution that we write as $\mathbb{P}(y \mid x)$. The way to read this is "what is the probability ($\mathbb{P}$) of the label y given ($\mid$) the inputs x).?"

If we already have the joint distribution, we can immediately recover the conditional distribution with one application of Bayes's rule:

$$\underset{D}{\underbrace{\mathbb{P}(y \mid x)}} = \frac{\overset{G}{\overbrace{\mathbb{P}(x, y)}}}{\mathbb{P}(x)}$$

The bottom missing term is not an issue because it can be computed as $\mathbb{P}(x) = \sum_{y \in Y} \mathbb{P}(x, y)$. So if we know G, we get a discriminator D for free! But there is no way to rearrange this equation to get G from D without having *something extra*. The problem of generation (joint distributions) is fundamentally more information and thus more difficult than discrimination (conditional distributions). This is why D has an easier task than G.

9.2   *Mode collapse*

The issue with our generator only producing some of the digits is a phenomenon called *mode collapse*. Because the generator has a harder problem to solve, it tries to find ways to cheat at the game. One way to cheat is to generate only the data that is *easy* and ignore other cases. If the generator can produce a perfect 0 every time that fools the discriminator, it will win the game—even if it can't generate any other digits! To make a better generator, we need to address this issue; in this section, we do another experiment to better understand it.

The easiest data points are usually associated with a *mode* of the data's distribution. The mode is the most common value found in a distribution. We use it to help understand the mode-collapse problem. To do this, we generate a grid of Gaussian variables. The following code does that such that the Gaussians are centered at zero:

```
gausGrid = (3, 3)              ◄─── How large should the grid be?
samples_per = 10000            ◄─── How many samples per item in the grid?
```

Next is some quick code that loops through every item in the grid and computes some samples. We use a small standard deviation in our samples so it is easy to see that there are nine well-separated modes:

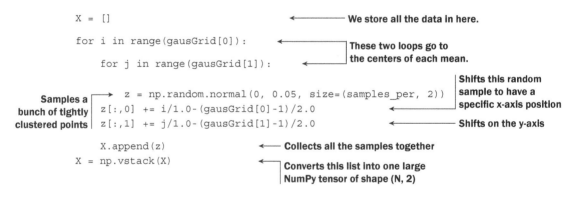

```
X = []                                        ◄─────────── We store all the data in here.

for i in range(gausGrid[0]):       ◄──────┐ These two loops go to
    for j in range(gausGrid[1]):   ◄──────┘ the centers of each mean.

        z = np.random.normal(0, 0.05, size=(samples_per, 2))
        z[:,0] += i/1.0-(gausGrid[0]-1)/2.0
        z[:,1] += j/1.0-(gausGrid[1]-1)/2.0

        X.append(z)            ◄─── Collects all the samples together
X = np.vstack(X)               ◄─┐ Converts this list into one large
                                 └ NumPy tensor of shape (N, 2)
```

Samples a bunch of tightly clustered points

Shifts this random sample to have a specific x-axis position

Shifts on the y-axis

Finally we can plot these samples! We use a kernel density estimate (kde) plot that smooths the visual of the 2D grid. We have enough samples that each mode looks *perfect*, and we can clearly see nine modes in a nice grid:

```
plt.figure(figsize=(10,10))
sns.kdeplot(x=X[:,0], y=X[:,1], shade=True, fill=True, thresh=-0.001)  ◄─┐
```

Plots perfect toy data

[18]: <AxesSubplot:>

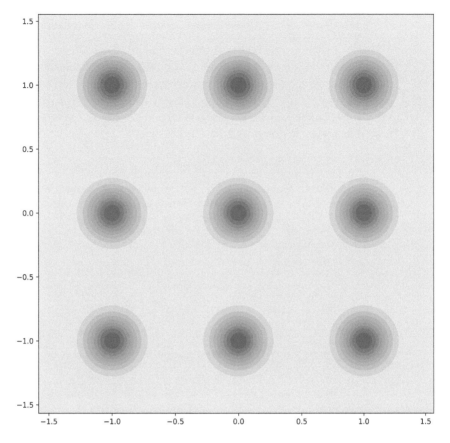

Now we have some nice simple data; surely our GAN should be able to solve this task. There are only two variables, and the distributions are Gaussians—practically the easiest and simplest distribution we could ever hope to have. Let's set up a GAN for this problem and see what happens! The following code quickly creates a dataset using the `TensorDataset` class. We are using 32 latent dimensions since this is a small problem that does not need 128, and we are using 256 neurons per layer. This should be more than necessary to learn the problem:

```
toy_dataset = torch.utils.data.TensorDataset(
    torch.tensor(X, dtype=torch.float32))
toy_loader = DataLoader(toy_dataset, batch_size=batch_size, shuffle=True,
    drop_last=True)
latent_d = 64
G, D = simpleGAN(latent_d, 512, (-1, 2))    ←——   A new GAN with just two output
                                                   features for our toy problem
```

With that in place, we can rerun the `for` loop we made to train our GANs for 100 epochs. Then we can generate some synthetic data, which we quickly do with another `no_grad` block:

```
with torch.no_grad():
    noise = torch.randn(X.shape[0], latent_d, device=device)
    fake_samples = G(noise).cpu().numpy()
```

Samples some random $z \sim \mathcal{N}(0, 1)$

⟵── **Creates the fake data** $G(z)$

Now let's visualize the generated samples with the following `kdeplot` call. Ideally, we should see the same image with a grid of nine circles. Instead, you usually see that only one or two of the nine Gaussians were generated by G! On top of that, the GAN does not always do a particularly good job of learning just one Gaussian. Instead of getting the larger shape and width, it learns a mode of the mode, focusing on the very center area with the most samples:

```
plt.figure(figsize=(10,10))
sns.kdeplot(x=fake_samples[:,0], y=fake_samples[:,1],
    shade=True, thresh=-0.001)          ⟵── Plots what G learned of our toy data
plt.xlim(-1.5, 1.5)      ⟵── Manually sets the x-axis to the range our dataset originally had
plt.ylim(-1.5, 1.5)      ⟵── Same for the y-axis
```

[23]: (-1.5, 1.5)

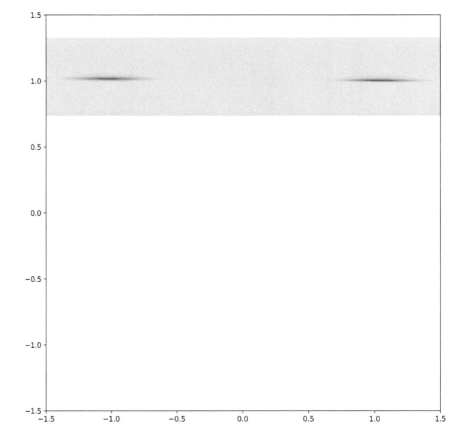

This behavior is an example of the mode-collapse phenomena. Instead of learning about the entire input space, the GAN picked the most convenient option for itself and overfit to just that. Hopefully, this toy problem shows you how easy it is for GANs to fall into the mode-collapse trap. All the tricks we learn in this chapter, and even the most cutting-edge approaches, only lessen this issue—we have not solved it. Even when you train a GAN that seems to work well on your problems, you should manually inspect the results and compare them against the real data. Look for patterns and styles that appear in the real data but not the generated outputs to identify whether mode collapse is happening and how severe it is. A GAN that generates good-looking outputs but has collapsed onto a few modes can easily trick you into thinking your results are better than they actually are.

9.3 Wasserstein GAN: Mitigating mode collapse

GANs are a highly active area of research right now, with many different approaches to deal with the mode-collapse problem. This section talks about one approach that has proven to be a reliable improvement and from which many others are building more sophisticated solutions. It is called the *Wasserstein GAN* (WGAN).[1] The name Wasserstein comes from the math for deriving this improvement, which we are not going to discuss. Instead, we will talk about the result and why it works.

As before, we will write the loss function in two parts: the loss for the discriminator and the loss for the generator. In this new solution, we do not use a sigmoid activation for the output of the discriminator D: that way, we have fewer vanishing gradient issues. The discriminator will still output a single value, though.

9.3.1 WGAN discriminator loss

The loss of the discriminator is the difference between D's score on fake data and D's score on real data. That looks like $D(G(z)) - D(x)$, so D wants to *minimize* this value as much as possible. This score can't saturate, which helps mitigate issues with vanishing gradients. More important, we will include a *penalty on the complexity of D*. The idea is that we want to handicap D so it has to work harder to learn more powerful models, which we hope makes the game between D and G a fair fight. We want to do this because D has the advantage of an easier problem. The discriminator's loss becomes

$$loss_D = \underbrace{D(G(z))}_{\text{G-score}} - \underbrace{D(x)}_{\text{D-score}} + \underbrace{\lambda \cdot \left(\|\nabla D\left(\epsilon \cdot x + (1 - \epsilon) \cdot G(z)\right)\|_2 - 1 \right)^2}_{\text{Complexity penalty}}$$

We annotate this equation in a moment, but first let's talk through it as you might see in a paper. Remember that by default, the goal is to minimize a loss function. What does minimizing this equation do? First, there is the subtraction of the G-score term and the

---

[1] Introduced by M. Arjovsky, S. Chintala, and L. Bottou, "Wasserstein generative adversarial networks," *Proceedings of the 34th International Conference on Machine Learning*, vol. 70, pp. 214–223, 2017. We show the version by I. Gulrajani, F. Ahmed, M. Arjovsky, V. Dumoulin, and A. C. Courville, "Improved training of Wasserstein GANs," *Advances in Neural Information Processing Systems*, vol. 30, pp. 5767–5777, 2017.

D-score term. G-score gives a score of how realistic the generator's output is, and D-score gives a score of how realistic real data looks. To minimize this, the discriminator D wants to minimize (large negative values!) the G-score and maximize (large positive values!) the D-score. So, large score values indicate more realism. Because the scores are not bounded by anything, we are really comparing the relative scores of fake data to those of real data. The important part here is that regardless of how well the discriminator is doing, the two values are just numbers subtracted, so the gradient should be easy to compute without any numerical concerns.

The other interesting addition is the *complexity penalty* term on the right side. How does this penalize complexity? It does so by taking the norm ($\| \cdot \|_2$) of the gradient (∇) of the discriminator D. The value ϵ is selected randomly in the range $[0, 1]$, so the penalty is applied to a random mix of real and fake data, which makes sure D can't cheat by learning simple functions for part of the data and complex functions for the other part. Finally, the value λ is a hyper-parameter we control. The larger we set it, the more we penalize complexity.

Now that we have walked through the parts of this new loss for D, let's repeat the equation with some color-coded annotations summarizing what is happening:

The discriminator D's loss is   trying to give negative scores to fake data from G

and positive scores to real data.   To avoid overfitting, a penalty is applied

on a random mix of real and fake data.   The discriminator's complexity

is penalized for becoming too complex or too simple.

$$loss_D = D(G(z)) - D(x) + \lambda \cdot \left(\left\| \nabla D\left(\epsilon \cdot x + (1-\epsilon) \cdot G(z) \right) \right\|_2 - 1 \right)^2$$

That our complexity term includes a gradient in the loss function means computing the loss requires taking the gradient of a gradient! Working out the math for that is difficult, but luckily PyTorch is here to do it for us. We can focus on understanding what this equation says and how to derive it.

A gradient tells you which direction to move in to minimize a function, and larger values mean you are at a steeper part of the function you are trying to minimize. A simple function that always returns the same value (i.e., no change) has a gradient of zero, which is the only way to get the complexity penalty to zero. So the further our function gets from simply returning the same value, the higher its penalty will be. That's the trick to how this part of the equation penalizes a complex model. Getting the penalty term to zero requires returning the same value under all circumstances, essentially ignoring the input. That is a uselessly simple function, but that will minimize that part of the loss: there is always a pull on D that wants it to move away from learning anything complex. In general, whenever you see something like $\|\nabla f(x)\|$ in a loss function, you should understand it as penalizing complexity.

9.3.2   *WGAN generator loss*

That was a lot of exposition about the discriminator and its fancy new loss function. The generator's loss, by comparison, is much simpler. The discriminator wants to maximize the G-score, and the generator wants to minimize the G-score! Our loss is the G-score with the sign flipped so G is minimized:

$$loss_G = -D(G(\boldsymbol{z}))$$

Why is the generator's loss so much simpler? It ties back to three reasons we have already discussed. First, the generator G does not care what D says about real data $\boldsymbol{x}$. This means we can remove the $D(\boldsymbol{x})$ term from the loss. Second, D has the advantage of an easier problem. The complexity penalty was to disadvantage D, and since we are talking about G's loss, we do not want to disadvantage G with an unnecessary penalty. Third, G's goal is to trick D. The only remaining part of the G-score is $D(G(\boldsymbol{z}))$. Since G has the opposite goal, we shove a negative sign in front, giving us the final loss $-D(G(\boldsymbol{z}))$.

9.3.3   *Implementing WGAN*

This new approach is often abbreviated WGAN-GP, where the GP stands for gradient penalty.[2] WGAN-GP helps solve the mode-collapse problem by reducing the opportunities for vanishing gradients and leveling the playing field between G and D so that G has an easier time keeping up with D. Let's train a new GAN with this approach on the toy grid and see if it helps.

   Since we will be using the WGAN-GP multiple times, we'll define a function `train_wgan` that does the work. This function follows the same setup and organization as our original GAN training loop, but each section of the function will have some changes. This includes the prep at the function start, giving the inputs to D and G, adding the gradient penalty, and computing the final WGAN-GP loss. We first define the function with arguments to take in the networks, the loader, the number of latent dimensions, how many epochs to train for, and the device to use.

UPDATING THE TRAINING PREP

This code uses a simple trick: if statements around `isinstance(data, tuple)` or `len(data)`. This way, we have a training loop that will work when the user gives a `Dataloader` with only the unlabeled data $\boldsymbol{x}$ or when given the data and labels y (but it won't use the labels; we just won't throw any errors about it):

```
def train_wgan(D, G, loader, latent_d, epochs=20, device="cpu"):
    G_losses = []
    D_losses = []

    G.to(device)
    D.to(device)
```

---

[2] There is a WGAN that came first, but I find WGAN-GP easier to use and more consistent in its behavior

```
optimizerD = torch.optim.AdamW(D.parameters(),    ◄── Sets up Adam optimizer for D
➡ lr=0.0001, betas=(0.0, 0.9))
optimizerG = torch.optim.AdamW(G.parameters(),    ◄── Sets up Adam optimizer for G
➡ lr=0.0001, betas=(0.0, 0.9))

for epoch in tqdm(range(epochs)):
for data in tqdm(loader, leave=False):
    if isinstance(data, tuple) or len(data) == 2:
        data, class_label = data
        class_label = class_label.to(device)
    elif isinstance(data, tuple) or len(data) == 1:
        data = data[0]
    batch_size = data.size(0)
    D.zero_grad()
    G.zero_grad()
    real = data.to(device)
```

UPDATING THE D AND G INPUTS

In the body of the loop, we compute the results of D on real and fake data. An important change here is that we are *not* calling the detach() function on fake when it goes into the discriminator, because we need to include G in the gradient penalty calculation in the next step:

```
D_success = D(real)    ◄─────────    Step 1: D-score, G-score,
                                     and gradient penalty. How well
                                     does D work on real data?

noise = torch.randn(batch_size, latent_d, device=device) ◄──  Trains with an all-fake
fake = G(noise)    ◄──                                        batch and generates a
                      Generates a fake image                  batch of latent vectors
                      batch with G

D_failure = D(fake)    ◄──
                          Classifies the all-fake
                          batch with D
```

CALCULATING THE GRADIENT PENALTY

With fake computed, we can compute the gradient penalty. First we select random values in the range of $[0,1]$ for ϵ in the eps variable. We have to make sure it has as many axes as the training data to make the tensors multiply together. So if our data is of shape (B, D), eps will have a shape of $(B, 1)$. If our data has a shape of (B, C, W, H), eps needs a shape of $(B, 1, 1, 1)$. This way, every item in the batch is multiplied by one value, and we can compute the mixed input that goes into D.

The next line of code has an autograd.grad function call. To be honest, this function frightens me, and I have to look it up every time I need to use it. It does the work of computing the gradient ∇ for us in a way that PyTorch can use to compute gradients.

Basically, this function does the same thing as calling .backward(), except it returns the object as a new tensor instead of storing it in the .grad field. It's OK if you don't understand this function, as it is niche in its use. But I'll give a quick high-level explanation for those who are interested. outputs=output tells PyTorch what we would have called .backward() on, and inputs=mixed tells PyTorch the initial inputs that gave this result. grad_outputs=torch.ones_like(output) gives PyTorch an initial value to start the gradient calculation with, which is set to all ones so we end up with our desired gradient for all parts. The options `create_graph=True`, `retain_graph=True` tell PyTorch that we want automatic differentiation to work on the result (this does the gradient of a gradient):

```
eps_shape = [batch_size]+[1]*(len(data.shape)-1)      Now calculate tensors
eps = torch.rand(eps_shape, device=device)            to use to compute the
mixed = eps*real + (1-eps)*fake                        gradient penalty term.
output = D(mixed)

grad = torch.autograd.grad(outputs=output, inputs=mixed,
    grad_outputs=torch.ones_like(output), create_graph=True,
    retain_graph=True, only_inputs=True, allow_unused=True)[0]

D_grad_penalty = ((grad.norm(2, dim=1) - 1) ** 2)

errD = (D_failure-D_success).mean() + D_grad_penalty.mean()*10    Calculates
errD.backward()                                                   D's loss
optimizerD.step()      ←—— Updates D
```

CALCULATING THE WGAN-GP LOSS

With the `grad` variable finally in hand, we can quickly compute the total loss. The `*10` is the λ term controlling how strong the penalty is. I've hardcoded it to 10 because that's a good default value for this approach, but better coding would make `lambda` an argument of the function with a default value of 10.

The second step computes the update to G in the final chunk of code, where we begin by re-zeroing out the gradients. This is a defensive coding step due to the trickiness of keeping track of when we have and have not altered the gradients. Then we sample a new latent z in the `noise` variable, compute `-D(G(noise))`, take the average, and do our updates:

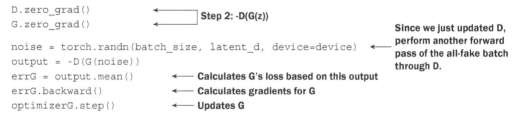

```
D.zero_grad()                          Step 2: -D(G(z))
G.zero_grad()
                                                        Since we just updated D,
noise = torch.randn(batch_size, latent_d, device=device)  ←  perform another forward
output = -D(G(noise))                                       pass of the all-fake batch
errG = output.mean()      ←—— Calculates G's loss based on this output  through D.
errG.backward()           ←—— Calculates gradients for G
optimizerG.step()         ←—— Updates G
```

We end the function by recoding the loss for each of G and D to look at later, and return those losses as the result of calling the function:

```
    D_losses.append(errD.item())
    G_losses.append(errG.item())
return D_losses, G_losses
```

With this new `train_wgan` function in hand, we can attempt to train a new Wasserstein GAN on the earlier toy problem with nine Gaussians in a 3×3 grid. We simply call the following code snippet:

```
G, D = simpleGAN(latent_d, 512, (-1, 2))
train_wgan(D, G, toy_loader, latent_d, epochs=20, device=device)
G, D = G.eval(), D.eval()
```

RESULTS WITH LESS MODE COLLAPSE

The following code generates some new samples. The results are not perfect, but they are *much* better than we got before. The GAN has learned to cover a wider portion of the input data, and the shape of the distribution is closer to the ground truth that we know. We can generally see all nine modes represented, which is good, although some are not as strong as the others:

```
with torch.no_grad():
    noise = torch.randn(X.shape[0], latent_d, device=device)
    fake_samples_w = G(noise).cpu().numpy()
plt.figure(figsize=(10,10))
ax = sns.kdeplot(x=fake_samples_w[:,0], y=fake_samples_w[:,1],
    shade=True, thresh=-0.001)
plt.xlim(-1.5, 1.5)
plt.ylim(-1.5, 1.5)
```

[27]: (-1.5, 1.5)

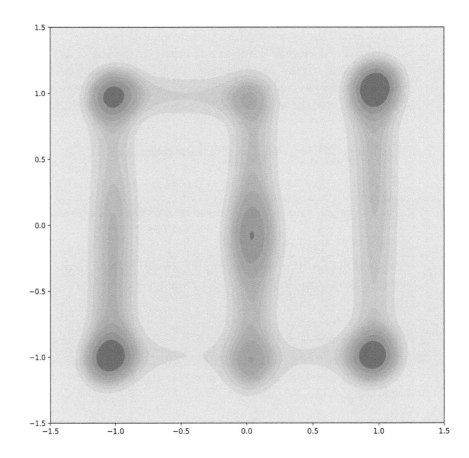

The mode-collapse issue is not solved by the Wasserstein approach, but it is greatly improved. A downside of the Wasserstein approach, and of most GANs, is that it requires many more iterations to converge. A common trick to improve WGAN training is to update the discriminator five times for every update to the generator, which further increases the total number of epochs to get the best possible results. You should do closer to 200 to 400 epochs for most problems to train a really good GAN. Even with WGAN, you will often see it collapse if you train it again. This is part of the notoriety of training a GAN, but more data and more training epochs will improve it.

With that said, let's go back to our original MNIST problem and see if our WGAN-GP improves the results. We redefine the latent dimension size as 128 and the output shape to match that of MNIST. Again we have a sigmoid output for G because MNIST values are all in the range of $[0, 1]$. The following code trains this with our new approach:

```
latent_d = 128
out_shape = (-1, 1, 28, 28)
G, D = simpleGAN(latent_d, neurons, out_shape, sigmoidG=True)

D_losses, G_losses = train_wgan(D, G, train_loader, latent_d, epochs=40,
    device=device)

G = G.eval()
D = D.eval()
```

> **NOTE** Why update the discriminator D more times than you update the generator G? So the discriminator has more changes to update and catch what the generator G is doing. That's desirable because G can only become as good as the discriminator D. This doesn't give too much of an unfair advantage to D, thanks to the complexity penalty.

Now we generate some synthetic data, but we won't look at the scores: the scores are no longer probabilities, so it is much harder to interpret them as a single value. This is why we made `scores` an optional argument for `plot_gen_imgs`:

```
with torch.no_grad():
    noise = torch.randn(batch_size, latent_d, device=device)
    fake_digits = G(noise)
    scores = D(fake_digits)
    fake_digits = fake_digits.cpu()
    scores = scores.cpu().numpy().flatten()
plot_gen_imgs(fake_digits)
```

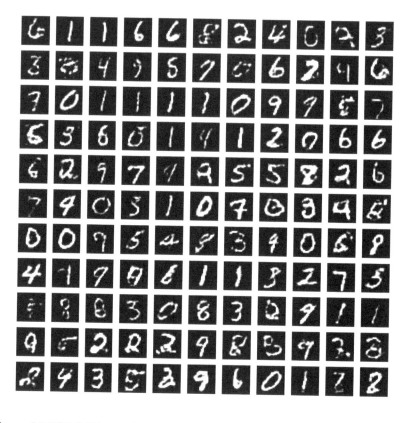

Overall, our MNIST GAN samples look much better than before. You should be able to find an example of all 10 digits in most samples, even if some of the digits are a little uglier or malformed. You should also see more variety of styles within a single specific digit! These are subjectively massive improvements in our GAN's quality. One downside is that our 0s, 3s, and 8s are not as crisp as they were when we had mode collapse: our WGAN-GP could use more training epochs, and it's doing *more* than it was before. When the original GAN collapsed, it got to use its entire network to represent only three digits. Now each digit has less of the network because we are representing all 10 digits. This is part of why I recommend comparing your generated results to your real data to decide if the results are good. High-quality collapsed results can lure you into a false belief about the quality of or GAN.

We can also plot the losses of both the discriminator and generator again. The following code does this and uses a convolution to smooth the average loss so we can focus on the trends. When interpreting the loss for a WGAN-GP, remember that the generator G wants a large loss, and the discriminator D wants a small loss:

```
plt.figure(figsize=(10,5))
plt.title("Generator and Discriminator Loss During Training")
plt.plot(np.convolve(G_losses, np.ones((100,))/100, mode='valid') ,label="G")
plt.plot(np.convolve(D_losses, np.ones((100,))/100, mode='valid') ,label="D")
plt.xlabel("iterations")
plt.ylabel("Loss")
plt.legend()
plt.show()
```

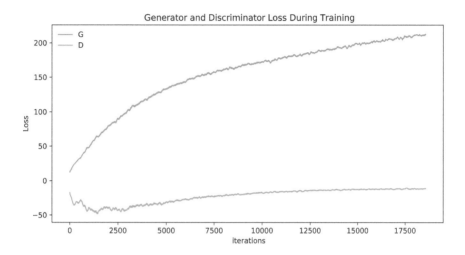

Interpreting this figure, G is improving with more training, which is good and a reason to keep training. But the discriminator D seems to have stopped improving, which may be a sign that D isn't strong enough to learn a better representation now. This is an issue because G's quality will only improve as D gets better at the task. A major change we can make is to implement a convolutional GAN so the generator (and discriminator) get the structural prior of convolutions and (we hope) both do better!

9.4 Convolutional GAN

As with most deep learning applications, the best way to improve your results with a GAN is to choose an architecture that makes sense for your problem. Since we are working on images, we can use a convolutional architecture to improve our results. This requires a bit of finagling around the latent representation z. Our code creates a vector of shape (B, D) for D dimensions in z. What shape should our latent be for a convolutional G?

9.4.1 *Designing a convolutional generator*

One approach is to make a latent tensor of shape (B, C', W', H'), so it is already shaped like an image but does not have the correct output shape of (B, C, W, H). We make the width and height of this latent smaller than the real data and use transposed convolutions to expand up to the size of our real data. But for C', we want to use more channels than our original data has. This way, the model can learn to interpret the latent channels as having different kinds of meaning, and having only one or three channels would likely be too small.

The following code sets up our parameters for training a *convolutional GAN*. First we determine the `start_size` that will be the initial width and height W' and H'. We make $W' = W/4$ so we can do two rounds of expansion with a transposed convolution. We can't make it any smaller without some ugly code because that gets us down to $28/4 = 7$ pixels: dividing by 2 again would be 3.5 pixels, and that's not something we can easily deal with. Next we define how many `latent_channels` C' as 16. This is a hyperparameter to choose, and I've simply chosen a small value that I would increase if my results did not work well. Since we have a latent variable with a shape of (B, C', W', H'), we define the `in_shape` tuple to represent this as the counterpart to the `out_shape` tuple we have been using. Our network will use `in_shape` to reshape the input to G; `out_shape` will still be used to reshape the output of G and the input to D:

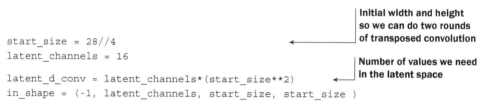

```
start_size = 28//4
latent_channels = 16

latent_d_conv = latent_channels*(start_size**2)
in_shape = (-1, latent_channels, start_size, start_size )
```

Initial width and height so we can do two rounds of transposed convolution

Number of values we need in the latent space

This code sets up the variables we need for our problem while also being easy to adjust for new problems. If you have larger images, experiment with more than two rounds of expansion and more than 16 latent channels, which can be easily achieved by altering the first two lines.

IMPLEMENTING CONVOLUTIONAL HELPER FUNCTIONS

Now we need a few variables before defining our convolutional architecture. We start our generator with `n_filters=32` filters, and we use a leak rate of 0.2 for our LeakyReLU activation. We also define the kernel size as `k_size=5`. Usually we use more depth with a kernel size of 3 for our CNNs. For GANs, I often find that a slightly larger kernel size improves results. Our transposed convolutions, in particular, will have smoother outputs if we use a kernel size that is a multiple of the stride, so we give them a separate kernel size of `k_size_t=4`. This helps ensure that when the transposed convolution expands the output, each location in the output gets an even number of contributions to its value:

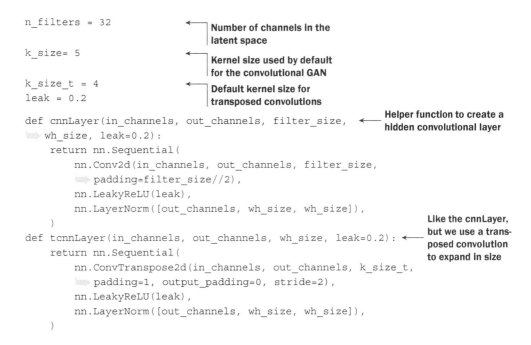

```
n_filters = 32                          Number of channels in the
                                        latent space

k_size= 5                               Kernel size used by default
                                        for the convolutional GAN

k_size_t = 4                            Default kernel size for
leak = 0.2                              transposed convolutions

def cnnLayer(in_channels, out_channels, filter_size,    Helper function to create a
    wh_size, leak=0.2):                                 hidden convolutional layer
    return nn.Sequential(
        nn.Conv2d(in_channels, out_channels, filter_size,
            padding=filter_size//2),
        nn.LeakyReLU(leak),
        nn.LayerNorm([out_channels, wh_size, wh_size]),
    )                                                   Like the cnnLayer,
def tcnnLayer(in_channels, out_channels, wh_size, leak=0.2):  but we use a trans-
    return nn.Sequential(                                     posed convolution
        nn.ConvTranspose2d(in_channels, out_channels, k_size_t,  to expand in size
            padding=1, output_padding=0, stride=2),
        nn.LeakyReLU(leak),
        nn.LayerNorm([out_channels, wh_size, wh_size]),
    )
```

IMPLEMENTING A CONVOLUTIONAL GAN

Now we define our CNN GAN. For G, we start with a View(in_shape) so the latent vector z becomes the desired input shape we specified: (B, C', W', H'). Next come a few rounds of convolutions, activation, and LN. Remember that for CNNs, we need to keep track of the width and height of the input, which is why we have the MNIST height of 28 by 28 encoded into our architecture. We follow our simple pattern of using two or three rounds of CNN layers before and after each transposed convolution:

```
G = nn.Sequential(
    View(in_shape),
    cnnLayer(latent_channels, n_filters, k_size, 28//4, leak),
    cnnLayer(n_filters, n_filters, k_size, 28//4, leak),
    cnnLayer(n_filters, n_filters, k_size, 28//4, leak),
    tcnnLayer(n_filters, n_filters//2, 28//2, leak),
    cnnLayer(n_filters//2, n_filters//2, k_size, 28//2, leak),
    cnnLayer(n_filters//2, n_filters//2, k_size, 28//2, leak),
    tcnnLayer(n_filters//2, n_filters//4, 28, leak),
    cnnLayer(n_filters//4, n_filters//4, k_size, 28, leak),
    cnnLayer(n_filters//4, n_filters//4, k_size, 28, leak),
    nn.Conv2d(n_filters//4, 1, k_size, padding=k_size//2),
    nn.Sigmoid(),
)
```

9.4.2 *Designing a convolutional discriminator*

Next, we implement the discriminator D. This takes a few more departures from our normal setup. Again, these are some tricks you can use to help improve your GANs:

- D and G are asymmetric. We can make D a smaller network than G to help give G an advantage in the competition. Even with the gradient penalty in WGAN-GP, D still has an easier job to learn. A rough rule of thumb I've found helpful as a starting point is D having two-thirds as many layers as G. Then plot the loss of D and G over a training run to see if D is getting stuck (loss does not decrease) and should become larger, or if G is stuck (loss does not increase), at which point maybe D should shrink or G should become larger.

- Switch to average pooling with `nn.AvgPool2d` instead of max pooling. This helps maximize gradient flow because every pixel contributes equally to an answer, so all pixels get a share of the gradient.

- End your network with some aggressive pooling, which is most easily done with the `AdaptiveAvgPool` or `AdaptiveMaxPool` function. This can help keep D from keying off the exact location of a value when what we really care about is the overall look of the content.

The following code incorporates these ideas into the definition of D. Again, we are using LN, so we need to keep track of the height and width, starting at full size and then shrinking. We use using 4×4 for the adaptive pooling size at the end, so the next linear layer has $4 \times 4 = 16$ values per channel to take as input. If we were doing this on 64×64 or 256×256 images, I might push the adaptive pooling up to 7×7 or 9×9:

```
D = nn.Sequential(
    cnnLayer(1, n_filters, k_size, 28, leak),
    cnnLayer(n_filters, n_filters, k_size, 28, leak),
    nn.AvgPool2d(2),                                       ← To avoid sparse gradients,
                                                             we are using average
                                                             instead of max pooling.
    cnnLayer(n_filters, n_filters, k_size, 28//2, leak),
    cnnLayer(n_filters, n_filters, k_size, 28//2, leak),
    nn.AvgPool2d(2),
    cnnLayer(n_filters, n_filters, 3, 28//4, leak),
    cnnLayer(n_filters, n_filters, 3, 28//4, leak),
    nn.AdaptiveAvgPool2d(4),                               ← This is adaptive pooling,
    nn.Flatten(),                                            so we know the size is
                                                             4 × 4 at this point to be
    nn.Linear(n_filters*4**2,256),                          more aggressive in
    nn.LeakyReLU(leak),                                      pooling (often helpful for
    nn.Linear(256,1),                                        convolutional GANs) and
)                                                            to make coding easier.
```

TRAINING AND INSPECTING OUR CONVOLUTIONAL GAN

By moving the `View` logic into the network instead of the training code, we can reuse the `train_wgan` function for our CNN GANs. The following code trains them up:

```
D_losses, G_losses = train_wgan(D, G, train_loader, latent_d_conv,
    epochs=15, device=device)

G = G.eval()
D = D.eval()
```

Ten epochs is not a lot of time for training a GAN, but next we visualize some random samples from the CNN GANs, and the digits look much better than they previously did. Again, it is not surprising that a convolutional approach works better on images, but we did need to learn a few extra tricks to make this work well:

```
with torch.no_grad():
    noise = torch.randn(batch_size, latent_d_conv, device=device)
    fake_digits = G(noise)
    scores = D(fake_digits)

    fake_digits = fake_digits.cpu()
    scores = scores.cpu().numpy().flatten()
plot_gen_imgs(fake_digits)
```

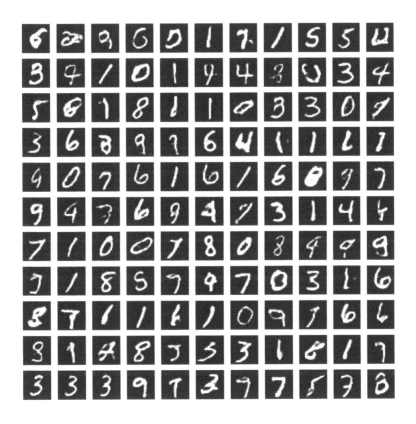

Would more epochs of training improve our WGAN-GP? The following code again plots a smoothed version of the G and D losses over every batch. There is a clear trend that G's score is increasing, which indicates that G is getting better at generating; but D's score is flat-lining (not getting better or worse). More training might improve this, but it's not a guarantee. It would be better if D's score was decreasing (because D wants negative values), making the graph expand in a funnel-like shape (the first 300 iterations have this shape). That would mean both G and D were improving, and we would be more confident that more epochs of training would improve the results of the GAN:

```
plt.figure(figsize=(10,5))
plt.title("Conv-WGAN Generator and Discriminator Loss")
plt.plot(np.convolve(G_losses, np.ones((100,))/100, mode='valid') ,label="G")
plt.plot(np.convolve(D_losses, np.ones((100,))/100, mode='valid') ,label="D")
plt.xlabel("iterations")
plt.ylabel("Loss")
plt.legend()
plt.show()
```

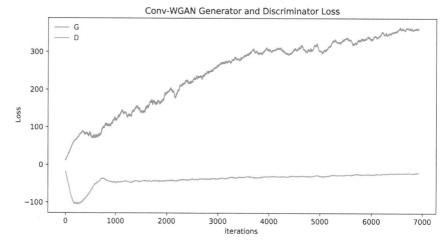

9.5   *Conditional GAN*

Another way to help improve the training of GANs is to create a *conditional GAN*. Conditional GANs are supervised instead of unsupervised because we use the label y that belongs to each data point x. This is a fairly simple change, as shown in figure 9.7.

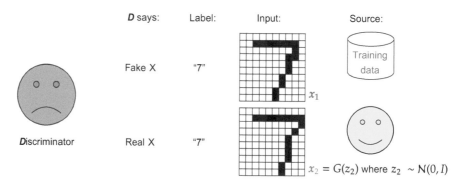

Figure 9.7   **Example of a conditional GAN where** D **made errors and** G **did well. The only change is that we include the label** y **of the data as an input to both** G **and** D. G **gets the label so it knows what to create, and** D **gets the label so it knows what it is looking for.**

Instead of asking the model to predict y from x, we tell G to generate an example of y. You can think of a normal GAN as asking the model to generate any realistic data and a conditional GAN as asking the model to generate realistic data that we can classify as y. This helps the model by giving it extra information. It doesn't have to figure out on its own how many classes there are because you are tell the model G what kind of data to generate by providing the label y. To make this happen, we also provide the information about y to the discriminator D.

Another way to think about this is that a conditional GAN allows us to learn a *one-to-many* mapping. All of our previous neural networks have been *one-to-one*. For any input x, there is one correct output y. But as figure 9.8 demonstrates, a conditional model lets us create many valid outputs for any one valid input.

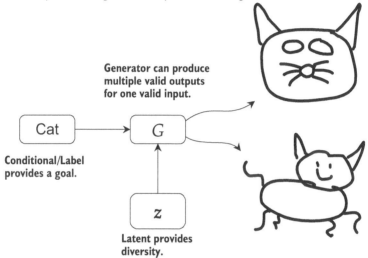

Figure 9.8 Example of how a conditional GAN is a one-to-many mapping. The input is "cat," and the output on the right shows multiple valid outputs. To get this diversity of outputs, the latent variable z gives G a way to create the multiple outputs.

Having a one-to-many mapping with conditional GANs also allows us to start manipulating what G produces. Given a single latent vector z, we can ask the model to produce a 1 using $G(z \mid y = 1)$ or a 3 by using $G(z \mid y = 3)$. If we do both of these things using the same value of z, the generated 1 and 3 will share similar characteristics like line thickness and slant.

9.5.1 Implementing a conditional GAN

We can implement a conditional GAN without much work. To do so, we first need to modify G and D to take two inputs: the latent z and a label y. Let's define a `ConditionalWrapper` class that does this for us. Our approach is that `Conditional-Wrapper` will take in a normal G or D network and use it as a subnetwork, similar to how we implemented U-Net. `ConditionalWrapper` takes z and y and combine them into a single new latent value $\hat{z}$. Then we pass the new latent $\hat{z}$ to the original network (either G or D).

The following `Module` definition implements this idea. In the constructor, we create an `nn.Embedding` layer to convert the labels y into vectors the same size as z. We also create a `combiner` network, which takes an input twice the size of the latent vector z and returns an output the same size as z. This network is intentionally small, with no more than two hidden layers, so it is just enough to combine our two input values z and y.

The `forward` function then gets to operate with very few steps. It embeds y into a vector. Since y's embedding and z have the same shape, we can concatenate them together to make a double-sized input. This goes into the `combiner` and then right into the original `net` (either G or D).

Here's the code:

```
class ConditionalWrapper(nn.Module):
    def __init__(self, input_shape, neurons, classes, main_network,
        leak=0.2):
        """
        input_shape: the shape that the latent variable z
            should take.
        neurons: neurons to use in hidden layers
        classes: number of classes in labels y
        main_network: either the generator G or discriminator D
        """
        super().__init__()

        self.input_shape = input_shape
        self.classes = classes
        input_size = abs(np.prod(input_shape))

        self.label_embedding = nn.Embedding(classes, input_size)

        self.combiner = nn.Sequential(
            nn.Flatten(),

            fcLayer(input_size*2, input_size, leak=leak),
            nn.Linear(input_size, input_size),
            nn.LeakyReLU(leak),

            View(input_shape),
            nn.LayerNorm(input_shape[1:]),
        )
        self.net = main_network

    def forward(self, x, condition=None):
```

Creates an embedding layer to convert labels to vectors → `self.label_embedding = nn.Embedding(classes, input_size)`

Figures out the number of latent parameters from the latent shape → `input_size = abs(np.prod(input_shape))`

In the forward function, we concatenate the label and original date into one vector. Then his combiner takes that extra-large tensor and creates a new tensor the size of just the original input_shape. This does the work of merging the conditional information (from label_embedding) into the latent vector.

One FC layer

A second FC layer, but first the inear layer and activation are applied

So we can reshape the output and apply normalizing based on the target output shape. This makes the conditio wrapper useful for linear and convolutional models.

The forward function takes an input and produces an output.

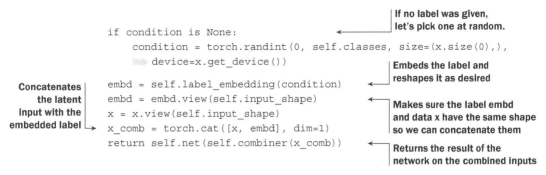

```
                      if condition is None:                          ← │ If no label was given,
                          condition = torch.randint(0, self.classes, size=(x.size(0),),  │ let's pick one at random.
                              device=x.get_device())                 ← │ Embeds the label and
                                                                        │ reshapes it as desired
Concatenates │        embd = self.label_embedding(condition)          ← │
the latent   │        embd = embd.view(self.input_shape)              ← │ Makes sure the label embd
input with the │      x = x.view(self.input_shape)                      │ and data x have the same shape
embedded label └──→   x_comb = torch.cat([x, embd], dim=1)             │ so we can concatenate them
                      return self.net(self.combiner(x_comb))          ← │ Returns the result of the
                                                                        │ network on the combined inputs
```

9.5.2 Training a conditional GAN

With this code, it is easy to convert our normal fully connected GANs to conditional GANs. The following snippet of code creates a new fully connected GAN. The only thing we change is to define the number of `classes=10` and wrap G and D independently using our new `ConditionalWrapper`:

```
latent_d = 128
out_shape = (-1, 1, 28, 28)
in_shape = (-1, latent_d)
classes = 10
G, D = simpleGAN(latent_d, neurons, out_shape, sigmoidG=True)

G = ConditionalWrapper(in_shape, neurons, classes, G)
D = ConditionalWrapper(out_shape, neurons, classes, D)
```

Now we need a way to train these conditional models, because the `train_wgan` function does not use the labels. This is another easy change. We can define a new function `train_c_wgan` that has the *exact* same code, except that any time we have `G(noise)` in our code, we change it to `G(noise, class_label)`. Similarly, any time we see something like `D(real)`, we change it to `D(real, class_label)`. That's it—we just add `, class_label)` any time we used `G` or `D`! This gives us the tools and code to create conditional GANs. The following block of code trains the ones we just defined:

```
D_losses, G_losses = train_c_wgan(D, G, train_loader, latent_d,
    epochs=20, device=device)

G = G.eval()
D = D.eval()
```

9.5.3 Controlling the generation with conditional GANs

Let's visualize the results of this new GAN and show how we can control the process at the same time. The following code generates 10 different latent vectors z and makes 10 copies of each z value. Then we create a `labels` tensor that counts from 0 to 9, covering all 10 classes. This way, we create $G(z \mid y = 0), G(z \mid y = 1), \ldots, G(z \mid y = 9)$.

Each digit is generated while using the same latent vector. Because the conditional controls the class that is generated, the latent z is forced to learn the *style*. If you look across each row, you will see that in each case, some basic styles are maintained across all the outputs, irrespective of the class.

Here's the code:

Counts from 0 to 9 and then wraps back around to 0. This is done 10 times.

```
with torch.no_grad():
    noise = torch.randn(10, latent_d, device=device).
        repeat((1,10)).view(-1, latent_d)
    labels = torch.fmod(torch.arange(0, noise.size(0),
        device=device), classes)
    fake_digits = G(noise, labels)
    scores = D(fake_digits, labels)
    fake_digits = fake_digits.cpu()
    scores = scores.cpu().numpy().flatten()
plot_gen_imgs(fake_digits)
```

Generates 10 latent noise vectors, and repeats them 10 times. We reuse the same latent codes.

The same latent in noise is used to generate 10 images, but we change the label each time.

When we plot the results, we should see a grid of digits from 0 to 9, where each row uses the same latent vector and shares similar visual properties.

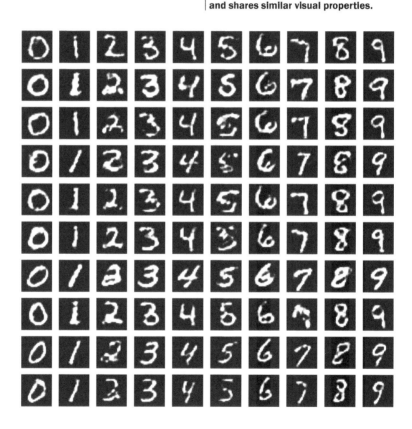

Notice that if the 0 at the start of a row has thick lines, all the digits in that row have thick lines. If 0 is slanted to the right, all the digits are slanted to the right. This is how conditional GANs let us control what is generated. We could extend this approach to even more conditioned properties, which would give us more control over what and how *G* generates its outputs. But this requires a lot of labeled outputs, which is now always a possibility.

9.6 Walking the latent space of GANs

We have seen that GANs can do an impressive job creating fake data, and the latent representation z begins to learn interesting properties about the data as it trains. This is true even when we don't have any labels. But we can also control the results generated by a GAN by altering the latent vector z itself. Doing so lets us manipulate images by labeling only a few of them so we can determine the right way to alter z.

9.6.1 Getting models from the Hub

Since training GANs is expensive, in this section we use the PyTorch *Hub* to download a pretrained GAN. The Hub is a repository where people can upload useful pretrained models, and PyTorch has built-in integration to download and use those models. We'll download an example trained on higher-resolution images of faces for something more fun to look at than MNIST.

First things first: we load the desired GAN model from the Hub. This happens with the `hub.load` function, where the first argument is the repository to load from, and the following arguments depend on the repository. In this case, we load a model called PGAN that was trained on a high-resolution dataset of celebrities. We also load the `torchvision` package, which has vision-specific extensions to PyTorch:

```
import torchvision
model = torch.hub.load('facebookresearch/pytorch_GAN_zoo:hub', 'PGAN',
    model_name='celebAHQ-512', pretrained=True, useGPU=False)
```

SPECIFICS OF THE PGAN HUB MODEL

The code loaded into the Hub defined a `buildNoiseData` function, which takes the number of samples we want to generate and produces noise vectors to generate that many images. We can then use the model's `test` method to generate images from the noise. Let's try it!

```
num_images = 2
noise, _ = model.buildNoiseData(num_images)
with torch.no_grad():
    generated_images = model.test(noise)
```

Using the `torchvision` helper function to plot the images, you should see a synthetically generated man and woman:

```
grid = torchvision.utils.make_grid(generated_images.clamp(min=-1, max=1),
    scale_each=True, normalize=True)
plt.imshow(grid.permute(1, 2, 0).cpu().numpy())
```

```
[50]:  <matplotlib.image.AxesImage at 0x7f2abd028f90>
```

Just as with our GANs earlier, these images were created by learning to convert noise into realistic-looking images! If we print the noise values, we see randomly sampled values from the Gaussian distribution (there is no magic hidden under the hood):

```
print(noise)

tensor([[-0.0766, 0.3599, -0.7820, …, -1.0038, 0.5046, -0.4253],
        [ 0.5643, 0.4867, 0.2295, …, 1.1609, -1.2194, 0.8006]])
```

9.6.2 *Interpolating GAN output*

A cool property of GANs is that the latent values z that are learned tend to be well behaved when you manipulate them mathematically. So if we take our two noise samples, we can interpolate between the noise vectors (say, 50% of one and 50% of the other) to produce interpolations of the images. This is often called *walking the latent space*: if you have one latent vector and walk some distance to a second latent vector, you end up with something that represents a mix of your original and destination latents.

If we apply this to our two samples, the male image slowly transitions to female, the hair darkens to brown, and the smile widens. In the code, we take eight steps in the latent space from the first image to the second, changing the ratio of how much each latent contributes to the result:

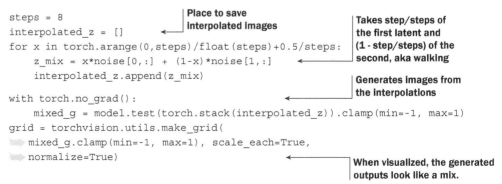

```
plt.figure(figsize=(15,10))
plt.imshow(grid.permute(1, 2, 0).cpu().numpy())
```

```
[52]:  <matplotlib.image.AxesImage at 0x7f2af48f42d0>
```

We can take this even further. If we are willing to label a few instances from our dataset, we can extract vectors with semantic meaning. Figure 9.9 shows how this might work at a high level.

GANs tend to learn a latent vector to represent different important concepts like "smiling," and if you can extract those vectors, you can manipulate the output to increase or decrease the latent properties.

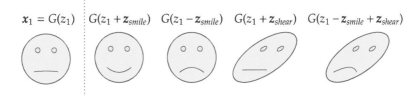

$$x_1 = G(z_1) \quad G(z_1 + z_{smile}) \quad G(z_1 - z_{smile}) \quad G(z_1 + z_{shear}) \quad G(z_1 - z_{smile} + z_{shear})$$

Figure 9.9 Example of a generated image and the kinds of semantic vectors you might be able to find. The left shows the original latent and associated output from G. By adding these semantic vectors, we can alter what is generated. These are called latent vectors because we didn't tell the GAN what they are: they were hidden from the GAN, and it had to learn them on its own from patterns in the data.

This basically means it is possible to find a vector z_{smile} that we can add to any other latent vector to make someone smile, or subtract from another latent vector to remove a smile. The great thing is that we *never told G about any of these latent properties*. G learns to do this on its own, and if we can discover the semantic vectors, we can make these alterations! To do this, let's first generate a bunch of random images of people to use:

```
set_seed(3)                                          ──────── Gets consistent results
noise, _ = model.buildNoiseData(8*4)                 ──── Creates random generations
with torch.no_grad():
    generated_images = model.test(noise)
grid = torchvision.utils.make_grid(
    generated_images.clamp(min=-1, max=1),
    scale_each=True, normalize=True)                 ──── Visualizes them
plt.figure(figsize=(13,6))
plt.imshow(grid.permute(1, 2, 0).cpu().numpy())
```

```
[53]: <matplotlib.image.AxesImage at 0x7f2abc505710>
```

9.6.3 Labeling latent dimensions

Now we have 32 example faces. If we can identify certain properties that we care about for each generated image, we can label them and attempt to learn what parts of the noise control different aspects of the output.[3] Let's identify the individuals who are male/female and those who are smiling or not. I created an array for each property, corresponding to each image, so we have 32 labels for "male" and 32 labels for "smiling." Essentially, we are creating our own labels y for properties we care about, but we will be able to extract these semantic[4] vectors with very few labeled examples. G has already done the hard work of learning the concept on its own:

```
male = [0, 1, 0, 0, 1, 0, 0, 0,
        1, 1, 1, 1, 0, 1, 0, 0,
        1, 0, 0, 1, 0, 0, 1, 0,
        0, 0, 0, 0, 0, 0, 1, 0]
smile = [1, 1, 0, 0, 1, 0, 1, 1,
         0, 0, 0, 0, 0, 1, 0, 0,
         1, 0, 1, 0, 1, 1, 1, 1,
         0, 0, 1, 1, 0, 0, 0, 1]
male = np.array(male, dtype=np.bool)
smile = np.array(smile, dtype=np.bool)
```

Labels for which images are apparently male or smiling. I went through the generated images manually to create these lists.

```
male = torch.tensor(np.expand_dims(male, axis=-1))
smile = torch.tensor(np.expand_dims(smile, axis=-1))
```

Converts the shape from (32) to (32, 1)

3 Better ways to do this is an active research problem, but our simple approach works shockingly well.

4 People have many different mental models of what they mean by *semantic*, and it's a pet peeve for many researchers. We are not going down that rabbit hole.

CALCULATING A SEMANTIC VECTOR

Now we want to calculate the average male and average non-male vector. We do the same thing for smiling, so let's define a simple function that uses the binary labels `male` and `smile` to extract the vector that represents the difference. The more labels we generate, the better the results will be:

```
def extractVec(labels, noise):
    posVec = torch.sum(noise*labels, axis=0)/torch.sum(labels)
    negVec = torch.sum(noise* labels, axis=0)/torch.sum( labels)
    return posVec-negVec
```

Gets the average of everything with class label 0 ◄─ (points to posVec line)

Average of everything with class label 1 ◄─ (points to negVec line)

Takes the difference between the averages to approximate the difference between the latent concepts ◄─ (points to return line)

MANIPULATING IMAGES WITH SEMANTIC VECTORS

Now we can use the `extractVec` function to extract a male gender vector. If we add it to any latent vector z, we get a new latent vector that becomes more male. Everything else in the generated image should generally stay the same, such as background, hair color, head position, etc. Let's try it:

```
gender_vec = extractVec(male, noise)          ◄── Extracts the gender vector
with torch.no_grad():
    generated_images = model.test(noise+gender_vec)   ◄── Generates new images
                                                           by adding the gender
                                                           vector to our original
grid = torchvision.utils.make_grid(                    latent vectors
    generated_images.clamp(min=-1, max=1),
    scale_each=True, normalize=True)          ◄── Plots the results
plt.figure(figsize=(13,6))
plt.imshow(grid.permute(1, 2, 0).cpu().numpy())
```

[56]:   <matplotlib.image.AxesImage at 0x7f2abc4f5850>

Overall, the results are pretty decent. Not perfect, but we did not use many examples to discover these vectors. We can also subtract this gender vector to remove male-ness from the images. In this case, we would be making each image appear more feminine. The following code does this by simply changing + to -:

```
with torch.no_grad():
    generated_images = model.test(noise-gender_vec)
grid = torchvision.utils.make_grid(generated_images.clamp(min=-1, max=1),
➥ scale_each=True, normalize=True)
plt.figure(figsize=(13,6))
plt.imshow(grid.permute(1, 2, 0).cpu().numpy())
```

```
[57]:  <matplotlib.image.AxesImage at 0x7f2abd67d590>
```

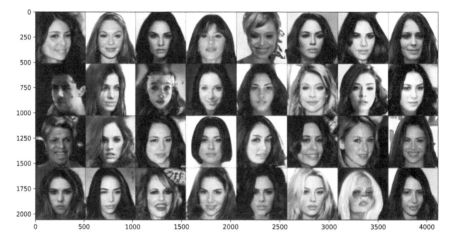

Maybe you want everyone to be happy! We can do the same thing with the `smile` vector we extracted to make everyone smile more:

```
smile_vec = extractVec(smile, noise)
with torch.no_grad():
    generated_images = model.test(noise+smile_vec)
grid = torchvision.utils.make_grid(generated_images.clamp(min=-1, max=1),
➥ scale_each=True, normalize=True)
plt.figure(figsize=(13,6))
plt.imshow(grid.permute(1, 2, 0).cpu().numpy())
```

`[58]:` `<matplotlib.image.AxesImage at 0x7f2ab47d0750>`

9.7 Ethics in deep learning

In chapter 4, we took a brief detour to talk about the importance of understanding how we are modeling the world and how using those models can impact the way others perceive the world. This is a conversation worth revisiting now that we have learned about GANs.

The semantic concepts GANs learn are based on data and do not necessarily represent the truth about how the world works. For example, most people identify and present as male or female, which is reflected in our data, so a GAN learns a somewhat linear relationship between male and female as a uniform spectrum. But that does not match the reality for many people who do not fit into a bucket of just male or female. The manipulation of gender in an image using GANs is thus something you should give thought to before exposing it as part of any system.

For any system (machine learning or otherwise) you build, you should ask yourself some simple questions: How will it impact the majority of people who use it? How will it impact the minority of people who use it? Are there people who benefit or are hurt by the system, and *should* those people receive that benefit or detriment? Could your deployment changes people's behavior in positive or negative ways or be misused by even well-intentioned users? Generally, think about *what could go wrong* at a micro and macro scale.

I'm not attempting to prescribe any philosophical or moral belief system on you. Ethics is a very complex topic, and I can't do it justice in a subsection of a chapter (and it is not the topic of this book). But with deep learning comes the ability to automate many different things. This can be a boon to society and free people from laborious and draining work, but it can also amplify and replicate undesirable inequalities at a newly efficient scale. For this reason, I want you to be aware and start training yourself to think about these kinds of considerations. Here are a few links to resources you can use to grow your understanding of these concerns:

- First, an older paper that captured many of these concerns in a broader perspective: B. Friedman and H. Nissenbaum, "Bias in computer systems," *ACM Trans. Inf. Syst.* vol. 14, no. 3, pp. 330-347, 1996, https://doi.org/10.1145/230538.230561, https://nissenbaum.tech.cornell.edu/papers/Bias%20in%20Computer%20Systems.pdf.

- I mentioned Kate Crawford (www.katecrawford.net) previously, and I also recommend Timnit Gebru (https://scholar.google.com/citations?user=lemnAcwAAAAJ) and Reuben Binns (https://www.reubenbinns.com/).

- In particular, I like the paper "Fairness in machine learning: lessons from political philosophy," R. Binns, *Proceedings of Machine Learning Research* vol. 81, pp. 1–11, 2018, http://proceedings.mlr.press/v81/binns18a/binns18a.pdf. It is accessible and poses different perspectives on what the tricky concept of fairness means.

You don't need to master these things to be a good deep learning researcher or practitioner, but you *should* learn to think about and consider them. If you know enough to simply say, "This might be a problem; we should get some guidance," you are better equipped than many practitioners today.

The ability to manipulate images, in particular, has led to a research area and problem known as *deep fakes*. GANs are a big component of this issue. They have been used to mimic voices and alter videos so the mouth movements match supplied audio, and they are a powerful tool to mislead others. You now know enough to start building or using systems that can do this, and with it comes a responsibility to consider those actions and ramifications. If you release code online, could it be easily misappropriated to harm others? What are the benefits of placing that code into the public, and do they outweigh the harms? These are situations where you may also want to think about how you could mitigate these harms. If you create a generator that could be misappropriated, perhaps you could work on a detector that can tell whether an image came from your model/approach and thus help detect any malignant use.

These may seem like abstract problems, but as you build your skills and abilities, they will be real concerns. For example, a recent report[5] has shown that deep fakes are being used to swindle people out of hundreds of thousands of dollars. My goal is not to force you into any particular action; as I said earlier, ethics is not a black-and-white issue with easy answers. But it is something you should begin to give thoughtful consideration when doing your work.

---

[5] L. Edmonds, "Scammer used deepfake video to impersonate U.S. Admiral on Skype chat and swindle nearly $300,000 out of a California widow," *Daily Mail*, 2020, http://mng.bz/2j0X.

Exercises

Share and discuss your solutions on the Manning online platform at Inside Deep Learning Exercises (https://liveproject.manning.com/project/945). Once you submit your own answers, you will be able to see the solutions submitted by other readers, and see which ones the author judges to be the best.

1 Another trick for improving a convolutional generator G is to start with one or two fully connected hidden layers and reshape their output into a tensor (B, C', W', H'). Try implementing this yourself. Do you think the results look better?

2 Our `combiner` network in the `ConditionalWrapper` class is designed for fully connected networks. This would be a problem for our discriminator D to use. Modify the `ConditionalWrapper` class to define a small CNN for the `combiner` when the `input_shape` indicates that the `main_network` is a CNN. Use this to train a conditional CNN GAN.

3 One challenge of manipulating a new image x is getting a latent vector z for it. Modify the `train_wgan` function to take in an optional network E that is the *encoder* network. E takes an image x and tries to predict the latent vector z that generates x. So it will have a loss of $\|E(G(z)) - z\|_2$. Test the encoder, and visualize the images generated by $G(z)$, then $G(E(G(Z)))$, and then $G(E(G(E(G(Z)))))$ (i.e., generate an image, then generate the encoded version of that image, and then generate the encoded version of the previous image).

4 You can make GANs that solve complex tasks like *inpainting*, where you need to fill in a missing part of an image. Replace generator G with the U-Net architecture from the previous chapter. Use `RandomErasing` transform to create noisy inputs $\tilde{x}$ that are the input to your GAN. The discriminator remains the same, and there is no longer a latent variable z. Train this model, and check how well it does at the inpainting task.

5 Once you get exercise 3 working, make a new version where your U-Net G takes in the noisy image $\tilde{x}$ and a latent vector z. How does this model behave differently than the first one?

6 **Challenging**: Read the paper "Image-to-Image Translation with Conditional Adversarial Networks" (https://arxiv.org/abs/1611.07004). It defines a GAN called pix2pix. See if you can understand most of the paper. If you feel daring, try to implement it yourself, as you have now learned about and used every component in the paper!

7 Using the PGAN model, generate more images and come up with your own semantic vectors to manipulate them.

Summary

- GANs work by setting up two networks that play a game against each other. Each helps the other learn.

- GANs are a generative modeling approach, which means the generator G model has a harder task than the discriminator D. This mismatch in difficulty contributes to a problem called mode collapse, where the generator focuses only on the easier parts of the data.

- A number of nuanced tricks to reduce vanishing gradients help us train GANs faster and better for both fully connected and convolutional architectures.

- GANs can suffer from mode collapse, causing them to over-focus on the most common or easiest thing instead of learning to generate a diversity of outputs.

- The Wasserstein GAN adds a penalty to the discriminator that prevents it from becoming too good at the GAN game, helping reduce mode collapse.

- We can condition the output of a GAN on some labels, allowing us to make one-to-many models and control what the GAN generates.

- GANs learn semantically meaningful latent representations. We can extract vectors that repeat a concept and use them to manipulate images.

- GANs have elevated the need to consider the ethical implications of your models, and you should always ask yourself what could go wrong when deploying a model.

Attention mechanisms

This chapter covers

- Understanding attention mechanisms and when to use them
- Adding context to an attention mechanism for context-sensitive results
- Handling variable-length items with attention

Imagine having a conversation with a couple of friends at a busy coffee shop. Around you are other conversations and people placing orders and talking on their cell phones. Despite all this noise, you, with your complex and sophisticated brain and ears, can pay *attention* to *only what is important* (your friends!), and selectively ignore the things occurring around you that are not relevant. The important thing here is that your *attention is adaptive* to the situation. You *ignore* the background sounds to listen to your friends only when there is nothing more important happening. If a fire alarm goes off, you stop paying attention to your friends and focus your attention on this new, important sound. Thus, attention is about adapting to the relative importance of inputs.

Deep learning models can also learn to pay attention to some input, or features, and ignore other features. They do this with *attention mechanisms*, which are another type of prior belief we can impose on our network. Attention mechanisms help us deal with situations where part of our input may be irrelevant, or when we need to focus on one feature of many features being fed into the model. For example, if you are translating a book from English to French, you do not need to understand the entire book to translate the first sentence. Each word you should output in the English translation will depend on only a few nearby words in the same sentence, and you can ignore most of the surrounding French sentences and content.

We would like to endow our networks with the ability to ignore superfluous and distracting inputs to focus on the most important portions, and that's the goal of an attention mechanism. If you believe some of your input features are more or less important than other features, you should consider using an attention-based approach in your model. If you want state-of-the-art results on speech recognition, object detection, a chat bot, or machine translation, for instance, you will probably be using an attention mechanism.

In this chapter, we see how attention works on some toy problems so that in the next chapter, we can build something far more sophisticated. First, we create a toy problem out of the MNIST dataset that is too hard for a normal network but is easily and better solved with a simple kind of attention that learns how to score the *importance* of each item in the input. Then we improve the simple attention into a full-fledged approach that takes into account some *context* to better infer the importance of items in the input. Doing so will also allow us to make the attention mechanism work with variable-length data so we can work on padded data.

10.1 *Attention mechanisms learn relative input importance*

Now that we've talked about the intuition behind attention, let's create a toy dataset. We will modify the MNIST dataset to create a new kind of task, so let's quickly load that up:

```
mnist_train = torchvision.datasets.MNIST("./", train=True,
    transform=transforms.ToTensor(), download=True)
mnist_test = torchvision.datasets.MNIST("./", train=False,
    transform=transforms.ToTensor(), download=True)
```

Attention mechanisms are most useful when we have *multiple items* as inputs into our model. Since MNIST is a single digit, we will augment each item in MNIST to become a bag of digits. We use fully connected layers for this (i.e., flattened MNIST, ignoring the image nature), so instead of having a batch of digits (B, D), we have T digits (B, T, D). So why did I call this a *bag* instead of a sequence? Because we don't care in what order the digits are presented in the tensor. We just need a tensor large enough to hold everything in the bag.

Given a bag of digits $x_1, x_2, \ldots, x_T$, we have a label y that is equal to the *largest* digit in the bag. If our bag contains 0, 2, 9, the label for the bag is "9." The following code implements a `LargestDigit` class to wrap an input dataset and create new items by randomly filling a bag of `toSample` items and selecting the maximum label value:

```
class LargestDigit(Dataset):
    """
    Creates a modified version of a dataset where some number of samples
    are taken, and the true label is the largest label sampled. When
    used with MNIST, the labels correspond to their values (e.g., digit
    "6" has label 6)
    """

    def __init__(self, dataset, toSample=3):
        """
        dataset: the dataset to sample from
        toSample: the number of items from the dataset to sample
        """
        self.dataset = dataset
        self.toSample = toSample

    def __len__(self):
        return len(self.dataset)

    def __getitem__(self, idx):
        selected = np.random.randint(0,
            len(self.dataset), size=self.toSample)
        x_new = torch.stack([self.dataset[i][0] for i in selected])
        y_new = max([self.dataset[i][1] for i in selected])

        return x_new, y_new
```

Randomly selects n=self.toSample items from the dataset

Stacks the n items of shape (B, *) into (B, n, *)

Label is the maximum label.

⟵ Returns (data, label) pair!

NOTE   Why not call this a *set* of items? A set implies that no repetitions are allowed, whereas a bag allows repetitions to occur. This matches the behavior of the Python set class, where duplicate items are automatically removed from the set. The type of problem we are creating is similar to a niche research area called multi-instance learning,[1] if you want to learn about other types of models that work on bags of data.

This is a much harder version of the MNIST dataset for a model to learn from. Given a bag with a label, the model has to infer, on its own, which item in the input is the largest, use that information to slowly learn to recognize all 10 digits, also learn that the digits are ordered, and return the largest digit in a bag.

10.1.1 Training our baseline model

The following block of code sets up our training/testing loaders and uses a batch size of $B = 128$ items and 10 epochs of training:

```
B = 128
epochs = 10
```

---

[1]   See J. Foulds and E. Frank, "A review of multi-instance learning assumptions," *The Knowledge Engineering Review*, vol. 25, no. 1, pp. 1–25, 2010, https://www.cs.waikato.ac.nz/~eibe/pubs/FouldsAndFrankMIreview.pdf.

```
largest_train = LargestDigit(mnist_train)
largest_test = LargestDigit(mnist_test)

train_loader = DataLoader(largest_train, batch_size=B, shuffle=True)
test_loader = DataLoader(largest_test, batch_size=B)
```

If we plot an item from the dataset, we should see the modified dataset correspond to what we have described. The following code samples a random item from the dataset and gets the digits 8, 2, and 6. The "8" is the largest label, so 8 is the correct answer. In this case, the digits 2 and 6 *do not matter* because 2 < 8 and 6 < 8. They could have been any digit less than 8, in any order, and the results would not change. We want our model to learn to *ignore* the smaller digits:

```
x, y = largest_train[0]

f, axarr = plt.subplots(1,3, figsize=(10,10))
for i in range(3):
    axarr[i].imshow(x[i,0,:].numpy(), cmap='gray', vmin=0, vmax=1)
print("True Label is = ", y)

True Label is = 8
```

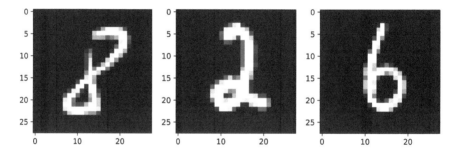

Now that we have this toy problem, let's train a simple fully connected network and treat this like any other classification problem we might attempt. This will be our baseline and show how hard the new version of MNIST is:

```
neurons = 256
classes = 10
simpleNet = nn.Sequential(
    nn.Flatten(),
    nn.Linear(784*3,neurons),      ←—— 784*3 because there are 784 pixels
    nn.LeakyReLU(),                       in an image and 3 images in the bag
    nn.BatchNorm1d(neurons),
    nn.Linear(neurons,neurons),
    nn.LeakyReLU(),
    nn.BatchNorm1d(neurons),
    nn.Linear(neurons,neurons),
    nn.LeakyReLU(),
    nn.BatchNorm1d(neurons),
    nn.Linear(neurons, classes )
)
```

```
simple_results = train_network(simpleNet, nn.CrossEntropyLoss(),
    train_loader, val_loader=test_loader, epochs=epochs,
    score_funcs='Accuracy': accuracy_score, device=device)
```

We have trained up the model and can plot the results. Since this is MNIST, we can get 98% accuracy without too much effort using just fully connected layers. But this bagged dataset results in a fully connected network barely reaching 92%, even with our fanciest tricks like LeakyReLUs and batch normalization:

```
sns.lineplot(x='epoch', y='val Accuracy', data=simple_results,
    label='Regular')
```

[11]:   `<AxesSubplot:xlabel='epoch', ylabel='val Accuracy'>`

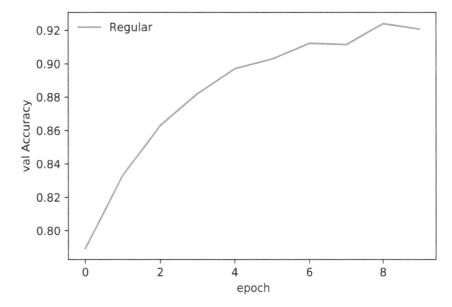

10.1.2 *Attention mechanism mechanics*

Next, we'll design a very simple kind of attention mechanism that takes a step toward the more complete attention we learn about later in this chapter. The primary tool we use is the softmax function $sm(x)$ from chapter 2. Remember that once we compute $p = sm(x)$, p represents a probability distribution. A probability distribution has all values greater than or equal to zero, and the sum of all the values is one. The mathy way to say this is $0 \leq p_i \leq 1$ and $\sum_i p_i = 1$. Remember that a primary function of attention is to ignore parts of the input, and we do that by multiplying the parts to ignore with small values at or near zero. If we multiply something by zero, we get zero, effectively erasing it from the input. Thanks to the softmax computation, we can learn to multiply inputs by small values at or near 0, effectively learning how to ignore them.

Figure 10.1 shows the three primary steps of an attention mechanism. The first two steps are trivial and will change depending on your network and problem: simply get your features into your network and have some initial hidden layers before the attention mechanism is applied so that they can learn a useful representation. Then the final steps occur that perform the attention:

1 Assign a score to every input x_t using a *score* function.

2 Compute a softmax over all scores.

3 Multiply each item by its softmax score, and then add all the results together into an output $\bar{x}$.

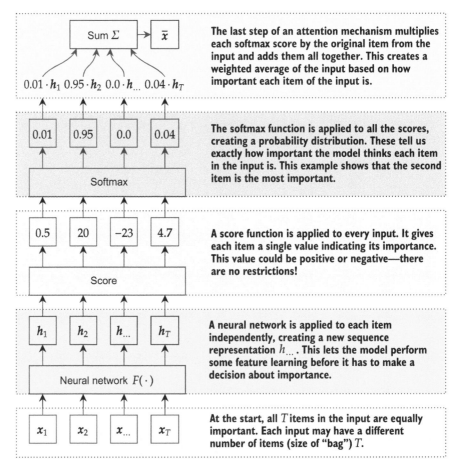

The last step of an attention mechanism multiplies each softmax score by the original item from the input and adds them all together. This creates a weighted average of the input based on how important each item of the input is.

The softmax function is applied to all the scores, creating a probability distribution. These tell us exactly how important the model thinks each item in the input is. This example shows that the second item is the most important.

A score function is applied to every input. It gives each item a single value indicating its importance. This value could be positive or negative—there are no restrictions!

A neural network is applied to each item independently, creating a new sequence representation $h_{...}$. This lets the model perform some feature learning before it has to make a decision about importance.

At the start, all T items in the input are equally important. Each input may have a different number of items (size of "bag") T.

Figure 10.1   Diagram of how attention mechanisms work. The input sequence x_t can be variable in number (i.e., you could have $T = 1$ items, $T = 13$, or $T =$ any number you like). A score function assigns a raw importance value to each item t. The softmax function creates relative scores. The output is then the weighted average of the inputs.

Let's restate some of this using a more mathematical notation to fill in some details. The way attention mechanisms usually work is that we represent the input as T different components $x_1, x_2, \ldots, x_T$, each of which has a tensor representation $x_t \in \mathbb{R}^D$. These T items could be natural breaks in the input (e.g., we naturally have different images in this toy problem), or they could be forced (e.g., we could split a single image into sub-images). Each input x_t is transformed into a new tensor $h_t = F(x_t)$, where $F(\cdot)$ is a neural network. This means the inputs to the attention do not have to be the first inputs into the model but can be the result after some computation that has already been done.

> **NOTE** This also means x_t does not have to be a one-dimensional tensor. For example, the network $F(\cdot)$ could be a CNN and $x_t \in \mathbb{R}^{(C,W,H)}$. We are making it 1D right now for simplicity. However, we generally do want h_t to be one-dimensional.

So the processed sequence $h_1, h_2, \ldots, h_T$ is the actual input to the attention mechanism. Next, we need to learn an importance score $\tilde{\alpha}_i$ for each input x_i. Let's say a different function $\tilde{\alpha}_i = \text{score}(F(x_i))$ learns to compute that. Again, the function $\text{score}(\cdot)$ is *another* neural network. That means our model itself will learn how to score the inputs for us.

Then we want to normalize the importances into a probability, so we get $\alpha = \alpha_1, \alpha_2, \ldots, \alpha_T = sm(\tilde{\alpha}_1, \tilde{\alpha}_2, \ldots, \tilde{\alpha}_T)$. With these combined, we can now compute a weighted average of the representations h_t. Specifically, we first compute the softmax scores represented by α:

$$\alpha = sm(\underbrace{\text{score}(\overbrace{F(x_1)}^{h_1})}_{\tilde{\alpha}_1}, \text{score}(F(x_2)), \ldots, \text{score}(F(x_T)))$$

Next we compute the output of the attention mechanism $\bar{x}$:

$$\bar{x} = \sum_{i=1}^{T} \alpha_i \cdot \underbrace{F(x_i)}_{h_i}$$

If the jth item x_j is not important, hopefully our network will learn to give the item j a value of $\alpha_j \approx 0$, in which case it will successfully ignore the jth item! This idea is not too complicated, especially compared to some of the early items like RNNs that we have learned about. But this simple approach has proven to be very powerful and can provide significant improvements to a number of problems.

10.1.3 Implementing a simple attention mechanism

Now that we understand how attention mechanisms work, let's work on implementing a simple one for our bagged MNIST problem. We are not considering the convolutional nature of our data yet, so if we want to convert our bag of images (B, T, C, W, H) into a bag of feature vectors $(B, T, C \cdot W \cdot H)$, we need a new version of the nn.Flatten function that leaves the first two axes of our tensor alone. This is pretty easy to do with the following Flatten2 class. It just creates a view of the input but explicitly uses the first two axes as the start of the view and puts all leftover values at the end:

```
class Flatten2(nn.Module):
    """
    Takes a vector of shape (A, B, C, D, E, ...)
    and flattens everything but the first two dimensions,
    giving a result of shape (A, B, C*D*E*...)
    """
    def forward(self, input):
        return input.view(input.size(0), input.size(1), -1)
```

The next step is to create some classes for implementing our attention mechanism. The primary thing we need is a `Module` that takes the attention weights α with the extracted feature representations $h_1, h_2, \ldots, h_T$ and computes the weighted average $\bar{x} = \sum_{i=1}^{T} \alpha_i \cdot h_i$. We call this the `Combiner`. We take in a network `featureExtraction` that computes $h_t = F(x_t)$ for each item in the input, and a network `weightSelection` that computes α from the extracted features.

DEFINING THE COMBINER MODULE

The forward function for this `Combiner` is pretty simple. We compute the `features` and the `weights` as we have described. We do a small amount of tensor manipulation to make sure `weights` is in a shape that will allow us to pairwise multiply with the features, because pairwise multiplication requires tensors to have the same number of axes. Also notice that we are making sure to add comments about the shape of each tensor on every line. Attention mechanisms involve many changing shapes, so it is a good idea for you to include comments like these:

```
class Combiner(nn.Module):
    """
    This class is used to combine a feature extraction network F and an
    importance prediction network W, and combine their outputs by adding
    and summing them together.
    """

    def __init__(self, featureExtraction, weightSelection):
        """
        featureExtraction: a network that takes an input of shape (B, T, D)
        and outputs a new
        representation of shape (B, T, D').
        weightSelection: a network that takes in an input of shape
        (B, T, D') and outputs a
        tensor of shape (B, T, 1) or (B, T). It should be normalized,
        so that the T
        values at the end sum to one (torch.sum(_, dim=1) = 1.0)
        """
        super(Combiner, self).__init__()
        self.featureExtraction = featureExtraction
        self.weightSelection = weightSelection
```

```
def forward(self, input):
    """
    input: a tensor of shape (B, T, D)
    return: a new tensor of shape (B, D')
    """
    features = self.featureExtraction(input)        ⟵ (B, T, D) $h_i = F(x_i)$

    weights = self.weightSelection(features)         ⟵ (B, T) or (B, T, 1) for $\alpha$

    if len(weights.shape) == 2:                      ⟵ (B, T) shape

    weights.unsqueeze(2)                             ⟵ Now (B, T, 1) shape

    r = features*weights                             ⟵ (B, T, D); computes $\alpha_i \cdot h_i$

    return torch.sum(r, dim=1)                       ⟵ Sums over the T dimension,
                                                        giving the (B, D) final shape
```

DEFINING A BACKBONE NETWORK

Now we are ready to define our attention-based model for this problem. First, we quickly define two variables—T for how many items are in our bag, and D for the number of features:

```
T = 3
D = 784
```

The first network to define is the feature extraction network. We could also call this the backbone network, as it follows the same intuition as the backbone from Faster R-CNN in chapter 8. This network will do all the heavy lifting to learn a good representation h_i for every item in the input.

The trick to making this easy to implement is to remember that the nn.Linear layer can work on tensors of shape (B, T, D). If you have an input of that shape, the nn.Linear layer will be applied to all T items *independently*, as if you wrote a for loop like this:

```
for i in range(T):
    h_i = linear(x[:,i,:])                ⟵ (B, D)
    h_is.append(h_i.unsqueeze(1))         ⟵ Makes (B, 1, D)
h = torch.cat(h_is, dim=1)                ⟵ (B, T, D)
```

So we can use nn.Linear followed by any activation function to apply this backbone to every input separately:

```
backboneNetwork = nn.Sequential(
    Flatten2(),                  ⟵ Shape is now (B, T, D)
    nn.Linear(D,neurons),    ⟵ Shape becomes (B, T, neurons)
    nn.LeakyReLU(),
    nn.Linear(neurons,neurons),
    nn.LeakyReLU(),
    nn.Linear(neurons,neurons),
    nn.LeakyReLU(),              ⟵ Still (B, T, neurons) on the way out
)
```

DEFINING AN ATTENTION SUBNETWORK

Now we need a network to compute the attention mechanism weights α. Following the backbone logic, we assume that the feature extraction network has done the heavy lifting, so our attention subnetwork can be on the small side. We have one hidden layer and then a second layer that explicitly has an output size of 1. We need this because every item in the input gets *one* score. Then we apply the softmax over the T dimension to normalize these scores over each bag's group:

```
attentionMechanism = nn.Sequential(
    nn.Linear(neurons,neurons),      ←── Shape is (B, T, neurons)
    nn.LeakyReLU(),
    nn.Linear(neurons, 1 ),          ←── (B, T, 1)
    nn.Softmax(dim=1),
)
```

TRAINING A SIMPLE ATTENTION MODEL AND RESULTS

With the feature extracting backbone and the weight computing attention mechanism, we can now define a complete attention-based network. It starts with a `Combiner` that takes in the two subnetworks we've defined, followed by any number of fully connected layers we desire. Usually the backbone has already done a lot of work, so you can often use just two or three hidden layers at this step. Then we train the model:

```
simpleAttentionNet = nn.Sequential(                    Input is (B, T, C, W, H). The
        Combiner(backboneNetwork, attentionMechanism), ←── combiner uses the backbone
        nn.BatchNorm1d(neurons),                           and attention to process.
        nn.Linear(neurons,neurons),                        The result is (B, neurons).
        nn.LeakyReLU(),
        nn.BatchNorm1d(neurons),
        nn.Linear(neurons, classes )
    )
simple_attn_results = train_network(simpleAttentionNet,
    nn.CrossEntropyLoss(), train_loader, val_loader=test_loader,
    epochs=epochs, score_funcs={'Accuracy': accuracy_score}, device=device)
```

With training complete, we can look at the accuracy of our model. After just one epoch, our simple attention network is already doing better than the regular network:

```
sns.lineplot(x='epoch', y='val Accuracy', data=simple_results,
    label='Regular')
sns.lineplot(x='epoch', y='val Accuracy', data=simple_attn_results,
    label='Simple Attention')
```

```
[18]:   <AxesSubplot:xlabel='epoch', ylabel='val Accuracy'>
```

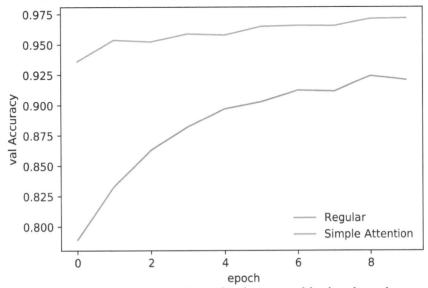

We can also select random samples from the dataset and look at how the attention mechanism selects the inputs. Here is some simple code to run a sample through; the following graphic shows the attention weight in red on top of each digit. With "0, 9, 0" as the input, the attention mechanism correctly placed almost all of the weight on the digit 9, allowing it to make an accurate classification:

```
x, y = largest_train[0]        ◀── Selects a data point (which is a bag)
x = x.to(device)               ◀── Moves it to the compute device
                                                                    Applies
with torch.no_grad():                                               score(F(x))
    weights = attentionMechanism(backboneNetwork(x.unsqueeze(0)))  ◀──
    weights = weights.cpu().numpy().ravel()    ◀── Converts to a NumPy array

f, axarr = plt.subplots(1,3, figsize=(10,10))  ◀── Makes a plot for all three digits
for i in range(3):
    axarr[i].imshow(x[i,0,:].cpu().numpy(),    ◀── Plots the digit
        cmap='gray', vmin=0, vmax=1)
    axarr[i].text(0.0, 0.5, str(round(weights[i],2)),  ◀──┐ Draws the attention
        dict(size=40, color='red'))                        │ score in the top left

print("True Label is = ", y)
```

True Label is = 9

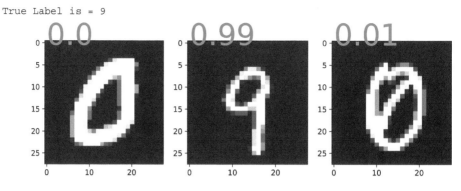

We have now seen how this simple attention can help us learn faster and better networks when only a subset of the inputs is important. But there are two lingering problems. First, we have the naive expectation that *everything* in a batch is the same size. We will need some padding to fix this, just as we used in our RNNs.

The second issue is that our scores lack *context*. The importance of one item depends on the other items. Imagine you are watching a movie. You pay attention to the movie and not the birds outside or the running dishwasher because the movie is more important. But that changes if you hear a fire alarm. Right now, our `attentionMechanism` network looks at each item independently, so both a movie and a fire alarm may receive high scores—but in reality, their scores should be relative to the other things that are present.

10.2 Adding some context

The first thing we improve about our approach to attention mechanisms is adding context to the scores. We leave all the other parts alone. By *context*, we mean the score for an item x_i should depend on all the other items $x_{j \neq i}$. Right now we have a backbone feature extractor $F(\cdot)$ and an importance calculator score$(\cdot)$. But that means the importance of any input x_i is determined without any context about what the other inputs are, because score$(\cdot)$ is applied to everything independently.

To get an idea of why we want context, let's return to that noisy coffee shop where you are chatting with friends. Why are you ignoring all the background noise? Because you have the *context* that your friend is talking and they are more important to you than other conversations. But if your friend is not present, you may find yourself listening in on random conversations around you.

In other words, the attention mechanism uses *global* information to make *local* decisions. The local decisions came in the form of the weights α, and the context provides the global information.[2]

How can we add context to the attention mechanism? Figure 10.2 shows how we make this happen.

---

[2] If you want to get fancy, the context can be *anything* you think is valid. But it's easiest to make the context a function of all inputs.

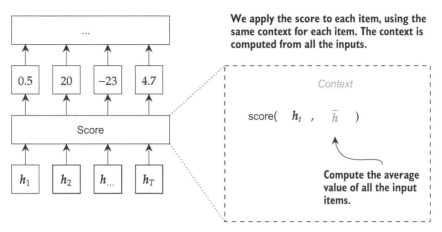

Figure 10.2 The attention mechanism process on the left remains unchanged except for the score component. The right is zoomed in on how scores work. The score block takes in the results $h_{...}$ from the backbone/feature extraction network. For each score $\tilde{\alpha}_t$, two inputs are used: h_t, for which we want to compute the score, and $\bar{h}$, which represents a context of all the inputs $h_{...}$. This context $\bar{h}$ can be a simple average of all the items.

We make score($\cdot, \cdot$) a network that takes in two inputs: the tensor of inputs (B, T, H) and a second tensor of shape (B, H) containing a context for each sequence. We use H here to represent the number of features in the states $h_t = F(x_t)$, to make them distinct from the size D of the original inputs x_i. This second context tensor of shape (B, H) has no time/sequence dimension T because this vector is intended to be used as the context for all T items of the first input. This means every item in a bag will get the same context for computing its score.

The simplest form of context we can use is the average value of all the features extracted. So if we have $h_i = F(x_i)$, we can compute the average $\bar{h}$ from all of these to give the model a rough idea of all the options it has to choose from. This makes our attention computation occur in three steps:

1. Compute the average of the features extracted from each input. This treats everything as being equal in importance:

$$\bar{h} = \frac{1}{T} \sum_{i=1}^{T} \underbrace{F(x_i)}_{h_i}$$

2. Compute the attention scores α for the T inputs. The only change here is that we include $\bar{h}$ as a second argument to each score computation:

$$\alpha = sm(\text{score}(h_1, \bar{h}), \text{score}(h_2, \bar{h}), \dots, \text{score}(h_T, \bar{h}))$$

3 Compute the weighted average of the extracted features. This part is identical to before:

$$\bar{x} = \sum_{i=1}^{T} \alpha_i \cdot \underset{\underset{\boldsymbol{h_i}}{\uparrow}}{F(\boldsymbol{x}_i)}$$

This simple process gives us a new framework for attention scores, allowing us to alter the score of an item based on the other items present. We still want our score networks to be very simple and lightweight, because the backbone $F(\cdot)$ will do the heavy lifting. There are three common ways to compute the score from the representation $\boldsymbol{h}$ and the context $\bar{\boldsymbol{h}}$, commonly called the *dot, general,* and *additive scores.* Note that none of these is generally considered better than the others—attention mechanisms are still very new, and each of the following approaches works better or worse than others in different situations. The best advice I can give you right now is to try all three and see which works best for your problem. We will talk about each of them, since they are simple, and then run all of them on our toy problem to see what happens. In the descriptions, I use H to refer to the number of dimensions/neurons coming into the attention mechanism.

10.2.1 Dot score

The dot score is one of the simplest scoring methods but can also be one of the most effective. The idea is that if we have an item $\boldsymbol{h}_t$ and a context $\bar{\boldsymbol{h}}$, we take their dot product, $\boldsymbol{h}_t^\top \bar{\boldsymbol{h}}$, to get a score. We take the dot product because it measures how aligned in direction and size two vectors are. In chapter 7, we talked about vectors being orthogonal: that concept can help you understand this. If two vectors are orthogonal, their dot product is 0, meaning they have no relationship. The less orthogonal they are, the larger the dot product. If it is a large positive value, they are very similar, and if it is a large negative value, they are very different. In addition to this trick, we divide the result by the square root of the dimension of the vectors H. That gives us the following equation for the dot score:

$$\text{score}(\boldsymbol{h}_t, \bar{\boldsymbol{h}}) = \frac{\boldsymbol{h}_t^\top \bar{\boldsymbol{h}}}{\sqrt{H}}$$

Why divide by $\sqrt{H}$? The concern is that the normal dot product calculation may lead to larger-magnitude values (very big positive or big negative values). Large values will cause vanishing gradients when the softmax is computed, just as we saw with the tanh and sigmoid (σ) activation functions. So we divide by $\sqrt{H}$ to try to avoid large values—the specific choice of using the square root was made heuristically because it tended to work.

Implementing this approach is pretty simple. We need to use the batch matrix multiply method `torch.bmm`, since we will compute the scores for all T time steps at once. Each item has a shape of (T, H), and the context—after we use the `unsqueeze` function to add a dimension of size 1 to the end of it—will have a shape of $(D, 1)$.

Multiplying two matrices of shapes $(T, H) \times (H, 1) = (T, 1)$, which is the shape we need: one score for each item. `torch.bmm` applies this for every item in the batch, so `torch.bmm((B, T, H), (B, H, 1))` has an output of shape $(B, T, 1)$. The following `DotScore` implements this as a reusable `Module`, where the `forward` function takes in `states` and a `context`. We'll reuse this pattern for the other two score methods:

```
class DotScore(nn.Module):

    def __init__(self, H):
        """
        H: the number of dimensions coming into the dot score.
        """
        super(DotScore, self).__init__()
        self.H = H

    def forward(self, states, context):
        """
        states: (B, T, H) shape
        context: (B, H) shape
        output: (B, T, 1), giving a score to each of the T items based
            on the context
        """
        T = states.size(1)
        scores = torch.bmm(states,context.unsqueeze(2)) \
            / np.sqrt(self.H)      ←—— Computes $h_t^\top \bar{h}$. (B, T, H) -> (B, T, 1).
        return scores
```

10.2.2 *General score*

Since the dot score is so effective, can we improve it? What if one of the features in $\bar{h}$ is not very useful? Can we learn to not use it as much? That's the idea behind the *general* score. Instead of simply computing the dot product between each item h_t with the context $\bar{h}$, we add a matrix W in between them. This gives us

$$\text{score}(h_t, \bar{h}) = h_t^\top \mathbf{W} \bar{h}$$

where $\boldsymbol{W}$ is a $H \times H$ matrix. The general score can be called a generalization of the dot product score because it can learn the same solution as the dot score, but the general score can also learn solutions the dot score can't. This occurs if the model learns to set $\boldsymbol{W}$ equal to the identity matrix, $\boldsymbol{I}$, because for any possible input $\boldsymbol{z}$, $\boldsymbol{Iz} = \boldsymbol{z}$.

Again, this implementation is simple because the general score has what is called a *bilinear relationship*. A bilinear function looks like

$$\boldsymbol{x_1}^\top \mathbf{W} \boldsymbol{x_2} + \boldsymbol{b}$$

where $\boldsymbol{x_1} \in \mathbb{R}^{H1}$ and $\boldsymbol{x_2} \in \mathbb{R}^{H1}$ are the inputs, and $\boldsymbol{b}$ and $\boldsymbol{W}$ are the parameters to learn. PyTorch provides a `nn.Bilinear(H1, H2, out_size)` function that can compute this for us. In our case, $H1 = H2 = H$, and our output size is 1 (a single score value for each item).

We need to know about two tricks to implement this in one call to compute all T scores. We have a tensor of shape (B, T, H) for our items $\boldsymbol{h}_1, \boldsymbol{h}_2, \ldots, \boldsymbol{h}_T$ but a tensor of only (B, H) for our context $\bar{\boldsymbol{h}}$. We need both tensors to have the same number of axes to be used in the bilinear function. The trick is to stack the context into multiple copies T times, so we can create a matrix of shape (B, T, H):

```
class GeneralScore(nn.Module):

    def __init__(self, H):
        """
        H: the number of dimensions coming into the dot score.
        """
        super(GeneralScore, self).__init__()
        self.w = nn.Bilinear(H, H, 1)            ⟵——— stores W

    def forward(self, states, context):
        """
        states: (B, T, H) shape
        context: (B, H) shape
        output: (B, T, 1), giving a score to each of the T items based
          on the context
        """
        T = states.size(1)
        context = torch.stack([context for _ in range(T)], dim=1)  ⟵
        scores = self.w(states, context)        ⟵
        return scores
```

Repeats the values T times. (B, H) -> (B, T, H).

Computes $h_t^\top W \bar{h}$. (B, T, H) -> (B, T, 1).

NOTE   We introduced `GeneralScore` as trying to improve `DotScore`, which is reasonable because of how related they are. Yet today, neither appears to be better than the other in practice. As we mentioned, attention mechanisms are very new, and we as a community are still figuring them out. Sometimes you'll see `Dot` do better than `General`, and sometimes not.

10.2.3 *Additive attention*

The last score we'll discuss is often called *additive* or *concat* attention. For a given item and its context, we use a vector **v** and a matrix **W** as the parameters for the layer, making a small neural network, as shown in the following equation:

The score between two inputs is computed by

combining both inputs into a single input,

pushing them through a single hidden layer of a neural network,

and then applying an output (linear) layer to produce the score.

$$\text{score}(\boldsymbol{h}_t, \bar{\boldsymbol{h}}) = \mathbf{v}^\top \; \tanh\left(W \; [\boldsymbol{h}_t; \bar{\boldsymbol{h}}] \; \right)$$

This equation is a simple one-layer neural network. W is the hidden layer, followed by tanh activation, and v is the output layer with one output,[3] which is necessary because the score should be a single value. The context $\bar{h}$ is incorporated into the model by simply concatenating it with the item h_t so that the item and its context are the inputs into this fully connected network.

The idea behind the additive layer is fairly simple: let a small neural network figure out the weighting for us. Implementing it requires a little cleverness, though. What operations would you expect to need? Both v and W can be taken care of with nn.Linear layers, and you need to use the torch.cat function to concatenate the two inputs h_t and $\bar{h}$ together, so you might annotate this previous equation as follows:

$$\text{score}(h_t, \bar{h}) = \underset{\substack{\downarrow \\ \text{nn.Linear(H,1)}}}{v^\top} \quad \tanh\left(\overset{\substack{\text{nn.Linear(2*H,H)} \\ \uparrow}}{W} \quad \underset{\substack{\downarrow \\ \text{torch.cat((}h_t,h\text{), dim=1)}}}{[h_t; \bar{h}]}\right)$$

While this would work as described, it would be computationally inefficient. It is slow because we don't have just h_t—we have $h_1, h_2, \ldots, h_T$ in one larger tensor of shape (B, T, H). So rather than split this into T different items and call the attention function multiple times, we want to implement this in such a way that the T attention scores are calculated all at once, and we can do this by using the same trick we used with the general score. Just be sure to do the concatenation after the stacking trick so the tensors are the same shape—and use dim=2 so they are concatenated along the feature dimension H rather than the time dimension T. A diagram of this process is shown in figure 10.3, and the following code shows how to implement it:

```
class AdditiveAttentionScore(nn.Module):

    def __init__(self, H):
        super(AdditiveAttentionScore, self).__init__()
        self.v = nn.Linear(H, 1)
        self.w = nn.Linear(2*H, H)          ←── 2*H because we
                                                 concatenate two inputs

    def forward(self, states, context):
        """
        states: (B, T, H) shape
        context: (B, H) shape
        output: (B, T, 1), giving a score to each of the T items based
            on the context
        """
        T = states.size(1)                  ←── Repeats the values T times

        context = torch.stack([context for _ in range(T)], dim=1)  ←──
                                                 (B, H) -> (B, T, H)

        state_context_combined = torch.cat(
            (states, context), dim=2)        ←── (B, T, H) + (B, T, H) -> (B, T, 2*H)
```

---

[3] Because v has one output, it is a common convention to write it as a vector instead of a matrix with one column.

```
scores = self.v(torch.tanh(
    self.w(state_context_combined)))        ◀——— (B, T, 2*H) -> (B, T, 1)
return scores
```

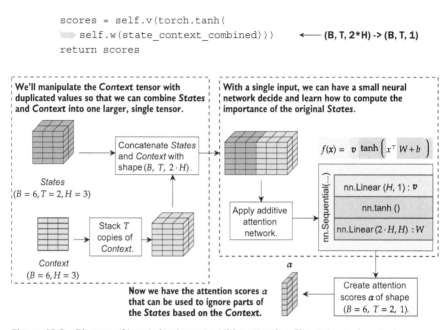

Figure 10.3 Diagram of how to implement additive attention. The states and context are represented on the left, and the context is reshaped (via copying) to have the same shape as the states. This make it easy to concatenate them together to then be fed into a neural network.

10.2.4 *Computing attention weights*

Now that we have the various attention scores we want, we'll define a simple helper Module that takes in the raw scores $\tilde{\alpha}$ and extracted representations $h_{\dots}$ and computes the final output $\bar{x}$. This will replace our Combiner module by adding one new step: applying a *mask* to the inputs.

Our toy MNIST example started with all bags having the same size, which never happens in real life. Any dataset you work with will most likely have inputs containing variable numbers of items (e.g., words in a sentence to translate), and if we train on batches of data, we have to deal with the inconsistency. This is why we need extra logic to compute the final weights α to take a Boolean *mask* as input. The mask tells us which parts of the input are real (True) and which are padded (False) to make the tensor shape consistent. This works almost the same as the RNNs in chapter 4 when we padded the smaller items to the same size as the largest bag/sequence in a batch. The mask replaces the role of the packing code.

The trick we use here is to manually set the score for every item that has a False value to be a very large negative number like –1000. We do this because $\exp(-1000) \approx 5.076 \times 10^{-435}$, so this will most likely underflow to zero and cause *desirable* vanishing gradients. When the calculation underflows to zero, its gradient and contributions are zero, effectively eliminating its impact from the model. The following code does this with a new ApplyAttention class:

```
class ApplyAttention(nn.Module):
    """
    This helper module is used to apply the results of an attention
    mechanism to a set of inputs.
    """

    def __init__(self):
        super(ApplyAttention, self).__init__()

    def forward(self, states, attention_scores, mask=None):
        """
        states: (B, T, H) shape giving the T different possible inputs
        attention_scores: (B, T, 1) score for each item at each context
        mask: None if all items are present. Else a boolean tensor of shape
            (B, T), with 'True' indicating which items are present / valid.

        returns: a tuple with two tensors. The first tensor is the
        final context
        from applying the attention to the states (B, H) shape. The
        second tensor
        is the weights for each state with shape (B, T, 1).
        """
        if mask is not None:
            attention_scores[ mask] = -1000.0
        weights = F.softmax(attention_scores, dim=1)

        final_context = (states*weights).sum(dim=1)
        return final_context, weights
```

Sets everything not present to a large negative value that causes vanishing gradients

Computes the weight for each score. (B, T, 1) still, but sum(T) = 1

(B, T, D) * (B, T, 1) -> (B, D)

Working with masks is very common with attention mechanisms. To make that easier, we can define a nice helper function for computing masks from any tensor with a shape $(B, T, \ldots)$. The idea is that we expect any missing item or non-present item to have its tensor filled with a constant value, usually zero. So we look for any dimension over time T that has values equal to this constant. If everything is equal to that constant, a value of False should be returned; otherwise, we want something that is True to indicate that the values present are good to use. The following getMaskByFill function does this. The input x is what we want to get a mask for, time_dimension tells us which dimension of the tensor is used to represent T, and fill indicates the special constant used to denote padding/invalid parts of the input:

```
def getMaskByFill(x, time_dimension=1, fill=0):
    """
    x: the original input with three or more dimensions, (B, ..., T, ...)
        which may have unused items in the tensor. B is the batch size,
        and T is the time dimension.
    time_dimension: the axis in the tensor 'x' that denotes the time dimension
    fill: the constant used to denote that an item in the tensor is not in use,
        and should be masked out ('False' in the mask).
```

```
return: A Boolean tensor of shape (B, T), where 'True' indicates the value
    at that time is good to use, and 'False' that it is not.
"""
```

Skips the first dimension 0 because that is the batch dimension →

```
to_sum_over = list(range(1,len(x.shape)))

if time_dimension in to_sum_over:
    to_sum_over.remove(time_dimension)
with torch.no_grad():
    mask = torch.sum((x != fill), dim=to_sum_over) > 0
return mask
```

(x!=fill) determines locations that might be unused because they are missing the fill value we are looking for to indicate lack of use. We then count the number of non-fill values over everything in that time slot (reducing changes the shape to (B, T)). If any entry is not equal to this value, the item represent must be in use and so returns a value of true.

Let's see a quick example of how this new function works. We create an input matrix with a batch of $B = 5$ inputs, $T = 3$ time steps, and a 7×7 image with one input channel. That's be a tensor of shape $(B = 5, T = 3, 1, 7, 7)$, and we make it so that the last item in the first batch is unused and the entire fourth item is unused. Our mask should look like this:

$$
\text{mask} = \begin{bmatrix}
\text{True} & \text{True} & \text{False} \\
\text{True} & \text{True} & \text{True} \\
\text{True} & \text{True} & \text{True} \\
\text{False} & \text{False} & \text{False} \\
\text{True} & \text{True} & \text{True}
\end{bmatrix}
$$

The following code creates this hypothetical data and computes the appropriate mask and then prints it out:

```
with torch.no_grad():
    x = torch.rand((5,3,1,7,7))
    x[0,-1,:] = 0            ←——————— Don't use the last item in the first input.
    x[3,:] = 0              ←——————— Don't use any of the fourth item!
    x[4,0,0,0] = 0          ←——————— Makes it look like we aren't using
                                       part of the fifth item, but we still are!
    mask = getMaskByFill(x)            This line was added to show that
print(mask)                            this works even on tricky inputs.

tensor([[ True, True, False],
        [ True, True, True],
        [ True, True, True],
        [False, False, False],
        [ True, True, True]])
```

The mask returned the correct output. This one function allows us to create masks for text sequences, sequences/bags of images, and just about any kind of unusual tensor shape.

10.3 Putting it all together: A complete attention mechanism with context

With a score method (e.g., dot), getMaskByFill function, and our new ApplyAttention function, we can define a complete attention-based network that is adaptive to the input. For most attention-based models, we do not use nn.Sequential for defining the main model because of all the non-sequential steps involved with attention. Instead, we use `nn.Sequential` to define and organize the subnetworks that our larger network uses.

Let's define a `SmarterAttentionNet` that is our entire network. Inside the constructor, we defines a network for our `backbone` that computes $h_i = F(x_i)$, and a `prediction_net` that computes our prediction $\hat{y} = f(\bar{x})$. The arguments `input_size`, `hidden_size`, and `out_size` define the number of features in the input (D), hidden neurons (H), and predictions our model should make (10 classes for MNIST). We also add an optional argument to choose which attention score is used as the `score_net`:

```python
class SmarterAttentionNet(nn.Module):

    def __init__(self, input_size, hidden_size, out_size, score_net=None):
        super(SmarterAttentionNet, self).__init__()
        self.backbone = nn.Sequential(
            Flatten2(),                              # ← Shape is now (B, T, D)
            nn.Linear(input_size,hidden_size),       # ← Shape becomes (B, T, H)
            nn.LeakyReLU(),
            nn.Linear(hidden_size,hidden_size),
            nn.LeakyReLU(),
            nn.Linear(hidden_size,hidden_size),
            nn.LeakyReLU(),
        )                                            # ← Returns (B, T, H)

        self.score_net = AdditiveAttentionScore(hidden_size) \  # ← Try changing this
            if (score_net is None) else score_net              #   and see how the
                                                               #   results change!
        self.apply_attn = ApplyAttention()

        self.prediction_net = nn.Sequential(         # ← (B, H), x̄ as input
            nn.BatchNorm1d(hidden_size),
            nn.Linear(hidden_size,hidden_size),
            nn.LeakyReLU(),
            nn.BatchNorm1d(hidden_size),
            nn.Linear(hidden_size, out_size )        # ← (B, H)
        )
```

Next we define the `forward` function that computes the result of the network. We compute the `mask` from the input followed by the hidden states $h_{...}$ from the backbone on the same input. We use the average vector $\bar{h}$ as the context `h_context`. Instead of computing this with `torch.mean`, we compute the mean ourselves in two steps so that we divide by only the number of valid items. Otherwise, an input with 2 valid items but 8 padded items would be divided by 10 instead of 2, and that's not correct. This calculation also include `+1e-10` to add a tiny value to the numerator: this addition is some defensive coding so that if we ever receive a bag of *zero* items, we do not perform a division by zero. That would produce a `NaN` (Not a Number), which would cause silent failures.

Here's the code:

```python
def forward(self, input):
    mask = getMaskByFill(input)
```

```
h = self.backbone(input)        ←—— (B, T, D) -> (B, T, H)

h_context = (mask.unsqueeze(-1)*h).sum(dim=1) ←——
h_context = h_context/(mask.sum(dim=1).unsqueeze(-1)+1e-10)

scores = self.score_net(h, h_context)        ←—— (B, T, H), (B, H) -> (B, T, 1)

final_context, _ = self.apply_attn(h, scores, mask=mask) ←—— Result is (B, H) shape

return self.prediction_net(final_context)    ←—— (B, H) -> (B, classes)
```

Divides by the number of valid items, plus a small value in case a bag was all empty →

h_context = torch.mean(h, dim=1) computes torch.mean but ignores the masked-out parts. First, add together all the valid items. (B, T, H) -> (B, H).

The last three lines of the `forward` function are again pretty simple. The `score_net` computes the `scores` α, the `apply_attn` function applies whichever attention function we have chosen, and `prediction_net` makes a prediction from the `final_context` $\bar{x}$.

Let's train up some better attention models. The following block creates an attention network for each option, `DotScore`, `GeneralScore`, and `AdditiveAttentionScore`:

```
attn_dot = SmarterAttentionNet(D, neurons, classes,
    score_net=DotScore(neurons))
attn_gen = SmarterAttentionNet(D, neurons, classes,
    score_net=GeneralScore(neurons))
attn_add = SmarterAttentionNet(D, neurons, classes,
    score_net=AdditiveAttentionScore(neurons))

attn_results_dot = train_network(attn_dot, nn.CrossEntropyLoss(),
    train_loader, val_loader=test_loader,epochs=epochs,
    score_funcs={'Accuracy': accuracy_score}, device=device)
attn_results_gen = train_network(attn_gen, nn.CrossEntropyLoss(),
    train_loader, val_loader=test_loader,epochs=epochs,
    score_funcs={'Accuracy': accuracy_score}, device=device)
attn_results_add = train_network(attn_add, nn.CrossEntropyLoss(),
    train_loader, val_loader=test_loader,epochs=epochs,
    score_funcs={'Accuracy': accuracy_score}, device=device)
```

All three results are plotted by the following code. The results follow a trend that all three improved attention scores have similar performance. They all start out learning faster and converging faster than the simple attention we started with, and maybe the new methods are converging to something better. You will see some variation from run to run, but this dataset is not big or difficult enough to cause really interesting changes in behavior:

```
sns.lineplot(x='epoch', y='val Accuracy', data=simple_results,
     label='Regular')
sns.lineplot(x='epoch', y='val Accuracy', data=simple_attn_results,
     label='Simple Attention')
sns.lineplot(x='epoch', y='val Accuracy', data=attn_results_dot, label='Dot')
sns.lineplot(x='epoch', y='val Accuracy', data=attn_results_gen,
     label='General')
sns.lineplot(x='epoch', y='val Accuracy', data=attn_results_add,
     label='Additive')
```

[29]: `<AxesSubplot:xlabel='epoch', ylabel='val Accuracy'>`

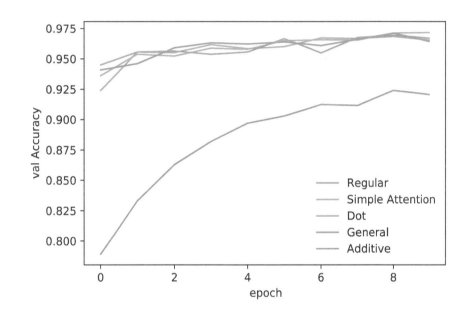

The other benefit of our new code is the ability to handle variable-sized inputs, where the shorter/smaller items are padded to match the length of the longest/largest item in a batch. To make sure it's working, we define a new `LargestDigitVariable` dataset that picks a random number of items to put in each bag, up to some specified maximum number. This will also make the training problem even more challenging because the network needs to determine whether there is any relationship between the number of items in a bag and the bag's label.

The following code does this, with only two real changes. First, our `__getitem__` method computes `how_many` items to sample. Second, we implement padding inside our dataset object for simplicity, so if `how_many < maxToSample`, we pad the input with zero values to get everything the same size:

```
class LargestDigitVariable(Dataset):
    """

    Creates a modified version of a dataset where some variable number of
    samples are taken, and the true label is the largest label sampled.
    When used with MNIST the labels correspond to their values (e.g.,
    digit "6" has label 6). Each datum will be padded with 0 values if
    the maximum number of items was not sampled.
    """

    def __init__(self, dataset, maxToSample=6):
        """
        dataset: the dataset to sample from
        toSample: the number of items from the dataset to sample
        """
        self.dataset = dataset
        self.maxToSample = maxToSample

    def __len__(self):
        return len(self.dataset)

    def __getitem__(self, idx):
        how_many = np.random.randint(1,self.maxToSample, size=1)[0]
        selected = np.random.randint(0,len(self.dataset), size=how_many)
        x_new = torch.stack([self.dataset[i][0] for i in selected] +
        [torch.zeros((1,28,28)) for i in range(self.maxToSample-how_many)])
        y_new = max([self.dataset[i][1] for i in selected])
        return x_new, y_new
```

Stacks the n items of shape (B, *) into (B, n, *). New: pad with zero values up to the max size.

New: how many items should we select?

Randomly selects n=self.toSample items from the dataset

Label is the maximum label.

Returns (data, label) pair

The next block of code creates the training and test set loaders and should look very familiar to you by this point in the book:

```
largestV_train = LargestDigitVariable(mnist_train)
largestV_test = LargestDigitVariable(mnist_test)

trainV_loader = DataLoader(largest_train, batch_size=B, shuffle=True)
testV_loader = DataLoader(largest_test, batch_size=B)
```

We would *usually* train our new models on this new dataset. But here is the cool thing: our new attention mechanism's design can handle a variable number of inputs thanks to padding, and the attention prior includes the concept that only a subset of the inputs are relevant. So even though our data now has a new, larger shape, with more possible inputs, we can reuse the same network we have already trained.

Instead of training a new model, the following code runs through the test set and makes predictions using one of our models trained on only bags of size 3, and it will hopefully work well on bags of size 1 through 6:

```
attn_dot = attn_dot.eval()

preds = []
truths = []
    with torch.no_grad():
        for inputs, labels in testV_loader:
            pred = attn_dot(inputs.to(device))
            pred = torch.argmax(pred, dim=1).cpu().numpy()

            preds.extend(pred.ravel())
            truths.extend(labels.numpy().ravel())
print("Variable Length Accuracy: ", accuracy_score(preds, truths))

Variable Length Accuracy: 0.967
```

You should see something around 96 or 97% accuracy on this new problem, and we trained on an easier version of it. This gives you an idea of how powerful the attention approach can be. It can often generalize very well to changes in the input data and sequence length, which is part of what has made attentions very successful. They have quickly become a go-to tool for most natural language processing tasks today.

It is not *always* possible to generalize like this. If we keep making the inputs longer than we trained on (increasing the maxToSample argument), the accuracy will eventually start to decrease. But we can counteract that by training on inputs that are as long as we expect to receive.

The important thing to be aware of here is that the attention approach can handle a variable number of inputs and generalize beyond what was given. This, combined with the ability to be selective with respect to the inputs, makes the approach very powerful.

Exercises

Share and discuss your solutions on the Manning online platform at Inside Deep Learning Exercises (https://liveproject.manning.com/project/945). Once you submit your own answers, you will be able to see the solutions submitted by other readers, and see which ones the author judges to be the best.

1. Train a new model for the LargestDigit problem that is convolutional. To make this work, you'll need to convert your data from shape (B, T, C, W, H) to $(B * T, C, W, H)$, essentially enlarging the batch size to run your 2D convolutions. Once you are done convolving, you can go back to a shape of (B, T, C, W, H). What accuracy are you able to get with this approach?

2. GeneralScore uses a matrix W that starts with random values. But you could instead initialize it as $W = I/\sqrt{H} + \epsilon$, where ϵ is just some small random values (say in the range of –0.01 to 0.01) to avoid hard zeros. This would make GeneralScore start with the behavior of DotScore. Try to implement this yourself.

3   Using the `tanh` activation in the additive attention score is somewhat arbitrary. Try multiple different versions of the additive attention by replacing the `tanh` activation with other options in PyTorch. Are there any activations you think may work particularly well or poorly?

4   Let's implement an even harder version of the `LargestDigitVariable` dataset. To determine the label of a bag, take the sum of the labels of the bag's contents (e.g., 3, 7, and 2 are in bag = "12"). If the sum is even, return the largest label; and if the sum is odd, return the smallest. For example "3"+"7"+"2" = 12, so the label should be "7." But if the bag was "4"+"7"+"2"= 13, the label should be "2."

5   You do not have to use the average of the inputs as your context; you can use *anything* that you think might work better. To demonstrate this, implement an attention network that uses an *attention subnetwork* to compute the context. This means there will be an initial context that is the average $\bar{h}$, which is used to compute a *new* context $\bar{x}_{cntx}$, which is then used to compute the *final* output $\bar{x}$. Does this have any impact on your accuracy in exercise 4?

Summary

- Attention mechanisms encode a prior that some items in a sequence or set are more important than others.

- Attention mechanisms use a context to decide which items are more or less important.

- A score function is needed to determine how important each input is, given the context. The dot, general, and additive scores are all popular.

- Attention mechanisms can handle variable-length inputs and are particularly good at generalizing over them.

- Like RNNs, attentions require masking to handle batches of data.

Sequence-to-sequence

This chapter covers

- Preparing a sequence-to-sequence dataset and loader
- Combining RNNs with attention mechanisms
- Building a machine translation model
- Interpreting attention scores to understand a model's decisions

Now that we have learned about attention mechanisms, we can wield them to build something new and powerful. In particular, we will develop an algorithm known as *sequence-to-sequence* (Seq2Seq for short) that can perform machine translation. As the name implies, this is an approach for getting neural networks to take one sequence as input and produce a different sequence as the output. Seq2Seq has been used to get computers to perform symbolic calculus,[1] summarize long documents,[2] and even translate from one language to another. I'll show you step by step how we can translate from English to French. In fact, Google used essentially the same approach as its production machine-translation tool, and you can read about it at https://ai.googleblog.com/2016/09/

---

[1] G. Lample and F. Charton, F. "Deep learning for symbolic mathematics," in Proceeds of ICLR 2020.
[2] A. See, P. J. Liu, and C. D. Manning, "Get to the point: summarization with pointer-generator networks," Association for Computational Linguistics, 2017.

a-neural-network-for-machine.html. If you can imagine your inputs/outputs as sequences of things, there is a good chance Seq2Seq can help you solve the task.

The astute reader may think, an RNN takes in a sequence and produces an output for every input. So it takes in a sequence and outputs a sequence. Isn't that "Seq-to-Seq"? You are a wise reader, but this is part of why I called Seq2Seq a design approach. You could hypothetically get an RNN to do anything Seq2Seq could do, but it would be difficult to get it to work. One problem is that an RNN alone implies that the output sequence is the same length as the input, which is rarely true. Seq2Seq decouples the input and output into two separate stages and parts and thus works much better. We get to how that happens shortly.

Seq2Seq is the most complex algorithm we implement in the book, but I'll show you how we can break it into smaller, manageable subcomponents. Using what we have learned about organizing PyTorch modules, this will be only a little painful. We walk through the task-specific setup with our dataset and `DataLoader` to prepare for training, describe the submodules of a Seq2Seq implementation, and end by showing how the attention mechanism lets us peer into the black box of neural networks to understand *how* Seq2Seq is performing the translations.

11.1 Sequence-to-sequence as a kind of denoising autoencoder

In a moment, we will go into the details of Seq2Seq, how to implement it, and how to apply it to translate English into French. But first, I want to show you an example of how well it can work and the explainability[3] that attention provides. A result of a large Seq2Seq translation model is shown in figure 11.1, translating from French to English. Each word in the output has a different attention applied to the original sentence, where black values indicate 0 (not important) and white values indicate 1 (very important).

For most items in the output, very few items from the input are relevant to getting the correct translation. But some cases require multiple words from the input to translate properly, and others need to be reordered. Classical machine translation approaches, which worked on a more word-by-word level, often had complex heuristic code to deal with situations that required multiple words of context and possibly unusual order. But now we can let the neural network learn the details for us and get an idea about how the model is learning to perform the translation.

---

[3]   What "explainability" is, or if it is even a real thing, is actually a fiery topic in many ML circles. For a great opinion piece, check out Zachary Lipton's "The mythos of model interpretability" at https://arxiv.org/abs/1606.03490.

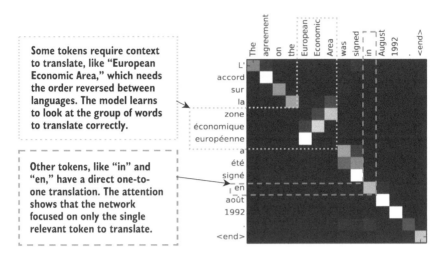

Some tokens require context to translate, like "European Economic Area," which needs the order reversed between languages. The model learns to look at the group of words to translate correctly.

Other tokens, like "in" and "en," have a direct one-to-one translation. The attention shows that the network focused on only the single relevant token to translate.

Figure 11.1 Results from the paper "Neural machine translation by jointly learning to align and translate" by Dzmitry Bahdanau, Kyunghyun Cho, and Yoshua Bengio. The input is on the left, and the output on the top. The attention result when trained on a larger corpus for more epochs results in a nice, crisp attention map.

How does Seq2Seq learn to do this? At a high level, the Seq2Seq algorithm trains a denoising autoencoder over sequences rather than static images. You can think of the original English as the noisy input and French as the clean output, and we ask the Seq2Seq model to learn how to remove the noise. Since we are dealing with sequences, this usually involves an RNN. A simple diagram is presented in figure 11.2. We have an encoder and decoder to convert inputs to outputs just like a denoising autoencoder; the difference is that a Seq2Seq model works over sequences instead of images or fully connected inputs.

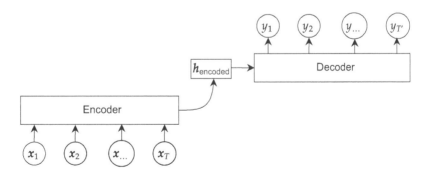

Figure 11.2 High-level depiction of the sequence-to-sequence approach. An input sequence $x_1, x_2, \ldots, x_T$ goes into an encoder. The encoder produces a representation of the sequence $h_{encoded}$. The decoder takes this representation and outputs a new sequence $y_1, y_2, \ldots, y_{T'}$.

Here we have some original input sequence $X = x_1, x_2, \ldots, x_T$, and the goal is to output a *new* sequence $Y = y_1, y_2, \ldots, y_{T'}$. These sequences do not have to be the same. $x_j \neq y_j$, and they can even be different lengths so $T \neq T'$ is also possible. We describe this as a denoising approach because the input sequence X gets mapped to a related sequence Y, almost as if X were a noisy version of Y.

Training a Seq2Seq model is no easy task. Like anything that uses RNNs, it is computationally challenging. It is also a difficult learning problem; the encoder RNN takes in X and produces a final hidden state activation h_T, which the decoder RNN must take as input to produce a new sequence Y. That requires packing a lot of information into a single vector, and we have already seen how RNNs can be difficult to train.

11.1.1 Adding attention creates Seq2Seq

The secret to getting a Seq2Seq model working well is adding an attention mechanism. Instead of forcing the model to learn one representation h_{encoded} to represent the *entire* input, we learn a representation h_i for each item x_i of the input sequence. Then we use an attention mechanism at each step of the output to look at all of the input. This is shown in more detail in figure 11.3, and we continue to expand the details of different parts of Seq2Seq until we can implement the entire approach. Notice that the last hidden state from the encoder, h_T, becomes the *initial* hidden state of the decoder, but we haven't indicted what the inputs to the decoder are at each time step. We get to that later in the chapter; there are too many parts to discuss all at once.

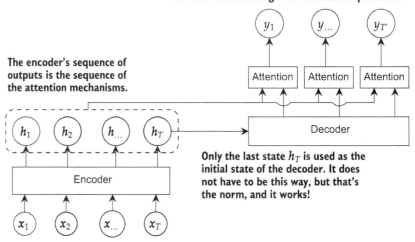

Figure 11.3   Deeper high-level diagram of how Seq2Seq operates. The first input to the decoder is the last output of the encoder. The decoder produces a sequence of outputs that are used as the contexts for an attention mechanism. By changing the context, we change what the model is looking for in the input.

Now let's talk about figure 11.1 and figure 11.3 together. The T inputs/hidden states from the encoder network in figure 11.3 would become the T rows of the original French in figure 11.1. Each attention block in figure 11.3 becomes one of the columns of figure 11.1. Because the attention outputs a score from 0 to 1 for every item in the input (filling a row), we can plot that in a heat map with dark values for low scores and white for high scores, showing which parts of the input were most important for producing each part of the output. Hence, we get figure 11.1 in its entirety. This also exemplifies how the attention captures the idea that importance is a *relative* concept. The importance of each word in the input changes depending on what we are trying to produce or what other words are present.

You may be wondering why the attention improves the RNN-based encoder and decoder: doesn't the gating mechanism from the long short-term memory (LSTM) do the same thing, selectively allowing/disallowing (gate on/off) information based on the current context? At a high level, yes, there is similarity to the approach. The key difference is the availability of information. If you did this as figure 11.2 depicts using just two RNNs for the encoder and decoder, the hidden state of the decoder RNN must learn how to represent (1), how far along it is with its creation of the output, (2) the entire original input sequence, and (3) how to not corrupt one with the other. By using an attention mechanism on the outputs of the decoder RNN, the RNN now only has to learn #1, as all of the original input items are available later for the attention, which alleviates #2 and also means #3 is a non-issue. While Seq2Seq is a complex algorithm, you have already learned and used *every* step that goes into implementing it. This is really an exercise in putting a lot of the building blocks of deep learning together into one powerful result.

11.2 Machine translation and the data loader

With the big-picture goal in mind—building a Seq2Seq translation model—we will work from the bottom up. The very bottom starts with defining what translation is and getting the data loaded. Then we can move on to how the input to a Seq2Seq model is handled, and finally add the attention mechanism to produce the outputs one at a time.

Broadly, machine translation is the name researchers use for studying how to get computers to translate from one language (e.g., English) to another (e.g., French). Machine translation as a problem will also help solidify how the inputs and outputs to the Seq2Seq model are different sequences of possibly different lengths.

The language that the input X is in—in our case, English—is called the *source* language. The destination language, French, is the *target* language. Our input sequence X might be the string "what a nice day," with a target string Y of "quelle belle journée." One difficult aspect of translation is that these sequences are not the same length. If we use words as our tokens (also called our alphabet Σ), our source sequence X and target sequence Y are:

$$\boldsymbol{X} = [\text{"what"}, \text{"a"}, \text{"nice"}, \text{"day"}]$$

$$\boldsymbol{Y} = [\text{"quelle"}, \text{"belle"}, \text{"journxe"}]$$

If we can successfully convert the sequence $\boldsymbol{X}$ into $\boldsymbol{Y}$, we will accomplish the task of machine translation. Several nuances can make this difficult:

- As already mentioned, the sequences may not be the same length.

- There may be complex relationships between sequences. For example, one language may put adjectives before nouns, and another may put nouns before adjectives.

- There may not be a one-to-one relationship. For example, "what a nice day" and "what a lovely day" can both have the same translation from English to French. Translation is usually a many-to-many task, where multiple valid inputs map to multiple valid outputs.

If you asked a natural language processing (NLP) researcher, they would give you an even longer list of why and how machine translation is challenging. But it's also a great opportunity to use Seq2Seq models because you do not need to look at the *entire* input to make decisions about each word of the output. For example, "journée" translates to "day" or "daytime"; it is not a homonym. Thus we can almost translate that word on its own without any other context. The word "amende" requires more context because it is a homonym for a "fine" and for "almond"; you can't translate it without knowing if someone is talking about food or money. Our attention mechanism can help us ignore the inputs that do not provide any helpful context for translation. This is part of why a Seq2Seq model can do very well at this task, even without us being able to enumerate all the reasons translation is difficult.

11.2.1 Loading a small English-French dataset

To build a machine translation dataset, we need some data. We'll reuse a small corpus of English-French translations. The following code quickly downloads it and does some minor preprocessing: removing punctuation and converting everything to lowercase. While it is possible to learn these things, doing so takes more data, and we want this example to run quickly with a limited amount of data:

```
from io import BytesIO
from zipfile import ZipFile
from urllib.request import urlopen
import re

all_data = []
resp = urlopen("https://download.pytorch.org/tutorial/data.zip")
zipfile = ZipFile(BytesIO(resp.read()))
```

```
for line in zipfile.open("data/eng-fra.txt").readlines():
    line = line.decode('utf-8').lower()           ◄─── Lowercase only, please.
    line = re.sub(r"[-.!?]+", r" ", line)          ◄─── No punctuation.
    source_lang, target_lang = line.split("\t")[0:2]
    all_data.append( (source_lang.strip(), target_lang.strip()) ) ◄─── (English,
                                                                         French)
```

To help give us some intuition, the following code prints the first few lines of the corpus to show the data. We already see a number of difficulties in the data. Words like "run" have more than one correct translation on their own, and some single English words can become one or more French words. This is before we even look at the longer sentences in the corpus:

```
for i in range(10):
    print(all_data[i])

('go', 'va')
('run', 'cours')
('run', 'courez')
('wow', 'ça alors')
('fire', 'au feu')
('help', "à l'aide")
('jump', 'saute')
('stop', 'ça suffit')
('stop', 'stop')
('stop', 'arrête toi')
```

To make training faster, let's limit ourselves to sentences that contain six or fewer words. You can try increasing this limit to see how the model does, but I want to make these examples train quickly. A real-world translation task could use the same code but would need more time and data to learn something more robust—but that could take days of training, so let's keep it short:

```
short_subset = []          ◄─── The subset we use
MAX_LEN = 6
for (s, t) in all_data:
    if max(len(s.split(" ")), len(t.split(" "))) <= MAX_LEN:
        short_subset.append((s,t))
print("Using ", len(short_subset), "/", len(all_data))

Using 66251 / 135842
```

BUILDING THE ALPHABET

Now the short_subset list contains all of the English-French translation pairs we will use, and we can build a vocabulary or alphabet for our model. As before, a vocabulary gives every unique string we use a unique ID as a token, starting from 0 and counting up. But we also add some special tokens to give our model helpful hints. First, because not all sentences are the same length, we use a PAD_token to denote padding, indicating that the value in a tensor is not used because the underlying sentence has already ended.

The two new things we introduce are *start of sentence* (SOS) and *end of sentence* (EOS) tokens. These are commonly found in machine translation, as well as many other NLP tasks. The SOS_token token is often placed at the beginning of the source sequence X

to indicate to the algorithm that translation has started. The EOS_token is more useful, as it is appended to the end of the target sequence Y to indicate that the sentence is complete. This is very useful later so the model learns how to end a translation. When the model is done, it outputs an EOS_token, and we can stop the process. You may think that punctuation is a good stopping point, but that approach would prevent us from extending our model to translate sentences or paragraphs at a time. Once every item in the batch has generated an EOS_token, we know it is safe to stop. This also helps because the outputs may have differing lengths, and the EOS marker helps us figure out how long each different generated sequence should be.

The following code defines our SOS, EOS, and padding markers and creates a dictionary word2indx to create the mapping. We are also defining PAD_token as mapping to index 0 so that we can use our getMaskByFill function easily. Similar to our autoregressive model, an inverted dictionary indx2word is created so that we can look at our results more easily when we are done (it is easier to read words than a sequence of integers):

```
SOS_token = "<SOS>"          ←—— "START_OF_SENTENCE_TOKEN"
EOS_token = "<EOS>"          ←—— "END_OF_SENTENCE_TOKEN"
PAD_token = "_PADDING_"

word2indx = {PAD_token:0, SOS_token:1, EOS_token:2}
for s, t in short_subset:
    for sentence in (s, t):
        for word in sentence.split(" "):
            if word not in word2indx:
                word2indx[word] = len(word2indx)
print("Size of Vocab: ", len(word2indx))
indx2word = {}                           ←——— Builds the inverted dictionary
for word, indx in word2indx.items():          for looking at the outputs later
    indx2word[indx] = word

Size of Vocab: 24577
```

IMPLEMENTING A TRANSLATION DATASET

Now we create a TranslationDataset object that represents our translation task. It takes in the short_subset as the underlying input data and returns PyTorch int64 tensors by splitting on spaces and using the vocabulary word2indx that we just created:

```
class TranslationDataset(Dataset):
    """
    Takes a dataset with tuples of strings (x, y) and
    converts them to tuples of int64 tensors.
    This makes it easy to encode Seq2Seq problems.
    Strings in the input and output targets will be broken up by spaces
    """

    def __init__(self, lang_pairs, word2indx):
        """
        lang_pairs: a List[Tuple[String,String]] containing the
            source,target pairs for a Seq2Seq problem.
```

```
        word2indx: a Map[String,Int] that converts each word in an input
        ➦ string into a unique ID.
        """
        self.lang_pairs = lang_pairs
        self.word2indx = word2indx

    def __len__(self):
        return len(self.lang_pairs)

    def __getitem__(self, idx):
        x, y = self.lang_pairs[idx]
        x = SOS_token + " " + x + " " + EOS_token
        y = y + " " + EOS_token

        x = [self.word2indx[w] for w in x.split(" ")]     ⟵┐ Converts to lists
        y = [self.word2indx[w] for w in y.split(" ")]     ⟵┘ of integers

        x = torch.tensor(x, dtype=torch.int64)
        y = torch.tensor(y, dtype=torch.int64)
        return x, y
bigdataset = TranslationDataset(short_subset, word2indx)
```

Seq2Seq tasks generally require a lot of training data, which we do not have right now because we want this example to run in 10 minutes. We will use more of the data (90%) for training and just 10% for testing.

IMPLEMENTING A COLLATE FUNCTION FOR TRANSLATION DATA

We also need to define a `collate_fn` function to create one larger batch from the inputs that are different lengths. Each item already ends with an `EOS_token`, so we just pad the shorter inputs with our `PAD_token` value to make everything the same length.

To make this compatible with our `train_network` function, we also need to be a little clever in how we return the results of `collate_fn`. We will return the data as a set of nested tuples, $((X, Y), Y)$ because the `train_network` function expects tuples with two items, $(input, output)$, and our Seq2Seq model requires both X and Y at training time. The reason is explained soon. This way, the `train_network` function will break up the tuple as

$$((\underset{\underset{\text{input}}{\downarrow}}{X, Y}),\ \underset{\underset{\text{output}}{\downarrow}}{Y}\ )$$

The following code does all the work. `pad_batch` is our collation function, which begins by finding the longest input sequence length `max_x` and the longest output sequence length `max_y`. Since we are padding (not *packing*, which is supported only by RNNs), we can use the `F.pad` function to do that. It takes the sequence to pad as the first input and a tuple telling it how much to pad to the left and how much to pad to the right. We only want to pad to the right side (end) of a sequence, so our tuples look like `(0, pad_amount)`:

```
train_size = round(len(bigdataset)*0.9)
test_size = len(bigdataset)-train_size
train_dataset, test_dataset = torch.utils.data.random_split(bigdataset,
    [train_size, test_size])

def pad_batch(batch):
    """
    Pad items in the batch to the length of the longest item in the batch
    """
    max_x = max([i[0].size(0) for i in batch])
    max_y = max([i[1].size(0) for i in batch])

    PAD = word2indx[PAD_token]

    X = [F.pad(i[0],(0,max_x-i[0].size(0)), value=PAD)
        for i in batch]
    Y = [F.pad(i[1],(0,max_y-i[1].size(0)), value=PAD)
        for i in batch]
    X, Y = torch.stack(X), torch.stack(Y)
    return (X, Y), Y

train_loader = DataLoader(train_dataset, batch_size=B, shuffle=True,
    collate_fn=pad_batch)
test_loader = DataLoader(test_dataset, batch_size=B, collate_fn=pad_batch)
```

> We have two different maximum lengths: the max length of the input sequences and the max length of the output sequences. We determine each separately and only pad the inputs/outputs by the exact amount we need.

> We use the F.pad function to pad each tensor to the right.

11.3 Inputs to Seq2Seq

When we are talking about a Seq2Seq model, there are two sets of inputs: the input to the encoder and the input to the decoder. To specify what goes into each part, we need to define what the encoder and decoder blocks of Seq2Seq are in figure 11.3. It should not surprise you that we use an RNN for each, and it is your choice if you want to use a gated recurrent unit (GRU) or LSTM. When we code this later, we'll use a GRU because it makes the code a little easier to read.

The inputs to the encoder are easy: we are just feeding in the input sequence $X = x_1, x_1, \ldots, x_T$. The decoder produces predictions of what it thinks the output sequence is: $\hat{Y} = \hat{y}_1, \hat{y}_1, \ldots, \hat{y}_{T'}$. We take the cross-entropy loss between $\hat{Y}$ and Y as the learning signal for training this network.

But we are missing a big detail: the inputs to the decoder. RNNs usually take in a previous hidden state (that would be h_{encoded} for the decoder) plus an input for the current time step. There are two options for the decoder's inputs: autoregressive style and teacher forcing. We will learn about both options because using both works better than using either one alone.

For both options, we use the last hidden state of the encoder (h_T) as the initial hidden state of the decoder ($h_{\text{encoded}} = h_T$). We do this instead of using the zero vector so that the gradient flows through the decoder and into the encoder, connecting them. More important, the last hidden state h_T is a summary of the entire input sequence, and that context of "what the input was" will help the decoder decide what the first part of the output should be.

11.3.1 *Autoregressive approach*

Figure 11.4 shows our first option for implementing the decoder's inputs, which we call the *autoregressive* option. For the autoregressive approach, we use the predicted token at time step t as the input for the next time step $t + 1$ (the dashed grey lines).

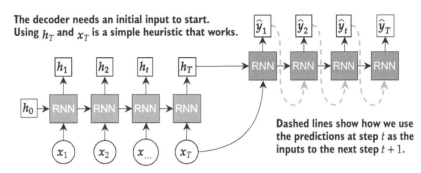

Figure 11.4 Example of an autoregressive approach to the decoding step. The first input to the decoder is the last input to the encoder. Every subsequent input to the decoder is the prediction from the previous step.

The other detail is what the *first* input should be. We have not made any predictions yet, so we can't use the previous prediction as the input. There are two sub-options, and both have very similar performance. The first option is to *always* use the SOS marker as the input, which is a very reasonable idea. Semantically, it makes sense as well; the first input says, "the sentence is starting," and the RNN must use the context to predict the first word. The second option is to use the last token of the input, which should be an EOS marker or a padding token. This ends up with the decoder RNN learning that the EOS and padding have the same semantic meaning as "sentence start." Either option is acceptable, and in practice the choice does not tend to make a noticeable difference. We will implement it so the last item from the encoder becomes the first input to the decoder, as I think it is a slightly more general approach.

Since the output of our model is a probability of the next word, there are two ways to select the next input $t + 1$: take the most likely token, or sample the next token based on the probabilities given. In chapter 6, when we trained an autoregressive model, selecting the most likely next word caused unrealistic output. So when we implement this, we will go for the sampling approach.

11.3.2 *Teacher-forcing approach*

The second option is called *teacher forcing*. The first input to the decoder is handled the exact same way as in the autoregressive approach, but the subsequent inputs are different. Rather than using the prediction $\hat{y}_t$ as the input for $\hat{y}_{t+1}$, we use the true correct token y_t, as shown in figure 11.5.

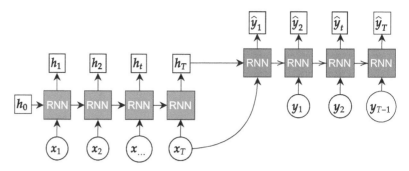

Figure 11.5   Example of teacher forcing. For the decoder, we ignore the predictions and at step t, we feed in the correct previous output y_{t-1}. The predictions are still used when the loss is computed.

This makes teacher forcing a little easier to implement because we don't have to guess what comes next: we have the answer. This is also why our code needs the true labels $\boldsymbol{Y}$ as input during training so that we can compute the teacher-forcing result.

11.3.3 *Teacher forcing vs. an autoregressive approach*

The teacher-forcing approach has the benefit of giving the network the *correct* answer from which to continue its predictions. This makes it easier to predict all subsequent tokens correctly. The intuition is simple: it is harder to be correct on the tth prediction if you have been wrong for all of the $t-1$ previous predictions. Teacher forcing helps the network by allowing it to learn simultaneously all the words it needs to predict.

The autoregressive approach can be slower to learn because the network has to learn to predict the first word correctly before it can focus on the second, and then the second before the third, and so on. But when we want to make predictions on new data, where we *do not know the answer*, teacher forcing is impossible: we have to make predictions in an autoregressive fashion, so it's good for the model to learn to make predictions this way.

The practical solution we use is to combine the autoregressive and teacher-forcing approaches. For each input, we randomly decide which approach we want to take, so we will train with both. But at prediction time, we only do the autoregressive option since teacher forcing requires knowing the answer. A fancier approach is to switch between teacher forcing and autoregressive in a single batch, but that's painful to implement. Picking one option per batch will make our code easier to write and read.

The use of teacher forcing is also why we made the target sequence $\boldsymbol{Y}$ part of the input to our network. We use the `self.training` flag to switch between different behaviors when training and predicting with our model.

11.4   *Seq2Seq with attention*

What we have shown and described so far is technically enough to implement a sequence-to-sequence-style model. However, it will not learn very well and will have poor performance. Including an attention mechanism is the key to making Seq2Seq work.

The attention mechanism can work with both teacher forcing and the autoregressive approach and will change how we make predictions about the current word at the tth step of the RNN. So rather than have the decoder RNN predict $\hat{y}_t$, we have it produce a latent value $\hat{z}_t$. The value $\hat{z}_t$ is our *context* for the attention mechanism. Figure 11.6 shows the process for predicting the tth word in four main components:

1. The encoder step learns a useful representation of the input.

2. The decoder step predicts a context for each item of the output.

3. The attention step uses the context to produce an output $\bar{x}_t$, which is combined with the context $\hat{z}_t$.

4. The prediction step takes the combined attention/context result and predicts the next token of the sequence.

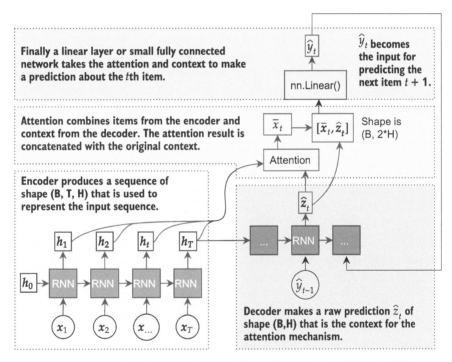

Figure 11.6 The process of applying attention to predict one item at a time of the output. Each highlighted region shows one of the four steps of encoding, decoding the context, attention, and prediction. This is repeated until an EOS token is found or a maximum limit is reached.

You can see that the attention block (which could use any of the three score functions we defined) takes the context $\hat{z}_t$ and the hidden states $h_1, h_2, \ldots, h_T$ from the encoder RNN as its inputs.

The attention mechanism, combined with the `apply_attn` module from before, produces a weight $\alpha_1, \alpha_2, \ldots, \alpha_T$ for each hidden state. We then use the hidden states and weights to compute a final context for the current time step t, $\bar{x}_t = \sum_{i=1}^{T} \alpha_i h_i$.

Since each h_i is most influenced by the ith input, this gives the Seq2Seq model a way to look at just a subset of the input sequence as being relevant to predicting the tth item of the output.

To complete this, we concatenate the attention output $\bar{x}_t$ with the local context $\hat{z}_t$, giving us a new vector

$$[\bar{x}_t, \hat{z}_t]$$

$$\downarrow$$

torch.cat(($\bar{x}_t$, $\hat{z}_t$),dim=1)

which we feed into a final fully connected network to transform into our final prediction, $\hat{y}_t$.

This may seem daunting, but you have already written or used code for all of these steps. The encoder uses a normal nn.GRU layer because it can return a tensor of shape (B, T, H) giving us all the outputs, which you learned to do in chapter 4. We use a nn.GRUCell for the context predictions $\hat{z}_t$ because it has to happen step by step; you used this in chapter 6 for the autoregressive model. In the same chapter, you used sampling to select the next token and trained the model using a teacher-forcing-like approach. We just learned and used the attention mechanism, and you learned about the concatenated output feed into another layer in chapter 7 for U-Net.

11.4.1 *Implementing Seq2Seq*

We're ready to implement the Seq2Seq model. To set up our constructor, let's talk about what components we need in the model itself.

First we need an nn.Embedding layer to convert tokens into feature vectors, similar to the char-RNN model from chapter 7. We use the padding_idx option to state which token value is used to indicate padding since there are multiple different sequence lengths.

Next we need an encoding RNN and a decoding RNN. We use the GRU because it's a little simpler to write code for compared to the LSTM. In particular, we will code each RNN differently. For the encoder, we use the normal nn.GRU module, which takes in a tensor of shape (B, T, D), since it expects all T items at once. This is easier to code and also lets us use the bidirectional option with ease. Since we have the entire input, the bidirectional option is a good choice.[4]

The decoder RNN can't be bidirectional because we are generating the output one item at a time. This also means we can't use the normal nn.GRU module, because it expects all T' items of the output to be ready at once, but we do not know how long each output is until we have encountered all the EOS tokens. To fix this, we use the nn.GRUCell. This will require us to keep track of the hidden states and multiple layers of the decoder manually, and we have to write a for loop to keep iterating over the predictions until we have a complete result.

---

[4] The biggest choice of a bidirectional RNN is usually "Do I have access to the future/whole sequence at test time?" For our translation task, this is true, so it's worth doing. But it's not always true! If we wanted to make a Seq2Seq model that took in *live speech* in real time, we would need to use a non-bidirectional model, because we would not know the speaker's future words.

To make sure we do not end up in an infinite loop in the case of a bad prediction, we include a `max_decode_length` to enforce a maximum number of decoding steps through the decoder RNN that we are willing to attempt. Finally, we need our `ApplyAttention` module with some `score_net` for computing the scores (we use the `DotScore`) and a small network `predict_word` to predict the next word. The following code snippet covers all the items we have discussed and creates the constructor for our Seq2Seq model:

```
class Seq2SeqAttention(nn.Module):

    def __init__(self, num_embeddings, embd_size, hidden_size,
        padding_idx=None, layers=1, max_decode_length=20):
        super(Seq2SeqAttention, self).__init__()
        self.padding_idx = padding_idx
        self.hidden_size = hidden_size
        self.embd = nn.Embedding(num_embeddings, embd_size,
            padding_idx=padding_idx)
        self.encode_layers = nn.GRU(input_size=
            embd_size, hidden_size=hidden_size//2,
            num_layers=layers, bidirectional=True)
        self.decode_layers = nn.ModuleList([
            nn.GRUCell(embd_size, hidden_size)] +
            [nn.GRUCell(hidden_size, hidden_size)
            for i in range(layers-1)])
        self.score_net = DotScore(hidden_size)
        self.predict_word = nn.Sequential(
            nn.Linear(2*hidden_size, hidden_size),
            nn.LeakyReLU(),
            nn.LayerNorm(hidden_size),
            nn.Linear(hidden_size, hidden_size),
            nn.LeakyReLU(),
            nn.LayerNorm(hidden_size),
            nn.Linear(hidden_size, num_embeddings)
        )
        self.max_decode_length = max_decode_length
        self.apply_attn = ApplyAttention()
```

We set the hidden size to half the intended length because we make the encoder bidirectional. That means we get two hidden state representations, which we concatenate together, giving us the desired size.

The decoder is uni-directional, and we need to use GRUCells so that we can do the decoding one step at a time.

predict_word is a small, fully connected network that converts the result of the attention mechanism and the local context into a prediction of the next word.

Now we can talk about how to implement the `forward` function of the Seq2Seq algorithm. Figure 11.7 outlines the process.

We will walk through these blocks in the order they would run according to our diagram, explain what is happening, and show the code to make it happen. Note that in the diagram, we have separated out two lists: `all_attentions` and `all_predictions`. These collect the attention and prediction scores so that we can make both available from the model to look at the attention scores and examine the predictions or pass them to any subsequent module we may want to use.

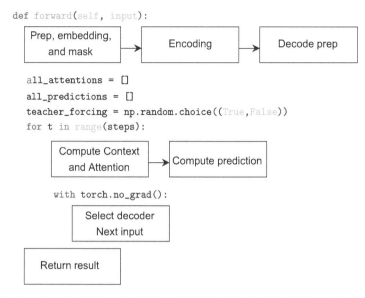

```
def forward(self, input):
```

```
all_attentions = []
all_predictions = []
teacher_forcing = np.random.choice((True,False))
for t in range(steps):
```

```
with torch.no_grad():
```

Figure 11.7 Outline of the forward function and the seven steps in its implementation. Each block shows one unit of work, and arrows show sequential tasks.

PREP, EMBEDDING, AND MASK BLOCK

The first thing we need to do in our function is some prep and organization. The input can be a tensor of shape (B, T) or a tuple of two tensors $((B, T), (B, T'))$, depending on whether we are in testing or training mode, respectively. We check what our input is and extract the `input` and `target` values appropriately. We `embd` all of the input values and compute useful things like our `mask`; and from the `mask`, we can determine how long each sequence is. The length is the number of `True` values, so we can get the `seq_lengths` with a simple `sum` call. We also grab the compute device being used, for later when we need to sample the next input for the decoder:

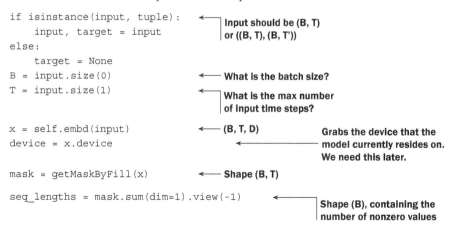

```
if isinstance(input, tuple):        Input should be (B, T)
    input, target = input           or ((B, T), (B, T'))
else:
    target = None
B = input.size(0)                   What is the batch size?
T = input.size(1)                   What is the max number
                                    of input time steps?

x = self.embd(input)                (B, T, D)     Grabs the device that the
device = x.device                                 model currently resides on.
                                                  We need this later.

mask = getMaskByFill(x)             Shape (B, T)

seq_lengths = mask.sum(dim=1).view(-1)          Shape (B), containing the
                                                number of nonzero values
```

ENCODING BLOCK

Now that our data and masks are ready, we need to push the data through our encoder network. To maximize throughput, we pack the input data before feeding it to the RNN, which is easy and fast to do since we computed the `seq_lengths` from the `mask`. In addition, `h_last` contains the last activation even with variable-length items, simplifying our code. We do need to unpack `h_encoded` for our attention mechanism later and reshape it to (B, T, D), since we are using a bidirectional model. Some similar shape manipulation will make sure `h_last` is of shape (B, D) instead of the default $(2, B, D/2)$ from our bidirectional approach.

Here's the code:

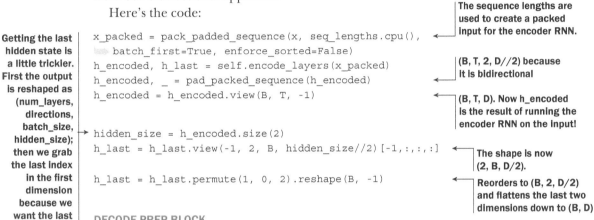

The sequence lengths are used to create a packed input for the encoder RNN.

Getting the last hidden state is a little trickier. First the output is reshaped as (num_layers, directions, batch_size, hidden_size); then we grab the last index in the first dimension because we want the last layer's output.

```
x_packed = pack_padded_sequence(x, seq_lengths.cpu(),
    batch_first=True, enforce_sorted=False)
h_encoded, h_last = self.encode_layers(x_packed)
h_encoded, _ = pad_packed_sequence(h_encoded)
h_encoded = h_encoded.view(B, T, -1)

hidden_size = h_encoded.size(2)
h_last = h_last.view(-1, 2, B, hidden_size//2)[-1,:,:,:]

h_last = h_last.permute(1, 0, 2).reshape(B, -1)
```

(B, T, 2, D//2) because it is bidirectional

(B, T, D). Now h_encoded is the result of running the encoder RNN on the input!

The shape is now (2, B, D/2).

Reorders to (B, 2, D/2) and flattens the last two dimensions down to (B, D)

DECODE PREP BLOCK

Before we start the decoding block, we need to do a little prep. First, we store a list of the previous hidden state activations of the decoder RNN. We do this because we are using GRUCells, which need us to keep track of hidden state activations so we can make sequential steps of the RNN run efficiently.[5]

To make our code simpler, we reuse the `embd` layer for encoding the inputs to the decoder. This is OK because the `embd` layer does very little work; most of it is done by the decoder layer. Since we will make the last input to the encoder be the first input to the decoder, we need to grab that. Doing `input[:, seq_lengths-1]` looks like it should work, but it returns a tensor that is of shape (B, B, D) instead of (B, D). To make this work the way we want, we need to use the `gather` function instead, which gathers the specified indices along the specified axis (`1`).

All of this is in the following code block for the decoder prep, which ends with figuring out the number of steps for which we need to run the decoder:

New hidden states for decoders

```
h_prevs = [h_last for l in range(len(self.decode_layers))]

decoder_input = self.embd(input.gather(1,
    seq_lengths.view(-1,1)-1).flatten())

steps = min(self.max_decode_length, T)
```

How many decoding steps should we do?

Grabs the last item from the input (which should be an EOS marker) as the first input for the decoder. We could also hardcode the SOS marker. (B, D).

---

5   If we wanted to switch this out with an `LSTMCell`, we would need another list for the LSTM's context states.

```
if target is not None:
    steps = target.size(1)
```
◄─── If we are training, the target value tells us exactly how many steps to take. We know the exact decode length.

COMPUTE CONTEXT AND ATTENTION BLOCK

Now we need to compute the context and attention results. This is running inside a `for` loop over `t` steps. The variable `decodr_input` has our current input to work on: the value selected from the previous prep step or the value we compute in the next two steps.

We have our `GRUCells` in a list of `decode_layers` that we iterate through to push the batch through the layers ourselves, just as we did in chapter 6 with the autoregressive model. Once done, our result $\hat{z}_t$ is stored in a variable called `h_decoder`. A call to our `score_net` gets the normalized scores, and then `apply_attn` returns the $\bar{x}_t$ and the softmax weights α in the variables `context` and `weights`, respectively. This is shown in the following chunk of code:

```
x_in = decoder_input   ◄─── (B, D)

for l in range(len(self.decode_layers)):
    h_prev = h_prevs[l]
    h = self.decode_layers[l](x_in, h_prev)

    h_prevs[l] = h
    x_in = h
h_decoder = x_in

scores = self.score_net(h_encoded, h_decoder)
context, weights = self.apply_attn(h_encoded, scores,
    mask=mask)

all_attentions.append( weights.detach() )
```

This is the attention mechanism. Let's look at all the previous encoded states and see which ones look relevant. (B, T, 1) $\hat{\alpha}$.

(B, D). We now have the hidden state for the decoder at this time step.

(B, D) for $\bar{x}$ and (B, T) for α

Saves the attention weights for visualization later. We are detaching the weights because we do not want to compute anything else with them; we just want to save their values to make visualizations.

COMPUTE PREDICTION BLOCK

With the previous task done, we can use `torch.cat` to combine $\bar{x}_t$ and $\hat{z}_t$ and feed the result to `predict_word` to get our final prediction $\hat{y}_t$ for the tth output:

Compute the final representation by concatenating the attention result and the initial context: (B, D) + (B, D) -> (B, 2*D).

```
word_pred = torch.cat((context, h_decoder), dim=1)
word_pred = self.predict_word(word_pred)
all_predictions.append(word_pred)
```

Get a prediction about what the next token is by pushing it through a small fully connected network: (B, 2*D) -> (B, V).

This is another situation where `nn.Sequential` helps make the code clean, since `predict_word` is an entire neural network that we do not need to think about.

SELECT THE DECODER'S NEXT INPUT BLOCK

We are almost done with Seq2Seq, with one last part to implement: selecting the next value for `decoder_input` at step $t + 1$. This is done in the `with torch.no_grad()` context so that we can do the work we need. First, we check whether the model is in self.training mode, because if it is not, we can bail out and simply select the most likely word. If we are in training mode, we check whether we should use teacher_forcing and defensively check that our target values are available. If both are true, we make the input for $t+1$ be the true output that should have occurred for the current time step t. Otherwise, we sample the next work in the autoregressive manner. Here's the code:

```
if self.training:
    if target is not None and teacher_forcing:
        next_words = target[:,t].squeeze()
    else:
        next_words = torch.multinomial(
            F.softmax(word_pred, dim=1), 1)[:,-1]
    else:
        next_words = torch.argmax(word_pred, dim=1)
```

Samples the next token based on the predictions made

We have the target and selected teacher forcing, so use the correct next answer.

We are trying to make an actual prediction, so we take the most likely word. We could improve this by using temperature and sampling, as we did for the char-RNN model.

There are two things worth noting that could be improved in this code. First, instead of taking the most likely next word at test time, we could do sampling as we did with the autoregressive model. Second, we could add a temperature option, as we used before, to change how often we chose the more likely words. I haven't made these changes to keep the code a little simpler.

Once the next_words are selected and we exit the with torch.no_grad() block, we can set decoder_input = self.embd(next_words.to(device)). We need to wait until the no_grad() context is gone so gradients are tracked for this step.

RETURN THE RESULT BLOCK

Finally we are at the end of our Seq2Seq implementation. The last step is to return our results. If we are in training mode, we just need to give back the predictions by stacking the predictions for all T' words together, giving us torch.stack(all_predictions, dim=1). If we are in evaluation mode, we also want to get the attention scores so that we can examine them. Similar to the predictions, they are stacked together:

```
if self.training:
    return torch.stack(all_predictions, dim=1)
else:
    return torch.stack(all_predictions, dim=1),
        torch.stack(all_attentions, dim=1).squeeze()
```

When training, only the predictions are important.

When evaluating, we also want to look at the attention weights.

11.4.2 *Training and evaluation*

We have defined a Seq2Seq model, and now we can try it. We use 20 epochs of training and a few layers. Since this is an RNN, we also use gradient clipping as part of our training. An embedding dimension of 64 and hidden neuron size of 256 is on the smaller side to make this run faster; I would prefer to set these values to 128 and 512 if I was willing to wait longer and had more data.

Here's the code:

```
epochs = 20
seq2seq = Seq2SeqAttention(len(word2indx), 64, 256,
    padding_idx=word2indx[PAD_token], layers=3, max_decode_length=MAX_LEN+2)
```

```
for p in seq2seq.parameters():
    p.register_hook(lambda grad: torch.clamp(grad, -10, 10))
```

DEFINING A LOSS FUNCTION

The last thing we need is a loss function to train our network. The standard `nn.CrossEntropyLoss` does not handle this situation where our output has a shape of (B, T, V), with V as the size of the vocabulary. Instead, we iterate through all T time steps of the output and slice off the correct piece of the input and labels that we can call `nn.CrossEntropyLoss` without any errors. This is the same kind of approach we used for training the autoregressive model in chapter 6.

The only change we make is the use of the `ignore_index` value. If the label `y=ignore_index`, the `nn.CrossEntropyLoss` does not calculate any loss for that value. We can use this to handle the padding tokens, as we do not want the network to learn to predict padding; we want it to predict the EOS token when appropriate and then be finished. This allows us to make our loss function understand that the output has padding, too:

```
def CrossEntLossTime(x, y):
    """
    x: output with shape (B, T, V)
    y: labels with shape (B, T')
    """
    if isinstance(x, tuple):
        x, _ = x
    cel = nn.CrossEntropyLoss(ignore_index=word2indx[PAD_token])   ◄─┐  We do not want
    T = min(x.size(1), y.size(1))                                     │  to compute a
    loss = 0                                                          │  loss for items
    for t in range(T):                                                │  that have been
        loss += cel(x[:,t,:], y[:,t])                                 ┘  padded!
return loss
```

With that, we can call the `train_network` function with our Seq2Seq model and our new loss function. We are not using the validation loss right now for a few reasons. We would need to add more code to our `train_network` function to support it, since our Seq2Seq model changes its output at evaluation time. A bigger issue is that the loss function we are using is not very intuitive to look at. Still, we plot the training loss afterward to make sure it's going down, to confirm that learning is happening:

```
seq2seq_results = train_network(seq2seq, CrossEntLossTime,
    train_loader,epochs=epochs, device=device)

sns.lineplot(x='epoch', y='train loss', data=seq2seq_results,
    label='Seq2Seq')
```

`[19]:` `<AxesSubplot:xlabel='epoch', ylabel='train loss'>`

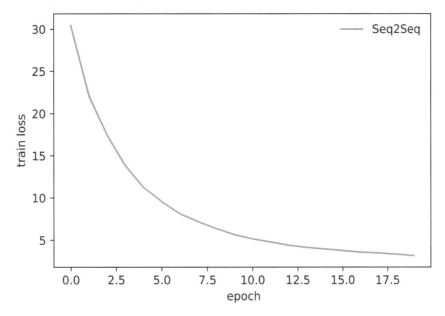

BLEU about validation loss?

Evaluating Seq2Seq models can be particularly challenging. How do you know if a translation is bad when there are multiple valid translations? This is something we are ignoring during training, yet somehow the model still works surprisingly well.

The loss function we used for training is what people use to train Seq2Seq models in general, but people tend to use different evaluation metrics to determine how good their model is. These evaluation metrics are fairly complicated, so we stick with a more subjective evaluation to avoid adding too much to this chapter. If you want to learn more, machine translation is normally evaluated against BLEU (https://en.wikipedia.org /wiki/BLEU) scores. But BLEU may not be the best metric if you are not doing a translation task, as BLEU is specifically designed for translation.

VISUALIZING ATTENTION SCORE MAPS

Looking at the loss of the network, we can clearly see that it has decreased during training. To help us evaluate the results, we can make some translations and look at the attention mechanism's results. This will be a subjective analysis, but I encourage performing a subjective evaluation whenever working with Seq2Seq models. Objective evaluations tend to be difficult when you have many-to-many mappings, so getting dirty with the data helps build an understanding of what is happening. At each time step t, the attention mechanism tells us which input words were considered important for predicting each output word. This can help us understand whether the model is learning something reasonable.

We define the following `plot_heatmap` function to quickly plot the attention results. The `results` function will use it to take in an input, translate it to French, and show the prediction, attention, and true translation:

```
def plot_heatmap(src, trg, scores):
    fig, ax = plt.subplots()
    heatmap = ax.pcolor(scores, cmap='gray')

    ax.set_xticklabels(trg, minor=False, rotation='vertical')
    ax.set_yticklabels(src, minor=False)
    ax.xaxis.tick_top()    ◄─────────  Puts the major ticks at the middle
    ax.set_xticks(np.arange(scores.shape[1]) + 0.5, minor=False)   of each cell and the x-ticks on top
    ax.set_yticks(np.arange(scores.shape[0]) + 0.5, minor=False)
    ax.invert_yaxis()

    plt.colorbar(heatmap)
    plt.show()
```

Before defining the results function, let's quickly put our `seq2seq` model into evaluation mode. This way, we get the attention maps. Then the function can use our inverse map `indx2word` to see what the original data and predictions should have been. We print out the input and target, along with `seq2seq`'s prediction. At the end, we show the heat map of the attention scores that will help us subjectively evaluate the results. The input to this function is simply the index into the test set that we want to consider:

```
seq2seq = seq2seq.eval().cpu()
def results(indx):
    eng_x, french_y = test_dataset[indx]
    eng_str = " ".join([indx2word[i] for i in eng_x.cpu().numpy()])
    french_str = " ".join([indx2word[i] for i in french_y.cpu().numpy()])
    print("Input:     ", eng_str)
    print("Target:    ", french_str)

    with torch.no_grad():
        preds, attention = seq2seq(eng_x.unsqueeze(0))
        p = torch.argmax(preds, dim=2)
    pred_str = " ".join([indx2word[i] for i in p[0,:].cpu().numpy()])
    print("Predicted: ", pred_str)
    plot_heatmap(eng_str.split(" "), pred_str.split(" "),
    ➥ attention.T.cpu().numpy())
```

Now we can look at some results. You may get slightly different results, depending on your model's training run. For the first sentence, I get the translation "les animaux ont peur du feu," which Google Translate says translates back into the English sentence "some animals are afraid of fire." In this case, the model had a different result that was *mostly* correct, but it used "les," which translates as "the" instead of the more appropriate "certain."

The attention map shows that "les" was indeed looking at the correct part of the input ("some") but maybe focusing too much on the start of the sentence. If I had to guess, "the" is just a more common start of a sentence than "some," and the network made the error based on that. But we can also see that "du feu" correctly attends to the "of fire" portion of the input to produce the correct output. While the math is not perfect, the model picked a word with a similar meaning for understandable reasons.

We can also see how we can use the action mechanism to better understand our model's results. This is something very powerful about attention mechanisms: they give us a degree of *interpretability* in our otherwise opaque neural networks. In this case, maybe we need to get more diverse sentences with a variety of starting tokens/phrases.

Here's the code:

```
results(12)

Input:      <SOS> some animals are afraid of fire <EOS>
Target:     certains animaux craignent le feu <EOS>
Predicted:  les animaux ont peur du feu <EOS> <EOS>
```

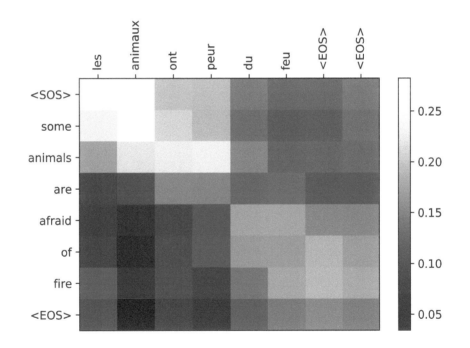

The next translation shows the result for a sentence for which I often see translations with greater differences. Here we get "quel temps fait il aujourd'hui" as the translation, changing the first four words from the original target of "comment est le temps." While different than the target, the result is still a reasonably correct translation. This shows both that Seq2Seq has some very difficult things to learn around and the power of this approach to successfully learn despite these issues. This is also why evaluating the equality of machine translation tasks can be very difficult. The attention mechanism is not quite as crisp in this example since no individual word used means "weather" in this case.

Here's the code:

```
results(13)

Input:      <SOS> what is the weather like today <EOS>
Target:     comment est le temps aujourd'hui <EOS>
Predicted:  quel temps fait il aujourd'hui <EOS> <EOS> <EOS>
```

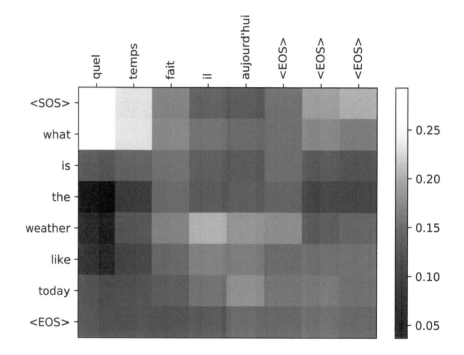

The next example shows another reasonable translation—Google Translate returns the same result for me. It looks like the model may have swapped out some synonyms or changed a gendered word, but I would need to know French to be sure. This is part of why I love machine learning—I can get computers to do the many things I'm incapable of on my own:

```
results(16)

Input:      <SOS> no one disagreed <EOS>
Target:     personne ne fut en désaccord <EOS>
Predicted:  personne n'exprima de désaccord <EOS>
```

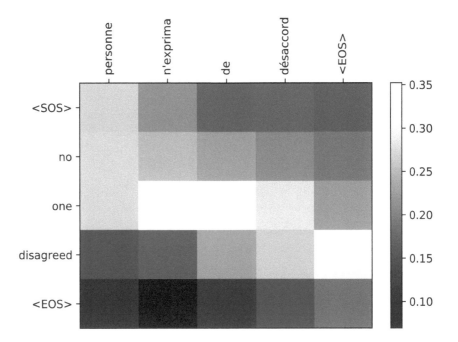

If you had the computational resources to do a larger training set and also had more time, you could get results like the translation we showed at the start of the chapter in figure 11.1. Not only does this show a longer sentence being converted from French to English, but a more refined output from the attention mechanism. It becomes obvious which exact word is being translated, and you can see the model correctly changes the order of "zone économique européenne" to "European Economic Area," adapting to the linguistic nuances of the language.

While the previous code is still missing one major trick to maximize performance, this is not a toy implementation. This same approach has been used in real-world machine translation systems and was only supplanted by new approaches in 2019.

Exercises

Share and discuss your solutions on the Manning online platform at Inside Deep Learning Exercises (https://liveproject.manning.com/project/945). Once you submit your own answers, you will be able to see the solutions submitted by other readers, and see which ones the author judges to be the best.

1. By default, the decoder users h_T as its initial hidden state. Try changing it to use an average of the decoder's outputs, $\frac{1}{T}\sum_{t=1}^{T} h_t$.

2. Our Seq2Seq was hardcoded to DotScore. Try using GeneralScore and your new initialization of GeneralScore on the translation task. Does your evaluation show one performing better or worse than the others?

3 **Challenging:** Create a new dataset for an image addition task. Make the input a random number of MNIST images and the output value a sequence of characters denoting the sum of the digits. So the input may be a sequence of the images for 6, 1, and 9, then the output should be the string "16." Then modify the Seq2Seq model to train and run on this problem. *Hint:* Modify the encoder and `collate_fn`.

4 Write out the reasons why the task in exercise 3 is challenging. What things will the network need to learn to solve the problem? Try to articulate how many different mental concepts and tasks exist to solve the problem and how they are explicitly or implicitly defined by the loss of the network.

5 Modify the Seq2Seq model to use LSTM layers instead of GRU ones. This will require some extra tracking for the LSTM's own context results.

6 Try training models that do not use *any* teacher forcing—only the autoregressive approach. How do they perform comparatively?

Summary

- We can train a denoising autoencoding-like model called sequence-to-sequence for solving problems with a many-to-many mapping.

- Machine translation is a many-to-many problem that we can implement and do well with a Seq2Seq model.

- Attention scores can be used as an interpretable output of the model, allowing us to better understand how the model makes decisions.

- The autoregressive approach can be combined with teacher forcing to help the model learn faster and better.

Network design alternatives to RNNs

Recurrent neural networks—in particular, LSTMs—have been used for classifying and working with sequence problems for over two decades. While they have long been reliable tools for the task, they have several undesirable properties. First, RNNs are just plain slow. They take a long time to train, which means waiting around for results. Second, they do not scale well with more layers (hard to improve model accuracy) or with more GPUs (hard to make them train faster). With skip connections and residual layers, we have learned about many ways to get fully connected and convolutional networks to train with more layers to get better results. But RNNs just do not seem to like being deep. You can add more layers and skip connections, but they do not show the same degree of benefits as improved accuracy.

In this chapter, we look at some methods that can help us with one or both of these problems. First, we tackle the slowness of RNNs by violating our prior beliefs. We use RNNs because we know the data is a sequence, but we pretend that it is not a normal sequence so we can do something faster—and potentially less accurate. Next, we look at a different way of representing the sequential component of our data to augment these faster alternatives and regain some of our accuracy.

Finally, we learn about transformers (no, not the copyrighted kind), which are even slower to train but scale much better with depth and powerful compute devices. Transformer-based models are quickly becoming foundational to the highest accuracy solutions for many tasks in natural language processing and are likely to become a large part of your life as a practitioner.

12.1 TorchText: Tools for text problems

To help us test the relative pros and cons of many alternatives to RNNs, the first thing we need is a dataset and some baseline results. For this chapter, I briefly introduce and use the `torchtext` package. Like `torchvision`, it is a subproject of PyTorch. Whereas `torchvision` provides extra tooling specifically for vision-based problems, `torchtext` provides extra tooling around text-based ones. We won't go into all the special features it contains; we are simply going to use it for easy access to a harder dataset.

12.1.1 Installing TorchText

The first thing to do is quickly make sure `torchtext` and the optional dependency `sentencepiece` are installed; otherwise, we won't be able to get all of our desired features to work. The following code installs both when run via Colab (or any Jupyter notebook):

```
# !conda install -c pytorch torchtext
# !conda install -c powerai sentencepiece
# !pip install  torchtext
# !pip install  sentencepiece
```

12.1.2 Loading datasets in TorchText

Now we can import `torchtext` and the associated `datasets` package, where we will load the AG News dataset. This dataset has four classes, and `torchtext` will provide the utilities to get us ready for training quickly. But first we import the package, get the dataset iterators (this is how `torchtext` likes to provide data), and place the train and test data in their own respective lists:

```
import torchtext
from torchtext.datasets import AG_NEWS

train_iter, test_iter = AG_NEWS(root='./data', split=('train', 'test'))
train_dataset = list(train_iter)
test_dataset = list(test_iter)
```

Now we have loaded the AG News dataset, which has four possible topic classes for each document: World, Sports, Business, and Sci/Tech. The following block of code prints out an example of this dataset. We have a `string` of words representing our input x and a label for the class y. `torchtext` unfortunately bucks the normal trend of returning tuples ordered by data/input first and label second (x, y) and instead swaps the order as (y, x):

```
print(train_dataset[0])

(3, "Wall St. Bears Claw Back Into the Black (Reuters) Reuters - Short-
sellers, Wall Street's dwindling\\band of
ultra-cynics, are seeing green again.")
```

We need to break up each sentence into a set of discrete tokens (i.e., words) and build a vocabulary (Σ) to map each word to a unique integer value, because the `nn.Embedding` layer only takes integer inputs. `torchtext` provides a few tools for making this pretty painless and working with some of the existing Python tooling. Python brings the `Counter` object to count how many times different tokens are seen, and `torchtext` provides a `tokenizer` and `Vocab` object to split up strings and do the bookkeeping for us:

```
from torchtext.data.utils import get_tokenizer
tokenizer = get_tokenizer('basic_english')

from collections import Counter
from torchtext.vocab import Vocab

counter = Counter()
for (label, line) in train_dataset:
    counter.update(tokenizer(line))
vocab = Vocab(counter, min_freq=10,
    specials=('<unk>', '<SOS>', '<EOS>', '<PAD>'))
```

Tokenizers break strings like "this is a string" into lists of tokens like ['this', 'is', 'a', 'string'].

We are fine with the default English style tokenizer.

How many lines in this dataset

We need to create a vocabulary of all the words in the training set.

Counts the number of unique tokens and how often we see them (e.g., we see "the" a lot, but "sasquatch" maybe once or not at all)

Loops through the training data

Creates a vocab object, removing any word that didn't occur at least 10 times, and adds special vocab items for unknown, start of sentence, end of sentence, and padding

Now we need two more helper functions to complete the `torchtext` specific setup. `text_transform` takes in a string and converts it into a list of integers based on the vocabulary Σ. The other, simpler item is `label_transform`, which makes sure the labels are in the right format (you may have to change this more for different datasets in torchtext):

```
def text_transform(x):
    return [vocab['<SOS>']] + [vocab[token]
        for token in tokenizer(x)] + [vocab['<EOS>']]

def label_transform(x):
    return x-1
```

String to a list of integers

vocab acts like a dictionary and handles unknown tokens. We can make it pre- and post-pend with the start and end markers, respectively.

Labels are originally [1, 2, 3, 4], but we need [0, 1, 2, 3].

```
print(text_transform(train_dataset[0][1]))
```
← Transforms the first data point's text into a list of tokens

```
[1, 434, 428, 4, 1608, 14841, 116, 69, 5, 851, 16, 30, 17, 30, 18, 0, 6, 434,
377, 19, 12, 0, 9, 0, 6, 45, 4012, 786, 328, 4, 2]
```

The torchtext specifics are basically out of the way now; we can do some initial PyTorch ceremony to get set up. We want to note how many tokens are in our vocabulary and the number of classes, and decide on the embedding dimension, batch size, and number of training epochs. I've chosen some arbitrary values for each in the following starting code. We also save the integer representing our padding token "<PAD>" because we will need it for batching up our datasets:

```
VOCAB_SIZE = len(vocab)
NUM_CLASS = len(np.unique([z[0] for z in train_dataset]))
print("Vocab: ", VOCAB_SIZE)
print("Num Classes: ", NUM_CLASS)

padding_idx = vocab["<PAD>"]

embed_dim = 128
B = 64
epochs = 15

Vocab:  20647
Num Classes:  4
```

We also define the function we use as our collate_fn for the DataLoader class in PyTorch. collate_fn is generally the best place to implement padding, as it allows you to pad by exactly the minimum amount needed for the current batch of data. It is also a convenient place to reverse the label and input order to match the standard (input, label) pattern we expect. That way, our returned batches will follow (x, y) like the rest of our code expects, and we can reuse everything we've done so far.

All of this is done in the pad_batch function, which follows a normal approach to padding. We first determine what the longest sequence is of all the items in the batch and store its value in the max_len variable. Then we use the F.pad function to pad to the *right* of each item in the batch. This makes all the items the same length so we can stack them into a single tensor. Notice that we make sure to use the padding_idx for the value to pad by:

```
def pad_batch(batch):
    """
    Pad items in the batch to the length of the longest item in the batch.
    Also, re-order so that the values are returned (input, label)
    """
    labels = [label_transform(z[0]) for z in batch]       ← Gets and transforms every label in the batch
    texts = [torch.tensor(text_transform(z[1]),           ← Gets and tokenizes every text and puts them into a tensor
        dtype=torch.int64) for z in batch]
    max_len = max([text.size(0) for text in texts])       ← What is the longest sequence in this batch?

    texts = [F.pad(text, (0,max_len-text.size(0)),        ← Pads each text tensor by whatever amount makes it max_len
        value=padding_idx) for text in texts]
```

Makes x
and y a
single
tensor

```
x, y = torch.stack(texts), torch.tensor(labels, dtype=torch.int64)
return x, y
```

Now we can build our `DataLoaders` as we have done many times before to feed data to our models. Thanks to the `Dataset` abstraction, we don't have to know the details about how `torchtext` implemented its loaders, and we can see that by setting `collate_fn=pad_batch`, we can work around any quirks a dataset may have by how it returns data. Instead of rewriting the dataset, our chosen `collate_fn` simply cleans up the output of the `Dataset` the way we want:

```
train_loader = DataLoader(train_dataset, batch_size=B, shuffle=True,
    collate_fn=pad_batch)
test_loader = DataLoader(test_dataset, batch_size=B, collate_fn=pad_batch)
```

12.1.3 *Defining a baseline model*

Now that we have our dataset collate function and loaders ready, we can train some models. Let's start by implementing a baseline RNN model to which we can compare each alternative, giving us a barometer to judge pros and cons. We'll use a gated recurrent unit (GRU)-based RNN with three bidirectional layers to try to maximize the accuracy we get. We're using a GRU here because it's faster than an LSTM, and we want to give it every chance it can get to win the runtime comparisons we will explore. While we could explore different hidden dimension sizes, learning rates, and other knobs, this is a pretty straightforward and standard first attempt I would use for an RNN. So let's pick our loss function and call our handy-dandy `train_network`:

```
gru = nn.Sequential(
    nn.Embedding(VOCAB_SIZE, embed_dim,              ←——— (B, T) -> (B, T, D)
        padding_idx=padding_idx),
                                                     (B, T, D) -> ( (B,T,D) , (S, B, D) )
    nn.GRU(embed_dim, embed_dim, num_layers=3,  ←
        batch_first=True, bidirectional=True),
                                                     We need to take the RNN output
                                                     and reduce it to one item, (B, 2*D).
    LastTimeStep(rnn_layers=3, bidirectional=True), ←
    nn.Linear(embed_dim*2, NUM_CLASS),          ←——— (B, D) -> (B, classes)
)

loss_func = nn.CrossEntropyLoss()
gru_results = train_network(gru, loss_func, train_loader,
    val_loader=test_loader, score_funcs={'Accuracy': accuracy_score},
    device=device, epochs=epochs)
```

Our first attempt's result is shown next and seems to be doing reasonably well, with some overfitting after the first few epochs but stabilizing around 91.5% accuracy. Through the rest of this chapter, as we develop new alternatives, we plot them onto the same figure to get an overall comparison. For example, we want to think about max accuracy (if we regularize better, what we might be able to achieve), stabilized accuracy (what can we get with little effort), and epochs until some level of accuracy (how long we need to train).

Here's the code:

```
sns.lineplot(x='epoch', y='val Accuracy', data=gru_results, label='GRU')
```

```
[16]:  <AxesSubplot:xlabel='epoch', ylabel='val Accuracy'>
```

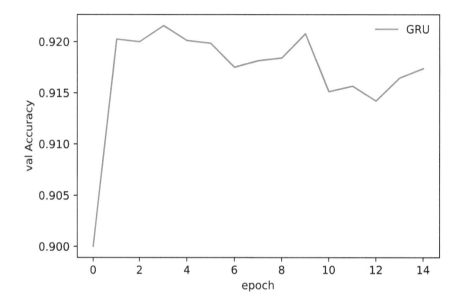

12.2 *Averaging embeddings over time*

The GRU baseline is ready for us to compare against, so let's learn our first new approach to handling a variable-length sequence classification problem. Instead of performing complex RNN operations over the time series, we just *average* all the items in the sequence. So if we have an input of shape (B, T, D), we compute the mean value along the second axis, creating a new tensor of shape (B, D). It has the benefit of being very simple to implement; it is fast; and it *removes the time dimension*, allowing us to then apply whatever approaches we desire (such as residual connections) after that point. Figure 12.1 shows what this looks like.

Because we are averaging over the time dimension, we ignore that there is an order to the data. Another way to say this is that we are *ignoring the structure* of the data to simplify our model. We *might* want to do this to make our training and prediction faster, but it could also backfire and give us worse-quality results.

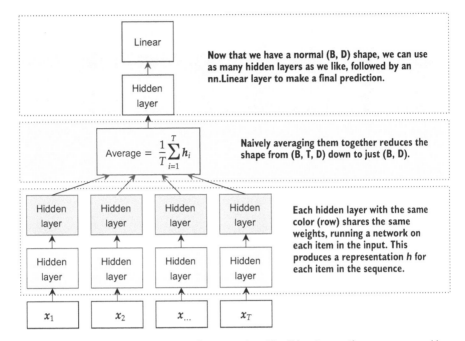

Now that we have a normal (B, D) shape, we can use as many hidden layers as we like, followed by an nn.Linear layer to make a final prediction.

$$\text{Average} = \frac{1}{T}\sum_{i=1}^{T} h_i$$

Naively averaging them together reduces the shape from (B, T, D) down to just (B, D).

Each hidden layer with the same color (row) shares the same weights, running a network on each item in the input. This produces a representation *h* for each item in the sequence.

x_1 x_2 $x_{...}$ x_T

Figure 12.1 Example of averaging embeddings over time. The T inputs over time are processed by the same neural network via weight sharing. Because there are no connections across time, the model is unaware that there is an order to them. The time dimension is resolved by simply averaging all of the representations so a regular fully connected network can run afterward to produce the output.

One simple way we can implement averaging over time is to use the adaptive pooling we learned about in chapter 8. Adaptive pooling works by taking the *desired output size* and adjusting the pooling size to force the output to have the desired size. The Faster R-CNN used adaptive pooling to shrink any input down to a 7×7 grid. Instead, we will be a little exploitive of how adaptive pooling works. If our input has a shape of (B, T, D), we want to perform adaptive pooling over the last two dimensions, so we use adaptive 2D pooling. We make the target shape for the pooling non-symmetric with a shape of $(1, D)$. Our input already has a shape of D in the last dimension, so the last dimension will not be altered. The time dimension shrinks down to 1, forcing it to be averaged over time. Because of its adaptive pooling, this code will work even if the value T changes between batches. We can define and try this model very quickly in the following code.

As mentioned before, this code relies on the fact that if you give a PyTorch nn.Linear layer a tensor of shape (B, T, D), it will apply the linear layer to all T different inputs independently, effectively performing weight sharing in a single call. We call nn.AdaptiveAvgPool2d with the explicit target shape of $(1, D)$ that reduces the input tensor from (B, T, D) down to $(B, 1, D)$. Then we can end with one hidden layer and a nn.Linear to predict the classes:

```
simpleEmbdAvg = nn.Sequential(
    nn.Embedding(VOCAB_SIZE, embed_dim, padding_idx=padding_idx),  ←⎤
    nn.Linear(embed_dim, embed_dim),                         (B, T) -> (B, T, D)
    nn.LeakyReLU(),
    nn.Linear(embed_dim, embed_dim),
    nn.LeakyReLU(),
    nn.Linear(embed_dim, embed_dim),
    nn.LeakyReLU(),
    nn.AdaptiveAvgPool2d((1,embed_dim)),      ←—— (B, T, D) -> (B, 1, D)
    nn.Flatten(),                             ←—— (B, 1, D) -> (B, D)
    nn.Linear(embed_dim, embed_dim),
    nn.LeakyReLU(),
    nn.BatchNorm1d(embed_dim),
    nn.Linear(embed_dim, NUM_CLASS)
)
simpleEmbdAvg_results = train_network(simpleEmbdAvg, loss_func, train_loader,
⟿ val_loader=test_loader, score_funcs={'Accuracy': accuracy_score},
⟿ device=device, epochs=epochs)
```

The next two lines of code plot the results. Looking at the accuracy of these two approaches, we see that the GRU performs better. If you run this multiple times, you might find that the average embedding approach sometimes starts to overfit the data. So at *first glance*, this alternative was not worthwhile:

```
sns.lineplot(x='epoch', y='val Accuracy', data=gru_results, label='GRU')
sns.lineplot(x='epoch', y='val Accuracy', data=simpleEmbdAvg_results,
⟿ label='Average Embedding')
```

```
[18]:  <AxesSubplot:xlabel='epoch', ylabel='val Accuracy'>
```

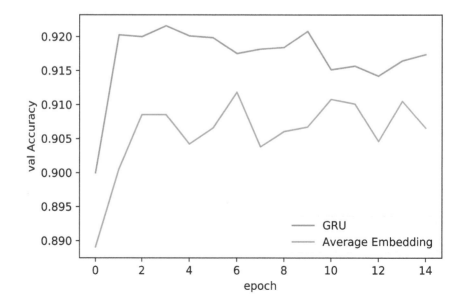

But we should ask why the averaged embeddings work at all. We implemented this approach by *ignoring* something we know to be true about the data: that it has a sequential order and that the order matters. You can't just rearrange the words in a sentence and get an intelligible result.

The averaged embedding approach can get reasonable accuracy because there are often ways to cheat at a problem. For example, the four classes of AG news are World, Sports, Business, and Sci/Tech. So if your model sees a sentence with the words "NFL," "touchdown," and "win," it does not really matter what order those words occurred in. You can probably guess from the existence of the words alone that this is a Sports article. Similarly, if you see the words "banking" and "acquisition," you can tell there is a good chance it's a Business article without knowing anything else about the sentence.

The average embeddings can get reasonable accuracy because we don't always *need* our prior to do OK. The potential benefit of the average embeddings comes into play when we look at the time it takes to train the model. The following code re-creates the figure but with `total_time` on the x-axis. This makes it clear that training the average embeddings is around three times faster than the GRU model. If you had a huge dataset where training a GRU could take a week, a 3× speedup becomes pretty attractive:

```
sns.lineplot(x='total time', y='val Accuracy', data=gru_results, label='GRU')
sns.lineplot(x='total time', y='val Accuracy', data=simpleEmbdAvg_results,
    label='Average Embedding')
```

[19]: <AxesSubplot:xlabel='total time', ylabel='val Accuracy'>

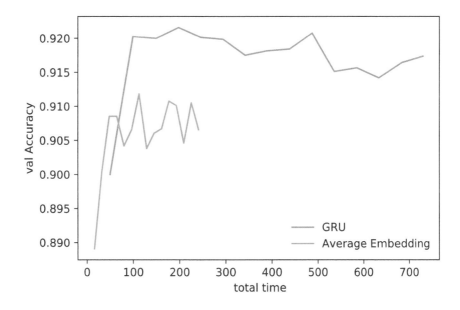

Averaging the embeddings ultimately violates a prior belief that the data has an order and the order is important, in exchange for a simpler and faster model. I often build models like this simply because I'm working on a large amount of data and I want to get some initial results more quickly. But this is also an exercise in a larger task: learning to recognize when you have an acceptable model that violates things you believe.

In this specific scenario, we can explain *why* a model that violates what we believe (time is important) works (single words are too informative). In the future, you may find that a dumber model like this performs suspiciously well, and a good practitioner shouldn't take good result at face value. If you can't rationalize *why* a model that violates this assumption is working, you should do a deep dive into your data until you can. Look at the examples the model gets correct and wrong, and try to figure out how the model is learning to do the job. Are there any obvious patterns to the data points the model gets wrong or right? Is there something in the input data that should not be there? Does something innocuous like the length correlate surprisingly well with the goal?

I can't tell you in advance *how* to do this process other than to be *incredulous* about your model's success. Put yourself in the mindset of a cheater, and try to figure out ways to cheat at the problem. Label some data by hand and see if you can come up with different ideas for getting answers, and look at how your approach matches your model's biases. For example, if you can label a sentence by picking out just a few keywords, the sequential order of the words isn't as critical as you thought.

In doing this process, you may come across a case of *information leakage*, where information about the label is erroneously or unrealistically seeping into your training data. Discovering this is a good thing and means you need to fix the information leakage before doing any more model development, because it will taint any model you try to build. In my experience, overly simple modeling that works far better than I expected almost always denotes leakage that I eventually find.

How does information leakage happen?

Information leakage can happen infinite possible ways when you're building your data if something strongly *correlated* with your label y exists in the data but the correlation does not naturally exist. Instead, it is an artifact of the process used to create and organize the data, often due to a bug in the data preparation. People often accidentally *place the label y into the input features x*, which the model quickly learns to exploit!

I'll give you an example from some of my published work on building malware detection models.[a] Many people were using data from a clean install of Microsoft Windows to represent benign or safe data. Then they found some malware online and built a classifier that appeared to have *near perfect* accuracy. When we dove into the data, we found that almost everything Microsoft releases comes with the string "Copyright Microsoft Corporation." This string ended up *leaking* information that the label was "benign" because it occurred only in benign data and never in malware data. But in reality, the string "Copyright Microsoft Corporation" has nothing to do with a file being malware or not, so the models would not work well on new data.

Information leakage can also occur in silly or subtle ways. There is an apocryphal tale (https://www.gwern.net/Tanks) about the military wanting to build an ML model to detect if a tank was present in an image sometime between 1960 and 2000. The story goes (as I first heard it) that they collected a bunch of images of tanks and images of empty fields and trained a network that got perfect accuracy. But every picture of a tank had the sun present in the image, and the non-tank images did not include the sun. The model learned to detect the sun instead of tanks, because it was easier to recognize. This never really happened, but the story is a fun tale about how information can leak in unexpected ways.

<hr>

[a] E. Raff et al., "An investigation of byte n-gram features for malware classification," *J Comput Virol Hack Tech*, vol. 14, pp. 1–20, 2018, https://doi.org/10.1007/s11416-016-0283-1.

12.2.1 *Weighted average over time with attention*

While the code we implemented earlier works, it is *slightly* incorrect. Why? Because `nn.AdaptiveAvgPool2d` has no idea about the padded inputs, which result in embeddings of the value 0. This has the impact of shrinking the magnitude of shorter sequences. Let's take a look at how. Suppose, for simplicity, that we are embedding tokens into just one dimension. So maybe we have three data points that look like this:

$$\begin{array}{cccccc} \boldsymbol{x}_1 = & 2 & 3 & 5 \\ \boldsymbol{x}_2 = & 4 & 2 & 4 & 6 & 1 \\ \boldsymbol{x}_3 = & 3 & 4 & 4 & 1 \end{array}$$

When we compute the average value for each item, we want to get this:

$$\begin{array}{lll} \bar{\boldsymbol{x}}_1 = & \frac{2+3+5}{3} & = 3.333\ldots \\ \bar{\boldsymbol{x}}_2 = & \frac{4+2+4+6+1}{5} & = 3.4 \\ \bar{\boldsymbol{x}}_3 = & \frac{3+4+4+1}{4} & = 3 \end{array}$$

But we have padded everything in this batch to have the same length as the longest item in the batch! The padding values are all zeros, so what is computed becomes

$$\begin{array}{lll} \bar{\boldsymbol{x}}_1 = & \frac{2+3+5+0+0}{5} & = 2 \\ \bar{\boldsymbol{x}}_2 = & \frac{4+2+4+6+1}{5} & = 3.4 \\ \bar{\boldsymbol{x}}_3 = & \frac{3+4+4+1+0}{5} & = 2.4 \end{array}$$

This has significantly changed the values of $\bar{\boldsymbol{x}}_1$ and $\bar{\boldsymbol{x}}_3$! To fix this, we need to implement the averaging ourselves in the same way we computed the context vector for our attention mechanism in the previous chapter.

But if we compute that context vector, why not apply the attention mechanism? The attention will learn a weighted average of all the input words and could hypothetically learn to ignore certain words based on all the information available.

To try this, we will implement a new `Module` that does the embedding and computes a mask based on which values were padded or not. Since the mask has a shape of (B, T), we can take the sum over the second time dimension to know how many valid items are in each batch. Then we can sum over all the items over time, divide by the appropriate value, and get the context vector to pass along to our previously defined attention mechanism.

The following code implements an `EmbeddingAttentionBad` class that does the work of putting each input token through an embedding layer, running some hidden layers (with shared weights across time), and then applying one of our attention mechanisms from chapter 10 to compute a weighted average result. It needs to know the `vocab_size` and the embedding dimension `D` as arguments, with an optional `embd_layers` to change the number of hidden layers and `padding_idx` to tell it what values are used to denote padding:

```python
class EmbeddingAttentionBag(nn.Module):

    def __init__(self, vocab_size, D, embd_layers=3, padding_idx=None):
        super(EmbeddingAttentionBag, self).__init__()
        self.padding_idx = padding_idx
        self.embd = nn.Embedding(vocab_size, D, padding_idx=padding_idx)
        if isinstance(embd_layers, int):
            self.embd_layers = nn.Sequential(          # ← (B, T, D) -> (B, T, D)
                *[nn.Sequential(nn.Linear(embed_dim, embed_dim),
                nn.LeakyReLU()) for _ in range(embd_layers)]
            )
        else:
            self.embd_layers = embd_layers
        self.attn = AttentionAvg(AdditiveAttentionScore(D))   # ← Functions defined in chapter 10

    def forward(self, input):
        """
        input: (B, T) shape, dtype=int64
        output: (B, D) shape, dtype=float32
        """
        if self.padding_idx is not None:
            mask = input != self.padding_idx
        else:                                          # All entries are True.
            mask = input == input                      #  mask is shape (B, T).
        x = self.embd(input)                           # ← (B, T, D)
        x = self.embd_layers(x)                        # ← (B, T, D)
        context = x.sum(dim=1)/(mask.sum(dim=1).unsqueeze(1)+1e-5)
        return self.attn(x, context, mask=mask)        # ← If we wanted to do normal averaging, we could return the context variable right now! ((B, T, D), (B, D)) -> (B, D).
```

Averages over time. (B, T, D) -> (B, D).

With this new module, we can build a simple new network in the following code block. It starts with the `EmbeddingAttentionBag` that computes the embedding, hidden layers shared over time, and attention. Then we follow up a hidden layer and `nn.Linear` to produce a prediction:

```python
attnEmbd = nn.Sequential(                              # ← Now we can define a simple model!
    EmbeddingAttentionBag(VOCAB_SIZE, embed_dim,
    padding_idx=padding_idx),                          # ← (B, T) -> (B, D)
    nn.Linear(embed_dim, embed_dim),
    nn.LeakyReLU(),
```

```
        nn.BatchNorm1d(embed_dim),
        nn.Linear(embed_dim, NUM_CLASS)
    )
attnEmbd_results = train_network(attnEmbd, loss_func, train_loader,
    val_loader=test_loader, score_funcs={'Accuracy': accuracy_score},
    device=device, epochs=epochs)
```

Now we can plot the results. The attention-based embedding takes a little longer to train but is still over 2× faster than the RNN. This makes sense since the attention version is doing more operations. We can also see that attention has improved our model's accuracy, getting very close to the GRU. It suffers from more overfitting as the attention embedding's accuracy begins to plummet with more updates:

```
sns.lineplot(x='total time', y='val Accuracy', data=gru_results, label='GRU')
sns.lineplot(x='total time', y='val Accuracy', data=simpleEmbdAvg_results,
    label='Average Embedding')
sns.lineplot(x='total time', y='val Accuracy', data=attnEmbd_results,
    label='Attention Embedding')
```

```
[22]:   <AxesSubplot:xlabel='total time', ylabel='val Accuracy'>
```

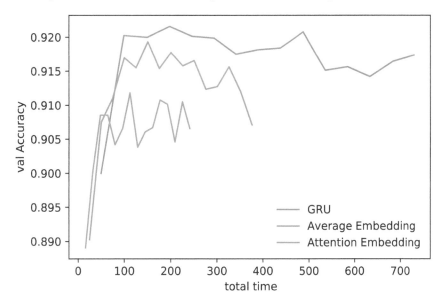

The biggest issue with the attention embedding is *still* that it lacks any sense about the order of words in the sentence. This is the time component of the model that is lacking. To further highlight it, let's show another way to look at the problem. Consider the input sentence "the red fox chased the blue dog." Our model embeds each word into its vector representation, and we are ultimately performing some kind of averaging over the embeddings (weighted or unweighted, depending on whether you used attention). Let's look at how this sentence works if we have an embedding dimension of $D = 1$ and the dimension's value is set to integers. That gives us the following setup:

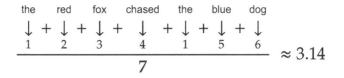

$$\frac{\underset{1}{\downarrow} + \underset{2}{\downarrow} + \underset{3}{\downarrow} + \underset{4}{\downarrow} + \underset{1}{\downarrow} + \underset{5}{\downarrow} + \underset{6}{\downarrow}}{7} \approx 3.14$$

This equation shows an unweighted average, but making it a weighted average would just change the value at the end—the fundamental flaw of not understanding the sequential nature of the data remains. So, for example, if we switch "fox" and "dog" in the sentence, the meaning changes—but the embedding approach will *return the same result*. This is shown in the following equation and demonstrates how the network cannot detect subtle changes in meaning:

the   red   dog   chased   the   blue   fox

$$\frac{\underset{1}{\downarrow} + \underset{2}{\downarrow} + \underset{6}{\downarrow} + \underset{4}{\downarrow} + \underset{1}{\downarrow} + \underset{5}{\downarrow} + \underset{3}{\downarrow}}{7} \approx 3.14$$

This can be a particular problem if there is a risk of very noisy data. The next example randomly rearranges all the words in the sentence. The meaning of the sentence is lost, but the model still insists that nothing has changed. All of these examples are equivalent to the embedding-based models:

the   chased   the   blue   red   dog   fox

$$\frac{\underset{1}{\downarrow} + \underset{4}{\downarrow} + \underset{1}{\downarrow} + \underset{5}{\downarrow} + \underset{2}{\downarrow} + \underset{6}{\downarrow} + \underset{3}{\downarrow}}{7} \approx 3.14$$

The more important sequence order is for solving a problem, the more the current approach of averaging the vectors will struggle to make a correct classification. This applies to the attention-based version as well, because it is not aware of order. Each word h_i is assigned a weight α_i based on a context $\bar{h}$, so it does not see the information that is missing! This makes the utility of the averaging approach very problem-specific for complex problems. Think about any situation where negation language like "not," "isn't," or "didn't" is used in a sentence. With negation, language order is critical. These are the kinds of things you should think about as the costs of getting faster training time with an embedding approach.

> NOTE Since I'm talking about the cons, it's still worth noting that the attention-based embeddings got *very* close to the GRU's accuracy. What does that mean? If I saw these results on a dataset, I would have two initial hypotheses: (1) the order of my data is not as important as I thought for the problem at hand, or (2) I need a larger RNN with more layers or more hidden neurons to capture the complex information present in the order of the data. I would investigate hypothesis #2 first

by training a bigger model, because that just takes compute time. Investigating hypothesis #1 takes my personal time to dig into the data, and I usually value my time over a computer's. If there is a way to answer the question by running a new model, I prefer to do that.

12.3 Pooling over time and 1D CNNs

Since we have identified the lack of sequence order information as a serious bottleneck to better results, let's try a different strategy that keeps *some* of the time information but not all of it. We have already learned about and used convolutions, which include a spatial prior: that things near each other are likely to be related. That captures a lot of the sequential ordering that our previous embedding approach lacked. RNNs and 1D convolutions operate on similarly shaped tensors, as shown in figure 12.2.

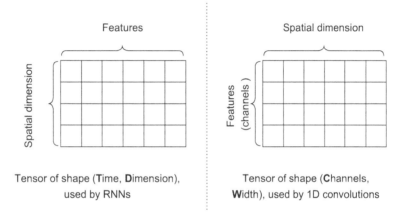

Figure 12.2 Example showing the tensor shapes used by RNNs (left) and 1D convolutions (right), without the first batch dimension. In each case, we have one axis for the tensor representing something spatial (T versus W) and one representing features at a location (D versus C).

This shows that 1D convolutions and RNNs have the same shape but slightly different meanings *assigned* to each axis. The RNN's *spatial* dimension is at index 1 for the time axis T. The 1D convolution's spatial dimension is at index 2 with the width of the input data (similar to the width of an image!). For the spatial prior, RNNs are assigning the belief that the exact order of all items is important. By contrast, a convolution is assigning the belief that only nearby items are related. Both an RNN and a CNN encode feature information about a specific item in the sequence; they simply assign different interpretations to that data.

The 1D convolution's sense of time and order is weaker than that of an RNN, but it is *better than nothing*. For example, negation words usually occur right before the word they are trying to negate, so 1D CNNs could capture that simple spatial relationship. If we can rearrange our tensor so that the spatial dimension matches what the convolution expects, we can use a 1D CNN to capture some information about time and use it as our classifier. Figure 12.3 shows that we can do this rearrangement by permuting the axes of the tensor.

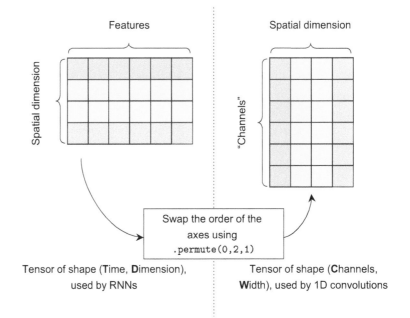

Figure 12.3 Features

Spatial dimension

Spatial dimension

"Channels"

Swap the order of the axes using `.permute(0,2,1)`

Tensor of shape (**T**ime, **D**imension), used by RNNs

Tensor of shape (**C**hannels, **W**idth), used by 1D convolutions

Figure 12.3   Converting an RNN's tensor shape into one suitable for use with a 1D convolution. We use the `.permute` function to swap the second and third axes (leaving the batch axis alone). This moves the spatial dimension into the location a 1D convolution would expect.

Instead of 2D convolutions over images, we can use 1D convolutions over words. The nn.Conv1d layer looks at data as (B, C, W), where B is still the batch size, C is the number of channels, and W is the width (or words) of the input. The result of an embedding layer is (B, T, D), where T is the length of the sequence. If we reorder the output to be (B, D, T), it will fit the general expectations of a 1D convolution. We can use this trick to change basically *any* problem for which we would use an RNN into one where we can apply a convolutional network.

But there is still one problem. For all the CNNs we have been working with, the input has been a fixed size: for example, MNIST is always a 28×28 image. But the sequence length T is variable for our problem! Again, we can use adaptive pooling to help us resolve this situation.

The final shape of our tensor, after rounds of 1D convolutions, activation functions, and normal pooling, will be (B, D', T'), where D' and T' indicate that the number of channels (D') and length of the sequence (T') may have been altered by our convolutions and normal pooling, respectively. If we use adaptive pooling over just the last dimension, we can reduce the shape to $(B, D', 1)$, which will be the same size regardless of how long the original input was. If we do this with adaptive *max* pooling, we select the largest activation for each channel as the representative of that channel for the final classification problem. That means we can switch to using a linear layer afterward and perform the classification problem we want, because the shape will be consistent from this point forward! The following code shows all of this put together to define a 1D CNN for classifying our sequences:

```
def cnnLayer(in_size, out_size):              I'm being lazy; we should
    return nn.Sequential(                      make k_size an argument, too.
        nn.Conv1d(in_size, out_size, kernel_size=k_size, padding=k_size//2),
        nn.LeakyReLU(),
        nn.BatchNorm1d(out_size))

k_size = 3
cnnOverTime = nn.Sequential(
    nn.Embedding(VOCAB_SIZE, embed_dim,
        padding_idx=padding_idx),              (B, T) -> (B, T, D)
    LambdaLayer(lambda x : x.permute(0,2,1)),  (B, T, D) -> (B, D, T)
    cnnLayer(embed_dim, embed_dim),            We pretend that D is the number
    cnnLayer(embed_dim, embed_dim),            of channels in this new
                                               interpretation of the data.

    nn.AvgPool1d(2),                           (B, D, T) -> (B, D, T/2)

    cnnLayer(embed_dim, embed_dim*2),
    cnnLayer(embed_dim*2, embed_dim*2),

    nn.AvgPool1d(2),                           (B, 2*D, T/2) -> (B, 2*D, T/4)

    cnnLayer(embed_dim*2, embed_dim*4),        Now that we have done
    cnnLayer(embed_dim*4, embed_dim*4),        some rounds of pooling and
                                               convolution, reduce the tensor
                                               shape to a fixed length.
    nn.AdaptiveMaxPool1d(1),                   (B, 4*D, T/4) -> (B, 4*D, 1)

    nn.Flatten(),                              (B, 4*D, 1) -> (B, 4*D)
    nn.Linear(4*embed_dim, embed_dim),
    nn.LeakyReLU(),
    nn.BatchNorm1d(embed_dim),
    nn.Linear(embed_dim, NUM_CLASS)
)
cnn_results = train_network(cnnOverTime, loss_func, train_loader,
    val_loader=test_loader, score_funcs={'Accuracy': accuracy_score},
    device=device, epochs=epochs)
```

NOTE   Normally, we can choose max or average pooling based on individual preference. In this case, there is a good reason to prefer `nn.AdaptiveMaxPool1d` instead of `nn.AdaptiveAvgPool1d`: not all items in the batch will have the same length, and the batch items that received padding will return a vector of zero values. That means the activations where padding occurred will likely have smaller values and thus not be selected by the max-pooling operations. This helps our architecture work properly even though we are ignoring different inputs having different lengths. This is a tricky workaround so we don't have to think about padding as much.

The strategy we just coded up, converting a sequential problem with an RNN into a 1D convolution, is *very* popular for classification tasks. It gets us a lot of spatial information while allowing us to train faster. The following code plots the results:

```
sns.lineplot(x='total time', y='val Accuracy', data=gru_results, label='GRU')
sns.lineplot(x='total time', y='val Accuracy', data=simpleEmbdAvg_results,
    label='Average Embedding')
sns.lineplot(x='total time', y='val Accuracy', data=attnEmbd_results,
    label='Attention Embedding')
sns.lineplot(x='total time', y='val Accuracy', data=cnn_results,
    label='CNN Adaptive Pooling')
```

```
[24]:    <AxesSubplot:xlabel='total time', ylabel='val Accuracy'>
```

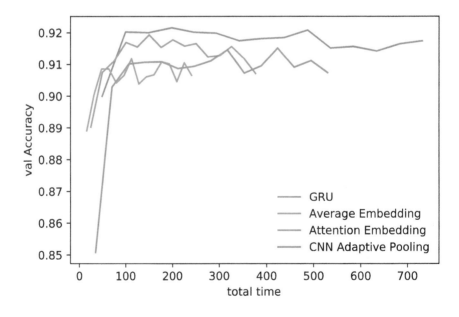

After running the CNN with adaptive pooling, some results show a variety of pros and cons. On the positive side, the CNN does not appear to be overfitting, meaning its performance may improve even more if we train for more epochs. This also means the final accuracy of the CNN is better than that of the averaged embeddings.

Our CNN is also pretty naive right now. Just as we improved 2D CNNs with more layers, residual connections, and other tricks, we could reimplement those methods (e.g., residual connections) and apply them here to get better results. This gives us an advantage over RNNs, which don't tend to improve much as we add all these bells and whistles we've learned about.

On the more disappointing side, the CNN's peak accuracy is not as good as either of the averaged embeddings *on this dataset*. We already know that the spatial nature of the data is not critical because of how well the naive embedding approach has done. The more important the spatial information is to the problem, the more we would expect this CNN approach to perform better than the embedding approach. But training both models can give you some initial information about how much order matters in your data.

12.4 *Positional embeddings add sequence information to any model*

RNNs capture all the sequential nature of the input data, and we've now seen that CNNs can capture some subset of that sequential-ness. Our embeddings are fast and potentially very accurate but often overfit the data since they lack this sequential information. This is hard to fix because the sequential information comes from our model design (i.e., using an RNN or CNN layer).

But instead of relying on the architecture to capture sequential information, what if there was a way to embed the sequential information into the embeddings? If the embeddings themselves contain information about their relative order, can we improve the results of our algorithms? That's the idea behind a recent technique called a *positional encoding*.

Figure 12.4 shows how this process works. We represent the location t (e.g., first, second, third, etc.) as a vector. Then we add those vectors to the inputs so the inputs contain themselves and information about where each item is in the input. This encodes sequential information into the network's inputs, and now it is on the network to learn how to extract and use the information about time.

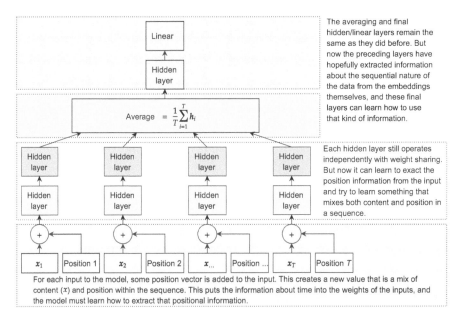

Figure 12.4   Average embedding approach that we started with, augmented with positional embeddings. Separate from the inputs, vector values encode information about our location within a larger sequence. This is added to the vectors representing the inputs, creating a mix of content and sequence information.

The big question is, how do we create this mythical encoding? It is a slightly mathy approach, but not too complicated. We need to define some notation so we can discuss it. Let's use $h_i \in \mathbb{R}^D$ to represent the embedding (from nn.Embedding) after feeding in token x_i. Then we have a sequence of embeddings $h_1, h_2, \ldots, h_t, \ldots, h_T$. We want a position vector $P(t)$, which we can add to our embeddings to create an improved embedding $\tilde{h}_t$ that contains information about the original content h_t and its location as the tth item in the input—something like this:

Our data that has its location as the tth item in a sequence is created by taking the original data and literally adding a new vector that represents the number/position t.

$$\tilde{h}_t = \quad h_t \quad +P(t)$$

Then we can proceed with $\tilde{h}_1, \tilde{h}_2, \ldots, \tilde{h}_t, \ldots, \tilde{h}_T$ as the inputs to the rest of our network, knowing that the sequential nature has been placed inside the embeddings! It turns out we can do this with a surprisingly simple approach. We define a function for $P(t)$ using the sin and cos functions, and we use the input to the sin and cos functions to represent the position of a vector t. To walk through how this works, let's plot what $\sin(t)$ looks like:

```
position = np.arange(0, 100)
sns.lineplot(x=position, y=np.sin(position), label="sin(position)")
```

[25]: <AxesSubplot:>

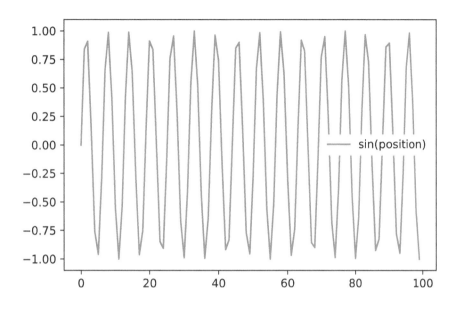

The sin function oscillates up and down. If we have computed $\sin(t) = y$, knowing y tells us something about what the input t may have been! Because $\sin(\pi \cdot c) = 0$ for all integers c, we can tell if we are some multiple of π in the sequence order (the $\pi \approx$ third item, or the $2\pi \approx$ sixth item, or the $2\pi \approx$ ninth item, etc). If $y = 0$, it is possible we were $t = 3 \approx \pi$ or $t = 6 \approx 2 \cdot \pi$, but we can't tell which of these specific positions we are in—only that we are in a position approximately a multiple of $\pi \approx 3.14$! In this example, we have 100 possible positions, so we can tell that we are in one out of ≈ 32 possible positions using this approach.

We can improve the situation by adding a second sin call, but with a frequency component f. So we compute $\sin(t/f)$ with $f = 1$ (what we have already plotted) and with $f = 10$:

```
position = np.arange(0, 100)
sns.lineplot(x=position, y=np.sin(position), label="sin(position)")
sns.lineplot(x=position, y=np.sin(position/10), label="sin(position/10)")
```

`[26]:   <AxesSubplot:>`

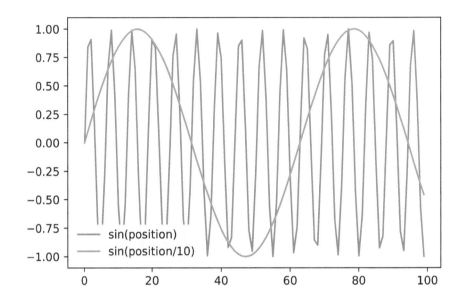

With two values of f, it is possible to uniquely identify some positions. If $\sin(t) = 0$ and $\sin(t/100) = 0$, there are only four possible positions we could be in, $t = 0, 31, 68, 94$, which are the only four positions where both cases are (approximately) true. If $\sin(t) = 0$ but $\sin(t/10) \neq 0$, then we know 0, 31, 68, and 94 are not options. In addition, the different values from the sin function are also informative about our position. If $\sin(t/10) = -1$, we know we must be at position 48, because it is the only option where we get -1 as the output, given a maximum time of $T = 100$.

This shows that if we keep adding frequencies f to the calculation, we can begin to infer from the combination of values our *exact* location within the input sequence. We define a position encoding function $P(t)$ that returns a D dimensional vector by creating sin and cos values at different frequencies $f_1, f_2, \ldots, f_{D/2}$. We only need $D/2$ frequencies because we use both a sin and cos value for each frequency. That gives us

$$P(t) = \begin{bmatrix} \sin\left(\frac{t}{f_1}\right) \\ \cos\left(\frac{t}{f_1}\right) \\ \sin\left(\frac{t}{f_2}\right) \\ \cos\left(\frac{t}{f_2}\right) \\ \vdots \\ \sin\left(\frac{t}{f_{\frac{D}{2}}}\right) \\ \cos\left(\frac{t}{f_{\frac{D}{2}}}\right) \end{bmatrix}$$

as the representation for our encoding vectors. But how do we define f_k? The paper[1] that originally proposed this recommended using the following:

$$f_k = 10000^{\frac{2 \cdot k}{D}}$$

Let's see a quick example of what this looks like. For simplicity, we use $D = 6$ dimensions and just plot the sin components so the plot is not too crowded:

```
dimensions = 6
position = np.expand_dims(np.arange(0, 100), 1)
div = np.exp(np.arange(0, dimensions*2, 2) *
     (-math.log(10000.0) / (dimensions*2)))    ← Computes the frequency f
                                                  In a numerically stable way
for i in range(dimensions):
    sns.lineplot(x=position[:,0], y=np.sin(position*div)[:,i],
        label="Dim-"+str(i))
```

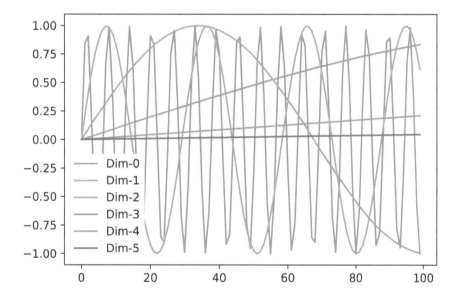

As we start adding more dimensions with more frequencies, it becomes easier to identify unique positions in time. Pick any location on the plot's x-axis, and you can identify a unique combination of values for all six dimensions that will not be shared by any other position on the x-axis. This is what our network will use to extract information about the location from the data.

This specific form of a positional encoding also has some nice mathematical properties that make it easier for neural networks to learn. For example, a single linear layer can learn to shift the position encoding by a fixed amount (i.e., move to the left or right by t units), helping a network learn to perform logic over the time component.

---

[1] A. Vaswani et al., "Attention is all you need," *Advances in Neural Information Processing Systems*, vol. 30, pp. 5998–6008, 2017.

12.4.1 *Implementing a positional encoding module*

We will add two more things to this approach that have been found helpful in practice. First, we do not want to give equal weight to both the content (original embedding h_t) and the position $P(t)$. So we use the following equation to up-weight the importance of the content over the position:

> Our data that has its location as the *t*th item in a sequence is created by taking the original data, but scaled up to make sure the focus is on the data, and literally adding a new vector that represents the position *t*.

$$\tilde{h}_t = \boxed{h_t \cdot \sqrt{D}} \ + P(t)$$

Second, we include a dropout on the resulting vector so we do not learn to overfit to the fixed values of the positional encoding $P(t)$. Now let's define a new PyTorch `Module` that applies this positional encoding for us. The current implementation requires knowing the maximum sequence length T in advance, using the `max_len` argument in the constructor. I've borrowed the code for this positional encoding from the PyTorch examples at http://mng.bz/B1Wl[2] and adapted it slightly:

```python
class PositionalEncoding(nn.Module):
    def __init__(self, d_model, dropout=0.1, max_len=5000, batch_first=False):
        super(PositionalEncoding, self).__init__()
        self.dropout = nn.Dropout(p=dropout)
        self.d_model = d_model

        pe = torch.zeros(max_len, d_model)
        position = torch.arange(0, max_len, dtype=torch.float).unsqueeze(1)
        div_term = torch.exp(torch.arange(0, d_model, 2).float() *
            (-math.log(10000.0) / d_model))
        pe[:, 0::2] = torch.sin(position * div_term)
        pe[:, 1::2] = torch.cos(position * div_term)      # Done so that when we call
        pe = pe.unsqueeze(0).transpose(0, 1)              # .to(device), this array will
        self.register_buffer('pe', pe)                    # move to it.
        self.batch_first = batch_first
                                                          # This code works on (T, B, D)
                                                          # data, so we need to reorder if
    def forward(self, x):                                 # the input is (B, T, D).
        if self.batch_first:                                        # Mixes the input
            x = x.permute(1, 0, 2)                                  # and positional
        x = x *np.sqrt(self.d_model) + self.pe[:x.size(0), :]       # information
        x = self.dropout(x)                               # Regularizes to avoid overfitting

        if self.batch_first:                              # Goes back to a (B, T, D) shape
            x = x.permute(1, 0, 2)
        return x
```

---

2 This code is under a BDS-3 license; check out the repo for this book for the license included.

12.4.2 Defining positional encoding models

With our new positional encoding, we can redefine the simple averaging approach from before by inserting our PositionalEncoding class directly after the nn.Embedding layer. It does not impact the tensor's shape in any way, so everything else can remain the same. It simply alters the values in the tensor with our new positional encoding $P(t)$:

```
simplePosEmbdAvg = nn.Sequential(
    nn.Embedding(VOCAB_SIZE, embed_dim, padding_idx=padding_idx),      ←──┐
    PositionalEncoding(embed_dim, batch_first=True),        (B, T) -> (B, T, D)│
    nn.Linear(embed_dim, embed_dim),
    nn.LeakyReLU(),
    nn.Linear(embed_dim, embed_dim),
    nn.LeakyReLU(),
    nn.Linear(embed_dim, embed_dim),
    nn.LeakyReLU(),
    nn.AdaptiveAvgPool2d((1,None)),        ←── (B, T, D) -> (B, 1, D)
    nn.Flatten(),        ←── (B, 1, D) -> (B, D)
    nn.Linear(embed_dim, embed_dim),
    nn.LeakyReLU(),
    nn.BatchNorm1d(embed_dim),
    nn.Linear(embed_dim, NUM_CLASS)
)
```

Adapting our attention-based embedding is also simple. When we defined EmbeddingAttentionBag, we added the optional argument embd_layers. If embd_layers is a PyTorch Module, it will use that network to run a hidden layer over the batch of (B, T, D) items. We define that Module ourselves, which will start with the PositionalEncoding module since the input to embd_layers is already embedded. That's done in the following code in two parts. First we define embd_layers as the positional encoding followed by three rounds of hidden layers, and then we define attnPosEmbd to be an attention-based network with positional encoding. Now we can train both of these new positional averaging networks and compare them with the original averaging and attention-based versions. If the accuracy improves, then we know that the information order was indeed important:

```
embd_layers = nn.Sequential(        ←── (B, T, D) -> (B, T, D)
    *([PositionalEncoding(embed_dim, batch_first=True)]+
      [nn.Sequential(nn.Linear(embed_dim, embed_dim), nn.LeakyReLU())
       for _ in range(3)])
)

attnPosEmbd = nn.Sequential(
    EmbeddingAttentionBag(VOCAB_SIZE, embed_dim,
      padding_idx=padding_idx,
      embd_layers=embd_layers),        ←── (B, T) -> (B, D)
    nn.Linear(embed_dim, embed_dim),
    nn.LeakyReLU(),
    nn.BatchNorm1d(embed_dim),
    nn.Linear(embed_dim, NUM_CLASS)
```

```
)

posEmbdAvg_results = train_network(simplePosEmbdAvg, loss_func,
    train_loader, val_loader=test_loader, score_funcs={'Accuracy':
    accuracy_score}, device=device, epochs=epochs)
attnPosEmbd_results = train_network(attnPosEmbd, loss_func, train_loader,
    val_loader=test_loader, score_funcs={'Accuracy': accuracy_score},
    device=device, epochs=epochs)
```

POSITIONAL ENCODING RESULTS

The following code plots the results for all the embedding models, with and without positional encodings. Our positional embeddings provide a significant benefit, accuracy is improved across the board, and there are less-severe dips in accuracy that indicate less overfitting. The impact on training time is also minuscule—the models take only a few more seconds to train than the originals:

```
sns.lineplot(x='total time', y='val Accuracy', data=simpleEmbdAvg_results,
    label='Average Embedding')
sns.lineplot(x='total time', y='val Accuracy', data=posEmbdAvg_results,
    label='Average Positional Embedding')
sns.lineplot(x='total time', y='val Accuracy', data=attnEmbd_results,
    label='Attention Embedding')
sns.lineplot(x='total time', y='val Accuracy', data=attnPosEmbd_results,
    label='Attention Positional Embedding')
```

```
[31]:  <AxesSubplot:xlabel='total time', ylabel='val Accuracy'>
```

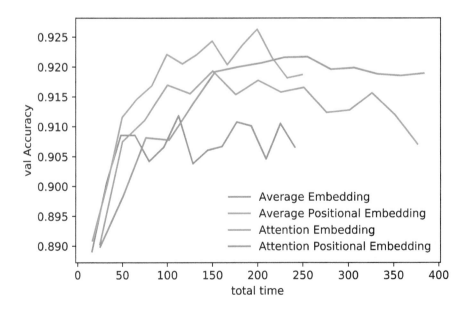

These results provide evidence that our hypothesis about sequence order helping prevent overfitting was also correct, particular with the attention-based approach. Both versions using the positional encodings still fluctuate but do not drop in accuracy as quickly with more epochs of training. This shows how we can use a completely different kind of approach to encode sequence information into our models.

Our attention-based embedding is definitely a better idea: let's compare just that to the earlier GRU results. With this combination, we begin to match or even outperform the GRU-based RNN in terms of accuracy, *and* it is over twice as fast to train! A pretty great combo. Here's the code:

```
sns.lineplot(x='total time', y='val Accuracy', data=gru_results, label='GRU')
sns.lineplot(x='total time', y='val Accuracy', data=attnEmbd_results,
     label='Attention Embedding')
sns.lineplot(x='total time', y='val Accuracy', data=attnPosEmbd_results,
     label='Attention Positional Embedding')
```

```
[32]:   <AxesSubplot:xlabel='total time', ylabel='val Accuracy'>
```

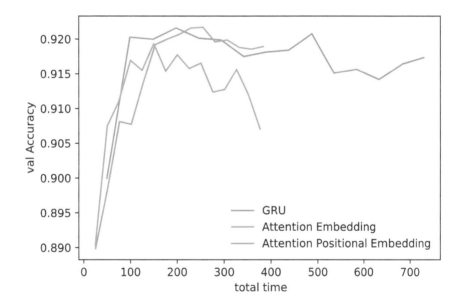

The takeaway is that positional encodings are a cheap, fast, and effective way to encode sequence information into our networks. Surprisingly, positional encodings were not invented on their own but rather in conjunction with the topic of the next section of this chapter: transformers. So in most current deep learning, you won't see a positional encoding used outside of transformers, but I have found them widely useful beyond transformers as a fast and easy way to endow a model with the concept of time/ordered data.

12.5 Transformers: Big models for big data

The last alternative to RNNs that we will learn about is the transformer architecture. It is built out of two primary subcomponents: positional encoding (which we just learned about) and *multiheaded attention*. Transformers are a very recent development and have become extremely popular due to some of their benefits. However, they tend to work best for big problems with *lots* of data (at least 50 GB, in my experience) and *lots* of compute (you'll want 4+ GPUs), so we won't see the full benefits in this chapter. Still, transformers are important to learn about and are the foundation for some of the current big advances in deep learning. The latest and greatest models for machine translation, question answering, few-shot learning, and dozens of NLP tasks are built with different transformer flavors. The goal of this section is to help you understand the standard, original, vanilla transformer with no special additions. After this chapter, I recommend reading Jay Alammar's blog post "The Illustrated Transformer" (http://jalammar.github.io/illustrated-transformer/) for a detailed step-by-step walk-through of a transformer.

12.5.1 Multiheaded attention

To understand how a transformer works, we need to understand *multiheaded attention* (MHA), which is an extension of the attention mechanisms we learned about in chapter 10. Like normal attention, MHA involves using the softmax function and `nn.Linear` layers to learn to selectively ignore or focus on different parts of an input. Our original attention mechanism has one context, which allows it to look for one kind of pattern. But what if you want to look for multiple different things at once (like a positive statement "good" preceded by a negation statement "not")? This is where multiheaded attention comes into play. Each "head" of the multi*head* attention can learn to look for different kinds of patterns, similar to how each filter in a convolutional layer can learn to look for different patterns. The high-level strategy of how MHA works is shown in figure 12.5.

At an intuitive level, you can think of MHA as answering questions or queries about a dictionary of key-value pairs. Since this is a neural network, both the keys and values are vectors. Because each key has its own value, the key tensor K and value tensor V must have the same number of items T. So both have a shape of (T, D) for D features.

Following this high-level analogy, you can ask as many or as few questions about the key-value dictionary as you like. The list of queries Q is its own tensor with a different length T'.

The MHA output has one response for each query, and it has the same dimension, giving us a shape of (T', D) for the output of the MHA. The z total heads of the MHA do not change the size of its output in the same way that changing the number of filters changes the number of channels in the output of a convolutional layer. That's just an oddity of how the MHA was designed. Instead, the MHA tries to mix all the answers together into a single output.

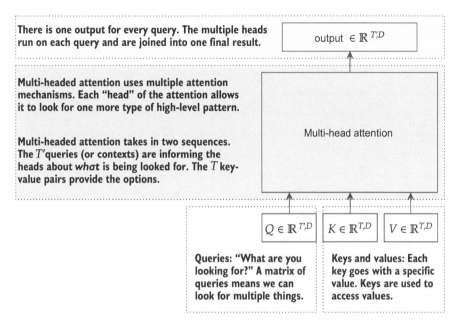

There is one output for every query. The multiple heads run on each query and are joined into one final result.

output $\in \mathbb{R}^{T,D}$

Multi-headed attention uses multiple attention mechanisms. Each "head" of the attention allows it to look for one more type of high-level pattern.

Multi-headed attention takes in two sequences. The T' queries (or contexts) are informing the heads about *what* is being looked for. The T key-value pairs provide the options.

Multi-head attention

$Q \in \mathbb{R}^{T,D}$ $K \in \mathbb{R}^{T,D}$ $V \in \mathbb{R}^{T,D}$

Queries: "What are you looking for?" A matrix of queries means we can look for multiple things.

Keys and values: Each key goes with a specific value. Keys are used to access values.

Figure 12.5 Outline of the multiheaded attention block. There are three sequences as inputs: the queries Q and the keys and values K, V, which are paired together. The MHA returns a D-dimensional vector that answers each query $q_i \in Q$.

As another way of explaining this analogy, we can think about MHA as a kind of deep learning alternative to the standard Python dictionary object. A dictionary d = {'key' : value} represents a set of keys, each with a specific value. You can then query that dictionary with something like d['query']. If query in d, you get its associated value, but if not you get None. An MHA layer has the same overall goals but does not require perfect matches between queries and keys as a dictionary does. Instead, it's a little soft, and multiple similar keys can respond to a single query, as shown in figure 12.6.

Your gut reaction may be to worry about giving answers when nothing looks similar to the query: isn't returning a gibberish answer/value bad? This is actually a good thing because the MHA can learn that it needs to adjust some of the keys/values during training. Remember in chapter 3 that we saw how to manually specify useful convolutions, but we instead let the neural network learn what convolutions should be used. The MHA works the same way: it starts out with randomly initialized and meaningless keys and values but learns to adjust them to something useful during training.

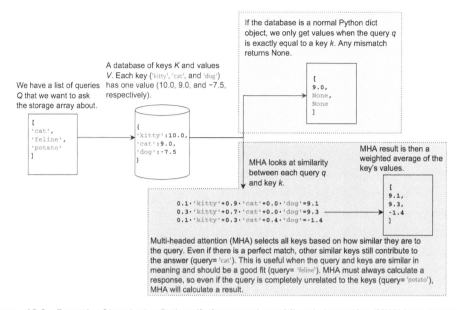

Figure 12.6   **Example of how both a Python dictionary and a multiheaded attention (MHA) have the concepts of queries, keys, and values. In a dictionary (top), a query and key must be a perfect match to get a value. In an MHA (bottom), each key contributes to answering each query based on how similar the key is to the query. This ensures that there is always an answer.**

Associative memories

The idea of querying a nebulous cloud of neurons and retrieving specific representations from it is quite old. This is a reasonable description of what is called an associative memory, and you can read a brief summary of some of its history at https://thegradient.pub/dont-forget-about-associative-memories.

In short, ideas related to associative memories go all the way back to the 1960s, which is fun for those who don't realize how old AI is as a field. While they are not currently in vogue among practitioners, there is still modern research on using them. I think they are also useful to learn about on your own to broaden how you think about problems and AI/ML. Many fields like cognitive science, psychology, neurology, and electrical engineering have helped shape early and foundational work, but sadly, associative memories do not often get the recognition they deserve today.

FROM ATTENTION TO MHA

The MHA can seem overly complex and opaque when we describe it on its own; instead, let's describe it using only the attention mechanisms we learned about from chapter 10. This is different from the way most works discuss MHA and takes a little longer, but I think it is easier to understand.

Let's start by writing out the equation for what our normal attention mechanism does. We have a score function that takes in two items and returns a value $\tilde{\alpha}$ that indicates the level of importance/similarity of that pair. The score function could be any of the dot, general, or additive scores we learned about—but everyone uses the dot score for MHA because that is just what people do.

We compute several scores for T different inputs, and they go into a softmax function to calculate a final vector of T scores α that says how important each of the T items was. Then we take the dot product between α and the original T items, which produces a single vector that is the result of our original attention mechanism. This is all shown in the following equation:

Given a set of T local states $h_1, \ldots, h_T$ and a global context $\bar{h}$ we can compute a weighted average of all the local states by computing a similarity score for each state against the global context,   normalizing the scores to sum to one,   and taking the product between each of the   scores and the states.

$$\left\langle \text{softmax} \left(\begin{bmatrix} \text{score}(h_1, \bar{h}) \\ \text{score}(h_2, \bar{h}) \\ \vdots \\ \text{score}(h_T, \bar{h}) \end{bmatrix} \right), \begin{bmatrix} h_1 \\ h_2 \\ \vdots \\ h_T \end{bmatrix} \right\rangle = \alpha_1 \cdot h_1 + \ldots + \alpha_T \cdot h_T = \sum_{i=1}^{T} \alpha_i \cdot h_i$$

Now let's make a few changes to how this works. First, let's rename our *context* vector $\bar{h}$ to our *query* vector q and make it an input to the score function. The context or query tells us what we are looking for. Instead of using $h_1, h_2, \ldots, h_T$ to determine the importances α *and* the output vectors, let's separate them into two different sets of tensors that do not have to be the same. By random happenstance, we call the tensors used for α the *keys* $K = [k_1, k_2, \ldots, k_T]$ and the *values* $V = [v_1, v_2, \ldots, v_T]$. Then we get the following three-argument score function that uses the original two-argument score function:

Given a query q and a set of T key ($K = [k_1, \ldots, k_T]$) value ($V = [v_1, \ldots, v_T]$) pairs, we can search for the response value by

computing a similarity score for each key K against the query q,

normalizing the scores to sum to one, and taking the product between each of the

scores against the value for each key. The response value is a weighted

average of all the values by how similar their keys were to the query.

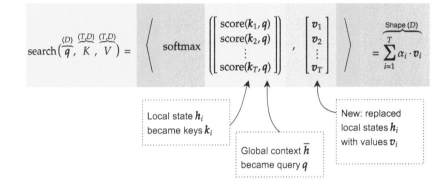

Local state h_i became keys k_i

Global context $\bar{h}$ became query q

New: replaced local states h_i with values v_i

All we have really done so far is *generalize* our score function to make it a bit more flexible. We can think of search (q, K, V) as addressing "Given this query q, give me the average value V from the dictionary based on its keys K." This is a generalization because if we called score $\left(\frac{1}{T} \sum_{i=1}^{T} h_i, [\ldots, h_i, \ldots], [\ldots, h_i, \ldots] \right)$, we would get the same result as before!

This gives us the result for *one* query. To extend this to multiple queries, we call the three-argument score function multiple times. This gives us the result for *one head* of an MHA and is usually denoted by a function named `Attention`:

Given a set of T' queries $Q = [q_1, \ldots, q_{T'}]$ and a set of T key ($K = [k_1, \ldots, k_T]$) value ($V = [v_1, \ldots, v_T]$) pairs, we can compute an attention function by

searching the key-value database for every query and stacking their results into one larger matrix.

$$\text{Attention}\big(\overset{(T',D)}{Q} , \overset{(T,D)}{K} , \overset{(T,D)}{V} \big) = \overset{(T',D)}{\begin{bmatrix} \text{search}(q_1, K, V) \\ \text{search}(q_2, K, V) \\ \vdots \\ \text{search}(q_{T'}, K, V) \end{bmatrix}}$$

This equation is a straightforward adaption of what we just did. We now have multiple queries $Q = [q_1, q_2, \ldots, q_{T'}]$, so we call `score` multiple times and stack the T' results into one larger matrix.

With that, we can finally define the MHA function. If we have z heads, you may have correctly guessed that we call the `Attention` function z times! But the input is still Q, K, and V. To make each head learn to look for something different, each head has three `nn.Linear` layers W^Q, W^K, and W^V. These linear layers have the job of preventing the multiple calls from all computing the exact same thing, because that would be silly. Then we concatenate all z results into one big vector and end with a final output `nn.Linear` layer W^O that has the sole job of making sure the output of MHA has D dimensions. This all looks like the following equation:

Multi-headed attention (MHA) also takes in queries Q and key-value pairs K and V as well as the number of heads z.

MHA concatenates the results of z different attention calls

and then applies a linear layer to avoid making the output z times larger.

To avoid getting duplicate answers for each attention call, the queries, keys, and values are altered. This provides diversity in answers.

$$\underbrace{\text{MuliHead}_z(Q, K, V)}_{\text{Output shape of } (T', D)} = \underbrace{\overbrace{\left[\text{head}_1 ; \text{head}_2 ; \ldots ; \text{head}_z\right]}^{\text{torch.cat}\left(\left[\text{head}_1, \text{head}_2, \ldots, \text{head}_z\right]\right).shape \to (T', z \cdot D)}} \overset{(z \cdot D, D)}{W^O}$$

$$\text{head}_i = \text{Attention}\left(QW_i^Q, KW_i^K, VW_i^V\right)$$

That gets us from our original attention mechanism to the more sophisticated MHA. Because the MHA is decently involved and has multiple layers, it does not need as many heads z as a convolutional layer needs filters C. Whereas we usually want somewhere between 32 and 512 filters (based on what gets the best results), for MFA, we usually want no more than $z = 8$ or $z = 16$ heads.

We won't implement the MHA function since PyTorch provides a good implementation for us. But let's quickly look at some pseudo-Python to get an idea of how it goes. First we create the W_i^Q, W_i^K, W_i^V layers and the output W^O. That happens in the constructor, and we can use the PyTorch `ModuleList` to store a list of modules that we want to use later:

```
self.wqs = nn.ModuleList([nn.Linear(D, D) for _ in range(z)])
self.wks = nn.ModuleList([nn.Linear(D, D) for _ in range(z)])
self.wvs = nn.ModuleList([nn.Linear(D, D) for _ in range(z)])
self.wo = nn.Linear(z*D, D)
```

Then we can move into the `forward` function. Let's assume an `Attention` function already exists, for simplicity. We basically just need to call this `Attention` function repeatedly, applying the linear layers defined in the constructor. The `zip` command can be used to make this pretty concise, giving us a triplet of W_i^Q, W_i^K, and W_i^V with the result appended to a list of `heads`. They are combined at the end with concatenation, and the final W^O layer is applied:

```
def forward(Q, K, V):
    heads = []
    for wq, wk, wv in zip(self.wqs, self.wks, self.wvs):
        heads.append(Attention(wq(Q), wk(K), wv(V)))
    return self.wo(torch.cat(heads, dim=2) )
```

Multiheaded attention standard equations

We used our score function from the last chapter to show how the MHA is really just an extension of what we have already learned. I think that journey helps to solidify what the MHA is doing. The MHA can also be expressed with fewer equations: I find them more opaque to understand, but it's worth showing them since that's how most people write them!

The main difference is how the `Attention` function is written. Normally it's the result of three matrix multiplications:

$$Attention(Q, K, V) = \text{softmax}\left(\frac{QK^\top}{\sqrt{D}}\right) V$$

This is equivalent to what I've already shown you, but it is not obvious how it does attention this way (in my opinion). This version is the preferred way to implement MHA because it runs faster.

12.5.2 *Transformer blocks*

Now that we know what the MHA block looks like, we can describe the transformer! There are two kinds of transformer blocks: an encoder and a decoder. They are shown in figure 12.7 and use the familiar concept of a residual connection.

The encoder block can be used in a network for almost any sequence-based architecture (e.g., sentiment classification); it does not need to be paired with a decoder. It begins with a residual connection with the MHA; the same input sequence is used for the queries, key, and values, so this is described as a self-attention layer because there is no external context or input. Then a second residual connection occurs that uses only a linear layer. You can repeat this encoder block multiple times to make a deeper and more powerful network: the original paper[3] used six of them, so that has become a common default.

---

[3] The "Attention Is All You Need" paper that introduced positional encodings! (See footnote 1.)

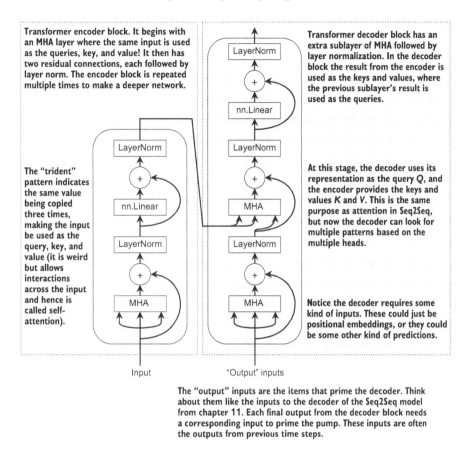

The "output" inputs are the items that prime the decoder. Think about them like the inputs to the decoder of the Seq2Seq model from chapter 11. Each final output from the decoder block needs a corresponding input to prime the pump. These inputs are often the outputs from previous time steps.

Figure 12.7 The two types of transformer blocks: the encoder (left) and decoder (right). Both use layer normalization, residual connections, and MHA layers. The first MHA in each is called self-attention because the same input is used for Q, K, and V.

The decoder block is almost always used with an encoder block and generally used for sequence tasks with multiple outputs (e.g., machine translation). The only difference is that a second MHA residual connection is inserted after the first one. This second MHA uses the output of the encoder block as the keys and values, and the previous MHA's result is used as the queries. This is done so that you can build either sequence-to-sequence-like models like chapter 11's or autoregressive style models.

You may notice in this design that there are no explicit time connections like those that our RNNs have. Transformers get *all* of their sequence information from positional encodings! This is why we needed to learn about positional encodings first, so we can reuse them to create a transformer model.

WARNING   The encoder and decoder look at and process all time steps simultaneously. This can be bad for autoregressive models where you are trying to predict the next item. Naively using a transformer for an autoregressive model means the transformer can look at future inputs, which is cheating when the goal is to predict the future! For such applications, you need to use a special mask to prevent the transformer from looking into the future. This mask has a triangular shape so that interactions are limited across time and is provided by the `generate_square_subsequent_mask()` method of the `Transformer` class.

The following block of code implements a simple approach to classifying the sequence with a transformer. It starts with an `Embedding` layer followed by a `PositionalEncoding` and then three `TransformerEncoder` layers. Ideally, we would use six layers here; but transformers are even *more* expensive than RNNs, so we have to handicap the model to make this example run quickly. After the transformer runs, we still get an output of shape (B, T, D): we use our normal attention to get that down to a single vector with shape (B, D) so we can make a prediction. Note in this code the weird quirk that transformers require their tensors to be organized as (T, B, D), so we need to reorder the axis a few times to make everything work out:

```
class SimpleTransformerClassifier(nn.Module):

    def __init__(self, vocab_size, D, padding_idx=None):
        super(SimpleTransformerClassifier, self).__init__()
        self.padding_idx = padding_idx
        self.embd = nn.Embedding(vocab_size, D, padding_idx=padding_idx)
        self.position = PositionalEncoding(D, batch_first=True)
        self.transformer = nn.TransformerEncoder(         ◀──┐ The main work for
            nn.TransformerEncoderLayer(                      │ our transformer
            d_model=D, nhead=8), num_layers=3)               │ implementation
        self.attn = AttentionAvg(AdditiveAttentionScore(D))
        self.pred = nn.Sequential(
            nn.Flatten(),                 ◀─── (B, 1, D) -> (B, D)
            nn.Linear(D, D),
            nn.LeakyReLU(),
            nn.BatchNorm1d(D),
            nn.Linear(D, NUM_CLASS)
        )

    def forward(self, input):
        if self.padding_idx is not None:
            mask = input != self.padding_idx
        else:
            mask = input == input        ◀─── All entries are True.
        x = self.embd(input)             ◀─── (B, T, D)
        x = self.position(x)             ◀─── (B, T, D)
        x = self.transformer(x.permute(1,0,2))  ◀──
        x = x.permute(1,0,2)             ◀─── (B, T, D)
        context = x.sum(dim=1)/mask.sum(dim=1).unsqueeze(1)  ◀─── Average over time
        return self.pred(self.attn(x, context, mask=mask))
```

Because the rest of our code is (B, T, D), but transformers take input as (T, B, D), we have to change the order of the dimensions before and after.

```
simpleTransformer = SimpleTransformerClassifier(  ←── Builds and trains this model
    VOCAB_SIZE, embed_dim, padding_idx=padding_idx)
transformer_results = train_network(simpleTransformer, loss_func,
    train_loader, val_loader=test_loader, score_funcs={'Accuracy':
    accuracy_score}, device=device, epochs=epochs)
```

Now we can plot the results of all our methods. Transformers hit the highest accuracy of all of them and are still improving as we keep training. If we did more epochs and used more layers, they would probably improve even more! But that increases training time, and the transformer is already slower than the GRU model:

```
sns.lineplot(x='total time', y='val Accuracy', data=gru_results, label='GRU')
sns.lineplot(x='total time', y='val Accuracy', data=attnEmbd_results,
    label='Attention Embedding')
sns.lineplot(x='total time', y='val Accuracy', data=attnPosEmbd_results,
    label='Attention Positional Embedding')
sns.lineplot(x='total time', y='val Accuracy', data=cnn_results,
    label='CNN Adaptive Pooling')
sns.lineplot(x='total time', y='val Accuracy', data=transformer_results,
    label='Transformer')
```

```
[34]:  <AxesSubplot:xlabel='total time', ylabel='val Accuracy'>
```

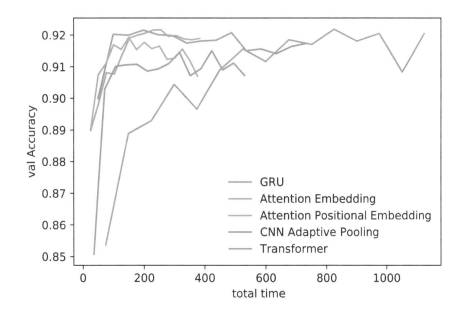

Where does this leave us with our results? By default, the attention-based embedding with positional encodings is a great tool. It doesn't always outperform a modern RNN like the GRU or a LSTM, but it's a good candidate that is faster to run. You can look at either approach for most problems. If you have excess compute, though, RNNs have the benefit of being more studied and understood, so it may be easier to trust your results with them.

Transformers are a tool that you bring out when you need the maximum possible accuracy and you've got oodles of GPUs available (and data) to pay their hefty price. RNNs have a bad habit of plateauing in accuracy after three to six layers, bucking the deep learning trend where more layers get you a more powerful model with better results. Transformers in total usually have 24+ layers and still gain accuracy from having more. That said, transformers can be more accurate *and* faster when you are working on massive datasets that *require* using multiple GPUs.

This is because transformers process all T items in a sequence *simultaneously*, whereas RNNs need to process them one at a time. Doing work this way makes transformers scale to multiple GPUs better because there is more work to split up and run simultaneously. With an RNN, you can't break up the work because one step depends on the previous step, so you have to wait. That being said, researchers and companies are using *hundreds to thousands of GPUs* to train a single model on hundreds of gigabytes or more of data. This tells you the kind of scale it takes to really see the benefits of transformers.

While transformers are not yet ready to replace RNNs, they are another approach that can be used. They currently hold the top slot to maximize accuracy when you have a large amount of data and compute available. In the next chapter, we learn how to extract the benefits of transformers for your own problems *without* needing a thousand GPUs!

Exercises

Share and discuss your solutions on the Manning online platform at Inside Deep Learning Exercises (https://liveproject.manning.com/project/945). Once you submit your own answers, you will be able to see the solutions submitted by other readers, and see which ones the author judges to be the best.

1 Use Optuna to try to optimize the attention-based averaged embedding classifier. Try to tune the initial dimension used by the nn.Embedding layer, the number of hidden neurons in all subsequent layers, the total number of hidden layers, and which of the score functions (dot, general, additive) to use on the AG News corpus. How much higher can you get the accuracy?

2 Going back to chapter 6, convert the ResidualBlockE and ResidualBottleNeck layers into their 1D counterparts ResidualBlockE1D and ResidualBottleNeck1D. Then use them to try to improve the 1D CNN from this chapter on the AG News corpus. How high can you get the accuracy?

3 Using your best 1D CNN for AG News, try adding positional encoding to the network. How does it impact your results?

4 PyTorch provides a `nn.MultiheadAttention` module that implements the MHA approach. Come up with your own modification to the attention-based averaged embedding classifier to use MHA, and try to get it to have better accuracy.

5 Transformers often work best with a learning rate schedule. Try the schedules we learned about in chapter 5 to see if you can reduce the number of epochs it takes `SimpleTransformerClassifier` to learn or increase its final accuracy.

Summary

- We can intentionally reduce how much our models understand the sequential nature of data to reduce runtime.

- We can encode positional information by modifying the inputs to the data instead of using an RNN or CNN that encodes positional information in their structure, which can endow other faster alternatives with sequential information or improve accuracy.

- The multiheaded attention is a generalization of the attention from chapter 10, which involves multiple contexts or queries and multiple results. It can obtain greater accuracy at a higher computational cost.

- Transformers are a powerful alternative to RNNs that can obtain high accuracies at a steep computational cost. They work best when you have large amounts of data and compute, because they scale up and out better than RNNs do.

Transfer learning

You now know a range of techniques for training models from scratch on new data. But what if you do not have time to wait for a big model to train? Or what if you do not have a lot of data to begin with? Ideally, we could use information from a bigger, well-curated dataset to help us learn a more accurate model in fewer epochs for our new, smaller dataset.

That is where *transfer learning* comes into play. The idea behind transfer learning is that if someone has gone through the effort of training a big model on a bunch of data, you can probably use that *already trained* model as a starting point for your problem. In essence, you want to *transfer* to your problem all the information that the model has extracted from some related problem. When that's possible, transfer learning can save you weeks of time, improve your accuracy, and just generally work better. This is especially valuable because you can get better results with less labeled data, which is a

486

big time- and moneysaver. This makes transfer learning one of the most practical tools you should know for on-the-job work.

Transfer learning works best when there are intrinsic similarities between the original larger set of data and the smaller target data you want to apply it to. This is particularly true for CNNs because of how intrinsically similar images are. Even if you have a source dataset of landscape photographs and a target dataset of cats and dogs, the structural priors we talked about in chapter 3 are still true: pixels near each other are related to each other, and far-off pixels have little bearing.

This chapter focuses on one particular type of transfer learning that reuses the literal weights and architecture from a previously trained network for a new problem. After we show how this works with CNNs for images, we see how to do transfer learning for text classification models using transformer-based models. Just a few years ago, transfer learning for text was not nearly as easy or successful. But transfer learning allows us to sidestep the enormous training costs of transformers, getting their benefits at little cost.

13.1 Transferring model parameters

The key to success in any new machine learning application is access to representative data that has been labeled accurately. But getting lots of labeled data requires time, effort, and money. Entire companies exist just to help people label their data using services like Amazon's Mechanical Turk. At the same time, we want evidence that our approach will work before we invest a large amount of time collecting and labeling a huge corpus. This puts us in a conundrum: we want to build a good initial model to see if a task is viable, but getting enough data to build a good first model is expensive.

We want to make an accurate model with less data and compute time by using *related* data to help us build the model. Essentially, we want to *transfer* things we have *learned* about one domain to a different, but related, domain. This is the idea behind *transfer learning*. Practically, transfer learning is one of the most useful approaches you should know about in your arsenal of deep learning tools. Especially if you are doing any work in a computer vision- or text-based application area, transfer learning can be very powerful.

One of the most successful approaches to transfer learning that we learn in this chapter is to transfer the *weights* θ from one model to another. The original model is trained on a large dataset of high-quality data, which shares some structural similarities with the smaller set of data that we really care about. For example, images have a lot of structural similarities—so we could take a model trained on almost any large image-classification task and use it to help us with a more nuanced task. To do this, we need to make the smallest possible modification or addition to the original model f to make it fit the new problem. This high-level approach is depicted in figure 13.1; we see in a moment how to perform the mechanical details.

13.1.1 Preparing an image dataset

To get started with transfer learning, we will download a Cats-vs-Dogs dataset that was organized as part of a Microsoft Kaggle competition (https://www.kaggle.com/

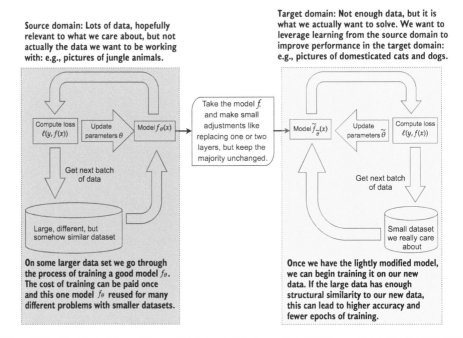

Figure 13.1   Training a big model on a big dataset. It is a one-time cost, because we can reuse the big model by transferring it to many different smaller tasks. This is done by editing the model but keeping almost all of the original architecture and weights θ intact. Then we train the modified model on the new dataset.

shaunthesheep/microsoft-catsvsdogs-dataset), so it will be a binary classification problem. This is our first time creating a new image-classification dataset in PyTorch, so we walk through the steps as a useful exercise. The following code snippet downloads the zip file containing the dataset and extracts it to a folder called PetImages. Note that two of the files in this zip file are unfortunately corrupted. We need to delete these two files for our data loader to work properly, which is why we have a `bad_files` list indicating the corrupted images and removing them. Here's the code:

```
data_url_zip = "https://download.microsoft.com/download/3/E/1/
   3E1C3F21-ECDB-4869-8368-6DEBA77B919F/kagglecatsanddogs_3367a.zip"
from io import BytesIO
from zipfile import ZipFile
from urllib.request import urlopen
import re

if not os.path.isdir('./data/PetImages'):        ◀──  Download this dataset if we
    resp = urlopen(data_url_zip)                       have not already done so!
    zipfile = ZipFile(BytesIO(resp.read()))
    zipfile.extractall(path = './data')

bad_files = [                                    ◀──  This file is bad and will
    './data/PetImages/Dog/11702.jpg',                 screw up the data loader!
    "./data/PetImages/Cat/666.jpg"
```

```
]
for f in bad_files:
    if os.path.isfile(f):
        os.remove(f)
```

Some of the images have corrupted EXIF data as well. The EXIF data is metadata about the image (such as where the photo was taken) and is not important for what we want to do. For that reason, we disable any warnings about this issue:

```
import warnings
warnings.filterwarnings("ignore",
    "(Possibly )?corrupt EXIF data", UserWarning)
```
Don't bother us about these bad files, thank you.

Now we use the `ImageFolder` class provided by PyTorch to create a `Dataset` for this class. The `ImageFolder` expects a root directory with one child folder for each class. The name of the folder is the name of the class, and every image in that folder is loaded as an example for the dataset with that specific class label; see figure 13.2.

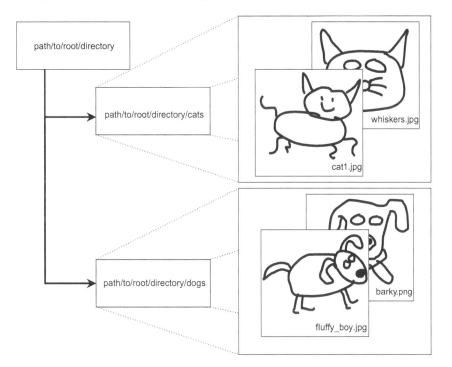

Figure 13.2 The `ImageFolder` class of PyTorch takes in a path to a root folder. It assumes every subfolder represents a class, and each subfolder should be filled with images of that class. This example shows two classes, cats and dogs, with very artistic drawings.

The `ImageFolder` class takes an optional `transform` object that we use to simplify the loading process. This `transform` is the same transformation class we used for data augmentation in chapter 3. Since the images are all of varying sizes, we can use a Compose transform to resize, crop, and standardize them to all have the same shape. This way, we can train on batches of data the same way we did on MNIST (all 28×28) and CIFAR-10 (32×32). Our Compose transform builds a pipeline of sub-transforms to run in order, which in this case will do the following:

1   Resize the image so the smallest dimension is 130 pixels. For example, a 260×390 image would become 130×195 (maintaining the same aspect ratio).

2   Crop out the center 128×128 pixels.

3   Convert the image to a PyTorch tensor, which includes normalizing the pixel values from $[0, 255]$ to $[0, 1]$.

In addition to the transforms, we make a train/test split with 80% of the data for training and the remaining 20% for our test set. The following code sets all this up with our dataset of cats and dogs:

```
all_images = torchvision.datasets.ImageFolder("./data/PetImages",
     transform=transforms.Compose(
         [                                          The smallest of width/height
             transforms.Resize(130),          ◄──  becomes 130 pixels.
             transforms.CenterCrop(128),      ◄──  Takes the center 128 × 128 image
             transforms.ToTensor(),           ◄──  Converts it to a PyTorch tensor
         ]))

train_size = int(len(all_images)*0.8)        ◄──  Picks 80% for training
test_size = len(all_images)-train_size       ◄──  20% remainder for testing

train_data, test_data = torch.utils.data.random_split   ◄──  Creates the random splits
     (all_images, (train_size, test_size))                    of the specified sizes
```

With the dataset in place, we can now create our DataLoaders for training and testing (using a batch size $B = 128$). This dataset has a little over 20,000 samples in the training set, making it smaller in the total number of images than MNIST, but the images are much larger than what we've previously worked with (128×128 instead of 32×32 or smaller):

```
B = 128
train_loader = DataLoader(train_data, batch_size=B, shuffle=True)
test_loader = DataLoader(test_data, batch_size=B)
```

We have a dataset and loader objects; let's take a look at the data. Class 0 is the cat class, and 1 is the dog class. The next block of code visualizes some of the data with the class number marked in the corner. This gives us an idea about the complexity of this dataset:

```
f, axarr = plt.subplots(2,4, figsize=(20,10))        ◀── Creates a grid of
for i in range(2):                                         eight images (2 × 4)
    for j in range(4):                      ◀── Rows
        x, y = test_data[i*4+j]             ◀── Columns
                                            ◀── Grabs an image from the test corpus
        axarr[i,j].imshow(x.numpy().transpose(1,2,0))    ◀── Plots the image

        axarr[i,j].text(0.0, 0.5, str(round(y,2)),       ◀── Draws the label in
            dict(size=20, color='red'))                      the top-left corner
```

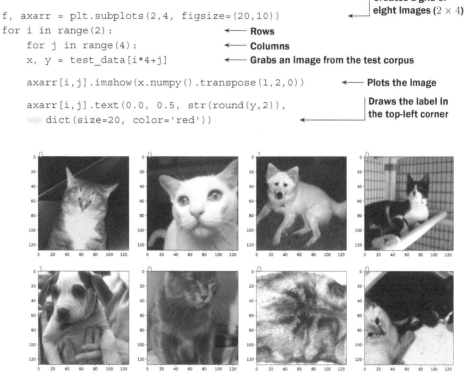

While there are only two classes, the content of the images is more diverse and complicated than other toy datasets we have used, like MNIST and CIFAR. The animals are in a variety of poses, cameras have over/underexposure, there may be more than one animal in the image with different backgrounds, and humans may appear in the photos as well. This complexity needs to be learned, but it will be a challenge to learn how to classify cats versus dogs using only 20,000 samples.

13.2 Transfer learning and training with CNNs

Let's train a model. In particular, we use the smaller ResNet architecture as our starting point. ResNet is the architecture that invented the residual connections we learned about in chapter 6, and ResNet-X usually refers to one of a few specific neural networks that use residual layers (e.g., ResNet-50 or ResNet-101). We use ResNet-18, which is the smallest of the (common) ResNets. We can grab an instance of the model using the torchvision.models class, which has a number of popular prebuilt architectures for various computer vision tasks.

ResNet uses adaptive pooling at the end of the network, which means we can reuse the ResNet architectures for classification problems with essentially any arbitrarily sized input image. The problem is that ResNet was designed for a dataset called ImageNet, which has 1,000 output classes. Since ImageNet and its 1,000 classes are what the ResNet models have been pretrained on, that makes ImageNet our source domain. So, the architecture will end with a `nn.Linear` layer with 1,000 outputs. Our target domain of cats versus dogs has two classes, so we want it to have only one or two outputs (for training with binary cross entropy and softmax, respectively). Figure 13.3 shows the situation and how we achieve transfer learning.

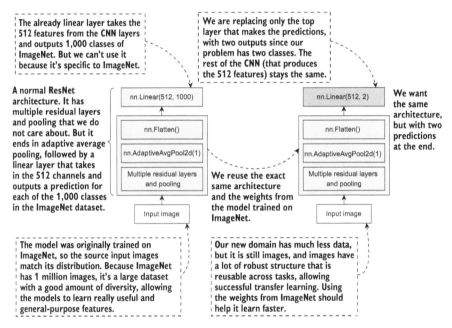

Figure 13.3   The left side shows a summary of ResNet. We want to alter it to look like the right side, where only the last `nn.Linear` layer has been changed. The input to each `nn.Linear` layer is 512 because the final convolutional layer has $C = 512$ channels, and using adaptive average pooling down to just 1×1 means there are only 512 values in the output, regardless of the size of the original image.

We can use the object-oriented nature of PyTorch to adapt the preexisting models to our new problem with relative ease. The finally fully connected layer in PyTorch's ResNet is named "fc," so we can reach into the network and replace the fc object! Since the `nn.Linear` layer keeps the number of inputs in an object called `in_features`, we can replace this last layer in a generic fashion that will work without us having to hardcode the number of inputs. The following code shows this process, which is often called *surgery* because we are chopping off part of the model and replacing it with a new part.[1] It takes two lines of code and is very easy to accomplish:

---

[1]   I've never had a surgery that quite worked that way, and I think I'm OK with that. Please note I am a PhD, not an MD, so my knowledge of proper surgery etiquette and how to chop things off safely is limited.

```
model = torchvision.models.resnet18()
model.fc = nn.Linear(model.fc.in_features, 2)      ◄── Performs some "surgery"
```

The two lines of code are summarized in figure 13.4. By default, the ResNet model has random weights, so this is basically giving us a new ResNet to train from scratch for our problem.

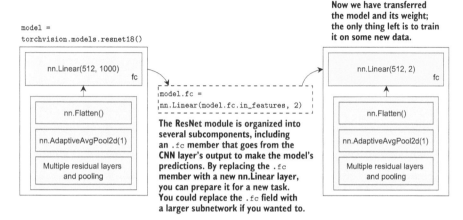

Figure 13.4 Demonstration of the mechanics of transferring a model via its weights in PyTorch. The original model has been initialized with a set of weights (random by default; potentially pretrained). We replace the top part of the model with a new version that fits our purpose.

This gives us a model we can train to predict whether an image is of a cat or a dog. The following code uses the standard `CrossEntropyLoss` that we have used many times now, and our regular `train_network` function. The network is larger than most of what we have built in this book, and the images are larger, too, so training this example takes a bit longer to run:

```
loss = nn.CrossEntropyLoss()
normal_results = train_network(model, loss, train_loader, epochs=10,
    device=device, test_loader=test_loader, score_funcs={'Accuracy':
    accuracy_score})
```

Now that we have trained the model, we can do our very well-trodden process of plotting the result of this regular approach to training a model. We are getting some decent results without having to do much thinking. We just took ResNet-18 and ran with it, which is a common approach that many people use to solve practical problems:

```
sns.lineplot(x='epoch', y='test Accuracy', data=normal_results,
    label='Regular')
```

[13]: <AxesSubplot:xlabel='epoch', ylabel='test Accuracy'>

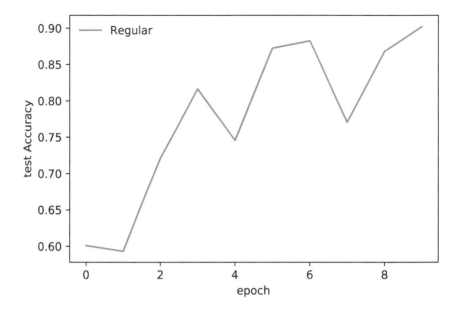

NOTE   Architectures like ResNet-18 and the others in the `torchvision.models` package have gone through a lot of testing and been found to work well across a variety of problems. So if you need to do any kind of image classification, this is almost always a good place to start, using the hard work others have done to design good architectures. But what we've done so far just creates a new version of ResNet with random initial weights. Transfer learning involves using a set of weights Θ that have already been trained on another dataset, which can significantly improve our results.

13.2.1 *Adjusting pretrained networks*

We have initialized a default ResNet module, performed surgery on it to adapt it to our classification task, and trained it using the same gradient descent tools we have used throughout this book. The only thing missing to turn this into real transfer learning is pretraining the ResNet model on a source domain (e.g., ImageNet) instead of randomly initializing it (the default).

Fortunately, that pretraining has already been done. All of the models provided by PyTorch under `torchvision.models` have an option to set a flag `pretrained=True`, which returns a version of the model that has already been trained on a designated original dataset. For ResNet, that original dataset is ImageNet. So let's quickly grab our new model. We have essentially the same two lines of code for our initial surgery on ResNet-18, except that we add the `pretrained=True` flag:

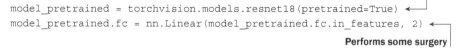

As before, we replaced the fully connected layer of this network with a new one. The original convolutional filters are pretrained, but the fully connected layer at the end is randomly initialized because we replaced it with a new `nn.Linear` layer—and by default, all modules in PyTorch start with random weights. The hope is that because ImageNet is such a large dataset, with 1 million training images, we can learn a better model more quickly. We may have to learn this `nn.Linear` layer from scratch, but all the preceding convolutional layers should be at a better starting place because they were trained on so much data.

WHY PRETRAINING WORKS

Before we train `model_pretrained` on our cat/dog problem, we should ask, "what is the intuition behind how this works?" *Why* does starting from the weights of an already-trained model help us on a new problem? In chapter 3, when we first talked about convolutional networks, we saw how convolutions can learn to find edges at different angles. Convolutions can also learn to find colors or changes in color, sharpen or blur an image, etc. All of these things are broadly useful to *any* image-based problem. So the crux of why pretraining works is that the things convolutions learn to detect on a large dataset are *probably* the same kinds of things we want to detect in any other image-based problem. If these are generally useful things for a CNN to learn how to detect, the CNN will probably learn them better from more data rather than less. Thus, the pretrained network from a larger dataset should hopefully have already learned to look for the kinds of patterns we care about, and the final `nn.Linear` layer simply needs to learn how to assemble these patterns into a decision. Training from scratch would require learning both the patterns and how to make a classification decision from them.

Transfer learning generally works best when the source dataset you want to transfer from is larger than the target dataset, because you need enough data to have an advantage over just training from scratch on the data you care about. There is also a factor of how relevant the source data is compared to the target domain you want to work on. If the data is relevant enough, the things the source model learns well (because it has more data) are more likely to be reusable on the target data. This balancing act is summarized in figure 13.5.

Luckily for us, almost any large image dataset tends to be relevant enough to put us in the top-right corner of figure 13.5: the structure of pixel correlations is very strong and generalizable, which is something easiest to visualize with the first layer of the network. Because the first convolutional layer takes in the image's red, green, and blue channels, we can treat each filter as an image and plot it to see what it is looking for. Let's do that for our pretrained model first to see what it has as a starting point. First we need to grab the weights for the filters from the first convolutional layer. For ResNet, this is defined as the `conv1` layer:

More source
data than
target data

The source domain is larger, giving it
an advantage of more information to
learn better weights. But if it's not
relevant enough to the problem at
hand, the things learned may not be
useful to the target domain.

The source domain is larger, giving it
an advantage of more information to
learn better weights. Being relevant to
the target domain makes it likely that
the weights are also useful to the
target domain.

Source domain is
unrelated to the
target domain.

Source domain is
more related to the
target domain.

*Transferring from a smaller data set is usually redundant: if
your target has more data it already has the advantage in
amount of information. This is a difficult space to operate in.*

Source data
smaller than
target

Figure 13.5   The tradeoff between source and target dataset size and relevance. The top-right corner
is the best place to be, and top-left is sub-optimal and won't always work. The bottom half is a uniformly
difficult place to do effective transfer learning.

```
filters_pretrained = model_pretrained.conv1.weight.data.cpu().numpy()  ◄───┐
```
Grabs the first convolutional filters
weights, moves them to the CPU,
and turns them into a NumPy tensor

The `filters_pretrained` object now has a copy of the weights used by the model. It
has a shape of $(64, 3, 7, 7)$ because ResNet-18's first layer has 64 filters and expects an
input with 3 channels (red, green, and blue), and the 64 filters are each 7×7 in width
and height. Since we want to plot these, let's first normalize the filters to the range $[0, 1]$,
since that is what Matplotlib expects for color images:

Shift so everything is in
the range [0, Max value]

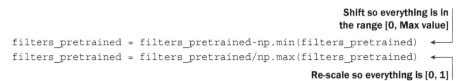

```
filters_pretrained = filters_pretrained-np.min(filters_pretrained)  ◄───┘
filters_pretrained = filters_pretrained/np.max(filters_pretrained)  ◄───┐
```
Re-scale so everything is [0, 1]

Matplotlib also expects images to be formatted as (W, H, C), but PyTorch uses (C, W, H). To fix this, we move the channel dimension (1, because dimension 0 has the number of filters) to the last position (-1) to match Matplotlib's expectations:

```
filters_pretrained = np.moveaxis(filters_pretrained, 1, -1)  ◄── The weights are shaped (#Filters, C, W, H), but Matplotlib expects (W, H, C), so we move the channel dimension.
```

LOOK TO THE FILTERS

Next we can plot the filters. You should see a number of common patterns among them, like white/black edges at different angles and frequencies (one white and one black line, versus several). These black-and-white filters act as edge detectors, detecting edges at different angles and patterns with different rates of repetition. You also see a few filters that have a single color like blue, red, purple, or green. These filters detect specific color patterns. If you have a large, diverse enough training set, you'll tend to see results like these in your first convolutional layer, even if it is a completely different problem:

```
i_max = int(round(np.sqrt(filters_pretrained.shape[0])))   ◄── Take sqrt(# items) to make a square grid of images
j_max = int(np.floor(filters_pretrained.shape[0] /          ◄── Divides by the # of rows
    float(i_max)))
f, axarr = plt.subplots(i_max, j_max,      ◄── Makes the grid in which to plot the images
    figsize=(10,10))
for i in range(i_max):                     ◄── Each row
    for j in range(j_max):                 ◄── Each column
        indx = i*j_max+j                   ◄── Indexes into the filters

        axarr[i,j].imshow(filters_pretrained[indx,:])    ◄── Plots the specific filter
        axarr[i,j].set_axis_off()          ◄── Turns off the numbered axis to avoid clutter
```

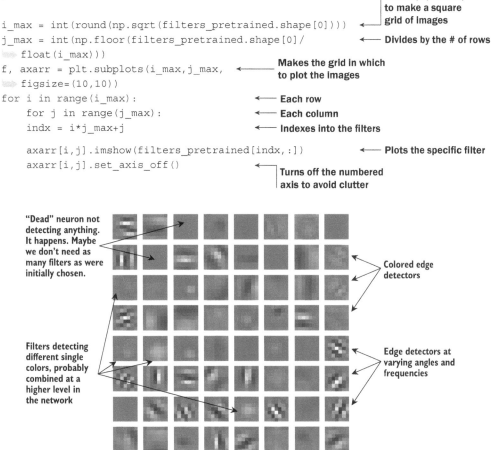

"Dead" neuron not detecting anything. It happens. Maybe we don't need as many filters as were initially chosen.

Colored edge detectors

Filters detecting different single colors, probably combined at a higher level in the network

Edge detectors at varying angles and frequencies

But we got that with ImageNet's 1 million training images. We have around 20,000, which is far fewer. What happens when we learn filters from scratch on this data? Let's take a look at the `model` we trained and find out. This uses the same code as before, but we wrap it in a function called `visualizeFilters` that takes in the tensor to visualize. We pass in the first `conv1` filters from the original `model` we trained from scratch, and we can see the filters that result:

```
filters_catdog = model.conv1.weight.data.cpu().numpy()    ◄── Filters from the model we trained at the start of this chapter
visualizeFilters(filters_catdog)    ◄── Plots the results
```

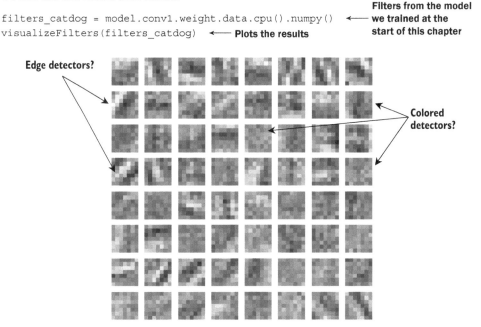

Edge detectors?

Colored detectors?

Pretrained ResNet-18 had nice, crisp filters, and it was easy to see what each had learned to detect. Here, the filters look like they contain noise. We see some evidence of black/ white edge-detection filters forming, but they are also tainted with color information. This means a filter that is working to detect edges will partially fire for items without edges but with the right color—which could cause issues down the line.

In general, you should not judge the quality of a model by what the filters look like but instead by the behavior of the model on realistic, diverse test data. In this case, we know what good filters *usually* look like in the first layer of an RGB image model and can make reasonable comparisons. These filters don't look good.

But just because the filters are different does not mean they are always worse. To judge that, we would need to train the pretrained network and compare the accuracy on the test data. If the pretrained model had better accuracy, the quality of the initial convolutional filters could be one valid explanation for why the performance was worse.

13.2.2 *Preprocessing for pretrained ResNet*

Now that we have some intuition as to *why* we want to use a pretrained network, let's train a new network and find out if it is any better. It is critically important that we make our input data match the pretrained model's expectations. In particular, the ImageNet models in `torchvision.models` use a standardization of zero mean and unit variance ($\mu = 0$, $\sigma = 1$) for each input color channel. The particular coefficients used are from ImageNet, so we quickly define a new `Module` to normalize the input before it's passed to the pretrained network.

> **WARNING** If you use transfer learning via a pretrained network, you *must* make sure your preprocessing of the data matches how the model was originally trained. Otherwise, the model will not get what it initially expects, and the weights become meaningless. The preprocessing used isn't always well documented, which can be annoying, and it's a critical gotcha detail to look out for.

The next block of code does this normalization. The entire model that does all the work is passed in as the `baseModel`, and we wrap it with a `Module` that pre-normalizes the input. This normalization is specified by how ResNet was originally trained, and we use `requires_grad=False` so the normalization isn't altered during training:

```
class NormalizeInput(nn.Module):
    def __init__(self, baseModel):
        """
        baseModel: the original ResNet model that needs to have its inputs
            pre-processed
        """
        super(NormalizeInput, self).__init__()          The model that we want to use.
        self.baseModel = baseModel       ◀────────────  We need to normalize its input first.
        self.mean = nn.Parameter(torch.tensor(
            [0.485, 0.456, 0.406]).view(1,3,1,1),    ◀──  The mean and standard
            requires_grad=False)                          deviation used for ImageNet
        self.std = nn.Parameter(torch.tensor(             normalization. We just have
            [0.229, 0.224, 0.225]).view(1,3,1,1),    ◀──  to accept these "magic"
            requires_grad=False)                          numbers that everyone uses.

    def forward(self, input):
        input = (input-self.mean)/self.std    ◀──  Normalizes the input and then feeds
        return self.baseModel(input)    ◀──────────  it into the model we want to use
```

`requires_grad=False:` we don't want these values to change during training!

> **WARNING** A lot of code you see online hardcodes this normalization step or hardcodes it into the data loader. I don't like either of these approaches. The normalization is *specific* to networks pretrained on ImageNet. That means it's not part of the data, so it shouldn't be part of the transforms used in the `Dataset` class. If you want to switch to something else, you may not want to use the same normalization. I prefer making the normalization part of the model because that's intrinsically where these normalization values came from! I appear to be in the minority on this, so be on the lookout when you read other people's code.

This `NormalizeInput` class performs the normalization used for the pretrained ResNet models in PyTorch. Now we can wrap our pretrained model with this normalizing `Module` to get the correct behavior. This way, there is no mismatch between how we have formatted our data and what the pretrained weights were expecting. I like this approach because it encapsulates the peculiarity of the preprocessing that is *specific to this circumstance* into its own class. If we want to change to a different model or augment the data loader with our own transformations, we can do so without worrying about the model-specific preprocessing that must occur, because the model-specific processing is part of the model. This happens here in a single line of code that wraps the pretrained model with this specific normalizer:

```
model_pretrained = NormalizeInput(model_pretrained)
```

Our model preprocessing matches what the pretrained model expects, and we can finally move on to training the network. There are two primary approaches to doing so, which we will discuss.

13.2.3 *Training with warm starts*

We have a pretrained model that is set to preprocess the data correctly, and we have our new data. The simplest way to go forward is to call `train_network` with `model_pretrained` and see what happens. The following line trains this model, and we can check the results and see how it did. We called these the `warmstart_results` because this approach to transfer learning is called a *warm start*:

```
warmstart_results = train_network(model_pretrained, loss, train_loader,
    epochs=10, device=device, test_loader=test_loader, score_funcs={'Accuracy':
    accuracy_score})
```

A nuanced point worth making is that warm starting and transfer learning are *not* synonyms. Training *any* model with a warm start is when you use *any* set of initial weight values Θ_{init} that you expect to be closer to your desired solution than using the default random values. Warm starts are a common optimization approach, and transfer learning is not the only situation where warm starts happen. So if someone tells you they are using a warm start, that does not necessarily mean they are doing any kind of transfer learning. In short, a warm start simply means you have an initial set of weights that you believe are better than random weights. It so happens that one approach to transfer learning is via this warm-start strategy.

Warm starts outside transfer learning

A common application of warm starts outside of transfer learning is hyperparameter optimization with linear models. Because linear models are often trained with exact solvers (you converge to the one true answer), their runtime depends in part on the values used at the start of the process. When you are training 10+ models, each with a different regularization penalty λ, the solution to the model with one value of λ is probably similar to the solution with a slightly different value $\lambda + \epsilon$. Since you will arrive at the correct answer regardless of starting point, you can warm-start the solution to $\lambda + \epsilon$ using the previous solution found for λ.

This technique is very popular with Lasso-regularized models and support vector machines because of their higher training costs and the need to do a hyperparameter search to get good results. This is what happens with tools like scikit's `LassoCV` class (http://mng.bz/nrB8).

Since our warm weights come from a model trained on another problem, the weights are how we *transfer* knowledge from the original domain to the new domain. Another name for this approach is *fine tuning*: we have something that is generically good, and we want to adjust it slightly to our specific problem.

By calling the `train_network` function with the pretrained weights, we are performing that slight adjustment, because gradient descent will alter every weight of the network to try to minimize the loss. When we plot the results to see if this was a good idea, a dramatic difference in accuracy occurs. The warm start didn't just reach a higher accuracy: it reached a higher accuracy after a *single* epoch. That means we could have made this whole process 10× faster by not training for 10 epochs. We obviously didn't know that in advance, but this illustrates the kinds of advantages you see when using pretraining. You converge faster, often to better solutions:

```
sns.lineplot(x='epoch', y='test Accuracy', data=normal_results,
    label='Regular')
sns.lineplot(x='epoch', y='test Accuracy', data=warmstart_results,
    label='Warm')
```

```
[24]:   <AxesSubplot:xlabel='epoch', ylabel='test Accuracy'>
```

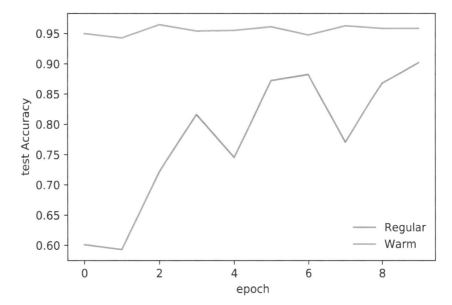

This double win of better accuracy in less time is part of why transfer learning is one of the most useful tools to tackle new problems. We can also get some intuition about how useful the warm start was by comparing the weights before and after fine-tuning. The following code again calls `visualizeFilters` to look at the convolutional filters after the fine-tuning of the ResNet-18 model. The filters are essentially identical to what we started with, which is a good indicator that they are indeed generically good filters for many problems. If they weren't, SGD would have altered them more to improve its accuracy:

Grabs the filters after fine-tuning the warm-started model

```
filters_catdog_finetuned = model_pretrained.baseModel.
    conv1.weight.data.cpu().numpy()
visualizeFilters(filters_catdog_finetuned)
```

Plots the filters, which look very similar to the pretrained model's initial filters

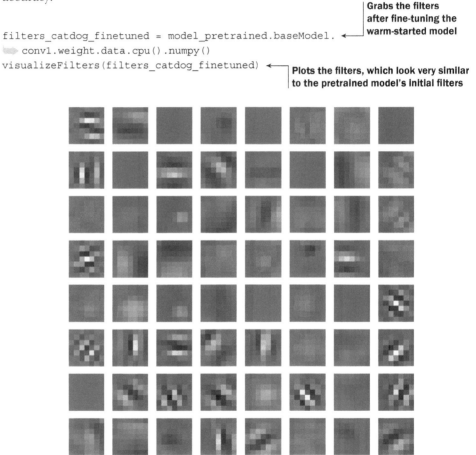

13.2.4 *Training with frozen weights*

We also have another option for transfer learning in this situation called *weight freezing* or using *frozen* weights. Weight freezing is when we decide not to alter the parameters/ coefficients of a layer. Gradients are still calculated and backpropagated through the layer, but when we perform gradient updates, we make no changes—as if we set the learning rate $\eta = 0$.

It is not possible to use weight freezing for *all* layers of the network; that would mean there is nothing to train! Training is only meaningful if we adjust at least some of the parameters of the model. A common approach is to freeze the weights for all the convolutional and normalizing layers and only change the weights of the fully connected layers. This implicitly assumes that the filters learned from the original domain are *as good as or better* than what we could learn on this new domain.

To do this, we start by setting the `requires_grad` flag for every parameter in our model to `False`. This way, no parameter saves a gradient after backpropagation, and thus no changes occur when the optimizer performs the update step. After freezing the entire model, we replace the model's fully connected layer, which by default has `requires_grad=True`. We want this since the new fully connected layer is the only layer we want to adjust. Then we can build and train the model just as we did with the warm-start approach. The following code does the freezing process and then trains the model:

```
model_frozen = torchvision.models.resnet18(pretrained=True)
for param in model_frozen.parameters():
    param.requires_grad = False
```

Turn off gradient updating for all parameters!

```
model_frozen.fc = nn.Linear(model_frozen.fc.in_features, 2)
model_frozen = NormalizeInput(model_frozen)
```

Our new fc layer has requires_grad = True by default.

```
frozen_transfer_results = train_network(model_frozen, loss, train_loader,
    epochs=10, device=device, test_loader=test_loader,
    score_funcs={'Accuracy': accuracy_score})
```

Next we plot the results. The frozen model is *very* stable in its results. That makes sense because it isn't adjusting nearly as many parameters. It performs just a smidge worse than the warm model but still far better than the naive approach of training from scratch:

```
sns.lineplot(x='epoch', y='test Accuracy', data=normal_results,
    label='Regular')
sns.lineplot(x='epoch', y='test Accuracy', data=warmstart_results,
    label='Warm Start')
sns.lineplot(x='epoch', y='test Accuracy', data=frozen_transfer_results,
    label='Frozen')
```

[27]: <AxesSubplot:xlabel='epoch', ylabel='test Accuracy'>

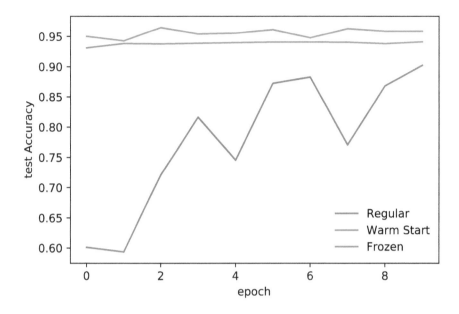

So which is better, warm or frozen weights? This single result seems to indicate a minor tradeoff: warm weights are more accurate, but frozen weights are more consistent. This is *true* but does not tell the full story. To hear that story, keep reading: the next section talks about the primary factor that can tip the scales in this tradeoff—*dataset size*.

13.3   *Learning with fewer labels*

So far, we have warm starting and frozen weights as our two primary methods of performing transfer learning. These are the most common and successful ways of doing transfer learning in practice. But when should you do which? You can always try both and see which works best, but frozen weights have a particular advantage when you have extremely small amounts of training data.

Why would that be? Imagine that a single ideal set of parameters Θ^* will give the best performance for a problem.[2] Your ability to find *any* set of parameters Θ depends on how much data (and compute resources) you can get. One *simplified* way to think about this is that your estimate of the true parameters is a noisy view of them:

$$\Theta \;=\; \Theta^* \;+\; \epsilon$$

Your best guess ⟶ | **the truth**   **noise**

---

2   This is often described as having an oracle that can magically deliver to you the *perfect* solution.

The more data you have, the better the model you can build, and $\epsilon \to 0$. If you have *no* data, you can only pick answers randomly because you can only pick Θ randomly, so $\epsilon \to \infty$. Clearly, the size of your training data N impacts how well you can estimate your parameters.

The other factor is how many parameters you have. Imagine if you had 1,000 data points about the height of random people. You could probably get a very accurate estimate about the average height and standard deviation of heights for people in general from this 1,000-person sample. But what if you want to document *1 trillion* different things, such as every possible interaction of DNA with height, weight, hair color, health, diseases, left-/right-handedness, propensity for making bad puns, and so on? There are too many interactions, and your ability to get an accurate answer for *every* one of those things from just 1,000 people will be astronomically low. The number of parameters D is a factor in how well you can estimate your model. Crudely, we could say

Your best guess of the model's parameters is equal to

the best possible solution for the parameters plus

some amount of noise that

is amplified (made worse) by having more parameters

but reduced (made easier) by having more data.

$$\theta = \theta^* + \frac{\epsilon \cdot D}{N}$$

This is a very rough intuitive form. There is no truly linear relationship between solution quality, the number of features D, and the number of data points N.[3] The point is to illustrate that if you do not have enough data N, and you have too many parameters D, you will not learn a good model.

This gives us more understanding of when to use warm versus frozen weights. When we freeze weights, they are no longer parameters we can modify, which effectively reduces the D term of the equation and better estimates the remaining parameters. This is also why the frozen approach is more stable than the warm approach: the noise factor is dampened by reducing the number of parameters D.

This is particularly valuable when we have less labeled data. To show how, we can simulate the situation with our cats versus dogs classifier by randomly sampling a small

---

[3] My oversimplification is very oversimplified, but the intuition is a good one to have. It is an intuition that will hold for most machine learning but not always for deep learning. It is very hard to prove things about deep learning: much progress has been made, but when D becomes large, you should always second-guess your intuitions. It is difficult to reason about such high-dimensional spaces. For more discussion of the weirdness of learning the parameters of neural networks, I encourage you to look at C. Zhang et al., "Understanding deep learning requires rethinking generalization," International Conference on Learning Representations, 2017.

portion to use for training: twice our batch size, for a total of 256 training images. This is normally *far* too little data to learn any kind of CNN from scratch:

```
train_data_small, _ = torch.utils.data.random_split(
    train_data, (B*2,len(train_data)-B*2))
train_loader_small = DataLoader(train_data_small,
    batch_size=B, shuffle=True)
```

Makes the small dataset = 2* the batch size

Makes the loader for this tiny dataset

Now we have a *much* smaller dataset. We can train a model using all three approaches: from scratch, using a warm start, and using frozen weights. Our first results showed a warm start performing slightly better than freezing. If our understanding is correct, freezing the weights should do better than a warm start in this scenario. To test this, let's train up each of these options:

```
model = torchvision.models.resnet18()                          ←— 1. Training from scratch
model.fc = nn.Linear(model.fc.in_features, 2)

normal_small_results = train_network(model, loss, train_loader_small,
    epochs=10, device=device, test_loader=test_loader,
    score_funcs={'Accuracy': accuracy_score})

model = torchvision.models.resnet18(pretrained=True)           ←— 2. Training the warm model
model.fc = nn.Linear(model.fc.in_features, 2)                  ←— Performs some surgery
model = NormalizeInput(model)

warmstart_small_results = train_network(model, loss, train_loader_small,
    epochs=10, device=device, test_loader=test_loader,
    score_funcs={'Accuracy': accuracy_score})

model = torchvision.models.resnet18(pretrained=True)           ←— 3. Training with frozen weights

for param in model.parameters():
    param.requires_grad = False

model.fc = nn.Linear(model.fc.in_features, 2)

model = NormalizeInput(model)

frozen_transfer_small_results = train_network(model, loss,
    train_loader_small, epochs=10, device=device, test_loader=test_loader,
    score_funcs={'Accuracy': accuracy_score})
```

Turns off gradient updating for all parameters

Our new fc layer has requires_grad = True by default.

Notice that we didn't change *any* of the code for each of these three options. They all operate mechanically the same way as before; the only difference is how little data we are giving each model. The results are plotted next, and we can see a huge impact that matches our understanding of how parameter count D and dataset size N affect learning with warm and frozen weights:

```
sns.lineplot(x='epoch', y='test Accuracy', data=normal_small_results,
    label='Regular')
sns.lineplot(x='epoch', y='test Accuracy', data=warmstart_small_results,
    label='Warm Start')
sns.lineplot(x='epoch', y='test Accuracy', data=frozen_transfer_small_results,
    label='Frozen')
```

```
[30]:    <AxesSubplot:xlabel='epoch', ylabel='test Accuracy'>
```

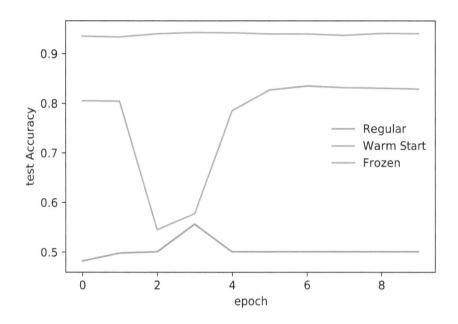

We see a *dramatic* difference in the results. Training from scratch is still the worst, barely getting above 50% accuracy on the test set. Using a warm start is better, with $\approx 80\%$ accuracy; but using frozen convolutional layers does best at $\approx 91\%$, almost as good as the results training on 20,000 samples. So the frozen approach is the best when we have a very limited amount of training data, but its ability for further improvement is also limited. That is where warm starts come in; warm models can start coming out ahead of frozen models if you have enough labeled data (but still not too terribly much).

> **NOTE**   If you are doing on-the-job work that is computer-vision-based, I would almost always recommend starting with pretrained models. The approach is so effective that there is limited reason to train a model from scratch if you want to use current tools and build a product. It's worth training one model from scratch to see if you have a rare problem where pretraining does not work, but otherwise, pretrained models will make your life easier. If you can build a viable solution with pretrained models, you can eventually build a data collection and labeling process to make your own large corpus that can help improve things; but that is a sizable investment. Pretraining helps you reach a viable first solution without having to pay that high cost.

While we have not shown it here, you can also balance between a warm start and a frozen start. As we mentioned earlier, the first convolutional layers of a computer vision task tend to learn filters that are generically useful across a wide array of problems. As you get deeper into the network, the filters become more specialized. In very deep models, the last convolutional filters are often only useful for the specific task at hand.

You can exploit that by freezing the initial layers of the network but allowing the later layers to be altered as a warm start. This hybrid approach can require a bit of trial and error to select the depth at which to stop freezing the weights, depending on your original model (i.e., which version of ResNet or some other architecture), how much data it was trained on, and your new target domain data. The adjustment of freezing versus not-freezing different layers essentially becomes your new way to modify the model when using a pretrained network since you can't add more neurons or layers to something that already exists. This won't always make a huge difference, so many people skip it to focus on designing more/better data-augmentation pipelines as a better return on their time.

13.4 Pretraining with text

The success of using pretrained networks to perform transfer learning depends on learning *robust* features/patterns that are widely applicable. Until recently, this approach had not been successful for natural language processing (NLP) related tasks. Thanks to new models like the *transformer* that we learned about in chapter 12, this situation is finally starting to change.

In particular, a family of transformer-based algorithms has significantly improved the quality of results we can achieve on text problems. The first of these pretrained models is called BERT[4] (yes, named after the character Bert on *Sesame Street*). To get started adjusting a pretrained BERT model, we will reuse the AG News dataset from the last chapter (loading `torchtext`, the `tokenizer` and `vocab` objects, and the `text_transform` and associated `label_transform`), and call the training and test set for AG News `train_dataset_text` and `test_dataset_text`, respectively).

The only real change is that we create a small version of the corpus with 256 labeled items. Learning with limited training data is where transfer learning gets the greatest return on results and also helps these examples run quickly:

```
train_data_text_small, _ = torch.utils.data.random_split(   ◄─── Slices off a
    train_dataset_text, (256,len(train_dataset_text)-256))       tiny dataset
```

Now we train the same GRU model from chapter 12 as a baseline. On the full dataset, a GRU was able to obtain 92% accuracy. With this smaller labeled set, we expect the accuracy to decrease. The following block of code reuses the same `pad_batch` function from the last chapter to train the same GRU model, but we have only 256 labeled examples:

---

[4] J. Devlin, M.-W. Chang, K. Lee, and K. Toutanova, "BERT: Pre-training of deep bidirectional transformers for language understanding," *Proceedings of the 2019 Conference of the North American Chapter of the Association for Computational Linguistics: Human Language Technologies, Volume 1 (Long and Short Papers)*, pp. 4171–4186, 2019.

```
embed_dim = 128
gru = nn.Sequential(
    nn.Embedding(VOCAB_SIZE, embed_dim),               ←—— (B, T) -> (B, T, D)
    nn.GRU(embed_dim, embed_dim, num_layers=3,
      batch_first=True, bidirectional=True),           ←—— (B, T, D) -> ( (B,T,D) , (S, B, D) )
                                                        ←—— Reduces the RNN output
    LastTimeStep(rnn_layers=3, bidirectional=True),          to one item, (B, 2*D)

    nn.Linear(embed_dim*2, NUN_CLASS),                 ←—— (B, D) -> (B, classes)
)


train_text_loader = DataLoader(train_data_text_small,  ⎤ Creates train and test
  batch_size=32, shuffle=True, collate_fn=pad_batch)   ⎦ loaders using collate_fn
test_text_loader = DataLoader(test_dataset_text, batch_size=32,
  collate_fn=pad_batch)
gru_results = train_network(gru, nn.CrossEntropyLoss(),
  train_text_loader, test_loader=test_text_loader,
  device=device, epochs=10,
  score_funcs={'Accuracy': accuracy_score})            ←—— Trains our baseline GRU model
```

13.4.1 Transformers with the Hugging Face library

Our baseline GRU is trained and represents the typical approach we would use. For the transfer learning version, we create a frozen BERT model to gain the benefits of this pretrained text model. The first thing we need is an implementation that contains some pretrained architectures. Lucky for us, the Hugging Face (https://huggingface.co/transformers) library has quickly become a de facto tool and repository for researchers to place the latest and greatest extensions to BERT. To install it, run the following command:

```
!pip install transformers
```

We will use a model called *DistilBERT*,[5] which is a version of the BERT model that has been distilled down into a smaller network with fewer parameters. This is just to make the example run faster, because transformer models in general are computationally expensive. Part of making BERT-type models successful is training large models using dozens of GPUs on hundreds of gigabytes of data. The fact that transformers continue to benefit from more layers and larger datasets, and parallelize well across many GPUs, to a much greater degree than RNNs is part of what makes transformers so powerful. But training a transformer/BERT model from scratch is simply too much investment for many people and teams today. The ability to use transformers for transfer learning is part of what makes them so relevant to the rest of us who don't have a dozen GPUs available at all times.

Because using pretrained BERT models is quickly becoming popular, the models also come with a handy `from_pretrained` function, which can take different strings specifying BERT models trained in different settings. For example, one may have been trained on case-sensitive inputs and another trained on case-insensitive input. The offi-

---

[5] V. Sanh, L. Debut, J. Chaumond, and T. Wolf, "DistilBERT, a distilled version of BERT : smaller, faster, cheaper and lighter," ArXiv e-prints, pp. 2–6, 2019, https://arxiv.org/abs/1910.01108.

cial documentation (https://huggingface.co/transformers/model_doc/distilbert.html) describes which options are available. We use the insensitive one since we have less data (fewer cases means fewer parameters and better performance in small datasets):

Loads the DistilBert classes

```
from transformers import DistilBertTokenizer, DistilBertModel   ◄──┘
tokenizer = DistilBertTokenizer.from_pretrained('distilbert-base-uncased')   ◄──
bert_model = DistilBertModel.from_pretrained('distilbert-base-uncased')
```

Initializes the tokenizer (converts strings to input tensors) and the model (input tensors to output tensors)

Notice that we have not just the `bert_model` but also a *new* tokenizer. This is so we can use the same encoding process used by the original BERT training to convert new strings into inputs for BERT. *We can't mix and match tokenizers between different models.* This is similar to how we used a specific normalizing mean and standard deviation when using the pretrained ResNet-18 model. We need the initial input to the model for our new target domain to be processed the same way as in the original domain. The `tokenizer` object takes raw strings as input and performs all the preprocessing that was used when the original model was trained in the same manner, making our lives easier.

The strategy for implementing our `collate_fn` for the BERT model looks very similar to our GRU model. Instead of calling `text_transform`, we call the `tokenizer` that Hugging Face provides on the original strings. In particular, there is a `batch_encode_plus` function that takes a list of strings and converts it into a batch of data ready for processing (with masks, if you so desire). We simply add the arguments `return_tensors='pt'` to let Hugging Face know we want PyTorch tensors (it supports TensorFlow, too) and the `padding=True` flag so the shorter sentences are padded to equal length:

```
def huggingface_batch(batch):
    """
    Pad items in the batch to the length of the longest item in the batch.
    Also, re-order so that the values are returned (input, label)
    """
    labels = [label_transform(z[0]) for z in batch]   ◄── The first three lines are
    texts = [z[1] for z in batch]                          the same as before.

    texts = tokenizer.batch_encode_plus(texts,   ◄── New: Hugging Face encodes
        return_tensors='pt', padding=True)['input_ids']   a batch of strings for us.

    x, y = texts, torch.tensor(labels, dtype=torch.int64)   ◄── Back to old code:
    return x, y                                                 stack them up and
train_text_bert_loader = DataLoader(                            return the tensors.
    train_data_text_small, batch_size=32, shuffle=True,
    collate_fn=huggingface_batch)   ◄── Makes our data loaders with the new collage_fn
test_text_bert_loader = DataLoader(test_dataset_text, batch_size=32,
    collate_fn=huggingface_batch)
```

Changed: Don't use the old text_transform; get the raw texts. →

13.4.2 *Freezing weights with no-grad*

The last thing we need is our BERT model with frozen weights. Since the output contains padding, we define a `Module` class to figure out the mask for the padding and use it as appropriate. BERT gives us an output tensor of shape (B, T, D), which we need to reduce to (B, D) to make a classification prediction. The `getMaskByFill` function from chapter 12 gives us the padding mask so that we can reuse the attention layers to average over only the valid (not padded) tokens. We can access the number of hidden neurons D that BERT is using with the `bert_model.config.dim` variable. Each model in Hugging Face has a `.config` variable with various information about how the model is configured.

We also use this as an opportunity to show a different approach to frozen weights. Instead of manually setting `requires_grad=False` for each parameter, we can use the `with torch.no_grad():` context instead. It has the same effect, computing gradients for any needed backpropagation but forgetting them immediately so they are not used during the gradient update. This is convenient if we want to make the freezing adaptive or make the code more explicit that gradients will not be used for a portion of it. The downside to this approach is that it's difficult to implement models with a mix of warm and frozen layers.

Here's the code:

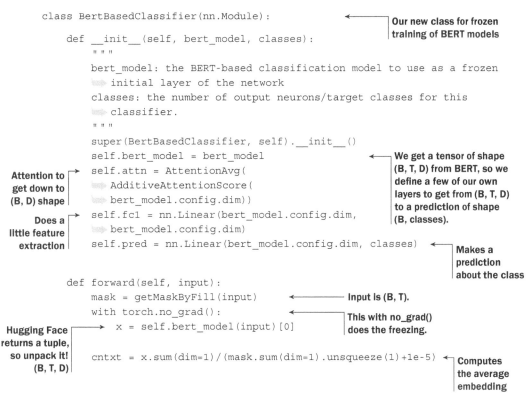

```
class BertBasedClassifier(nn.Module):          ◄─────── Our new class for frozen
    def __init__(self, bert_model, classes):           training of BERT models
        """
        bert_model: the BERT-based classification model to use as a frozen
        ⮑ initial layer of the network
        classes: the number of output neurons/target classes for this
        ⮑ classifier.
        """
        super(BertBasedClassifier, self).__init__()
        self.bert_model = bert_model               ◄─── We get a tensor of shape
        self.attn = AttentionAvg(                       (B, T, D) from BERT, so we
            AdditiveAttentionScore(                     define a few of our own
            bert_model.config.dim))                     layers to get from (B, T, D)
        self.fc1 = nn.Linear(bert_model.config.dim,     to a prediction of shape
            bert_model.config.dim)                      (B, classes).
        self.pred = nn.Linear(bert_model.config.dim, classes)   ◄─── Makes a
                                                                     prediction
                                                                     about the class

    def forward(self, input):
        mask = getMaskByFill(input)        ◄─────── Input is (B, T).
        with torch.no_grad():              ◄─── This with no_grad()
            x = self.bert_model(input)[0]        does the freezing.

        cntxt = x.sum(dim=1)/(mask.sum(dim=1).unsqueeze(1)+1e-5)   ◄─── Computes
                                                                       the average
                                                                       embedding
```

Attention to get down to (B, D) shape

Does a little feature extraction

Hugging Face returns a tuple, so unpack it! (B, T, D)

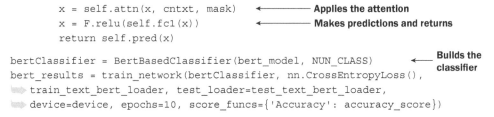

```
        x = self.attn(x, cntxt, mask)        ←——————— Applies the attention
        x = F.relu(self.fc1(x))              ←——————— Makes predictions and returns
        return self.pred(x)
```

```
bertClassifier = BertBasedClassifier(bert_model, NUN_CLASS)    ←—— Builds the
bert_results = train_network(bertClassifier, nn.CrossEntropyLoss(),    classifier
➥ train_text_bert_loader, test_loader=test_text_bert_loader,
➥ device=device, epochs=10, score_funcs={'Accuracy': accuracy_score})
```

As before, we can train this BERT-based classifier using our handy `train_network`
function:

```
sns.lineplot(x='epoch', y='test Accuracy', data=gru_results,
➥ label='Regular-GRU')
sns.lineplot(x='epoch', y='test Accuracy', data=bert_results,
➥ label='Frozen-BERT')
```

[41]:   <AxesSubplot:xlabel='epoch', ylabel='test Accuracy'>

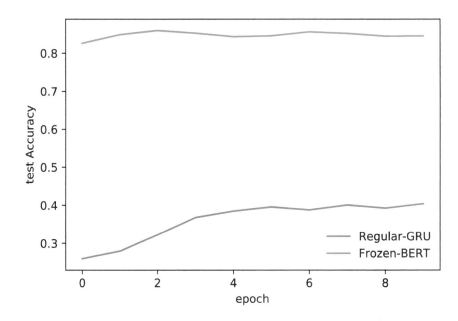

Looking at the results, we can see that the GRU is learning, but very slowly. The GRU
tops out at ≈ 40% accuracy, less than half of the 92% it can achieve on the full training
set. Our frozen BERT model gets ≈ 84%, which is a significant improvement. There is
a higher price in this case, though. As we mentioned earlier, BERT-style models tend
to be very large and thus computationally expensive. Training and applying our BERT
classifier was about 10× slower than the GRU.

From a model accuracy perspective, it is clearly a net win since the GRU will never get
to 84% accuracy on its own. The BERT-based model may be too slow to apply in practice,
though. It depends on the resources available and the specifics of the problem at hand.

This is an important tradeoff to be aware of, and it is not uncommon when using the pretraining approach. Intrinsically, we want to use the pretrained model because it was already trained on a larger dataset, but that also means the models become larger to maximize accuracy.

In my personal experience, I've found that pretrained transformers often start to lose their advantage as you build up the labeled dataset for your problem. Whereas pretrained CNNs almost always outperform those trained from scratch, I often find that with transformers, there isn't such a clear-cut, consistent result. Sometimes they are better, sometimes not. This is especially true compared to non-deep approaches like Lasso-penalized logistic regression, which performs very competitively on many text datasets.

Still, using a pretrained model for textual data is now a possibility. It will likely improve with time and is a powerful tool when you have very few training samples. Keep it in your toolbox, but explore the alternatives if you have a text-based problem.

Exercises

Share and discuss your solutions on the Manning online platform at Inside Deep Learning Exercises (https://liveproject.manning.com/project/945). Once you submit your own answers, you will be able to see the solutions submitted by other readers, and see which ones the author judges to be the best.

1. Use the `dir` command to explore the subcomponents of the PyTorch `resnet18` model, and write your own function `def warmFrozenResnet18(num_frozen)` that freezes only the first `num_frozen` convolutional layers in the network.

2. Using your `warmFrozenResnet18` function, explore the tradeoffs between the degree of warm versus frozen layers when using $N = 256$, $N = 1,024$, and $N = 8,192$ labeled training samples.

3. Repeat the previous two exercises, but use the `MobileNet` class instead.

4. Go back to chapter 8, where we trained Faster R-CNN to detect the location of MNIST digits. Do your own pretraining of the backbone network as an MNIST classifier, and then use that pretrained backbone to train Faster R-CNN. Test the results on a number of images, and describe any differences you see in the results. *Note:* This will be easier if you make the `backbone` have two parts: one that is the larger feature processing subnetwork containing only convolutional layers and pooling, and a second prediction subnetwork that does any final pooling (optional), flattening, and prediction of the class label. Then you can use just the feature processing subnetwork for the Faster R-CNN.

5. You can use autoencoders to do unsupervised pretraining when you have a lot of data but most of it is unlabeled. Write a denoising autoencoder for the cats versus dogs problem that is trained on the entire dataset, and then use the encoder

portion as the warm start for a classifier. You can think of the encoder feature as the processing backbone, and you need to add a prediction subnetwork on top.

6 Hugging Face has special classes to make it easier to use pretrained models. Look up the documentation for the `DistilBertForSequenceClassification` class, and replace our approach for the AG News dataset with the Hugging Face API's built-in approach. How do they compare?

Summary

- You can transfer knowledge by reusing the weights of a network that has already been trained on one dataset, applying them to a new dataset, and performing surgery on the final layer of the network to make it match your problem.

- The weights of a pretrained model can be warm (allowed to change) or frozen (kept constant) during training, providing different benefits when you have more or less data, respectively.

- The benefits of transfer learning are greatest when we have very little labeled data.

- Pretraining for convolutional networks and computer vision problems is extremely effective, whereas pretraining for text problems is still useful but has more tradeoffs due to differences in model size and compute time.

- Pretraining for text is best done with transformer-type models trained on large corpora.

Advanced building blocks

The exercises in this book have thus far been designed so that you can learn about *real* techniques in a minimal amount of compute time. But when you work on real-world problems, they often require hundreds of epochs and models that are deeper than what you have trained so far, and they must process larger inputs than the examples in this book.

When tackling these larger data sets, it sometimes takes extra tools to get the best results. This chapter covers some of the latest and greatest techniques that researchers have developed to improve deep learning models: techniques that often work best when training on larger data sets for many epochs. We focus on approaches that are simple, broadly useful, effective, and easy to implement. For these more advanced techniques, you often will not see the full benefit on smaller models or by training for only 10 to 20 epochs as we have for most of the book. In practice, these techniques bear the greatest fruit when training for 100 to 300 epochs. I have designed experiments to show some of the benefits in a relatively short amount of time, but you should expect more significant benefits on bigger problems.

We cover three approaches that you can safely add to almost any model and get a tangible improvement. Anti-aliasing pooling improves on the pooling operation we have been using, making it better for almost any CNN application. This pooling increases accuracy by better handling small shifts in the content of an image. Next, we look at a newer approach to residual connections called ReZero, allowing our networks a little more flexibility to decide when and how to use a skip connection. As a result, they are more accurate and converge in fewer epochs, simultaneously making learning faster. Finally, we talk about a new way to construct our loss functions: MixUp, the foundation for a growing approach to improving almost any neural network's results by reducing overfitting.

14.1 Problems with pooling

Pooling was an early component of CNNs and has seen the least change over the years. As we discussed in chapter 3, pooling layers help us endow our models with translation invariance: they produce the same or a similar answer when we shift the content of an image up/down or left/right. They also increase the receptive field of postceding layers, allowing each convolutional layer to view more of the input at once and gain additional context. Despite their ubiquity, a subtle flaw has plagued CNNs for decades, and only recently have we noticed it and devised a simple solution. The crux of the problem is that naive pooling loses more information than necessary and introduces noise as a result. We walk through an example that demonstrates how this loss of information happens, and then we discuss the solution and develop a new pooling layer to fix it.

For the problem demonstration, we will download an image of a zebra from Wikipedia.[1] The fact that this is a zebra is important, as you'll see in moment. The following code downloads the image from the given URL and converts it to a Python Imaging Library (PIL) image:

```
import requests
from PIL import Image
from io import BytesIO

url = "https://upload.wikimedia.org/wikipedia/
    commons/9/9c/Zebra_in_Mikumi.JPG"

response = requests.get(url)
img = Image.open(BytesIO(response.content))
```

Now we resize the image to 1,000 pixels on the shortest dimension and crop out the center content. The primary purpose of this step is to alter the code so you can try different images yourself afterward. The `ToTensor` transform then converts the PIL image to an appropriate PyTorch `Tensor` with its values scaled to the range $[0, 1]$:

---

[1]   Image by Sajjad Fazel: https://commons.wikimedia.org/wiki/User:SajjadF.

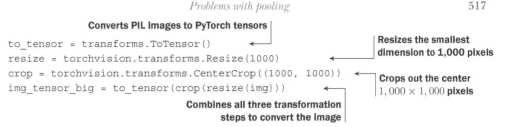

```
to_tensor = transforms.ToTensor()
resize = torchvision.transforms.Resize(1000)
crop = torchvision.transforms.CenterCrop((1000, 1000))
img_tensor_big = to_tensor(crop(resize(img)))
```

Converts PIL Images to PyTorch tensors

Resizes the smallest dimension to 1,000 pixels

Crops out the center $1,000 \times 1,000$ **pixels**

Combines all three transformation steps to convert the image

Next, a simple application of ToPILImage converts the image back into the original PIL image object. Jupyter notebooks are smart enough to display these images automatically, and you should see two zebras in the image. Notice that while the background content is fuzzy and out of focus, the zebras are crisp and well captured. Their fur and black-and-white stripes are clear and easy to see, including the more dense collection of stripes on their faces:

```
to_img = transforms.ToPILImage()
to_img(img_tensor_big)
```

Now we use max pooling to shrink the image by a factor of four. We are shrinking it by four times instead of two to exacerbate the issue with pooling. The following code does the pooling and then prints the image, allowing us to see that something is definitely off:

```
shrink_factor = 4                                     How much pooling to perform
img_tensor_small = F.max_pool2d(img_tensor_big,
    (shrink_factor,shrink_factor))                    Applies pooling
to_img(img_tensor_small)                              Resulting image
```

While the background still looks fine, the zebras have many pixelated patterns in their stripes, often called *jaggies*. The jaggies get worse where the black-and-white stripes are denser. They are noticeable, but not horrific, near the zebra's rump; they're distractingly bad toward the chest; and the faces look seriously garbled and lack any of the detail from the original photo.

This issue is called *aliasing*. A simplified explanation is that aliasing occurs when you try to *sample* fine, detailed information into a smaller space. We are emphasizing the word *sample* here because aliasing occurs when we are *selecting exact values* from a larger representation to fill out a smaller representation. This means many different inputs can result in the same block-like jaggies, and the more you try to shrink the input, the worse the problem gets.

Let's look at a toy example of how aliasing occurs. Figure 14.1 shows three different one-dimensional patterns. The first has black and white blocks in a fixed pattern, alternating one after the other. The second shows the blocks in pairs of two, and the third has a pair of adjacent white blocks but no adjacent black blocks. Even though the patterns are different, simple max-pooling gives the same output for all of them.

This is not great. But is it a problem? We have built several CNNs that seem to work fine, and people have been using max pooling for decades. Maybe this is not a big deal unless we want to build zebra detectors. While our CNNs work, the aliasing problem is real and gets worse every time we add another pooling layer to our architectures. By understanding why aliasing is a problem, we can build up the knowledge we need to understand how to fix the problem.

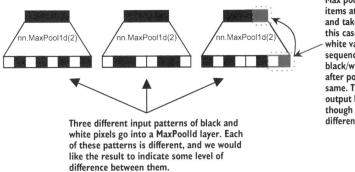

Max pooling looks at two items at a time in the input and takes the maximum (in this case, a black value > white value). Because every sequence of two pixels is a black/white pair, the result after pooling is always the same. This makes every output look identical even though the inputs are different.

Three different input patterns of black and white pixels go into a MaxPool1d layer. Each of these patterns is different, and we would like the result to indicate some level of difference between them.

Figure 14.1 Example of how the aliasing problem can lose information. Three different inputs go into the max-pooling layer, but we obtain three identical outputs. This is an extreme case, but it demonstrates the fundamental problem.

14.1.1 Aliasing compromises translation invariance

To show why aliasing is an issue, we'll use the CIFAR-10 data set due to its greater complexity compared to MNIST. CIFAR images have 32×32 height and width, but we select a smaller block of 24×24 pixels by taking a random crop of the image. (When taking smaller sub-images, it's common practice to use a random crop for training for more diversity and a center crop for the test set to get consistent results.) This way, we can test our CNN on shifts of up to eight pixels top/down or left/right to see the impact that translating the image's content has on the CNN's predictions. Pooling is supposed to improve translation invariance (i.e., you get the same result even if you shift things around), but we'll show how aliasing prevents us from getting the full benefit.

> **NOTE** Training on crops that are slightly smaller than the original image size is a fairly common practice with images 128×128 or larger. Doing so provides extra diversity to your model's inputs, avoids showing the exact same image multiple times as you progress through multiple epochs of training, and gives the model a little more realism (data is rarely nicely centered). We wouldn't normally do this for an image as small as 32×32 because of how little content there is, but we need to so that we have pixels to shift.

The next block of code sets up CIFAR-10 with the sub-images we described. We use a random 24×24 crop during training, and we create two different versions of the same test set. In general, your test should be deterministic—you want to get the same results if you do the same thing. It would be very hard to determine whether a model change yielded any improvement if running the same model with the same weights gave a different test result each time. To make our test deterministic, our test loader takes a center crop so the test images are the same every time. But we also want to look at some of the results as different shifts occur, so we make a second version that returns the original 32×32 images: we can manually crop them to look at how shifts change the model's predictions:

```
B = 128
epochs = 30

train_transform = transforms.Compose(          ← Transform for training:
    [                                             random crop to PyTorch tensor
        transforms.RandomCrop((24,24)),
        transforms.ToTensor(),
    ])
test_transform = transforms.Compose(           ← Transform for testing:
    [                                             crops the center to a PyTorch tensor
        transforms.CenterCrop((24,24)),
        transforms.ToTensor(),
    ])

trainset = torchvision.datasets.CIFAR10(root='./data', train=True,
    download=True, transform=train_transform)
train_loader = torch.utils.data.DataLoader(trainset, batch_size=B,
    shuffle=True, num_workers=2)
testset_nocrop = torchvision.datasets.CIFAR10(          ← A version of the test set with
    root='./data', train=False, download=True,            full 32 × 32 images, so we
    transform=transforms.ToTensor())                      can test specific crops

testset = torchvision.datasets.CIFAR10(root='./data', train=False,
    download=True, transform=test_transform)
                                                       The test loader used
test_loader = torch.utils.data.DataLoader(testset,  ← during evaluation is the
    batch_size=B, shuffle=False, num_workers=2)        deterministic center crop.
cifar10_classes = ('plane', 'car', 'bird', 'cat',   ← Maps the class index back to
    'deer', 'dog', 'frog', 'horse', 'ship', 'truck')   their original names for CIFAR-10
```

Let's see what the data looks like with our random cropping. The following code selects the same image from the training set four times and then plots it with the class label. Each time, the image is shifted a bit, adding extra complexity:

```
f, axarr = plt.subplots(1,4, figsize=(20,10))      ← Makes a 1 × 4 grid
for i in range(4):                                   Grabs a specific item from
    x, y = trainset[30]                            ← the training set (I like planes)
    axarr[i].imshow(x.numpy().transpose(1,2,0))    ← Reorders to the (W, H, C)
    axarr[i].text(0.0, 0.5,cifar10_classes[y].upper(),  shape that NumPy and
        dict(size=30, color='black'))                   Matplotlib like for images
```

Plots with the class name in the corner

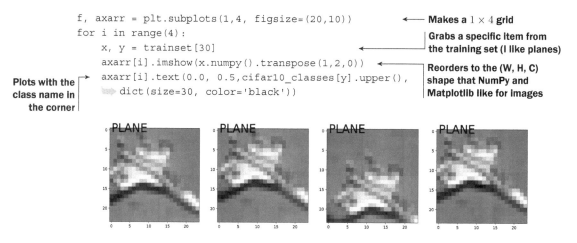

Now let's train a simple network using convolutions and the allegedly flawed max pooling. We use just two rounds of max pooling here, equivalent to the same amount of pooling we used for the example with the zebra. This is enough to demonstrate the problems with pooling even on non-zebra inputs. In general, the issues become worse with even more pooling. In this code, and throughout this chapter, we add our trusty `CosineAnnealingLR` scheduler from chapter 6. It helps maximize the results and allows us to show in only 30 epochs some behaviors that are usually seen only after 100 epochs of training (that doesn't mean you shouldn't do 100 epochs on a real production problem, just that we can show the kind of behavior more quickly this way). Here's the code:

```
C = 3                ◄───── Number of input channels
h = 16               ◄───── Number of channels in the hidden layer
filter_size = 3
pooling_rounds = 2

def cnnLayer(in_size, out_size, filter_size):   ◄──  Helper function as we
    return nn.Sequential(                           have done many times
        nn.Conv2d(in_size, out_size, filter_size, padding=filter_size//2),
        nn.BatchNorm2d(out_size),
        nn.ReLU())

normal_CNN = nn.Sequential(          ◄──  A normal CNN with blocks of two CNN
    cnnLayer(C, h, filter_size),         layers separated by max pooling
    cnnLayer(h, h, filter_size),
    nn.MaxPool2d(2),
    cnnLayer(h, h, filter_size),
    cnnLayer(h, h, filter_size),
    nn.MaxPool2d(2),
    cnnLayer(h, h, filter_size),
    cnnLayer(h, h, filter_size),
    nn.Flatten(),
    nn.Linear(h*(24//(2**pooling_rounds))**2,
    ▒▒ len(cifar10_classes))
)

loss = nn.CrossEntropyLoss()

optimizer = torch.optim.AdamW(normal_CNN.parameters())  ◄──┘ performance
scheduler = torch.optim.lr_scheduler.CosineAnnealingLR(optimizer, epochs)

normal_results = train_network(normal_CNN, loss,    ◄───── Trains our model as usual
    ▒▒ train_loader, epochs=epochs, device=device,
    ▒▒ test_loader=test_loader, optimizer=optimizer,
    ▒▒ lr_schedule=scheduler,
    ▒▒ score_funcs={'Accuracy': accuracy_score})
```

Annotations in the code:
- `# channels · ( 24 pixels / 2 rounds of pooling )² =` number of inputs to final layer
- Sets up our optimizer with a learning rate scheduler to maximize performance

We have trained our model, and currently nothing *seems* out of place. The accuracy increased regularly with each epoch of training, which is normal and good. This data set is more challenging than MNIST, so getting 74.35% accuracy is reasonable. The issue occurs when we look at different versions of the same image:

```
sns.lineplot(x='epoch', y='test Accuracy',
             data=normal_results, label='Regular')
```

[13]: <AxesSubplot:xlabel='epoch', ylabel='test Accuracy'>

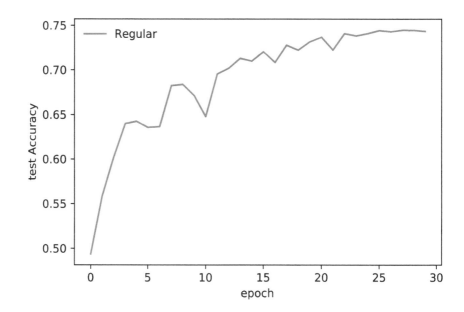

The following code takes one of the full 32×32 images from the test set and makes a prediction on all 64 possible 24×24 sub-images. That's done with the x_crop variable that is passed into the network, and the probability of the correct class is computed with prob_y:

```
test_img_id = 213                          ◀── Test image to grab
x, y = testset_nocrop[test_img_id]         ◀── Gets the original 32 × 32 image
offset_predictions = []                    ◀── Saves the prediction for each 24 × 24 sub-image
normal_CNN = normal_CNN.eval()
for i in range(8):              ◀── For up/down shifts
    for j in range(8):          ◀── For left/right shifts

        x_crop = x[:,i:i+24, j:j+24].to(device)    ◀── Grabs the cropped image
        with torch.no_grad():                            Classifies the image and
            prob_y = F.softmax(normal_CNN(      ◀──     gets the probability
              x_crop.unsqueeze(0)), dim=-1)            of the correct class
              .cpu().numpy()[0,y]
            offset_predictions.append((x_crop, prob_y))  ◀── Saves the resulting score
```

Now we plot all 64 images, and above each image, we show the model's probability of predicting the correct class. Visually, these images are almost identical because they are all sub-images of the same original input. We should get similar predictions for *all* of them because they are essentially the same:

```
f, axarr = plt.subplots(8,8, figsize=(10,10))        ◄── 8 × 8 grid of images
for i in range(8):        ◄── For each row
    pos = 0        ◄── Keeps track of which specific
                       shift we are accessing

    for x, score in offset_predictions[i*8:][:8]:     ◄── Grabs the next eight images
                                                          to fill out the columns

        axarr[i, pos].imshow(x.cpu().numpy().transpose(1,2,0))  ◄──
        axarr[i, pos].text(0.0, 0.5,        Plots the 24 × 24 sub-image
            str(round(score,2)),
            dict(size=20, color='green'))
        pos += 1        ◄── Moves to the next image position
```

Prints the probability of the correct class in the top left

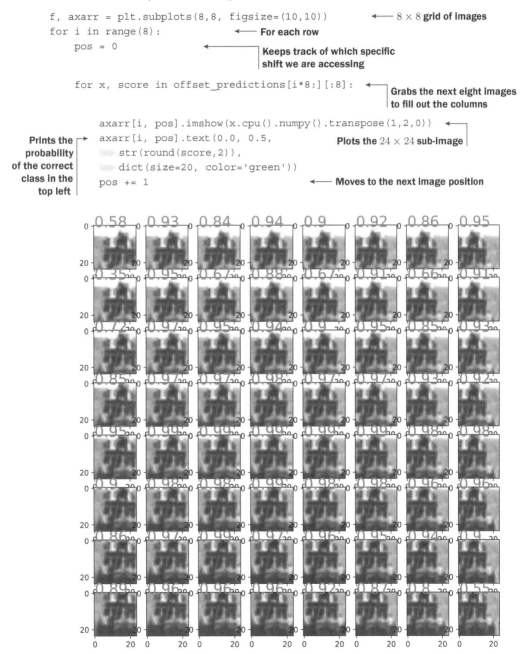

Can you see the problem? While the model is always *correct* (this time), its confidence can change dramatically, fluctuating from 34.84% to 99.48% confidence about the image being a truck. This is the problem with max pooling: it's not *actually* translation-invariant. If it was, we'd get the same confidence score for each of these images. You can try changing the `test_img_id` variable to see this occurs with other test images as well. Now we know that max pooling does not provide good translation invariance; the degree of failure is much larger than we would like.

14.1.2 *Anti-aliasing by blurring*

We can build a better version of pooling if we don't *just* select the maximum value. Remember back in chapter 4 when we used a handcrafted convolution to blur the input? Blurring has the effect of mixing information between adjacent locations. If we first do some blurring to mix information, we can get our pooling to differentiate between patterns that would typically cause aliasing. Let's walk through how blurring can help us build a better pooling operation that is robust against the aliasing problem and can be used as a drop-in replacement for max pooling.

Figure 14.2 shows how we can use blurring for the same 1D sequences we showed in figure 14.1. Remember that these patterns originally all resulted in the same output when we used standard max pooling. In this case, we will still use max pooling, but we will use `stride=1` (with padding) so the output is the same size as the input. This gives us a new representation that returns the maximum for every possible local area.

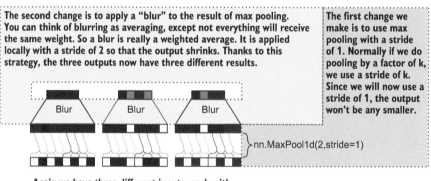

Figure 14.2   An approach to max pooling that helps mitigate aliasing: also called anti-aliasing. First we do max pooling with a stride of 1 to get an output the same size as the input. Then we apply a blurring kernel/convolution with a stride of 2, which shrinks the output to the desired size and maintains the behavior of max pooling but allows us to delineate that the three outputs came from three different inputs. This approach captures more information than naive max pooling.

Normal max pooling takes every other max value because we use 2 as the input to say we want to reduce each dimension by a factor of 2. Instead, we *average* the max values in groups to select the final representation. For the left-most example, this has no impact on the output. But it does change the other two examples: the middle example's output now has a black-and-gray pattern corresponding to the locations with more white cells. This allows us to better differentiate these similar patterns and reduce the aliasing issues that occur.

We need a function that performs blurring. As we saw in chapter 3 on CNNs, it is possible to perform blurring using a convolution with the right kernel. Which one should we choose? Richard Zhang, who showed how to fix this problem,[2] used a binomial filter slightly larger than the pooling size. A binomial filter puts the majority of weight in the center and decreases the weight for items that are further away so the blurring focuses on items at the current location instead of far-away cases. For a 1D filter with a size of k, the ith binomial filter value is equal to

$$\text{filter}_i = \frac{\binom{i}{k}}{2^i}$$

For $k = 2$ to $k = 7$, the following table shows the filter values. The largest values are always in the middle, and the values decrease toward the edges. The result is a weighted average that puts the most emphasis on the values where the filter is currently located, slowly decreasing to further-away items. That's what yields the blurring effect that will help us resolve the aliasing issue:

```
k = 2 :                        1     1
k = 3 :                    1     2     1
k = 4 :               1     3     3     1
k = 5 :           1     4     6     4     1
k = 6 :       1     5    10    10     5     1
k = 7 :   1     6    15    20    15     6     1
```

Lucky for us, this pattern matches what is known as the *binomial distribution* (after we divide by the sum of all k values so they add up to 1.0), which is conveniently implemented in the SciPy library. We can thus use this to implement a new `BlurLayer`. We give it an input option for D, the number of dimensions in our input data (one, two, or three), a `kernel_size` that tells how wide to make the binomial filter kernel, and a `stride` that controls how much to shrink the input. Both `kernel_size` and `stride` act the same way convolutional layers do.

---

[2] R. Zhang, "Making convolutional networks shift-invariant again," in *Proceedings of the 36th International Conference on Machine Learning*, vol. 97, pp. 7324–7334), 2019.

Here's the code:

```
class BlurLayer(nn.Module):
    def __init__(self, kernel_size=5, stride=2, D=2):
        """
        kernel_size: how wide should the blurring be
        stride: how much should the output shrink by
        D: how many dimensions in the input. D=1, D=2, or D=3 for tensors of
           shapes (B, C, W), (B, C, W, H), (B, C, W, H, Z) respectively.
        """
        super(BlurLayer, self).__init__()

        base_1d = scipy.stats.binom.pmf(list(range(
            kernel_size)), kernel_size, p=0.5)

        if D <= 0 or D > 3:
            raise Exception()

        if D >= 1:
            z = base_1d

        if D >= 2:
            z = base_1d[:,None]*z[None,:]

        if D >= 3:
            z = base_1d[:,None,None]*z

        self.weight = nn.Parameter(torch.tensor(z,
            dtype=torch.float32).unsqueeze(0),
            requires_grad=False)
        self.stride = stride

    def forward(self, x):
        C = x.size(1)
        ks = self.weight.size(0)

        if len(self.weight.shape)-1 == 1:
            return F.conv1d(x, torch.stack(
                [self.weight]*C), stride=self.stride,
                groups=C, padding=ks//self.stride)
        elif len(self.weight.shape)-1 == 2:
            return F.conv2d(x, torch.stack(
                [self.weight]*C), stride=self.stride,
                groups=C, padding=ks//self.stride)
        elif len(self.weight.shape)-1 == 3:
            return F.conv3d(x, torch.stack(
                [self.weight]*C), stride=self.stride,
                groups=C, padding=ks//self.stride)
        else:
            raise Exception()
```

Makes a 1D binomial distribution. This computes the normalized filter_i value for all k values.

z is a 1D filter.

Invalid option for D!

We are good.

The 2D filter can be made by multiplying two 1D filters.

The 3D filter can be made by multiplying the 2D version with a 1D version.

Applying the filter is a convolution, so we save the filter as a parameter in this layer. Requires_grad=False because we don't want it to change.

How many channels?

How wide was our internal filter?

All three calls are the same: we just need to know which conv function to call.

The groups argument is used to apply the single filter to every channel, since we don't have multiple filters like a normal convolutional layer.

We should never reach this code: if we do, we know we have a bug!

With this `BlurLayer`, we can implement the strategy we discussed for fixing max pooling's aliasing problem. First, let's try it on the original zebra image to show that it works. We again call `max_pool2d`, but we set `stride=1` so the image is not made any smaller. After that, we create a `BlurLayer` and make the kernel size as large as or larger than the factor we want to shrink by. That means if we want to pool by a factor of z, our blurring filter should have a `kernel_size`$\geq z$. The `stride` of the `BlurLayer` is then set to how much we want to shrink by:

```
                                          Applies max pooling with a stride of 1
tmp = F.max_pool2d(img_tensor_big, (shrink_factor,shrink_factor), ←┘
     stride=1, padding=shrink_factor//2)
img_tensor_small_better = BlurLayer(kernel_size=int(1.5*shrink_factor), ←┐
     stride=shrink_factor)(tmp.unsqueeze(0))         Blurs the max pooling result

to_img(img_tensor_small_better.squeeze())         ←── Shows the result
```

The image of the zebra is much cleaner. Ugly jaggies no longer cover the zebras (there are still some blocks, but not nearly as many as in the original). If we look at the zebra's mane or face, it is difficult to tell how dense the stripe pattern is, but it at least looks smooth. Also, before, it was hard to see any difference between the pattern on the zebra's face and that on its chest and front legs—the blocky output made it difficult to tell what was going on. With anti-aliasing, we can distinguish that the face must have a very fine level of detail and a dense pattern, and the torso's pattern has more changes in angle.

It is also worth noticing the grass and the trees in the background. The trees look similar in both images because they were out of focus in the original image: they were effectively pre-blurred. The grass in the foreground looks subtly different than the original pooled image, again because our new approach is anti-aliasing the image.

14.1.3 Applying anti-aliased pooling

Now that we have shown that max pooling has a problem, we can create a new `MaxPool2dAA` (the AA stands for anti-aliasing) to use as a drop-in replacement for the original `nn.MaxPool2d`. The first argument is how much we want to pool by, just like in the original. We also include a `ratio` that controls how much larger the blur filter should be than the shrinking ratio. We set it to a reasonable default of $1.7\times$ larger. This way, if we want to pool by a larger amount, the code will automatically select a larger filter size for the blurring:

```
class MaxPool2dAA(nn.Module):
    def __init__(self, kernel_size=2, ratio=1.7):
        """
        kernel_size: how much to pool by
        ratio: how much larger the blurring filter should be than the
        ➥ pooling size
        """
        super(MaxPool2dAA, self).__init__()

        blur_ks = int(ratio*kernel_size)                    ◀─┤ Makes a slightly larger
                                                              │ filter for blurring
        self.blur = BlurLayer(kernel_size=blur_ks,   ◀──── Creates the blur kernel
        ➥ stride=kernel_size, D=2)
        self.kernel_size = kernel_size                 ◀──── Stores the pooling size

    def forward(self, x):
        ks = self.kernel_size
        tmp = F.max_pool2d(x, ks, stride=1, padding=ks//2)  ◀── Applies pooling
                                                                 with stride=1
        return self.blur(tmp)          ◀──── Blurs the result
```

Next we can define the `aaPool_CNN` model from our first network, except that we replace every pooling operation with our new anti-aliasing version. The rest of the training code is also identical:

```
aaPool_CNN = nn.Sequential(              ◀──┤ Same architecture as usual,
    cnnLayer(C, h, filter_size),            │ but replaces pooling with
    cnnLayer(h, h, filter_size),            │ our anti-aliased version
    MaxPool2dAA(2),
    cnnLayer(h, h, filter_size),
    cnnLayer(h, h, filter_size),
    MaxPool2dAA(2),
    cnnLayer(h, h, filter_size),
    cnnLayer(h, h, filter_size),
    nn.Flatten(),
    nn.Linear((24//(2**pooling_rounds))**2*h, len(cifar10_classes))
)
```

```
optimizer = torch.optim.AdamW(aaPool_CNN.parameters())
scheduler = torch.optim.lr_scheduler.CosineAnnealingLR(optimizer, epochs)

aaPool_results = train_network(aaPool_CNN, loss, train_loader,
    epochs=epochs, device=device, test_loader=test_loader,
    optimizer=optimizer, lr_schedule=scheduler,
    score_funcs={'Accuracy': accuracy_score})
```

When we look at the training results, the anti-aliased model is almost always ahead of the regular version of the network. Both models have the same number of layers and the same number of parameters to learn, so this impact is due entirely to changing the pooling operation:

```
sns.lineplot(x='epoch', y='test Accuracy', data=normal_results,
    label='Regular')
sns.lineplot(x='epoch', y='test Accuracy', data=aaPool_results,
    label='Anti-Alias Pooling')
```

[22]: <AxesSubplot:xlabel='epoch', ylabel='test Accuracy'>

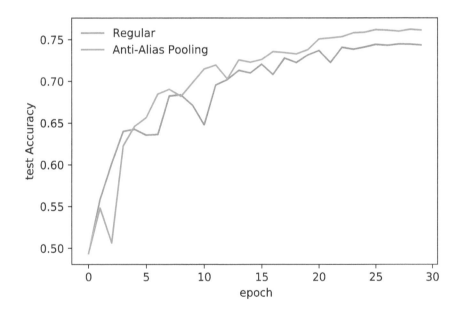

The new `aaPool_CNN` converges to a better solution more quickly: it reaches 76.14999999999999% accuracy after 30 epochs. That alone is a reason to use this approach as a replacement for regular pooling. But we do not know if it solved the translation problem.

Now let's look at how shifting the image changes the predictions of our new model. The following code runs the same test on `test_img_id` from the test set, calculating the model's confidence of the correct class for all 64 possible shifts. Then we plot the probability of the correct class on the y-axis; the x-axis shows how many pixels we have shifted. Ideally, we should see a solid line vertically across the plot, indicating that the model consistently returns the same result:

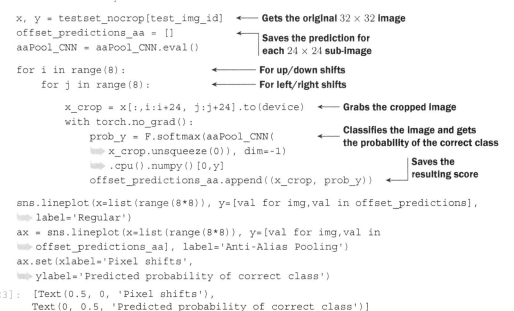

```
x, y = testset_nocrop[test_img_id]     ←── Gets the original 32 × 32 image
offset_predictions_aa = []                 ┌ Saves the prediction for
aaPool_CNN = aaPool_CNN.eval()             └ each 24 × 24 sub-image

for i in range(8):                     ←──── For up/down shifts
    for j in range(8):                 ←──── For left/right shifts

        x_crop = x[:,i:i+24, j:j+24].to(device)   ←── Grabs the cropped image
        with torch.no_grad():                         ┌ Classifies the image and gets
            prob_y = F.softmax(aaPool_CNN(         ←──┘ the probability of the correct class
              x_crop.unsqueeze(0)), dim=-1)
              .cpu().numpy()[0,y]                     ┐ Saves the
            offset_predictions_aa.append((x_crop, prob_y))  ←──┘ resulting score
sns.lineplot(x=list(range(8*8)), y=[val for img,val in offset_predictions],
    label='Regular')
ax = sns.lineplot(x=list(range(8*8)), y=[val for img,val in
    offset_predictions_aa], label='Anti-Alias Pooling')
ax.set(xlabel='Pixel shifts',
    ylabel='Predicted probability of correct class')
```

```
[23]:  [Text(0.5, 0, 'Pixel shifts'),
        Text(0, 0.5, 'Predicted probability of correct class')]
```

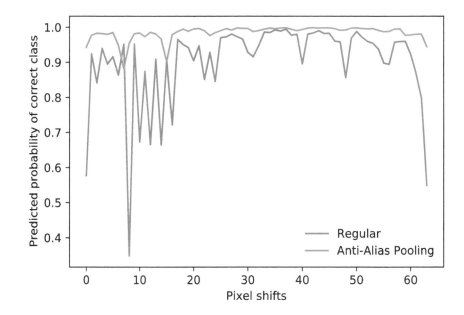

In this plot, `aaPool_CNN` does much better. While it does not solve the aliasing problem perfectly, the predictions returned are more consistent than the original model. If you try changing the `test_img_id`, you should see that this is usually the case, but not always. If we trained for more epochs, say 100, the consistency of the `aaPool_CNN`'s predictions would continue to increase, while the original CNN would always suffer from aliasing problems.

> **NOTE** When you tackle specific problems like translation invariance, results can improve in sometimes unintuitive ways. Maybe the original model fluctuated between 60 and 95% probability, but the new model steadily returns a 40% probability of the correct class. That means the original model was *more accurate* on that sample, but the new model is *more consistent*. This can happen, but we make the change in the belief that greater consistency and robustness to translations *should* be correlated with better results *most* of the time.

These aliasing problems can also occur when we use a convolution with a stride ≥ 2 or with average pooling. The `nn.AvgPool2d` layers can be replaced with a `BlurLayer` to reduce the impact. Strided convolutions (i.e., `stride=s`) are fixed the same way we fixed max pooling: replace the convolution's original stride with `stride=1`, apply any normalization and activation function, and then end with a `BlurLayer` with `kernel_size=s`.

This approach to fixing max pooling is very recent, invented in 2019 and published in a top-tier conference's proceedings. If you made it this far and felt like you understood, congratulations—you can now comprehend and appreciate cutting-edge deep learning research!

14.2 Improved residual blocks

The next two techniques require larger networks and problems to see their full benefit. We still use CIFAR-10 and can show some of their improvements, but they are even more successful on larger and more challenging problems. We will start with improved residual blocks, which we first learned about in chapter 6. The residual strategy generally looks like the equation

$$h = \text{ReLU}\left(x + F(x)\right)$$

where $F(\cdot)$ represents a small sequence of convolutions, normalization, and activation functions repeated twice. This creates skip connections in the network, which makes it easier to learn deeper networks with more layers. These deeper networks also tend to converge faster and to a better-quality solution.

There is nothing particularly wrong with residual connections. As we mentioned before, they are very effective and have been adapted to many other architectures (e.g., U-Net and transformers). But a few small adjustments can provide a consistent improvement in results with a nice intuitive logic.

A technique called *ReZero*[3] can further improve the residual approach to converge even faster and to even better solutions. The approach is shockingly simple and easy to integrate into your residual block's definition. The idea is that the path $F(x)$ is noisy and may add unnecessary complexity to our computations, at least early on. We would rather the network start simple and gradually introduce complexity as needed to solve the problem at hand. Think of it like building a solution one piece at a time rather than trying to build everything at once.

This is accomplished using the following equation, where α is a parameter learned by the network, but we initialize $\alpha = 0$ at the start of training:

$$h = x + \alpha \cdot \text{ReLU}\left(F(x)\right)$$

Because $\alpha = 0$, at the start we get the simplified network $h = x$. *This has done nothing to the input.* If all of our layers looked like this, then they might as well not exist—we would get the same answer if they were removed, since nothing was altered. But during gradient descent, the value of α is altered, and suddenly the inner term of $\text{ReLU}\left(F(x)\right)$ activates and begins to contribute to the solution. The network can choose how much emphasis to put on the nonlinear operations in this term or focus on the original value x by changing the magnitude of α (positive or negative). The larger it gets, the more the network uses the computations in $F(\cdot)$.

14.2.1 *Effective depth*

The benefits of ReZero are subtle, so let's annotate the equation and walk through it in more detail before we implement it. We have the ReZero residual equation as

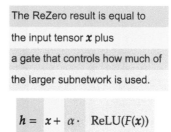

The ReZero result is equal to

the input tensor *x* plus

a gate that controls how much of

the larger subnetwork is used.

$$h = x + \alpha \cdot \ \text{ReLU}(F(x))$$

---

[3]   T. Bachlechner et al., "ReZero is all you need: fast convergence at large depth," https://arxiv.org/abs/2003.04887, 2020.

The fact that we set $\alpha = 0$ at the start of training, instead of a random value, is the critical thing here. If $\alpha = 0$, we get $h = x$, which is the simplest possible function because it *does not do anything*. How can this be helpful? Let's study the architecture created by ReZero in figure 14.3 to understand how this is a benefit. At first glance, it seems very similar to regular residual connections.

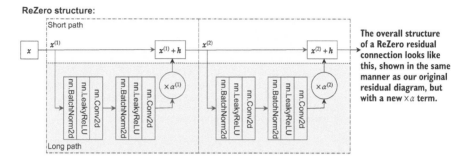

Figure 14.3 Architecture of ReZero for two layers of a network. The shortcut path at the top allows easy gradient flow to the layers, and the long path at the bottom does all heavy work. Instead of simply adding back in the results of the subnetworks from the long path, we multiply them by α before adding them back in.

The elegance is that this does not do anything *at first*. Because the α value is set to $\alpha = 0$ at the start, the subnetworks are all effectively gone, leaving us with a *linear* architecture, as demonstrated in figure 14.4. This is one of the simplest possible architectures we could create, which means initial learning happens very quickly because the total number of effective parameters is minimized.

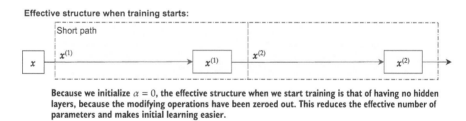

Because we initialize $\alpha = 0$, the effective structure when we start training is that of having no hidden layers, because the modifying operations have been zeroed out. This reduces the effective number of parameters and makes initial learning easier.

Figure 14.4 ReZero's behavior at the start of training for two layers of a network. The shortcut path at the top make a single linear layer ($x^{(1)} = x^{(2)}$) because nothing is added into them. The subnetworks in the long path are effectively gone because their contributions were multiplied by $\alpha = 0$.

But as training happens, the gradient descent process may alter the α values. Once α is altered, the subnetwork $F(x)$ begins to contribute. So the approach begins as a linear model (all $\alpha = 0$ and does nothing) and slowly becomes more complex over time. The impact is shown in figure 14.5.

Effective structure after epochs of training:

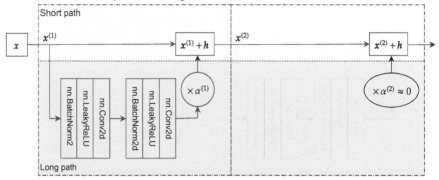

After several epochs of training, we have the resulting "effective" structure. Each residual block's α value may have learned a different value, deciding when to start contributing to the solution. This also means a value of alpha may still be near zero, so it effectively does not exist. ReZero allows our network to decide on its own how many layers of residual blocks to use and when to use them.

Figure 14.5   ReZero architecture with several epochs of training. As the model trains, it can learn to change each α independently, slowly adding hidden layers back into the network. This way, it gradually learns to use the depth and select the total effective depth it desires based on the data. In this case, ReZero learned that it only needed one of its layers; for the second, it learned to keep $\alpha \approx 0$.

After several epochs of training, we have the resulting effective structure. Each residual block's α value may have learned a different value, deciding when to begin contributing to the solution. This also means a value of alpha may still be near zero, so it effectively does not exist. ReZero lets our network decide on its own how many layers of residual blocks to use and when to use them. It may choose not to set *any* of the α values to be near zero, which is also fine. Sometimes it is easier to learn how to use all the layers by starting small and growing more complex over time, which ReZero allows.

14.2.2 *Implementing ReZero*

That's the secret to the ReZero trick! The original discoverers had more math to show theoretically *why* it helps, but we can focus on implementing it. Our improved residual block incorporates this change as an option to choose from. We compartmentalize the function $F(\cdot)$ into its own nn.Sequential module, and if the ReZero flag is set to True, we make self.alpha a Parameter of the network that can be learned. Like the original residual connection we learned about, we also use a shortcut object when the number of channels or stride changes so that we can use 1×1 convolutions to make the shapes match:

```
class ResidualBlock(nn.Module):
    def __init__(self, in_channels, channels, kernel_size=3, stride=1,
        activation=nn.ReLU(), ReZero=True):
        """
        in_channels: how many channels come into this residual block
        channels: the number of output channels for this residual block
        kernel_size: the size of the filters to use in this residual block
```

```
    stride: the stride of the convolutions in this block. Larger
      strides will shrink the output.
    activation: what activation function to use
    ReZero: whether or not ReZero style initializations should be used.
    """
    super().__init__()

    self.activation = activation
    pad = (kernel_size-1)//2
    filter_size = (kernel_size,kernel_size)

    self.F = nn.Sequential(
        nn.Conv2d(in_channels, channels, filter_size,
          padding=pad, bias=False),
        nn.BatchNorm2d(channels),
        activation,
        nn.Conv2d(channels, channels, filter_size, padding=pad,
          stride=stride, bias=False),
        nn.BatchNorm2d(channels),
    )

    self.alpha = 1.0
    if ReZero:
        self.alpha = nn.Parameter(torch.tensor([0.0]),
          requires_grad=True)




    self.shortcut = nn.Identity()

    if in_channels != channels or stride != 1:
        self.shortcut = nn.Sequential(
            nn.Conv2d(in_channels, channels, 1, padding=0,
              stride=stride, bias=False),
            nn.BatchNorm2d(channels),
        )

def forward(self, x):
    f_x = self.F(x)
    x = self.shortcut(x)

    if isinstance(self.alpha,nn.Parameter):
        return x + self.alpha * self.activation(f_x)

    else:
        return self.activation(x + f_x)
```

How much to pad by so W/H stays the same

Complex branch of the network that applies two rounds of layers

Alpha is a float if we are not using ReZero, or a parameter if we are

Shortcut is the identify function. It returns the input as the output unless the output of F will have a different shape due to a change in the number of channels or stride: in that case, we make the shortcut a 1×1 convolution as a projection to change its shape.

Computes the results of F(x) and x, as needed

ReZero

Normal residual block

That was a simple change to include; now let's try it. First we train a relatively deep network for CIFAR-10. The following module contains 28 `ResidualBlocks`, each of which contains 2 layers of convolutions, giving a total of 56 convolutional layers. This is much deeper than most of our networks in this book due to the need to make examples run quickly so you can change them. But ReZero's benefit comes from being able to learn extremely deep networks. You could push this to thousands of hidden layers, if you wanted to, and it would still learn.

Here's the code:

```
resnetReZero_cifar10 = nn.Sequential(          ⟵  Trains a new residual network
    ResidualBlock(C, h, ReZero=True),              using the ReZero approach
    *[ResidualBlock(h, h, ReZero=True) for _ in range(6)],
    ResidualBlock(h, 2*h, ReZero=True, stride=2),    ⟵          Instead of pooling,
    *[ResidualBlock(2*h, 2*h, ReZero=True) for _ in range(6)],  let's use a strided
    ResidualBlock(2*h, 4*h, ReZero=True, stride=2),             convolution layer.
    *[ResidualBlock(4*h, 4*h, ReZero=True) for _ in range(6)],  This keeps the skip
    ResidualBlock(4*h, 4*h, ReZero=True, stride=2),             connections intact
    *[ResidualBlock(4*h, 4*h, ReZero=True) for _ in range(6)],  without extra code.
    nn.AdaptiveAvgPool2d(1),
    nn.Flatten(),                                 We used adaptive pooling down to
    nn.Linear(4*h, len(cifar10_classes)),  ⟵  1 × 1, so it's easier to compute the
)                                             number of inputs to the final layer.

optimizer = torch.optim.AdamW(resnetReZero_cifar10.parameters())
scheduler = torch.optim.lr_scheduler.CosineAnnealingLR(optimizer, epochs)
resnetReZero_results = train_network(resnetReZero_cifar10, loss,
    train_loader, epochs=epochs, device=device, test_loader=test_loader,
    optimizer=optimizer, lr_schedule=scheduler,
    score_funcs={'Accuracy': accuracy_score})
```

That trained our ReZero model. Next, we repeat the same network but set `ReZero=False` to make a more standard residual network to compare against. The only difference between these two networks is the simple multiplication by α as a parameter that starts at 0. We'll skip the code since it is identical other than the `ReZero` flag.

Now we can plot the results. Both residual networks perform significantly better than the simple approach, which we expect. You may find that ReZero does worse than other options for the first epoch: its initial behavior is that of a linear model, as all the subnetworks are blocked by $\alpha = 0$. But as training progresses, ReZero starts converging toward a solution more quickly, often in half as many epochs on big data sets or with 100+ layers. Since our networks are still small to normal size, we don't see as large a difference as is possible. But the deeper we make this network, with more parameters, the more significant a difference we see between the two methods.

Here's the code:

```
sns.lineplot(x='epoch', y='test Accuracy', data=normal_results,
    label='Regular')
sns.lineplot(x='epoch', y='test Accuracy', data=resnet_results,
    label='ResNet')
sns.lineplot(x='epoch', y='test Accuracy', data=resnetReZero_results,
    label='ResNet ReZero')
```

```
[27]:  <AxesSubplot:xlabel='epoch', ylabel='test Accuracy'>
```

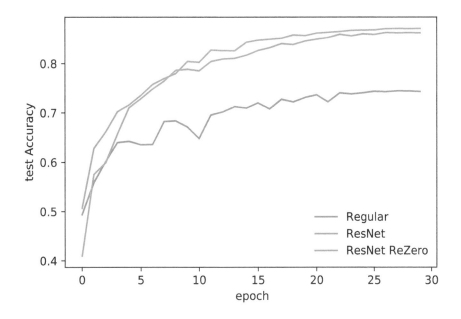

The ReZero approach can be used beyond residual network-style architectures. The original paper's authors have shared code at https://github.com/majumderb/rezero so you can use their ReZero-enhanced transformer to improve the training of transformer-based models. This is particularly valuable since transformers take a long time to train and often require more sophisticated tricks with learning rate schedules to maximize their performance. The ReZero technique helps minimize this complexity. I've personally had a lot of success with ReZero's approach as a simple, easy-to-add method that makes things a little faster and better with almost no effort.

14.3 MixUp training reduces overfitting

The last method we learn about helps mitigate overfitting. Say we have two inputs, x_i and x_j, with corresponding labels y_i and y_j. If $f(\cdot)$ is our neural network and ℓ is our loss function, we normally compute our loss as

$$\text{total loss} = \underbrace{\ell(f(\boldsymbol{x}_i), y_i)}_{\text{Loss on first data point}} + \underbrace{\ell(f(\boldsymbol{x}_j), y_j)}_{\text{Loss on second data point}}$$

This has served us well thus far, but sometimes models learn to overfit the data. Most approaches to regularization involve applying a penalty to the network itself. Dropout, for example, alters the network's weights by randomly forcing some to be zero so the network can't rely on a specific neuron being present to make its decision.

MixUp[4] takes a different approach. Instead of altering or penalizing the network, we alter the loss function and the inputs. This way, we can change the incentives (the model is always trying to minimize the loss) instead of handicapping the model. Given two inputs $\boldsymbol{x}_i$ and $\boldsymbol{x}_j$, we *mix* them together into one new input $\tilde{\boldsymbol{x}}$ with a new label $\tilde{y}$. We do this by taking a random value $\lambda \in [0, 1]$ and taking a weighted average between the two:

$$\tilde{\boldsymbol{x}} = \lambda \boldsymbol{x}_i + (1 - \lambda) \boldsymbol{x}_j$$
$$\tilde{y} = \lambda y_i + (1 - \lambda) y_j$$

Writing the equation this way feels odd at first. We average two images together and feed the averaged image into the network? It makes sense that if an image was 75% cat and 25% zebra, the answer should be 75% cat and 25% zebra, but how do we deal with an averaged label? In practice, we do something that is mathematically equivalent and use both labels y_i and y_j with the new input $\tilde{\boldsymbol{x}}$. We compute our loss as

$$\text{total mixup loss} = \lambda \cdot \ell(f(\tilde{\boldsymbol{x}}), y_i) + (1 - \lambda) \cdot \ell(f(\tilde{\boldsymbol{x}}), y_j)$$

So we have an input $\tilde{\boldsymbol{x}}$ that is the weighted average between y_i and y_j, and we take the weighted loss between both possible predictions. This gives us an intuition as to how to implement the MixUp loss in practice.

Let's dive into this with the example shown in figure 14.6. We have the logits: the output of the neural network *before* the softmax function turns them into probabilities. Then we have the softmax results computed from those logits. If the correct class is class 0, its logit value does not need to be much larger than the others to get high confidence. But softmax *never* assigns a 100% probability, so the loss for a data point *never goes to zero*. As a result, the model constantly gets a small but consistent incentive to push the logit for class 0 *higher* to push the score for the correct class ever higher. This can push the model into unrealistically high scores to eke out small increases in the softmax result.

---

4   H. Zhang et al., "Mixup: beyond empirical risk minimization," ICLR, 2018.

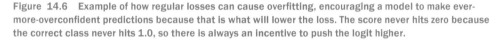

Logits	Softmax result	
[5, −2, −1]	[0.9966 … , 0.0009, 0.0025]	At first the model learns a good prediction (the logits), which maps to a high probability of the correct class.
[9, −2, −1]	[0.99994 … , 0.00002, 0.00005]	
[19, −2, −1]	[0.999999997 … , 0.00 … , 0.00 …]	

But the model wants to lower the loss. One way to do that is to keep driving the correct class's logit into disproportionately higher and higher values. This starts to overfit in order to achieve this "last mile" point.

Figure 14.6 Example of how regular losses can cause overfitting, encouraging a model to make ever-more-overconfident predictions because that is what will lower the loss. The score never hits zero because the correct class never hits 1.0, so there is always an incentive to push the logit higher.

MixUp instead helps the model learn to modulate its predictions, making them only as large as there is reason to believe—rather than going all in on what it believes, as demonstrated in figure 14.7. It's like a betting site that allows users to gamble on an event. You don't want to offer 1 million to 1 odds just because the event is *more* likely—you want the odds to reflect a realistic assumption about how likely you are to be correct.

If we apply mixup with 99% class 0 and 1% class 2, we can avoid degrading to overconfidence (going "YOLO ALL IN ON BLACK") and forcing the logit at index 0 needlessly high. The model will instead try to balance out its degree of predicting both classes to match the goals of 99% and 1%, respectively. This forces the model to predict in moderation by lowering (↓) the logit at index 0 and raising (↑) the logit at index 2.

Figure 14.7 With MixUp, there is not the same incentive to overpredict. Instead, the model tries to reach a target percentage based on how much of two different classes was selected. MixUp mixes the labels and the inputs so there is a signal for each class proportional to the MixUp percentage λ.

If we have a mix of $\lambda\%$, the model will need to learn to predict specifically $\lambda\%$ and $(1-\lambda)\%$ to maximize its score (minimize loss). Thus there is no incentive for the model to ever go all in on any prediction.

14.3.1 *Picking the mix rate*

The only thing left to decide is how to pick λ. It needs to be in the range of $[0, 1]$ to make sense as an average, but we do not necessarily want to pick λ uniformly in this range. When we actually use our network $f(\cdot)$, images will come in with no mixing. They will be normal images, so we want to train with a lot of $\lambda \approx 0$ and $\lambda \approx 1$, as these two cases correspond to no mixing. If we sample λ uniformly from $[0, 1]$, this is unlikely to happen. It's OK that λ is near the extreme values because it will still limit all-in behavior and penalize overly confident predictions.

We use what is known as the *beta distribution*. The beta distribution usually takes two arguments, a and b, and we denote a sample drawn from the distribution as $\lambda \sim$ Beta(a, b). If $a = b$, then the beta distribution is symmetric. If the value is $a = b < 1$, the distribution is a U shape, making values of $\lambda \approx 0$ and $\lambda \approx 1$ more likely and $\lambda \approx 1/2$ less likely. This is what we want, so the model is good at making predictions on clean inputs at test time but is trained to be more robust with slightly noisy values and occasionally very noisy values.

The original paper by Hongyi Zhang et al. suggests using a value of $\alpha \in [0.1, 0.4]$ and setting both beta parameters to this value ($a = b = \alpha$). The following bit of code from SciPy shows what this distribution looks like. The x-axis is the value of λ, and the y-axis is the probability density function (PDF), giving the relative probability of each value of λ:

```
range_01 = np.arange(100)[1:]/100          ⟵ Takes 100 steps along the x-axis for plotting
for alpha in [0.1, 0.2, 0.3, 0.4]:         ⟵ Four hyperparameter values to demonstrate

    plt.plot(range_01, scipy.stats.beta(alpha, alpha).⟵
        pdf(range_01), lw=2, ls='-', alpha=0.5,          Plots the beta distribution
        label=r'$\alpha='+str(alpha)+"$")                for each option
plt.xlabel(r"$\lambda \sim Beta(\alpha, \alpha)$")
plt.ylabel(r"PDF")
plt.legend()
```

```
[28]:  <matplotlib.legend.Legend at 0x7fb37a70f590>
```

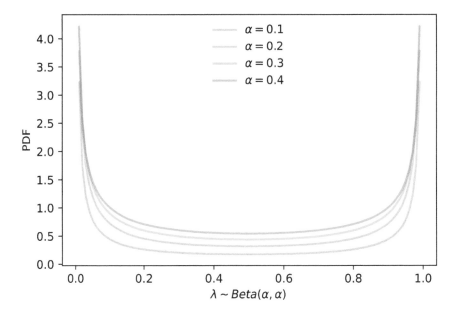

14.3.2 *Implementing MixUp*

Now we understand the mathematical form of MixUp and how we sample λ. Let's talk about the implementation strategy. First we need the loss function, which we'll call ℓ_M. We need four things to implement this function: our predictions $\hat{y}$ from our network processing the mixed data $\tilde{x}$ (i.e., $\hat{y} = f(\tilde{x})$) will be the first input. Our true label y is composed of the three other components: the original labels y_i, y_j and the mixing value λ. Using the original loss function $\ell(\cdot, \cdot)$, we can write this out as

The mixup loss takes in   the model's prediction

and the labels of the two data points that were mixed together, and the percentage of mixing that occurred.

It is equal to λ% of the loss predicting the first original label plus

$(1-\lambda)$% of the loss predicting the second original label.

$$\ell_M\left(\ \hat{y},\ \underbrace{y_i, y_j, \lambda}_{"y"}\ \right) = \lambda \cdot \ell(\hat{y}, y_i) + (1-\lambda) \cdot \ell(\hat{y}, y_j)$$

Using this, we can think of $\hat{y}$ as our normal outputs/predictions and y_i, y_j, λ as a label tuple. So we define a `MixupLoss` function that takes $\hat{y}$ and y. If y is a Python `tuple`, we know that we need to compute the MixUp loss ℓ_M. And if it's a normal tensor, we are computing the original loss function ℓ:

```
class MixupLoss(nn.Module):
    def __init__(self, base_loss=nn.CrossEntropyLoss()):
        """
        base_loss: the original loss function to use as a sub-component of
            Mixup, or to use at test time to see how well we are doing.
        """
        super(MixupLoss, self).__init__()
        self.loss = base_loss

    def forward(self, y_hat, y):
        if isinstance(y, tuple):                    ←—— We should be doing MixUp!

            if len(y) != 3:                          There should be a tuple of
                raise Exception()                ←— y_i, y_j, and lambda!
            y_i, y_j, lambda_ = y              ←—— Breaks the tuple into its components
            return lambda_ * self.loss(y_hat, y_i) +
                (1 - lambda_) * self.loss(y_hat, y_j)

        return self.loss(y_hat, y)            ←—— Else, y is a normal tensor and a normal
                                                  set of labels! Compute the normal way.
```

Now we have a loss function that can take in a normal batch of data and give us the normal loss. But at training time, we need to provide a tuple of y_i, y_j, λ to trigger the MixUp loss, and we need to somehow create a batch of mixed inputs $\tilde{x}$. In particular, we need to get a batch of B data points $x_1, x_2, \ldots, x_B$ with labels $y_1, y_2, \ldots, y_B$ and mix them with a new batch of data to create $\tilde{x}_1, \tilde{x}_2, \ldots, \tilde{x}_B$, which seems to require a complicated change to our loader.

Rather than deal with getting a new batch of data, we'll shuffle just one batch of data and treat the shuffled version as a new batch. The high-level summary of how this is organized is shown in figure 14.8. If we only need one batch of data, we can alter the `collate_fn` to modify the batch. The common mathematical notation for this shuffled ordering is $\pi(i) = i'$, where $\pi(\cdot)$ is a function that indicates a *permutation* (i.e., a random shuffling) of the data.

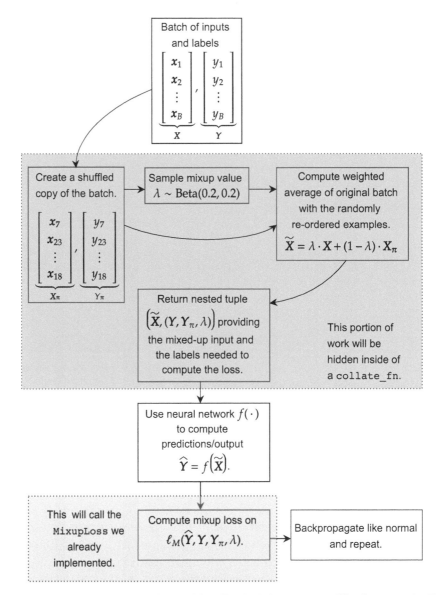

Figure 14.8 Process to implement MixUp training. The shaded areas are modifications we make. Everything else remains the same as training and implementing any other neural network.

For example, say we have a batch of $B = 4$ items. The values

$$\boldsymbol{x}_{\pi(1)}, \boldsymbol{x}_{\pi(2)}, \boldsymbol{x}_{\pi(3)}$$

may give any one of these possible $3! = 6$ orderings:

$$\boldsymbol{x}_1, \boldsymbol{x}_2, \boldsymbol{x}_3$$

$$\boldsymbol{x}_1, \boldsymbol{x}_3, \boldsymbol{x}_2$$

$$\boldsymbol{x}_2, \boldsymbol{x}_2, \boldsymbol{x}_1$$

$$\boldsymbol{x}_2, \boldsymbol{x}_1, \boldsymbol{x}_2$$

$$\boldsymbol{x}_3, \boldsymbol{x}_2, \boldsymbol{x}_1$$

$$\boldsymbol{x}_3, \boldsymbol{x}_1, \boldsymbol{x}_2$$

The function `torch.randperm(B)` will give us an array of length B that is a random permutation $\pi(\cdot)$. Using a random reordering of each batch, we can use the `collate_fn` of the `DataLoader` to alter the batch of training data with a random grouping of the same data. It is exceedingly unlikely that a data point will be paired with itself, and if it is, this process will just temporarily degrade to normal training. So, we get a new batch of training data:

$$\text{New Batch } \tilde{\boldsymbol{X}} = \lambda \cdot \begin{bmatrix} \boldsymbol{x}_1 \\ \boldsymbol{x}_2 \\ \vdots \\ \boldsymbol{x}_B \end{bmatrix} + (1 - \lambda) \cdot \begin{bmatrix} \boldsymbol{x}_{\pi(1)} \\ \boldsymbol{x}_{\pi(2)} \\ \vdots \\ \boldsymbol{x}_{\pi(B)} \end{bmatrix}$$

Once the batch is altered and contains a collection of mixed training instances $\tilde{\boldsymbol{X}}$, we can return a tuple y for the label:

$$\text{tuple label } y = \left(\begin{bmatrix} y_1 \\ y_2 \\ \vdots \\ y_B \end{bmatrix}, \begin{bmatrix} y_{\pi(1)} \\ y_{\pi(2)} \\ \vdots \\ y_{\pi(B)} \end{bmatrix}, \lambda \right)$$

Now we can define `MixupCollator` as our special `collate_fn`. It takes a `collate_fn`, which is the method a user can specify to change how batches are created. `MixupCollator` is also responsible for sampling a new value of λ for each batch, so it needs to take the variable α as a second argument to control how aggressive the mixing is. We provide reasonable default values that sample batches the regular way and are in the middle range of mixing aggressiveness:

```
from torch.utils.data.dataloader import default_collate

class MixupCollator(object):
    def __init__(self, alpha=0.25, base_collate=default_collate):
        """
        alpha: how aggressive the data mixing is: recommended to be
in [0.1, 0.4], but could be in [0, 1]
        base_collate: how to take a list of datapoints and convert them
into one larger batch. By default uses the same default as
PyTorch's DataLoader class.
        """
        self.alpha = alpha
        self.base_collate = base_collate
    def __call__(self, batch):
        x, y = self.base_collate(batch)
        lambda_ = np.random.beta(self.alpha, self.alpha)
        B = x.size(0)
        shuffled_order = torch.randperm(B)


        x_tilde = lambda_ * x + (1 - lambda_) * x[shuffled_order, :]

        y_i, y_j = y, y[shuffled_order]
        return x_tilde, (y_i, y_j, lambda_)
```

The batch comes in as a list. We convert it into an actual batch of data. → `x, y = self.base_collate(batch)`

Samples the value of lambda to use. Note the "_" at the end, because lambda is a keyword in Python. → `lambda_ = np.random.beta(self.alpha, self.alpha)`

Creates a random shuffled order pi → `shuffled_order = torch.randperm(B)`

Computes the mixed version of the input data → `x_tilde = lambda_ * x + (1 - lambda_) * x[shuffled_order, :]`

Gets the labels → `y_i, y_j = y, y[shuffled_order]`

Returns a tuple of two items: the input data and another tuple of three items that MixupLoss needs

With these two classes, we can easily incorporate the MixUp approach into almost any model. A new training loader needs to be built with `collate_fn=MixupCollator()`, and we need to pass `MixupLoss()` to our `train_network` function as the loss function to use. All the rest of our code works just as before, but with the addition of MixUp training:

Replaces the data loader with a new one that uses our MixupCollator

```
train_loader_mixup = torch.utils.data.DataLoader(trainset, batch_size=B,
    num_workers=2, shuffle=True, collate_fn=MixupCollator())

resnetReZero_cifar10.apply(weight_reset)

optimizer = torch.optim.AdamW(
    resnetReZero_cifar10.parameters())

scheduler = torch.optim.lr_scheduler.CosineAnnealingLR(optimizer, epochs)

resnetReZero_mixup_results = train_network(resnetReZero_cifar10,
    MixupLoss(loss), train_loader_mixup, epochs=epochs,
    device=device, test_loader=test_loader,
    optimizer=optimizer, lr_schedule=scheduler,
    score_funcs={'Accuracy': accuracy_score})
```

Resets the weights too, out of laziness

The optimizer and scheduler remain unchanged.

Wraps our normal loss with our new MixupLoss since we are training with MixUp

If we plot the accuracy, we see that our ResNet ReZero model combined with MixUp has further improved the rate of convergence, and the final accuracy is 88.12%:

```
sns.lineplot(x='epoch', y='test Accuracy', data=normal_results,
    label='Regular')
sns.lineplot(x='epoch', y='test Accuracy', data=resnet_results,
    label='ResNet')
sns.lineplot(x='epoch', y='test Accuracy', data=resnetReZero_results,
    label='ResNet ReZero')
sns.lineplot(x='epoch', y='test Accuracy', data=resnetReZero_mixup_results,
    label='ResNet ReZero + MixUp')
```

```
[32]:   <AxesSubplot:xlabel='epoch', ylabel='test Accuracy'>
```

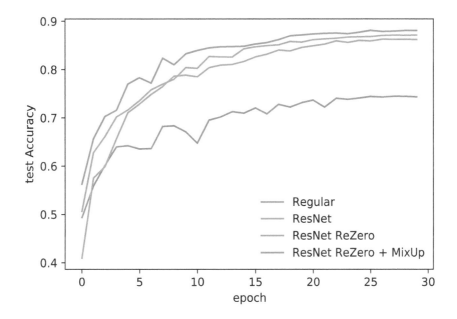

Looking at the results as a function of time, we see that the ReZero and MixUp methods are only incremental increases in runtime. Just using a deeper model with the ResNet approach is where most of the computational cost comes from. So if you are building a deeper network, both of these approaches are easy to add and can increase your model's accuracy.

> **WARNING** The first two approaches we learned in this chapter are almost always worth using without worry. MixUp sometimes hurts accuracy but is usually a decent improvement, so it's worth trying a new architecture once with and without MixUp to see how it does for your problem. MixUp is also trickier to apply to things like transformers and RNNs, although its extensions will help (with some uglier code). I'm sticking with standard MixUp for simplicity for now, but I know I can look at its extensions if I need to.

The only downside to these approaches is that their benefit is often only seen when working with bigger models or when we are already at risk of overfitting due to the complexity of our networks. If they hurt your accuracy, there is a good chance you need to make your network deeper and/or widen the layers in order for them to help.

Exercises

Share and discuss your solutions on the Manning online platform at Inside Deep Learning Exercises (https://liveproject.manning.com/project/945). Once you submit your own answers, you will be able to see the solutions submitted by other readers, and see which ones the author judges to be the best.

1. We looked at the change in probability of translating (shifting) CIFAR-10 images for a specific example. Instead, compute the median deviation of change in class probability over all of the test set of CIFAR-10 for both the original CNN and the anti-aliased version (i.e., for every image, compute the 64 probability values and the standard deviations of those probabilities. Compute that value for every image, and take the median). Does the result show what you expect, that anti-aliasing reduces the median change in probability?

2. Implement the anti-aliased version of strided convolution and average pooling based on the descriptions in this chapter. Then implement new convolutional networks that replace max pooling with the standard and anti-aliased versions of strided convolution and average pooling. Test them yourself using the same CIFAR-10 example we used for `MaxPool2dAA`.

3. Implement a ReZero version of the bottleneck class from chapter 6 and a ReZero version of a fully connected residual block. Test them both on CIFAR-100 and see how they compare to non-ReZero counterparts.

4. Our ReZero residual network has 6 blocks of residual layers between each section of its definition. Try training both a ReZero and a normal residual block with 18 blocks, instead. How does the performance of each approach change?

5. Implement the anti-aliased version of strided convolution for the ReZero residual network, and train it on CIFAR-10. How does it impact accuracy and convergence?

6. **Challenging:** The paper "Manifold mixup: better representations by interpolating hidden states"[5] describes an improved version of MixUp that performs the mixing at a randomly selected hidden layer of the network rather than at the input. Try to implement this yourself, and test it on CIFAR-10 and CIFAR-100. Hint: this will be easier to do by defining a custom `Module` for the network and using a `ModuleList` to store the sequence of layers that are candidates for mixing (i.e., you don't need *every* possible hidden layer to be an option).

---

[5]   V. Verma et al., *Proceedings of the 36th International Conference on Machine Learning*, vol. 97, pp. 6438–6447, 2019.

Summary

- Aliasing occurs when naive pooling is used. It interferes with a model's translation invariance.

- Incorporating a blur operation helps mitigate the aliasing problem, which in turn helps improve our model's accuracy.

- Adding a kind of gate α to the subnetwork of a residual block gives the model a chance to incorporate complexity over time, improving convergence speed and causing the model to converge to more accurate solutions.

- Cross-entropy and other losses can overfit when they get overconfident about predicting classes.

- MixUp combats overconfident predictions by penalizing them, forcing the model to learn how to hedge its bets.

- Anti-aliased pooling, ReZero residuals, and MixUp are widely useful and can be used together, but their strength is most apparent with large data sets and when training for 100+ epochs.

appendix A
Setting up Colab

All of the code in this book is written using Python 3 as a Jupyter notebook. While you can set up Jupyter and the software libraries on your own computer using Anaconda (www.anaconda.com/products/individual), this book takes the approach of using Google's Colab service (https://colab.research.google.com). Google Colab has all the needed software libraries preinstalled and provides access to a free graphics processing unit (GPU) for limited periods. This is enough for you to get started learning without having to invest hundreds or thousands of dollars in a computing setup. This appendix walks through how to get set up with Google Colab; I encourage you to get the Pro version, which is currently only a few dollars a month. This is not a sponsored recommendation—I don't get a kickback, and I've never worked for Google. It's just a product I like that I think is making deep learning more accessible.

A.1 Creating a Colab session

Go to https://colab.research.google.com/notebooks/intro.ipynb, which gives you a default introductory notebook, as shown in figure A.1. Click the Sign In button in the top-right corner to sign in to Colab so you can save your work and use the GPUs.

When you click Sign In, you'll be presented with Google's standard login screen (figure A.2). If you already have a Google account, you can log in with that; otherwise, click the Create Account button, and you will be guided through the account creation process.

Once signed in, you'll go back to the first screen in figure A.1. This first notebook Colab shows you is also a mini-tutorial about Colab and Jupyter, if you aren't familiar with them.

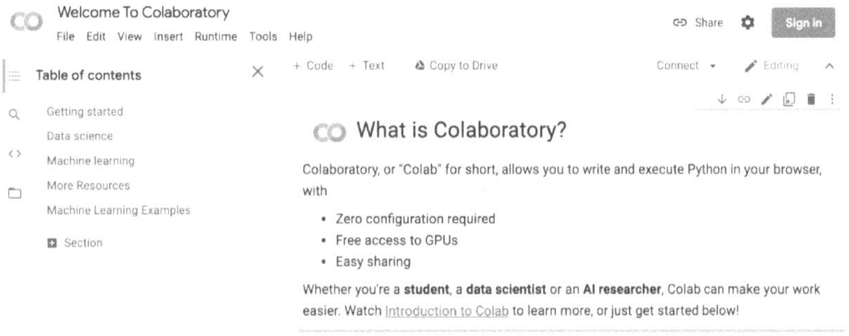

Figure A.1   The first screen you should see when you go to Colab for the first time. The Sign In button is in the top-right corner.

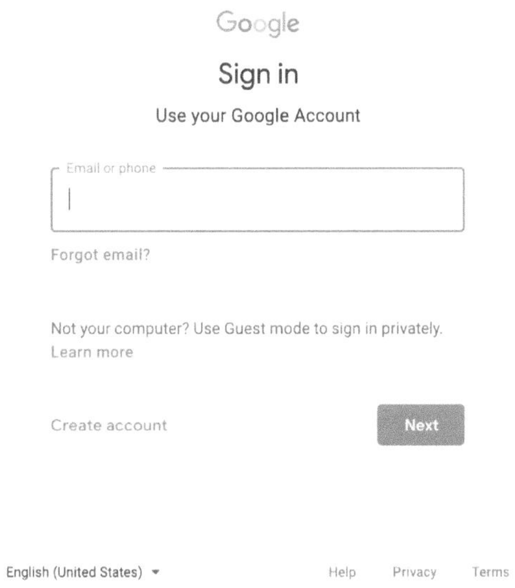

Figure A.2   Google's standard sign-in page is used for Colab. Use your current Google account if you have one, or click Create Account to be guided through creating an account.

Adding a GPU

Now let's talk about the free GPU. Colab does not *guarantee* you a GPU, and no GPU is provided by default. You must explicitly request that a GPU be attached to your notebook. To access a GPU with Colab, choose Runtime > Change Runtime Type from the menu at the top of the web page (figure A.3).

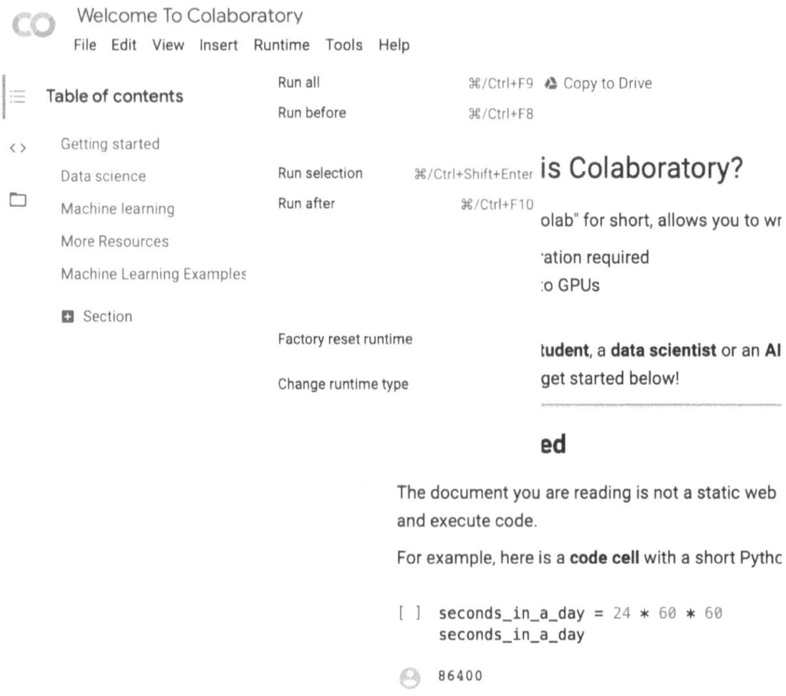

Figure A.3   To attach a GPU to your notebook, choose Runtime > Change Runtime Type.

In the next window, the Hardware Accelerator list gives you the options None, GPU, and TPU, as shown in figure A.4. The None option means CPU-only and is the default. GPU and TPU add resources on top of the existing CPU. Both GPUs and TPUs are called *co-processors* and provide more specialized functionality. Currently, TPU support in PyTorch is very new, so I recommend selecting the GPU option (as I've done for this entire book). Doing so restarts the notebook (you'll lose any work you've done, so do this early), and it should return with a GPU present and ready to use.

GPUs are expensive and in-demand commodities, so you do not have *unlimited* access to this GPU. There is no public formula, but current demand for GPUs and how much you personally are using GPUs will impact the quality of the GPU you get. Colab has a priority queue system to even out the resources for everyone—if demand is very high, you may not be able to get a GPU when you request one. If you can't get a GPU (or one that is as fast as you would like), wait a few hours (or potentially a day, depending on your usage and Colab's demand) and try again.

As I mentioned earlier, while doing so is not required, I encourage you to sign up for Colab Pro to make your life easier (https://colab.research.google.com/signup). The Pro version does not fundamentally change how Colab works, but it gives you higher priority for GPU access and longer runtimes when using Colab. Colab Pro is only $10 a month: it's a pretty good deal for portable GPU access and far cheaper than diving into new hardware. In my experience, I found Colab Pro has always meant that I got a GPU without issue.

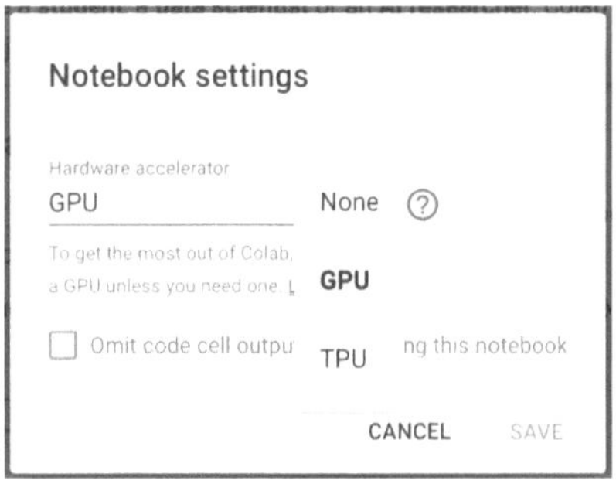

Figure A.4 The None option means CPU-only. Both other options also have a CPU. Select the GPU option to add a GPU to your notebook.

Testing your GPU

Click the Save button in the Notebook Settings window, and you'll have access to an Nvidia GPU in your Colab session! You can double-check this by running the following command:

```
!nvidia-smi
```

The ! is a special function of a Jupyter notebook. Instead of running Python code, it runs the code on the command line of the host computer. nvidia-smi is a program that gives you information about all the GPUs running in your computer and their current utilization. I ran this command and got the output shown in figure A.5, indicating that a Tesla P4 with 7.6 GB of RAM was allocated for my use. You may get different results when you run this, and that's OK. Not having exact control is the price we pay for a free GPU.

```
+-----------------------------------------------------------------------------+
| NVIDIA-SMI 440.82       Driver Version: 418.67       CUDA Version: 10.1     |
|-------------------------------+----------------------+----------------------+
| GPU  Name        Persistence-M| Bus-Id        Disp.A | Volatile Uncorr. ECC |
| Fan  Temp  Perf  Pwr:Usage/Cap|         Memory-Usage | GPU-Util  Compute M. |
|===============================+======================+======================|
|   0  Tesla P4            Off  | 00000000:00:04.0 Off |                    0 |
| N/A   32C    P8     7W /  75W |      0MiB /  7611MiB |      0%      Default |
+-------------------------------+----------------------+----------------------+

+-----------------------------------------------------------------------------+
| Processes:                                                       GPU Memory |
|  GPU       PID   Type   Process name                             Usage      |
|=============================================================================|
|  No running processes found                                                 |
+-----------------------------------------------------------------------------+
```

Figure A.5 Example output of the nvidia-smi command. If you see something similar to this, everything is ready to use.

That's all you need to do to get ready to run code with Colab. It comes with most machine learning libraries preinstalled and ready to go. For example, this book uses seaborn and Matplotlib for easy plotting/visualization of our results, NumPy for initial data loading and to work with arrays, and pandas to examine our results. The tqdm library is another useful utility that provides easy access to progress bars with an estimated completion time, as shown in figure A.6.

Epoch: 8%   4/50 [00:25<04:55, 6.43s/it]

Train Batch: 83%   194/235 [00:04<00:00, 42.18it/s]

Figure A.6   The training code in this book creates progress bars like this for every call. This is useful because training a neural network can take a while, and you can judge how long you have left. Five minutes? Grab a coffee. An hour? Read another chapter of a riveting book about a man with a hat and cool outfit espousing tidbits of learning wisdom.

We can simply import these libraries, and they are ready to go. On occasion, you may need to install a package, which can be done with the standard `pip` command using the same ! trick. The command is shown when needed through the book. All the libraries I've mentioned are common tools in a machine learning practitioner's toolbelt, and you should have at least some familiarity with them before diving into this book.

index

RELATED MANNING TITLES

Deep Learning with Python, Second Edition
by Francois Chollet

ISBN 9781617296864
504 pages, $59.99
October 2021

Grokking Deep Learning
by Andrew W. Trask

ISBN 9781617293702
336 pages, $39.99
January 2019

Deep Learning with PyTorch
by Eli Stevens, Luca Antiga, and Thomas Viehmann
Foreword by Soumith Chintala

ISBN 9781617295263
520 pages, $39.99
July 2020

For ordering information go to www.manning.com